PSYCHODIAGNOSIS IN SCHIZOPHRENIA

PSYCHODIAGNOSIS IN SCHIZOPHRENIA

IRVING B. WEINER, Ph. D.

Assistant Professor of Psychiatry (Psychology)
University of Rochester School of Medicine and Dentistry

JOHN WILEY & SONS, INC., NEW YORK · LONDON · SYDNEY

Library of Congress Catalog Card Number: 66–26761
Printed in the United States of America

To Jacob H. Weiner

(1905–1963)

PREFACE

Schizophrenia is one of the most prevalent and perplexing psychological disturbances in our society. Statistical reports from clinics and hospitals attest its widespread occurrence, and a voluminous literature bears witness to extensive exploration of its etiology, diagnosis, and treatment. Questions about schizophrenia frequently arise in clinical settings, in which crucial decisions concerning patient care hinge on careful diagnostic evaluation, and the psychologist's psychodiagnostic skills are often enlisted to answer such questions. This state of affairs places the psychologist in an unenviable position. If he is conversant with the literature, he is aware that the etiology and phenomenology ∨ of schizophrenia are not yet conclusively established and that experimental demonstration of the diagnostic validity of psychological tests lags behind the use to which experienced clinicians feel justified in putting them.

As a responsible professional person, however, the clinical psychologist recognizes that, in spite of our limited knowledge, diagnostic judgments involving aspects of schizophrenia are necessary for adequate treatment planning. He is furthermore cognizant that he will be called on to apply psychological test data to such judgments. To respond effectively, he must be able to relax his scientific stance sufficiently to concern himself with the job that needs to be done. That is, it is necessary for the clinician to focus on the single case and seek conclusions that are practically useful, even if they admit of exception or cannot be thoroughly documented. Without losing sight of the issues that remain unresolved, he must employ what information and skills are available to him to perform his functions as helpfully as he can. Skepticism should not cloud his judgment, nor should the lack of definitive answers paralyze his capacity to venture an opinion.

This book is written to answer the following question: given present knowledge, in what ways can the psychologist utilize test data to make diagnostic judgments about schizophrenic persons? The book is addressed to graduate students in psychology, for whom it can serve as an advanced text and reference source, and to the practicing clinician, for whom it will provide an integrated summary of the literature in this area and an opportunity to compare his experience with various psychodiagnostic guidelines to be proposed. Basic familiarity with the administration, scoring, and interpretation of psychological tests is assumed in the presentation. The book is intended as a clinical handbook, and its main purpose is to categorize test behaviors that facilitate differential diagnosis in schizophrenia.

However, no clinician should be satisfied to have in his hands a skeletonized cookbook. Psychodiagnosis requires the psychologist to infer from raw test data general statements about personality functioning and from these statements to draw conclusions about the presence or absence of various pathologic states. To do so in a flexible and sophisticated manner, he needs to be broadly familiar with the subject matter of psychopathology, with conceptual frames of reference linking psychopathologic behavior to psychological test variables, and with research findings pertinent to the clinical use of psychological tests. Accordingly, this book stresses a conceptual orientation to personality assessment, expressed largely in the language of psychoanalytic ego psychology, and discusses problems of differential diagnosis in terms of general behavioral constructs, psychological test variables that assess these constructs, and relevant empirical data.

The book is divided into four parts. Part 1 includes three introductory chapters, the first of which is devoted to a historical overview of various approaches to the study of schizophrenia and considers the influence of a number of pioneering contributors on current issues and lines of investigation. Chapter 2 sketches an ego-disturbance model of schizophrenia that is amplified in Chapters 4 to 12. Chapter 3 reviews the history of the application of three clinical tests—the Rorschach, the Draw-a-Person, and the Wechsler Adult Intelligence Scale—to the diagnostic study of schizophrenia and describes the bases on which these three measures are selected for detailed discussion in Parts 2 and 3.

Part 2, entitled Psychodiagnosis of Schizophrenia: Assessment of Disturbances in Ego Functioning, is comprised of nine chapters that survey test indicators of various ego disturbances associated with schizophrenia. These chapters describe correlates of healthy and schizophrenic ego functioning and their manifestations on the three tests mentioned above. Test variables identifying characteristics of schizophrenia are illustrated with case excerpts. Additionally, relevant normative data and experimental findings are cited, and, although evaluative reviews of the research literature are not undertaken, certain issues in the assessment and planning of validating studies are explored. The presentation in Part 2 is of necessity uneven. In some instances available empirical findings are sufficient to confirm psychodiagnostic recommendations derived from conceptual frames of reference; in other cases such data are lacking or inconclusive, and the conclusions drawn rest heavily on logical inference and the accumulated clinical experience reported in the literature.

Part 3, Differential Diagnosis in Schizophrenia, is devoted to several of the difficult questions that arise in clinical practice. These include whether the schizophrenic patient's disturbance is acute or chronic in nature (Chapter 13), whether he is on the verge of becoming increasingly disturbed or is in the process of remitting (Chapter 15), and whether there are paranoid or affective components to his condition (Chapters 14 & 17). Other challenging problems discussed are the identification of borderline and pseudoneurotic schizophrenia (Chapter 16) and the discrimination between schizophrenia and turmoil in adolescents (Chapter 18). In each of these chapters the clinical literature on the various diagnostic subcategories is reviewed and test indices significant for differential diagnosis are considered. These particular diagnostic categories do not correspond to any standard nomenclature, nor do they necessarily represent distinctions clearly defined by clinical and research findings. Rather, their selection rests with their being in the author's clinical experience the questions most frequently asked about schizophrenic patients. Detailed case studies are included to illustrate each of the diagnostic subcategories.

Part 4 is devoted to a brief consideration of scientific and professional issues impinging on psychodiagnostic practice. Chapter 19 outlines the requirements for a reliable, valid, and useful psychodiagnostic procedure and assesses the extent to which the clinical test battery satisfies these requirements. Attention is also given to problems of research design in validational studies of psychodiagnostic techniques and to the extant controversy between proponents of the clinical and statistical methods of prediction in personality study. Finally, some remarks are offered on the status and rewards of psychodiagnostic activity.

Some additional comment is necessary concerning the examples and case material utilized in the text. No special effort was made to obtain test data from schizophrenic patients clearly identified as typifying certain diagnostic subcategories. To have done so would have provided material representative for schizophrenic patients in generally but hardly representative of schizophrenic patients *referred for psychological examination.* The cases and examples included in this book are chosen from actual clinical files and illustrate the performance of patients who posed diagnostic problems of sufficient difficulty and significance to warrant detailed psychological examination.

This selection of material from actual files of referred patients has important implications. It must be recognized, for example, that test discriminators derived from comparisons between normal persons and random or block samples of hospitalized schizophrenic patients, most of whom are obviously or seriously disturbed, may be useful for research purposes but have little promise of clinical utility. Although such test discriminators will be efficient where tests are extraneous, that is, when the patient's condition can be readily diagnosed without recourse to testing, there is no guarantee that they will be of value for the patient whose disorder is mild, borderline, incipient, or mixed in some way.

Much of the early work on psychodiagnosis in schizophrenia, including virtually all of the contributions mentioned in Chapter 3, was conducted with chronic, hospitalized, seriously disturbed persons. It is not too surprising, then, that attempts to validate indicators of schizophrenia derived in these studies have often been of limited success with clinic populations and among acutely schizophrenic patients. It is unfortunate that inconclusive results in such cases have led many critics to impugn the possible utility of psychological tests rather than to seek out discriminating variables in populations similar to those in which they are to be applied. This matter is touched on at several points in the text, particularly in the introduction to case studies in Chapter 13 and the section on validity in Chapter 19.

Also important is the fact that the examples presented in the following chapters, having been drawn from actual case files, are the productions of patients of somewhat uncertain diagnostic status. Although these examples may therefore on occasion lack clarity, they provide a representative picture of the manner in which various test indices associated with schizophrenia are likely to be manifest in an actual population of referred patients. Finally, it should be noted that the material presented is applicable primarily to adult groups; diagnosis of schizophrenia in adolescents is treated separately in Chapter 18, and the evaluation of childhood disturbances is not included in the current presentation.

I would like to express my appreciation to the many people who helped me to prepare this book. Dr. David Shakow was kind enough to read and comment on the manuscript, and I benefited from valuable suggestions by Dr. John Romano, chairman, and Dr. Norman Harway, Dr. Leonard Salzman, and Dr. Robert Goldstein of the Department of Psychiatry in the University of Rochester School of Medicine and Dentistry. Background and follow-up information for some of the case presentations was furnished by Dr. Elmer Gardner and Dr. Haroutun Babigian through a cumulative psychiatric case register, which is supported by the National Institute of Mental Health, Grant OM-381 (C2), and the Milbank Memorial Fund, and by Dr. W. Twitty Carpenter, Dr. Douglas Evans, and Dr. Edwin Freeman. For her long and faithful service I should like to thank Miss Jane Widman, who typed the bulk of the manuscript in its several revisions. I am additionally grateful for the secretarial assistance provided during my work by Mrs. Shirley Miller, Mrs. Rita Searle, Miss Christine Agnew, Miss Patricia Bauer, Miss Mary Lou Mariani, and Miss Mildred Randall.

I would also like to pay my deepest respects to the memory of Gordon Ierardi, whose informed and encouraging editorship inestimably aided my work.

Various copyrighted materials are quoted in the text by the kind permission of Basic Books, Inc., the *British Journal of Medical Psychology*, the *Bulletin of the Menninger Clinic*, Charles C Thomas, Publisher, Grune and Stratton, Inc., Harcourt, Brace and World, Inc., International Universities Press, Inc., the *Journal of Clinical Psychology*, the *Journal of Projective Techniques and Personality Assessment*, Logos Press, Inc., W. W. Norton and Co., and the *Psychiatry Digest*. Appreciation is also expressed to Sigmund Freud Copyrights Ltd., Mr. James Strachey, and the Hogarth Press Ltd. for permission to quote from "Analysis Terminable and Interminable" in Volume XXIII (1937–1939) of the Standard Edition of *The Complete Works of Sigmund Freud*.

IRVING B. WEINER

Rochester, New York
August 1966

CONTENTS

PART IV. CONCLUSION

PART ONE

 INTRODUCTION

1

BASIC APPROACHES TO SCHIZOPHRENIA: HISTORY AND CURRENT ISSUES

THE clinical picture of schizophrenia was initially labeled as a syndrome by the Belgian psychiatrist Morel, who in 1860 introduced the term *dementia praecox* (*démence précoce*) to describe an insidious, progressive personality decompensation in a 14-year-old boy. However, the formal study of schizophrenia did not receive a major impetus until Emil Kraepelin published his classical discussion of dementia praecox in 1896. Kraepelin's contribution was based on earlier descriptions of three conditions, *hebephrenia, catatonia,* and *paranoia,* that had previously been considered distinct and unrelated syndromes. Kahlbaum in 1863 had referred to a condition occurring in puberty as *paraphrenia hebetica,* and Hecker in 1871 had labeled this condition *hebephrenia* and characterized it in terms of fluctuating melancholia, mania, and confusion. In 1874 Kahlbaum had provided the first clinical description of *catatonia,* in which he stressed the muteness, postural rigidity, impaired volition, and occasional waxy flexibility associated with this disorder. The term *paranoia,* which dates at least from Hippocrates, had been used during the eighteenth and nineteenth centuries in a variety of senses, often as a name for delusional and delirious disorders (Cameron, 1959).*

EMIL KRAEPELIN (1856-1926) AND THE DESCRIPTIVE APPROACH

Emil Kraepelin included in the fifth edition of his *Textbook of Psychiatry,* published in 1896, the first attempt to synthesize the nomen-

---

* A recent paper by Wender (1963) is recommended for a fuller review of pre-Kraepelinian descriptions of schizophrenic disturbance.

clature of schizophrenia. In this text Kraepelin concluded that because hebephrenia, catatonia, and paranoia were all characterized by progressive decay and eventual dementia they should be identified as forms of a single disorder, dementia praecox, the fundamental criterion for which is its outcome, dementia. Kraepelin defined dementia praecox as a syndrome consisting of hallucinations, delusions, incongruous affectivity, impaired attention, negativism, stereotyped behavior, and progressive dilapidation, and he designated the type of dementia praecox as hebephrenic, catatonic, or paranoid, depending on which symptoms were predominant. Kraepelin believed that the clinical features of the disorder were caused either by a degenerative disease of the brain or by metabolic disturbances, and he was critical of any attempt to interpret the behavior of the afflicted person in psychological terms.

Kraepelin's approach has often been subjected to harsh criticism. Arieti (1959a, p. 456) maintains that Kraepelin's contributions are "outdated," and Zilboorg (1941, p. 150) states that Kraepelin's concentration on the description of external deviations, rather than on the understanding of inner personality, "threatened to eliminate the very foundation of clinical psychiatry." Nevertheless, a survey of current literature reveals far-reaching influences of Kraepelinian concepts that justify Wender's (1963, p. 1148) complaint that Kraepelin "is as frequently belittled as he is infrequently read." In addition to the widespread utilization of Kraepelin's classificatory scheme, at least three of his major ideas figure prominently in contemporary approaches to the study of schizophrenia.

First, Kraepelin's emphasis on description is thoroughly endorsed by many researchers who feel that the basic task in behavioral science is classification. Eysenck (1961a), for example, subscribes to the dictum that "nosology precedes etiology." He credits Kraepelin with introducing the application of experimental psychological methods to the study of abnormal behavior and dedicates to him his *Handbook of Abnormal Psychology*. Katz and Cole (1963), in a recent paper with the very Kraepelinian title, "A Phenomenological Approach to the Classification of Schizophrenic Disorders," stress continued descriptive work as necessary to further understanding of the etiology of schizophrenia. Beck (1954), Guertin (1952), Lorr, Klett, and McNair (1963), Wing (1961), Wittenborn (1951), and others who are studying schizophrenia by applying factor analytic techniques to phenomenological data are also operating in the Kraepelinian tradition. The viability of descriptive efforts emerges particularly clearly in the following remarks by Shakow (1966, pp. 150–151):

I do not understand how a psychologist can adopt a professional orientation which does not acknowledge classification as fundamental in dealing with the multiplicity of phenomena involved in the diagnosis of mental disorder. Classification is essential whether it is being made for therapeutic or for research purposes. . . . Science is not possible without classification.

Second, Kraepelin's emphasis on brain disease and metabolic dysfunction as likely etiologic agents in schizophrenia has remained viable. Biochemical and metabolic functioning in schizophrenic patients, as reviewed by Kety (1960) and Freeman (1958), are under extensive examination, and many workers are attempting to demonstrate that psychological problems in schizophrenia are secondary to a primary neurologic deficit (Bender, 1953; Leach, 1960; Pasamanick & Knobloch, 1961).

Third, Kraepelin's use of expected outcome as a diagnostic criterion is retained in current studies employing such prognostic measures as the Elgin Prognostic Rating Scale (Wittman, 1944) as differential indices of the acute-chronic and process-reactive dimensions of schizophrenia (Herron, 1962a; see Chapter 13). The rationale in these studies is but one step removed from Kraepelin: to Kraepelin a poor prognosis indicated schizophrenia and a good prognosis, its absence; currently, good prognosis is often used to identify a reactive and poor prognosis a process schizophrenic disturbance.

EUGEN BLEULER (1857-1939) AND FORMAL PSYCHOLOGICAL ANALYSIS

In 1911 Eugen Bleuler published his classic work, *Dementia Praecox or the Group of Schizophrenias,* a text that remains today as significant for the understanding of schizophrenic disorders as any other single work. Bleuler accepted Kraepelin's classification scheme and even suggested an additional form of schizophrenia, the *simple,* which Kraepelin later included among his categories. However, Bleuler was dissatisfied with Kraepelin's dementia praecox concept, partly because it gave little credence to psychodynamic considerations and partly because Bleuler's own clinical observations revealed that the condition neither necessarily began in early adolescence nor invariably led to dementia. Bleuler felt that the disorder could best be characterized as a splitting of the basic functions of the personality, and from the Greek words *schizin* (to split) and *phren* (mind) he coined the name *schizophrenia,* with which he recommended that the term dementia praecox be replaced.

According to Bleuler, the formal mechanism underlying all schizophrenic symptoms is a loosening in the continuity of associations. Also characteristic of the disorder are ambivalence, disturbances of affectivity, and *autism*, a term Bleuler proposed to describe detachment from reality. By emphasizing connections between schizophrenic symptomatology and psychological processes within the personality, Bleuler introduced to the study of schizophrenic disturbance the type of formal psychological analysis that has inspired such significant contributions as Von Domarus' (1944) discussion of predicate logic, Cameron's (1939a) observations on overinclusive thinking, Goldstein's (1944) analysis of impaired concept formation, and Lorenz' (1961) description of the expressive functions of schizophrenic language.

Bleuler also introduced the following extremely important interrelated notions about schizophrenic disturbances: (a) these disturbances range over a wide continuum, from the hardly noticeable to the blatant and florid; (b) the diagnostic label schizophrenia may be applicable not only to grossly disturbed patients who require hospital care but also to many nonpsychotic persons who are making reasonable life adjustments outside an institution; and (c) social restitution may occur quite frequently in acute psychotic episodes, but underlying schizophrenic mechanisms that dispose a person to such episodes persist and are never fully restituted. Like Kraepelin, Bleuler believed that organic processes are the fundamental cause of schizophrenia; however, in disagreement with Kraepelin, he felt that personal, psychogenic factors shape the clinical picture of a schizophrenic psychosis.

The current significance of these Bleulerian concepts is extensive. Bleuler's position on the diagnosis of schizophrenia in nonpsychotic states, for example, is still a subject of discussion and concern. Polatin (1948) stresses that early recognition and diagnosis of schizophrenia in mild cases is necessary for the prompt institution of appropriate therapeutic measures, but, as Zilboorg (1941) points out, many clinicians persist in utilizing other euphemistic diagnoses until advanced states of the illness are reached. Edelston (1949) also suggests that the change from Kraepelin's term dementia praecox to Bleuler's schizophrenia has unfortunately been one of nomenclature only, with the basic idea of schizophrenia remaining Kraepelinian. It remains the case that associations of schizophrenia with negative prognosis and social stigma, however unjustified, often conduce to conservative diagnostic attitudes in clinical practice: "Some do not believe in schizophrenia; others assume that with this diagnosis all therapeutic . . . efforts are handicapped or even made illusory" (Kinross-Wright & Kahn, 1958).

In addition, by proposing an interaction between organic processes and psychogenic influences in schizophrenia, Bleuler looked beyond controversies between organically and psychologically oriented theorists and anticipated such sophisticated interaction hypotheses as those presented by Fessel (1964), Meehl (1962), and Rosenthal (1963), who put forward conceptions of schizophrenia embracing genetic, neurophysiological, and experiental variables. Meehl, for example, hypothesizes that schizophrenia derives from a neural integrative defect, labeled *schizotaxia,* that is transmitted through the genes. Persons with schizotaxia acquire a personality organization called *schizotypy* that is characterized by four core behavior traits: *cognitive slippage, anhedonia, interpersonal aversiveness,* and *ambivalence.* These schizotypic traits are universally learned by all schizotaxic persons, regardless of their social learning history. Whereas most schizotypes remain compensated, those who are confronted with certain causal environmental influences, the most important of which may be a schizophrenogenic mother, are likely to decompensate into clinical schizophrenia.

ADOLF MEYER (1866-1950) AND THE EXPERIENTIAL EMPHASIS

Adolf Meyer (1907, 1910), in contrast to both Kraepelin and Bleuler, emphasized the importance of psychological factors in the etiology of schizophrenia. He felt that schizophrenia was not a disease entity, but rather a maladaptation determined by life experiences, and he advanced the idea that longitudinal study of the schizophrenic individual would reveal progressive development of "faulty habits." According to Meyer, an unfortunate combination of inadequate coping behaviors and acute situational stress could cause an individual to suffer a "schizophrenic reaction," which he conceived as a habit disorganization that sometimes eventuates in pervasive personality disorganization and withdrawal.

In asserting that schizophrenia could be a "reaction" rather than an insidious, progressive illness, Meyer was agreeing with Bleuler that schizophrenia can occur in mild forms and have a favorable prognosis for social restitution. Meyer's description of how acute schizophrenic episodes can develop in response to environmental stress, together with his focus on the reactive nature of the condition and its psychological origins, significantly stimulated therapeutic efforts with schizophrenic patients. It should also be noted that Meyer's emphasis on habit formation is an indirect but clearly recognizable antecedent of learning theory approaches to psychopathology, and his views are currently mirrored in the efforts of Bateson and his co-workers (1956) to demonstrate that schizophrenia is a coping behavior learned in response to repeated exposure to inconsistent, or "double-bind," situations.

Meyer's insistence that schizophrenia should not be considered a disease entity continues to command considerable attention. Szasz (1961), for example, maintains that all emotional and behavioral disturbances independent of demonstrable organic lesions are "problems in living" and should not be considered disease. He outlines (1957a) a conception of schizophrenia "unburdened by medieval disease models" and based on hypotheses of deficient internal objects and impeded symbol formation. In a similar vein Laing and Esterson (1964, p. 4) contend that the diagnosed schizophrenic is not suffering from a disease but rather "is someone who has queer experiences and/or is acting in a queer way."

These elaborations of Meyer's point of view have evoked some ringing rebuttal. Ausubel (1961) challenges the tenability of Szasz' basic propositions. He concludes that Szasz' view, by treating personality disorders as problems of morality rather than illness, would "turn back the psychiatric clock twenty-five hundred years." Engel (1962), who, like Szasz, criticizes historical disease models for their institutional quality and failure to focus on the patient, argues that disease is a natural phenomenon, broadly applicable to maladjustments in living, that merits a definition sufficiently general to encompass a wide range of organic and functional impairments. Carefully reasoned statements by Guttmacher (1964), Herron (1963), and Reid (1962) also support the use of the term *disease* to describe mental abnormality.

Although the many substantive considerations adduced to buttress these opposing opinions are outside the focus of this discussion, it should be noted that some writers (e.g., Matarazzo, 1965, p. 437) regard the disease-maladaptation controversy in psychopathology as "partisan debates" that little benefit the suffering patient. Though not necessarily endorsing this latter position, the presentation in this book does not join the disease question. Schizophrenia is referred to as *disturbance* or *disorder*, and it is left to the individual reader whether he wishes to consider disturbed or disordered psychological functioning as disease.

CARL JUNG (1875-1961) INTRODUCES A PSYCHOSOMATIC HYPOTHESIS

Carl Jung's 1903 book, *The Psychology of Dementia Praecox*, is the original effort to apply psychoanalytic concepts to schizophrenia. Jung's primary interests were in symbolism and unconscious processes, and he concerned himself with the psychogenesis of schizophrenia for many years (e.g., Jung, 1939). However, an interesting and often overlooked aspect of his early book was his mention of a psychosomatic mechanism in schizophrenia. As noted by Arieti (1955, p. 28), Jung suggested here that an emotional disorder can produce metabolic changes that in turn induce physical damage to the brain and cause schizophrenic disorder.

Jung's early hypothesis is reflected in more recent contributions by

Leopold Bellak (1949, 1955), who delineates a multiple-factor, psycho-somatic approach to schizophrenia. Noting that many diverse causative agents may participate in producing a schizophrenic disorder, Bellak concludes that the unifying similarity among schizophrenic conditions is disturbed ego functioning (see Chapter 2). Relevant to Bellak's position is a recent paper by Krapf (1964) in which he argues convincingly that the psychopathologic unity of schizophrenia, as first conceptual-ized by Bleuler, is neither inconsistent nor incompatible with the apparent fact of its causal diversity.

SIGMUND FREUD (1856-1939) AND PSYCHOANALYTIC INTERPRETATION

It is difficult to summarize the contributions of Sigmund Freud to the study of schizophrenia, both because he did not often write directly about schizophrenia and because much of his work nevertheless has considerable relevance to the interpretation of schizophrenic phenomena. Among Freud's fundamental achievements was his recognition that psychological symptoms serve a defensive function for the personality. As early as 1894, in his paper "The Defense Neuro-psychoses," Freud described a patient in whom unacceptable thoughts were defended against by a hallucinatory psychosis: "One is therefore justified in saying that the ego has averted the unbearable idea by a flight into psychosis" (p. 74). Two years later, in "Further Remarks on the Defense Neuro-psychoses," Freud (1896) introduced the concept of projective defense to explain delusional illness, and in his famous case analysis of Schreber's memoirs (Freud, 1911a), he presented a detailed explanation of paranoid symptom formation as a defensive operation of the personality.

A second major contribution by Freud to the understanding of schizophrenia appears in *The Interpretation of Dreams*, first published in 1900. In Chapter VI of this book, entitled "The Dream-Work," Freud discusses the operation of condensations, displacements, and symbolic representations in determining the often illogical, unrealistic, and apparently meaningless manifest content of dreams. In Chapter VII, "The Psychology of the Dream Process," he adds a section on the differential characteristics of primary and secondary process thinking. These discussions are the first to provide a basis for understanding schizophrenic symptoms not only in terms of formal mechanisms but also in relation to underlying needs and attitudes having deep psychological significance to the individual.

Freud's third contribution is found in his discussion of the role of narcissism in schizophrenia in his 1914 paper, "On Narcissism: an Introduction." Attempting to account for schizophrenic disturbance in terms of his libido theory, Freud suggested in this paper that the withdrawal of cathexes from the external world and their direction onto the ego lead to a state of heightened narcissism characterized by megalomania and diminished interest in people and things. By noting that such a state can also be observed in children and in primitive peoples, Freud introduced as an explanatory concept in the study of schizophrenia the notion of regression to primitive modes of function.

The concept of regression is basic to many contemporary theories of schizophrenia. Arieti (1955, p. 384), for example, defines schizophrenia as consisting of "the adoption of archaic mental mechanisms, which belong to lower levels of integration," and he refers to the form assumed in schizophrenia as a "progressive teleologic regression" (1959a, p. 475). Heinz Werner (1948, Chapters 12 & 13) emphasizes regressive perceptual functioning in his analysis of schizophrenia. For Werner, increasing capacity to differentiate and integrate perceptual stimuli is a central element in cognitive ontogenesis, and psychotic disorder is characterized by primitive, childlike limitations of the ability to analyze and synthesize perceptual fields.

A fourth and somewhat later Freudian contribution initiated consideration of the role of the ego in schizophrenia. In *The Ego and the Id* Freud (1923) suggests that psychoses result from disturbances in the relationship between the ego and its environment, and in two 1924 papers, "Neurosis and Psychosis" and "The Loss of Reality in Neurosis and Psychosis," he speaks of the ego's tendency in schizophrenia to withdraw from reality and form substitute realities. Many current efforts to conceptualize schizophrenia and utilize psychological tests in its diagnosis derive from the proposition that disturbed ego functioning is a basic aspect of schizophrenia. Hartmann (1953), one of the chief architects of contemporary psychoanalytic ego psychology, presents an excellent review of the importance of the ego in schizophrenia, and Holt (1960) spells out some implications of the ego psychoanalytic approach for psychodiagnosis. Although some theorists (e.g., Pious, 1949; Wexler, 1952) emphasize the role of superego operations in schizophrenia, contemporary literature on schizophrenia remains predominantly ego-oriented and generally consistent with Wyatt's (1953) view that psychopathology can be described in terms of the cognitive events of the ego.

HARRY STACK SULLIVAN (1892-1949) AND THE INTERPERSONAL APPROACH

A final basic approach to schizophrenia to be mentioned in this brief overview is that of Harry Stack Sullivan, whose early papers on schizophrenia have recently been collected in the volume *Schizophrenia as a*

Human Process (1962). In his first paper on schizophrenia, published in 1924 with the title "Schizophrenia: Its Conservative and Malignant Features," Sullivan (1962, Chap. 1) took issue with Bleuler's emphasis on impaired association and argued that the primary disorder in schizophrenia is a regression to infantile levels of mental function. Sullivan's position in this first paper has much in common with regressive views of schizophrenia, but with his 1929 paper, "Research in Schizophrenia," Sullivan (1962, Chap. 6) began to introduce the basic concepts of his interpersonal approach to schizophrenia.

In his 1929 paper Sullivan contended that the earlier genetic, organic, and psychoanalytic interpretations of schizophrenia were inadequate and misleading, inasmuch as they did not view the schizophrenic as a total person. Although schizophrenia is characterized by a "regressive preponderance" of fantasy life and irrational activity, says Sullivan, the fundamental problem of the schizophrenic is "an underlying extraordinary preponderance of certain motivations normally accorded by occasional expression in life." These motivations, he says, have their origin in prenatal and childhood environmental factors that previous theorists have underemphasized. Sullivan concluded that the major focus of attention in efforts to understand and treat schizophrenic patients should be on interpersonal rather than intrapsychic factors. In later contributions he further described the derivation of schizophrenic symptomatology from motivational difficulties (Sullivan, 1953, Chapters 19–21) and the schizophrenogenic role of parent-child relationships that prevent a child from acquiring anxiety-eliminating response patterns and generate distorted perceptions of interpersonal relationships (Sullivan, 1946, Lectures III-V).

Sullivan's interpersonal emphasis has had a major influence on theoretical conceptions of schizophrenia and on the emergence of new treatment methods and research directions. Clearly in the Sullivanian tradition is Cameron's (1947, Chap. 15) focus on "desocialization" as the primary causative factor in schizophrenia. Cameron asserts that the schizophrenic is a person who lacks the requisite social skills for meeting the challenges of complex interpersonal relationships and who consequently withdraws into a "pseudocommunity" in which real-world role-taking is replaced by relationships to fantasied objects. Cameron's psychosocial approach implies a conception of schizophrenic pathogenesis quite different from Bleulerian notions. Whereas Bleuler views the schizophrenic's withdrawal and inability to maintain effective social communication as secondary to disordered thinking, Cameron is suggesting that autistic thought is only a secondary consequence of the withdrawal occasioned by inadequate object relations.

The conviction that interpersonal aversion is the core of schizophrenia to which other aspects of the disorder are secondary has major implications for its treatment. Sullivan's attention to interpersonal factors in his work with schizophrenic patients, as reflected in his own writings and his influence on such later contributors as Fromm-Reichman (1959) and Searles (1960), has been central to the development of techniques for intensive psychotherapy in schizophrenia. Sullivan's views also imply that efforts to understand and prevent schizophrenia should focus on aspects of parent-child relationships that conduce to maladaptive behavior patterns, and this focus has prompted such research into the role of the family in the etiology, onset, and course of schizophrenia as the studies of Lidz and Fleck (1960) and Wynne and Singer (1963a).

SCHIZOPHRENIA AS A DIAGNOSTIC LABEL

This chapter has briefly surveyed the history and current significance of several approaches to the study of schizophrenia. Although further elaboration of this introductory material is outside the focus of this book, the references cited are recommended as basic readings with which the clinician who diagnoses, treats, or studies schizophrenic patients should be familiar. One issue that does require further discussion at this point is whether the label schizophrenia should be used at all in clinical psychodiagnosis. Some psychologists consider it "a dubious procedure for psychologists to fit their personality descriptions to the straightjacket of vague and unreliable psychiatric diagnoses" (Sacks & Lewin, 1950, p. 481), and others disparage research uses of psychiatrically diagnosed criterion groups (G. F. King, 1954). Among psychiatrists there are some who denigrate the concept of schizophrenia itself. Menninger (1959, p. 517) believes that "no such disease as schizophrenia can be clearly defined or identified or proved to exist," and Szasz (1957b) considers schizophrenia a harmful and misleading term that, like "the ether," is used to fill a scientific void and will gradually disappear as more of the "real facts" are comprehended.

However, these opinions can be challenged on several grounds. First, it is an error to dismiss schizophrenia as a psychiatric term that is secondary or peripheral to the psychologist's clinical endeavors. Schizophrenia is a shorthand notation for a disorder of functioning having significant psychological concomitants, and terminologically it belongs not to psychiatry but to behavioral science. Furthermore, the sophisticated clinician does not assume the stance of fitting his test data directly to nosological categories. He may communicate with such metonyms as "schizophrenic indicators," but in actual practice he operates by identifying from test protocols certain personality characteristics from which he secondarily draws inferences about the likely presence or absence of various psychopathologic syndromes. As Schafer (1948, p. 63) has remarked, "A pattern of test results does not indicate schizophrenia; it indicates an identifying characteristic of schizophrenia."

Second, there is good reason to believe that the notion of diagnostic unreliability is largely a myth when applied to schizophrenia. Schmidt and Fonda (1956), comparing diagnostic judgments by pairs of psychiatrists on 426 state hospital patients, found agreement concerning a schizophrenic-nonschizophrenic distinction for 90% of the patients. Even when nonpsychotic patients were eliminated from the sample and the psychiatrists were asked to discriminate only between schizophrenic and nonschizophrenic psychotic patients, they achieved a 78% agreement rate. Sandifer, Pettus, and Quade (1964) report on the conference presentation of 91 patients to 10 diagnosticians, who achieved a 74% reliability figure for schizophrenic diagnoses and whose independent judgments were in agreement more frequently in regard to schizophrenia than concerning any other diagnostic category.

Not all studies have so successfully demonstrated the reliability of schizophrenic diagnosis, but none provides a rebuttal for impressive data recently reported by Babigian, Gardner, Miles, and Romano (1965). In a longitudinal study of 1215 patients in a case-register project, they found that 70% of patients diagnosed as schizophrenic received that same diagnosis on subsequent psychiatric contacts. These authors were able to conclude that, although the usefulness of diagnostic classification varies considerably from one major category to another, the category schizophrenia has considerable diagnostic consistency.

Third, we live in a real world. In the United States it is a world in which 50% of all persons being treated for mental and emotional disturbances in hospitals carry a diagnosis of some schizophenic disorder (Lemkau & Crocetti, 1958). Nearly 25% of the patients seen in ambulatory clinics throughout the United States are diagnosed schizophrenic (*Outpatient Psychiatric Clinics*, 1963, pp. 150–151). For these patients the diagnostic label and certain adjectives accompanying it—for example, chronic, paranoid, remitted—convey significant information concerning their treatment and prognosis. Hence the professional person who is to participate in mental health efforts, whether in hospital or clinic, must be prepared to deal with schizophrenia as a diagnostic label. As Hathaway (1959, p. 200) comments concerning psychologists' reluctance to use tests to support diagnostic classifications, ". . . as clinical psychology accepts more real clinical responsibility, this aloof position is untenable."

Finally, Szasz's views on the history of science do not appear satisfactory. Schizophrenia might better be compared to "gravity" than to "the ether," a term with little specificity. The advent of relativity theory has led to extensive revisions of the Newtonian concept of gravity and major reformulations of Newton's calculations. Yet the term gravity, because of its widespread applicability and the degree of information it communicates, remains in use, and new knowledge is utilized to expand and sharpen the concept of gravity rather than eliminate it. The future of schizophrenia seems comparable. The nature of its evolution, the volume of significant clinical and laboratory research conducted in its name by a host of disciplines, and its broad familiarity to behavioral scientists and laymen make it likely that further knowledge will be used not to replace but to clarify and expand the utility of the term.

► 2

THE EGO-DISTURBANCE MODEL
OF SCHIZOPHRENIA

BEHAVIORAL scientists typically emphasize those of the many extant definitions of schizophrenia that are most compatible with their particular theoretical orientations and lines of investigation. Psychodiagnosis relates closely to the following conception of schizophrenia outlined by Bellak (1958, pp. 4, 52):

> The somewhat variable symptoms generally associated with this diagnostic label must be understood as the final common path of a number of conditions which may lead to and manifest themselves in a severe disturbance of the ego . . . the concept of the schizophrenias as disorders of many etiologies but with a shared final common path of ego disturbance leads quite logically to the concept that the diagnosis of schizophrenia at present can best be made on the basis of the degree of ego disturbance in a given patient.

The major premise of this book is that the diagnosis of schizophrenia is essentially a phenomenological diagnosis based on observable impairments of ego functions.

For assessment purposes it is useful to divide the functions of the ego into the following six: thought processes, relation to reality, object relations, defensive operations, autonomous functions, and synthetic functions. This categorization of ego functions, as summarized below, is derived largely from the formulations of David Beres (1956), with certain changes in content and emphasis made to increase the relevance of the ego-disturbance model to psychodiagnosis. Like all models, the following model comprises a series of constructs arbitrarily created for purposes of conceptualization. Its value lies solely in its utility for organizing and communicating data, and it does not imply any reification of ego functions into immutable or mutually exclusive phenomena.

THOUGHT PROCESSES

The thought processes consist primarily of *cognitive focusing, reasoning,* and *concept formation.* These processes in the psychologically healthy person are marked by the capacities (a) to scan information selectively, attending to essential and ignoring irrelevant stimuli, (b) to draw logical inferences about the relationships between objects and events, and (c) to interpret experience at appropriate levels of abstraction. These capacities correspond to the psychoanalytic conception of secondary process thinking, and their impairment, as described by Holt (1956), is manifest in such formal characteristics of primary process thinking as loose and nonsensical associative links and autistic logic. The nature of disturbed thinking and its psychodiagnostic assessment are the subjects of Chapters 4, 5, and 6.

RELATION TO REALITY

Relating to reality is basically a perceptual process with two major components, the capacity to test reality and the capacity to maintain an adequate sense of reality. *Reality testing* consists of accurate perception of the environment, and its impairment is identified by autistic perceptions, poor judgment, and inability to recognize conventional modes of response. *Reality sense* is based on a person's perception of his body, and its disturbance is reflected in indefinite ego boundaries and distorted body imagery, as discussed by Schilder (1935), Federn (1952), and Fisher and Cleveland (1958). The psychopathology and assessment of impaired relation to reality are detailed in Chapters 7 and 8.

OBJECT RELATIONS

The psychologically healthy individual is able to form and maintain satisfactory relationships with people. The person who lacks sufficient social skill to engage comfortably in interpersonal relations is likely to withdraw from the human environment, and declining contacts with people, increasingly restricted social life, seclusion, reticence, and waning interest in the outside world have been identified as significant indicators of early schizophrenia (Weiner, 1958). Chapter 9 presents test indices of deficient social skill and interpersonal aversion.

DEFENSIVE OPERATIONS

The defensive operations of the ego provide the healthy individual with control and stability in his life adjustment. The controlling aspects of ego defense relate to the operation of repression, which normally prevents primitive, anxiety-provoking thoughts and wishes from reaching consciousness. Impairment of repressive barriers is identified by the conscious awareness of sexual and aggressive fantasies and impulses that violate personal or social standards. The stabilizing aspects of defensive operations lie in the formation and maintenance of a characterological defensive style that promotes consistent and organized patterns of dealing with people, affects, and life situations. Unstable defensive patterns are manifest in poorly integrated affective expression and inconsistent response style. The evaluation of disturbed defensive operations is the subject of Chapter 10.

AUTONOMOUS FUNCTIONS

The autonomous functions of the ego, usually defined as those that, although influenced by intrapsychic and interpersonal conflict, develop or originate independently of such conflict (Hartmann, 1939), include intelligence, perception, intention, thinking, language, memory, productivity, motor development, and the learning capacity inherent in them. Schizophrenia has typically been considered a disorder in which these basic capacities are not impaired (Bleuler refers to them as "the intact simple functions"), and differential diagnosis from organic brain syndromes usually hinges on the schizophrenic's retention of these elemental skills. However, there is accumulating research evidence that certain impairments of intellectual ability, vocabulary skill, learning capacity, and psychomotor reactivity are associated with schizophrenia independently of motivational and institutional variables. These findings and their relevance to psychodiagnosis in schizophrenia are considered in Chapter 11.

SYNTHETIC FUNCTIONS

The synthetic functions of the ego largely overlap and summarize the five previously discussed functions. Synthetic operations constitute an individual's capacity to organize and integrate his cognitive skills, his ability to relate to reality, his capacity for object relatedness, and his defensive resources in the service of a healthy and rewarding life. The unique factor introduced by the synthetic function is the organizing capacity itself, and schizophrenia is in part characterized by an inability to synthesize experience and integrate functioning effectively. Chapter 12 deals with the assessment of synthesizing capacity and with some related global indices of ego functioning.

The phenomenology of schizophrenia can, with few exceptions, be described in terms of these six ego functions. Not every schizophrenic manifests disturbance of all of them, and, as they are overlapping rather than discrete functions, more than one may be involved in certain aspects of schizophrenic behavior. As elaborated in Part Two, however, each of the six functions contributes something unique and essential to the evaluation of possible schizophrenia.

⮞ 3

PSYCHODIAGNOSTIC TECHNIQUES
IN SCHIZOPHRENIA:
A BRIEF HISTORY

ALTHOUGH this book is concept- rather than test-oriented, certain tests have been selected for discussion with an eye to the needs of the practicing clinician. If, after a number of schizophrenic characteristics had been identified, the literature were combed for tests and scales that best assess each of them, the result would be a formidable and clinically impracticable conglomeration of measures. Shakow (1963), for example, lists 12 areas of psychological deficit in schizophrenia, his assessment of which involves more than a dozen complex techniques. It seems necessary, therefore, to sacrifice some ideal considerations to utility, and this presentation focuses on psychodiagnostic indicators of schizophrenia that occur within the context of a representative clinical battery.

Recent publications by Murstein (1963, pp. 64–68) and Sundberg (1961) suggest as a representative clinical battery the Rorschach, the Draw-a-Person (DAP), and the Weschler Adult Intelligence Scale (WAIS). From Murstein's review of categorizations of diagnostic tests, it is apparent that two major distinctions recognized by psychologists contrast "objective" with "projective" (Rosenzweig, 1942) and "surface" with "depth" measures (Stone & Dellis, 1960). Data concerning the frequency with which various tests of these types are used are summarized by Sundberg, who surveyed testing practices in 181 agencies in the United States.

According to Sundberg's report, the two psychological tests used most frequently in clinical services are the Rorschach and DAP. The

19

Bender-Gestalt and Thematic Apperception Test rank third and fourth, respectively, and the fifth most widely used test is the WAIS. A battery of the Rorschach, DAP, and WAIS thus includes the two most frequently used tests, both of which are depth-projective measures, and the most frequently used surface-objective test.[1] This three-test battery is the focus of subsequent discussion, and the history of each test's application to the diagnosis of schizophrenia is briefly reviewed in the following pages.

RORSCHACH'S TEST

The Rorschach test was the creation of the Swiss psychiatrist, Hermann Rorschach, and the ten inkblots currently in use are essentially the same ten he selected from the many with which he experimented between 1911, the year of his original experiments, and 1922, the year of his untimely death at age 37.[2] In his major publication, the *Psychodiagnostics*, published in 1921, Rorschach emphasized the differential diagnostic features of the test, and 188 of the 405 patients he studied in preparing his monograph were schizophrenic. Hence the application of the Rorschach to the diagnosis of schizophrenia dates from the construction and first uses of the test.

For several years following Rorschach's death, however, little attention was paid to the Rorschach diagnosis of schizophrenia. In the meantime, Rorschach testing was introduced to the English-speaking countries. David Levy learned of the test in Europe from Oberholzer, Rorschach's co-worker, and on his return to the United States encouraged Samuel Beck to study the technique. Beck (1930a) described the Rorschach method to the convention of the American Orthopsychiatric Association and in the same year published his first research with the test, a study of feeble-minded children at the New York City Children's School on Randall's Island (Beck, 1930b). Beck's papers were the first on the Rorschach to apear in American journals. The Rorschach was introduced in England in a series of papers, the earliest

[1] It should be noted that objective and projective are convenient, approximate labels for tests, and not absolute or mutually exclusive definitions of them. For example, Mayman, Schafer, and Rapaport (1951) discuss the projective application of intelligence tests, and some aspects of Rorschach response, as seeing Card V as a butterfly or identifying a red area as a red object, represent fairly objective apperception.

[2] Experimental use of inkblot tests prior to Rorschach's work is reviewed by Tulchin (1940).

being a bibliographic article, by Vernon (1933, 1935) and Guirdham (1935). Until the late 1930's, however, the bulk of the work on the test appeared in German-language publications. An excellent 1935 review by Marguerite Hertz surveys the early European papers on problems of Rorschach administration, scoring, reliability, and validity.

Interest in diagnosing schizophrenia with the Rorschach was rekindled in 1934 by Skalweit, who attempted to demonstrate progressive personality deterioration in schizophrenic patients by means of repeated Rorschach testings over a period of years. In 1935 papers by Dimmick and Hackfield introduced Rorschach diagnosis of schizophrenia to the American literature, and the majority of work in this area has since appeared in American journals.

The year 1938 was marked by three major contributions which greatly stimulated clinical use of the Rorschach: a monograph by Beck, *Personality Structure in Schizophrenia,* which grew out of a multidisciplinary investigation of schizophrenia at the Boston Psychopathic Hospital; a study by Rickers-Ovsiankina, "The Rorschach Test as Applied to Normal and Schizophrenic Subjects"; and an article by Benjamin and Ebaugh affirming the diagnostic validity of the Rorschach in schizophrenia. Salient aspects of these contributions are presented in subsequent chapters. For a detailed review of this early work the reader is referred to Klopfer and Kelley's 1942 text, *The Rorschach Technique,* and to a 1943 paper by Beck.

THE DRAW-A-PERSON TEST (DAP)

Interest in artistic productions and expressive movements as personality indicators has a long history, [3] and the formal clinical application of human figure drawings dates at least from Florence Goodenough's introduction of the Draw-a-Man Test in 1926. Goodenough developed this test primarily to measure intelligence in children, and she indicates that attempts to relate children's drawings to their mentality had their beginnings in England as early as 1885. One year before the appearance of Goodenough's book, Lewis (1925) noted that it had long been recognized that graphic art, like dream material, reflects unconscious processes, and he suggested the use of formal figure drawings in the clinical setting to aid therapists in identifying the conflicts and attitudes of their patients.

[3] An excellent bibliography covering the history of psychological study of artistic productions and expressive movements is provided by Levy (1950).

During the 25 years following these two contributions, however, interest in the clinical use of figure drawings was focused primarily on the evaluation of intelligence and personality attributes in children, and little effort was made to apply them either to adults or to clinical psychodiagnosis. Some early interest in mounting such an effort developed from a series of review articles prepared by Anastasi and Foley in the late 1930's and early 1940's. In these papers Anastasi and Foley addressed themselves to theoretical relationships between art and insanity, to case studies and biographies of artists who had been institutionalized for mental illness, and in a 1941 paper to the nature of spontaneous art productions in abnormal persons. Anastasi and Foley (1944) subsequently undertook an experimental comparison of the drawings of normal and abnormal persons, as did Chase in a 1941 study.

The first major stimulus to the clinical use of human figure drawings with adults was Karen Machover's 1949 book, in which she introduced the DAP in its current form and outlined a framework for its interpretation. Although Machover did not attempt an integrated presentation of DAP indicators of schizophrenia, her material encouraged other clinicians to begin exploring the potential value of the test for diagnosing schizophrenia. Albee and Hamlin (1949, 1950) presented early evidence that global assessments of adjustment based on the DAP had sufficient validity to warrant further study of the technique as a psychodiagnostic tool, and Holzberg and Wexler (1950a) reported the initial attempt to derive specific DAP indicators of schizophrenia. Reviews by Swenson (1957) and Jones and Thomas (1961) summarize the first several years' research with the DAP.

THE WECHSLER ADULT INTELLIGENCE SCALE (WAIS)

The WAIS is the 1955 standardization of the Wechsler-Bellevue (W-B) test introduced by David Wechsler in 1939 to provide a valid and reliable measure of global intellectual capacity in adults. The demands of World War II soon extended the use of the W-B beyond Wechsler's original purpose, however, and the 1944 edition of the W-B manual finds him stating his aim to broaden the test's clinical applicability, particularly to meet the needs of the military, and devoting considerable attention to differential diagnosis.

Nevertheless, relatively little investigative work on the relationship between W-B performance and schizophrenia was reported before 1945. Five papers of historical interest are an article by Gilliland

(1940), which was the first to identify W-B scatter as a pathologic indicator, two contributions by Rabin (1941, 1942), which were the earliest to examine specific W-B patterns in schizophrenia, and reports by Gilliland, Wellman, and Goldman (1943) of scatter patterns in various psychoses and by Reichard and Schafer (1943) concerning the technique of profile and scatter interpretations.

The major impetus to assessing schizophrenia with the W-B was the first volume of Rapaport, Gill, and Schafer's *Diagnostic Psychological Testing*, which appeared in 1945. This book includes a detailed rationale for the various W-B subtests and profile analyses for diverse groups of schizophrenic, neurotic, and normal subjects. Many details of the Rapaport et al. contribution are presented in subsequent chapters. The early work with the W-B is summarized in a 1945 review by Rabin, who with his co-workers has published subsequent reviews of research with the W-B and WAIS in 1951, 1956, and 1962, the latter two with Guertin as senior author.

PART TWO

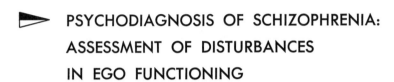 PSYCHODIAGNOSIS OF SCHIZOPHRENIA:
ASSESSMENT OF DISTURBANCES
IN EGO FUNCTIONING

▶ 4

THOUGHT PROCESSES:
I. COGNITIVE FOCUSING

DISTURBED thinking is generally considered the distinctive and most prominent feature of schizophrenic disorder. Bleuler (1911), though he included ambivalence, autism, and affective disorder among the fundamental symptoms of schizophrenia, designated thought disorder, defined as a disruption in the continuity of associations, as the primary identifying characteristic of schizophrenia. Meehl (1962) similarly points out that although ambivalence, anhedonia, and interpersonal aversiveness are important aspects of schizophrenia, cognitive slippage is usually the most heavily weighted factor in clinical judgments. This and the following two chapters are concerned with the nature of disturbed thinking and encompass the bulk of psychodiagnostic indicators most distinctively associated with schizophrenic disturbance.

Thinking entails the scanning of stimuli impinging on the perceptual apparatus, reasoning about the relationships between these stimuli, and the formation of concepts that integrate these relationships. Correspondingly, thought processes in the normal individual are characterized by the following three capacities: (a) the capacity to scan information selectively, establishing and maintaining focus on that which is relevant and preventing the intrusion of irrelevant material; (b) the capacity to reason logically about the relationships between objects and events; and (c) the capacity to interpret experience at appropriate levels of abstraction. These three chapters on thought processes are devoted, respectively, to these capacities.

THE ROLE OF IMPAIRED COGNITIVE FOCUSING
IN SCHIZOPHRENIC DISTURBANCE

This chapter considers the relationship of impaired cognitive focusing to schizophrenic disturbance. Bleuler (1911, p. 356) touched on the notion of cognitive focusing by suggesting that loose associative links result when "the goal of a thought is not kept constantly in mind." The role of impaired cognitive focusing in schizophrenia was first clearly stated by Cameron (1939a,b), however, who observed in his early experiments with schizophrenic subjects their propensity for *overinclusion,* which he defined as the "inability to select and restrict and to eliminate the less closely related elements from the conceptual structure."

The performance of schizophrenic subjects on various cognitive, perceptual, and motor tasks has led numerous other writers to call attention to the importance of impaired cognitive focusing in schizophrenic behavior. Shakow (1950), for example, concludes from many years' research that an especially significant aspect of schizophrenic disorganization is the inability to maintain a *major set.* Shakow (1962) states that the major set always stands in contrast to many possible intruding minor sets and that the schizophrenic's difficulty "lies in not being able to keep to the major set and being drawn to the adoption of minor ones."

Payne, Mattusek, and George (1959), adducing strong experimental support for Cameron's theory of overinclusion, formulate schizophrenic cognition in terms of a *filter mechanism.* Like Shakow's major set, Payne et al.'s filter mechanism normally facilitates purposeful behavior by inhibiting irrelevant stimuli and promoting efficient information processing. In schizophrenia, however, the filter mechanism is faulty and fails to prevent extraneous stimuli from intruding on and disrupting cognitive focusing.

Weckowicz and Blewett (1959) hypothesize from studies of schizophrenic thinking that cognitive processes are more global, less selective, and less analytical in schizophrenic than in normal persons because the former are unable to limit appropriately the breadth of their attention. *Overbroad attention,* like overinclusion, poor set maintenance, and faulty information filtering, is defined primarily by the inability to shut off information that is irrelevant to the task at hand. Similarly invoking the concept of attention, Rashkis and Singer (1959) and Singer (1960) infer from available data that schizophrenia is a psychological disorganization characterized chiefly by inability to pay attention to and coordinate stimuli from various internal and external systems.

These analyses of the role of impaired cognitive focusing in schizophrenia constitute what has been called the *interference* theory of schizophrenic psychological deficit. As recently stated by Buss and Lang (1965, p. 20), the interference theory runs as follows:

> This theory assumes that when a schizophrenic is faced with a task, he cannot attend properly or in a sustained fashion, maintain a set, or change the set quickly when necessary. His ongoing response tendencies suffer interference from irrelevant, external cues and from "internal" stimuli which consist of deviant thoughts and associations. These irrelevant, distracting, mediated stimuli prevent him from maintaining a clear focus on the task at hand, and the result is psychological deficit.

On the basis of an exhaustive survey of laboratory studies of psychological deficit in schizophrenia, Lang and Buss (1965, p. 97) conclude that interference theory is the only extant theory sufficiently comprehensive to account for known data. The relationship of interference theory to other explanations of schizophrenic performance is considered for a variety of cognitive deficits in portions of Chapters 6, 9, and 11. Theoretical issues aside, however, experimental findings clearly demonstrate that schizophrenic persons have difficulty in focusing on relevant and excluding irrelevant stimuli, in shifting set as the occasion demands, in inhibiting the expression of deviant and idiosyncratic associations, in pacing themselves, and in sustaining efficient performance. Each of these five deficits in cognitive focusing has counterparts in the psychodiagnostic test battery, and the following sections relate each to psychodiagnostic indices that in turn identify schizophrenic ego impairment. Of the five deficits, the first two pertain primarily to *failure to establish* and the latter three to *failure to maintain* appropriate cognitive focus, and the following discussion is organized accordingly.

FAILURE TO ESTABLISH FOCUS

Extensive research work, much of it reviewed by Lang and Buss (1965), indicates that schizophrenic persons have difficulty selecting for their attention the most relevant aspects of a stimulus field and adjusting their attention to accord with changes in the situation to which they are responding. Effectively demonstrating these phenomena are studies by McGhie and Chapman (1961) and Chapman and McGhie (1962), in which schizophrenic subjects proved particularly distracted by various sensory inputs irrelevant to tasks on which they were working; by Weckowicz (1960), in which schizophrenic subjects were relatively unable to differentiate figure from ground sufficiently to identify embedded figures; and by Draguns (1963) and Lang and Luoto (1962), in which on both picture interpretation and paired-associate learning tasks schizophrenic subjects continued to respond in terms of previously presented stimuli to the detriment of their performance on subsequent portions of the tasks.

Four psychodiagnostic indices that reflect such failures to establish focus on appropriate stimuli are *unusual location choice* and *figure-ground blurring* on the Rorschach, *Picture Completion deficiency* on the WAIS, and *perseveration* on either Rorschach or WAIS.

UNUSUAL LOCATION CHOICE

Location choice in the Rorschach test involves selective focusing of attention on certain configurational elements of the stimulus field, and impaired ability to identify the essential elements of a situation is likely to result in location choices that deviate from normal expectancy. Normal expectancy is defined largely by the basic principles of location choice scoring outlined by Beck et al. (1961, pp. 12–31). Beck begins by pointing out that the portions of the inkblots selected by subjects for their responses fall into the two broad categories of *wholes* and *parts*. Of the whole (W) responses, Beck continues, some are simple and common and others are difficult and less common. Of the part responses, some are based on common details (D) and others on rare details (Dd), with common and rare details distinguished by their relative frequency of occurrence in records of normal subjects.

Inherent in these definitions is the expectation that the normal subject will give the largest percentage of his responses to D's, all of which are common, a lesser proportion to W's, only some of which are common, and the smallest percentage to Dd's, all of which are rare. Impaired ability to establish focus on essential stimuli is therefore likely to be reflected in a relatively low D% and a corresponding elevation of W% and/or Dd%.

A number of studies support this conclusion. Beck (1938) found a significantly [1] greater frequency of Dd responses in the records of 81

---

[1] Specific significance levels are generally not indicated for the findings presented in this book, and those labeled *significant* have reported probabilities of .05 or less. This method of presentation touches on the relative merits of accepting or rejecting the null hypothesis according to preset confidence limits (Lindquist, 1953, p. 49) versus reporting the actual probability value at which the null hypothesis may be rejected (Siegel, 1956, p. 8), but further consideration of this issue is outside the focus of this book.

schizophrenic than of 64 control subjects, and, consistent with the notions of cognitive focusing presented here, he concluded from his data that schizophrenics are often sensitive to the usually overlooked details of daily life and relatively unresponsive to obvious stimuli commonly attended to by normal persons. Rickers-Ovsiankina (1938) came to a similar conclusion on the basis of her early work, and she added that a marked *W-Dd* sequence and a focus on inconspicuous *Dd* are particularly likely to be associated with schizophrenia.

More recent studies by Friedman (1953) and Knopf (1956), examining *W*, *D*, and *Dd* frequency expressed as percentages of total response (*R*), have confirmed the relative elevation of *W* and *Dd* locations among schizophrenic subjects. Friedman, comparing 30 schizophrenic with 30 normal control subjects, found median *W%*'s of 46 and 25 in the two groups, respectively, and median *D%*'s of 45 and 67. For both *W%* and *D%* the differences were significant. In an analysis of *Dd%*'s Knopf obtained significantly different median values of 15.0% for 100 schizophrenics and 6.5% for a mixed group of 100 nonschizophrenic psychiatric patients.

Normative Data for Location Choice. These group differences in location choice do not, however, provide adequate basis for clinical interpretation. In order to judge the possible pathologic significance of a test variable and to establish criteria for its application in the individual case, it is requisite to consult normative data. The Rorschach performance of normal persons has been examined in several studies, the results of which are utilized throughout this book in the derivation of clinical guidelines. Normative studies contributing information about location choice include the following: Beck, Rabin, Thiesen, Molish, and Thetford (1950), 157 men and women; Brockway, Gleser, and Ulett (1954), 126 men; Cass and McReynolds (1951), 104 men; Gardner (1936), 100 men and women; and Phillips and Smith (1953), 250 men.

These normative studies indicate that the average Rorschach record has 20–30 responses with a *W%* ranging from 20–45, a *D%* from 45–60, and a *Dd%* from 5–15. Additional analyses by Fiske and Baughman (1953) of the Beck et al. data and by Phillips and Smith (1953, pp. 11–12) reveal the following relationships between total *R* and location choice percentages: as *R* increases above expectancy, both *D%* and *Dd%* normally increase, whereas *W%* remains constant or decreases; with decreasing *R*, *W%* and *D%* increase slightly and *Dd%* tends to drop out. Finally, and particularly important for the brief record, Phillips and Smith (1953, p. 196) report that *W*'s occurring as the sole mode of response are common on Cards I and V but very rare on II, III, VIII, IX, and X; D's as the sole location choice occur fairly frequently on the five chromatic cards but seldom on I and V.

These data suggest the following conclusions regarding unusual location choice: $D\%$ below 45 with $W\%$ above 45 and/or $Dd\%$ above 15 in a record of average length begins to suggest impaired cognitive focusing; low $D\%$ is particularly deviant in a long record; high $Dd\%$ is of especial diagnostic significance in a brief record; and both Dd as the sole mode of approach to a card and a D orientation on Cards I and V, with W's on the chromatic cards, suggest disturbance, even when over-all location choice percentages are within normal expectancy.

General Considerations in the Interpretation of Location Choice. Although the unusual location-choice patterns that are described above increase the likelihood of schizophrenia, specific clinical interpretation of location choice involves some general psychodiagnostic considerations applicable to all test indicators. First, it must be recognized that, although the presence of unusual location choice patterns suggests schizophrenia, their absence does not rule out the diagnosis. There are ego disturbances other than thought disorder, thought processes other than cognitive focusing, and indices of impaired cognitive focusing other than unusual location choice. Hence not every schizophrenic manifests thought disorder, not every schizophrenic with thought disorder displays impaired cognitive focusing, and not every schizophrenic whose cognitive focusing is impaired evinces unusual location choice.

These facts imply that the diagnostic validity of deviant location choice patterns, and of other schizophrenic indicators as well, requires not that most schizophrenic subjects manifest them but rather that relatively few nonschizophrenic persons do. In other words, a number of indicators, each of which characterizes some meaningful proportion of schizophrenic but very few nonschizophrenic subjects, can be combined to yield a thoroughly satisfactory test battery. Research and clinical emphases should accordingly be vested in those schizophrenic indicators that yield few false positives, and a relatively small yield of true positives should not be considered automatically to vitiate the utility of a diagnostic index.[2]

Second, specific clinical interpretation of many psychodiagnostic indicators hinges on a number of scoring and diagnostic refinements elaborated in later chapters. With regard to location choice, it is clear that a poorly articulated, amorphous, or inaccurately perceived W response has different implications from a well-integrated, realistic W

---

[2] These and other issues germane to the validity and utility of psychodiagnostic tests are considered more fully in Chapter 19.

percept (Friedman, 1953; see Chaps. 8 & 12). It has also been demonstrated that acute may differ from chronic (Rapaport, Gill, & Schafer,
1946; see Chap. 13) and paranoid from nonparanoid schizophrenics
(Siegel, 1953; see Chap. 14) in their location choices. Hence the relationship between location choice percentages and cognitive focusing
exhausts neither the diagnostic significance of location choice scores
nor the manner in which location choice relates to other ego functions
and to subcategories of schizophrenic disturbance.

FIGURE-GROUND BLURRING

As mentioned on page 28, Weckowicz and Blewett (1959) suggest
that the schizophrenic's in ability to shut off information irrelevant to
the task at hand leads him to perceive in a more global and less selective manner than the normal person. Because the schizophrenic is at
the mercy of all environmental stimulation, they continue, and is consequently unable to concentrate on one part of the visual field to the
exclusion of others, he will have difficulty discriminating figure from
ground in a perceptual task. Weckowicz (1960) confirmed this hypothesis in an experiment in which he presented an embedded-figures
task to schizophrenic, normal, and nonpsyschiatric patient groups. The
99 schizophrenics in his study performed significantly less well in discriminating the embedded figures than his 62 normal and patient
controls.

Blurring of figure and ground is reflected in the psychodiagnostic
battery by Rorschach WS responses, which represent failure to differentiate space from the gray or colored aspects of the blots. WS responses are illustrated by Phillips and Smith (1953, p. 16) with "black
and white butterfly" and "white smoke and black smoke." As Phillips
and Smith point out, the WS must be distinguished from responses in
which space is responded to as a gap ("a butterfly with holes in its
wings"), as a color differentiated from the gray or colored details
("snow"), or as an independent contour ("a top"). These three types
of white-space usage (S) do not constitute a blurring of figure-ground
differentiation, and no particular frequency of total S has been associated with schizophrenia (Fonda, 1960). It is specifically the failure
to discriminate any figure from ground, not merely figure-ground reversal, that indicates impaired cognitive focusing.

However, although indices of impaired cognitive focusing are primarily a schizophrenic phenomenon, figure-ground blurring is not
unique to schizophrenia. Organic brain syndromes are marked by
many perceptual difficulties, and work summarized by Teuber (1950,
p. 35) has demonstrated the relative inability of brain-damaged subjects to differentiate figure from ground. Hence, when other data make

it possible to rule out organicity, the WS response is particularly likely to identify a schizophrenic impairment of cognitive focusing. The WS response is extremely rare in all adult groups, and it represents so great an impairment of cognitive focusing that in the absence of brain damage even a single occurrence of such a percept suggests schizophrenic thought disorder.

PICTURE COMPLETION DEFICIENCY

The Picture Completion (PC) subtest of the WAIS measures the ability to differentiate essential from nonessential elements of a situation. According to Wechsler (1958, p. 175), schizophrenic subjects tend to perform poorly on this test because they are "oblivious to details." Deficient PC performance is defined by a discrepancy between PC attainment and general intellectual capacity as indicated by the WAIS Vocabulary score. [3] Rogers (1951), comparing 100 neurotic with 83 schizophrenic subjects of comparable intelligence, found almost three-quarters of the schizophrenics but fewer than half of the neurotics to display such discrepancies.

However, available statistical data recommend a more stringent quantitative criterion for Picture Completion deficiency than merely a PC score falling below Vocabulary. A table by Wechsler (1958, p. 164) indicates that a difference between PC and Vocabulary of at least two scale scores is necessary for significance at the 15% level. McNemar (1957) states that WAIS scale score differences must be at least 2.5 times greater than the standard error of difference scores between the scales to guarantee nonchance occurrence. According to McNemar's tables, a PC-Vocabulary difference of slightly more than three points is required for significance.

These data suggest as one criterion for Picture Completion deficiency a PC score falling more than three points below Vocabulary. In a comparison approximating this criterion Rapaport et al. (1945, p. 243) found that more than half of a sample of acute and chronic schizophrenic subjects had PC-Vocabulary discrepancies of three or more points, whereas 76% of a normal control group had discrepancies of two points or fewer. The magnitude of their PC-Vocabulary discrepancies significantly differentiated these schizophrenic from the control subjects. [4]

---

[3] Issues concerning the adequacy of vocabulary skill as an index of intellectual capacity against which impairment of other abilities can be measured are discussed in Chapter 11.

[4] The Rapaport et al. (1945, 1946) studies include extensive WAIS and Rorschach comparisons among diagnostic groups and are cited at many points in this book.

A Picture Completion deficiency suggesting impaired cognitive focusing may be indicated by the quality as well as the number of PC errors made by a subject. Specifically, the more an incorrect PC response deviates from types of error commonly made on this subtest, the greater the likelihood of disordered thinking. The qualitative evaluation of PC errors is facilitated by Table 1, which is based in part on a report by Wolfson and Weltman (1960) of PC errors made by 110 normal subjects and 110 hospitalized psychiatric patients, 82 of whom were schizophrenic. The table lists the errors found by Wolfson and Weltman to occur commonly in both normal and patient groups and also includes illustrative unusual errors this author has drawn from records of schizophrenic patients. Any accumulation of such unusual responses reflects impaired capacity to identify the essential elements of a situation and suggests schizophrenia.

PERSEVERATION

Adaptive cognitive focusing requires the capacity to shift focus as the stimulus characteristics of a situation change. When an individual is unable to alter his focus, he continues to respond in terms of previously important stimuli that are no longer relevant to the situation at hand. This inappropriate persistence and repetition of ideas is usually referred to as perseveration and was described by Bleuler (1911, p. 27) as a common phenomenon in schizophrenia. Perseveration, unlike the three preceding indices of impaired cognitive focusing, is a general phenomenon that can be defined independently of the psychodiagnostic test battery. Within the test framework, however, perseveration has

---

It must therefore be acknowledged that they have been criticized for such methodological flaws as small subsample size and failure to control adequately for age, sex, and socioeconomic status. Although the former difficulty can be circumvented by lumping certain diagnostic subgroupings into broader categories, the control problem defies ready resolution. As summarized by Rabin and Guertin (1951), some writers seize on the limited controls of the Rapaport et al. work as grounds for mistrusting its significant results and decrying its rationale. However, it seems equally reasonable to conclude with some other writers (e.g., Wechsler, 1958, pp. 162–163) that heterogeneity of experimental groups *obscures* significant differences among them and that failure to include adequate controls in psychodiagnostic research leads if anything to inaccurate negative, not misleading positive, results. From the latter point of view, better controls in the Rapaport et al. study would be expected to have yielded even clearer diagnostic differentiations than did emerge. These and similar considerations pertain to much of the research literature surveyed in this book and are noted at several points. Methodological matters are reserved primarily to Chapter 19, however, which deals in part with problems of validational research in psychodiagnosis.

clear manifestations in Rorschach and WAIS behavior that facilitate the identification of thought disorder.

TABLE 1

COMMON AND SCHIZOPHRENIC ERRORS ON THE WAIS PICTURE COMPLETION TEST

Item	Errors common to normal and patient groups [1]	Illustrative errors of schizophrenic patients [2]
1. Knob	None	Key
2. Tail	Food	Udders, tongue, sex organs, trough, mud
3. Nose	Ear	Rest of her body
4. Handles	Wheels	Exhaust, hubcaps, steering wheel, driver
5. Diamond	None	Other 48 cards
6. Water	Person to hold	Spout
7. Nose Piece	Part of nose	Eyes, lapels, a smile, part in hair
8. Peg	Bow, strings	Violinist, sounding holes
9. Oar Lock	Person	Motor, life jackets, anchor
10. Base Thread	Socket	Piece of tungsten, lamp, glare from bulb
11. Stars	Pole, stripes	Red on flag, a stand
12. Dog Tracks	Foot, boots, shoes	Gun, leash
13. Florida	States, names	Canada, Alaska, Panama
14. Stacks	Sails, deck, top	Water, paddles, the captain, people
15. Leg	Tail, eyes, head	Scales, person to eat it
16. Arm Image	Arm, part of chair or table	Woman's legs, lamp
17. Finger	Pockets, ear	Coat, zipper, cap, cuffs on pants
18. Shadow	Path, hand, ground, grass	Woman
19. Stirrup	Person, saddle horn	Ear, penis, other eye
20. Snow	Chimney, fence	Trail, people, lightning rod, path
21. Eyebrow	Ear, shoulder	Necklace, other eye, ribbon in hair

[1] From Wolfson and Weltman (1960), based on 110 patients and 110 normal subjects.
[2] From case files.

Klopfer and Spiegelman (1956, pp. 285–287), discussing Rorschach diagnosis, delineate two types of perseveration that appear in test responses, "magic wand" and "fixed concept." In "magic wand" perseveration there is no correspondence between the blots and the percepts repetitively projected onto them. This type of perseveration is common in very young children but occurs in adults only in the context of advanced mental deterioration. In "fixed concept" perseveration a response that accurately corresponds to a blot when first given is repeated on subsequent blots without regard for actual blot qualities. It is this second type of perseveration that is likely to occur in the records of schizophrenics who are unable to shift their focus of attention adaptively.

Perseveration has been associated with organic brain disease as well as schizophrenia (Evans & Marmorston, 1964; Piotrowski, 1937) however, and recourse to other test data may be necessary to determine whether Rorschach perseveration is due to a schizophrenic or organic impairment of flexibility. Of interest in this regard is Levine's (1943) use of a graphic Rorschach technique in which subjects are asked to make drawings of their Rorschach percepts. Levine found that schizophrenic patients often produce drawings that accurately depict their responses but have no resemblance to any identifiable Rorschach detail, whereas many brain-damaged subjects make drawings that meticulously replicate the Rorschach details to which they have responded but poorly represent the objects they have reported seeing.

Hence the schizophrenic and organic may perseverate in a phenomenologically similar manner, but for different reasons: the schizophrenic is fixed on his train of thought and unable to take account of the changing stimulus properties of his environment; the brain-damaged individual is fixed on the exact stimulus properties of his environment and unable to modify his ideation. It is therefore in the schizophrenic's preoccupation with his own imagery, regardless of changing stimuli, that he is likely to display pathologically inflexible cognitive focusing. [5]

Several methods of scoring Rorschach perseveration have been employed in clinical research. Friedman (1953) assigned a value of 1.0 to each repetition of a scorable response during free association and a value of 0.5 both to responses that repeated some element of a previous response and to repetitive additional responses. He found that perseveration scores based on these weights and expressed as percentages of total R significantly discriminated schizophrenic from normal groups, which had median perseveration scores of 22.6 and 13.9%, respectively.

Friedman's method is somewhat gross, however, in that it does not (a) distinguish between the repetition of common responses (e.g., "bat" to Cards I and V) and unusual responses, (b) assign any heavier weight to a third or fourth than to a second repetition of a percept, or (c) recognize Bohm's (1958, p. 117) caution against confusing schizophrenic perseveration with certain preoccupations associated with neurotic conflicts. Becker (1956), on the other hand, scores a Rorschach record perseverative only when a response is given *three or more times* without regard for formal blot qualities. Becker's method of scoring perseveration has been used successfully in diagnosing organicity (Fisher, Gonda, & Little, 1955) and in differentiating process from reactive schizophrenics (Brackbill & Fine, 1956; see Chap. 13).

[5] Additional psychodiagnostic similarities and differential considerations in schizophrenia and organic brain disease are discussed in portions of Chapters 6, 7, 8, 9, 10, and 12.

When a stringent criterion for scoring perseveration is applied, as when only perceptually inaccurate repetitions of Rorschach responses are scored, the appearance of any clearly perseverative response is grounds for suspecting thought disorder. The more frequently perseverations occur, especially when they constitute the sole or predominant method of dealing with one or more Rorschach cards, the more severe the thinking disturbance suggested and, barring evidence of organic brain disease, the more likely is schizophrenia.

That perseverative tendencies may also appear in response to WAIS items is illustrated by a schizophrenic young man who answered "South" when asked the direction of travel from Chicago to Panama and responded to the next Information item ("Where is Brazil?") with "Southeast." Sequences of this type exemplify inflexible cognitive focusing, with inability to alter sets as the demands of the situation change. A chronic schizophrenic adolescent girl stated on WAIS Similarities that axe and saw are *"equipment to cut things down with"* and table and chair are *"equipment to sit down on."* Such *automatic repetition* of imprecise words or phrases is also a subtle but important clue to pathologic perseverative tendencies (Piotrowski, 1936–1937, 1940).

Two other types of perseverative verbal response are *echolalia* and *clang association,* both of which are included by Bleuler (1911, pp. 24–29) in his discussion of secondary symptoms in schizophrenia. In echolalia the subject's verbatim repetitions of the examiner's statements suggest that he is unable to shift his focus from the stimulus properties of what he is hearing to the formulation of an appropriate reply. A recent review of the literature on echolalia by Carluccio, Sours, and Kolb (1964) establishes the association of echolalia with severe personality disturbance.

Clang associations involve a persistent focus on the sound rather than on the meaning of verbal productions. Clang associations sometimes occur to a subject's own comments when the sound of some word he has used becomes fixed in his associations. A highly intelligent schizophrenic graduate student responded to "What is ethnology?" as follows: "The study of ethnic groups—or of birds—Lorenz is one, he wrote a book about wrens." In other instances clang associations may be elicited by test items themselves, although such occurrences are unusual except in the context of vocabulary and word association tests ("head-bed," "betrayed-beloved," "room-boom," "diamond-dynamo"). The pathologic significance of both echolalia and clang association is such that even a single occasion of either in the clinical battery strongly suggests thought disorder.

FAILURE TO MAINTAIN FOCUS

Adaptive cognitive focusing entails not only the establishment of an appropriate focus of attention but also the maintenance of that focus for the duration of the task at hand. As indicated on page 29, failure to maintain appropriate focus consists of the intrusion of irrelevant external or internal stimuli on a previously established set and conduces to the overt expression of idiosyncratic associations, inconsistencies in the rate and flow of associations (impaired "pacing"), and inconsistent cognitive efficiency. In the following sections each of these failures to maintain cognitive focus is related to psychodiagnostic indices that facilitate the diagnosis of schizophrenic thought disorder.

Overt Expression of Idiosyncratic Associations

There is considerable research evidence that schizophrenic, more than normal persons, are given to unique, uncommon associations to their experiences and are unable to prevent such deviant associations from intruding on and disrupting their response processes. In studies of word association, for example, Johnson, Weiss, and Zelhart (1964), Moran (1953), and Sommer, Dewar, and Osmond (1960) found the responses of schizophrenic subjects to be less common and less related to the stimulus words than those produced by normal subjects. Spence and Lair (1964) affirmed the schizophrenic's inability to inhibit overt expression of intruding associations by finding that among schizophrenic and normal groups making equivalent numbers of errors on a paired-associate learning task the normals tended to err more by omissions and the schizophrenics more by offering inappropriate responses.

Two psychodiagnostic variables that assess these consequences of failure to maintain adaptive cognitive focus are *dissociation* and *deviant verbalization*. Like the previously discussed perseveration, these two pathologic behaviors are general rather than test-specific phenomena. However, both may appear at any point in a subject's verbal response to the test battery and thus provide psychodiagnostic evidence of disordered thinking.

DISSOCIATION

Dissociation, which was delineated by Bleuler as a fundamental symptom of schizophrenia, is a disconnection and apparent lack of relation between ideas. Arieti (1955, pp. 253–264) employs principles of *similarity* and *contiguity* to analyze the formal qualities of dissociated thinking. He suggests that whereas the normal person associates ideas on the basis of their similarity and contiguity the schizophrenic not only *associates* ideas that are similar or contiguous but *assumes identity* among them. For example, the normal person is likely to associate Washington and Eisenhower on the basis of their both having been generals and presidents; the schizophrenic, however, may assume an identity on the basis of these similarities so that when asked "Who was the first president of the United States?" he replies "Eisenhower." In the same vein, if a schizophrenic thinks of the White House whenever he thinks of the presidency, he may when asked to name three Presidents say "Washington, Eisenhower, and White House." Underlying such responses is so complete an identification of similar or contiguous ideas that they become interchangeable, regardless of their relative pertinence to the question at hand.

As these examples suggest, dissociation resulting from inappropriate assumption of identity frequently determines irrelevant answers to WAIS Information items. Some dissociated Information responses reflect inappropriate identity between numbers and dates that have some broad similarity, as in the following answers by schizophrenic patients: for number of weeks in a year, "352" (a partial identification of number of weeks with number of days in a year); for Washington's birthday, "October 12" (Columbus Day, like Washington's birthday, is a holiday commemorating a famous man); for distance from Paris to New York, "5280 miles" (identification of distance measures with the number of feet in a mile); for the boiling point of water, "32 degrees" (identity is assumed between the two physical values for water, boiling and freezing point).

Other dissociated responses indicate inappropriate identity between proper nouns, as in these responses by schizophrenic patients: for the capital of Italy, "Paris" (also a capital city); for the author of *Hamlet*, "Julius Caesar" (another of Shakespeare's plays); for the location of Egypt, "Israel" (a contiguous Mediterranean country). Such dissociated responses, apparently derived from inappropriate assumption of identity between similar or contiguous concepts, strongly suggest thought disorder, most particularly when they occur on items well within the subject's demonstrated intellectual capacity.

Cameron (1944), on the basis of his experimental observations of schizophrenic subjects (1938, 1939a, 1939b), describes certain other types of dissociation as *asyndesis*. *Asyndetic thinking*, according to Cameron, is a paucity of causal links in a train of associations, and the asyndetic thinker is prone during his verbalizations to lose his focus and express trains of irrelevant and loosely connected thoughts. Some test responses illustrating such dissociation are the following: distance from Paris to New York—"I've always gone by ship, and it took four or five days; I don't know how many knots the ship went, but it's probably about as far as from here to Los Angeles"; lost in a forest—"I have a poor sense of direction; I once took my aunt 200 miles out of her way"; similarity between North and West—"It's a little cooler (?) I don't know, but how about the East, is it cold or warm there?"; to Card V—"That's a bat, isn't it? Mr. Brown shot one up at our club; I think everyone should belong to a club, don't you?"

Less pronounced asyndesis may become apparent only in the course of inquiry about WAIS and Rorschach responses, with the asyndetic thinker missing the point and replying to questions in an oblique or irrelevant fashion. In cases of mild thought disturbance the examiner's only clue to asyndesis may be very subtle discontinuities between the foci of his questions and the subject's answers. Such pathologic asyndetic interchanges as the following may initially give the examiner the mistaken impression that he merely has been misheard or misunderstood: *What does this saying mean, "One swallow doesn't make a summer"*—"swallows flying around are a sign of rain"; *What's missing in this picture* (PC 17, man missing finger)—"one of his hands is bigger than the other"; Card I—"I see a person here (*where do you see it?*) it looks like it's up in a tree actually, actually it's a woman (*what helps you see it as a woman?*) actually she looks like a witch, here's her broomstick (*could you show me the parts you're describing?*) what is it you'd like to know about it?"

In severe schizophrenic disorganization intrusions on cognitive focusing may become so pervasive that irrelevant associations not only interfere with communication but completely dominate the response process. When a person's thinking is disrupted to this extent, elements of external tasks are subordinated to his preoccupations, and the examiner may not be able to keep him sufficiently focused on the test situation to conduct an adequate examination. Such a degree of dissociation, to which Cameron (1944) refers as *interpenetration of themes*, usually leaves little question about the presence of schizophrenic disturbance.

DEVIANT VERBALIZATION

Disturbances of thought and language are so closely related that many aspects of disordered thinking are reflected in deviant verbal productions. However, this discussion follows Holt and Havel (1960, pp. 293–294) in limiting the definition of deviant verbalization to instances of distorted language, as opposed to distortions of either the content or structure of thought. Deviant verbalizations, then, are language distortions that result from the intrusion of idiosyncratic modes of expression and impede verbal communication.

Deviant verbalizations may usually be categorized as either *queer* or *peculiar*. The distinction between queer and peculiar responses to tests, as first suggested by Rapaport et al. (1946, pp. 344–350) for the Rorschach, is somewhat arbitrary and has not been examined experimentally. Nevertheless, deviant verbalizations in the psychodiagnostic situation do take two somewhat different forms to which these labels can be conveniently assigned. In some instances a subject may make a remark that would be appropriate in some contexts but in one way or another is inappropriate to the test situation; at other times he may indulge in language that would be unusual in any context and has no test-specific deviance. As illustrated below, these two forms of deviant verbalization correspond to the categories of queer and peculiar responses, respectively.

Queer Verbalizations. Queer verbalizations, according to Holt and Havel (1960), result from failure to maintain an appropriate set in talking about what one is responding to. The normal person in the Rorschach situation, for example, is able to maintain a set appropriate to the subject matter, to his level of knowledge, and to his relationship with the examiner. Loss of these sets may result in (a) unusual ways of approaching the Rorschach task ("a crab, I was hoping for an octopus"; "a French poodle, I hope they haven't clipped it"; "old shoes, preferably cowboy boots"), (b) stilted and pretentiously pedantic communications ("artistic design of a fly's foot"; "biological cross section of a male, showing his penile projection and his anal capacity"), and (c) language inappropriate to a professional situation ("a twat"; "two skeletons screwing on a tin can").

Queer verbalizations are fairly easy to identify, and when given seriously in the absence of obvious attempts to provoke or leg-pull they are strongly suggestive of thought disturbance. In the Rapaport et al. (1946, Appendix I) study queer verbalizations occurred exclusively among schizophrenics. None of 54 normal and 95 neurotic and depressed subjects gave a single queer response, whereas 26 (40%) of the 65 paranoid and undifferentiated schizophrenics in the study gave one or more.

Peculiar Verbalizations. Peculiar verbalizations are less dramatic and less deviant than queer verbalizations, but they similarly constitute odd language usage that cannot be justified in terms of subcultural idiom or unfamiliarity with English. The oft-quoted example of a *peculiar* Rorschach response, "part of a lady's vagina," is not *queer*, inasmuch as it represents an appropriate approach to the Rorschach task and is couched in language appropriate to the testing situation. Yet the unnaturally stilted description of feminine sexual anatomy as "a lady's vagina" and the strange specificity in the phrase "part of" stamp this response as *peculiar*. Other examples of peculiar language usage in Rorschach responses of schizophrenic subjects are the following: "X-ray of somebody's self"; "something in a *biography* lab"; "a matched brace of stomachs with the food gullets attached"; "a male penis"; "a big *phanton*"; a "rhinocerous and its *probiscus*"; two dogs with their *snoods* together."

Because mildly stilted and pedantic language may be associated with obsessive-compulsive defenses independent of disordered thinking, the frequency of peculiar Rorschach responses and the degree to which they deviate from conventional language usage must be carefully considered. The larger the number of peculiar responses in a record, the greater the percentage of the total response they constitute, and the more they interfere with communication, the more likely the presence of schizophrenia rather than obsessive-compulsive neurosis. Nevertheless, the implications of peculiar responses for schizophrenia are most clear in records that do not otherwise suggest an obsessive-compulsive defensive style. [6]

These cautions concerning the interpretation of peculiar Rorschach responses notwithstanding, available data indicate (a) that the occurrence of even a single peculiar response is much more likely to characterize schizophrenic than nonschizophrenic conditions and (b) that the presence of more than two peculiar responses is exceedingly rare in other than schizophrenic subjects. Rapaport et al. (1946, Appendix I) report the complete absence of peculiar response in all but 11 (8%) of their 132 normal and neurotic subjects, whereas 39 (60%) of their 65 paranoid and undifferentiated schizophrenics gave one or more peculiar responses. Only slightly more than 2% of the normals and neurotics, but 32% of the schizophrenics, had two or more peculiar responses. These findings indicate that the presence in a Rorschach record of even one and especially more than one instance of clearly peculiar language usage is likely to indicate schizophrenia.

Peculiar language usage may also appear on the WAIS, as the fol-

---

[6] For an elaboration of Rorschach indices of obsessive-compulsive defense, the reader is referred to Schafer (1954, Chap. 10).

lowing illustrative Information, Comprehension, and Similarities answers by schizophrenic subjects demonstrate:

INFORMATION. VATICAN: "Seat of the centerpost of the Catholic church, located in a small principality outside the outskirts of Rome." YEAST: "Spores in yeast actuate from the moisture in the bread." BLOOD VESSELS: "Capillary, ordinary, and tertiary."

COMPREHENSION. BAD COMPANY: "May have a deteriorating influence." MOVIES: "Run to a fire-box." DEAF: "Aren't able to be familiar with the audible part of their own anatomy." CITY LAND: "Because of all the vertical and horizontal construction"; "City has more vicinities to go to"; "The mercenary value is higher."

SIMILARITIES. EYE-EAR: "Members of the head"; "Part of sensory system"; "Sensual parts of your being." AIR-WATER: "Biological factors of the outdoors." POEM-STATUE: "Creations of man's creativity and creative ability."

Instances of such peculiar responses on the WAIS suggest thought disorder, and, as in the case of peculiar Rorschach responses, the more frequent they are, the more they· deviate from conventional language usage, and the less basis there is for attributing them to an obsessive-compulsive orientation, the stronger is the likelihood of schizophrenia.

Also helpful in identifying instances of peculiar language usage is Cameron's (1944) description of the manner in which improper use of *metonymy* may determine personally idiomatic expressions. Metonymy is a figure of speech in which one word is substituted for another that it suggests, as in "the *pen* is mightier than the *sword*." Metonyms usually vivify speech and have no necessary relationship to psychopathology. Cameron, however, calls attention to the use of metonyms that are so imprecise that they interfere with normal communication and require continual translation, as in "I have *menu* three times a day," in which *menu* is used for *meals*, and "*business walks* as usual," in which the peculiar phase *business walks* is employed to express the general idea of how things are going. Use of such imprecise metonyms and personal idioms, singly or combined into sentences, results in peculiar, strange, and sometimes incomprehensible verbal productions that imply thought disorder.

It should be emphasized finally that deviant verbalizations may be extremely subtle, especially in instances of mild disturbance. Recognizing deviant verbalizations in such cases requires a vigilant ear for stilted, strained, and unusual expressions, and often only thorough familiarity with the vocabulary, syntax, and modes of expression conventionally elicited by the various test stimuli provides a basis for determining that a particular verbal production is queer, peculiar, or personally idiomatic.

Inconsistency in the Rate and Flow of Associations

The preceding section has dealt with direct manifestations of the inroads of intrusive elements on cognitive focusing. The operation of intrusive elements can also be inferred from their indirect manifestation in the form of inconsistency in the rate and flow of associations. Three indices of such inconsistency that identify thought disorder are *blocking, thought pressure,* and *deviant tempo.*

BLOCKING

In blocking, which Bleuler (1911, p. 33) considered "the most extraordinary formal element of schizophrenic thought processes," associative activity seems to come to an abrupt and complete standstill. Usually an unpleasant and anxiety-provoking experience perceived as a "thought deprivation," blocking is described by Bleuler (pp. 35–37) as follows:

At times the patient is able to speak easily and readily, move quite freely, and then again thinking or movements will halt, freeze, coagulate. . . . Partial blocking . . . can manifest itself in other ways, too. It is not at all rare that speech is blocked while the thought process continues to be expressed in the form of a brief series of gestures which serve to complete the sentence already begun.

Blocking, like dissociation, is not a test-specific phenomenon, but it is indicated by any verbal test behavior that resembles Bleuler's description. The subject who responds haltingly, alternating long pauses with clipped phrases, whose minimal replies are accompanied by strenuous efforts to focus productively on the test materials, who seems constantly on the verge of saying something, though no words come forth, and who is clearly distressed by his lack of fluency is manifesting schizophrenic blocking. At times the blocked subject expresses his difficulty directly with such statements as "I just can't think," "I can't seem to keep my mind working," or, after a long pause, "I've lost track of where I was—what's the question again?" In other instances blocking can be inferred from such strained, disconnected responses as the following reaction to Card VIII by a schizophrenic young woman: "Looks like a bad dream . . . two animals here . . . an X-ray . . . it clashes . . . the colors . . . I don't . . . colored inkblots . . . there is something about them I don't care for too much."

In addition to such general qualitative clues, two quantitative psychodiagnostic variables may be helpful in identifying blocking. As elaborated below, these variables are specific to the Rorschach and involve aspects of card *rejection* and *reaction time*.

Rejection in Schizophrenia. The rejection of Rorschach cards has been related by Bohm (1958, p. 269) to schizophrenic blocking, and Rorschach (1921, p. 22) originally reported a noteworthy frequency among schizophrenics of failure to respond, particularly on "easy" cards. However, clinical experience and research findings indicate that there is no one-to-one relationship between rejection and schizophrenia, and, as suggested by the following brief review of studies in this area, certain kinds of rejection are likely to indicate blocking and other kinds are not.

Brockway et al. (1954) found a definite tendency for records of normal subjects to be freer from rejections than those of psychiatric patients, but both Tamkin (1958) and Mensh and Matarazzo (1954) have reported no differences in rejection frequency between neurotic and psychotic patient groups. These two negative studies involve somewhat unique samples: 43% of Tamkin's patients rejected one or more cards, which is unusually high in view of McKeever and Gerstein's (1959) normative finding of only a 25% rejection rate among 693 patients; and the psychotic patients in the Mensh and Matarazzo study who did not reject any cards had an unusually high mean response total of 55.5. Nevertheless, there is no convincing evidence in the literature to recommend *gross rejection frequency* as an adequate criterion of schizophrenic blocking.

However, attention to the loci of rejections and to the length of the record in which they occur appears to have diagnostic potential. Sisson, Taulbee, and Gaston (1956), for example, found that schizophrenics reject Cards V, VII, VIII, IX, and X significantly more often than normals, and McKeever and Gerstein (1959) report that Cards I, III, and VIII are significantly less likely to be rejected than all other cards except V, which also is seldom rejected. Finally, according to a study cited by Piotrowski (1957, p. 312), likelihood of rejection decreases as total R increases.

Therefore, although the mere occurrence of rejection may not be diagnostically significant for schizophrenia, there is some basis for interpreting rejection of Cards I, III, V, and VIII, especially in the context of good responsivity on the other cards, to indicate blocking. It is additionally helpful to recognize that, although inability to form a response may be associated with the lethargy or ideational impoverishment of a depressive disorder, rejections resulting from such impairments are most likely to occur on those cards that are normatively most difficult. The depressed subject, as well as the guarded, inhibited subject and the mentally defective subject, tends to give his few responses where responses are most easily formulated. Hence, rejection of easy cards with adequate response to difficult ones differentiates schizophrenic blocking from depressive incapacity, intellectual limitation, and guardedness.

This actuarial approach still does not take into account some important qualitative aspects of rejection. As Siegel (1948, p. 125) points out, "Quality of refusal must be carefully evaluated, and withdrawal associated with emotional blocking must be distinguished from that which stems from negativistic defiance." Negativism and poor cooperation may reflect psychopathology, but unlike blocking they are not distinctively schizophrenic phenomena. More specifically, rejections given by surly or passive-aggressive subjects who make little effort to cooperate with the test administration, who accord the cards only a cursory glance, and who display minimal concern over their failure to respond are unlikely to have particular diagnostic significance for schizophrenia. On the other hand, when a subject who is participating actively in the examination professes with dismay and after a lengthy study of a Rorschach card that he is unable to see anything, especially when the card is a relatively easy one, he is probably blocked and suffering a pathologic impairment of his capacity to maintain an adaptive cognitive focus.

Reaction Time in Schizophrenia. Assessment of reaction time, the second quantitative Rorschach variable related to blocking, also requires careful consideration of research and clinical findings. Matarazzo and Mensh (1952), in a study of normals and psychotic, neurotic, and organic patients, found none of these groups to be faster or slower in responding than any other. However, they were able to demonstrate that Cards I, II, III, V, and VIII typically have relatively short and IV, VI, VII, IX, and X relatively long reaction times. This result was replicated by Meer (1955) in a sample of 50 normal subjects. The 104 normal adults studied by Cass and McReynolds (1951) had median reaction times of 13 seconds for the achromatic cards and 14 seconds for the chromatic cards, and from the performance of 50 subjects Sanderson (1951) obtained the following normal ranges of reaction times for the cards, expressed in seconds: I, 5–11; II, 5–18; III, 5–14; IV, 8–18, V, 4–15; VI, 4–25; VII, 7–22; VIII, 4–19; IX, 5–27, and X, 5–22.

Although, as indicated by the Matarazzo and Mensh study, average reaction time may not discriminate diagnostic groups, individual reaction times exceeding the normally observed ranges often suggest blocking. As with rejection, however, it is again important to approach the data clinically as well as actuarially. [7] For example, a long reaction time attributable to a subject's purposeful inattention to a blot is quite different from a delay during which he is intently focused on the card and striving to produce a response. Although the latter may constitute blocking, distractibility and poor cooperation do not, even though they may have other psychopathologic implications.

Furthermore, long latencies in apparently cooperative subjects in turn comprise subtle subcategories having different diagnostic implications. In some instances a subject engages in lengthy, silent study of a card before any verbalization. Delayed reactions of this type usually identify either lethargy and retardation associated with a depressive disorder or a guarded approach in which the subject is carefully sifting and censoring his impressions before sharing them with the examiner. In other cases a subject displays a lengthy reaction time during which he gestures or verbalizes haltingly in an apparent effort to keep his attention focused on his responses. It is the latter pattern of delay that most particularly suggests blocking.

THOUGHT PRESSURE

Thought pressure, the obverse of blocking, is a surfeit of associative activity in which ideas are formulated faster than they can be meaningfully integrated and expressed more rapidly than they can be logically organized. The subject with thought pressure feels compelled to think, sometimes to the point of being exhausted by his relentless, racing stream of ideation.

The verbal productions of schizophrenic patients with thought pressure often resemble the flights of ideas observed in connection with manic psychosis. In discriminating these phenomena, Bleuler (1911, pp. 304–306) concluded that because a flight of ideas cannot itself lead to "loosening of habitual concepts" or "falsification of logical functions," the presence of bizarre associations and violations of logic uniquely identifies schizophrenic thought pressure. According to Bleuler, all the symptoms of manic-depressive psychosis can appear in schizophrenia,

---

[7] Issues involving the relative merits of clinical and actuarial interpretation of psychodiagnostic data are discussed in Chapter 19.

but the possibility of manic psychosis is eliminated as soon as any schizophrenic features are observed. [8]

In common with blocking and deviant verbalization, thought pressure is a general pathologic phenomenon that is not defined by psychodiagnostic tests but may be manifest at any point in a subject's verbal response to them. The Rorschach test in particular, by virtue of its relative lack of structure and minimal restrictions on the subject, [9] is particularly fertile ground for the evocation of thought pressure. Thought pressure usually appears on the Rorschach in the form of an extremely long and complex record. Although highly intelligent, obsessive subjects may give large numbers of responses, such persons characteristically achieve a long record through a carefully organized and systematic approach to the blots in which all blot areas are taken into consideration by a series of fairly discrete responses. The pressured subject, on the other hand, is likely to present his responses in a slap-dash fashion, embellishing and interweaving them more quickly than the examiner can record. On occasion he will produce a record in which it is difficult even to identify or score any discrete responses.

Thought pressure is sometimes evidenced on the Rorschach by such direct statements as "I'm getting more ideas about these things than I can keep track of." More commonly, however, it must be inferred as described above from such complex responses as the following rapidly delivered interpretation of the lower central details of Card VIII by a schizophrenic man:

This small yellow area could be a woman, and these two arms are reaching out toward her or putting something on her head; it's some kind of saintly process, a figure standing between two mountains, and arms reaching down to bestow something. (?) It looks like a woman, with her face turned, and I'm looking at her back; the woman is in a bathing suit or is suntanned, so her breasts are lighter than the rest of her body; she's kneeling and facing me, but she's upright on her knees; this yellow area that she's kneeling in looks almost fluid; she could be bleeding, I guess, the outline of her legs is red; in between her legs is a couple of drops of blood, so she could be bleeding; but down here it's yellow, so she could be urinating; it looks like she's at the top of a hill, looking down over everything, and she's producing this stream which comes down.

The presence in a record of such pressured streams of thought, especially when they involve such loosely connected and bizarre associa-

---

[8] The differential diagnosis of affective disturbance is discussed further in Chapter 17.

[9] The diagnostic significance of structural differences among the tests in the psychodiagnostic battery is considered in detail in Chapter 15.

tions as are contained in the above example, identifies thinking disturbance and suggests schizophrenia.

DEVIANT TEMPO

Deviant tempo is a pathologic variation of association rate marked by alternations of blocking and thought pressure with one another or with normal response rates. Beck (1961, p. 229) attempted to quantify deviant tempo on the Rorschach by computing average fluctuation of numbers of responses and reaction times over the ten cards. Although neither mean fluctuation in productivity nor mean fluctuation in initial response time has been found to discriminate schizoprenic from normal groups (Beck, 1954, p. 211), Beck's fluctuation formulas suggested to Weiner (1962, 1965b) a modified measure of deviant tempo that has proved helpful in identifying schizophrenia.

Recognizing that Beck's formulas do not take into account the normative data concerning card difficulty (see pp. 46–48), Weiner hypothesized that four specific deviations from normally expected Rorschach response rate might be particularly sensitive to schizophrenic associational disturbance: (a) more responses to V than to IV; (b) more to V than to VI; (c) more to IX than to VIII; and (d) more to IX than to X. These specific indices were chosen because they represent marked deviations from normal expectancy and involve comparisons over successive cards and between chromatic or achromatic cards only. In two samples comprising 61 schizophrenic and 104 nonschizophrenic psychiatric patients, the presence of any one or more of these indices of deviant tempo significantly discriminated the schizophrenic from the nonschizophrenic patients and achieved a 67% classification accuracy (Weiner, 1962).

Psychiatric follow-up data available on 89 of these patients two to five years after the original study revealed a significant relationship between these response rate indices of deviant tempo and subsequent diagnosis of schizophrenia (Weiner, 1965b). Hence there is both concurrent and predictive evidence that deviant tempo, as defined by the presence of one or more of the four response-rate indices, is a valid indicator of schizophrenia. Although reaction times have not been studied in light of normative card difficulty, it follows that similarly derived reaction-time indices of deviant tempo might also identify a pathologic inconsistency in the rate and flow of association.

Inconsistent Cognitive Efficiency

Impaired capacity to maintain the focus of attention often leads to certain inconsistencies of cognitive efficiency that indirectly reflect the presence of thought disorder. Three categories of inconsistent test performance that indicate impaired cognitive efficiency are *intratest scatter, intertest scatter, and variable response quality.*

INTRATEST SCATTER

Intratest scatter is defined by a performance pattern that is inconsistent with the relative difficulty of test items. In the psychodiagnostic battery intratest scatter is measured by the extent to which easy items are failed and difficult ones are passed within the various subtests of the WAIS. Gross assessment of whether scatter is present within a WAIS subtest is facilitated by the fact that the relative difficulty of most WAIS items corresponds closely to their numerical order (Wechsler, 1958, pp. 247–249). The Information, Comprehension, Picture Completion, and Object Assembly subtests are perfectly ordered in terms of increasing difficulty; Arithmetic, Similarities, Block Design, and Picture Arrangement are, with only a single exception, correctly ordered, and Vocabulary has 12 misplaced items. Normally, then, two-point, one-point, and zero-credit answers should follow in approximate sequence as the administration of a subtest proceeds, and deviations from such a sequence will identify intratest scatter.

Intratest scatter suggests the interference of intrusive elements with a subject's ability to maintain his focus of attention, and Rapaport et al. (1945, Chap. II) present impressive evidence that such scatter discriminates schizophrenic from neurotic and normal persons. These authors calculated for each subtest of the Wechsler the percentage of errors occurring on easy, intermediate, and difficult terms. Using percentage of errors on easy items as the index of intratest scatter, they found that a significantly larger proportion of their total schizophrenic sample than of either their neurotic or normal groups displayed scatter on Information, Comprehension, and Similarities; their acute and chronic schizophrenic subjects were significantly more often scattered than their normals and neurotics on Arithmetic, Picture Completion, and Picture Arrangement; and on Vocabulary, the schizophrenics' tendency to scatter exceeded that of both the normal and neurotic groups, but to a significant extent only for the normal.

For the Digit Span test Rapaport et al. assessed scatter by comparing Digits Forward with Digits Backward. If the Digits Forward was less than or more than two points greater than Digits Backward, they scored the Digit Span sequence as *irregular.* Digit Span irregularity thus scored occurred significantly more frequently in their schizophrenic than in their normal groups.

Unfortunately, with the following exceptions little effort has been made to quantify intratest scatter since the time of the Rapaport study. Holzberg and Deane (1950) calculated a scatter coefficient by first subtracting the total number of items for which any credit is given on a subtest from the number of the last item for which any credit is given and then dividing this remainder by the total raw score of the subtest. In their initial study with this coefficient Holzberg and Deane found significant scatter differences between schizophrenic and neurotic subjects on Comprehension, Picture Completion, and Block Design.

Watson (1965) has recently assessed WAIS intratest scatter by measuring the *number of runs* (sets of consecutive correct and consecutive incorrect responses) and *proportion of correct responses* (correct responses divided by the total number of responses) occurring in the various subtests. His work to date with these two measures suggests that patients with organic brain disease may produce an extent of intratest scatter comparable to that observed in schizophrenics. Accordingly, it may be that intratest scatter most clearly suggests a schizophrenic impairment of thought processes when cerebral pathology is not otherwise in evidence.

Further studies of these various approaches to scatter have not appeared, and for clinical purposes the inference of cognitive inefficiency from intratest scatter rests primarily with qualitative inspection of subtest performance. However, Wechsler's convenient ordering of the test items and the Rapaport unequivocal findings notwithstanding, adequate inspection for intratest scatter requires careful attention to two important parameters of WAIS subtest performance, namely, *normative irregularity* and *factorial composition*.

Normative Irregularity. Certain normative irregularities in the adequacy of WAIS response have been pointed out by Fink and Shontz (1958). In examining the intratest scatter of WAIS Vocabulary in 100 nonpsychiatric patients, they found the same linear order of difficulty reported by Wechsler, but they also discovered that certain words tend significantly often to yield partial (one-point) rather than full (two-point) credit. These words are "winter," "slice," "enormous," "sentence," "regulate," and "remorse." Fink and Shontz conclude that a one-point answer on these items should not be taken to indicate intellectual inefficiency, regardless of the total Vocabulary score. Although normative data concerning full and partial credit responses to scales other than Vocabulary have not been published, the possibility of item pull is germane to most WAIS subtests, and partial credit answers must therefore be interpreted cautiously in estimating intratest scatter.

Factorial Composition. Factor analyses of the Information, Arithmetic, and Picture Completion subtests reported by Saunders (1960a,

1960b) demonstrate that these scales are not factorially pure. Items of the Information scale, for example, load highly on five different factors, which Saunders names General, Contemporary, Cultural, Scientific and Numerical. Most people, of course, are likely as a consequence of their personal and professional backgrounds to be more informed in some than in other of these areas, independent of any psychopathology they may suffer. A social studies teacher, for example, might miss relatively easy scientific items but deal facilely with difficult items having contemporary referents, whereas a mechanic would probably display a better grasp of scientific than of general information. Hence the most diagnostically significant instances of intratest scatter are those in which successes on difficult items follow failures on factorially related easier items.

Saunder's findings facilitate such careful evaluation for the three WAIS subtests he studied. As already noted, he identified five factorial groupings of Information items. These factors, with the items highly loaded on them listed in order of increasing difficulty, are General Information (PRESIDENTS, POPULATION, GENESIS, TEMPERATURE, ILIAD, KORAN), Contemporary Affairs (HEIGHT, ITALY, PARIS, EGYPT, KORAN), Cultural Information (VATICAN, GENESIS, FAUST, APOCRYPHA), Scientific Information (CLOTHES, YEAST, TEMPERATURE), and Numerical Information (WASHINGTON, POPULATION, SENATORS).

Pass-fail sequences on Information that violate order of difficulty within these factorial groups clearly indicate inconsistent cognitive efficiency. For example, an intelligent schizophrenic woman who failed only five of the 29 Information items revealed her disordered thinking (a) by giving the correct number of senators after stating that Washington was born on February 29 and that the population of the United States is two and a half million and (b) by correctly identifying the Koran after giving "Asia Minor" as the location of Egypt. If, on the other hand, this woman's five errors had occurred on HEIGHT, ITALY, PARIS, EGYPT, and KORAN, one might conclude that she was relatively uninformed in contemporary affairs rather than that her cognitive functioning was inconsistent.

The factorial composition of the Arithmetic subtest is less complex than that of Information, but Saunders did extract from it three factors potentially useful in evaluating cognitive inconsistency: Scientific Information, with high loadings of items 9 and 12; Numerical Information, with high loadings of items 5, 6, 9, 10, 12, and 14; and Numerical Operations, with high loadings of items 5, 8, 10, 11, and 14.

Saunders extracted three factors from his analysis of the Picture Completion subtest. The items loading highly on each, presented in order of increasing difficulty, are the following: Factor I—OAR LOCK,

DOG TRACKS, LEG, ARM IMAGE, SHADOW, and SNOW; Factor II—HANDLES, WATER, PEG, OAR LOCK, BASE THREAD, and FLORIDA; and Factor III—TAIL, HANDLES, WATER, BASE THREAD, STACKS, and FINGER.

The utility of these factorial groupings in assessing inconsistent Picture Completion performance is demonstrated by the following two cases of women in their twenties, both of whom had raw scores of 11 on Picture Completion and whose 10 errors were scattered throughout the test. One of these women had a three-year history of recurrent decompensation, was seen in the hospital, and was eventually diagnosed as having an overt chronic schizophrenic condition; the other woman had experienced a transient psychotic episode and at the time of testing was ambulatory and considered well compensated. On Picture Completion the more seriously disturbed woman, after missing DOG TRACKS and LEG, passed ARM IMAGE (see Factor I); after missing WATER, PEG, and BASE THREAD, she passed FLORIDA (see Factor II); and after missing BASE THREADS and STACKS, she passed FINGER (see Factor III). This patient thus displayed inconsistency within all three of the factorial groups identified by Saunders.

The relatively intact woman, on the other hand, had three of her 10 misses on items not included in any factorial grouping (DIAMOND, NOSE PIECE, and STARS), and her other seven errors occurred only on the more difficult items within the factorial groups (SNOW from Factor I; PEG, OAR LOCK, BASE THREAD, and FLORIDA from Factor II; and STACKS and FINGER from Factor III). Hence this second patient's apparently irregular sequence of successes and failures was on closer inspection relatively mildly deviant and less indicative of inconsistent cognitive efficiency than the pattern of the first woman.

These examples clarify the importance of factorial composition in decisions concerning whether inconsistent efforts on WAIS subtests reflect intrusions on adaptive cognitive focusing. Further data are needed to facilitate the diagnostic interpretation of intratest scatter on WAIS subtests other than Information, Arithmetic, and Picture Completion. As much as possible, estimates of intratest scatter should proceed in terms of judgments about item comparability, and research studies of scatter indices that ignore such meaningful subtleties of item content should be viewed with caution.

INTERTEST SCATTER

Intertest scatter is defined by relatively good performance on certain tests and relatively poor performance on others. General interest in variability across tests has had a long history and encompassed a number of psychometric scales and behavioral tasks. Fiske and Rice (1955), who extensively review experimental studies of intraindividual response variability, note for example that reports of enhanced variability among schizophrenic subjects have appeared since 1909 (pp. 240–241). Taylor, Rosenthal, and Snyder (1963) also comment on the frequency with which schizophrenic subjects are observed to be excessively variable in task performance.

Interest scatter is measured in the psychodiagnostic battery by the degree of variability across the various subtests of the WAIS. Extreme discrepancies between high and low subtest attainments suggest the inroads of intrusive elements on cognitive focusing, and intertest scatter is therefore an important indirect index of impaired capacity to maintain focus. However, some difficulties arise in quantifying intertest scatter and determining what extent of variability is sufficient grounds for inferring thought disorder. Much of this difficulty derives from the sketchy and inconsistent nature of research efforts in this area, a review of which will help to elucidate some guidelines for efficient psychodiagnostic utilization of intertest scatter.

The first evaluation of Wechsler-Bellevue scatter as a diagnostic indicator was contributed by Gilliland (1940), who reported that intertest variability was 35% greater in a group of psychotic subjects than would be predicted from Wechsler's standardization data. In a subsequent study, however, Gilliland, Wellman, and Goldman (1943) were unable to replicate this finding.[10] In two later studies Olch (1948) reported significantly greater intertest variability in a schizophrenic than in a normal control group, whereas Garfield (1948) found no differences in scatter between samples of schizophrenic and nonschizophrenic patients.

To some extent the failure of these studies consistently to confirm intertest scatter as a schizophrenic indicator is attributable to their use of *vocabulary scatter*, which is the mean of subtest deviations from Vocabulary score, as their scatter index and to their failure to control for intelligence. French and Hunt (1951) report that there is a positive relationship between intelligence level and degree of vocabulary scatter, and large scale studies of college students by Estes (1946) and Merrill and Heathers (1952) indicate that a fair amount of vocabulary scatter is normal in persons of above average and superior intelligence. Monroe (1952), moreover, found evidence of strong interaction between adjustment and intelligence in their influence on Wechsler-Bellevue deviations from Vocabulary. It is therefore likely that intertest

---

[10] Considerable psychometric work on scatter, much of it involving the Stanford-Binet, appeared before these Wechsler studies. For summaries of this earlier work the reader is referred to reviews by Hunt (1936) and Mayman (1945a).

scatter when measured by subtest deviations from Vocabulary score will yield many false positive diagnoses of psychopathology, particularly in intelligent subjects, and succeed only sporadically in differentiating patient from control groups.

For these reasons a number of investigators have assessed intertest scatter in terms of *mean subtest scatter*, which is the average of subtest deviations from the mean subtest score. Gilhooly (1950a, 1950b) found a correlation of —.03 between *IQ* and this measure of intertest variability, which indicates that the diagnostic use of mean subtest scatter is relatively unlikely to be contaminated by intellectual level. Furthermore, this measure of intertest scatter has the advantage of being readily applicable to various short-form administrations of the WAIS in which Vocabulary is not included.

Studies by Wechsler (1958, p. 163) and Trehub and Scherer (1958) affirm the diagnostic validity for schizophrenia of subtest deviations from mean subtest score. Wechsler reports comparisons between 58 consecutively examined schizophrenic patients and 58 matched normal controls. The mean of the average deviations of the schizophrenic subjects was significantly larger than that of the controls. Trehub and Scherer devised a scatter index based on mean subtest scores which is very easy to use when a full WAIS is available. After averaging each subject's 11 scale scores, they added absolutely the differences of all subtest scores from this mean value. Applying their index to a sample of 166 schizophrenic and 103 nonschizophrenic psychiatric patients, Trehub and Scherer were able with a cutting score of 19 to classify 66% of their subjects correctly as schizophrenic or nonschizophrenic.

Even though these studies demonstrate the association of extensive scatter around the mean of WAIS subtest scores with schizophrenia, it cannot be ignored that many psychodiagnostic investigations of scatter have yielded discouraging results. Early work by Harris and Shakow (1937, 1938) seriously challenged the diagnostic utility of scatter measures on the Stanford-Binet, and Guertin, Rabin, Frank, and Ladd (1962, p. 16), in the most recent of their several surveys of the WAIS literature, conclude that although measures of intersubtest variability distinguish schizophrenic from normal groups, they are not unique to schizophrenia and may not discriminate reliably in the individual case.

The generally observed variability of schizophrenic persons nevertheless suggests that adequately defined and investigated measures of intertest scatter can contribute consistently to psychodiagnostic judgments. This prospect rests primarily with some demonstrated qualities of the WAIS that have seldom been incorporated into research and clinical studies of intertest scatter. First, there is evidence that discrepancies between the verbal subtests of the WAIS and the subtests of perceptual and manipulative abilities must be interpreted with caution, because sociocultural orientations, educational background, and vocational experiences can markedly influence relative performance on these two types of task. Levinson (1958), for example, found that 64 Yeshiva students, steeped in traditional Jewish values that stress verbal and discount manual skills, earned a mean WAIS verbal *IQ* of 125.6 but a performance *IQ* of only 105.3. Since disparities between verbal and performance attainments may often occur for such reasons, independently of psychological disturbance, even large variations between these two types of task cannot be expected necessarily to reflect disordered thinking.

These considerations suggest that WAIS intertest scatter is most likely to indicate impaired cognitive focusing and concomitant thought disorder when (a) one or more of the verbal subtest scores deviates widely from the general level of verbal attainment, (b) one or more of the perceptual and manipulative subtest scores deviates widely from over-all achievement on the performance scales, and/or (c) either the verbal or the performance subtest scores generally show extreme variability. This approach to scatter measurement was approximated by Rapaport et al. (1945, p. 71), who computed a *total mean scatter* by adding the variability of the subtest scores around the verbal (omitting Arithmetic and Digit Span) and performance means, respectively. Rapaport's 63 paranoid and undifferentiated schizophrenic subjects received significantly higher total mean scatter scores than both their 59 neurotic and 54 control subjects. However, it is important to note that a sample of psychotically depressed subjects in the Rapaport population also displayed relatively large scatter scores. Elevated intertest scatter therefore appears more likely to indicate schizophrenic disturbance when serious depression is not in evidence.

The assessment of intertest scatter can be sharpened even more, however, by taking into account the implications of some relevant factor analytic data. Although Frank (1956) extracted only two factors in an analytic study of the WAIS, which he labeled Verbal and Performance, most other factor analytic studies, including work by Cohen (1957a, 1957b) and Berger, Bernstein, Klein, Cohen, and Lucas (1964), identify *three* WAIS factors in addition to a dominant general factor. These three factors and the subtests that load highly on them are Verbal Comprehension (Information, Comprehension, Similarities, and Vocabulary), Perceptual Organization (Picture Completion, Block Design, Picture Arrangement, and Object Assembly), and Memory (Arithmetic and Digit Span).

These findings reveal that to measure intertest scatter merely within verbal and performance scales cuts across some subtests that may normally bear little interrelationship. The factorial structure of the WAIS suggests rather that inconsistent cognitive functioning is most clearly assessed from intertest scatter when the scatter occurs within the four subtests of Verbal Comprehension, the four subtests of Perceptual Organization, or the two subtests of Memory. Variability across rather than within these factorial groups, on the other hand, may well be related less to psychopathology than to patterns of interest and background experience, as suggested by the Levinson (1958) study. For example, poor Comprehension in comparison to good Information and Similarities is probably more likely to indicate pathologic inconsistency than are discrepancies between Comprehension and Block Design or between Similarities and Picture Completion.

Also relevant to psychodiagnostic use of intertest scatter are reports by Cohen (1952) and Berger et al. (1964) that indicate that the factorial structure of the Wechsler scales is largely invariant over groups of normal, schizophrenic, neurotic, and brain-damaged persons. The factorial structure of the WAIS is also stable over various age groups, according to these studies, with the exception that for the 18-, 19-, and above-60-year-old groups the memory factor tends to lose separate identity and coalesce with the verbal skills. Hence it is not deviation from normal factorial structure that characterizes the WAIS performance of schizophrenic subjects, but rather inconsistent attainment within factorially related groups of subtests, and the factorial structure against which such deviance can be judged is not inordinately influenced by age or diagnostic status.

As already noted, these factorial considerations have seldom been incorporated into research designs, and the material presented in this section suggests that studies measuring scatter *within the context of factorially related subtests* might expand the body of evidence validating intertest scatter as a schizophrenic indicator.

VARIABLE RESPONSE QUALITY

A third and very important psychodiagnostic manifestation of inconsistent cognitive functioning is wide variation in the quality of Rorschach responses, which Rorschach (1921, p. 157) found particularly indicative of schizophrenia. Variable response quality is measured primarily in terms of form and organization levels, and although the broad topics of perceptual accuracy and organizing capacity are treated in Chapters 7 and 12, respectively, abrupt variation in their levels is primarily an index of cognitive inconsistency.

Klopfer and Kelley (1942, p. 352) and Piotrowski (1945) both report that abrupt variations in form level are unique to and diagnostic of schizophrenia, and Rickers-Ovsiankina (1938) concluded as follows on the basis of her research:

> Probably more significant than the total score of a schizophrenic subject is the variation within a single record. In the same person may be found very poor and frequently absurd responses as well as ordinary good ones, or even responses which are considerably above the average with respect to fine and differentiated form perception.

Rapaport et al. (1946, p. 150) emphasize the particular importance of the quality of the W responses in a record and conclude from their data that the coexistence of vague or arbitrary W's with W responses of good quality is frequently an indication of schizophrenia.

Although there are few recent research data in this area, the earlier work suggests that sudden shifts from highly differentiated $F+$ to vague or absurd $F-$ or from amorphous or inaccurate to highly integrated W's are likely to identify pathologically inconsistent cognitive functioning.

► 5

THOUGHT PROCESSES:
II. REASONING

INABILITY to reason logically about the relationships between objects and events is a major aspect of schizophrenia, and unconventional modes of drawing inferences about the meaning of one's experience usually identify a significant disturbance of thought processes. Arieti (1955, pp. 189–273) devotes considerable attention to the schizophrenic's tendency to "retreat from reason," and a review of his excellent discussion will provide a good introduction to psychodiagnostic indicators of pathologic reasoning.

Arieti bases his analysis of disturbed reasoning on the concept of *predicate thinking* formulated by Von Domarus (1944). According to this concept, the schizophrenic reasons illogically because he accepts identity on the basis of identical *predicates,* whereas according to conventional, Aristotelian logic, identity is justified only by identical *subjects.* In conventional logic, for example, if all dogs have four legs and Fido is a dog, then Fido may be assumed to have four legs; *Fido* and *four legs* can be identified because they are aspects of the same subject, *dogs.* Following predicate logic, however, if dogs have four legs and horses have four legs, then horses are dogs because they share the same predicate, *four legs.* Arieti (1955, p. 195) quotes the predicate thinking of a woman who thought she was the Virgin Mary: "The Virgin Mary was a virgin; I am a virgin; therefore, I am the Virgin Mary."

The three major types of predicate that become involved in predicate thinking are *quality, spatial contiguity,* and *temporal contiguity.* Predicates of quality are illustrated by the examples just given: having four legs and being a virgin describe qualities intrinsic to dogs and women.

60

Predicates of spatial contiguity are operating when a man sees several people standing in front of a police station and concludes they are all policemen or decides that the tops of objects are cold because the tops of maps designate north and northern countries are cold. Predicate thinking based on temporal contiguity is demonstrated when a person observes that a light is extinguished just as he closes a door and concludes that his closing the door doused the light or receives a telephone call while thinking about the caller and infers that his thoughts determined the caller's actions.

Mild and transient instances of predicate thinking may occur in other than schizophrenic persons. Glasner (1966) refers to such apparent reasoning disturbances in otherwise intact, nonpsychotic individuals as "benign paralogical thinking," and he suggests for them the designation *benign paralogia*. Benign paralogia was clearly differentiated from schizophrenia in the patients Glasner studied, in that the reasoning peculiarities associated with it did not involve any falsification of reality, scattering of thought, or abnormality of thought content. The following general guideline for the interpretation of predicate thinking is emphasized in this chapter: the greater the extent to which predicate logic violates realistic considerations, the more widely it is manifest, the longer it persists, and the more it is refractory to controverting evidence, the stronger the likelihood of schizophrenic thought disorder.

Regarding the analysis of predicate thinking, it is sometimes difficult to identify the specific predicates on which it is based in a given instance, inasmuch as most subjects have an enormous number of potential predicates. Hence, as Arieti points out, predicate thought, in addition to being bizarre, is often individualistic and incomprehensible. Consider, for example, a patient of Von Domarus who identified Jesus, cigar boxes, and sex because each had the characteristic of being encircled.

More to the point of phenomenological analysis, however, is the fact that predicate thinking frequently involves partial rather than total identities. Arieti suggests that a schizophrenic who considers strength one of the characteristics of a horse and regards one of his acquaintances as being strong may visualize this person as consisting of part man and part horse. The experienced clinician will recognize in this and the preceding examples of predicate thinking much that is relevant to test indicators of impaired reasoning. The relationship of impaired reasoning to specific types of deviant test behavior is further explicated in discussions by Rapaport, Gill, and Schafer (1946, p. 329) of *appropriate distance from the test situation* and by Holt and Havel (1960) of *primary and secondary process thinking*.

Appropriate Distance from the Test Situation

The central hypothesis advanced by Rapaport et al., with particular reference to the Rorschach, is that the individual whose reasoning capacity is impaired is unable to maintain appropriate distance from the test situation. Normally, they point out, subjects conceive the Rorschach to require two tasks: (a) formulating responses that are justifiable in terms of the perceptual qualities of the inkblots and (b) subjecting their associations to the blots to critical, reality-bound judgments. When a subject does not sufficiently concern himself with perceptual justification of his responses, he is showing too little regard for the inkblot, that is, he is too distant from it and is likely to produce responses with excessive associative elaborations. If, on the other hand, he becomes so absorbed in the stimulus qualities of the inkblots that he is unable to make critical judgments about the plausibility of the associations they suggest, he tends to take the blots as an immutable reality (loss of appropriate distance) and to base his responses on an excessively literal interpretation of what he sees.

The following elaborate, perceptually unjustified response to Card I illustrates increased distance: "Two men fighting over something, attempting to grab it away from each other; it may be money there in the middle, because men usually fight over money; it's a stack of twenty-dollar bills they've been saving to invest, and now they can't agree what to do with it; they'll probably never speak to each other again." Loss of distance, with inappropriate interpretation of Rorschach card relationships as real relationships, is indicated by such replies as "a big ape (Card IV), big because it fills almost the whole card" and "the North Pole (Card X, top central detail), because it's at the very top."

In actuality, most poorly reasoned responses are complex products in which both increased and decreased distance can be identified. The influence of increased and decreased distance on specific types of poorly reasoned Rorschach responses is explored more fully in the course of subsequent examples.

Primary and Secondary Process Thinking

Holt and Havel undertake to operationalize the classical psychoanalytic concepts of primary and secondary process thinking. They stress the following three points as basic to their approach: (a) the more primary a person's thinking, the greater his preoccupation with instinctual aims and the prominence of uncontrolled libidinal and aggressive urges; the more the secondary process prevails, the greater the evidence of the operation of sublimation and countercathectic controlling structures, as inferred from such relatively autonomous drive derivatives as interests, values, and highly socialized desires; (b) the ascendance of primary process thinking is manifest in certain formal thought characteristics, including autistic logic and loose and nonsensical associative links; and (c) primary process thinking may be productive as well as pathologic, depending on the degree to which a person is able voluntarily and reversibly to surrender secondary process standards for primary process freedom and fluidity.

Although these aspects of primary and secondary process thinking have implications for a number of ego functions, Holt and Havel's elaboration of them emphasizes parameters of disturbed reasoning. Specifically, Holt and Havel link several categories of reasoning disturbance to particular types of Rorschach responses in terms of the mechanisms of the dream work outlined by Freud (1900, pp. 277–381) in his initial description of primary process thinking. These mechanisms are *condensation*, the fusion of two or more ideas or images, *displacement*, a shift of emphasis or interest from one mental content to another, and *symbolization*, the replacement of one idea or image by another. With reference to these three mechanisms, Holt and Havel develop a formal scoring scheme to measure primary process thinking on the Rorschach. Although their scales are not specified in detail here, the conceptualization of various test indices of impaired reasoning proposed by Holt and Havel is reflected in many sections of this chapter.

This chapter, then, considers a number of test variables indicative of impaired reasoning and explores the processes that contribute to them. Most of these variables are specific to the Rorschach, and in each some variation of predicate thinking, some failure to maintain appropriate distance from the test stimuli, or some manifestation of primary process thinking is recognizable. These test indices of disturbed reasoning can be roughly grouped under the three headings of *overgeneralized thinking*, *combinative thinking*, and *circumstantial thinking*.

OVERGENERALIZED THINKING

A prominent feature of impaired reasoning in schizophrenia is a predilection for overgeneralized thinking. Overgeneralized thinking consists of jumping to erroneous conclusions on the basis of minimal evidence and investing experiences with elaborate meanings not justified by their actual stimulus properties. Three types of Rorschach response that indicate overgeneralized thinking are *Fabulization, Confabulation,* and *absurd Dd.*

FABULIZATION

Fabulization is defined by greater affective elaboration or greater specificity of Rorschach responses than is realistically justified by actual blot stimuli. The following three types of Fabulization can be identified. Although each exemplifies increased distance from the card, they have somewhat different diagnostic implications.

Noun, Verb, and Adjectival Fabulization. The mildest type of Fabulization, as described by Phillips and Smith (1953, pp. 153–155), consists of the use of certain elaborative words or phrases, including adjectival elaborations ("fearful man," "threatening posture"), verbs of action ("yelling," "glaring"), and nouns that condense a basic percept into an elaboration ("bum," "head-hunter"). Such Rorschach response elaborations, however, are scored as Fabulization only when they are unique or extremely rare, convey some aura of emotional intensity, and represent motives, feelings, or attitudes that cannot reasonably be inferred from the blot. Fabulization should not be scored for elaborations that are relatively neutral or common ("dancing" on Card III) or for superior elaborations that are justified by reference to actual blot characteristics: Card IX, side pink detail—"Looks like the head of a little old German man, looks a little like Albert Einstein (?) the outline suggests a shaggy head like old Albert Einstein, with what looks like a turned-down moustache here"; Card V, top details—"Looks like the legs of a rather overweight ballet dancer on her toes (*overweight?*) the girth of the legs in proportion to the length indicates it."

Although noun, verb, and adjectival Fabulizations depart from the reality of the card, they do not necessarily indicate disturbed thinking. On the contrary, as Rapaport et al. (1946, p. 332) point out, such Fabulizations are frequently given by normally imaginative, sensitive people who employ language colorfully. Whether these Fabulizations identify pathologic reasoning depends on the attitudes with which they are expressed, their relative frequency in a record, and the degree to which they distort reality.

The normal individual who fabulizes tends to do so in a fanciful manner, fully aware of the liberties he has taken and quite able to recount the eccentricities of his associations if asked about them. The schizophrenic subject, on the other hand, is likely to fabulize with an air of reality and the emotion-laden conviction that no explanation of his response is necessary. Whereas a normal individual may fabulize occasionally, repetitive Fabulization, even if seemingly whimsical, indicates a disruptive proclivity for overgeneralized thinking. Finally, the schizophrenic more than the normal person is prone to distort reality in his fabulized responses. The Fabulization of "fearful man," for example, presents a plausible event and has little significance for disturbed reasoning. On the other hand, percepts like "a fur-lined nest" and "pregnant males" are relatively unconsonant with reality, and such responses as "profile of a child who is three years old" and "a hole chiseled in something about three inches thick and five inches long" are unusually specific descriptions hardly justified by the blot stimuli.

Hence the more that Fabulizations are given seriously and without justification, tend to dominate the response process, and distort reality, the greater is the likelihood of thought disturbance.

Extended Fabulization. A second type of Fabulization consists not merely of phrases but of extended associative elaborations that weave the basic percept into a complex narration. These Fabulizations can be easily identified by their resemblance to how a subject might be expected to respond if he were asked to make up a story about what he sees. The fabulizing subject not only reports content, locations, and determinants, but also offers detailed, unsolicited accounts of prior, present, and future circumstances impinging on his percepts. Although this type of Fabulization was originally subsumed by Rapaport et al. (1946, pp. 333–335) under the heading of Confabulation, the presentation here follows Holt and Havel (1960, pp. 294–295) in defining Confabulation to exclude extended elaborations of responses (see pp. 67–69).

The extended type of Fabulization is illustrated by the following four responses of schizophrenic subjects, the last of which is also notable for its dissociated, pressured quality:

I see a cross between a spider and a crab (Card III, reversed position, all of black) sitting in a crevice or a cave; it's just dropped its meal (center red detail) and is looking out at something more attractive it's contemplating attacking; the picture as a whole is deceptive and menacing, with overtones of danger; it's caught in a moment of arrest, a split second before the attack.

Two people lying on their backs (Card V); one is a woman and the other a man; they have just had intercourse and now they are sleeping.

There are two elephants here (Card IX, green detail); it's a mother and a child; the child wants to go out and play; it's his first real glimpse of freedom; the mother is concerned about the danger of the outside world, but she knows he needs the experience of being on his own, so she'll let him go.

Two women looking at each other (Card III, popular); they're about 60 years old, and they do that all the time, look at each other; they're sitting on these things, modern furniture, which isn't very comfortable; the whole thing looks like a messy home; the two ladies are talking and the home is a mess; my wife works for the SPCC and tells me about situations like this; here the kids have thrown ketchup bottles at the walls (reference to side red details), and it's running down; they're talking about promiscuous affairs, describing their various lovers; in the background (center detail) is the families of the two mothers; they're thinking they better clean up because the lady from the SPCC is going to be here soon.

The diagnostic significance of extended Fabulizations, like that of noun, verb, and adjectival Fabulizations, depends on the degree to which they are unrealistic or dominate the subject's thinking. A normal person may for his own enjoyment and with full cognizance of his overgeneralization occasionally indulge in flights of association such as the following response to Card VII by a man who clearly was not schizophrenic: "A funny idea occurs to me about this one; I can imagine two female dogs, all dressed up with full skirts, bustles, and waistcoats, who have just discovered to their chagrin that they're wearing the same thing." On the other hand, the more such elaborations violate realistic considerations and the more the subject appears mastered by, rather than master of, such fantasies, unable either to check or critically evaluate them, the more likely is the presence of thought disorder.

Self-Reference. A third type of Fabulization is *self-reference,* in which the response specificity or elaboration is referred by the subject directly to himself, with almost total loss of distance from the card. Self-reference responses nearly always suggest thought disorder and have classically been associated with schizophrenic disturbance (e.g., Bohm, 1958, p. 271). In some self-reference responses the subject perceives in the inkblot some part of himself or something belonging to him: "It's me with my pony tail up in the air"; "A separated penis, severed from the body, with semen dropping out of it—maybe it's my penis"; "That's my dog." In others the subject relates to himself some activity attributed to his percepts: "An insect crawling toward me"; "A bat, with his eyes piercing out at me." These types of bizarre self-reference, distinguished from extraneous self-referential comments ("caterpillars just like we have in our garden") and reminiscences ("I remember seeing a bat once that looked just like that"), neither of which implies thought disorder, are highly unlikely to occur in other than a schizophrenic context.

CONFABULATION

Confabulation is an excess of distance from a Rorschach inkblot in which a content based on only a small part of the blot is inappropriately attributed to a larger area. As mentioned on page 65, some writers have defined Confabulation to include certain types of associative elaboration here labeled as Fabulizations. Inasmuch as Confabulation is typically equated with specific *DW*, *DdW*, and *DdD* scores (see below), it minimizes confusion if the scoring of Confabulation is explicitly restricted to these types of response.

Confabulation, when scored according to stringent criteria recommended by Klopfer, Ainsworth, Klopfer, and Holt (1954, pp. 64–69), clearly indicates pathologically overgeneralized thinking. According to the Klopfer et al. recommendations, Confabulation is scored for those generalizations from small to larger blot areas in which the response inaccurately matches the shape of the larger area and is justified by the subject only in terms of the smaller one. The three scoring categories for Confabulation are *DW*, in which the generalization is made from a common detail to the whole blot; *DdW*, in which the generalization is from an uncommon detail to the whole; and *DdD*, in which a generalization from an uncommon to a common detail is made. All *DW*'s, *DdW*'s and *DdD*'s involve clearly inaccurate form perception, and accurately perceived and vague responses cannot constitute Confabulation. In addition, responses that involve the combination of a number of details in an unrealistic fashion are combinative (see pp. 69–82), rather than overgeneralized and should not be scored Confabulation.

The following examples from Klopfer et al. clarify these scoring rules. Card IV seen as a "snake" because the left side projection is "the head and neck" is a Confabulation; the subject overgeneralizes from the detail to the whole, which he uses as "the rest of the snake," in violation of its actual form properties. Card I seen as a crab "because of its claws" (center top projections) is not a Confabulation, since the shape of the whole blot is not incompatible with the shape of a crab. All of Card VIII interpreted as "a couple of mice climbing the side of a wall" is not scored Confabulation, inasmuch as (a) only the mice are seen clearly, with the wall remaining a vague background element, (b) the response as a whole does not do violence to the formal realities of the blot, and (c) if anything the response is combinative rather than overgeneralized.

The confabulated response can be understood as a manifestation of predicate thinking ("snakes have heads, this has what looks like a snake's head on it, therefore this is a snake"), although explicit expressions of *autistic logic* (see pp. 83–84) seldom accompany Confabulations. Like other consequences of predicate thinking, Confabulations vary qualitatively in their significance. As Phillips and Smith (1953, p. 20) point out, the smaller the area from which generalizations are made and the less important the content of this area to the eventual percept, the greater the degree of thought disturbance suggested.

Any Confabulation indicates a fairly significant reasoning impairment, but confabulated responses are by no means limited to the records of grossly disturbed schizophrenic subjects. The following three examples of Confabulation helped to identify subtly disordered thinking in persons who were not blatantly schizophenic: Card I—"A toad, because of the way these eyes pop out here" (top central details); Card IV—"The whole thing is a flower (?) because there's a bud here" (top detail); Card V—"A lady's hat (?) these two (side details) could be the hat pins, so the rest would fit in."

Research evidence has consistently demonstrated Confabulation to be a valid indicator of schizophrenia and to occur very rarely in normal and neurotic subjects. Beck (1938) found Confabulations in the records of 39 (48%) of 81 schizophrenics but only seven (11%) of a mixed control group of 64 normal persons and nonschizophrenic psychiatric patients. In a later comparison Beck (1954, pp. 210–212) reported a significantly greater frequency of Confabulations in the records of 60 schizophrenic subjects than those of 157 normals, whose mean DW was only .02.

Beck's schizophrenic populations were limited to hospital patients, but Rieman (1953), comparing the Rorschachs of neurotic and schizophrenic patients being treated in an outpatient clinic, also found the presence of Confabulation to discriminate significantly between groups in his two separate samples of 50 schizophrenics and 50 neurotics. Siegel (1953) found that 50% of a group of 30 diagnosed hebephrenic and catatonic schizophrenics gave Confabulations, whereas none of 30 paranoid schizophrenics and 30 normal adults confabulated.

From these data it is clear that, although not all schizophrenics confabulate, the presence of even a single Confabulation is extremely unlikely in the record of a normal or neurotic person and strongly suggests pathologically impaired reasoning. The possibility raised by Siegel's data that the paranoid subgroup of schizophrenia may also be relativley unlikely to confabulate is considered further in Chapter 14.

ABSURD Dd

Although a high percentage of *Dd* response may point to impaired cognitive focusing (see pp. 30–33), *absurd Dd* responses are primarily indicative of pathologic reasoning. The absurd *Dd* response is the investment of tiny Rorschach details with specific and elaborate meanings so far beyond justification that they constitute complete disregard for the reality of inkblot stimuli. Absurd *Dd*'s are similar to Fabulizations but merit separate consideration because they are *extreme* overgeneralizations that, unlike Fabulized responses, seldom occur in other than schizophrenic subjects.

Even a single instance of the extreme overgeneralization represented by an absurd *Dd* response indicates disordered thinking, and the smaller and less distinct the *Dd* and the greater its elaboration, the more severe the thought disorder suggested. The following are examples of extremely overgeneralized responses that are scored as absurd *Dd* and identify pathologic reasoning: Card VIII, two arbitrary inner details on either side of center "rocket" detail at top—"On one side a child, crying; on the other side another child, just standing and looking at the one who's crying; he's indifferent, doesn't care that the other one is crying"; Card X, center tiny part of "wishbone" detail—"It's a woman, a little on the heavy side, wearing a long flowing gown, like she's waiting for someone at a ball."

COMBINATIVE THINKING

A significant consequence of reasoning impairment is combinative thinking, which demonstrates the primary process mechanism of condensation. In combinative thinking perceptions and ideas are inappropriately condensed into impressions and conclusions that violate realistic considerations. Combinative thinking is illustrated by three types of Rorschach response in which unrealistic relationships are inferred between images, blot qualities, objects, or activities attributed to objects: *Incongruous Combination, Fabulized Combination,* and *Contamination.*

INCONGRUOUS COMBINATION

An Incongruous Combination is a Rorschach interpretation that unrealistically condenses qualities of blot details or of images they suggest into a single, incongruous percept. This type of condensation appears in several forms, each of which can be seen to reflect predicate thinking and a subject's increased and/or decreased distance from the test material. In producing an Incongruous Combination, the subject links blot characteristics and/or his associations to them solely on the basis of their contiguity, thereby losing distance from the card and inappropriately taking Rorschach relationships as real relationships. Additionally, he is likely to embellish his combination with perceptually unjustifiable meaning, thus inappropriately increasing his distance from the realistic qualities of the test stimuli. Four forms of Incongruous Combination response, each reflecting predicate thinking and inappropriate distance from the stimuli, are *composite, arbitrary form-color, inappropriate activity,* and *external-internal* responses.

Composite Responses. The nature of the composite response is delineated by Holt and Havel (1960, p. 286), who describe it as a combination of parts from two or more separate percepts into a "hybrid" creature. For example, the center detail of Card V can realistically be seen as a rabbit and the side details of the card as a bat's wings; however, the response "a rabbit with bat's wings" to the entire card is an Incongruous Combination in which the juxtaposition of the rabbit and the wings is unreasonably accepted as sufficient basis for reporting a composite percept that does not exist in nature. Similarly illustrative of the composite response are "wolves with the face of a mouse," "an elephant with sheep's ears," "two people with tails on their heads," "people with heads of a chicken," and "tree branches with hands on them." Also scored in this category are percepts of persons and animals with supernumary parts; for example, "Some beast with four legs—it's a chicken." The composite form of Incongruous Combination is also exemplified by hybrid figure drawings on the Draw-a-Person, as of a man's body with a dog's head, but such bizarre renderings are seldom encountered.

Composite responses reflect impaired reasoning, and when they are strictly scored their presence, even in small numbers, suggests disordered thinking. Composite responses should not be scored for perfectly congruous Rorschach combinations ("man with shoes on") or for images that are justified in art or mythology ("a three-headed dog—Cerberus"; "it's half man and half horse, like one of those centaurs"; "a Medusa, a woman with snakes for hair"; "body of a man with the head of a dog, like those old Egyptian drawings"). Responses of these latter types do not necessarily indicate faulty reasoning and are not composite in the technical, pathologic sense of the term.

Furthermore, as pointed out by Klopfer and Spiegelman (1956, pp. 282–285), even responses that are unequivocally composite will vary in their diagnostic significance. For one thing, composite responses may differ in how "far-fetched" they are, and Klopfer and Spiegelman note that the more such a combination deviates from any possible justification, realistic or aesthetic, the more seriously it represents pathologic reasoning. In addition, the less a subject expresses awareness of the poorly reasoned quality of a composite response he gives and the less he manifests any spirit of enjoyment or whimsy in giving it, the more serious are its pathologic implications.

In most instances careful inquiry into a subject's response is necessary to apply these scoring and qualifying considerations to a possibly composite percept. For example, when an obsessive-compulsive man who reported a beetle with butterfly wings on Card I was pointedly asked if it was one figure, he was able to reply, "No; the parts look as I described them, but of course they couldn't go together as a single creature." Similarly, a subject who seriously maintains even on inquiry that the figures on Card III are persons with both breasts and penises is more likely to have a thought disorder than one who has given the same response laughingly and when asked to account for it says, "It could be natives doing some kind of ritual dance and wearing a ritual costume having bisexual representations."

Arbitrary Form-Color Responses. Whereas composite responses involve only the form qualities of the blots, arbitrary form-color responses are condensations embracing two modalities. Incongruous Combination of form and color, as in "red bears," may be assumed to derive from the following predicate syllogism: "This detail looks like a bear; this detail is red; therefore, this detail must be a red bear." These condensations of form and color qualities may occur in responses of definite form (*FCarb*: "blue monkeys"; "green rabbits") or in vague percepts (*CFarb*: "green clouds"; "orange smoke"), but in both cases the essential criterion for scoring the response as *arbitrary* is that the object seen does not naturally exist in the color attributed to it (Klopfer et al., 1954, p. 178). Arbitrary form-color should not be scored for natural color use or for *F/C* and *C/F* responses in which color is employed to mark off subdivisions in a percept or to represent the color use found in maps or anatomical drawings (Holt & Havel, 1960, p. 288).

As Rapaport et al. (1946, pp. 231–232) state, because clear *FCarb* and *CFarb* responses are given almost exclusively by schizophrenics, an examiner should inquire carefully into apparent instances of such responses before scoring them. Most subjects who intend arbitrary descriptions humorously will readily explain their behavior on inquiry: "Of course there is no such thing as a green elephant"; "I was just thinking of a fairy tale where there is a red wolf"; "I could see it as a mask, just painted that way with yellow eyes and a green moustache." Others are able to account for seemingly arbitrary color use in a strained but still realistic manner: "The clouds aren't really red, but it's like a sunset with the glow from the sun's rays reflected on the clouds." On the other hand, a person who condenses form and color and fails either to demonstrate awareness of the inappropriateness of his combination or to exercise critical judgment in regard to the reality of his percept is likely to be suffering a schizophrenic impairment of his reasoning capacity.

Inappropriate Activity Responses. In inappropriate activity responses the condensation occurs between an object, usually a human or animal figure, and some activity incongruously ascribed to it. It is as if the subject, thinking of some behavior (e.g., "praying") coincidentally with his perception of some object on the Rorschach (e.g., "a witch"), combines the two ("a witch praying") without exercising any critical judgment concerning the incongruity of attributing prayerful activity to a witch. Although such responses also have a Fabulized quality, the inappropriateness of the ascribed activity provides the basis for considering them combinative as well as overgeneralized interpretations.

Holt and Havel (1960, p. 293) interpret inappropriate activity responses according to the degree to which they are unlikely, that is, distort reality, and the extent to which these responses distort reality determines their pathologic significance. For example, "two snakes sitting on a river bank" and "a lion baying at the moon" are Incongruous Combinations, inasmuch as snakes do not "sit" and lions do not "bay," but such responses only mildly stretch the limits of the animals' actual behaviors. Similarly unlikely but not impossible are such incongruous percepts as "a king playing leapfrog" and "a little baby driving a car." However, replies like "two beetles doing a Charleston" and "a man giving a mating call" attribute entirely inappropriate, nonexistent activities to the respective objects and suggest reasoning impairment. As with other qualitative indices, however, the implications of such inappropriate activity responses for thinking disturbance are attenuated when they are given humorously or are rationalized by references to mythological, cartoon, or fairy tale figures.

External-Internal Responses. External-internal condensation is indicated by percepts in which both external and internal body parts are identified in a realistically impossible manner (Holt & Havel, 1960, p. 285). Gross instances of this form of Incongruous Combination ("here's a man and this shaded part is his heart"; "the vagina of a woman and these would be her ovaries"), unless justified by specific reference to X-rays or anatomical drawings, strongly suggest thought disorder.

Less gross external-internal combinations are illustrated by *transparencies,* in which a subject reports details that would realistically be obscured by other aspects of his percept. These transparencies in Rorschach responses most usually involve clothing, as in a description of the center detail of Card I as a woman with the outer contours of the detail seen as her dress and the inner shaded detail described as her legs, in spite of the fact that at least the upper portion of the legs would not realistically be visible through the dress unless the dress were transparent. Such transparencies do not violate reality as seriously as combinations of internal and external organs; nevertheless, they constitute Incongruous Combinations, and their accumulation in a record suggests reasoning disturbance.

Incongruous Combinations of external and internal details may also occur on the Draw-a-Person (DAP). On the DAP as on the Rorschach, the most pathologic external-internal combinations are figures to which clear anatomical indications of internal organs have been added. Machover (1949, p. 74) reports that such drawings are rarely rendered by other than schizophrenic subjects. Machover also describes less autistic external-internal combinations in which a transparent effect is created by the addition of clothing that fails to conceal previously drawn body parts. Most frequently such drawings involve male figures in which the legs show through the pants and female figures with body contours visible through the skirt or blouse. In the same category are drawings in which the body line shows through the arms, or the hair or the outline of the forehead appears through a hat. Although Machover considers these transparencies less serious indicators of psychopathology than the appearance of internal organs, she nevertheless views them as reflecting faulty perspective and poor judgment (1949, p. 103).

Two research studies provide evidence that DAP transparency is a valid indicator of schizophrenia. Holzberg and Wexler (1950a), comparing 78 student nurses with 38 female schizophrenic patients, found transparencies in the drawings of one-third of the schizophrenics but only 10% of the normal group, which constitutes a significant difference. Hozier (1959) noted transparencies in the drawings of 20 or 25 hospitalized schizophrenics but in only six of 25 normal controls, which is also a significant finding. These data suggest that the appearance of transparencies in figure drawings is very rare in normal subjects and likely to be associated with schizophrenia.

Figures 1-4 are drawings rendered by adult schizophrenic patients who were not grossly disturbed but whose clinical history and eventual course, as well as other test data, strongly suggested thought disorder. Each drawing demonstrates transparency. Figure 1, the most childish and blatantly transparent of the four drawings, was completed by the addition of the trousers with complete lack of concern for the appearance of the leg and trunk through the clothing.

Figure 2 began as a stick figure, and when the patient was asked to draw a full person, he proceeded blandly to do so around the stick figure with no attempt to erase or cover the previous lines.

Figure 3 was originally sketched with rough circles and ellipses, much as an art student would approach a figure drawing, but was completed with the addition of the transparent skirt without any justification by the patient of the unlikely appearance of the final drawing.

Figure 4, which was rendered by a relatively intact young woman who had manifested only some transient indications of incipient schizophrenic disturbance, contains only a very subtle transparency effect, namely, the visibility of the lines of the skirt through the forearm, wrist, and hand.

FABULIZED COMBINATION

In the Fabulized Combination response unrealistic relationships are posited between two or more percepts solely on the basis of their spatial contiguity. It is as if the subject reasons that because two blot details are adjacent there must be some explicable connection between them. Although all Fabulized Combinations demonstrate a tendency to take Rorschach relationships as real relationships, Holt and Havel (1960, pp. 286–288) identify three variations of Fabulized Combination, *arbitrary linkage, unlikely combination,* and *impossible combination,* that differ in pathologic significance.

Arbitrary Linkage. Arbitrary linkage responses are minor difficulties in keeping distinct images apart or in separating a distinct image from a vague background. Arbitrary linkage is exemplified by "Siamese-twin" percepts (Card VII—"these are two women, but they're joined or stuck together in some way") and by strained efforts to account for the juxtaposition of distinct images: "A man, as if he's been tacked onto a pole or something"; "A penis, with the foreskin attached to it." Linkage of a clear percept with a vague background is apparent in the following response to Card VI: "A chameleon crawling along (top) with all this scum (rest of card) stuck to his hind legs."

Even though such arbitrary linkages should be distinguished from more natural integrations such as "two people holding on to a post" and "women picking up a kettle," they are not particularly significant

Figure 1

Figure 2

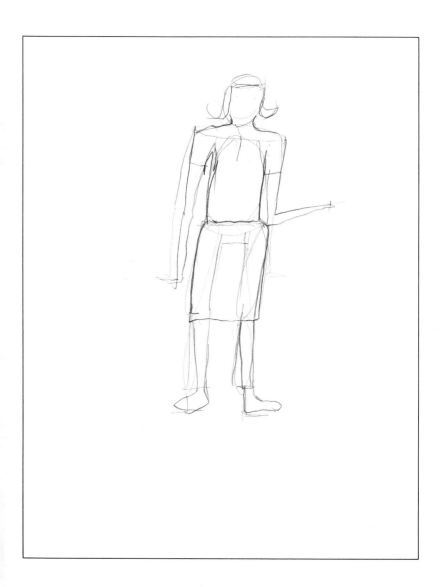

Figure 3

Figure 4

for impaired reasoning. Arbitrary linkages are not unusual in the records of imaginative and intellectually oriented subjects who are intent on integrating aspects of their experience, and unless they should happen to constitute the primary mode of response in a brief record, they do not imply disordered thinking.

Unlikely Combinations. Unlikely combinations are responses in which relationships other than mere linkage are attributed to contiguous details in a manner that stretches but does not completely violate realistic considerations: "Two elephants standing on two other elephants"; "Monkeys balancing rabbits on their heads"; "A dog and a lion rubbing noses." These types of response, when carefully differentiated from combinations that can reasonably be expected to occur in reality ("a man riding a horse"; "two wolves fighting over a piece of meat"), begin to suggest pathologic reasoning.

Impossible Combinations. Impossible combination is the type of Fabulized Combination that most definitely points to a schizophrenic impairment of reasoning. Responses of this type clearly distort reality by positing relationships that are impossible in one of three ways. First, some of these Fabulized Combinations involve impossible size discrepancies between objects or blot details. With loss of distance from the test stimuli a subject may, for example, perceive a relatively large detail as a dog and an adjacent smaller detail as a butterfly and report "a dog climbing on a butterfly," ignoring the fact that the actual relative size of dogs and butterflies makes such a relationship between them impossible. If a subject instead takes increased distance, he may, for example, describe the side orange and green details of Card IX as "a man walking his dog," which is a possible event in nature but involves perceiving the dog in a blot area that is actually larger than the one seen as a man. A man exceeded in size by his dog is an implausible state of affairs.

Second, a Fabulized Combination may be impossible by virtue of combining objects that do not ordinarily occur together in nature. Examples of such responses to Card III are "two monkeys fighting over a bow tie"; "two chickens rolling bowling balls." Although responses of this kind often involve inappropriate activities (e.g., chickens do not customarily bowl), they are Fabulized Combinations rather than merely Incongruous Combinations because they condense two or more *separate objects.* Whereas "chickens bowling" with no reference to bowling balls would be an Incongruous Combination, "chickens rolling bowling balls," in which both the bowling balls and the chickens are seen as distinct percepts, is a Fabulized Combination. Furthermore, chickens and bowling balls are unlikely to coexist, whether or not any interaction is attributed to them; that is, chickens and bowling balls seldom appear together in any setting, aside from that fact that chickens make poor bowlers.

The third type of impossible Fabulized Combination is one that mixes natural and supernatural frames of reference. A response illustrating such a combination is the following interpretation of Card III: "Two natives brewing something over a pot; the red represents little demons, and they're talking to them, and they'll hit them over the head if they don't follow instructions." In reality, of couse, one does not see such actual representations of supernatural creatures or forces interacting with corporeal objects. From this and the preceding examples, however, it is clear that impossible Fabulized Combinations may also include features that are merely unlikely. The following response by a schizophrenic man to Card X illustrates an unlikely but not impossible interaction between images, together with a clearly impossible size relationship between blot details: "The center blue spots are two men, and the two pink are women; these men have their hands on the pubic region and are holding onto the vaginas of the women."

Although the presence of impossible Fabulized Combinations strongly suggests thought disorder, the content of combinative responses should be carefully analyzed before they are labeled *impossible*. As indicated above, Fabulized Combination responses differ in the degree to which they distort reality, and arbitrary linkage and unlikely combination responses, the milder variations of Fabulized Combination, may occur in the records of nonschizophrenic persons who utliize an intellectual defensive style. Rapaport et al. (1946, p. 335) and Schafer (1954, p. 383) comment on the frequency in obsessive-compulsive neurotics of Fabulized Combination responses with basically good form quality and minimal reality distortion.

Furthermore, it is important with Fabulized as with Incongruous Combinations to determine through careful inquiry a subject's capacity to judge critically and to justify his combinative responses. The following replies of a young woman illustrate the usefulness of the inquiry in attenuating somewhat the pathologic implications of clearly impossible Fabulized Combinations: "I see a girl sitting on a couch (Card V, center detail), and it looks like two demons or something on the sides that are worshiping her (*demons are worshiping her?*) it could be something you would see in Greek mythology"; "I see mice here (Card VIII, popular), and on the inside (center white spaces) I can see two men . . . the mice look like they're going to eat them, they're trying to get at them . . . it looks like the mice are five or six times larger than the men (*how could the mice be so much larger?*) it would have to be a dream or a surrealistic painting." Had the patient responded to these inquiries about her responses with such remarks as "it just looks that way" or "I don't know how to account for it," she would have been displaying more serious thinking disturbance than is indicated by the comments she did make.

It should be emphasized, therefore, that it is the *impossible* Fabulized Combination, especially one inferred from vague or inaccurately perceived details and in no way justified by qualifying references, that is particularly likely to indicate pathologic reasoning and be associated with schizophrenia.

CONTAMINATION

Contamination responses are condensations that not only fuse certain aspects of two percepts, as do Incongruous Combinations, and posit some type of relationship between percepts, as do Fabulized Combinations, but totally fuse overlapping images into a single percept. Contaminated responses result when a subject blends two or more separate responses to the same Rorschach location into a single response, and they usually can be readily identified by their bizarre quality and their tendency to lead to neologisms. Rorschach's (1921, p. 38) classic example of Contamination was given by a subject who apparently perceived Card IV as both an organ of the body and as an authoritarian male figure and responded, "The liver of a respectable statesman." A classic illustration of neologistic Contamination, also involving Card IV, is the condensation of impressions of the fronts of a bug and an ox into "the front of a bug-ox." Another graphic example, offered by Rapaport et al. (1946, p. 388), is "bloody island" to the outer red areas of Card III seen as both looking bloody and as representing an island.

As the "bloody island" example makes clear, Contamination is an extreme instance of the violation of realistic considerations through utilization of predicate thinking: "This detail looks bloody and it looks like an island, so it must be a bloody island." Rapaport's (1946, p. 339) description of these condensations clarifies further the relationship between predicate thinking and inappropriate distance from Rorschach stimuli: ". . . we see that in all of them [contaminations] some form of objective spatial contiguity in the card is taken too seriously, with too much reality-value; and this loss of distance opens the door for schizophrenic autistic thinking and irrealistic conclusions."

Clinical and research reports leave little doubt that Contamination represents a severe impairment of the thinking process and indicates schizophrenia. Rorschach (1921, p. 38) states on the basis of his samples that "contaminated whole answers are found only in schizophrenia." Bohm (1958, p. 270) concludes from his review of the literature that "contaminated W (and occasionally even D) actually seem to be a specific symptom of schizophrenic thinking, with its condensations." Rapaport et al. (1946, Appendix I) found that Contamination responses occurred almost exclusively in their schizophrenic subjects.

Although Contaminations are infrequent—Goldfried (1962) found only six contaminated responses in the Rorschachs of 110 hospitalized psychiatric patients—they may in some cases provide crucial evidence in an otherwise uncertain diagnostic picture. The following four Contamination responses helped to identify thought disorder in patients about whom the question of schizophrenia was in sufficient doubt to warrant psychological consultation: Card V—"A bird and a woman; it's a bird flying through a woman"; Card VI—"This part looks like a catfish with whiskers, but it has wings too, so the whole thing must be a *catbird*"; Card VI—"It reminds me of a dog and also of a rug, so it's a *dogrug*"; Card X—"The whole things looks like a monster; these look like spiders; it's a monster *with spiderish hands*."

CIRCUMSTANTIAL THINKING

Circumstantial thinking is an orientation toward and the basing of conclusions on incidental, tangential, and nonessential aspects of a situation. In an investigation of circumstantiality in psychiatric patients Peck (1962) concludes that circumstantiality is a unique type of thought disorganization, the presence of which may be considered presumptive evidence of schizophrenia. In psychodiagnostic language circumstantial thinking consists of inferring real relationships from coincidental aspects of either the test stimuli or the associations they suggest. Circumstantial thinking is implicit in overgeneralized and combinative thinking, which are indirect expressions of predicate logic and of failure to maintain appropriate distance from test stimuli. As Rapaport et al. (1946, p. 341) and Holt and Havel (1960, p. 291) point out, however, circumstantial thinking differs from these other indicators of impaired reasoning in that it includes an *explicit* statement of fallacious reasoning.

Whereas the types of deviant response presented in the preceding sections of this chapter frequently justify *inferring* the presence of thought disorder, responses included under circumstantial thinking are cast in a syllogistic form that *clearly explicates* the subject's failure to endorse conventional modes of logic. For purposes of discussion, it is helpful to separate circumstantial thinking into *autistic logic* and *position/number response*, the latter being a specific and strictly scored example of autistic logic.

AUTISTIC LOGIC

Autistic logic is indicated by any response in which there is an explicit statement of predicate thinking. If, for example, the subject who gave the "chickens rolling bowling balls" response quoted on page 79 had actually said, "These look like chickens and these like bowling balls, and since the chicken part is touching the bowling ball part, the chickens must be rolling the bowling balls," he would have manifested *autistic logic* as well as a Fabulized Combination. Such a distinction is important because the explicit statement of autistic logic, as opposed to an unelaborated Fabulized Combination, represents a conscious, purposeful predilection to faulty, often irrefutable reasoning. Peck (1962) reports that such circumstantiality, although not necessarily a negative prognostic sign, tends to be associated with poor insight and a chronic, intermittent course of psychological disturbance. Generally speaking, then, autistic logic is likely to constitute a more serious and refractory deviation from normal thinking than do the less explicit indicators of pathologic reasoning.

The circumstantial evidence presented by the autistic thinker may be more or less relevant to the conclusions he has drawn. In relatively mild instances autistic logic may be expressed only in relation to size coincidences (Card X, inner yellow detail—"A small lion, small because it's only a little part of this whole picture"; Card III, bottom center detail—"A big beetle (*big?*) it's big in proportion to these two men here") or to fairly reasonable spatial contiguities (Card VII— "These two things are rabbits and the bottom part is lettuce (*lettuce?*) it's next to the rabbits and lettuce is what rabbits eat, the two go together").

At other times autistic logic is offered in a strained and unsuccessful attempt to justify the response given, as in the following examples: Card I, center detail—"A man and woman, embracing (*one a man, other a woman?*) because they're together, men and women belong together"; Card III—"Two people bending over a stove (*stove?*) it looks like the two people are bending over to warm their hands, so it must be a stove"; Card V, large side details—"Heads of a couple old men, with long white beards ("leg" detail) on their chins (*white beards?*) they have to have white beards because they're old"; Card VIII— "Two rats, climbing on a pile of garbage (*garbage?*) nothing particular about it, I just imagine that where rats are, there's garbage."

Autistic logic, like Contamination, occurs infrequently but is highly suggestive of thought disorder when it does. Rapaport et al. (1946, Appendix I) found one or more instances of autistic logic in 15 (23%) of their paranoid and undifferentiated schizophrenics but not a single occurrence in any of their nonschizophrenic groups.

POSITION/NUMBER RESPONSE

Position (*Po*) and *Number* (*No*) responses are specific instances of autistic logic that involve coincidental interpretation of the relative position or number of Rorschach details. The following three responses illustrate *Po* interpretation: Card VII—"Angels here, with the Earth down below here (*angels?*) because they're way up, above the Earth"; Card III, center red detail—"A heart because it's right in the middle of everything"; Card III, bottom central detail—"This reminds me of a pelvis, and these are ovaries (*ovaries?*) because they're on opposite sides of the pelvis."

No interpretations are exemplified by these two responses: Card VII—"Looks like part of a Latin fable (?) like the story of Romulus and Remus (?) there were two of them and there are two of these shapes"; Card X—"Two people (pink details), and the tan, yellow and green suggest to me they're the children of the two people (?) there's no real form, it's just that there are two people, husband and wife for instance, like me and my wife, and we have three children and there are three of these."

As Beck (1961, pp. 214–216) points out in a discussion of *Po* responses, the scoring of *Po* and *No* should be restricted to instances in which *position* or *number* is the dominant or sole basis for the percept and should not be extended to percepts that are also justified by realistic references to the shape or color of the blot area. Definite *Po* and *No* responses strongly suggest reasoning impairment, and most writers (e.g., Piotrowski, 1957, p. 84) consider them pathognomonic of schizophrenia. The infrequency of these responses poses some problems in research design, and in most studies they are lumped with the broader category of autistic logic (e.g., Rapaport et al., 1946; Watkins & Stauffacher, 1952). One interesting exception is Rickers-Ovsiankina's (1938) report of finding *Po* in the records of nine of 37 schizophrenics but none of a normal control group, which represents a significant difference.

6

THOUGHT PROCESSES:
III. CONCEPT FORMATION

CONCEPT formation in the normally functioning person is marked by the capacity to interpret experience at appropriate levels of abstraction. It is generally agreed that schizophrenia is characterized by impaired cognitive focusing (see Chap. 4) and disturbed reasoning (see Chap. 5), but divergent opinions exist as to (a) whether schizophrenic persons suffer any basic deficit in abstracting ability and (b) whether such deficits, even if present, differ in any diagnostically useful way from the conceptual impairments demonstrated by persons with organic brain disease. It is therefore helpful to introduce this chapter with a brief review of the major theoretical positions and experimental data concerning conceptual deficit and abstract thinking in schizophrenia.

CONCEPTUAL DEFICIT IN SCHIZOPHRENIA

GOLDSTEIN'S POSITION

Kurt Goldstein has been the leading proponent of the view that schizophrenics suffer impaired capacity to assume the abstract attitude. In the late 1930's Goldstein became interested in the similarity of the conceptual deficits he had noted in his studies of brain-damaged persons to those observed by Vigotsky (1934) and Kasanin and Hanfmann (1938) in their administration of sorting tasks to schizophrenics. On the basis of a study with Bolles (Bolles & Goldstein, 1938) Goldstein concluded, "There is no question that a very great concreteness is characteristic for the behavior of schizophrenics."

In a classic 1944 paper Goldstein pointed out that whereas the normal individual is capable of shifting at will from concrete to abstract attitudes according to the demands of the situation, both the organic and the schizophrenic are governed to an abnormal degree by concrete thinking and behavior. Goldstein added that although it was not yet possible to decide whether impairment of the abstract attitude is an organic phenomenon, the clinical picture of schizophrenia nevertheless suggests disturbed functioning of the brain apparatus.

A number of studies have adduced support for Goldstein's position. First, in the area of sorting behavior more refined and reliable measures than those used in the early studies have consistently identified a conceptual deficit in schizophrenic subjects. Feldman and Drasgow (1951) developed a visual-verbal test on which subjects are asked to form concepts encompassing three or four objects depicted on test cards. In well-controlled comparisons of normal and schizophrenic samples on this test, in which they repeatedly found no overlap between groups, the schizophrenics consistently displayed relative inability to formulate abstract concepts. Fey (1951) reports similar results with a modified card-sorting test in which even young, fairly well integrated schizophrenic subjects performed at lower conceptual levels than normal controls.[1]

Another task on which conceptual deficit has been observed in schizophrenics is proverb interpretation. Benjamin (1944) stimulated both clinical and research use of formal proverb administration and scoring with observations that schizophrenic subjects, regardless of their intelligence, are prone to literal interpretations of proverbs. Gorham, who has constructed a standardized Proverbs Test (Gorham, 1956a, 1963), reports impressive evidence that low abstraction scores validly differentiate schizophrenic form normal groups of comparable intelligence (Gorham, 1956b).[2]

A third measure that has been utilized to study the conceptual thinking of schizophrenics is vocabulary definition. Feifel (1949) compared the conceptual level of vocabulary definitions of a number of abnormal groups, including schizophrenics, with that of normal sub-

[1] For a fuller summary of research on the performance of schizophrenics on sorting and other conceptual tasks, excellent reviews by Rabin and King (1958, pp. 230–242), Payne (1961, pp. 239–250), and Buss and Lang (1965) are recommended. The early investigations in this area are described in a classic 1944 review by Hunt and Cofer.

[2] Recent work by Shimkunas, Gynther, and Smith (1966), however, suggests that the responses of schizophrenic subjects to the Proverbs Test are less distinctive for their levels of abstraction and concreteness then for the high incidence of idiosyncracy, bizareness, and inappropriateness in them.

jects equated for age, education, and raw vocabulary score. He found that the abnormals produced significantly fewer *synonym* definitions than the normals and significantly more that merited scores of *use and description, explanation,* or *inferior.* Harrington and Ehrmann (1954) similarly found a group of schizophrenics to be significantly less abstract in their verbal definitions than a paired group of normals. Moran, Moran, and Blake (1952b), however, scoring verbal definitions according to Feifel's criteria, found no differences in any scoring category among 63 schizophrenic and normal matched pairs. As these studies illustrate, vocabulary definitions have only inconsistently demonstrated conceptual impairment in schizophrenics.[3]

CAMERON'S POSITION

Considerable additional research bearing on the conceptual performance of schizophrenics on sorting, proverbs, and vocabulary tasks has been stimulated by theoretical positions critical of Goldstein's views. Cameron (1944), in particular, has contended that schizophrenia is *not* characterized by any basic defect in the capacity to assume the abstract attitude. Consonant with his belief that schizophrenia proceeds primarily from "social disarticulation" (Cameron, 1947, Chap. 15), he argues that the schizophrenic person typically retains a high degree of abstracting ability, even though the personality disorganization he has suffered as a consequence of his impaired social skills may impede his performance on conceptual tasks.

Whereas Cameron stresses the *etiology* of poor conceptual performance in schizophrenics, many researchers have pursued the implication of his approach that *actual test performance* is influenced by the relative emphasis in the test materials on social and affective factors. Whiteman (1954), for example, hypothesized that if Cameron's view that schizophrenic thinking is a product of social disarticulation is more accurate than Goldstein's conclusion that schizophrenic conceptual deficit results from basic impairment of abstracting capacity, then schizophrenics should exhibit greater decrements, relative to normals, on tests of social than on test of formal concepts. Administering both a social-concept test and conceptual tasks involving formal, impersonal concepts to matched (age, education, Wechsler-Bellevue Vocabulary) schizophrenic and nonschizophrenic patients, Whiteman found, as predicted, a greater decrement for schizophrenics relative to the controls on the social rather than on the formal-concept tests. Nevertheless,

[3] The related question whether vocabulary skills are sufficiently resistant to the inroads of thought disturbance to be a reliable index of premorbid intellectual potential is considered further in Chapter 11.

Whiteman's schizophrenic subjects also manifested a significant decrement on the formal tests.

Richman (1957), comparing the ability of deteriorated and less deteriorated schizophrenics to define standard and emotionally toned vocabulary words, found that the same movement from abstract to inferior definitions associated with deterioration was also associated with the degree to which the words were emotionally toned. Feffer (1961) reported that schizophrenics who were pathologically concrete on conceptual tasks displayed greater tendencies to avoid affective stimuli than did either less concrete schizophrenics or normal subjects. Also of interest is a study by Lewis, Griffith, Riedel, and Simmons (1959) in which proverbs having oral, anal, and phallic content were given to schizophrenics and matched controls. The schizophrenics abstracted significantly less well on oral than on anal and phallic proverbs; however, their *over-all* performance relative to the normal controls clearly indicated impaired abstracting capacity.

These several studies lend support to the view that a social or affective context may accentuate the performance deficit of schizophrenics on conceptual tasks, but they also indicate that conceptual deficit appears on formal measures as well. It should be recognized, moreover, that it is erroneous to draw any conclusions about the relative accuracy of Goldstein's and Cameron's positions on the basis of such findings. Cameron asserts that deficits on conceptual tasks are the result of a personality disorganization that is in turn secondary to impaired social communication. The schizophrenic's greater impairment on social than on formal tasks is consistent with Cameron's approach, but the observation of decrements even on formal tasks does not necessarily challenge his argument. There is no reason to assume that personality disorganization, once derived from social disarticulation, may not become sufficiently autonomous to impair performance on any kind of task. Hence the finding of decrements on formal tasks does not automatically controvert Cameron's emphasis on social etiologic factors.

On the other hand, finding greater deficits in schizophrenic subjects on social than on formal tasks does not necessarily vitiate Goldstein's hypothesis of impaired abstracting capacity. Any impairment of functioning may be exacerbated in situations in which the impaired person is faced with distressing affects. Because an aphasic patient has greater difficulty with language when he is anxious than when he is relaxed does not mean he is without organic defect. For most schizophrenics interpersonal settings are anxiety-provoking and likely to compound their thinking difficulties, no matter whether or not these difficulties originate in organic defect. Therefore poorer conceptual performance on social than on formal tasks does not negate the possibility of basic incapacity.

OTHER APPROACHES

Several other types of study have evolved from theories that follow Cameron in emphasizing factors other than loss of abstracting capacity to account for deficient conceptual performance in schizophrenia. One such theory, invoking the notions of cognitive focusing outlined in Chapter 4, suggests that the schizophrenic's poor performance on conceptual tasks results from his inability to focus on the test material and avoid being distracted by irrelevant stimuli.

Chapman (1956) tested such an hypothesis by administering card-sorting tests containing distracter figures to normal and schizophrenic subjects. The schizophrenics but not the normals made increasing numbers of errors as the distracter figures increased in number, thus confirming the hypothesis of the schizophrenic's relative distractability. However, in a later study of verbal concept formation, in which he varied both the associative strength of the distracter element and the difficulty of the task, Chapman (1958) found that the schizophrenics' error frequency exceeded the normals' as a function not only of distracter elements but of task difficulty as well, independent of the role of the distracter.

The focusing concept has led to numerous studies in which subjects have been given "enriched" tasks designed to reduce distractability and enhance focus on the appropriate stimuli. Blaufarb (1962) in one such study gave proverbs to schizophrenics and matched (WAIS Vocabulary) normals in two sessions. In the first session he used a standard administration of single proverbs, but in the second session he gave subjects a series of cards, each having on it three proverbs with the same meaning. Although the normals abstracted the singly administered proverbs better than the schizophrenics, their superiority to the schizophrenics disappeared with the administration of the enriched proverb sets. However, Gorham's (1956b) data indicate that a similar effect does not hold for multiple-choice administration of proverbs; the multiple-choice form of his Proverbs Test reveals significant schizophrenic impairment to the same extent as the standard administration.

Multiple-choice forms of vocabulary tests have also been used in an effort to demonstrate that schizophrenics have basically adequate abstracting skills that can be elicited under properly simulating conditions. Harrington and Ehrmann (1954) found that groups of schizophrenic and normal subjects who differed in the conceptual level of their definitions on a standard vocabulary test performed at equal levels of abstraction on the less complex task of multiple-choice vocabulary. Chodorkoff and Mussen (1952), however, reported schizophrenic subjects to choose significantly more definitions of a lower conceptual level than a normal group on a multiple-choice vocabulary measure, and both Flavell (1956) and Milgram (1959) observed schizophrenics to select fewer abstractly related words than normals on a multiple-choice test of word meanings.

Another interpretation of schizophrenic conceptual performance has focused on motivational variables. Cavanaugh (1958), for example, administered concept formation tasks involving social and formal concepts to normal and schizophrenic groups under usual conditions and under an experimental condition in which performance was rewarded by escape from an aversive stimulus. He found that schizophrenics taking the tests under usual conditions performed at inferior levels both to normal subjects and to schizophrenics "motivated" by the escape condition, whereas the "motivated" schizophrenics approximated normal performance.

Considerable research of this type has been stimulated by Rodnick and Garmezy (1957), who attribute much of the cognitive deficits observed in schizophrenic subjects to the schizophrenics' sensitivity to social censure and rebuff. Work in this area and issues concerning the role of social-motivational variables in schizophrenic behavior are considered further in Chapter 9. Also of note is an effort by Mednick (1958) to account for the inefficiency of schizophrenic subjects on conceptual tasks in terms of a Hullian-type learning theory approach to schizophrenia. Mednick hypothesizes that schizophrenia is marked by intense anxiety, the high-drive properties of which lead to excessive stimulus generalization and associative generalization that in turn impair task performance. As reviewed by Buss and Lang (1965, pp. 85–88), however, the assumptions on which Mednick bases this theory have not received strong experimental support.

It is a challenging task to summarize the above diverse findings in a manner that provides guidelines for clinical psychodiagnostic evaluation of schizophrenia. Nathan's (1964) view of the studies in this area is that they confirm Cameron's belief that schizophrenics are ultimately capable of abstract conceptual thinking but are able to display this capacity only under certain fortuitous circumstances that seldom characterize an actual testing situation. Rabin and King (1958, p. 241), however, conclude that these research findings "generally point to the presence of a deficit in the conceptual thinking of schizophrenics."

The latter opinion appears more consonant with reported data. Although there seems little question that schizophrenics may be adversely affected, and to a greater degree than other persons, by interpersonal, affect-arousing, or nonmotivating aspects of a testing situation, the studies by Whiteman, Lewis et al., Gorham, Chodorkoff and Mussen, and others have revealed schizophrenic deficits even under test conditions that control for such factors. As Meehl (1962) points out, even though enhanced motivation may attenuate and affect-arousal may exacerbate cognitive performance deficits, the fact remains that such deficits are observed to a greater degree in schizophrenic than in nonschizophrenic persons.

However, not to be ignored is the implication of those studies that have elicited essentially normal conceptual ability from schizophrenic subjects: that is, not all schizophrenics necessarily suffer conceptual deficits. Behind group averages are impressive data (e.g., Lothrop, 1960) to indicate that some schizophrenics manifest conceptual impairments and others do not. Hence, although conceptual impairments, like other diagnostic indicators, may help to identify schizophrenia when they are present, their absence does not rule out the diagnosis.

Finally, it is interesting to note that both Goldstein and Cameron have in recent years modified their views, perhaps in response to the research findings their original work stimulated. In a 1959 paper Goldstein resolves some of the questions he had left open earlier (see p. 86) and approaches Cameron's views by stressing anxiety rather than basic defect as the source of conceptual performance decrements in schizophrenia:

> The abnormal concreteness of the schizophrenic appears thus as a secondary phenomenon; it is not the effect of an organic defect; it does not represent a damage of abstraction, a deterioration of the mind, or a defect in thinking. It is an expression of the restriction in the use of the highest mental capacity.

Cameron, in the meantime, has come to emphasize less his earlier commitment to an interpersonal approach and has moved generally toward an ego psychoanalytic interpretation of behavior pathology. In his most recent text, *Personality Development and Psychopathology* (1963, Chap. 17), Cameron makes no reference to "social disarticulation" and, as in the organization of this book, discusses schizophrenic concept formation as an aspect of disordered thinking.

DISTINCTIVE FEATURES OF ABSTRACT THINKING IN SCHIZOPHRENIA

Although there is consensus that schizophrenics display performance deficits on conceptual tasks, and although the bulk of evidence suggests that these deficits are not merely situational or motivational arti-facts, additional controversy exists concerning the distinctive features of abstract thinking in schizophrenia. One prominent view, promul-gated by Goldstein (1944), holds that schizophrenics are excessively concrete, are unable to think symbolically, and do poorly on conceptual tests because they inappropriately restrict the scope of their thinking and commit errors of overexclusion. This conception is endorsed by Benjamin (1944) and Arieti (1955, pp. 209–215). Benjamin feels that the main feature of schizophrenic concept formation is the literalness with which tasks are interpreted. Arieti asserts that schizophrenics think concretely because they have lost their capacity to connote and are capable of dealing only with the denotative and verbal aspects of symbols.

A diametrically opposed interpretation of schizophrenic deficits on conceptual tasks has developed from Cameron's (1944) notion of over-inclusion in schizophrenia. Cameron's concept of overinclusion, which describes the schizophrenic's general difficulty in focusing his atten-tion on the most salient and relevant aspects of his environment, relates primarily to the cognitive focusing aspects of the thought process discussed in Chapter 4. Later writers, however, have seen in Cameron's term a specific explanation of schizophrenic conceptual errors, namely, that schizophrenics inappropriately enlarge conceptual categories, thereby making errors of overinclusion.

The alternative hypotheses of a restricted, overexclusive, overly lit-eral versus an enlarged, overinclusive, overly abstract approach as the explanation of schizophrenic impairment on conceptual tasks have stimulated considerable research. Two representative studies in this area are reported by Epstein (1953) and Chapman and Taylor (1957). Epstein, administering a pencil-and-paper concept-formation test (the Inclusion Test) to schizophrenic and normal groups, found (a) that the normals made approximately equal numbers of errors resulting from excessively narrow and excessively broad conceptual frames of reference, whereas the schizophrenics averaged twice as many errors of overinclusion than of underinclusion, and (b) that, although the schizophrenics overincluded significantly more frequently than the controls, the two groups did not differ in the frequency with which they underincluded.

Chapman and Taylor used a similar task in which subjects were asked to select from a group of items those belonging to a common conceptual category. In agreement with Epstein, they found no dif-ferences between schizophrenic and normal groups in a measure of overexclusive thinking—that is, conceptualizing from an excessively narrow base—but they did confirm their prediction that schizophrenics would use inappropriately broad, or overinclusive, bases for grouping. In this vein, Goldman (1960) found that group agreement on the meaning given symbols is lower among schizophrenics than among normals and that schizophrenics tend more than normals to relate a given symbol to divergent referents.

In summarizing these and other similar studies, Payne, Mattusek, and George (1959, p. 629) conclude that the theory of overinclusion has received strong experimental support and that studies of concreteness "have not succeeded in demonstrating that schizophrenics are unable to make abstract generalizations, although there is ample evidence that the generalizations they do make tend to be unusual."

Implications for Psychodiagnostic Indicators. The apparent fact that schizophrenics may err in being overly abstract as often as, if not more frequently than, overly concrete, suggests that psychodiagnostic indicators of *overinclusive concept formation* are the most efficient means of differentiating schizophrenic conceptual performance from that of both normal and brain-damaged persons. Research findings confirm that, on tests measuring only errors of underinclusion (e.g., responses to the Proverbs Test and tests of word meaning, scored only along a dimension from concrete to appropriately abstract), organic and schizophrenic groups tend to demonstrate similar deficits in comparison with normals and differ little from one another (Elmore & Gorham, 1957; Milgram, 1959). Furthermore, Salzman, Goldstein, Atkins, and Babigian (1966) have recently found psychotically depressed and hospitalized neurotic as well as schizophrenic patients to exhibit impaired capacity to abstract proverbs. It may therefore be that loss of the abstract attitude is *generally* associated with severe psychological disturbance and that indices of overly concrete thinking will contribute minimally to the differential diagnosis of schizophrenia.

However, on tasks in which the inappropriately overly abstract end of the conceptual continuum can be scored, meaningful differences of schizophrenic from both normal and organic groups are likely to appear. Two representative studies in this area, both of which employ a full range of conceptual scores from overexclusive through appropriate to overinclusive concept formation, are reported by Tutko and Spence (1962) and by Chapman (1961).

Tutko and Spence administered a sorting task in which subjects were asked to explain why groups of common objects belonged together. Those responses that were considered inadequate were scored according to whether they represented inability to specify a common property or whether they resulted from specification of properties that were excessively broad, vague, or idiosyncratic. Tutko and Spence found that normal subjects were superior to schizophrenic and brain-damaged subjects in the number of adequate responses they made and tended to make equal numbers of the two types of error when their responses were inadequate. Brain-damaged subjects, however, made errors primarily of inability to specify a common property, whereas reactive schizophrenics made errors primarily of too broad, vague, or idiosyncratic specification. It is interesting to note that a group of process schizophrenics made no more frequent errors than the reactive schizophrenics, but when they were in error they tended to respond more like the brain-damaged than the reactive schizophrenic group.[4]

These data indicate that, although some schizophrenics may demonstrate a concreteness similar to that of organic subjects on conceptual tasks, *the presence of overabstraction is a distinctive and diagnostically useful feature of schizophrenic concept formation.* This conclusion is supported by Chapman's (1961) study, in which he cross-validated the finding that schizophrenics make relatively more errors of over-inclusion and organics relatively more errors of overexclusion on conceptual tests. Chapman also points out, however, that inasmuch as schizophrenics may at times display either type of error the main factor in their poor performance is their tendency to use concepts of a specific preferred breadth, regardless of their appropriateness to the task.

Chapman's hypothesis concerning the inappropriate use of concepts of a specific preferred breadth is consonant with the suggestion on page 85 that normal concept formation is defined by the capacity to interpret experience at appropriate levels of abstraction. The data reviewed thus far suggest that the schizophrenic subject is deficient in this capacity and is likely to employ various inappropriate levels of abstraction: at those points at which he is overly concrete he reveals information that differentiates him from the normal but not necessarily from the brain-damaged person; at those points at which he is overly abstract he provides information that distinguishes his conceptual performance from that of both normal and organic persons. These conclusions point to several test behaviors that frequently identify a schizophrenic impairment of concept formation.

---

[4] Implications of this and other differences between process and reactive schizophrenics are discussed in Chapter 13.

PSYCHODIAGNOSTIC INDICATORS OF CONCEPTUAL
DEFICIT IN SCHIZOPHRENIA

Although proverbs and vocabulary definitions have figured prominently in research studies of abstract thinking, neither the WAIS Vocabulary items nor the three proverbs on the WAIS Comprehension subtest are particularly useful for the clinical evaluation of schizophrenic conceptual deficit, primarily because they provide relatively little opportunity for inappropriate overabstraction. Distinctive schizophrenic features may appear on proverb interpretations and vocabulary definitions, including dissociation, deviant verbalizations, and circumstantial reasoning, yet the conceptual impairments displayed by schizophrenic subjects on these items are unlikely to be discernible from those observed in brain-damaged and some psychotically depressed subjects.

Consider, for example, the following three responses given by schizophrenic patients to the proverb, "Strike while the iron is hot": "What you do depends on what you're striking"; "An iron has to be hot to iron clothes with"; "Strike while you're mad instead of waiting till you cool down." These answers represent concrete associations to the concepts *strike, iron,* and *hot,* respectively, but as such they do not differ from types of error produced by persons with organically determined conceptual impairments. On rare occasions a schizophrenic subject may formulate an overly abstract proverb interpretation that aids the identification of his thinking disturbance, as in this reply to the proverb, "One swallow doesn't make a summer," by an intellectualized schizophrenic man: "Atmospherically speaking, I guess you just can't depend on the weather or on humanity." On closer analysis, however, the subject's response is significant more for its irrelevance and peculiar language ("atmospherically speaking") than for the level of conceptualization he employs.

Specific diagnostic use of the three Comprehension proverbs is further complicated by the fact that two of them are relatively difficult items. In Wechsler's (1958, p. 247) standardization sample only 38% of subjects achieved even partial credit on BROOKS and only 22% did so on SWALLOWS. Hence the majority of normal persons are likely to err on these proverbs, and the diagnostic significance of any but grossly deviant interpretations of them is accordingly minimized.

Although the diagnostic utility of proverbs and vocabulary definitions as measures of conceptual impairment is thus limited in the clinical battery, there are three test behaviors that do suggest distinctively schizophrenic conceptual deficit: *variable Similarities* on the WAIS and *idiosyncratic symbolism* and *abstract preoccupation* on the Rorschach. Each of these indicators of disordered thinking consists of overly abstract, overly symbolic interpretations of stimuli and/or the coexistence of overexclusive and overinclusive levels of concept formation.

VARIABLE SIMILARITIES

The WAIS Similarities items may be responded to at many levels of conceptualization, and the schizophrenic person whose conceptual thinking is impaired is likely to vary considerably on this subtest from extremely concrete to excessively abstract interpretations. Such uneven concept formation, encompassing both ends of the conceptual continuum, is distinctively a schizophrenic phenomenon and differs both from the normal expectation of appropriate abstraction and from the brain-damaged or psychotically depressed person's concrete error tendencies. However, it is important to recognize that when such deficits are present they are manifest primarily as a *distinctive variability* of the Similarities performance and not necessarily as a lowered total score.

This latter point is adequately confirmed by research findings. Tolor (1964) administered the WAIS Similarities to groups of brain-damaged, schizophrenic, and normal subjects approximately matched in vocabulary scores and education. The organic patients earned significantly lower Similarities scores than the other two groups, but the total Similarities score did not discriminate schizophrenics from normals. Rapaport, Gill, and Schafer (1945, pp. 158–163), moreover, found no differences between normal and schizophrenic subjects in Similarities scatter from either vocabulary or mean subtest score.

Hunt, French, Klebanoff, Mensh, and Williams (1948a, 1948b), in both an initial and a cross-validating study, did find a greater frequency of poor Similarities performance relative to Vocabulary in schizophrenic than in normal groups; however, they also found a similar frequency of such differences in groups of normal elderly persons. The Hunt et al. studies suggest that even if in certain instances schizophrenic persons do earn relatively low Similarities scores their raw subtest scores alone are not likely to differentiate them from persons with structural brain changes due to the aging process or to specific brain syndrome.

In order to determine whether a subject's Similarities answers are pathologically variable, it is necessary to compare them with adequate criteria for appropriate, overly abstract, and overly concrete response.

Appropriately abstracted answers are relatively easy to identify from Wechsler's scoring criteria in the WAIS manual (1955, pp. 60–62). With rare exception, responses that merit two-point credit are entirely appropriate abstractions and indicate normal conceptual functioning.

One-credit answers are for the most part reasonable conceptual efforts that fall a little short of the mark. Partial-credit responses to very easy items well within a subject's demonstrated intellectual capacity begin to suggest conceptual impairment, but such responses tend to be only mildly overly abstract or overly concrete and seldom reflect pathologically uneven concept formation. Furthermore, one-credit responses are not unusually given by normal persons who happen to be relatively disinclined toward intellectual activity and verbal problem solving. Partial-credit responses on such items of intermediate difficulty as EYE-EAR ("organs of body"), AIR-WATER ("elements"), and EGG-SEED ("produce life"), for example, occur commonly and do not suggest conceptual deficit even in the records of highly intelligent people.

Although such partial-credit answers may generally indicate a subject's preference for concrete or abstract levels of interpretation, it is the zero-credit, failed items that crucially distinguish pathologically overexclusive and overinclusive thinking. In an overly concrete or overexclusive interpretation the subject selects for his response one or more highly specific functional or structural similarities between the objects that may correctly describe both but are not particularly relevant to identifying them and do not capture their basic essence. For example, it is true that both dogs and lions have four legs, tails, fur, eat meat, and can make a lot of noise, but these are specific fragments of their natures; to compare them in terms of such specific details does not grasp the broader feature of their structural unity that constitutes the most meaningful similarity between them, that is, that they are animals.

In contrast, an overly abstract or overinclusive interpretation begins with and takes for granted the essential unity of the objects and, without fragmenting them, attempts to subsume them under some very broad conceptual category. Excessively broad categories, even if accurate, overlook the more delimited and significant similarity interrelating the objects in question. The overincluding subject does not concern himself with the various structural and functional details of dogs and lions that are similar, for example, nor does he stop with the recognition that they are animals; rather, he is likely to take their being animals as a starting point for an inappropriately broad interpretation as "they are members of the animal kingdom created by God" or "they are among the creatures that inhabit our earth."

With these basic distinctions between overexclusive and overinclusive concept formation in mind, it is not difficult to identify the direction of the error in failed Similarities items. Table 2 provides additional examples of overly abstract and overly concrete responses to the Similarities items; although some of the examples are taken from Wechsler's scoring criteria, the majority are drawn by the author from clinical records of schizophrenic patients. Noteworthy in each case is that the response is not incorrect or irrelevant *as far as it goes* but is conceptually deficient in failing to achieve a level of abstraction optimally appropriate to the item.

TABLE 2

OVERLY CONCRETE AND OVERLY ABSTRACT RESPONSES BY SCHIZOPHRENIC
PATIENTS TO WAIS SIMILARITIES ITEMS

Item	Overly Concrete Responses	Overly Abstract Responses
1. Orange-banana	Contain calories	Nature's produce
2. Coat-dress	Have buttons; have a skirt part	Maintain human modesty
3. Axe-saw	Have edges; are sharp	Building blocks of modern society
4. Dog-lion	Bark; bite; tear meat	Creatures of God
5. North-west	Have timberlands; can be cold	Map-makers' terms; means of orienting oneself
6. Eye-ear	Have an opening; made of tissues	Allow man to deal with his environment
7. Air-water	Contain moisture	Substances; matter; compose the earth; part of universe
8. Table-chair	Have legs; can be made of wood	Items utilized by human beings; used for personal comfort
9. Egg-seed	Can be eaten; have same shape	Are germ cells; germinate their species; beginnings
10. Poem-statue	Poem is words and statues have words on them	Objects at which people look; sources of pleasure
11. Wood-alcohol	Come from trees	Useful compounds; chemical materials
12. Praise-punishment	Start with a p	Actions; help form the human mind; people are sensitive to them
13. Fly-tree	Have limbs; secrete	Made by God; occupy space in our world

There are no research data, aside from the few findings on Similarities scatter (see p. 51), that assess how many inappropriately abstracted responses or how great a variability between overly abstract and overly concrete responses constitute evidence for thought disorder. In general, however, the more a subject's abstracting efforts vary between overexclusive and overinclusive thinking, with emphasis on the latter, the greater and more grandiose the breadth of his overinclusiveness, and the more his errors of overinclusion appear on relatively easy items within his intellectual capacity, the greater the likelihood that he has a schizophrenic thought disorder.

IDIOSYNCRATIC SYMBOLISM

Inappropriate conceptualization appears in two types of symbolic Rorschach response, one involving symbolic interpretation of color or shading and the other consisting of the use of concrete images to represent abstract ideas. As elaborated below, responses of these types do not necessarily imply disordered thinking, but when they take *idiosyncratic* rather than *conventional* forms they are likely to be associated with a schizophrenic impairment of concept formation.

Regarding symbolic responses based on the color and shading qualities of the inkblots, it should first be noted that these responses may be more or less integrated with definite form perception. Klopfer, Ainsworth, Klopfer, and Holt (1954, Chap. 6) indicate separate scoring for *FCsym* (Card III—"Two rejected suitors . . . red part symbolizes heartbreak"), *CFsym* (Card II—"They have just murdered someone . . . above them is a symbol written in blood of what they have done"), and *Csym* (Card IX—"Life fighting against death; the orange is life and it's being swallowed up by the green"), and similar scoring refinements can be specified for shading symbolism. However, the pathologic significance of symbolic color and shading responses depends not so much on their extent of form integration as on the manner in which they are expressed and the degree to which they are idiosyncratic.

As Rapaport et al. (1946, p. 237) point out, in some cases a symbolic response emerges only at the conclusion of or in addition to an already carefully elaborated response an 1 is given with an air of fancy (e.g., "Let's say that this red in the middle stands for the love they bear for each other"). Such responses are not unusual in the records of normal persons who are highly imaginative and tend to deal with their affective experience in an intellectual fashion. On the other hand, as Rapaport et al. also indicate, symbolic responses offered as the initial or dominant response to a Rorschach area and expressed with an air of considerable reality (e. g., "This red in the middle *must* stand for some attraction between these two things on the side") are unusual in other than schizophrenic subjects.

Concerning the distinction between conventional and idiosyncratic symbolic interpretation of Rorschach qualities, Holt and Havel (1960, pp. 290–291) provide the following useful guideline. Conventional color or shading symbolism they define as the expression of culturally shared, stereotyped meanings of color or shading; for example, blue as coldness, red as anger, green as envy, or black as evil. Responses involving such conventional symbolism are not particularly suggestive of inappropriate concept formation and, as Klopfer et al. (1954, pp. 286–287) also note, are often associated with a nonschizophrenic intellectual defensive style.

Idiosyncratic symbolic responses, on the other hand, are based on symbolic referents unique to the thinking of the particular subject: "The red reminds me of prostitution"; "The black indicates confusion"; "Looks like an atom bomb explosion, and the red represents the death and destruction it caused"; "It depicts masculinity and femininity—the dark colors indicate stability, which is a masculine quality, and the lighter colors are instability, which is feminine." The use of such idiosyncratic symbols in the interpretation of color or shading suggests a pathologic tendency for overly abstract thinking.

Similar considerations apply to those responses in which concrete images are used to represent abstract ideas. They may involve conventional image symbols, as in "The bow gives a feminine touch" or "There's a dove at the top, signifying that all is peaceful"; or they may constitute idiosyncratic interpretations, as "Rats, symbolic of the nibbling away of the good green earth, of the good by the evil," or "Two people, with a cloud behind them indicating they're angry."

It is the latter, idiosyncratic use of concrete images as abstract symbols that suggests thought disorder, and the presentation of such responses with an air of reality and/or as the sole or most salient impression of a Rorschach area increases the likelihood of a schizophrenic impairment of concept formation. However, the pathologic significance of these responses, like that of color or shading symbolism, is attenuated when they are offered as purposefully fanciful additions to an otherwise appropriate response, as in the following interpretation of Card VIII: "Two animals, climbing up something; I could think of it as personifying something, perhaps the idea of trying to achieve, that is, trying to climb higher in what you do."

ABSTRACT PREOCCUPATION

Overinclusive thinking is indicated on the Rorschach not only by specific use of idiosyncratic symbols but also by preoccupation with highly abstract ideas. Exaggerated concern with abstract meanings at the expense of adequate attention to lower-level abstractions that are equally or more relevant to the situation at hand identifies inability to interpret experience at appropriate levels of abstraction.

Three types of abstract (*Ab*) response with different diagnostic implications appear on the Rorschach. One type, as described by Klopfer et al. (1954, p. 202), involves vague impressions of "powers" or "forces" with no specific content. Responses of this type are scored *impressionistic* by Piotrowski (1957, p. 356: "It gives me a feeling of power"; "It's depressing and gloomy") and by Holt and Havel (1960, p. 289: "Gives me the feeling of horizon"). Amorphous responses like "turmoil," "death," "autumn," and "gaiety," some of which may involve color or shading symbolism as well, also illustrate impressionistic *Ab*. Responses of this type occurring singly or in small numbers are not necessarily related to thought disorder, but in instances in which they dominate the response process and replace appropriate, more concrete responses they begin to suggest a pathologic preoccupation with abstraction.

A second type of abstract preoccupation, more serious than abstract impressions of Rorschach stimuli, is a highly fabulized response in which abstract concepts and events are described as if they were real objects. The following examples of such *Ab* responses, selected from the records of schizophrenic subjects, identify pathologic preoccupation with abstractions: Card V—"The two ends look like the tail and rear leg of something diving into something, diving into eternity, coming out of this world and going into nothing"; Card VII—"Looks like a representation of the environment closing in on you"; Card IX—"It gives me a feeling of nature up here and of Hell down here, with the beauty of nature confronting the evil depths of base emotion and indicating an approaching sense of the ultimate of extremely high ideals"; Card X—"In the center is something very desirable, and all these on the outside are forces trying to get at what's in the middle, but the pink is a protective device, protecting the important thing." The presence in a record of *Ab* responses involving such Fabulization and Fabulized Combination points to a pathologic impairment of conceptual thinking.

A third type of *Ab* response, most strongly indicative of thought disorder, is the specific designation of abstract symbols on the Rorschach. Phillips and Smith (1953, p. 123) score such responses *Alphabet* (*Al*) and illustrate them with "W," "A," "7," "3," "square," and "point." They report that such responses are extremely rare in all clinical groups and are associated with severe psychopathology when they occur. Orme (1963) confirmed this conclusion in a study of 1311 Rorschach records routinely collected in a clinical setting. Only 16 of these records contained *Al* responses, but 13 of the *Al* responders were schizophrenic, and the frequency of *Al* was significantly greater among the schizophrenic than the nonschizophrenic patients. It is therefore highly likely when an *Al* response appears in a subject's record that he is experiencing a schizophrenic preoccupation with abstractions.

7

RELATION TO REALITY:

I. REALITY TESTING

THE preceding chapters on cognitive focusing, reasoning, and concept formation have considered aspects of schizophrenic ego functioning related to disturbed *thinking*. This and the following chapter deal with a person's relation to reality and features of schizophrenia that derive from disturbances of *perception*. Schizophrenia is characterized by a detachment from reality that Bleuler originally labeled autism, and detachment from reality is basically a malfunctioning of the perceptual processes. This view is expressed by a number of researchers (e. g., Klein, 1951) who stress that perceptual investigation is important to personality research precisely because perception represents an individual's point of contact with reality.

Bleuler's (1911, p. 373) statement of the relationship between disturbed perceptual functioning, impaired relation to reality, and schizophrenic behavior remains as cogent as any in the literature:

The schizophrenic loosening of logical processes leads to the exclusion of all associations conflicting with emotionally charged complexes. The need which is present in all human beings, to seek a substitute in fantasy for the unsatisfactory reality, can be satisfied in this way without meeting any resistance. No matter how much the products of fantasy are in contradiction to reality, they certainly do not come into any conflict with reality in the patient's brain. Indeed, they are brought into as much harmony as possible with the patient's affective needs. In severe cases, the whole of reality, with its never ceasing perceptive-sensory stimulations, is blocked off; at the very most reality exists only in its most banal relationships: in eating, in drinking, in getting dressed. Thus the autistic thought content remains incorrigible and assumes complete reality-value for the patients, while the subjective reality-value of actuality is reduced to zero.

In this statement Bleuler anticipates by many years the "new look" in perception that became prominent on the psychological scene in the late 1940's and early 1950's with the development of the notions of need-influenced perception (Bruner & Goodman, 1947) and perceptual defense (Eriksen, 1951; McGinnies, 1949). Bleuler is essentially describing the same psychological processes that in these studies led impoverished children to overestimate the size of coins and normal adults to avoid conscious perception of tachistiscopically presented taboo words. Bleuler's observations, however, pertain to extreme instances of perceptual distortion in which the objective influence of stimulus input is so subordinated to subjective needs that it constitutes "a detachment from reality, together with the relative and absolute predominance of the inner life" (Bleuler, 1911, p. 63).

Bleuler considers autism a fundamental symptom of schizophrenia the presence of which clearly points to the diagnosis. Although less psychologically oriented theorists than Bleuler might take issue with his need-conflict interpretation of autism, those who argue that impaired perceptual functioning is primarily attributable to structural or physiological brain defects nevertheless typically agree that such impairments are characteristic in schizophrenia. Heath (1960), for example, who considers schizophrenia a genetically determined metabolic disease, delineates as its usual secondary manifestations the same disturbances outlined by Bleuler as the fundamental symptoms of the disorder.

The perceptual prosesses on which adequate relation to reality depends have two broad aspects, accurate perception of one's environment and accurate perception of one's body. Accurate perception of one's body is the essence of the *sense of reality,* which is the topic of Chapter 8. The present chapter concerns *reality testing,* which is defined primarily by accurate perception of one's environment. Deficiencies in basic reality testing skills are manifest in inaccurate perception and impaired judgment, psychodiagnostic indicators of which are presented below.

INACCURATE PERCEPTION

Perception is accurate to the extent that percepts are determined by the realistic qualities of the stimuli that elicit them. Schizophrenics have been found to be less accurate than normal persons in making even simple psychophysical judgments on a variety of perceptual tasks (Chambers, 1956; Cooper, 1960). In the clinical battery the objectivity of perceptual functioning is measured by the form quality of Rorschach responses. The greater the correspondence of a subject's Rorschach percepts to the actual shape of the blot areas to which he is responding, the stricter his allegiance to the objective, realistic qualities of his experience; the more his responses deviate from the forms represented by the blots, on the other hand, the less firm his grasp on reality.

The importance to intact ego functioning of perceptual accuracy as measured by Rorschach form quality is widely recognized. Beck (1948), for example, avers that accurate form perception is the sine qua non of adequate ego functioning. Klopfer, Ainsworth, Klopfer, and Holt (1954, p. 587) hold that the form level of Rorschach responses is the main clue to the ego's capacity for reality testing. Korchin (1960, p. 111) offers the following concise statement of the relationship between accurate form perception and the ego's reality testing operations:

> Mature ego functioning involves a capacity for undistorted perception. . . . This dimension of Rorschach performance—the degree to which the subject is attentive to, or departs from, the "reality" represented in the blots—has often been taken as a measure of the subject's ability to deal with, and his respect for, reality in general. In this sense, it becomes a measure of ego strength.

Two Rorschach scores, *low F+%* and *low R+%*, reflect perceptual inaccuracy and suggest a schizophrenic impairment of reality testing capacity.

LOW F+%

Low F+% is an index of the degree of detachment from reality manifest in a Rorschach record. Inasmuch as several different methods of scoring form level have been advocated, it is instructive to survey briefly the major approaches to form-level scoring before considering the research literature and related clinical recommendations for psychodiagnostic utilization of the $F+\%$ index.

Scoring Form Level. The scoring of form responses as "+" or "−" was introduced by Rorschach (1921), who determined form level by a combined actuarial and subjective approach. After designating those form responses occurring frequently in the records of approximately 100 normal subjects as $F+$, Rorschach subsequently scored $F+$ for form responses that appeared to correspond to the blots as well as or better than this basic list and $F-$ for form responses that in his judgment were inferior to it.

Some later workers expressed concern that Rorschach's method allowed too much room for subjective judgment without specifying adequate standards for good and poor form responses. Beck, for one, recommended using response frequency to establish definite form standards and thus eliminate as much as possible the necessity for subjective judgments, and his earlier form-level tables (Beck, 1950, pp. 158–195) have been widely employed. Hertz (1942) similarly used frequency of occurrence as the standard of accuracy to develop form-level norms for Rorschach responses.

Other clinicians have argued that reliance on frequency tables may blur the meaningful connection between form perception and reality testing and lead to logical inconsistencies. Piotrowski (1957, pp. 111–112), for example, contends that such tables err in emphasizing verbal rather than perceptual content. As a case in point, Beck's early tables scored $F+$ for all of Card V seen as an "insect" but $F-$ for the response "beetle" to same location, because "beetle" is infrequently given by normal persons. Piotrowski observes that the visual correspondence of the shape of a beetle is no worse a fit to Card V than the image of an insect.

In a different vein, Klopfer and Kelley (1942, pp. 154–157) express general dissatisfaction with Rorschach's effort to score all form responses as "$+$" or "$-$". They note that many form responses represent vague or indefinite concepts and lack the specificity necessary to characterize them as accurate or inaccurate. Klopfer and Kelley recommend scoring such responses merely as F, reserving $F+$ for clearly defined responses of superior accuracy and $F-$ for definite images that in the examiner's judgment are markedly discrepant from the form qualities of the blot. Klopfer et al. (1954, pp. 207–239) subsequently worked out a more elaborate numerical system of form-level rating, similarly based on judgment of the examiner, that will not be reviewed here.

Rapaport, Gill, and Schafer (1946, pp. 186–188) also emphasize subjective evaluation of form level. Although they agree with Rorschach that any response given frequently by normal people merits an $F+$ scoring, they argue that sophisticated clinical interpretation of form level requires the examiner to make several qualitative judgments. First, they recommend identifying not only forms corresponding well ($F+$) and poorly ($F-$) to the inkblots, but also "$\pm$" (essentially good with some traces of weakness of perceptual organization) and "$\mp$" (essentially poor with some traces of good perceptual organization) responses. Second, with regard to form definiteness, they offer the following scheme: sharp, definitive, and convincing form responses they score *special* $F+$; definitive but arbitrary and unconvincing form responses they score *special F*—; vague responses they score *Fv*; and mediocre but acceptable form responses they score *Fo*.

Piotrowski (1957, p. 112) similarly endorses subjective judgments by the examiner to determine form level, but he follows Rorschach fairly closely in suggesting that Popular responses should serve as the criterion against which form accuracy is judged. When a response fits the blot area to which it is given at least as well as the Popular responses match their respective areas, Piotrowski scores *F*+; when the fit falls short of the Popular standard, *F*— is scored. Piotrowski also suggests that responses containing images of objects of indeterminate shape, such as clouds, islands, rocks, etc., should be scored neither "—" nor "+," but as F±.

This material should suffice to demonstrate that differences of opinion have somewhat muddied the form-level waters.[1] That these controversies are not completely sterile is revealed in a study by Walker (1953). Walker had 100 normal persons unfamiliar with the Rorschach judge the correspondence to the blots of 191 *plus* and 108 *minus* W responses taken from Beck's 1950 tables. Although the group's judgments of *F*+ and *F*— were significantly related to Beck's, there were important differences between the two form-level lists: *F*+% scores derived from the group criteria significantly differentiated a normal adult sample from a group of paranoid schizophrenic subjects, whereas *F*+%'s computed from Beck's tables did not.

Recognizing some of the problems with his earlier tables, Beck, in preparing the most recent edition of his basic text (1961, pp. 130–207), utilized the reported experiences of about 200 practicing psychologists to revise his scoring lists. In the current tables such inconsistencies as the *insect-beetle* scoring cited by Piotrowski are largely eliminated, and general "+" and "—" categories for most locations are added, thus rectifying the earlier overemphasis on specific verbalization rather than perceptual content. However, these improvements notwithstanding, Beck adds that neither recourse to his tables nor to a compendium of tables such as that prepared by Small (1956) abolishes the necessity for frequent subjective form-level judgments by the examiner.

Further Recommendations for Scoring Form Level. The scoring procedure recommended in this book and used in case illustrations in later chapters is eclectic and derives from the following line of reasoning: the psychodiagnostic utility of any scoring scheme must be judged in

---

[1] The reader who is interested in a fuller discussion of historical developments and practical issues in the scoring of Rorschach form level is referred to two papers by Kimball (1950a, 1950b) and a summary by Bell (1948, pp. 99–110).

reference to the personality variables it is intended to assess. If form-level scoring is undertaken to evaluate reality testing—that is, the degree to which perception is accurate—it is of little value, as Klopfer and Kelley and Piotrowski argue, to attempt to score as "$+$" or "$-$" those indefinite forms that cannot be interpreted to indicate either clearly accurate or clearly inaccurate perception. Clouds, islands, and rocks, for example, can exist in almost any imaginable shape.

Rather, it is important to identify those form percepts that are clearly defined and, by comparing them with available standards when possible and relying on subjective judgment when necessary, to score them $F+$ or $F-$. Wherever possible, mediocre forms that depict objects of definite shape should also be scored $F+$ or $F-$, to give the fullest possible representation of a subject's level of perceptual accuracy.

A form-level scoring system, however, cannot ignore that the construction of a perceptual image from the formal stimulus qualities of an inkblot is influenced not only by the *accuracy* of a subject's perception but also by the degree of *articulation, differentiation,* and *integration* that characterize his perceptual functioning. However, although articulation, differentiation, and integration of perceptual impressions are major aspects of ego functioning, they are not primarily related to reality testing. Perceptual articulation is an index of the sense of reality, and its impairment as manifest in vague and amorphous percepts is discussed in Chapter 8 in reference to inadequate ego boundedness. Differentiation and integration of percepts relate primarily to the synthetic, organizational capacity of the ego, which is the subject of Chapter 12. As suggested above, therefore, the goal of evaluating perceptual accuracy through form-level rating seems best served by scoring clearly defined responses as $F+$ or $F-$ and assigning indefinite responses to a category that is excluded from over-all form-level evaluation, such as $F\pm$.

Scoring $F+\%$. Several slightly different procedures have been used to determine $F+\%$. $F+\%$ is computed by Rorschach and Beck as the ratio of $F+$ to the sum of $F+$ and $F-$ responses and by Rapaport et al. as the percentage of $F+$ and $F\pm$ responses, taken together, in all F responses. Piotrowski gives all $F\pm$ responses the weight of two thirds of an $F+$ and also includes form level scoring for shading, achromatic color, and FM responses in his computation of $F+\%$, which means that his $F+\%$ is more similar to $R+\%$ (see pp. 114–115) than to Beck's $F+\%$. Other scoring recommendations have appeared, but inasmuch as there are no vital issues to which they have been addressed they will not be pursued further here except to point out the obvious fact that research literature and normative standards can be no more consistent than the scoring procedures on which they are based. Fortunately, as the following research reports indicate, the minor variations in methods of computing $F+\%$ have not precluded fairly consistent investigative outcomes.

Low F+% in Schizophrenia. Low $F+\%$ is an identifying characteristic of schizophrenic disorder, demonstrating as Schafer (1948, p. 69) points out "the breakdown of reality-testing and the suffusion of apperception with pathologically autistic thought content." Research evidence attests that *low* $F+\%$ validly differentiates schizophrenic from normal and neurotic persons and is more reliably indicative of a schizophrenic diagnosis than any other single test variable.

Virtually all studies of $F+\%$ in schizophrenic and control groups have replicated the findings presented by Beck and Rickers-Ovsiankina in their historically significant 1938 contributions (see Chap. 3). Rickers-Ovsiankina compared the records of 37 schizophrenics and 20 normal controls of similar age, sex, and education and found mean $F+\%$'s of 66.9 in the schizophrenic and 87.3 in the control group. The difference between these means was significant, and all but one of the normal subjects had an $F+\%$ greater than the median schizophrenic $F+\%$ of 75. Beck studied 81 schizophrenic subjects and a control group consisting of 33 normal persons and 31 nonpsychotic psychiatric patients. He obtained mean $F+\%$'s of 61.5 for the schizophrenics and 83.9 for the controls, which closely approximates Rickers-Ovsiankina's findings.

Beck (1954, pp. 211–212) later reported Rorschach comparisons between 157 normal adults and schizophrenic and neurotic groups of 60 subjects each. The mean $F+\%$ for the normal group (79.2) was significantly larger than that of the neurotics (68.5), which in turn significantly exceeded that of the schizophrenics (61.2). Other studies have fairly uniformly observed average $F+\%$'s of around 60 for schizophrenic and around 80 for normal subjects. Friedman (1952b) obtained median $F+\%$'s of 61 from 30 schizophrenics and 84 from 30 normal controls. Berkowitz and Levine (1953) reported mean $F+\%$'s of 60.0 for 25 schizophrenic patients and 80.0 for 25 neurotic patients. In both studies the schizophrenics were significantly lower than the control subjects in $F+\%$.

These data demonstrate the validity of $F+\%$ for discriminating schizophrenia from normal and neurotic persons, and they suggest 60% as a criterion score for *low* $F+\%$ below which a schizophrenic impairment of reality testing is indicated. In addition, $F+\%$'s falling in the 60–70 range appear to represent a sufficient extent of perceptual inaccuracy to raise the possibility of schizophrenia, perhaps in a mild or incipient form. The schizophrenic subjects in these studies were all hospitalized patients, many of whom could be presumed to be chronically disturbed (see Chap. 13), and Rapaport et al. (1946, pp. 200–201) found a clear superiority of acute over chronic schizophrenic subjects in $F+\%$. Hence it may be that the frequently observed $F+\%$ of 60 in schizophrenic groups is primarily characteristic of relatively seriously disturbed persons, whereas a less deficient $F+\%$, in the 60–70 range, may be associated with mild or ambulatory schizophrenia.

There are no data that evaluate the efficacy of 60–70 $F+\%$ as a suggestive clue to schizophrenia, but the cutting point of 60 is well established as strongly indicative of the diagnosis. Berkowitz and Levine (1953) found a significant association between an $F+\%$ of 60 or less and schizophrenia; only three of their 25 neurotic subjects were this low in $F+\%$. Knopf (1956), comparing records of 100 schizophrenics with those of 131 neurotics, also found that a contingency table utilizing an $F+\%$ of 60 as the cutting score yielded a significant χ^2. Phillips and Smith (1953, p. 27), referring to their sample of 250 normal adult males, report that an $F+\%$ below 60 occurs in only 5% of normal subjects, and they concur that 60% $F+$ should be considered the lower limit for normality.

Low $F+\%$ in Nonschizophrenic Conditions. Although *low $F+\%$* validly discriminates schizophrenic from normal and neurotic persons, it should be recognized that indices of impaired relation to reality, unlike many of thought disorder, are not *distinctively* related to schizophrenia. $F-$ responses can be determined by a number of mechanisms, and perceptual inaccuracy characterizes certain nonschizophrenic conditions that must be considered in the differential diagnostic interpretation of *low $F+\%$*.

As summarized by Korchin (1960, pp. 119–123), there are basically four psychological mechanisms that conduce to $F-$ responses. The first mechanism is a conflict between needs and/or defenses that interferes in a *personal* manner with perceptual accuracy. In some instances of personal interference a subject's internal needs so overwhelm his capacity to control their expression that he responds primarily in terms of them, with correspondingly minimal concern for the objective qualities of the Rorschach stimuli; at other times the inkblots themselves cue off anxiety-provoking associations, the expression of which is defended against by a flight into harmless but hastily conceived and shoddy responses.

In both instances the resulting $F-$ is what Beck (1952, p. 21) calls a *personal F—*, "a misshaping of reality as dictated by personal need." Beck points out that *personal F—* responses are the type produced by normal and neurotic persons when they occasionally give $F-$ responses. However, *personal F—* responses clearly capture that aspect of poor reality testing that Bleuler had in mind when he coined the term *autism*, and their accumulation in a record suggests schizophrenia.

A second mechanism underlying $F-$ responses is a basic lack or impairment of perceptual ability that obtains independently of whether or not the blots stimulate threatening fantasy. Those $F-$ responses that result primarily from basic perceptual impairment are called *impersonal* (Beck, 1952). *Impersonal F—* responses, in addition to being given frequently by schizophrenics, are a major consequence of organic brain disease. The brain-damaged person, whose basic capacity to organize his visual field is likely to be impaired, when pushed to give other than obvious responses often produces large numbers of $F-$ responses of little personal significance. The relevance of *low F+%* in diagnosing organicity has been demonstrated by Piotrowski (1936–1937, 1937), who includes $F+\%$ below 70 among his positive Rorschach indicators of organicity, and, more recently, by Evans and Marmorston (1964), who found $F+\%$ below 70 to occur significantly more frequently in the records of 139 brain-damaged subjects than of 136 organically ill patients without cerebral pathology.

Unfortunately, it is not always possible to differentiate *personal* from *impersonal F—*, nor is there any fixed relationship between schizophrenia and *personal F—* on the one hand and organicity and *impersonal F—* on the other. The main points to recognize are (a) that *low F+%* may characterize brain-damaged as well as schizophrenic persons, (b) that a clear predominance of *impersonal F—* may point to organicity rather than schizophrenia, and (c) that *low F+%* is most useful in identifying schizophrenia when other test data are free from signs of cerebral pathology.[2]

---

[2] It is also important to recognize that the labels *cerebral pathology* and *organic brain disease* cover a variety of syndromes. The perceptual impairments that lead to *low F+%* are likely to characterize persons having chronic brain syndromes with irreversible structural brain changes and persons suffering those acute brain syndromes that are accompanied by *delirium*. Delirium, as described by Romano and Engel (1944), is a fluctuation in the level of awareness attributable to temporary disturbances in brain metabolism. Although diminished perceptual awareness is likely to increase $F-$ responsivity, it should be noted that not all acute brain syndromes are attended by delirium. Amphetamine-induced psychoses, for example, are difficult to diagnose precisely because they mimic schizophrenia and are typically not characterized by delirium (Weiner, 1964a). The fact that patients with amphetamine psychosis are not delirious suggests that they might not display

A third mechanism that may be involved in poor form perception is paucity of associational material for constructing responses. A subject whose experience is limited and whose perceptual contact with the world is minimal has relatively little basis for arriving at accurate interpretations of the inkblot shapes. Such limitations are primarily characteristic of feeble-minded persons, and associations between mental deficiency and *low F+%*, as summarized by Davidson and Klopfer (1937), are among the earliest experimental findings in the Rorschach literature. Hence the value of *low F+%* as a schizophrenic indicator is minimal in the evaluation of mentally defective persons.

The fourth mechanism affecting a subject's use of good and poor forms is his attitude toward the testing situation and the examiner. Because this variable cuts across pathologic and normal states, it is discussed in the following section on general factors that influence the interpretation of *low F+%*.

Factors Influencing the Interpretation of Low F+%. Beyond the specific inroads of brain damage and mental deficiency several general factors affect *F—* responsivity and influence the interpretation of *low F+%*. First, the dynamics of the subject's interaction with the examiner and the testing situation, as explicated by Sarason (1954, pp. 7–105) and Schafer (1954, pp. 1–73), must be taken into account. Those attitudes most relevant to a subject's form level concern (a) the manner in which he wishes to present himself and (b) his perception of what the examiner would like from him.

Some subjects, of course, do not wish to present themselves at all; they come for testing grudgingly at best, are angry, resentful, or frightened, and respond in a guarded manner. Such persons usually aim at presenting a "good" picture of themselves, with "good" meaning "healthy," "sane," or "don't need to be in a hospital." A similar effort to give a good account of themselves characterizes those subjects who, although basically as concerned and guarded as the hostile, blatantly uncooperative subject, utilize an exaggerated display of cheerfulness, self-confidence, and cooperation to convince the examiner of their good health.

At the other end of this dimension are subjects who are intent on presenting a "bad" picture of themselves. These people often are seeking incapacity in a regressive attempt to provoke dependent gratification from their environments, although such behavior at times repre-

---

poor form perception on the Rorschach. Weiner (1965c) has in fact reported differences in *F+%* between schizophrenic and amphetamine-psychotic patients that facilitate differential diagnosis of the two conditions.

sents an appropriate cry for help from a person who feels the extent of his distress is not sufficiently recognized by others.

With regard to the examiner's demands, some subjects perceive testing as an authoritarian situation in which they are expected to do exactly as they are told, no more and no less, and in which the examiner will be pleased if they follow instructions, keep strictly to the task, avoid irrelevancies, and respond as accurately as they can. Other subjects, in contrast, interpret psychological testing as a situation in which the examiner is most desirous that they give their imaginations free rein, expressing whatever thoughts come to their minds and using the test stimuli only as rough guides to their associations.

The implications of these attitudes for form level are obvious. The subject who wants to present a good impression of himself and who perceives the examiner as valuing accuracy will do his best to give accurate form interpretations. However, a subject with good intentions who construes the testing as a free associative task is likely to exert relatively little conscious control over his percepts, even if he is capable of doing so, and to indulge in numerous fanciful $F-$ responses. Correspondingly, the subject who wants to appear disturbed will focus on $F-$ if he structures the testing authoritatively and on banal $F+$ if he sees it as a measure of imaginative capacity.

Therefore the significance of *low F+%* for psychopathology is *attenuated* in cases of subjects who are seeking to impress the examiner and structure the situation liberally and for those who wish to appear disturbed and interpret the testing in an authoritarian fashion; it is *enhanced* in cases of well-intending subjects with authoritarian structure and for ill-intending subjects with liberal interpretation. For further elaboration on the identification and significance of the subject's attitudes toward the examination situation, the reader should review the contributions of Sarason and Schafer and also a classical paper by Schachtel (1945) on the effects of various subjective definitions of the test situation.

A second factor influencing the interpretation of *low F+%* is the degree to which $F-$ responses violate the formal reality of the inkblots. Phillips and Smith (1953, pp. 34–38) define four levels of $F-$ response, extending from responses that only minimally violate $F+$ criteria to those that grossly diverge from any form conceivably attributable to the particular Rorschach area. They report their experience that a striking relationship exists between the level of a subject's $F-$ responses and the degree of his psychopathology and that grossly discrepant $F-$ responses are extremely rare in the records of normal persons. Therefore on occasion the presence in a record of a few extremely inaccurate form perceptions suggests impaired reality testing even when the over-all $F+\%$ appears adequate; correspondingly, there are instances in which a *low* $F+\%$ determined solely by $F-$ responses that deviate only minimally from standards of accuracy must be conservatively interpreted.

Finally of significance in evaluating a *low* $F+\%$ is the length of the record in which it occurs. Fiske and Baughman (1953) found a significant negative correlation between $F+\%$ and total R, and their normative data suggest that *low* $F+\%$ is particularly deviant in a brief record and less so in a lengthy one. Since the number of accurate responses that can be given to a Rorschach card is considerably fewer than the possible number of inaccurate interpretations, it is understandable that as a normal person continues to respond beyond expectancy he is likely to give increasing numbers of poor, though not markedly poor, responses. A subject who is giving relatively few responses, on the other hand, normally focuses his attention on the more obvious, accurate forms.

The length of a Rorschach record does not appear to affect the validity of *low* $F+\%$ as a diagnostic indicator for schizophrenia. Sherman (1952), dividing a group of 71 schizophrenic and 66 normal subjects into high and low responders, found that both $F+\%$ and number of $F-$ responses significantly discriminated the schizophrenics from the normals in both high and low responding groups. Nevertheless, in view of the available normative data, it may be necessary in the evaluation of the individual case to adjust the criterion for *low* $F+\%$ upward in evaluating brief records and downward in considering lengthy ones.

In summary, then, although *low* $F+\%$ may be taken to indicate a schizophrenic impairment of reality testing in the absence of evidence of cerebral pathology and mental deficiency, its implications are attenuated (a) when a subject who interprets the situation liberally is attempting to give a good account of himself, (b) when a subject who structures the situation in an authoritarian manner is attempting to give a poor account of himself, (c) when the $F-$ responses given represent only mild deviations from $F+$ criteria, and (d) when the *low* $F+\%$ appears in the context of a lengthy record. The obverse of each of these factors enhances the pathologic significance of *low* $F+\%$ correspondingly and increases the likelihood of schizophrenia.

LOW R+%

Low $R+\%$ is a variant of *low* $F+\%$ that provides an alternate and sometimes more reliable index of perceptual inaccuracy than *low* $F+\%$.

$R+\%$ is determined by the same scoring procedures as $F+\%$, with the additional utilization of form-level scoring for form-dominated responses other than F, namely, M, FM, Fm, Fk, FK, Fc, FC', and FC. $R+\%$ is thus the percentage of all accurate responses in these nine categories among all responses scored "$+$" or "$-$." $R+\%$ is essentially the score used by Rapaport et al. (1946) as the "denominator" in their summary of form level (with $F+\%$ as the "numerator") and which Schafer (1954) later referred to as "extended $F+\%$."

In many cases $R+\%$ duplicates the information contained in $F+\%$, and the two ratios have in fact been found to be highly correlated (beyond .80) in both normal and neurotic groups (Feldman, Gurrslin, Kaplan, & Sharlock, 1954). However, since $R+\%$ represents a larger number of responses than $F+\%$, it may be the more reliable index, and for brief records or records with relatively few F responses, only the $R+\%$ provides a meaningful measure of perceptual accuracy.

Values for $R+\%$ are generally somewhat higher than those for $F+\%$. Cass and McReynolds' (1951) 104 normal adults had a median $R+\%$ of 84, with an $R+\%$ of 80 falling at the thirtieth percentile and an $R+\%$ of 70 at the fifth percentile. Piotrowski (1957, p. 117), whose scoring of $F+\%$ includes animal movement, shading, and achromatic color responses, hence approximating $R+\%$, states that the typical percentage in the adult of average intelligence is 80, with bright persons ranging between 85% and 90%. These ratios are roughly 10 percentage points higher than the normal adult range of 75–85% given by Beck (1961, p. 135) for $F+\%$, and Piotrowski suggests that an $R+\%$ below 70 is grounds for suspecting mental disturbance. In an experimental study Rieman (1953) used an $R+\%$ cutting score of 82 in comparing two groups of 50 schizophrenic and neurotic subjects. He found this $R+\%$ criterion to differentiate the diagnostic groups significantly in both original and replicating studies.

In individual psychodiagnosis it appears warranted to consider any $R+\%$ falling below 70 as a *low $R+\%$* indicating impaired reality testing. *Low $R+\%$* can result from the several previously discussed mechanisms (see pp. 110–112) that contribute to inaccurate perceptual functioning, and *low $R+\%$* is therefore likely to characterize the records of brain-damaged and mentally deficient as well as schizophrenic subjects. Furthermore, the significance of *low $R+\%$* is similarly attenuated or enhanced by the factors that influence the interpretation of *low $F+\%$* (see pp. 112–114).

IMPAIRED JUDGMENT

Good judgment is the capacity to comprehend the demands of a situation and evaluate correctly the degree to which alternative behaviors correspond to them. Judgment can be adequate only to the extent that the environment and the impact of various actions on it are accurately perceived. Hence, when reality testing is deficient, impaired judgment is likely to ensue and be reflected in failure to recognize conventional modes of response, misinterpretation of the implications of social situations, and incorrect evaluation of the appropriateness and consequences of behavior.

Impaired judgment is a significant aspect of schizophrenic disturbance, and there is no more graphic a description of such impairment than that by Bleuler (1911, pp. 90–94), from whose discussion of activity and behavior in schizophrenics the following excerpts are taken:

Outspoken schizophrenic behavior is marked by . . . disregard of many factors of reality. . . . Every day we observe ill-considered attempts at escape of apparently lucid patients which they will execute before the very eyes of the attendants, or by dashing out of their room into the corridor, from where they would still have to pass several locked doors. The patients' goals are often in obvious contradiction, not only with their actual abilities, but also with their mental predispositions in general. . . . In the moderate and severe cases it is the desultoriness in the intellectual sphere which often is most noticeable. An educated lady writes a number of letters, marks them "registered mail," and then does not mail them. . . . A sales clerk rides back and forth on the train . . . because he had heard that some people had become engaged to nice young women while riding on the night trains. A man takes off all his clothes outdoors in winter, walks naked through the village in order to take a dip in a river which lies a half-hour's distance away. A young girl sews stockings upon a rug.

Two test indicators that relate to poor judgment and suggest impaired reality testing are *low P* on the Rorschach and *Comprehension deficiency* on the WAIS.

LOW P

Rorschach workers concur that the Popular response (P) is an index of ability to recognize and endorse conventional modes of response. For Rorschach (1921, p. 198) P "represents the share in the collective or common way of sensing or perceiving things"; Beck (1952, p. 24) considers P a "measure of the ability to recognize the most common percepts of one's milieu"; Piotrowski (1957, p. 108) sees P as indicating "the degree to which the subject shares the common ideas of his social group"; and Molish (1951) interprets P as the "ability to adapt one's thinking to that of one's fellow man." Inasmuch as adequate judgment is based on accurate perceptions, any failure to share common ways of perceiving, recognize common percepts, share common ideas, or adapt one's thinking to that of others is likely to be associated with poor judgment:

The P responses have been considered to represent compliance with the thinking of the community—in other words, the capacity for thinking in conventional and stereotyped terms. Such a capacity is essential for balanced and realistic thinking, and the lack of it indicates a degree of lack of "common sense" and of understanding of the simple and common routes of thinking (Rapaport et al., 1946, p. 315).

There are several published lists of P responses that overlap but recommend different numbers of responses as P. Klopfer et al. (1954, pp. 70–79) suggest 10 P responses, Piotrowski (1957, p. 107), 13, and Beck (1961, pp. 208–211) and Hertz (1951), 21. Research literature must therefore be evaluated and clinical standards for clinical application established in terms of the particular P list that is used. As the following normative data fortunately indicate, however, results obtained with the various lists have proved fairly uniform.

P in Normal and Schizophrenic Groups. The highest normative average P reported in the literature is a mean P of 7.0 observed in the records of 157 normal adults scored according to the Beck criteria (Beck et al., 1950). Brockway et al. (1954), examining Hertz' P list in a sample of 151 normal men, obtained a median P of 5.7; a P of four fell at the twentieth percentile and a P of eight at the eightieth percentile for this group. Studies of the briefer Klopfer list have yielded a somewhat lower range of normative values. Klopfer et al. (1954, p. 312) suggest five as the average number of P in a record of medium length scored by their system. Cass and McReynolds (1951), following Klopfer's scoring with 104 records, obtained a median P of 5.5, which approximates the Brockway et al. median for the longer Hertz list; Cass and McReynolds report 3.5 as the twentieth percentile value for P, 3.0 as the tenth percentile, and 2.0 as the fifth percentile.

Several studies demonstrate that P validly discriminates schizophrenic from normal and neurotic persons. In his early study (1938) of 81 schizophrenics and a control group composed of 33 normal persons and 31 nonpsychotic psychiatric patients Beck obtained mean P's

of 3.95 for the schizophrenic and 5.92 for the control group and median
P values for the two groups, respectively, of 4.19 and 6.30. Both the
mean and median values represented significant differences between
the groups. Beck (1954) later reported comparisons between the previously mentioned mean P of 7.0 in 157 normal persons and the mean
P's of 60 neurotic (5.5) and 60 schizophrenic (4.9) subjects. Both the
normals and the neurotics significantly exceeded the schizophrenics in
mean P.

Friedman (1952b) scored the records of 30 schizophrenics and 30
normal controls according to Beck's list and obtained median P's of
4.25 and 5.38, respectively, in the two groups. Knopf (1956), using
Hertz' list, observed mean P's of 4.0 in a group of 100 schizophrenics
and of 5.0 in the records of 131 neurotics. In a study using Klopfer's
list, Berkowitz and Levine (1953) found mean P's of 3.84 and 4.88,
respectively, in groups of 25 schizophrenic and 25 neurotic subjects.
The difference between groups was significant in each of these three
studies.

Defining Low P. Assuming that a subject whose reality testing is
intact should give a P frequency at least as high as the average value
observed in schizophrenics and not much lower than the twentieth
percentile value for normal persons, these data suggest that a P less
than five (i. e., four or fewer), using Beck or Hertz scoring, and a P
less than four (i. e., three or fewer), with the Klopfer scoring, represent
a *low P* suggestive of a schizophrenic impairment of reality testing.

Successful discrimination with the Klopfer list has actually been
reported for both higher and lower cutting scores than four P. Vinson
(1960) found 22 of 30 schizophrenics but only 11 of 30 normal control
subjects to have fewer than three P, with the difference between the
groups being significant. Berkowitz and Levine (1953) significantly
distinguished 25 schizophrenic from 25 control subjects using five as
the cutting score for P. However, the bulk of available data points to
the less-than-four criterion for *low P* with Klopfer scoring.

In regard to the diagnostic implications of *low P*, there is some evidence to suggest that failure to give sufficient P responses is associated
primarily with moderate or severe rather than mild psychopathology.
Warner (1951) was unsuccessful in trying to differentiate nonhospitalized schizophrenic from neurotic patients on the basis of P, and the
data of Rapaport et al. (1946, p. 318; see Chap. 13) indicate significant
differences in P between acute and chronic schizophrenics.

Low P in Nonschizophrenic Conditions. As stated previously, indications of impaired reality testing are not unique to schizophrenia. *Low P*

like *low F+%* and *low R+%* may occur in brain-damaged and mentally defective persons, most of whom suffer perceptual impairments or limitations. Piotrowski (1936, 1937) and Evans and Marmorston (1964) found a low percentage of *P* in the total response (less than 25.0) to differentiate significantly brain-damaged from cerebrally intact subjects, and Davidson and Klopfer (1937–1938) summarize reports of few *P* in the records of feeble-minded persons. Utilization of *low P* as a schizophrenic indicator is accordingly facilitated when organic brain disease and mental deficiency can be ruled out.

Factors Influencing the Interpretation of Low P. Also paralleling the discussion of *low F+%* are certain factors that influence the interpretation of *low P*. First, Fiske and Baughman (1953) found a significant positive relationship approaching .40 between *P* and total *R* in their analysis of the 157 cases in Beck's normal group. Although the median *P* frequency in records of 20–24 responses was 6.9 and increased to 9.0 for records of more than 50 *R*, the median *P* in records of 10–14 *R* was only 3.8, which falls below the criterion recommended above for *low P* with Beck's scoring. Hence the pathologic implications of a *low P* vary with the number of responses, thus representing relatively less impairment in a brief record and relatively greater disturbance in a longer one.

Second, impaired reality testing may be suggested by a subject's failure to acknowledge particular *P* responses, regardless of his overall number of *P*. Such a possibility derives from a report by Molish (1951) that certain *P* responses are given significantly more frequently by normal than schizophrenic subjects. The two most prominent are the human figures to Card III and the animals to the lateral details of Card VIII. Among the *P*'s that discriminated the normals from the schizophrenics in Molish's analysis, these were the two most frequently given by the normals. Failure to recognize these two *P* percepts on Cards III and VIII, then, suggests difficulties in reality testing even when an adequate number of other *P*'s is present. Similar significance may attach to the omission of the bat or butterfly to Card V, which is the most common of all *P* percepts.

Finally, those aspects of subjects' attitudes toward the testing situation that influence *F+%* and *R+%* (see pp. 112–114) similarly affect *P*. Subjects wishing to give a good account of themselves who perceive the task as a free associative one and subjects wishing to appear disturbed who construe the test in an authoritarian manner are likely to shun the obvious *P* responses even if they are capable of identifying them, and their consequent *low P*'s must be interpreted cautiously.

Correspondingly, for subjects with the opposite combinations of attitudes a lowered P takes on increasing significance as an indicator of impaired reality testing.

COMPREHENSION DEFICIENCY

The Comprehension subtest of the WAIS measures the capacity for practical judgment. Rapaport et al. (1945, pp. 110–114), who consider in detail the relationship between the Comprehension items and situations calling for judgment, point out that both require accurate perception of the problem at hand, delay of first impulses, enumeration of possible modes of response, and careful determination of appropriate behavior. Although there is no guarantee that a subject who answers the Comprehension items correctly would behave judiciously if faced with comparable situations, it is unlikely that a person who fails to demonstrate adequate judgment on the Comprehension items will be able to respond appropriately in actual situations of the type they represent. Hence, although Comprehension proficiency does not guarantee good judgment, *Comprehension deficiency* suggests impaired judgmental capacity.

Defining Comprehension Deficiency. Consistent with the hypothesized relationship of impaired judgment to both schizophrenia and deficient WAIS Comprehension performance, studies by Olch (1948) and Senf, Huston, and Cohen (1955) have demonstrated relatively poor Comprehension attainment in schizophrenic as opposed to normal and neurotic groups. Other work has suggested that a diagnostically useful criterion for Comprehension deficiency applicable to the individual case may reside in the comparability of a subject's Comprehension with his other WAIS subtest scores. Garfield (1948), comparing 67 schizophrenics with 46 nonschizophrenic psychiatric patients, found the schizophrenics significantly more frequently than the controls to have Comprehension scores below their mean subtest score. Rogers (1951) observed Comprehension scores below Vocabulary in 49% of 83 schizophrenic but only 19% of 100 neurotic subjects, which represented a significant difference. Jastak (1953), rank ordering the mean scale scores of 40 schizophrenic and 40 neurotic patients, found that the schizophrenics' Comprehension performance was relatively poor (rank of six for male and 10 for female subjects), whereas in the neurotics Comprehension remained relatively high (ranks of three and one).

Although these data were obtained within patient populations, where discrimination is often more difficult to achieve than in comparisons between schizophrenics and normal controls, they indicate sufficient overlap between groups to question the adequacy of either Comprehension-below-Vocabulary or Comprehension-below-mean-subtest-score as a diagnostic criterion for Comprehension deficiency. The statistical data of Wechsler (1958, p. 104) and McNemar (1957) utilized earlier (see p. 34) help to resolve this difficulty. Wechsler indicates that a scale score difference of three between Comprehension and Vocabulary represents significance at the 15% level. Computations based on McNemar's recommendations yield a Comprehension-Vocabulary scale score difference of four as constituting a non-chance occurrence. Accordingly, Comprehension deficiency should be defined as a Comprehension score falling more than three and especially more than four points below Vocabulary, and a discrepancy of this extent is likely to identify pathologically impaired judgment.

Supporting this hypothesis are some findings reported by Rapaport et al. (1945, pp. 124–125) that affirm the diagnostic utility of Comprehension deficiency thus defined. Rapaport et al. compared the percentage of subjects in several diagnostic groups having Comprehension scores three or more points below Vocabulary or below mean subtest score. For both comparisons their schizophrenic groups displayed this degree of Comprehension deficit significantly more frequently than all their nonschizophrenic groups with the exception of depressed subjects, the significance of whose performance is discussed below. Also consistent with the recommended criterion for Comprehension deficiency is a description by Merrill and Heathers (1952) of 429 normal college students who were considered to have a fair degree of intertest scatter but of whom only 7% had Comprehension scores three or more points below vocabulary.

Comprehension Deficiency in Nonschizophrenic Conditions. In the preceding discussions of *low F+%*, *low R+%*, and *low P* it has been indicated that indices of impaired reality testing are not unique to schizophrenia and must be interpreted with adequate cognizance of certain nonschizophrenic conditions. As elaborated below, however, because Comprehension performance differs in certain important respects from Rorschach form level and *P* responses, Comprehension deficiency has somewhat different implications for differential diagnosis from the other three indices of impaired reality testing.

Inherent in the definition of reality testing with which this chapter was introduced is the fact that perception and judgment are interrelated rather than discrete functions. Thus, although *low F+%* and *low R+%* are presented here as specific indicators of perceptual inaccuracy and *low P* as an index of impaired judgmental capacity, all three indices involve primarily the perception of the external environment prior to and independent of any action by the individual, and all three emphasize *visual* perception. Comprehension items, in contrast, are given *orally* by the examiner, and the stimulus qualities of the situation are clearly indicated by him to the subject. The subject is not asked to visualize his environment; rather, he is required to judge the consequences or significance of behavior in already accurately defined situations.

Because of this difference between the two types of task, certain groups of persons who perform similarly to schizophrenics in form level and *P* may appear normal on Comprehension. Brain-damaged subjects, for example, often demonstrate *low F+%, low R+%,* and *low P,* presumably as a consequence of the general decrement in visual-organizational skills that accompanies organic brain disease (see pp. 111 and 119). The Comprehension subtest, however, does not call for the subject to visualize, and, being a measure of social comprehension and judgment, it is the very type of test on which brain-damaged subjects experience relatively little difficulty:

> Organic patients should not fail them, for these tests appear to require relatively little conceptual capacity or new learning, and the old social habits upon which the correct responses are based are relatively untouched by cerebral damage (Hunt & Cofer, 1944, p. 986).

Wechsler (1958, p. 171) confirms that most subjects with organic brain disease are unlikely to display decrements on WAIS Comprehension.

With regard to mentally defective persons, in whom *low F+%, low R+%,* and *low P* are also often observed (see pp. 112 and 119), it is important to note that these scores are judged *low* in comparison to normative expectancy. Whereas feeble-minded subjects will obviously earn lower than normal scores throughout the WAIS, Comprehension deficiency is not a normative but an ipsative evaluation. That a mentally defective person will have less judgmental capacity than a person of normal intelligence does not imply that he will perform less well on Comprehension than on any other WAIS subtest. Wechsler (1958, p. 172) reports that mental defectives are in fact not prone to display Comprehension deficits in relation to their Vocabulary or mean subtest scores.

Identification of a schizophrenic impairment of reality testing on the basis of Comprehension deficiency is therefore unlikely to be contaminated by organic brain disease or mental deficiency; yet relatively poor Comprehension performance may, as noted above, appear in many depressed persons. Rapaport et al. (1945, pp. 124–125) found that Comprehension scores three or more points below Vocabulary or below mean subtest score occurred significantly more frequently in their depressed than in their normal subjects and no less frequently in the depressives than in the schizophrenics.

There is a rationale for this finding that is consistent with the fact that depressed patients usually do not manifest the *low F+%*, *low R+%*, or *low P* indices of impaired reality testing. Recent research by Friedman (1964) demonstrates that depressive disorders, to the extent of their severity, are characterized not only by disturbances of mood and affect but also by psychomotor slowing and impaired capacity for short-term concentration. A depressed person faced with the Rorschach typically musters only enough interest and energy to give easy and obvious responses, many of which are *P* and most of which are *F+*. Only in instances in which a depressed person is preoccupied with anatomical concerns is he likely to stray from accurate, banal, and stereotyped percepts (Schafer, 1948, pp. 57–61). [3]

Comprehension items, on the other hand, call for active reasoning and concentration, and depressed persons, unable to mobilize energy for such a task, frequently give sketchy, superficial, and ill-considered responses to them. This adverse impact of depression on Comprehension performance is relatively less likely to appear on subtests such as Vocabulary that are based more on learned information than on active reasoning. Because Comprehension deficiency may therefore be expected to accompany pronounced depressive disorder, it most clearly indicates a schizophrenic impairment of judgment in those cases in which other data are adequate to rule out significant depression.

Other Comprehension Clues to Impaired Judgment. In addition to the fact that a relatively low total Comprehension score is likely to indicate impaired judgment, extremely poor responses on certain of the Comprehension items may suggest deficient reality testing even when the total subtest score is fairly well retained. The Comprehension subtest is clearly not a pure measure. Three of the Comprehension items are proverb interpretations that assess concept formation rather than judgment (see Chap. 6), and, leaving aside the first two seldom-administered items, CLOTHES and ENGINE, the remaining nine items are of two types: ENVELOPE, MOVIES, and FOREST ask what action should be taken in a given situation; BAD COMPANY, TAXES, CHILD LABOR, DEAF, CITY LAND, and MARRIAGE ask why a given state of affairs does or should obtain. In view of the nature of the relationship between impaired judgment

---

[3] Psychodiagnostic indicators of depressive disorder are considered further in Chapter 17.

and schizophrenic behavior, the three "What would you do . . .?" items would seem particularly likely to measure the judgmental lapses of a schizophrenic person.

Indeed, although there is no confirmatory research data to this effect, it is the author's impression from his review of several hundred records in the preparation of this book that performance on ENVELOPE, MOVIES, and FOREST is very sensitive to the inroads of schizophrenic disturbance on judgmental capacity. Gross errors on these three items, especially when their level of difficulty is within the subject's demonstrated intellectual capacity, are often associated with poor reality testing even when the over-all Comprehension score is not deficient. The following answers by schizophrenic subjects, whose ineptness could not be accounted for on a purely intellectual basis, illustrate the types of gross error that suggest impaired judgment: ENVELOPE: "Leave it alone, it's someone else's"; Try to get it postmarked." MOVIES: "Get up and leave"; "Try to lead people out as fast as I could"; "Probably ignore it and think it was cigarettes"; "Get everyone out safely." FOREST: "Try to find a home with people in it"; "Call for help"; "Run all over the place, it has to end somewhere"; "Listen for some signs of life"; "Follow my own scent (?) I use a strong cologne, I'd leave my own spoor behind."

It is interesting to note that these responses illustrate poor judgment and impaired reality testing independent of the presence of thought disorder. They contain little suggestion of dissociation or deviant verbalization, each being a relevant attempt to answer the question and couched in appropriate, comprehensible language. The only tendency toward peculiar language occurs in the last example, with the unusual use of the word *spoor* to describe a human scent. Furthermore, none of the responses demonstrates arbitrary or circumstantial reasoning.

Rather, these illustrative responses are obviously and strikingly deviant because they involve poor perception of reality and endorsement of maladaptive behavior that would fail to resolve the depicted situation satisfactorily. The sight of smoke and fire in the movies is highly unlikely to result from cigarettes, for example; the person who perceives his environment accurately is aware not only that smoking is forbidden in most theaters but also that cigarettes do not produce fire. Similarly, calling for help is a wise action in many situations of distress, but it is highly unlikely to yield salutary results when a person is lost in a forest, any more than would listening for signs of life. The endorsement of such actions, then, points to impaired judgmental capacity and suggests poor reality testing.

▷ 8

RELATION TO REALITY:
II. REALITY SENSE

THE sense of reality is predicated on accurate perception of the body and its boundaries. When reality sense is impaired, self-perception is characterized by indefinite ego boundaries and distorted body imagery. The study of inaccurate body perception has a long and interesting history, much of which is summarized in good reviews by Fisher and Cleveland (1958, pp. 3–53) and Kolb (1959). These papers and earlier important contributions by Schilder (1935) and Bychowski (1943) document the frequent clinical observation of disturbed body perceptions in schizophrenic persons. As these writers note, however, the description of phenomena related to impaired reality sense originated with neurologists, and schizophrenic disturbances of body perception are similar to and difficult to distinguish from those that accompany neurological disease. Accordingly, the differentiation of schizophrenia from organic brain syndrome figures prominently in the interpretation of psychodiagnostic indicators of impaired reality sense.

Schizophrenic phenomena deriving from inaccurate body perception fall generally into the two categories of *indefinite ego boundaries* and *distorted body imagery*. The person with indefinite ego boundaries is likely to feel that there is no clear demarcation between his body and that of others, so that what happens to him happens to others and vice versa, or that his body is physically vulnerable, so that he is coming apart, about to disintegrate, or so defenseless against bodily assault that even a slight physical stimulus might penetrate and destroy him.

Symptoms associated with distorted body imagery include sexual confusion, unusual sensations concerning body parts, and depersonalization. The person whose body image is distorted may be unable to recognize his or her masculinity or femininity and may develop convictions of looking like or having some body parts of the opposite sex; he may feel that some of his body parts are missing, diseased, changed in size or strength, or being subjected to unusual tortures or duress; or he may deny the reality of his body and experience various of his body parts as alien, nonexistent, or belonging to someone else.

Several experimental studies have affirmed the relative inaccuracy of schizophrenic persons in perceiving their bodies. Weckowicz and Sommer (1960), using a number of procedures to study body perception in schizophrenics, nonschizophrenic psychiatric patients, and normals, found that their schizophrenics significantly more often than their control subjects underestimated the size of the distal parts of their bodies. One hundred schizophrenics studied by Cleveland, Fisher, Reitman, and Rothaus (1962) were similar to a control group of neurotic and normal subjects in estimating the sizes of nonbody objects but overestimated the size of their body parts significantly more frequently than the controls. Cleveland et al. ascribe the differences between their findings (overestimates) and those of Weckowicz and Sommer (underestimates) to certain differences in methodology and subject population.

Fisher (1964a) and Fisher and Seidner (1963) describe research with a Body Experience Questionnaire (BEQ), which is an 82-item "Yes-No" checklist scored for nine categories of body-perception disturbance. In their studies with the BEQ Fisher and Seidner found that both schizophrenic men and schizophrenic women reported a larger number of distorted body experiences than normal men and women. For both sexes the experience categories of *small body size, loss of body boundaries, blocking of body openings,* and *perception of the body as dirty* significantly differentiated the schizophrenic from the normal subjects.

Clinical and research findings thus attest the validity of impaired reality sense, as manifest in inaccurate body perception, as an identifying characteristic of schizophrenia. Psychodiagnostic indicators of the two main categories of inaccurate body perception, *indefinite ego boundaries* and *distorted body imagery,* are presented below.

INDEFINITE EGO BOUNDARIES

The concept of ego-boundedness as a defining characteristic of psychological health has derived primarily from the contributions of

Federn (1952, Chaps. 8, 10, and 11). Federn takes issue with the classical psychoanalytic view that schizophrenia is a narcissistic illness accompanied by a hypercathexis of the ego and a corresponding withdrawal from the environment. Rather, Federn asserts, schizophrenia is a state of ego weakness in which there is a failure to cathect the ego and its boundaries adequately. Federn maintains that impairment of ego boundaries is not only a *symptom* of schizophrenia but the *basic process* of the disturbance during its entire course; and he attempts to demonstrate that deficient ego-boundary cathexis can determine all the phenomena observed in schizophrenia. Bychowski (1952, pp. 55–59) similarly considers poor differentiation of the ego from the external world to account for much of schizophrenic symptomatology, and he suggests the concept of "fluid" ego boundaries to describe the characteristic ego weakness associated with schizophrenia.

Zucker (1958) and Fisher and Cleveland (1958) have translated the ego-boundary concepts of Federn and Bychowski into psychodiagnostic test language. Zucker developed five "facets" for scoring the Rorschach, Mosaic, and Draw-a-Person (DAP) that incorporate a variety of deviant test behaviors into an ego-boundary frame of reference. Particularly relevant to the evaluation of indefinite ego boundaries of Zucker's facet of *fluid contours*, which is defined by vague, fluid Rorschach percepts and broken DAP contours. Fisher and Cleveland have devised a scoring scheme for two Rorschach variables, *Barrier* and *Penetration*, which assesses the definiteness of the body-image boundary. *Vague, fluid* Rorschach percepts, *low Barrier* and *high Penetration* scores, and *broken DAP contours* are the major psychodiagnostic indicators of indefinite ego boundaries.

VAGUE, FLUID PERCEPTS

Schafer (1960) has suggested that the Rorschach inkblots may be viewed as bodies that are relatively formless, meaningless, and poorly articulated. The normally functioning person creates a well-demarcated, integral percept by projecting onto the blots his own sense of ego-boundedness; that is, the person who perceives himself as a unitary, well-defined physical object distinct from other objects is likewise able to perceive delimited, meaningful forms in the Rorschach blots. On the other hand, the person who is experiencing difficulty in clearly identifying himself and other objects is likely to be threatened by the formlessness of the blots and unable to articulate them. Hence, as Schafer concludes, vague and fluid Rorschach percepts reflect indefinite ego boundaries and indicate impaired reality sense.

The assessment of vague Rorschach perception is facilitated by a

Developmental Level scoring system constructed by Friedman (1952a, 1953). The Developmental Level system defines the degree to which Rorschach responses articulate, differentiate, and synthesize the ink-blot stimuli. Whereas differentiation and integration of Rorschach stimuli are aspects of the synthetic functions of the ego discussed in Chapter 12, perceptual articulation relates meaningfully to the adequacy of ego boundaries and is relevant to this chapter.

Friedman scores failures to articulate Rorschach percepts as either *vague* or *amorphous*. A vague response, according to Friedman, is one "in which there is a diffuse general impression of the blot" and form elements are "of such an unspecific nature that almost any perceptual form is adequate to encompass the content." Vague responses thus include all *F* responses so indefinite that they merit an $F\pm$ scoring (island, clouds, rocks, etc.; see p. 107) and all responses in which form is present in a minor capacity (mF, kF, KF, cF, $C'F$, and CF). Amorphous responses are those "in which the shape of the blot plays no determinable role," namely, m, k, K, c, C', and C percepts.

Criteria for identifying pathologic degrees of vague and amorphous perception emerge from the following summaries compiled from studies by Friedman (1953) of 30 normal and 30 hebephrenic and catatonic schizophrenic subjects, by Siegel (1953) of 30 paranoid schizophrenics, by Frank (1951) of 30 neurotics, by Pena (1953) of 30 brain-damaged persons, and by Rosenblatt and Solomon (1954) of 80 mentally defective subjects.

Vague Responses. Vague W responses (Wv) are unusual in normal, neurotic, and mentally defective adults, with fewer than half the subjects in these groups giving even a single Wv response. In hebephrenic-catatonic, paranoid, and brain-damaged groups, on the other hand, the observed median proportions of Wv in all W ($Wv/W\%$) are 17.0, 26.5, and 22.2% respectively. The second and third percentages represent a significant difference from normal performance and the first approaches significance.

Vague D responses (Dv) hardly ever appear in brain-damaged or mentally defective subjects but occur relatively more frequently than Wv in normals and neurotics, with the respective median $Dv/D\%$'s observed in these two groups being 5.0 and 7.0. However, in schizophrenic subjects Dv's are relatively less frequent than Wv's, and the reported median $Dv/D\%$'s for hebephrenic-catatonic and paranoid schizophrenics are, respectively, 11.5 and 5.5. Only the first figure approaches a significant difference from normal performance.

Dv responses are therefore only slightly more unusual in the records of normal, neurotic, and mentally defective than of schizophrenic and brain-damaged subjects. The $Wv/W\%$ index, on the other hand, appears to be a sensitive measure of vague perceptual functioning, and the foregoing data suggest that any proportion of Wv in all W responses greater than 25% indicates a pathologic extent of ego-boundary indefiniteness. The tendency of brain-damaged subjects to produce this great a frequency of vague responses appears consistent with the disturbances in body perception and visual organization previously noted to accompany organic brain disease (see pp. 111 and 125). A $Wv/W\%$ greater than 25.0, occurring when other findings make it possible to rule out organicity, thus strongly suggests schizophrenia.

Amorphous Responses. Both amorphous $W(Wa)$ and amorphous $D(Da)$ responses are rare; the median $Wa/W\%$'s and $Da/D\%$'s for all groups studied are zero. However, although the reported percentages of normal, neurotic, and mentally defective subjects giving any Wa responses at all are only 0.0, 3.0, and 6.0, respectively, 17% of the paranoid schizophrenics, 20% of the brain-damaged subjects, and 37% of the hebephrenic and catatonic schizophrenics studied gave one or more Wa. The differences of the schizophrenic and brain-damaged groups from the other groups in tendency to give one or more Wa attain or approach significance in each case. Da is more frequent than Wa among normal, neurotic, and mentally defective groups but not in schizophrenic and brain-damaged subjects. Hence the various diagnostic groups display relatively little difference in Da tendency. These findings for amorphous percepts suggest that the presence in a record of one or more unequivocal Wa responses reflects a pathologic degree of indefinite ego-boundedness and, when brain damage is not otherwise in evidence, is likely to indicate schizophrenia.

Unfortunately, there are few additional data from which the validity of these recommended diagnostic criteria for vague and amorphous responses can be assessed. There are, however, other Rorschach clues to indefinite ego boundaries that often reduce the necessity for relying on strictly numerical criteria. One such clue is the *fluid* response, in which the boundaries of a subject's percept are in such a state of flux that he cannot assign it any stable identity. The content of fluid responses often changes so rapidly during the response process that the examiner is uncertain about what has been described to him. The following response by a schizophrenic woman to Card III illustrates such fluidity:

At the two sides I see two monsters warming their hands over a fire. The center looks like two more people, joined together. Sticking out of each of these monsters are breasts. (*Describe monsters?*) Look like—uh—two huge dogs (*dogs?*) the shape of them. (*Describe people?*) They're not people, they're somewhat like fish (*fish?*) no, more like dogs or bears (*not people, then?*) it's mostly the shape, there's the profile of a person there. (*Breasts?*) They're part of the dogs or the monsters or the people or whatever they are.

The specific content of vague and amorphous responses, particularly when the subject explicitly states his inability to impose any definite form on the inkblots, may also reveal indefinite ego boundaries. The following two case excerpts illustrate the types of inadequately demarcated response that often appear in the records of persons who are experiencing pathologic ego-boundary indefiniteness:

A 39-year-old schizophrenic woman included among her 30 Rorschach responses these seven: "An explosion of some kind"; "Some weird shape with shadings of black and gray in it (*shape of what?*) not of anything"; "A formation, ice and snow"; "The shadings of light gray are like dirty snow"; "Gives me a feeling of the outer crust of something (*?*) just a fragmentary shape, nothing definite"; "Looks like dripping wet paint"; "Gives me a fragile, breakable feeling, like coral with a delicate laciness."

A 24-year-old schizophrenic woman gave the following 12 responses in her 45-response record: "A stain, smeared in all directions, it doesn't stay in one place"; "Modern art, with no real appearance, could have any meaning"; "Blood"; "Dark areas are parts of the sea"; "Looks like mist, almost seems to flow"; "Muddy water"; "An abstract painting which isn't anything"; "Blue water"; "A sunset"; "Looks like something's torn (*what?*) could be anything"; "Another sunset"; "Smeared colors from a paint brush."

The accumulation in a record of such vague, poorly defined responses strongly suggests a serious incapacity of the subject to define his ego boundaries and in the absence of cerebral pathology points to schizophrenia.

LOW BARRIER AND HIGH PENETRATION

Fisher and Cleveland (1958), on the basis of comparisons between normal subjects and patients with psychosomatic illness, primarily rheumatoid arthritis, have devised a Rorschach system for scoring *Barrier* and *Penetration*. They conceive of the Barrier score as a positive assertion of body-boundary definiteness and the Penetration score as a feeling that the body exterior is easily penetrable and of little protective value. Hence, to the extent that their scoring system is valid, a combination of low Barrier and high Penetration scores is likely to reflect the poor differentiation of self from not-self, the minimal feelings of bodily integrity, and the fears of physical vulnerability that characterize impaired reality sense. The scoring, personality correlates, and psychopathologic significance of Barrier and Penetration scores are outlined in the following sections.

Scoring Barrier and Penetration. The following eight categories of responses are assigned Barrier scores by Fisher and Cleveland (1958, pp. 59–61): (a) *separate* articles of clothing (except for the frequent bowtie on Card III and boots on Card IV), clothing worn by animals and birds, and *distinctive* clothing worn by persons that is unusual or particularly decorative: (b) animals or creatures with distinctive or unusual skins (an inclusive list of 35 animals is given), animal skins other than the popular bearskin of which the surface qualities are emphasized, and shelled creatures except for crabs and lobsters; (c) references to enclosed openings in the earth (valley, mine shaft, well, etc.); (d) references to unusual animal containers (kangaroo, bloated cat, etc.); (e) references to overhanging or protective surfaces (umbrella, awning, shield, etc.); (f) references to things that are armored or dependent on their surfaces for protection (tank, rocket ship in space, man in armor, etc.); (g) references to things being covered, surrounded, or concealed; and (h) references to things with unusual container-like shapes or properties (bagpipes, throne, etc.). Each response falling into any one or more of these categories is given a score of one, and the total Barrier score is equal to the number of such responses.

The Penetration score is determined from the following seven categories of response (Fisher & Cleveland, 1958, pp. 61–63): (a) references to the mouth being opened or being used for intake or expulsion; (b) references to evading, bypassing, or penetrating through the exterior of an object and getting into the interior (X-ray, inside of the body); (c) references to the body wall being broken, fractured, injured, or damaged (mashed bug, person bleeding, bullet penetrating flesh, etc.) and to degeneration of surfaces (diseased skin, withered leaf, etc.); (d) openings in the earth that have no set boundaries or from which things are being expelled (bottomless abyss, fountain shooting up, etc.); (e) all openings (anus, window, doorway, etc.); (f) references to things that are insubstantial and without palpable boundaries (cotton candy, soft mud, etc.); and (g) references to transparency. The total number of responses falling into any one or more of these categories constitutes the Penetration score. For a complete exposition of Barrier-Penetration scoring the reader is referred to Fisher and Cleveland's book and the scoring examples in their appendix (pp. 371–390).

In their initial studies with the Barrier and Penetration scores Fisher and Cleveland discovered them to correlate significantly with total R. To control for this possible source of contamination, they decided to determine Barrier and Penetration scores from 25 responses only, the first three responses to Cards I-V and the first two responses to Cards VI-X. In the event that a given card lacks the specified number of responses, additional responses are selected from the next card in sequence on which there are more than the requisite number.

Fisher and Cleveland found that Barrier and Penetration scores based on the imposed limit of 25 responses are fairly independent of intelligence level, verbal productivity, and usual Rorschach determinants. Normatively, they obtained in one sample of 50 college students a median Barrier score of four and a median Penetration score of two. In another instance, administering a group Rorschach with the number of responses set at 24, they achieved very stable results in three successive normal samples, with the 200 subjects in these samples receiving median Barrier and Penetration scores of four and two, respectively.

Research with Barrier and Penetration Scores. Research findings as summarized by Fisher (1963) have confirmed the relationship of Barrier and Penetration scores to body attitudes and other personality variables. High Barrier and low Penetration scores are associated with an emphasis on exterior layers of the body, as manifest in such psychosomatic conditions as rheumatoid arthritis and contact dermatitis and in relatively high muscle (EMG) and skin (GSR) reactivity to stress. Low Barrier and high Penetration scores, on the other hand, are found in connection with interior body reactivity, as reflected by stomach ulcer and by relatively great increase in heart rate subsequent to stress.

Consistent with these findings, Fisher and Fisher (1964) have observed a high Barrier score to be associated with selective recall for verbal material referring to exterior rather than interior body sensations and with a focus on exterior as opposed to interior body sensations in reporting current and past body experiences. High Barrier scores have also been found to be directly related to ability to adjust to the stress of body disablement as measured in paraplegic men and pregnant women (Landau, 1960; McConnell & Daston, 1961). In addition, the studies summarized in Fisher's review and a more recent report by Fisher (1964b) indicate that a high Barrier score is associated with ability to communicate in an interpersonal setting, likelihood of communicating with other group members in a direct and active rather than passive or self-depreciatory manner, degree of insight into the individual's own behavior, and the clarity of his identity.

Interscorer reliabilities for Barrier and Penetration scores in several studies have ranged from .82 to .97 (Fisher, 1963), and Daston and McConnell (1962), who retested patients with long-term physical disorders, found a high degree of objectivity and stability for the two scores. Also of interest is a factor analysis reported by Holtzman, Thorpe, Swartz, and Herron (1961, pp. 146–172) of 23 indices, among them Barrier and Penetration as defined by Fisher and Cleveland, scored on the Holtzman inkblots in 16 different samples. Barrier scores were highly loaded on Factor I (median loading in the 16 samples was .60), which also was highly loaded on by Movement, Integration, Human, and Popular scores and was defined as indicating "well organized ideational activity, good imaginative capacity, well differentiated ego boundaries, and awareness of conventional concepts." In contrast to the loading of the Barrier score on a factor suggesting ego strength, the Penetration score loaded primarily on factors related to disturbance and defined by indicators of immaturity, somatic concerns, and psychopathology.

Barrier and Penetration Scores in Schizophrenia. In their book Fisher and Cleveland (1958, pp. 235–236) report comparisons between 50 normal, 40 neurotic (anxiety reaction), 40 undifferentiated schizophrenic, and 40 paranoid schizophrenic subjects. For the Barrier score they obtained median values of three for both the normal (range 0–6) and neurotic (range 0–9) groups and of two for the paranoid (range 0–10) and undifferentiated (range 0–6) schizophrenics. The normal and neurotic groups combined were significantly higher in Barrier score than the schizophrenic groups, but the only subgroup comparisons that attained significance were those of the undifferentiated schizophrenics and the paranoid schizophrenics with the neurotics.

For the Penetration score Fisher and Cleveland found medians of one for the normals (range 0–5), two for the neurotics (range 0–5), three for the paranoid schizophrenics (range 0–9), and four for the undifferentiated schizophrenics. The combined schizophrenic groups were significantly higher in Penetration score than the normal and neurotic subjects, and, whereas neither the two schizophrenic nor the two nonschizophrenic groups differed from one another, the normals and the neurotics were both significantly lower in Penetration score than either the undifferentiated or the paranoid schizophrenics.

Later work by Cleveland (1960) bears out the particular sensitivity of the Penetration score to the inroads of schizophrenic disturbance.

In one group of 25 acutely disorganized schizophrenics, followed over 13 weeks of treatment, Cleveland found significant interrelationships between decline in the Penetration score, decreased ratings of morbidity, and likelihood of being considered ready for discharge from the hospital. In a second group of 45 schizophrenics he again found a significant decline in Penetration score among those patients who were rated improved, but no diminution of Penetration in the unimproved patients. In both samples the Barrier score was unrelated to the criteria of patient change.

These data suggest that the most diagnostically meaningful Barrier and Penetration scores are the high ones. Whereas a high Barrier appears to indicate good ego strength, low Barrier is not clearly associated with schizophrenia and appears frequently in normal and neurotic persons. High Penetration scores are also associated with schizophrenia and decrease commensurately with clinical improvement, but a low Penetration score, although identifying relative freedom from concern about body boundary definiteness, does not necessarily rule out schizophrenia. In view of the available norms, the presence in a record of more than four and especially more than five clear Penetration responses is likely to reflect a pathologic indefiniteness of ego boundaries. Moreover, the pathologic implications of a high Penetration score are enhanced when the Barrier score is low; that is, in instances in which Penetration emphasis is not to some extent balanced by Barrier emphasis, the subject may be particularly prone to feelings of indefinite body boundedness.

Unfortunately, to this date Barrier and Penetration scores have not been studied in brain-damaged subjects. Baker (1956), however, in a careful analysis of the psychodiagnosis of organic brain disease, concludes that concern about the body image, as inferred primarily from types of Rorschach responses that would merit Penetration scoring, is among the most dependable signs of brain damage. Evans and Marmorston (1963, 1964) have demonstrated Baker's scoring for body image concern to discriminate significantly between brain-damaged subjects and cardiac patients without known cerebral pathology.

Also significant for the differential interpretation of Barrier and Penetration scores is a report by Orbach and Tallent (1965) of Rorschach findings in 31 patients tested five to 10 years after they had undergone colostomy. The Rorschach responses of those subjects revealed that conceptions of bodily damage, mutilation, and violation were central to their adaptation. Specifically, these colostomized subjects received significantly lower Barrier scores (the group mean was less than one) than the Fisher and Cleveland normal sample, and their mean Penetration score was 3.0, which approaches the Penetration elevation observed by Fisher and Cleveland in schizophrenic groups. It follows from these data that a high Penetration score will probably best identify a schizophrenic impairment of reality sense when questions of organic brain disease are not at issue and actual bodily damage has not recently or permanently been incurred.

The following Rorschach record graphically illustrates the contribution of low Barrier and high Penetration scores to the diagnosis of schizophrenia. This record was given by a 26-year-old housewife who had failed to improve during several weeks of hospital care subsequent to an acute onset of anxiety symptoms that were initially felt to represent a situational reaction. During her hospitalization she had become increasingly somatically preoccupied and had begun to express concern about her daughter's defenselessness in the face of physical assaults to which the patient fantasied she might be subjected by her husband and sons during her, the patient's, absence from the home. In capsule form, her Rorschach consisted of the following 22 responses, scored where indicated for Barrier (B) and Penetration (P) according to Fisher and Cleveland:

CARD I. Part of a woman, the backside; looks like she's deformed (P). A weird creature. A whole woman here, fatter than the other one.

CARD II. Looks like a broken heart (?) like a heart that's been stepped on, it's broken and bleeding (P). Two baby sheep. An arm or hand; it's a bloody mess and I don't want to look at it (P).

CARD III. People, but they're not all there; they've been deformed in some way (P). An X-ray of the chest, showing the heart inside (P). A girl's hair bow.

CARD IV. A man, like an acrobat, bent over and looking backward through his legs. Some kind of creature.

CARD V. A butterfly or an insect with wings.

CARD VI. Looks like something that's been torn apart; it's ripped down the middle and still suffering; it's still alive (P). A man's furry jacket (B).

CARD VII. Looks like deformed babies, almost like something that's been torn apart, that I wouldn't want to see (P).

CARD VIII. Animals on each side. The gray looks like a mountain. A little girl's dress that's all torn up; by the looks of the dress she's really been hurt bad (P).

CARD IX. Reminds me of blood dripping down, like from a cut (P). The green and yellow look like a volcano erupting (P).

CARD X. A lot of insects eating something (P). This looks like a hunk of meat, with blood on it, and these here, like spiders, are tearing it up (P).

This record, which contains 12 Penetration and only a single Barrier score, clearly demonstrates the patient's fear of physical vulnerability, her concomitant ego-boundary indefiniteness, and the corresponding impairment of her reality sense.

BROKEN CONTOURS

The normal person with a clear conception of his body as a unitary structure and a certain conviction of where he leaves off and external reality begins is likely to render figure drawings with closed, continuous contours. This inference hinges largely on Machover's (1949, p. 35) assertion that a subject projects aspects of his own body image onto his drawings of the human figure. Although Machover's position has at times been challenged (see below), research findings attest numerous relationships between body image and DAP parameters.

Figure Drawings as Representations of the Body Image. Several studies lend support to Machover's hypothesis that a subject's figure-drawing performance will to some extent reflect the image he has of his own body. Kotlov and Goodman (1953), comparing obese women with women of ideal weight, noted that most of the DAP differences between them occurred on their drawing of the female and not the male figure. Berman and Laffal (1953) rated as endomorphic, mesomorphic, or ectomorphic the body types of 39 male subjects and their male figure drawings. They found a significant positive correlation (.35) between the body types of the subjects and the body types of their drawings. Lehner and Silver (1948) and Giedt and Lehner (1951) both observed a significant relationship between the subjects' ages and the ages they ascribed to their figure drawings.

Swenson (1957, p. 437), who mentions these four studies in a review of DAP research, nevertheless concludes on the basis of the pre-1948 (i.e., pre-DAP) literature and one negative body-image study with hemiplegics that "there is slight basis for believing that the figure drawn usually represents the S's own body." However, other work in addition and subsequent to that reviewed by Swenson further justifies interpreting figure drawings as at least partial projections of the subject's body image.

Holtzman (1952), for example, found significant sex-related differences between the figure drawings of male and female subjects, with women drawing more feminine human figures than men. Abel (1953), examining the drawings of facially disfigured persons seeking plastic surgery, observed an association between degree of a subject's disfigurement and the likelihood of its being reflected in his drawings. Schmidt and McGowan (1959) were able to discriminate figure drawings by persons with visible physical disabilities from those by control subjects. Craddick (1963) asked fifth-grade children and college sophomores first to draw a person and then to draw a portrait of themselves. In both samples the two drawings were significantly related in size, placement on the page, and sex, and Craddick interpreted his data as supporting Machover's body-image hypothesis.

Broken Contours in Schizophrenia. In view of the apparent relationship between body image and figure drawings, it follows that fragmented drawings with broken contours are likely to reflect indefinite ego boundaries. Therefore, in the absence of possible organic brain disease to account for this index of disturbed body perception, broken contours on DAP figures suggest a schizophrenic impairment of reality sense.

Figures 5 and 6 are drawings of the female figure by schizophrenic women that illustrate broken contours. Figure 5 was drawn by a 28-year-old housewife who had been hospitalized after an eight-month period of progressive inability to remember and concentrate, with increasing preoccupation and difficulty carrying on routine daily functions. Other psychological test data and other diagnostic procedures yielded no evidence of cerebral pathology, and a diagnosis of schizophrenia was eventually made. At first glance her drawing appears relatively free from signs of disturbance. Yet a closer look reveals she has failed to close essential parts of the body boundary, leaving large gaps between the lines of the arms and the trunk and allowing the legs and the trunk to hang in midair.

Figure 6 is the product of a 34-year-old married woman who was admitted to the hospital with a six-month history of confusion, difficulty in thinking, and feelings of unreality. Her drawing contains several peculiarities, including the unusual combination of stick-figure legs with an otherwise full-figure rendition and the transparency of the chin with the line of the shoulder showing through. The clue to her indefinite ego boundaries is her blatant failure to close the lines of the arm and shoulder in her drawing.

In interpreting the broken contours clue to impaired reality sense, however, it is also necessary to consider the manner in which the subject has rendered his figure drawings. The more a person has for one reason or another drawn his figures carelessly and hurriedly, paying scant attention to his work and displaying little interest in the adequacy of his final product, the less unequivocally can his failure to close body contours be taken to indicate indefinite ego boundaries. On the other hand, broken contours assumes enhanced pathologic significance the more the subject labors conscientiously at his task, appears concerned

Figure 5

Figure 6

that his drawing represent his best effort, and expresses satisfaction with the quality of his completed figures. Similar considerations obtain for the DAP indicators of distorted body imagery presented below.

DISTORTED BODY IMAGERY

Distorted body imagery is an identifying characteristic of impaired reality sense that is often reflected in human figure drawings. Unfortunately, the value of the DAP in indicating other than gross distortions of body imagery is limited by the fact that many DAP variables are prone to contamination by diagnostically irrelevant factors, the most significant of which is artistic ability. A brief review of studies concerning the relationship of artistic ability to DAP performance will help to define those DAP indices of distorted body imagery that most reliably indicate psychopathology independently of drawing skill.

Figure Drawings as Artistic Productions. Although a subject's figure drawings are likely to reflect his image of his body, it is obvious that incapacity to project a normal body image onto drawings may be determined by lack of artistic ability as well as by psychological disturbance. There is considerable experimental evidence that clinicians have been inclined erroneously to base diagnostic judgments on DAP features that reflect limited drawing skill rather than disturbed body imagery.

Whitmyre (1953), in the first study to this effect, found psychologists' ratings of adjustment from drawings by psychiatric patients and normal controls to correlate nearly .80 with independent ratings of the drawings for artistic merit but only around .20 with the actual patient-nonpatient status of the subjects. Sherman (1958b), comparing artists' ratings of good-poor quality with psychologists' estimates of patient-nonpatient status for 52 sets of drawings, observed greater association of the psychologists' judgments with artistic quality than with actual patient-nonpatient status.

Nichols and Strümpfer (1962) factor analyzed a number of global ratings and specific scores for the figure drawings of 107 college students and a group of 90 hospital patients, including 30 nonpsychiatric, 30 neurotic, and 30 schizophrenic patients. Reanalyzing the 15 variables that had high communalities in a preliminary analysis, they found the largest factor for the patient group to be one of Quality. Rated artistic quality loaded .82 on this Quality factor, and adjustment as rated by the Albee and Hamlin (1949) scale loaded .85. Further studies of over-all quality ratings of figure drawings by Strümpfer and Nichols (1962) and Lewinsohn and May (1963) have detected no difference in the Quality factor among normal, neurotic, and schizophrenic groups in one case and between schizophrenic and nonschizophrenic psychiatric patients in the other.

The psychodiagnostic implications of these findings is clear: if body imagery is represented in the DAP and the artistic merit of subjects' drawings is unrelated to their behavioral adjustment, the identification of pathologic body imagery is possible only by focusing on those DAP distortions *that are relatively independent of artistic talent.* In other words, the available data suggest that, although DAP variables related to artistic ability may have minimal utility in the assessment of impaired reality sense because of their ambiguous etiology, deviant features of DAP performance that have little to do with drawing ability per se may correctly identify disturbed body perception. Two DAP indicators of distorted body imagery that satisfy this criterion are *undifferentiated sexuality* and *physical omission.*

UNDIFFERENTIATED SEXUALITY

Confusion about sexual identity is a salient aspect of distorted body imagery, and the projection onto figure drawings of poor sexual differentiation is likely to identify a schizophrenic impairment of reality sense. Several studies have demonstrated the diagnostic validity for schizophrenia of poor sexual differentiation on the DAP, as inferred from failure to indicate sex-appropriate differentiating features. Modell (1951), for example, administering repetitive DAP's to a group of seriously disturbed schizophrenic patients over a one-year period, found not only that the drawings of the group were initially characterized by poor differentiation between the male and female figures but also that during the course of the year the drawings of those patients who were considered recovering took on increasingly appropriate and differentiated sexual characteristics. However, those of the unimproved patients did not.

Swenson (1955) developed a five-point scale for scoring sexual differentiation on the DAP with which he was initially successful in discriminating hospitalized from ambulatory psychiatric patients. His scale of sexual differentiation is based on the following criteria: female with longer hair and definite feminine hair styling; male with angular body and female with rounded body, including both rounded hips and presence of breasts; male and female figures wearing sex-appropriate clothing; and minor details, such as eyes, mouth, earrings, etc., clearly sex-appropriate to the figure on which they are drawn. Cutter (1956), applying Swenson's scale to groups of sexual offenders and normal, neurotic, and psychotic subjects, found lack of sexual differentiation related to "personality disorganization," independent of sexual deviation.

Other work, however, has revealed that at least some aspects of Swenson's scale are heavily influenced by artistic ability. Sherman (1958a) was unable to distinguish schizophrenic from control subjects with Swenson's sexual differentiation scale and found the scale to be significantly related to ratings of artistic quality. In Nichols and Strümpfer's (1962) analysis the Swenson sexual differentiation score loader higher on the Quality factor (.76) than on the factor most associated with behavioral maladjustment (.31). These data suggest that the Swenson scale includes both features that are determined primarily by artistic ability—hence are of little psychodiagnostic value —and features that are independent of drawing ability and relate to maladjustment.

A study by Feldman and Hunt (1958) facilitates the determination of DAP features of sexual undifferentiation least dependent on drawing talent and consequently most likely to indicate disturbed body imagery. Feldman and Hunt asked art instructors to rate body parts for the ease or difficulty of learning to draw them. The artists included among the more difficult body features to render the eyes, the mouth, and the distribution of the hair over the head, all of which are basic items in Swenson's scale. They rated as relatively easy to draw those body parts relating to the general contour of the body, including breasts, chest, waist, hips, and body build.

It appears, therefore, that failure to differentiate the general body contours of male and female figures is the major DAP index of undifferentiated sexuality that is relatively independent of drawing ability. Such failure is thus likely to reflect disturbed body imagery. The greater the tendency of drawings to be shapeless, or the more the male figures take on soft, rounded contours and the female figures sharp, angular ones, the greater the degree of sexual confusion suggested and the more probable an impairment of reality sense.

PHYSICAL OMISSION

Physical omission is the failure to indicate the presence of major body parts, and those omissions most suggestive of impaired reality sense are complete failures to indicate hair, shoulders, arms, hands, legs, and feet. Each of these omissions significantly differentiated schizophrenic from normal subjects in the previously mentioned studies by Holzberg and Wexler (1950a) and Hozier (1959).

Both Holzberg and Wexler and Hozier also include in their DAP sign lists for schizophrenia scores pertaining to the position and flexibility (i.e., indication of joints) of arms, hands, and legs. However, Feldman and Hunt's art instructors rated the adequate representation of arms, hands, and legs as relatively difficult. Position and flexibility variables in figure drawings may therefore be inordinately influenced by artistic ability. Physical omission, on the other hand, if it is scored only when a subject makes no effort whatsoever to indicate certain body parts and is not scored when there is any representation of them, no matter how poor its quality, clearly indexes disturbed body imagery rather than drawing ineptness.

Hozier additionally proposes three DAP scores for schizophrenia that involve the proportion of various body parts, and Baldwin (1964) found an overemphasis on head in relation to body size to differentiate the drawings of schizophrenic from normal women. Levy, Lomax, and Minsky (1963), however, report a correlation of .85 between the proportional accuracy of figure drawings and their rated artistic merit. Hence poor proportionality like poor representation of certain body parts may result from limited drawing skill as well as from distorted body imagery, and only for subjects with obvious artistic ability should distorted body imagery be inferred from poorly proportioned figure drawings.

The following four drawings illustrate physical omission as observed in various degrees of schizophrenic disorder. Figure 7 was drawn by a 28-year-old woman who was functioning on an ambulatory basis and applied for outpatient psychotherapy in connection with some interpersonal difficulties. Her exaggerated hysterical behavior patterns raised question about possible underlying schizophrenic pathology, and on testing her Rorschach was found to contain frequent instances of circumstantial thinking, arbitrary reasoning, and inaccurate perception. Her drawing is notable both for its line gaps, which demonstrate broken contours, and her failure to make any effort to indicate the hands, which constitutes physical omission.

Figure 8 was produced by a 24-year-old single woman who was also maintaining an ambulatory adjustment but presented obvious signs of cognitive defect on interview. She was referred for testing not because the extent of her psychopathology was in question but to differentiate uncertain organic and schizophrenic etiology. Although cognitive examination revealed no evidence of cerebral pathology, her figure drawing reflects markedly distorted body imagery. Her failure to indicate the hands and her apparent lack of concern about including the trunk and legs are physical omissions. Furthermore, in addition to the fragmented line quality of the drawing, the disproportionality of the figure

Figure 7

Figure 8

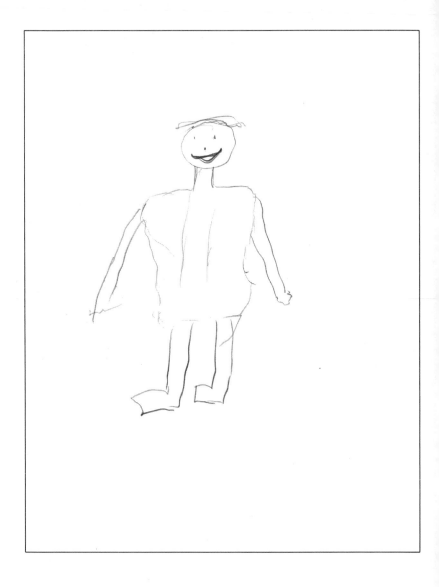

Figure 9

146

Figure 10

and its generally ghastly appearance seem beyond any defect that could be attributed to limited artistic talent.

Figures 9 and 10 were drawn by a 30-year-old professional man who was not brain-damaged and was admitted to the hospital in an acute state of confusion and disorganization. On examination he displayed considerable evidence of thought disturbance and poor reality testing. The extent of his impaired reality sense is apparent in these two drawings, particularly Figure 10, the sketchy and bizarre drawing of the female figure, in which there is no indication of arms and no effort to close the gaps in the legs.

Distorted Body Imagery in Nonschizophrenic Conditions. Figure drawings characterized by undifferentiated sexuality and physical omission may also occur in three nonschizophrenic conditions known to be accompanied by distorted body imagery. First, persons with organic brain disease, as mentioned earlier, manifest a wide range of disturbed body perceptions, and Reznikoff and Tomblen (1956) report a greater prevalence of DAP indicators of disturbance among brain-damaged than among either neurotic or schizophrenic subjects. Second, as also stated earlier, peculiarities are not unusual in the drawings of persons with visible physical defects. Levy (1950, p. 285), for example, includes in a review article figure drawings by a below-the-knee amputee in which the legs are omitted.

Finally, Gilbert and Hall (1962), using a 71-point qualitative scale to evaluate the figure drawings of 210 schizophrenics and 400 normal persons aged 10–91, found that with advancing age there is an increasing tendency for drawings to become absurd, incongruous, fragmented, and primitive. In their study schizophrenics were significantly inferior to normals at all ages sampled, but there was a marked similarity between the drawing disturbances found in the young and middle-aged schizophrenics and in the normal elderly persons. Therefore undifferentiated sexuality and physical omission are most likely to indicate a specifically schizophrenic impairment of reality sense in young and middle-aged persons who have no visible physical defects and present no evidence in cerebral pathology.

► 9

OBJECT RELATIONS

THE psychologically healthy individual is able to establish and maintain satisfactory relationships with people. Although maladaptive interpersonal relationships of various kinds mark neurotic as well as schizophrenic disturbances, schizophrenia is distinctively characterized by a withdrawal from object relatedness. Theorists following in the tradition of Sullivan and Cameron (see pp. 10–12) interpret schizophrenia *primarily* as a social disorder determined by inadequate channels for interpersonal communication. Will (1961), for example, ascribes considerable psychogenetic significance in schizophrenia to ineffective techniques for dealing with anxieties engendered by social situations. The person who as a result of unfortunate learning experiences fails to develop such techniques, says Will, experiences an inordinate amount of anxiety in his interactions with people and is likely to protect himself by withdrawing from the human environment.

One may or may not wish to accept an interpersonal formulation as adequate to account for the genesis and symptomatology of schizophrenia. Evidence cited in Chapter 6 (see p. 91) and the arguments of interaction theorists (Fessel, 1964; Meehl, 1962) incline toward the view that hypotheses derived solely from sociogenetic frameworks do not fully explain the various parameters of schizophrenic disturbance. Phenomenologically, however, there is little question that withdrawal and disturbed object relationships are salient features of schizophrenia. Weiner (1958, pp. 112–113) summarizes the clinical literature concerning object relations in schizophrenia as follows:

> Characteristically, there is a progressive decline in relationships to and contact with others. Social life becomes increasingly more restricted; the patients became more reticent and seclusive; withdraw into themselves;

149

and evidence no overt love for others; their interest in the world outside wanes. A history of protracted seclusiveness, a feeling of being alone in a crowd, of lacking feelings, and of persons appearing distant may be most suggestive in establishing a diagnosis.

In addition the disturbed object relations observed in schizophrenic persons may take the form of *emotional* withdrawal rather than the *physical* withdrawal stressed by Weiner. Whereas some schizophrenics physically isolate themselves to escape the frustration and rejection they anticipate in social situations, others, dreading the loneliness of social isolation, actively mingle with other people. These latter schizophrenics, however, although preserving an illusory appearance of social engagement, typically protect themselves against the vicissitudes of interpersonal relationships by assiduously avoiding any emotional involvement with the people with whom they interact. Thus both the physically isolated schizophrenic and the apparently socially engaged but emotionally withdrawn schizophrenic experience the feelings of social distantiation described by Weiner. It is usually only at the price of intense, poorly moderated, and anxiety-laden attachments that the schizophrenic can relax his pathologic emotional insulation.

The nature of a person's object relations, in contrast to the quality of his thinking and perceptual functioning, is sometimes more clearly indicated by his social history than by his response to psychodiagnostic tests. The test battery may consequently play a relatively minor role in the clinical assessment of disturbed object relations. Nevertheless, numerous relationships have been demonstrated between poor social skills and inefficient task performance, and the following brief review of work in this area suggests some potentially useful psychodiagnostic indicators of impaired object relations.

INTERPERSONAL FACTORS IN SCHIZOPHRENIC PERFORMANCE

Although rewarding relationships with others foster a positive interpersonal orientation, the individual who as a result of deficient social skills is unable to avoid anxiety in social situations is likely to become interpersonally aversive. At the same time, the person who avoids contact with others diminishes his opportunity for developing those social skills necessary for comfortable interpersonal relationships. Limited social skill and interpersonal aversion thus are sides of the same coin, and experimental indices of both have been associated with schizophrenic disturbance.

LIMITED SOCIAL SKILL

Of those social skills necessary for comfortable interpersonal relationships, the one most frequently studied is empathy, the ability to put oneself in another person's shoes and comprehend his needs and feelings.[1] Setting aside the issue of whether impaired empathy is a cause or an effect of schizophrenia, it is fairly well established that schizophrenics perform less well on measures of empathic capacity than normal persons. Jackson and Carr (1955), for example, asked 20 schizophrenic and 20 normal women to describe psychotic and normal women whom they met in a brief interview. When the subjects' predictions of how the women they had been asked to describe would rate themselves on a 40-item trait scale were compared with how these women actually rated themselves, the schizophrenics were found to be significantly less empathic than the normal subjects. Helfand (1956) asked schizophrenic and nonschizophrenic subjects to Q-sort 80 items to describe a former patient whose autobiography they were given to read. Discrepancies between the sorts and the former patient's actual self-description on the same measure revealed greater empathy among the normal than the schizophrenic subjects.

In another study Milgram (1960) gave a multiple-choice test to schizophrenic, brain-damaged, and normal subjects on which they were required to indicate the responses they felt would be typical of men as opposed to women and of adults as opposed to children. As judged from available normative standards of response to this test by men, women, and children, both the schizophrenic and brain-damaged groups were inferior to the normals in role-taking. Furthermore, when role-taking performance on the test was controlled for certain cognitive deficits observed in the brain-damaged subjects, their empathy scores approached the normal level and exceeded those of the schizophrenics.

These experimental demonstrations of relatively poor empathy among schizophrenic subjects should not be confused with the heightened sensitivity of schizophrenic patients frequently observed in the clinical setting. Fromm-Reichmann and others who have engaged in intensive therapeutic work with schizophrenics have noted them to be exquisitely sensitive to verbal and nonverbal aspects of their therapist's behavior and, once they have surrendered their strong resistance to emotional involvement, to be capable of intense transference reactions. However, as Fromm-Reichmann (1939, p. 416) points out, the schizophrenic

---

[1] For a concise review of concepts of empathy and a bibliography of related research the reader is referred to a recent paper by Buchheimer (1963).

patient typically distrusts and misinterprets the cues to which he is sensitive:

. . . the schizophrenic patient and the therapist are people living in different worlds and on different levels of personal development with different means of expressing and of orienting themselves. . . . So we should not be surprised that errors and misunderstandings occur when we undertake to communicate and strive for rapport with him.

The schizophrenic patient's sensitivity, in other words, is not accompanied by the accuracy of interpersonal perception that defines empathy, and his clinically noted misconceptions of the therapeutic relationship are consistent with the experimental evidence of limited empathic ability in schizophrenic subjects.

INTERPERSONAL AVERSION

Interpersonal aversion is most frequently operationalized for experimental purposes by comparing subjects' performance on neutral, impersonal tasks with their success on affect-laden, socially contextual tasks of equal difficulty. Several studies of the influence of social context on concept formation were cited in Chapter 6 to affirm that conceptual deficits are observed in schizophrenic subjects beyond whatever effects may be attributable to their interpersonal difficulties. However, in this chapter it is relevant to return to other aspects of these same and additional studies that indicate a particular susceptibility among schizophrenic persons to impaired cognitive functioning on tasks with prominent social referents.

Whiteman (1954, 1956) stimulated research in this area by demonstrating that socially oriented tasks can sensitively discriminate schizophrenic from nonschizophrenic subjects. Administering reasoning tests involving formal and social concepts to hospitalized schizophrenics and nonpsychotic controls matched in age, education, and intelligence, Whiteman found that, although the schizophrenics did less well than the controls on both types of test, their performance decrements were significantly greater on the social-concept than on the formal-reasoning task. Specifically, these schizophrenics displayed in their social-concept performance relatively large numbers of rejections, explicitly formulated concepts, and individualistic, physicalistic, and inappropriate responses.

Subsequent studies have consistently confirmed Whiteman's findings. Davis and Harrington (1957) presented to hospitalized schizophrenics and normal subjects two sets of pictures, one heavily weighted with and the other devoid of human content. For each set subjects were asked to choose correct pictures on the basis of information provided by the experimenter. When the subjects were matched on their ability to make accurate selections for the nonhuman picture set, the schizophrenics were found to perform significantly less well than the controls on the human content pictures.

Moriarity and Kates (1962) also gave a problem-solving task based on socially contextual pictures to schizophrenic and control subjects who were matched in conceptual ability on formal tasks. Their findings revealed the schizophrenics to have a selective performance impairment on the social materials. Brodsky (1963) administered to schizophrenic subjects and both hospitalized nonpsychiatric and nonhospitalized normal controls five card-sorting tasks; two tasks involved neutral stimuli and the other three presented pictures of people designed to elicit interpersonal attitudes. The schizophrenics earned poorer scores than the control subjects on all five tasks, but they did much less well in relation to the controls on the three interpersonal tasks than on the two neutral ones.

The basic design of these studies has been extended to other diagnostic groups and other methods. Bernstein (1960), for example, used neutral and socially contextual concept-formation tasks to study brain-damaged as well as schizophrenic and normal subjects. He found that when the brain-damaged and schizophrenic groups were equated for their performance on the neutral concept-formation task, the schizophrenics did significantly less well than the organics in social concept formation. Senf, Huston, and Cohen (1955) developed a Personal Discrepancy score based on the relative adequacy of response to personal and impersonal stems of a sentence completion test. When the test was administered to chronic schizophrenic, early schizophrenic, depressed manic-depressive, and neurotic subjects, the performance of the schizophrenics was judged significantly poorer on the personal than on the impersonal items, whereas no such Personal Discrepancy was observed for manic-depressive and neurotic groups.

Feldstein (1962) and Johannsen (1961) studied social disability in schizophrenia by varying the method of administration rather than the nature of the task. Feldstein manipulated the experimenter's interpersonal involvement with subjects who were given a picture interpretation test and found that schizophrenics, but not nonschizophrenic controls, displayed an increasing proportion of irrelevant verbal productions as the examiner increased the extent of his interaction with them.

Johannsen devised a button-pressing task in which subjects were informed about their performance either socially, by the examiner telling them their score of "rights" and "wrongs," or nonsocially, with feedback information communicated by patterns of flashing lights. Under conditions of nonsocial feedback normal, paranoid schizophrenic, and nonparanoid schizophrenic subjects performed equally well. With social feedback, however, the normals performed significantly better than they had under the nonsocial conditions, the paranoid schizophrenics remained about the same, and the nonparanoid schizophrenics performed significantly worse. Aside from possible differences between paranoid and nonparanoid schizophrenia (see Chap. 14), these several studies clearly attest the relative functioning disability experienced by schizophrenic persons in situations requiring them to deal with social contexts and interpersonal interactions.

SOCIAL MOTIVATION IN SCHIZOPHRENIA

The schizophrenic's demonstrated aversion to interpersonal situations has led some researchers to hypothesize that the primary source of performance decrements in schizophrenic subjects is deficient social motivation stemming from fears of criticism or rebuff in social situations. Such an interpretation of schizophrenic functioning received initial support from Rodnick and Garmezy (1957), who observed the performance of schizophrenics on stimulus generalization and concept formation tasks to decline markedly following censure by the experimenter; for example, "You're not doing very well."

Subsequent work, however, has cast doubt on both the nature of the schizophrenic's reaction to censure and the generality of low social motivation as an identifying characteristic of schizophrenia. Olson (1958), using a digit symbol task, noted that praise had a more salutary effect than censure on the performance of schizophrenic subjects, but he also found, in contrast to Rodnick and Garmezy, that censure *enhanced* rather than attenuated the schizophrenics' performance. Cavanaugh, Cohen, and Lang (1960) similarly report improved performance by schizophrenic relative to control subjects following censure on a reaction time test, with no change occurring subsequent to approval by the examiner. Goodstein, Guertin, and Blackburn (1961) also noted failure instructions to be more effective than success instructions in stimulating the reaction times of schizophrenics, but these investigators failed to find any differences between schizophrenic and control subjects in performance increments subsequent to either approval or censure.

Similarly inconsistent data have derived from studies in which attempts were made to replace the schizophrenic's presumably deficient social motivation with biological motivation. Pascal and Swenson

(1952) and Cavanaugh (1958), for example, employed escape from shock as a primary incentive to reward schizophrenic subjects for good performance. Pascal and Swenson found that schizophrenics approached normal performance on a complex discrimination reaction-time type of learning task when learning was followed by escape from such an aversive stimulus, and Cavanaugh similarly reports that "motivated" schizophrenics, that is, those subjected to an aversive stimulus, equaled the performance of a normal control group on a concept formation task.

Cohen (1956), however, giving motor-learning tasks to schizophrenic and normal groups under both shock and nonshock conditions, found that on some tasks the schizophrenics made fewer errors and had fewer trials to extinction under shock than under nonshock conditions, but on other tasks the normals and not the schizophrenics performed better under shock. Rosenbaum, Grisell, and Mackavey (1957) observed that, although schizophrenic subjects improved more than normals on a reaction-time task when shock was introduced, this group characteristic was not true for the female schizophrenic subjects nor for some of the male schizophrenics.

Hence experimentally induced motivation, whether by praise, censure, or shock, neither consistently nor uniformly minimizes schizophrenic deficits on cognitive tasks. It may be that the response of schizophrenic persons to censure and praise is determined by factors unrelated to their psychological disturbance, much as the Zeigarnik effect was found to be transcended by individual differences in subjects' attitudes toward achievement (Atkinson, 1953). If idiosyncratic personality dynamics determine whether individual attainment is encouraged more by praise for success or censure for failure, and if these dynamics operate independently of schizophrenic disturbance, then no consistent differences between schizophrenic and control subjects would be expected to emerge from such studies of motivational behavior.

As suggested by Buss and Lang (1965), moreover, it is possible that the effects of such manipulations on schizophrenic functioning are related more to their arousal and focusing functions (see Chap. 4) than to their incentive or reinforcement properties. At any rate, there clearly is insufficient basis for considering low social motivation, either generally or distinctively, to characterize schizophrenia. Indeed, the overlap between schizophrenic and normal subjects in the various studies cited is more striking than any differentiation realized in them. It therefore appears that indices of social motivation do not accurately reflect the interpersonal aversion that characterizes schizophrenia.

However, such a conclusion is not inconsistent with the notion that schizophrenic withdrawal is a defensive reaction to socially experienced failure or the view that deficient social skills aid identification of schizophrenic disturbance. The crux of the matter is that although deficient social skills are accompanied by behavioral withdrawal, they may or may not be associated with low social motivation. As pointed out on page 150, for some schizophrenics the defensive withdrawal occasioned by their inadequate social skills is manifest in decreased attention to people; for others, whose withdrawal is primarily into fantasy, human objects remain of considerable interest. The latter type of schizophrenic often devotes much thought to people and may derive satisfaction from manipulating, pleasing, or being attended to by others, even though, like the disinterested type, he is too threatened by interpersonal situations to initiate or reach out for human contacts on an adaptive emotional level.

PSYCHODIAGNOSTIC INDICATORS OF IMPAIRED OBJECT RELATIONS

The preceding brief review and formulation of literature concerning interpersonal factors in schizophrenic performance indicates that, although the mere presence or absence of interest in or ideation about people is not a useful clue to schizophrenia, indices of poor empathic capacity and particular susceptibility to impaired functioning in interpersonal situations can facilitate the diagnosis of schizophrenia. Among the following psychodiagnostic clues to disturbed object relations, the first two, *low M* and *low H* on the Rorschach, identify limited empathic skill and the third, *elevated Block Design* on the WAIS, reflects impaired interpersonal functioning.

LOW M

The Rorschach human movement response (M) is a multiply determined phenomenon, and Klopfer, Ainsworth, Klopfer, and Holt (1954, pp. 254–264) introduce hypotheses relating M both to empathy and to intelligence, imagination, inner stability, value systems, and self-acceptance as well. In a review of the movement score Piotrowski (1960) adduces evidence to support the two general notions that (a) M emphasis is associated with a preference for ideational as opposed to motoric activity and (b) M and M content are related to the handling of interpersonal relationships. The M response, in other words, is partly an index of interest in the needs and attitudes of others. Since persons who display little such interest tend to be minimally empathic, it follows that subjects who give few M are frequently deficient in the empathic skills on which good object relations depend.

Although few M may therefore indicate a pathologic impairment of the capacity to establish and maintain good object relations, it is important to note that an abundance of M has no necessary relationship to adaptive interpersonal behavior. As implied on page 156, good object relationships and effective social skills tend to contraindicate schizophrenia, but heightened interest in people does not. Many M reflects considerable attention to human attributes and motivations, *but it does not guarantee empathic ability.* Empathy is the accurate comprehension of the feelings and attitudes of others. Many M indicates only that the subject is *attempting* to comprehend the motives of other people; it does not ensure that he can do so accurately. Many M, therefore, does not necessarily identify good empathic capacity, even though few M suggests deficient empathy. The subject with many M may or may not have good social skills and he may or may not be schizophrenic.

If this formulation is correct, it should be demonstrable (a) that social withdrawal can be accompanied by few or many M, (b) that some schizophrenics give few and others many M responses, and (c) that efforts to separate schizophrenic from normal groups on the basis of numbers of M responses yield inconsistent results, depending on the composition of the schizophrenic sample. The literature in fact confirms all three of these deductions. Regarding (a), Beck (1954, p. 55) has observed that the social withdrawal associated with schizophrenic disturbance may take the form of a withdrawal into autistic fantasy, with many M, or may result in a narrowing of the range of interest, without M. In a later paper (1960), elaborating his SR-2 type of schizophrenia, Beck states that such schizophrenic persons are characterized both by "bankrupt object relations" and by withdrawal into ideational activity, that is, M responses.

Concerning (b), clinicians since Rorschach (1921, p. 28) have noted that some schizophrenics give few and others many M responses, and there is widespread agreement with Rorschach's conclusion that M's are likely to occur frequently in the records of schizophrenics with prominent ideational symptoms, particularly those with paranoid tendencies (Bohm, 1958, p. 270; Rapaport, Gill, & Schafer, 1946, p. 220; see Chap. 14). In a related experimental study King (1960) compared the Rorschach records of 14 matched pairs of paranoid schizophrenic subjects, half of whom had interpersonal delusions and the other half, somatic delusions. He found significantly more M responses among the interpersonally than the somatically deluded subjects. Similarly relevant is a study by Brecher (1956) of maternally overprotected and maternally rejected male schizophrenics in which she found twice as many M in the overprotected (average of 5.4 M) as in the rejected (average of 2.1 M) subjects.

Finally, in regard to (c), comparisons between schizophrenic and control groups in average M have yielded inconsistent findings. In one study Beck (1938) reports no differences between schizophrenics, nonpsychotic psychiatric patients, and normal subjects in M, but in another comparison (1954, p. 212) he notes a significantly higher frequency of M in 157 normal subjects than in 60 schizophrenics. Sherman (1952) found significantly more M in normals than in schizophrenics among subjects giving fewer than 20 responses, but no difference in M between normal and schizophrenic subjects with 20 or more responses. Knopf (1956), who compared 100 schizophrenics with 106 nonschizophrenic psychiatric patients, conducted two analyses of his data to identify those of his results that were stable; in one analysis the schizophrenics were significantly lower in M than the controls, but in the other they were not.

These clinical and experimental findings and the likely relationship between M and empathy indicate that, although the presence of many M does not rule out schizophrenia, few M may be an important clue to the deficient social skills that characterize schizophrenic disturbance. The following sections review normative data for M responses and quantitative and qualitative considerations relevant to a diagnostically useful definition of *low M*.

Normative Data for M Responses. Brockway et al. (1954) and Cass and McReynolds (1951) both report median M values of 2.0 for samples of 151 and 104 normal adults, respectively. The eightieth percentile points for M in these two studies were 3.4 and 4.5, respectively, and the twentieth percentile points were 0.9 and 1.0. An M of zero fell at the tenth percentile in the Cass and McReynolds sample. Beck et al. (1950) found a mean M of 3.50 for 157 normal adults, but Fiske and Baughman's (1953) analysis of the Beck et al. data reveals that this mean value is inflated by the large number of M's given by subjects who produced lengthy records. Fiske and Baughman found a correlation of .41 between M and R for the Beck et al. sample, and they report the following median frequencies of M within certain ranges of R: for 30–34 R, 3.0 M; for 25–29 R, 2.7 M; for 20–24 R, 2.1 M; and for both 15–19 R and 10–14 R, 0.7 M.

Low M in Schizophrenia—Quantitative Considerations. The above normative data indicate that normal subjects giving records of average and especially below average length may often produce relatively few M responses. Hence the only quantitative criterion for M likely, with any consistency, to distinguish schizophrenic from normal subjects is the total absence of M, which falls at the tenth percentile for normal persons. Rickers-Ovsiankina's (1938) work lends some support to such a strict criterion. She found no difference in mean M between schizophrenic and normal groups, but noted that 15 of her 37 schizophrenic subjects but only four of 20 normals had zero M (p approaching significance). Nevertheless, this *low* M criterion cannot be expected to differentiate all groups of schizophrenics from normals. Paranoid schizophrenics, for example, are, as indicated on page 157, unlikely to omit M responses (see also Chap. 14); and Rapaport et al. (1946, p. 220) and Piotrowski (1945) present evidence that absence of M is associated primarily with chronic rather than acute schizophrenic disorder (see Chap. 13).

For cases in which impaired social skills are reflected in failure to give M responses the Fiske and Baughman data also relevantly indicate that lack of M assumes enhanced significance as a record increases in length. Because of the high positive correlation between M and R, few M is relatively more deviant in long than in brief records, and one or two M in a very long record may be as diagnostically significant as total lack of M in a record of average length.

Low M in Schizophrenia—Qualitative Considerations. M is a gross scoring category applicable to responses with diverse content and varying perceptual accuracy. Certain qualitative as well as quantitative criteria for *low* M may therefore help to identify deficient social skills. First, the person whose interest in human attributes is associated with a fragmentary, depreciatory view of people or focused on nonhuman objects is unlikely to have social skills adequate to maintain good interpersonal relationships. On the Rorschach, then, M responses limited to (H), Hd, (Hd), A, (A), Ad, and (Ad) contents are only slightly less significant for limited empathic capacity than complete absence of M. The conclusions of Klopfer et al. (1954, p. 164) are relevant in this regard:

Subjects who lack closeness to other people may turn the usual human figures into animals and give M responses with (A) content. Content with Hd, (H), or (Hd) indicates hostile and critical tendencies, which are believed to obstruct free-flowing empathy and to indicate self-preoccupations that interfere with warm interpersonal relationships.

Second, the person whose interests in human attributes are focused on people but who is prone to inaccurate and unrealistic interpretations of interpersonal situations is also nonempathic, as was pointed out earlier. Hence M responses with minus form level $(M-)$ are as likely to be associated with deficient social skills and poor interpersonal relationships as the failure to produce any M. While the minus element of an $M-$ response is to some extent reflected in the form-level scores discussed in Chapter 7, $M-$ responses merit additional emphasis beyond that assigned to $F+\%$ and $R+\%$. Phillips and Smith (1953, pp. 70–71), on the basis of the approximately 1500 adult records they utilized in preparing their book, make the following observations:

> Empirically, form inadequacy is of far greater clinical significance in movement responses than in responses in which form is the only determinant. . . . $F-$ indicates inadequate judgment, and when it occurs in a movement response, suggests a faulty assessment of the social realities. Therefore, the presence of two or more $M-$ in a record of normal length suggests that social roles are played on the basis of a distorted perception of interpersonal relationships and will very likely be inappropriate.

Therefore the absence of either M with H content or $M+$, even in the presence of M's with other content or minus form level, indicates *low M* and suggests impaired capacity for effective interpersonal relationships. These qualitative considerations explain further why a large number of M responses does not necessarily rule out the possibility of deficient social skills. That is, a high M score based on movement ascribed to non-H or to minus form contents points to disturbed rather than adaptive objection relations. In this regard, Phillips and Smith (1953) propose as a quantitative index of the adequacy of M responses that any record in which $M-$ responses constitute one-fourth or more of all M's given should be considered indicative of psychosis.

Low M in Nonschizophrenic Conditions. Piotrowski (1960) indicates that the production of M responses requires both a certain level of ideational activity and a certain degree of interest in the needs and attitudes of other people, and to these two requisites Klopfer et al. (1954, p. 254) add a third, the ability to perceive in a differentiated and well-integrated fashion. The association of *low M* with schizophrenia derives primarily from those aspects of M production that pertain to interpersonal relationships; however, the fact that three nonschizophrenic conditions, depressive disorder, repressive defensive style, and organic brain disease, may also be characterized by *low M* is attributable to the other two elements of M production, ideational activity and differentiated perception.

Because lack of energy for ideational activity is a major feature of depression (see p. 123), it is to be expected that depressed and particularly severely depressed subjects will give few M. A similar expectation holds for persons who rely heavily on repressive defenses and accordingly evince a hysterical personality, because a repressive defensive style is typically accompanied by a preference for motoric and expressive behavior with correspondingly little interest in ideational or reflective activity (Levine & Spivack, 1964, pp. 136–147). Consistent with these expectations, only three of 52 depressed and hysterical subjects studied by Rapaport et al. (1946, Appendix I) gave more than a single M response.

In the case of zero M, therefore, reference to other indicators may be necessary to discriminate depressive lethargy and hysterical unreflectiveness from schizophrenic withdrawal. With one or even two M, however, there is an additional parameter of M response that often distinguishes the schizophrenic's difficulty in social relationships from the depressed subject's impoverished ideation and the hysteric's disinterest in ideational activity. This parameter is the distribution of the M responses over the 10 Rorschach cards. Normative expectancies for M distribution have been observed by Phillips and Smith (1953, pp. 66–68) and Rapaport et al. (1946, p. 222). On the basis of 250 normal records Phillips and Smith report that M responses occur most frequently on Card III, next most frequently on Card II, and also relatively frequently on Cards VII and IX. Least likely to elicit M's, according to both the Phillips and Smith and Rapaport et al. data, are Cards VI and VIII.

It is logical to expect that subjects who have little energy for or interest in ideational activity but who nevertheless produce an M or two will give their M's where M responses are most easily perceived. Equating ease of perception with frequency of occurrence, it follows that depressed and hysterical subjects will produce their occasional M responses primarily to Card III, somewhat less often to Card II, rarely to Cards VII and IX, and hardly ever to the other cards. Therefore, a single M response that occurs on other than Cards II or III, or the presence of two M's, neither of which is on Cards II, III, VII, or IX, is unlikely in normal, depressed, and hysterical subjects and raises the possibility of schizophrenia.

Brain-damaged subjects, on the other hand, are likely to give few M's not because of their level of ideational activity, which may or may not be low, but in relation to their inadequately differentiated and integrated perceptual functioning. Fewer than two M responses is one of the Rorschach signs validated by Piotrowski (1937, 1940) as discriminating brain-damaged from control subjects, and Evans and Marmorston (1964) have more recently found brain-damaged significantly more often than control subjects to give zero M. Because the brain-damaged person's difficulty in producing M rests with basic perceptual impairments, he tends to give those *M*'s of which he is capable where *M* responses are most easily seen. Hence brain-damaged, like depressed and hysterical subjects, will give their *M*'s primarily on Cards II, III, VII, and IX, and one or two *M*'s occurring elsewhere, in the context of a pathologic record, differentiates schizophrenia from organicity as well as from depression and hysteria.

In summary, then, *low M* most clearly indicates a schizophrenic impairment of social skills when other data make it possible to rule out depression, repressive defensive style, and brain damage. Additionally, when only a few *M* are present and they occur to cards other than those that frequently elicit *M*, namely II, III, VII, and IX, schizophrenia rather than these other conditions is suggested.

LOW H

The Rorschach *H* response, like the *M* response, reflects interest in people. As with *M*, a large number of *H* responses does not guarantee good interpersonal relationships (see p. 157); the interests indicated by *H* responses may be expressed in fantasy rather than social contact, and they may comprise negative, hypercritical, and distorted rather than positive and adaptive attitudes toward others. Consistent with this formulation, virtually no studies have found differences between schizophrenic and nonschizophrenic groups in average number of *H*.

On the other hand, the absence of *H* suggests limited empathic capacity and is an alternative to *low M* as an index of deficient social skill. *M* and *H* are highly correlated (Wishner, 1959), but in those instances where *M*'s occur primarily in *Hd* and *A* contents, the absence of *H* may be the more useful quantitative index of social withdrawal. Furthermore, since *H* production requires less ideational activity and less perceptual differentiation than *M* production, the absence of *H* in a record with zero *M* helps further to discriminate schizophrenia from depression, hysteria, and brain damage. Although subjects with these latter three conditions tend to produce banal Rorschach content with high *A%*'s, Rapaport et al.'s (1946, Appendix I) depressed and hysterical subjects were less likely to give zero *H* than zero *M*, and absence of *H* is not among the various Rorschach criteria for organic brain disease summarized by Burgemeister (1962, pp. 33–37) and Evans and Marmorston (1964).

Normative Data for H Responses. Normative data suggest diagnostic criteria for *H* similar to those applicable with *M*. Brockway et al. (1954) found a median of 2.6 *H* in their normative study, with twentieth and eightieth percentile scores of 0.9 and 4.6 *H*, respectively. Cass and Mc-

Reynolds (1951) obtained a median H of 2.5 from their normal sample, with 1.0 and 5.0 H falling respectively at the twentieth and eightieth percentiles. Fewer than five percent of the Cass and McReynolds sample failed to give at least one H response. Beck et al. (1950) noted a mean of 4.02 H in their normal sample, but the analysis of their data by Fiske and Baughman (1953) revealed a correlation of .49 between H and total R and the following median H scores in records of average and below average length: for 30–34 R, 3.4 H; for 25–29 R, 3.6 H; for 20–24 R, 2.6 H; for 15–19 R, 1.4 H; and for 10–14 R, 0.8 H.

Diagnostic Interpretation of Low H. The above data indicate that H occurs somewhat more frequently than M (see p. 158) and is very seldom totally absent from normal records. Hence failure to give H, even more than omission of M, indicates a pathologic deficiency of empathic capacity. In view of the positive relationship between H and R, *low H*, like *low M*, takes on increasing pathologic significance as a record increases in length. The Fiske and Baughman data imply that even one or two H in a long record is sufficiently deviant to suggest impaired empathy. Finally of note is Rapaport et al.'s (1946, p. 116) analysis of $H\%$ in various diagnostic groups, which suggests that *low H* is particularly likely to characterize chronic as opposed to acute schizophrenic disturbance (see Chap. 13).

Rorschach Empathy-Object Relationship (RE-OR) Score. A Rorschach Empathy-Object Relationship (RE-OR) scale recently devised by Pruitt and Spilka (1964) is of interest to mention here even though little is yet known of its utility. The RE-OR scale largely overlaps what has already been presented concerning numbers and quality of M and H responses, but it additionally takes into account the degree to which human figures are sex-specified and placed in contemporary and appropriate spatial-temporal settings. Pruitt and Spilka employ an 18-point scoring scale to measure the degree of empathic capacity represented by each Rorschach response, and the total RE-OR score is determined by cumulating the scoring weights assigned and dividing by total R.

Although the diagnostic validity of this scale and the degree to which it is influenced by R have not yet been established, the data reported by Pruitt and Spilka are promising. They compared the RE-OR scores of two primarily schizophrenic patient groups, one receiving group psychotherapy and the other not, with those of normal controls. The subjects in the patient groups were tested twice, once before the inception and again following termination of the treatment program.

Initially, the nontreated patient group, the treatment patient group, and the normal group had respective mean RE-OR scores of 2.1, 2.3, and 2.7, the F-ratio for which was not significant. At the termination of the group therapy program, however, the mean RE-OR scores were 1.5 in the nontreatment and 2.9 in the treatment group, which in comparison with the normal subjects' mean score of 2.7 yielded a significant F-ratio. Inasmuch as the improvements presumably associated with the treatment program were reflected in increasing RE-OR scores, the low end of the Pruitt and Spilka scale may provide an additional quantitative index of the impaired empathic capacity associated with schizophrenia.

ELEVATED BLOCK DESIGN

The WAIS, like the experimental measures of interpersonal aversion that differentiate schizophrenic from control subjects (see pp. 152–154), comprises subtests fairly heavily laden with social content, as well as formal, impersonal tasks that require little social judgment and minimal interaction with the examiner. Of the WAIS subtests, the two least likely to be affected by impaired social skills and concomitant interpersonal aversion are Block Design and Digit Symbol. In both the subject deals with abstract symbols that have no conventional reference to human attributes or social relationships, and in neither is he required to verbalize his responses to the examiner.

Digit Symbol, however, differs from Block Design in certain important respects that question its utility for indicating freedom from a schizophrenic impairment of object relatedness. Digit Symbol correlates less highly with the other nonverbal subtests than they do with each other (Wechsler, 1955, p. 16), and factor analytic studies reveal that Digit Symbol tends to load less highly on a Perceptual Organization factor than any of the other nonverbal subtests and by itself to constitute a separate factor (Berger, Bernstein, Klein, Cohen, & Lucas, 1964; Cohen, 1952). These facts and the nature of the Digit Symbol task suggest it may be more adversely influenced than the other nonverbal subtests by psychomotor inefficiency, which has been demonstrated to characterize schizophrenia (see Chap. 11). At any rate, schizophrenic subjects have consistently been found to perform less well on Digit Symbol than on any Wechsler subtests (Garfield, 1949; Jastak, 1953; Olch, 1948) and to earn lower Digit Symbol scores than neurotically depressed and anxious subjects of comparable intelligence (Beck, Feshbach, & Legg, 1962).

Block Design, on the other hand, appears unlikely to be affected by impaired social skills and relatively insensitive to distinctively schizophrenic cognitive deficits. Garfield (1949) found Block Design the third highest Wechsler scale score among 109 schizophrenic subjects. Olch (1948) observed Block Design to be the second highest Wechsler scale in a group of young schizophrenics and the fourth highest among older schizophrenic subjects. Garfield (1948), comparing the subtest deviations from mean subtest score of 67 schizophrenic and 46 non-schizophrenic psychiatric patients, found the largest difference between them on Block Design, with the schizophrenic group displaying fewer negative and more positive Block Design deviations from mean sub-test score than the nonschizophrenic group.

Defining Elevated Block Design. To translate the usually well-re-tained Block Design scores of schizophrenic subjects into a diagnostic index of interpersonal aversion, it is necessary to compare them with scores on other WAIS subtests that are normally highly correlated with and factorially related to Block Design but, in contrast to Block De-sign, are heavily laden with social and interpersonal referents and are demonstrably sensitive to the inroads of schizophrenic disturbance. The three WAIS subtests most highly correlated with and factorially related to Block Design in normal samples are Picture Completion (PC), Picture Arrangement (PA), and Object Assembly (OA) (Berger et al., 1964; Cohen, 1957a; Wechsler, 1955, p. 16). Of these the least sensi-tive to schizophrenia is OA, which has been found to remain relatively high in the performance of schizophrenic subjects in general (Gar-field, 1949; Olch, 1948) and of chronic schizophrenics in particular (Rapaport et al., 1945, p. 270).

Both PC and PA, however, are socially contextual tasks that have proved adversely affected by schizophrenic disturbance. The relatively poor performance of schizophrenic subjects on PC is reviewed in the earlier discussion of this subtest's relevance to cognitive focusing (see pp. 34–35), and available data concerning PA indicate that it is one of the lowest Wechsler scale scores among schizophrenic subjects (Garfield, 1949; Jastak, 1953). PA furthermore tends in schizophrenics to be particularly impaired in relation to other performance subtests (Rapaport et al., 1945, p. 230) and significantly more often than in normal subjects to fall below Vocabulary (Rogers, 1951).

PC and PA thus qualify as appropriate subtests against which to compare Block Design in determining whether the latter is patho-logically *elevated.* Block Design has in fact frequently been observed to be higher than both PC and PA in schizophrenic subjects (Garfield, 1948; Olch, 1948; Wechsler, 1958, p. 191). However, the mere superi-ority of Block Design to PC and PA does not provide a satisfactory diagnostic indicator. Garfield (1948) found no greater frequency of Block Design-greater-than-PC in schizophrenic than in control subjects, and inspection of the Rapaport et al. data (1945, Appendix II) reveals that, although 31 (49%) of 63 schizophrenic subjects had Block Design scores in excess of both PC and PA, 51 (35%) of 144 depressed, neurotic, and normal subjects did also, and the difference between these groups is not significant.

To establish a diagnostically useful definition of elevated Block Design, it is necessary to refer to the McNemar (1957) and Wechsler (1958, p. 164) tables utilized in earlier discussions. These tables indicate that discrepancies of Block Design from PA and PC must exceed three scale scores to approach significance and four scale scores to ensure a nonchance difference. Hence elevated Block Design should be inferred only when the Block Design score is four or more and especially five or more scales scores above either PC or PA, and it is most clearly demonstrated when Block Design exceeds both PC and PA to this extent.

Implications of Elevated Block Design for Schizophrenia. To summarize the preceding discussion, a Block Design score exceeding PC and/or PA by four or more scale scores (a) is unlikely to constitute a chance occurrence, (b) represents pathologically impaired functioning in situations involving social and interpersonal contexts, and (c) suggests interpersonal aversion and deficient capacity for comfortable object relations. No specific studies have assessed the validity of this elevated Block Design criterion for diagnosing schizophrenia. However, additional analysis of the Rapaport et al. data (1945, Appendix II) reveals that 25 (40%) of 63 paranoid and undifferentiated schizophrenics but only 26 (18%) of 144 depressed, neurotic, and normal subjects displayed a Block Design four or more scale scores above either their PC or PA, and this degree of association between schizophrenia and elevated Block Design yields a significant χ^2.

The diagnostic utility of elevated Block Design is further enhanced by its potential for discriminating schizophrenia from organic brain disease. As frequently mentioned in Chapters 7 and 8, most psychodiagnostic indicators of impaired relation to reality are as likely to identify brain damage as schizophrenia. However, as indicated in the discussion of Comprehension deficiency on page 122, tasks comprising concrete and socially relevant stimuli usually allow a brain-damaged subject to utilize his previous social learning to earn higher scores than he can achieve on abstract tests of concept formation and visual organization that provide him no such clues.

Accordingly, brain-damaged persons, in contrast to schizophrenics, tend to perform better on PC and PA than on Block Design. Rappaport (1953) has demonstrated a significant Block Design superiority of schizophrenic over organic subjects of comparable vocabulary skill, and Wechsler (1958, p. 174) suggests that inability to execute the Block Design task is the most significant WAIS clue to organic brain disease. More detailed studies by Reitan (1955) and by Matthews, Guertin, and Reitan (1962), however, indicate that the patterning of cognitive performance in brain-damaged subjects is less uniform than was once thought and is significantly influenced by the locus of the lesion. Specifically, Wechsler's criteria for organicity—Performance IQ below Verbal IQ with particular impairment on Block Design—are most likely to characterize persons with right hemispheric brain damage, whereas left hemispheric lesions are associated primarily with impairment of verbal skills. Elevated Block Design, therefore, will most effectively discriminate schizophrenia from organic brain syndromes when the latter involve right hemispheric or bilateral foci.

► 10

DEFENSIVE OPERATIONS

EFFECTIVE psychological adaptation requires the availability to a person of various defensive operations that assist him to control his ideation and integrate his affective experiences in a stable and consistent manner. Defensive operations viewed in this way are not pathologic phenomena but rather define a person's life style, that is, the particular compromises he has worked out between his needs and the limitations imposed on him by his behavioral standards, his environmental situation, and his mental and physical assets. When these operations falter, a person cannot prevent primitive, disrupting thoughts from impinging on his conscious awareness and is unable to integrate his emotional reactions in the service of a consistent response style.

Defensive inadequacies are thus manifest primarily in poor ideational control and emotional instability. Psychodynamically, ideational control can be related to the specific defense mechanism of repression, and emotional stability, to some consistent defensive style, repressive or otherwise, that promotes adaptive integration of affective experience. *Failure of repression* and *inconsistent affective integration* are therefore complementary clues to inadequate defensive resources, and the following sections consider psychodiagnostic indices of these impairments in schizophrenic disturbance.

FAILURE OF REPRESSION

The concept of *repression* was first elaborated as such in a 1915 paper by Freud, who stated, "The essence of repression lies simply in the function of rejecting and keeping something out of consciousness"

(p. 86). In this paper, however, Freud used repression synonymously with the term *defense*, which he had earlier employed to describe the process he had observed in patients whose "ego was confronted by an experience, an idea, a feeling, arousing an affect so painful that the person resolved to forget it, since he had no confidence in his power to resolve the incompatibility between the unbearable idea and his ego by the processes of thought" (1894, pp. 61–62).

Later, in *The Problem of Anxiety,* Freud (1926, pp. 110–112) distinguished between defense and repression, proposing defense as the general designation for all of the techniques employed by the ego to deal with conflicts and repression as the label for one particular mode of defense. [1] Anna Freud (1936) subsequently defined the particular repressive mode as "the withholding or expulsion of an idea or affect from the conscious ego" (p. 55), and went on to delineate the nature and significance of such other defense mechanisms as regression, reaction-formation, isolation, undoing, projection, introjection, turning against the self, reversal, and sublimation.

Although the relative prominence of these several defenses may contribute secondarily to the clinical picture of a schizophrenic disorder, it is the inadequate operation of repression that distinctively identifies schizophrenia. Kant (1940) and Hartmann (1950), among others, have emphasized the diagnostic significance for schizophrenia of failure to maintain repressive barriers, as manifest in conscious awareness of sexual and aggressive thoughts that violate personal or social standards. Kant avers that the ready accessibility of such thoughts early in a treatment situation identifies loss of repressive ability and differentiates schizophrenic from neurotic disturbance. Hartmann calls attention to the many libidinal and aggressive features of schizophrenic disturbance that are attributable to the deficient repressive capacity of the ego in this condition.

The role of repressive failure in schizophrenic disturbance is particularly clear in instances of homosexual panic reactions, which Glick (1959) describes as a form of acute schizophrenic reaction. Both Glick (1959) and James (1947) relate homosexual panic primarily to inability to repress unacceptable sexual impulses and a consequent excess of poorly controlled homosexual ideation.

Failure of repression is most clearly indicated in the psychodiagnostic test battery by deviant Rorschach content. The relationship of repressive defense to thematic material is explicated by Schafer (1954) in the following remarks:

---

[1] Contributions by Brenner (1957) and Madison (1961) provide an extended and scholarly review of Freud's concepts of repression.

Repression holds a special position as a defense, namely, it appears to be ubiquitous and prominently so. That is to say, everyone seems required to expend a more or less significant amount of psychic energy ("counter-cathexis") in keeping inevitably persisting and disturbing infantile strivings and their derivatives out of consciousness. Psychoanalytic theory and observation indicate that repressive defense is to be accepted as a part of normal development and normal adult personality organization (p. 193). . . . Failure of repression in the test situation usually reflects acute or chronic general ego weakness. When repressions fail, perverse, morbid and fantastic thoughts and fantasies tend to flood consciousness. Themes of torture, rape, incest, mutilation, sexual aberrations and frustration, freakishness and the like pour out . . . (p. 54).

Two recent contributions, an analysis of Rorschach content variables by Holt and Havel (1960) and the development by Levine and Spivack (1964) of a Rorschach Index of Repressive Style (RIRS), elaborate further the relationship between repressive failure and specific types of Rorschach content.

Rorschach Indices of Drive-Dominated Ideation. Holt and Havel (1960, pp. 270–284) utilize content variables heavily in outlining a scheme for Rorschach assessment of primary process thinking. As mentioned on page 62, these writers identify as one of the characteristics of primary process thinking the domination of ideational activity by drives: the more the content of a Rorschach response directly reveals a basic drive, that is, "the less neutralized is the energy of the drive," the less controlled the primary process tendencies. Holt and Havel separate the drives into two categories, one relating to libidinal aims and the other to aggressive aims, and they score responses falling into these categories on two levels: *Level 1* is scored for the more direct, intense, and blatant expressions of drives, and *Level 2* is used to indicate drive expressions that are in some way muted, socialized, or sublimated.

The domination of ideational activity by drives represents repressive failure, and those Rorschach responses that Holt and Havel score as *Level 1* are particularly likely to indicate impaired defensive operations. Responses reflecting libidinal aims and scored at *Level 1* include the following content areas:

ORAL: mouth, lips, tongue, breasts, and udders of a cow, all of which are scored at *Level 1* only when seen in isolation.

ANAL: buttocks seen in isolation and any reference to excretory organs, defecation, or feces.

SEXUAL (*i.e., phallic-genital*): genitals whether seen in isolation or as part of a person or animal, and indirect references to sexual organs.

EXHIBITIONISTIC-VOYEURISTIC: any specific spontaneous reference to nudity.
HOMOSEXUAL (*sexual ambiguity*): uncertainty, ambiguity, or changing mind about sex of genitalia.

Responses reflecting aggressive aims and scored at *Level 1* are divided by Holt and Havel into the following types:

POTENTIAL-SUBJECT: vivid sadistic fantasies portraying events about to happen—"Yawning, grasping mouth, going to bite off this part."
POTENTIAL-OBJECT: menaced or frightened figures.
ACTIVE-SUBJECT: primitive annihilation of an object—"Witches, tearing a woman apart."
ACTIVE-OBJECT: "Sharp instrument going through the penis."
RESULTS: aftermaths of sadistic, violent action, especially mutilated persons or animals.

The Rorschach Index of Repressive Style (RIRS). Levine and Spivack (1964) have developed an elaborate scoring scheme for identifying the degree to which a subject's Rorschach responses reflect the operation of repressive defenses. Using a broad interpretation of the concomitants of repressive defense, they base their scores on the following seven principles (pp. 17–32): specificity, elaboration, impulse responses, primary process thinking, self-references, movement, and organization. Most of these categories are treated in the chapters of this book that deal with the thinking, perceptual, object relations, and synthetic functions of the ego, to which they appear more intimately related than to defensive operations. However, germane to repressive defense as conceived in this chapter is Levine and Spivack's *impulse* category, which they introduce as follows (p. 25):

Any direct reference to sexuality, hostility, anality, or dependency in a response reflects lessened repressive functioning. It is assumed that repressions are maintained to keep just such impulse derivatives from consciousness. The presence of such ideation in the Rorschach thus implies a lessening of repressive functioning.

Levine and Spivack outline scoring criteria for four types of impulse response that indicate repressive failure:

SEX: any sex content, e.g., *penis, vagina;* sex content in a verb, e.g., *masturbating.*
DEPENDENCY: direct oral references such as *food, mouth,* or *breast;* dependency content in a verb, e.g., *sucking, eating.*
ANAL: direct anal references such as *anus* and *feces* and such responses as *mud* or *dirt.*
HOSTILITY: any reference to attack, fighting, blood, mutilation, war scenes, etc.

Psychodiagnostic Indicators of Repressive Failure

The experienced clinician will have recognized in the Holt and Havel and Levine and Spivack examples some responses that are unlikely to occur in other than schizophrenic subjects and others that have no particular implications for such a diagnosis. Both methods of analysis are intended as research rather than clinical tools, however, and the above sketchy summaries serve primarily to identify guidelines for diagnostic utilization of Rorschach content categories. Two indicators of repressive failure that emerge from these scoring schemes are *sexual preoccupation* and *aggressive preoccupation,* each of which as defined below has been demonstrated to suggest schizophrenic disturbance.

SEXUAL PREOCCUPATION

As Rapaport, Gill, and Schafer (1946, p. 304) point out, society promulgates certain taboos that are especially applicable to communication with a relative stranger, as in the testing situation. Inasmuch as the normal subject can accordingly be expected to approach testing with taboos that prevent him from associating along sexual lines, sexual preoccupation, as manifest in an accumulation of Rorschach responses having overt sexual content, indicates a failure of repression.

Sexual Preoccupation in Schizophrenia. In conventional Rorschach scoring Sex content scores are assigned to responses that refer to sexual organs (penis, vagina, breast, anus, testicles, etc.) or to sexual acts (intercourse, masturbation, fellatio, etc.). There is abundant evidence that such *Sex* responses occur more frequently in the records of schizophrenic than of nonschizophrenic subjects. Beck (1954, p. 212) reports the mean number of *Sex* responses in the records of schizophrenics to be significantly greater than the mean number given by samples of neurotic and normal persons, and Knopf (1956) has observed a larger mean number of *Sex* responses in schizophrenic than in nonschizophrenic psychiatric patients.

Other data from normal and patient groups suggest that the presence in a record of even a single *Sex* response is a diagnostically valid criterion for sexual preoccupation. In the first place, *Sex* responses are very rarely given by normal persons. Beck et al. (1950) found a mean frequency of 0.02 *Sex* responses in 157 normal subjects, and Fiske and Baughman's (1953) analysis of this sample revealed the median number of *Sex* responses even in very long records (more than 50 R) to be zero. Brockway et al. (1954) also found a median of zero

Sex responses in a normal sample of 126 subjects, with a *Sex* frequency of 0.3 responses falling at the eightieth percentile.

Second, numerous studies attest that *Sex* responses, even occurring singly, validly discriminate schizophrenic from nonschizophrenic subjects. Orme (1962), reviewing 1010 Rorschach records given in the course of routine psychological consultations, found that the percentage of subjects giving one or more *Sex* responses was significantly greater among schizophrenic than among alcoholic, melancholic, psychopathic, neurotic, or organic patient groups. Vinson (1960) also reports the presence of any *Sex* responses significantly more frequently to characterize the records of schizophrenic than normal subjects, and Rapaport et al. (1946, p. 312) found that any number of *Sex* responses greater than zero significantly discriminated both paranoid and undifferentiated schizophrenic subjects from depressed, neurotic, and normal control groups. Interestingly, Rapaport et al. also noted a greater tendency for *Sex* responses to occur in groups of "preschizophrenic" subjects than among overt schizophrenics. Zucker (1958, p. 82) similarly reports a greater frequency of *Sex* responses in ambulatory than in hospitalized schizophrenic patients. Other differences between overt, incipient, and borderline schizophrenic persons are discussed in Chapters 15 and 16.

Factors Influencing the Interpretation of Sexual Preoccupation. Although the presence of one or more *Sex* responses thus appears validly to discriminate schizophrenic from nonschizophrenic subjects, efficient diagnostic interpretation of *Sex* responses requires adequate consideration of the manner in which they are given and the locations to which they occur. With regard to manner of expression, Rapaport et al. (1946, p. 304) point out that *Sex* responses are occasionally offered by nonschizophrenic persons who are either relatively uninhibited or are professionally or psychologically sophisticated; in such instances, however, the *Sex* responses given usually occur in the context of an otherwise dilated and expressive record, and they are delimited responses couched in technically correct language.

On the other hand, *Sex* responses erupting in the setting of a constricted record strongly suggest psychopathology, especially when they demonstrate any of the following characteristics: vague, halting, verbalization ("the bottom parts of a woman . . . er . . . her private parts"); incorrect terminology (e.g., *womb* where *vagina* is clearly meant); fabulized or queer elaborations ("a penis in a state of erection"; "a lady's vagina, but it doesn't look like anyone I know"); and reference to sexual acts (e.g. "intercourse") rather than to sexual anatomy.

Concerning locations to which *Sex* responses occur, those few nonschizophrenic subjects who give *Sex* responses are likely to do so exclusively to those blot areas that most frequently stimulate sexual associations. These areas and the responses they elicit have been studied normatively by Shaw (1948) and Pascal, Ruesch, Devince, and Suttell (1950). Shaw asked 50 college men to study the Rorschach cards and indicate any areas that appeared to them to pertain to sex, sex organs, or sex acts. Pascal et al. repeated Shaw's method with 237 subjects, including normal, neurotic, and psychotic persons of both sexes. The following 10 *Sex* responses were reported by 20% or more of the subjects in both studies and may be considered *Sex* "populars":

CARD I: *breast* or *vagina* to top middle rounded bulges.

CARD II: *vagina* to lower red detail; *penis* to conelike detail at upper middle.

CARD III: *penis* to projection on usual leg detail; *breast* to projection on usual chest detail.

CARD IV: *vagina* to top center detail.

CARD VI: *penis* to upper portion of middle black column, with or without side details.

CARD VII: *vagina* to dark area at middle bottom.

CARD VIII: *vagina* to lighter orange-pinkish portions at middle bottom.

CARD X: *penis* to upper grey column, with or without side details.

Although these 10 responses are "populars" among possible *Sex* responses, it should be kept in mind that they were elicited in these studies under specific sex-arousal instructions and not under normal testing conditions. In the opinion of Rapaport et al. (1946, p. 304), under usual circumstances only five of these responses, those to Cards II, IV, VI, and VII, are likely to be given by other than disturbed subjects. These contributions imply that, although a nonschizophrenic subject may on occasion give one or more of these five *Sex* responses, any spontaneously given *Sex* response other than these five, and most particularly one not included among the 10 "populars" listed above, suggests repressive failure and possible schizophrenic disturbance.

The following case illustrates several clues to sexual preoccupation that identified repressive failure and helped to confirm a diagnosis of schizophrenia. The patient was a woman whose history suggested a chronic, borderline adjustment of many years' duration but who first required hospitalization at age 41, following an apparently acute onset of delusional and hallucinatory phenomena. Her Rorschach record on admission to the hospital contained 26 responses but in most respects was constricted ($F\%$ was 70). Yet her protocol included the following five *Sex* responses:

CARD II, black details with center white space: Looks like a picture I've seen in books, what do you call it, an *embryo*. [In later responses it became clear that she was using *embryo* where she meant *vagina*; hence this response indicates incorrect terminology as well as minus form level and an unusual location choice for a *Sex* response].

CARD IV, top center detail: This looks like the other picture [reference to Card II] . . . but I don't know the word for it (?) the *embryo* part again . . . or do you want me to say *vagina*? That's what it really looks like. [This response illustrates vague and halting verbalization].

CARD VI, top middle portion: Could look like a penis here. [This response is a *Sex* popular and if given as the patient's only *Sex* response would not necessarily indicate repressive failure].

CARD VII, bottom central details: This is some more of the *embryo* pictures. (*How does it compare with the others?*) Something is added to it, this other little part; I suppose it could be intercourse going on. [She again uses an incorrect word for *vagina*, but more significantly, she apparently sees an adjacent male genital organ in an unusual location and subsequently infers a sexual activity].

CARD X, top center detail: The same thing again as in the other picture, the suggestion of intercourse.

These five responses demonstrate most of the qualities that distinguish disturbed *Sex* responses from those that may occur in non-schizophrenic subjects. First, this woman's five *Sex* responses are far in excess of normal frequency, particularly in view of the fact that her record was only of average length and was not otherwise dilated or expressive. Second, she expresses her *Sex* responses haltingly and frequently uses incorrect terminology, even though in the course of the record it becomes clear that she was aware of the correct names of the organs she was describing. Third, she reports seeing not only sexual anatomy, but sexual activity as well. And, last, two of her *Sex* responses are inaccurately perceived and reported to locations that do not commonly elicit sexual associations. These features of her *Sex* responses clearly identify sexual preoccupation and a failure of repressive barriers.

It is finally of interest regarding *Sex* responses to note that their frequency and location do not appear influenced by the sex of either the subject or the examiner. Pascal et al. (1950) found no relationship between number of *Sex* responses obtained and sex either of subject or examiner. With standard clinical administration of the Rorschach Alden and Benton (1951) observed no relationship of sex of examiner to incidence of *Sex* responses, and Orme (1962) found in his sample that neither the type of *Sex* response given nor the card to which it was given was related to the subject's sex.

Nudity as an Additional Clue to Sexual Preoccupation. An additional clue to sexual preoccupation that validly differentiates schizophrenic from nonschizophrenic subjects is *nudity*. Although reference to nudity is included by Holt and Havel among Rorschach indices of primary process dominance, available validating data for nudity concern primarily the drawing of nude figures on the DAP. Holzberg and Wexler (1950a) found that nude drawings occur significantly more frequently among schizophrenic subjects (39%) than among normal controls (5%). Hozier (1959) quite similarly observed nude figure drawings in 40% of schizophrenic and only 4% of normal subject samples.

Unusual or excessive emphasis on sexual organs in nude figure drawings is especially suggestive of failure of repressive defenses and usually indicates schizophrenia (Machover, 1949, p. 74). Figures 11 and 12 illustrate such excessive sexual emphasis. These drawings were rendered by a 38-year-old married man whose general demeanor was conservative, polite, and soft-spoken. He was maintaining a tenuous ambulatory adjustment and had applied for outpatient help in connection with two distressing and pervasive preoccupations: (a) intense feelings of rage against his wife, who reportedly made him feel worthless by constantly comparing him to his sister's husband with such statements as, "You're not good enough to be tied to his tail"; and (b) a compulsion to seek extramarital sexual relations with as many women as possible. His drawings clearly demonstrate both broken contours and physical omission (see Chap. 8), and other features of his test data pointed clearly to schizophrenic disturbance. However, even in the absence of other data, the repressive failure indicated by the blatant sexual emphasis in these drawings would suggest the diagnosis.

AGGRESSIVE PREOCCUPATION

Aggressive preoccupation, defined as pressing conscious awareness of primitive aggressive fantasies and urges, indicates a failure of repressive defenses and suggests schizophrenic disturbance. Unfortunately, specific Rorschach scoring and interpretive considerations discriminating schizophrenic from nonschizophrenic subjects have not been so thoroughly explored for aggressive as for sexual responses. There is no specific *Agg* content score comparable to the *Sex* score, and most scoring systems employed to assess hostility from Rorschach content are based on such a variety of responses that they blur the differences between diagnostic groups.

A Rorschach Hostility score devised by DeVos (1952), for example, involves seven categories of content: depreciation of figures, oral aggression (*biting, yelling*), direct hostility (*fighting, arguing*), indirect

Figure 11

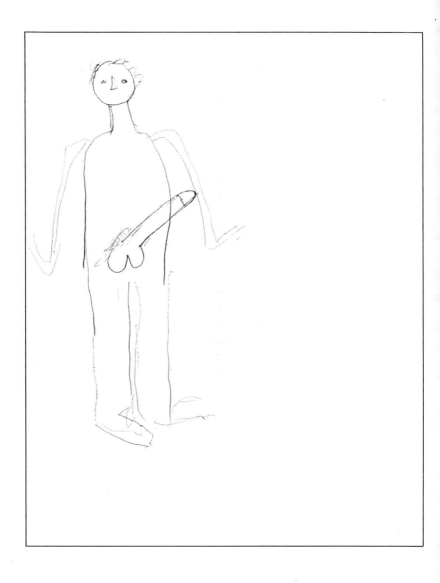

Figure 12

hostility (*knife, fort*), figures deformed or with parts missing, responses indicative of inner tension, and sadomasochistic responses. These content categories are sufficiently broad to include both primary process types of responses that result from a failure of repressive defenses and relatively bland responses that have no implications for psychopathology. As would therefore be expected, DeVos found no differences between normal, neurotic, and schizophrenic subjects in hostility as scored by his scale.

There are, however, two Rorschach manifestations of aggressive preoccupation that do appear to identify pathologic repressive failure. The first comprises those aggressively toned responses that are sufficiently blatant and deviant to leave little question that the subject is experiencing a loss of ideational control; that is, the more clearly an aggressive response falls into the *Level 1* category for primary process dominance outlined by Holt and Havel (see p. 170), the more an impairment of defensive operations is clearly indicated.

For example, such aggressively toned responses as "Two men fighting," "An animal biting into a piece of meat," "A person bleeding from an injury," and "A woman who has been tied to a post" do not suggest any major failure of repressive capacity. On the other hand, consider the following versions of these responses: "Two men fighting, killing each other; they're tearing each other to pieces;" "A predator, sinking his fangs into an innocent victim; he's crushing its bones and sucking its blood out"; "A person who has been hurt in some terrible accident, like he's just been run over by a train and it's cut off his arms and blood is dripping from the stumps"; "This woman has been tied to a post; it's part of some primitive ritual and she's going to be tortured and burned with hot coals."

Responses of the latter kind, which graphically portray gory and morbid fantasies, reflect gross inability to prevent primitive aggressive impulses from reaching conscious awareness. Frequently the distaste and discomfort induced in the examiner by such responses aid him in judging the degree to which they deviate from secondary process ideation and represent repressive failure. The more primitive the aggression expressed in such responses and the more frequently they occur, the greater the likelihood of a schizophrenic impairment of defensive operations.

It should be noted, however, that the significance of a subject's aggressive responses for repressive failure varies with the nature of his approach to the testing situation. As reviewed in Chapter 7 in relation to Rorschach form level, certain test behaviors take on increased pathologic implications the more they emerge in the setting of a constricted response to tests by a subject who structures the examination situation authoritatively and is striving to convince the examiner of his psychological adequacy (see pp. 112–113). Conversely, the schizophrenic implications of many deviant test indices, including blatantly aggressive Rorschach responses, are attenuated somewhat if they appear in the context of a highly expressive record given by a subject who interprets the testing situation as an occasion to exercise his associative capacity freely and/or evidences a need to impress others with the extent of his psychological distress.

Anatomy Responses as Indicators of Aggressive Preoccupation. The second and a less direct Rorschach manifestation of aggressive preoccupation is the *Anatomy (At)* response. According to Phillips and Smith (1953, pp. 123–129), *At* responses relate primarily to the handling of aggressive urges. *Bony At* responses, Phillips and Smith hypothesize, indicate the extent to which a person fears loss of control of hostile impulses and is engaged in preventing their expression; *visceral At* responses represent open expression and failure to repress aggressive urges. A relationship between internal *At* responses, whether bone or viscera, and difficulty in handling aggressive urges has been experimentally demonstrated by Sandler and Ackner (1951). In a factorial study of Rorschach content categories and psychiatric rating scales they found the positive pole of one of the four separate factors that emerged to be defined primarily by the perception of internal anatomical objects and to correlate with marked aggressive tendencies as psychiatrically rated. Ratings for overt aggressive behavior and for complaints of feelings of aggression loaded .53 and .41, respectively, on the anatomy factor.

This relationship between *At* responses and aggressive concerns suggests that an accumulation of *At* responses may reflect aggressive preoccupation. The hypothesized relationships between schizophrenia and aggressive preoccupation on the one hand and aggressive preoccupation and *At* responses on the other are substantiated by evidence that a high *At* score is associated with schizophrenia. Knopf (1956) found a significant difference in *At* between 100 schizophrenic subjects and 106 nonschizophrenic psychiatric patients, whose mean numbers of *At* responses were 2.6 and 1.7, respectively. Shereshevski-Shere, Lasser, and Gottesfield (1953), comparing *At* responses in the records of 36 schizophrenic and 36 normal subjects, found that although the presence of one or more *At* responses characterized more than half of the normals and did not distinguish them from the schizophrenics, the presence of two or more, of three or more, and of four or more *At* all significantly discriminated the schizophrenic from the normal subjects. Their most efficient criterion score was three or more *At*, which was demonstrated by 61% of the schizophrenic but only 14% of the normal subjects.

These data suggest that the occurrence in a record of three or more *At* responses is likely to be associated with schizophrenia. However, the diagnostic significance of frequent *At* responses is influenced by the length of the record in which they occur and the possible relationship of an elevated *At* score to certain nonschizophrenic conditions. With regard to record length, Fiske and Baughman (1953) report a significant correlation between *At* and total *R*, with the median *At* score in normal subjects running from 0.1 in records of 10–14 *R* to 2.8 in records of more than 50 *R*. Hence the criterion for a pathologic frequency of *At* varies somewhat with the length of the record, with several *At* being within normal limits in very long records and only one or two *At* suggesting deviance in very brief ones.

Concerning nonschizophrenic conditions, many *At* responses are observed to occur in subjects who for reasons other than repressive failure are preoccupied with bodily organs and their function. Although such preoccupation frequently characterizes schizophrenia, it is also notable in persons with specific physical defects or psychosomatic illnesses or who are facing or have recently undergone surgical procedures (e.g., see Orbach & Tallent, 1965). In addition, subjects whose work, schooling, or profession is related to anatomy may normally produce numerous *At* responses as a consequence of their special interests. The *At* responses produced by nonschizophrenic physicians, nurses, medical students, and biological scientists, however, are typically accurately perceived, correctly labeled, and carefully specified. Several inaccurate, uncertain, and confused *At* responses in a Rorschach record, on the other hand, are as likely to identify psychological disturbance in biologically sophisticated as in unsophisticated subjects.

In general, then, the implications of a large number of *At* responses for schizophrenia are greater the larger the percent of the total *R* they constitute and the less in evidence are actual physical or medical situations to which they might be attributed.

Combined Sex-At Scores in Schizophrenia. Finally of interest in specifying Rorschach content indices of repressive failure are combined *Sex-At* scoring scales devised by DeVos (1952) and Thiesen (1952). DeVos' scale is intended to assess body preoccupation and is based on the following kinds of responses: bone anatomy, flesh anatomy, internal sexual anatomy, sexual organs and intercourse, anal or fecal responses, disease, and childbirth or pregnancy. Some responses falling into these categories might relate more clearly to a person's perception of his body (see Chap. 8) than to his defensive operations, but, as demonstrated in previous examples, certain kinds of *Sex* and *At* responses are most notable for the degree to which they reveal inability to repress primitive, unacceptable impulses. At any rate, DeVos found mean scores on his Body Preoccupation Scale of 4.1 in 60 normal subjects, 9.3 in 30 neurotics, and 19.3 in 30 schizophrenics, with each group being significantly different from the other two.

Thiesen developed several Rorschach patterns for diagnosing schizophrenia, one of which is based on the number of *Sex* and *At* responses occurring in a record. This pattern is scored when *both* three or more *At* and one or more *Sex* responses are given. Working with the Beck et al. (1950) and Beck (1954) samples, Thiesen found that this *Sex-At* pattern occurred in the records of 12 of 60 schizophrenics but only one of 157 normal subjects. He interprets this significant difference between the groups to indicate a relationship between the *Sex-At* pattern and the somatic preoccupation and release from culturally determined inhibitions associated with schizophrenia.

Thiesen's data suggest that the *Sex-At* pattern occurs infrequently but, when present, almost always indicates schizophrenia. This conclusion is supported in a cross-validating study by Taulbee and Sisson (1954), who observed Thiesen's *Sex-At* pattern in the records of only five of 62 schizophrenics but not in any of a much larger sample of normal subjects. Rubin and Lonstein (1953) report only one instance of the *Sex-At* pattern in a sample of 42 schizophrenic subjects, which further points up the rarity of this pattern but does not negate its serious implications for schizophrenia when it appears.

INCONSISTENT AFFECTIVE INTEGRATION

Whereas ideational control relates to the specific mechanism of repression, the capacity for adaptive integration of affective experience is determined by the general adequacy of defensive operations. The individual who lacks a stable defensive style is unable to integrate his emotional life in a consistent fashion, and inconsistent affective integration is an identifying characteristic of schizophrenia. Hartmann (1953, p. 179), in fact, considers defensive instability the most obvious ego weakness in schizophrenia, and Bleuler (1911, pp. 363–373) states that affective disturbance resulting from inadequate resources for dealing with emotional experience is a fundamental characteristic of schizophrenia independent of thinking disturbance. Consistent with Bleuler's view, the S-2 type of schizophrenia delineated by Beck (1954, p. 131) is defined primarily by affect-dominated behavior and inability to control and direct emotional expression.

The adequacy of resources for integrating affective experience is indicated in the psychodiagnostic test battery primarily by the handling of color on the Rorschach. A number of interpretive frameworks have been proposed to account for this relationship between Rorschach color use and affective style, and a brief review of the major contributions in this area introduces the test assessment of inconsistent affective integration.

Relationships between Rorschach Color Use and Affective Style

A relationship between Rorschach color use and affective style was initially posited by Rorschach (1921, pp. 29–35). Rorschach observed that most of his subjects who gave few color responses were either depressed or were pedantic persons seldom inclined to express their feelings; those with many color responses, on the other hand, typically were elated in mood or clinically remarkable for their prominent affective discharge or scatter. From these clear empirical differences between subjects with few and many color responses, Rorschach inferred that a person's response to color must bear a strong relationship to the manner in which he handles his affective experience.

Rorschach (p. 98) also pointed out, however, that this sound empirical basis for inferring a color-affect relationship did not constitute a fully satisfactory explanation of the phenomenon. He made some tentative attempts to unravel the etiology of the color-affect relationship, primarily by referring to the connection in common parlance between various colors and affective experience, for example, the equation of cheerfulness with seeing the world "through rose-colored glasses." Similar in this regard are such expressions as "seeing red" and "being green with envy" and the identification of some colors as "cool" and others as "warm."

But it remained for later writers to pursue a more sophisticated explanation of the basic processes of Rorschach color use. The three major themes that have emerged from subsequent formulations of the interpretive significance of Rorschach color responses are (a) that color perception is a passive phenomenon resembling affective experience, (b) that color complicates the perceptual task and initiates emotional reactions in the perceiver, and (c) that color is a specific case of the general class of strong stimulations that require the perceiver to exercise his available resources and preferred style for integrating strong stimuli.

The importance of passivity in Rorschach color perception was first explored by Schachtel (1943), who focused on the degree to which color impinges on a subject's perception and captures his attention. Unlike form, which "the eye grasps," color "seizes the eye," says Schachtel, and color perception is analogous to emotional experience in that in both the subject is the passive recipient of direct and immediate sense data. In another early contribution Rickers-Ovsiankina (1943) similarly posited that the unique feature of color perception, as opposed to form and movement, is that it requires little active effort on the part of the subject to articulate or organize his impressions; that is, color is a direct sense datum of which a subject becomes immediately aware without having to organize, evaluate, or reflect on his associations.

Rickers-Ovsiankina extended her analysis one step further by suggesting that colors impress themselves on people not only in an immediate, but in a personal manner. The impact of colors is seldom neutral, she points out, but rather strikes people as pleasing or displeasing in some way. Hence, she concludes, Rorschach colors may be expected to initiate an emotional experience in the perceiver. She has recently (1960, p. 13) restated her formulation of the relationship between color and affect in the following way:

. . . chromatic colors affect us with quite individualized, directed, and provocative qualities, and we know from general psychology that the experience of being affected in such ways by an environmental event is considered by authorities on the subject to be equivalent to experiencing emotion.

With regard to the potential of color to initiate affective experience, Siipola (1950) has emphasized the degree to which the presence of color in the inkblots complicates the subject's perceptual task. According to Siipola it is the difficulty of the task posed by the colored cards, rather than any specific significance of color itself, that underlies the color-affect relationship:

. . . the mere presence of color in a blot does not endow it automatically with magic, affect-arousing properties. . . . arousal of affective attitudes can be explained in terms of the greater degree of affective involvement, pleasant or unpleasant, whenever a task becomes more difficult. . . .

Other writers have disdained efforts to formulate color perception as either a passive or affect-arousing experience and have stressed instead the extent to which a person's handling of color on the Rorschach reveals the nature and adequacy of his resources for integrating strong stimulation in general. Such a formulation was first spelled out by Rapaport et al. (1946, pp. 234–241), who state that the fact that colors have an impact on the associative processes similar to that of affects demonstrates the existence of but does not *explain* the color-affect relationship. Focusing on the *reaction to* rather than the *initiation of* emotional experience, Rapaport et al. maintain that the impact of color on the perceptual and associative processes demands significant activity by the subject, namely, the activity required to integrate the chromatic stimuli impinging on him. He may do so by ignoring the color or by responding to it freely, by subjugating color to other blot qualities or other blot qualities to color; whatever the subject does, however, reflects certain decisions he has made about how to handle the color.

The interpretive significance of color responses for Rapaport et al. lies in the fact that the subject brings to the testing situation his characterological style of organizing and controlling his affective experience. Accordingly, handling of color is related to affective style not because color produces an impact analogous to that of emotional stimulation but because color is a strong stimulus to which a subject responds with his available resources and preferred techniques for dealing with strong stimulation. The nature and adequacy of the subject's integration of the chromatic stimuli therefore directly indicate his resources for dealing with affective experience.

Rapaport et al.'s stress on the relationship of color use to the adequacy of resources for integrating affective experience has been widely endorsed. Klopfer, Ainsworth, Klopfer, and Holt (1954, pp. 275–278), for example, center their discussion of the color-affect relationship around the challenge faced by the subject to integrate color within the framework of the Rorschach task. They subscribe to the hypothesis that "the way in which the subject handles color gives an indication of his mode of reacting to an emotional challenge from his environment which taxes his skill in integrating an outside influence with his activity-in-progress." Shapiro (1960), seeking a perceptual understanding of the color response, also emphasizes the integrating activity required by chromatic stimuli. According to Shapiro, handling of color and affect are related because both are cases of the general class of perceptual organization, impairment of which leads to poorly controlled, inadequately integrated expressive functions.

Psychodiagnostic Indicators of Inconsistent Affective Integration

There are two Rorschach indicators of inadequate resources for integrating affective experience that validly discriminate schizophrenic from nonschizophrenic subjects. The first is *elevated C*, which identifies inability to maintain sufficient perceptual integration of color stimuli. The second pertains not to deficient integrating ability but to failure to utilize a consistent, stable style of integrating color and can be labeled *color stress*. The definition and interpretation of these two indicators is amplified below.

ELEVATED C

The scoring of Rorschach color responses, as outlined in detail by Klopfer et al. (1954, pp. 171–198), is comprised of three major categories that indicate the degree to which color is integrated with the form qualities of the inkblots: *FC* is scored for colored objects of definite form; *CF* is scored for colored objects of vague or indefinite form; and *C* is scored for responses in which color is used but form is nonexistent. As these definitions imply, the *FC-CF-C* scoring scheme represents a continuum from most to least perceptual integration of color. In view of the preceding discussion, it would be expected that the more a subject's responses tend toward pure *C*, the less adequate are his defensive operations for integrating affective experience and the more likely he is to be schizophrenic.

Available experimental and clinical data confirm this expectation. Sorting studies have demonstrated that schizophrenic subjects, in contrast to normals, tend to sort objects primarily or exclusively on the basis of their color rather than their form (Hanfmann & Kasanin, 1942), and clinical research has consistently noted the relative prominence of *C* and the relative absence of *FC* responses in schizophrenic as opposed to normal and neurotic subjects. In the following discussion of these clinical findings pure *C* is defined to include in addition to *C* those responses scored as color naming (*Cnam*), color description (*Cdes*), and color symbolism (*Csymb*). Because of the serious implications of clear instances of these kinds of responses, the examiner should adhere strictly to the stringent scoring criteria recommended for them by Klopfer et al. (1954, pp. 190–198). Particular care should be taken to differentiate *Csymb* from *FCsymb* and *CFsymb* responses. Large numbers of the latter two types of responses may suggest abstract preoccupation (see Chap. 6), but they do not share with *Csymb* the implication of inadequate perceptual integration.

Consistent with the *FC-CF-C* continuum of integrative adequacy,

Phillips and Smith (1953, p. 44) report from their data that *CF* responses occur with similar frequency in normal and schizophrenic groups, whereas *FC* responses are more characteristic of normals and pure *C* responses of schizophrenics. This conclusion accords with Beck's (1938) earlier findings for 81 schizophrenic subjects and a mixed control group of 64 persons, including both normals and nonpsychotic psychiatric patients. For the schizophrenic group the median numbers of *FC*, *CF*, and *C* responses were 0.71, 1.67, and 1.02, respectively; the comparable median scores for the control group were 1.36, 1.50, and 0.60. The median *CF* scores of the groups are similar, whereas their *FC* and *C* scores differ markedly in the same directions noted by Phillips and Smith.

Hertz and Paolino (1960) also found significantly more pure *C* among 35 schizophrenic than 35 neurotic subjects, and they suggest that the relatively large numbers of pure *C* responses in schizophrenics reflect a "tendency to infuse organizational acts with . . . diffuse, primitive, and inappropriate emotions" (p. 385). Fortier (1953, p. 53) similarly concludes in a review of the relationship of color response to ego functions that the relative frequency of poorly integrated color responses in schizophrenic subjects indicates "that the schizophrenic is considerably influenced by the environmental configuration in which he finds himself" and "that his perception of affective life in others and his affective reaction to the environment are undifferentiated and gross."

Defining Elevated C. Available normative data indicate that the presence of one or more pure *C* responses is a diagnostically useful definition for elevated *C*. Brockway et al. (1954) and Cass and McReynolds (1951) both report a median *C* of 0.0 in their normal samples. In the Brockway et al. study the eightieth percentile for *C* was 0.2 responses, and for the Cass and McReynolds group any incidence of *C* greater than 0.0 did not appear below the ninetieth percentile rank. In the Fiske and Baughman (1953) analysis of Beck et al.'s 157 normal subjects *C* was significantly correlated with total *R* (.34), but only for those subjects with more than 50 responses was the median frequency of *C* as great as 1.0. For subjects with 30–34 *R* the median *C* was 0.5, and for all remaining levels of *R* it was 0.3 or less. The appearance of even one and especially more than one pure *C* response is therefore highly unusual in normal persons and is likely to suggest a pathologic impairment of the capacity to integrate affective stimulation.

Elevated C in Schizophrenia. There is considerable evidence that elevated *C* as defined by the presence of one or more pure *C* responses validly discriminates schizophrenic from nonschizophrenic subjects.

Rickers-Ovsiankina (1938) found one or more pure C responses in 18 of 30 schizophrenic subjects but only one of 20 normal controls. Vinson (1960) similarly reports the presence of pure C in 18 of 30 schizophrenic but only one of 30 nonschizophrenic subjects. The group differences in both studies are statistically significant. Weiner (1964b), reviewing the records of 172 fairly intact, mostly ambulatory psychiatric patients, found only 21 patients to have given pure C responses; however, 16 of these patients were schizophrenic, and the presence of pure C significantly discriminated the schizophrenic from the nonschizophrenic patient group.

Rapaport et al. (1946, p. 258), who interpret C as evidence for abandonment of control over affects, also report valid discrimination of schizophrenic from nonschizophrenic groups on the basis of elevated C as defined here, and they additionally identify important subgroup differences among schizophrenic persons. They observed one or more pure C in 76% of their undifferentiated schizophrenics, 48% of their paranoid schizophrenics, 30% of their neurotic subjects, 24% of their depressed subjects, and 11% of their nonpatient controls. Although both schizophrenic subgroups gave pure C more frequently than the nonschizophrenics, the undifferentiated subgroup differed significantly from both the nonschizophrenics and the paranoid schizophrenics in frequency of pure C (see Chap. 14).

Factors Influencing the Interpretation of Elevated C. In view of these findings, elevated C appears validly to indicate a schizophrenic impairment of defensive operations, particularly in association with a nonparanoid schizophrenic illness. However, the implication of pure C responses for impaired defensive operations is influenced by several factors, including the length of the record in which they appear, the locations to which they are given, the contents to which they pertain, and the degree to which they are balanced by FC responses. With regard to record length, the low normative frequency of C for records of all lengths (see p. 187) indicates that total R generally has little bearing on the significance of elevated C. In some extremely long records, however, it is possible that one or two C may occur independently of defensive inadequacy.

Concerning the location of pure C responses, useful normative data by Gardner (1936) on 100 and by Phillips and Smith (1953, p. 43) on 250 normal adults reveal that Cards VIII and X normally elicit FC responses primarily, with normal persons who do give C doing so mainly on Card IX and to a lesser extent on Card II. Therefore in instances of a single pure C given to Card IX or even two C's limited to Cards II and IX the implication of elevated C for schizophrenia is somewhat attenuated. A C response to Cards VIII or X, on the other hand, or multiple C's, none of which is given to Cards II or IX, is highly unlikely to occur in normal persons and suggests schizophrenia.

Rapaport et al. (1946) discuss the diagnostic significance of both the sequence of color responses (pp. 261–263) and their content (pp. 258–261). They indicate that two types of color response have considerably less pathological significance than other pure C's, namely, *blood* to the red areas of Cards II or III and some variation of *palette* or *paint* on either of the last three cards. In the Rapaport et al. studies the pure C responses occasionally given by depressed and neurotic subjects were almost entirely of those two types, and the exclusion of such responses strikingly sharpened the differentiation of schizophrenic from nonschizophrenic subjects on the basis of pure C. Hence the diagnostic significance of elevated C is attenuated when the pure C's given are of these types, and it is correspondingly enhanced by the presence of other kinds of pure C response.

Finally, the implication of elevated C for schizophrenia is influenced by the degree to which pure C responses are balanced by FC responses. Schizophrenics have been noted to produce significantly fewer FC responses than normals (Beck, 1954, p. 212), and, although the presence of many FC's does not serve to rule out schizophrenia, the absence of this indicator of integrative skill heightens the significance of the presence of any pure C responses for impaired defensive operations. An analysis by Rapaport et al. (1946, p. 258) of the relative prominence of C in relation to CF and FC responses demonstrates the importance of this consideration. They found 53% of their undifferentiated and 33% of their paranoid schizophrenic subjects to have a frequency of C responses equal to or greater than their combined number of CF and FC responses, whereas only 18% of their depressed, 6% of their neurotic, and 4% of their normal subjects displayed this degree of C prominence. Both the undifferentiated and paranoid schizophrenic subgroups differed significantly from the nonschizophrenic subjects in this analysis.

Color Naming (Cnam) in Organic Brain Disease. The color naming (*Cnam*) variant of the pure C response is occasionally found in conjunction with organic brain disease rather than schizophrenia. The appearance of *Cnam* in persons whose perceptual functioning is impaired by brain damage is consistent with the hypothesized relationship between pure C and inadequate perceptual integration (see p. 186). The presence of *Cnam* was found by Piotrowski (1937) to differentiate brain-damaged from control subjects, and Aita, Armitage, Reitan, and Rabinowitz (1947), though observing *Cnam* to occur less frequently than Piotrowski's other organic indicators, also recommend its usefulness in identifying brain damage.

To some extent, then, elevated *C* most clearly reflects a schizophrenic impairment of integrative capacity when organic brain disease can be ruled out. However, the findings of some investigators suggest that this differential problem seldom arises. Baker (1956), for example, concludes from her work that *Cnam* is extremely rare in brain-injured subjects and much more likely to indicate schizophrenia than organicity when it occurs. Evans and Marmorston (1964) observed *Cnam* responses in only three of 139 brain-damaged subjects and were not able to differentiate them from their control subjects on the basis of this variable.

COLOR STRESS

Color stress is a pattern of Rorschach color use that differentiates schizophrenic from nonschizophrenic psychiatric patients and appears to represent failure to exercise a consistent, stable style of integrating affective experience. This pattern was initially described by Weiner (1961a), who in an investigation unrelated to schizophrenia incidentally found that three Rorschach color scores—one or two *CF*, *Sum C* 1.5–3.0, and *C* or *CF* without *C'*—were significantly associated with the severity of his subjects' psychopathology. Subsequently evaluating these three scores in two samples of hospitalized and ambulatory psychiatric patients, Weiner (1961b) found each score to occur significantly more frequently in the records of schizophrenic subjects than in those of persons with diagnosed neuroses or character disorders; a criterion score of two or more of these signs correctly identified 38 of the 49 schizophrenic and 71 of the 92 nonschizophrenic subjects in these samples, for an over-all diagnostic accuracy of 77%.

Weiner's (1961b, 1965b) tentative rationale for the color stress pattern derives from the probable defensive styles of two types of person who are *unlikely* to manifest these color scores. One such type is the subject who either avoids color entirely or employs it only in connection with highly structured (i.e., *FC*) percepts. As described by Schafer (1954, p. 341), subjects responding in this way tend to have prominent intellectual defenses and to exercise strict control of their affective experience. The other type of person unlikely to receive color stress signs is one who uses chromatic and achromatic colors freely. Subjects who respond in this manner, as Schafer (1954, p. 196) points out, are primarily persons with repressive defensive styles who deal with affect in a labile and spontaneous fashion. In both cases, avoidance of color and free use of it, the subject is demonstrating a more or less consistent defensive style according to which he integrates his affective experience.

The person who receives signs of color stress, on the other hand, is apparently unable to utilize either of these two defensive styles consistently. He can neither avoid nor strictly control his reactions to color, nor can he respond freely and fully to the colors. Rather, he vacillates between these alternatives and by so doing reveals an inconsistent style of integrating affective experience. This hypothesized relationship between the color stress signs and inconsistent affective integration accounts for their association with schizophrenia.

Several subsequent studies have affirmed the psychodiagnostic validity of color stress for schizophrenia. In an additional sample of 83 clinic patients Weiner (1964b) observed the presence of two or more of the three color signs mentioned above to differentiate significantly schizophrenic from nonschizophrenic patients. Because pure C shares with color stress implications for inadequate affective integration, Weiner (1965b) in a follow-up study included a pure C criterion for color stress. This follow-up study was based on independent diagnostic judgments that became available for 89 of his original subjects in a psychiatric case register two to five years after their initial testing. For these subjects color stress, defined as the presence of either one or more pure C *or* two or more of the previously used signs (1-2 CF, *Sum C* 1.5-3.0, C or CF without C'), significantly discriminated subsequently diagnosed schizophrenic from nonschizophrenic patients. This study demonstrated the color stress variable to have correctly predicted the schizophrenic-nonschizophrenic status of 64% of these subjects two to five years following their testing.

Some additional support for the diagnostic validity of color stress for schizophrenia appears in studies by Klinger and Roth (1964) and Orme (1964). Klinger and Roth, in a study of *Sum C*, found 71% of 126 nonschizophrenic psychiatric patients to have *Sum C*'s outside the color stress criterion range of 1.5-3.0, which is consistent with Weiner's findings. On the other hand, because only 31% of their 69 schizophrenic subjects had *Sum C*'s between 1.5 and 3.0, Klinger and Roth raise some question about the usefulness of the *Sum C* index. As Weiner (1965a) has pointed out, however, the Klinger and Roth data yield a significant difference between borderline schizophrenic and nonschizophrenic subjects, indicating that even partial scoring of color stress, utilizing only the *Sum C* sign, can discriminate an important category of schizophrenic disturbance.

Orme, examining the records of 50 schizophrenic and 50 neurotic subjects, found that all three of the original color stress signs occurred more frequently among the schizophrenics, and he reports a positive, but not statistically significant, trend for the schizophrenics more often than the neurotics to evince any *one* or more of these signs. Orme does not indicate why he chose to assess the validity of *one or more* of the signs rather than of the *two-or-more* criterion recommended by Weiner. Nevertheless, as further analyzed by Weiner (1965a), Orme's findings, even with the loose one-or-more criterion, clearly satisfy conventional significance requirements when the one-tail tests appropriate to such replication studies with unidirectional hypotheses are employed.

► 11

AUTONOMOUS FUNCTIONS

THE concept of autonomous ego functioning was formulated by Hartmann (1939, pp. 3–21; 1950) to describe those aspects of a person's adaptation to his environment that are constitutionally determined and develop independently of conflict. As Rapaport (1951a, pp. 364–367) points out in his commentary on Hartmann's work, the notion of an autonomously developing and conflict-free sphere of ego operations represented a new direction in psychoanalytic thinking about mental functioning. Whereas classical psychoanalytic theory postulates that the ego and its various activities originate as a secondary consequence of the frustration of primary instinctual drives, Hartmann maintains that certain ego operations, including perception, intention, object comprehension, thinking, language, recall phenomena, productivity, motor development, and the learning processes implicit in all of these arise independently of need deprivation.

A brief review of Freud's thinking about cognitive ontogenesis will help to clarify the nature of Hartmann's contribution. In 1911 Freud delineated as the two main parameters of mental functioning the *pleasure principle* and the *reality principle*. According to Freud, the newborn child is governed entirely by the dictates of the pleasure principle, which takes no cognizance of reality and strives exclusively for direct and immediate need gratification. However, Freud continues, the inevitable frustration of an infant's primary needs induces him to seek a conception of real-world circumstances in order that he may alter them in his favor. As a by-product of this process, Freud states, the pleasure principle gradually gives way to the reality principle and several new functions are instituted in the mental apparatus, including attention, notation, memory, judgment, action, and thought.

In the 1920's, with the advent of his structural model for intrapsychic processes, Freud delegated the influence of the pleasure principle to the *id* and the operation of the reality principle to the *ego*. However, the new model did not alter Freud's view that those functions associated with the reality principle and now designated as *ego functions* are secondary and fortuitous derivatives of primary id processes. In *The Ego and the Id*, for example, Freud (1923, pp. 15 & 29) makes the following statements:

. . . in every individual there is a coherent organization of mental processes, which we call his *ego*. . . . It is easy to see that the ego is that part of the id which has been modified by the direct influence of the external world acting through the Perceptual-Conscious.

Freud (1937, p. 240) later added that some aspects of ego function may be determined more by constitutional and maturational than by experiential factors:

We have no reason to dispute the existence and importance of original, innate distinguishing characteristics of the ego. . . . Each ego is endowed from the first with individual dispositions and trends. . . . But we shall not overlook the fact that id and ego are originally one; nor does it imply a mystical overvaluation of heredity if we think it credible that, even before the ego has come into existence, the lines of development, trends and reactions which it will later exhibit are already laid down for it.

However, in his final work, *An Outline of Psychoanalysis*, Freud (1938, p. 15) left little doubt concerning his belief that ego functions are a secondary rather than autonomous development:

Under the influence of the real external world which surrounds us, one portion of the id has undergone a special development. From what was originally a cortical layer, provided with organs for receiving stimuli and apparatus for protection against excessive stimulation, a special organization has arisen which henceforth acts as an intermediary between the id and the external world. This region of our mental life has been given the name of *ego*.

In contrast to these views, Hartmann's thesis is that, although some ego functions do derive from frustration-induced modifications of id impulses, others develop or originate independently of conflicts between a child's basic needs and his ability to gratify them. Rapaport (1951b) similarly argues that certain features of the mental apparatus must be viewed as congenitally rather than ontogenetically given. According to Rapaport, psychological observation of general principles underlying perceptual and motor phenomena in all persons demonstrates that such apparatuses are "inborn and characteristic of the species and the biological individual, before they become expressive of conflict and experience" (p. 117).

Rapaport also indicates in his paper that *autonomy* is a relative concept: autonomous ego functions are defined as such because drives do not determine their course and because they operate even in circumstances in which they do not facilitate primary need gratification; on the other hand, autonomous ego functions are involved in executing the actions that gratify drives, and they may secondarily become involved in and influenced by conflict situations.

As discussed by Rapaport (1960, pp. 54–55) in a later paper, Hartmann's contributions to the metapsychology of ego functioning have two implications for psychoanalytic structural theory. First, to recognize that certain ego operations are constitutionally determined implies that the ego does not derive exclusively from the id, as Freud had maintained, but rather that both id and ego "emerge from the common undifferentiated matrix of the first extrauterine phase of ontogenesis." Second, to conceptualize such constitutionally given apparatuses as the memory, motor, and perceptual systems within a psychoanalytic framework establishes them as relevant and necessary areas of investigation for the ego psychologist.

The efforts of Hartmann and Rapaport thus legitimized the autonomous ego functions as appropriate concerns of psychoanalytic ego psychology, but these functions have figured prominently in conceptions of schizophrenia at least since Bleuler's 1911 monograph. In Bleuler's view only certain functions of the mental apparatus, notably association and affective integration, are "altered" in schizophrenia; others, including sensation and perception, orientation, memory, consciousness, and motility, remain "intact." Bleuler's "intact" functions closely resemble those operations later identified by Hartmann as "autonomous," and he maintains that, although a schizophrenic person's dissociation, preoccupation, and autism may secondarily handicap his ability to exercise these "intact" functions, schizophrenia does not entail any basic impairment of the capacities they represent (1911, p. 55).

Bleuler's views concerning the intactness of the autonomous ego functions in schizophrenia are implicitly endorsed by the many later writers who attribute the subnormal performance of schizophrenic subjects on intellectual and perceptual-motor tasks to such psychological phenomena as distractibility, inability to maintain set, poor cooperation, and low motivation (see Chaps. 4, 6, & 9). On the other hand, theorists more thoroughly committed than Bleuler to an organic interpretation of schizophrenic behavior aver that performance decrements observed in schizophrenic subjects derive from basic impairments of the mental faculties similar to those associated with organic brain disease (see Chaps. 1 & 13). This issue is further discussed in this chapter, but available data do not resolve whether impairments of autonomous ego functioning in schizophrenia are *basic* or *secondary*.

It is generally agreed, however, that, whether for primary or secondary reasons, schizophrenic persons perform relatively poorly on measures of autonomous ego functions, and many such measures have been found to discriminate schizophrenic from control subjects in the laboratory (e.g., Shakow, 1963). These measures have not yet been widely studied clinically, nor have they yet been validated for individual as well as group discriminations. Hence this chapter on autonomous functions is not focused specifically on the psychodiagnostic assessment of identifying features of schizophrenic disturbance but rather is devoted to an overview of the literature concerning schizophrenic performance in the five most frequently studied areas of autonomous ego functioning: general intellectual level, vocabulary skill, psychomotor speed, perceptual constancy, and learning ability. The inclusion of this material despite its lack of specific relevance to the clinical test battery reflects the author's conviction that these experimental findings are required knowledge for the clinician who attempts to comprehend and psychodiagnose schizophrenic disturbance.

GENERAL INTELLECTUAL LEVEL

Studies of general intellectual level in schizophrenia have been addressed primarily to three questions: (a) whether general intellectual ability declines in the *course* of schizophrenic disturbance, (b) whether general intellectual performance is impaired by the *onset* of schizophrenic disturbance, and (c) whether premorbid level of intellectual functioning is related to *susceptibility* to schizophrenia. Research findings in this area can be summarized in reference to these three issues.

Intellectual Deterioration during the Course of Schizophrenic Disturbance

Although many earlier investigators had attempted to demonstrate intellectual deterioration in schizophrenia by comparing the intelligence test performance of normal and psychopathologic subjects (see Hunt & Cofer, 1944, pp. 974–975), Trapp and James (1937) were the first to report a *longitudinal* study of intellectual functioning in schizophrenic patients. Trapp and James administered the Stanford-Binet to 41 hospitalized schizophrenics who had been similarly tested at the time of their hospital admission four months to 13 years earlier. They found a mean drop of 7.6 *IQ* points in these patients between the first and second testings, with a correlation of .39 between *IQ* drop and length of hospitalization, and they concluded from their data that schizophrenia is accompanied by a progressive deterioration of general intellectual ability.

However, subsequent experimental results have challenged the generality of the Trapp and James conclusion. Rabin (1944), reexamining 30 schizophrenic subjects with the Wechsler-Bellevue from one to 35 months after their initial testing on hospital admission, found only six subjects to have lost five or more *IQ* points, whereas more than half the group had gained five or more *IQ* points. Rabin therefore rejects the notion of intellectual deterioration in schizophrenia. It should be noted, however, that Rabin's subjects were not particularly comparable to those from whom Trapp and James drew their conclusions. Rabin describes most of his subjects as having been rated clinically "improved" by the time of retesting, whereas many of the Trapp and James subjects had been hospitalized without remission for a number of years.

In this regard, Haywood and Moelis (1963) have recently confirmed a difference between improved and unimproved schizophrenics in test-retest *IQ*'s. They found 20 clinically improved schizophrenics to have gained an average of 7.30 *IQ* points during their hospitalization, whereas 20 unimproved schizophrenics had lost an average of 2.65 *IQ* points. Both the gain in the improved group and the loss in the unimproved group were significantly different from chance. Haywood and Moelis conclude from these data that intellectual deficits appearing in schizophrenia are reversible but increase in magnitude in direct relation to the intensity and persistence of the psychotic symptoms. This hypothesis would account for the differences between the Trapp and James and the Rabin results.

Nevertheless, more recent findings reported by Smith (1964) indicate that even with extended disorder and hospitalization intellectual decline as measured by standard intelligence tests is not inevitable. Smith retested 24 schizophrenic patients eight years after they had been given the Wechsler-Bellevue and other scaled measures on admission to the hospital. Although these patients had been continuously hospitalized during the eight-year interval, they evinced negligible retest changes on all measures.

Thus there is no single answer to the question whether general intellectual ability declines in the course of schizophrenic disturbance.

Available data suggest that declining performance on measures of general intelligence is unlikely to occur in recently hospitalized or remitting schizophrenic patients; that with increasing length of disturbance and hospital stay progressive deterioration in test performance is increasingly likely to appear; and that such deterioration is nevertheless not inevitable and does not characterize all schizophrenic patients.

Intellectual Impairment Secondary to the Onset of Schizophrenic Disturbance

As summarized by Payne (1961, p. 197), some 30 studies comparing the observed *IQ* scores of schizophrenic and nonschizophrenic persons clearly identify relative intellectual limitations in schizophrenics: the mean *IQ*'s reported for 1284 schizophrenics and 987 neurotics are 96.08 and 105.01, respectively. Payne (p. 200) also reports differential *IQ*'s for the traditional subgroups of schizophrenia, as demonstrated by the following mean scores over the various studies: paranoid schizophrenics, 94.84; simple schizophrenics, 88.23; catatonic schizophrenics, 82.80; and hebephrenic schizophrenics, 80.60. However, without attempting to draw inferences from these data, Payne correctly points out that they are highly ambiguous, in that they do not indicate whether schizophrenic disturbance *produces* intellectual impairment in a previously normal person or whether schizophrenia *happens to occur* primarily among persons of relatively limited intellect.

Several investigators have attempted to assess the first of these alternatives, that general intellectual performance is adversely affected by the onset of schizophrenia, by comparing intelligence test scores of schizophrenic persons with some measure of their premorbid functioning. Rappaport and Webb (1950), administering to 10 hospitalized schizophrenic patients an *IQ* test identical to one the patients had taken in high school before their onset of disturbance, found a significant mean drop of more than 30 *IQ* points for the group after they had become schizophrenic. However, because most of these subjects had been hospitalized for a period of years, it is not possible to determine from the Rappaport and Webb data whether the intellectual decline they observed resulted from the *onset* or the *persistence* of schizophrenia.

An interesting but similarly equivocal study is reported by Schwartzman and Douglas (1962), who readministered an army induction test battery to 80 veterans, 30 of whom were schizophrenic and had been in a veterans hospital for six months or longer, 20 of whom were schizophrenic but had been discharged from the hospital 12 months or more before the retesting, and 30 of whom had no history of psychiatric disorder. On retesting the hospitalized schizophrenic group displayed a significant mean drop of 15.2 *IQ* points, the remitted schizophrenics had a smaller but still significant loss of 5.1 *IQ* points, and the control group had a significant mean gain of 11.8 *IQ* points.

Although these results suggest both that schizophrenic disturbance produces intellectual deficits not observed in normal persons and that such deficits are greater in continuously hospitalized than in remitted schizophrenic patients, they fail, as do the Rappaport and Webb data, to clarify the extent to which the *onset* rather than the course of schizophrenia impairs intellectual performance. It is unclear (a) whether the patient and former-patient groups in the Schwartzman and Douglas study suffered deficits at the time of their admission to the hospital or developed them in the course of their illness and (b) whether the differential decline in the patient and former-patient groups was present at admission or developed during hospitalization as one group improved and the other did not.

Other researchers have tried to separate onset from persistence factors by testing subjects as early as possible in their hospital course. Lubin, Gieseking, and Williams (1962) administered the Army Classification Battery (ACB) to 159 schizophrenic soldiers within the first three months after their admission to the hospital and compared these patients' scores with their performance on the same test at the time of their induction into the service. These men were found to have suffered a significant decline in intellectual ability subsequent to the onset of schizophrenia, as evidenced by score drops from one-sixth to one-third of a standard deviation on the second testing.

Although the Lubin et al. findings seem fairly straightforward, an equally well-designed study by Griffith, Estes, and Zerof (1962) yielded completely opposite results. Griffith et al. compared scores on one of the Wechsler forms (Wechsler-Bellevue I, Wechsler-Bellevue II, or WAIS) of 65 schizophrenic veterans, most of whom were tested within one month of their admission to the hospital, with their induction performance on the Army General Classification Test (AGCT). Equating the WAIS and AGCT scales by conversion to standard scores, they found a *significant net gain in intellectual performance* subsequent to the onset of schizophrenia, equivalent to about three Wechsler *IQ* points per subject. Although it might be tempting to attribute this result to structural and administrative differences between the WAIS and the AGCT, Griffith et al. present convincing evidence that the two measures are highly correlated (around .85) and that, if anything, the AGCT is the easier of the two, a fact that enhances the significance of the Griffith et al. results.

The difference between the Lubin et al. and Griffith et al. findings leaves unresolved the question of whether general intellectual performance is impaired by the onset of schizophrenic disturbance. Griffith et al. even advance the hypothesis that for some people a schizophrenic breakdown represents a resolution of tensions and inhibitions that had previously impeded intellectual functioning, with the result that an individual, now free from such inhibitions, is able to earn higher scores on intelligence tests.

Albee, Lane, Corcoran, and Werneke (1963), however, question the value of studying differences between the intellectual ability of schizophrenic subjects and test scores they have earned during a premorbid stage of their adult lives. They present data relating to *early* premorbid history that cast doubt on whether any significant changes in general intellectual level occur secondarily to the onset of an overt schizophrenic disturbance in adulthood. Albee et al. compared the Wechsler *IQ* scores of 112 hospitalized schizophrenic patients with public-school records of their performances on both group and individual intelligence tests taken when they were in the sixth grade. They found no significant differences between these subjects' early premorbid *IQ's* and their scores following the onset of schizophrenia. Albee et al. accordingly conclude that general intellectual decline does not accompany the onset of schizophrenia in adulthood, and they suggest that observed differences in general intellectual level between schizophrenic and normal subjects are not results of the short-term effects of schizophrenia but rather of long-term personality characteristics that from childhood on both depress a person's intellectual functioning and dispose him to become schizophrenic.

Intellectual Impairment Prior to the Onset of Schizophrenic Disturbance

The Albee et al. data and the inconsistency of efforts to demonstrate intellectual decline subsequent to the onset of schizophrenia point to the second of the alternatives mentioned on page 198: that lower levels of intellectual functioning are observed in schizophrenic than in normal populations because schizophrenia occurs primarily among persons of relatively limited intellect. Put in a slightly different way, this alternative involves the questions of (a) whether low intellectual performance is predictive of susceptibility to schizophrenia and (b) whether, as Albee et al. hypothesize, such intellectual limitations far antedate the onset of disorder and are one facet of a schizophrenic predisposition.

Regarding question (a) above, studies by Mason (1956) and Miner and Anderson (1958) on military personnel have clearly demonstrated below-normal intellectual functioning in army inductees who later became schizophrenic. Mason compared the AGCT scores of 510 veterans hospital patients, 368 of whom were schizophrenic, with a normal control group of more than 290,000 inductees. Although Mason does not report specific *IQ* scores, his table reveals that those men who later proved susceptible to schizophrenic breakdown earned significantly lower AGCT scores than the control group. It is further of interest that those men later diagnosed as paranoid schizophrenic differed less from the normal group than did those assigned to other schizophrenic subcategories.

Miner and Anderson compared the induction AGCT scores of 61 men who became psychotic in the service with the scores for all men inducted during a nine-month period. The psychotic group was found to have earned significantly lower AGCT scores than the control group. These three studies suggest that, other things being equal, the less intelligent of two people is the more likely to become schizophrenic and furthermore that the more intelligent of two potentially schizophrenic persons is the more likely to develop a paranoid than a nonparanoid form of schizophrenia.

Concerning question (b) above, there is little relevant work before that of Albee et al. (1963). Two exceptions are contradictory reports by Gardner (1931) and Birren (1944). Gardner reviewed the school records of 100 adult schizophrenic patients and concluded that they had generally performed less well than their classmates. Birren compared records obtained from a child-guidance clinic of 38 children who later became psychotic with 53 who did not and reported that the prepsychotic children did not differ in intelligence from the controls.

More recently, Lane and Albee (1963, 1964) have carefully investigated the association between childhood intellectual impairment and adult schizophrenia. In the first of these studies they were able to locate 153 adult schizophrenics on whom two sets of public school test data were available, one from early (ages 5–8) and one from late (ages 11–14) childhood. On both individual (Stanford-Binet) and group tests these adult schizophrenics had as children displayed a significant drop in *IQ* between the early-childhood and late-childhood testings. In contrast, a control group of 872 children in the same schools gained in scores over this period, and, as Lane and Albee indicate, test-retest studies of the Stanford-Binet normally show relatively little loss between these ages.

In the second study Lane and Albee considered the problem of whether children who later become schizophrenic not only demonstrate an abnormal decline in *IQ* between early and late childhood, but also are from the beginning below their peers in intellectual ability. They compared second-grade *IQ* tests of 36 children who became adult schizophrenics with the *IQ*'s of their siblings tested with the same tests in the same grade. The potentially schizophrenic children were found to have been significantly below their siblings in *IQ*, whereas control children matched for *IQ* and neighborhood did not differ significantly from the average *IQ*'s of their siblings. Heath, Albee, and Lane (1965) have subsequently demonstrated that such relative intellectual limitations in early childhood are particularly likely to characterize persons who as adults become *process* schizophrenics, whereas *reactive* schizophrenics appear not to have been significantly less intelligent than their siblings as children (see Chap. 13).

These results suggest that intellectual deficits exist, long before the overt onset of their disorder, in many persons who become schizophrenic. Although such a phenomenon is not inconsistent with the possibility of intellectual deterioration during the course of schizophrenic disturbance, it mitigates the likelihood that intellectual decline occurs in schizophrenia only subsequent to and as a direct consequence of its onset. On the other hand, the Lane and Albee work does not imply a necessary *causal* relationship between low *IQ* and schizophrenia; rather, their data suggest that a relative impairment of a child's intellectual capacity, as manifest in his performing less well than his siblings on intellectual measures and declining in performance between early and late childhood, is one of the *associated* consequences of whatever organic, psychological, interpersonal, or interactional influences determine schizophrenia.

VOCABULARY SKILL

There is considerable evidence that vocabulary skill, as measured by standard tests of word definitions, is relatively unaffected by the onset of schizophrenia and less likely than other aspects of intellectual functioning to deteriorate during the course of schizophrenic disturbance. Beginning with a 1920 study by Wells and Kelley, groups of mentally disturbed persons have consistently been found to earn their highest scores on the vocabulary subtests of intelligence test batteries and to differ less from normal subjects in vocabulary skill than in any other intellectual ability. [1] Most of the recent investigations of vocabu-

[1] For an enumeration of studies in this area beyond those reviewed in the following pages, the reader is referred to Brody (1942), Payne (1961, pp. 204–209), and Roe and Shakow (1942).

lary skill in schizophrenia, as reviewed below, have been addressed to the relative merits of hypotheses advanced by Babcock, Yacorzynski, and Yates concerning the role of vocabulary measures in psychodiagnosis.

Babcock's Hypothesis

The suggestion by Wells and Kelley that degree of impairment in psychotic persons could be measured by the drop of other test scores below vocabulary was first operationalized by Babcock (1930), who proposed that, in view of the resistance of vocabulary skills to the inroads of mental disorder, performance on vocabulary tests can provide both a good index of intellectual functioning before the onset of disturbance and a baseline against which other intellectual abilities can be compared to determine the extent of deterioration that has taken place during the course of disturbance.

Babcock (1933) accordingly devised a test of mental efficiency in which deterioration is estimated from the discrepancy between vocabulary skill and performance on subtests of learning, memory, and motor skills. Early studies with the Babcock Test, as reviewed by Mayman (1945b), confirmed that the total efficiency scored derived from the test is lower in schizophrenic than in normal subjects and is inversely related to clinical impressions of extent of deterioration.

Yacorzynski's Hypothesis

Although many tests of mental efficiency have been based on Babcock's hypothesis, Yacorzynski (1941) has questioned whether vocabulary skill is an accurate index of premorbid intelligence and an adequate baseline for estimating mental deterioration. Yacorzynski contends that vocabulary skill does *not* resist deterioration in mental disturbance and that any observed stability of vocabulary scores in psychotic persons is more *apparent* than *real*. The mentally disturbed subject may remain able to satisfy the gross correct-incorrect scoring criteria employed in conventional vocabulary tests, Yacorzynski continues, but he suffers conceptual impairments in vocabulary skill that are revealed when word definitions are scored according to important qualitative criteria. Hence, Yacorzynski concludes, since vocabulary skills *do* decline with psychosis, they cannot be considered to reflect premorbid intelligence accurately.

A number of studies (see Chap. 6) support Yacorzynski's hypothesis. Feifel (1949) scored the vocabulary definitions of 185 mental patients and 185 normal controls according to five qualitative categories suggested by Yacorzynski: *synonym, use and description, explanation, inferior,* and *error.* He found the patients, who were equated with the controls in age, education, and raw vocabulary score (i.e., the number of correct definitions), to give significantly fewer *synonym* definitions than the normals and significantly more *use and description, explanation,* and *inferior* definitions. Harrington and Ehrmann (1954), employing a similar experimental design, also observed schizophrenic subjects, equated with normal controls in gross vocabulary score, to give conceptually inferior vocabulary definitions.

Chodorkoff and Mussen (1952) found comparable qualitative differences between the performance of schizophrenic and normal subjects on a multiple-choice test of word definition. Subjects were provided four alternate choices for each word, representing *class, description, example,* and *function* definitions. The schizophrenic subjects chose a significantly greater number of *function* and *example* definitions than normal subjects of equal gross vocabulary skill, whereas the normals significantly more frequently selected *class* definitions.

Studies by Moran (1953) and Chapman (1960), utilizing measures of word usage rather than conceptual level of definitions, have adduced further support for the Yacorzynski hypothesis. Moran, working with 40 pairs of schizophrenic and normal subjects matched in raw vocabulary scores, found that, although the schizophrenics had apparently been able to define a list of words as well as the controls, they were less well able to differentiate further the meanings of these words and to use them in communicating and reasoning.

Chapman devised a multiple-choice test of word usage in which subjects are asked to explain the meaning of such expressions as "David turned yellow when he faced the enemy" and "Miss Bailey's illness turned her yellow." Each statement is accompanied by three alternative explanations, one correct, one irrelevant, and one erring in employing either a too literal ("David's skin became discolored") or a too figurative ("Miss Bailey became cowardly") interpretation of the words used. Chapman found schizophrenic subjects to make more errors of both figurative and literal types on this test than normal subjects.

However, not all of the work in this area has affirmed Yacorzynski's hypothesis. Moran, Moran, and Blake (1952b), in a study of 63 schizophrenic and normal pairs matched for age, education, and raw vocabulary scores, failed to find any differences in the conceptual level of their definitions as scored for Yacorzynski's categories. Eliseo (1963), commenting on Chapman's study, observes that Chapman's schizophrenic subjects had spent most of the preceding 10 years in the hospital and were significantly lower than his normal controls in functioning vocabulary level. When Eliseo repeated Chapman's experiment with schizophrenic subjects newly admitted to the hospital and a control group equivalent in word knowledge, he found no differences between the groups in word usage.

In view of the Moran et al. and Eliseo findings, Yacorzynski's hypothesis cannot be regarded as definitely substantiated even though many studies appear to bear out his point of view. On the other hand, it should be recognized that even eventual confirmation of the Yacorzynski hypothesis would not vitiate Babcock's recommendations for the clinical utilization of vocabulary tests. Yacorzynski is stating in effect that vocabulary definitions as conventionally scored are *too easy* a task; that is, by failing to take into account qualitative features of word usage, such measures fail to reveal the language impairment accompanying schizophrenia and consequently yield *overestimates* of the schizophrenic's capacity. Whether or not this is the case has little bearing on whether vocabulary performance *as conventionally scored* on measures of word definition resists decline in schizophrenia and is therefore a useful index for assessing intellectual potential and deterioration. In other words, even if schizophrenic persons suffer a decline in the conceptual level of their vocabulary skill as Yacorzynski avers, their ability to define words correctly may, as Babcock suggests, remain sufficiently intact to reflect their intellectual capacity.

Yates' Hypothesis

A criticism of the Babcock principle more relevant than Yacorzynski's hypothesis to such clinically used measures of vocabulary skill as the WAIS Vocabulary is raised by Yates (1956). Noting that a large number of factors unrelated to psychopathology have been observed to depress vocabulary performance, Yates concludes in effect that standard vocabulary measures are *too difficult* to assess intellectual capacity reliably; that is, contrary to Yacorzynski's concern with *overestimation,* Yates asserts that standard vocabulary measures *underestimate* functioning potential. Specifically, Yates criticizes the use of vocabulary tests to measure premorbid ability in mental patients on the grounds that vocabulary skill is adversely affected by institutional variables. Because vocabulary skill declines in schizophrenic persons in relation to their length of hospitalization, Yates argues, such skill is useful neither as an estimate of previous functioning levels nor as a baseline against which to judge deterioration.

Rabin, King, and Ehrmann (1955) report data that confirm both the relative difficulty of standard vocabulary definitions and the adverse influence of institutionalization on vocabulary performance. Rabin et al. administered three tests to 25 long-term hospitalized schizophrenics, 25 short-term hospitalized schizophrenics, and 25 nonpsychiatric medical patients equated for age and education: a conventional measure of word definitions (Wechsler-Bellevue Vocabulary), a vocabulary recognition task not requiring verbal responses (the Ammons Full Range Picture Vocabulary), and a measure of communication skill (inquiry on the Ammons). Their nonschizophrenic and short-term schizophrenic subjects performed similarly on all three measures; on all three measures the long-term schizophrenics were significantly inferior to the other two groups. However, the long-term schizophrenics were less impaired in relation to the other groups on the nonverbal than on the verbal vocabulary measures.

These findings support the view that vocabulary performance is impaired by hospitalization and is consequently of limited value for estimating previous functioning level except for schizophrenics in early stages of their disturbance. Hamlin and Jones (1963) obtained similar results in comparing remitted with unimproved schizophrenic patients of equal age and education. Those patients who remained in the hospital performed significantly less well on WAIS Vocabulary than those who had improved sufficiently to be discharged. Additionally, the Rabin et al. data suggest that performance on some measures that are less difficult and complex than vocabulary definitions, such as recognition or picture-vocabulary tests, may be more likely to reflect intellectual capacity.

Longitudinal Studies and Implications for the Individual Case

Before these various studies are invoked to denigrate such measures as WAIS Vocabulary as an index of premorbid intellectual functioning and a baseline for estimating deterioration, however, it should be recognized that none of them is *longitudinal;* they are *comparative* studies and as such only indirectly confirm the Yates hypothesis. Contrary to Yates' views, recent reports of longitudinal studies of schizophrenic patients have in fact directly demonstrated relative resistance to decline of vocabulary performance in chronic, hospitalized schizophrenics.

In one such study, Moran, Gorham, and Holtzmann (1960) reexamined after a six-year interval the chronic schizophrenics who had been tested in Moran's (1953) earlier studies of vocabulary knowledge and usage. They gave the Wechsler-Bellevue Vocabulary and seven special tests of word usage, including synonyms, sentence construction, similarities, analogies, and word association, to 35 of the original 40 subjects who were still in the hospital at the time of the follow-up study. These subjects displayed a remarkably stable performance over the six years; there was among them no significant change in scores on any of the measures, and those minimal declines that were in evidence were clearly attributable to the normal aging process.

Ginett and Moran (1964) later conducted a similar study, this time readministering the Wechsler-Bellevue Vocabulary to 67 chronically hospitalized schizophrenic patients who had taken the same test 13 years earlier. They found no significant decline in vocabulary performance for these patients. On the strength of these longitudinal data it seems justified to conclude, in disagreement with inferences based on the earlier comparative studies, that performance on standard measures of vocabulary skill is stable over time and during schizophrenic disturbance.

Although there is therefore reason to believe that standard vocabulary measures like the WAIS Vocabulary are in general relatively resistant to deterioration during the course of schizophrenic disturbance, two other considerations influence the utility of such measures for estimating intellectual potential in the individual case. First, though vocabulary skill is a *good* baseline against which to estimate impairment of other functions, it is not necessarily the *best* such baseline.

As discussed in regard to intertest scatter (see Chap. 4), cultural educational, and personal factors unrelated to psychopathology often affect the pattern of WAIS subtest scores. Although Vocabulary is *in general* more highly correlated with Full Scale IQ than any other WAIS subtest except Information (Wechsler, 1958, p. 99), many nonverbal, nonintellectually oriented persons may normally earn lower scores on Vocabulary than on the perceptual and manipulative subtests of the WAIS. For such persons deterioration during mental disturbance may involve a drop of their previously well-developed perceptual-motor skills to the level of their normally low vocabulary skills, in which case using WAIS Vocabulary as a baseline for estimating deterioration would fail to reveal the extent of their functioning loss.

Hence in the individual case a number of methods of estimating intellectual potential from the WAIS other than from Vocabulary score should be considered. Among other such methods proposed are the following: prorating from the highest or two highest subtest scores (Brown & Bryan, 1957; Thorp & Mahrer, 1959); prorating from the three highest subtest scores weighted 2.5, 1.5, and 1.0, respectively, from highest to lowest (Thorp & Mahrer, 1959); and repeatedly administering the verbal subtests, urging the subject to give multiple answers and scoring only the best one (Mahrer & Bernstein, 1958).

Second, in estimating intellectual potential the examiner needs to keep in mind the implications of theoretical and practical differences between intellectual *potential* or *capacity* and intellectual *ability*. Following Shakow (1946), a subject's ability is his current functioning level as defined by his actual performance on a given measure; his potential or capacity is his physiological limit, defined as the level at which he would be able to perform on the given measure in the absence of all the characterological and situational factors that are operating to depress his functioning level.

These definitions suggest that, although attempts to evaluate severity of disturbance from differences between capacity and ability are of definite practical value, efforts to identify "premorbid intelligence" may be rather meaningless. To estimate a schizophrenic patient's intellectual potential gives no indication of the extent to which his actual functioning level ever approached his capacity before the onset of his disorder. Indeed, the Albee and Lane data discussed previously suggest that differences between ability and capacity observed at the time of onset of schizophrenia have often been present from early childhood on. Consequently, an estimate of intellectual capacity does not necessarily represent a previously attained level of functioning and cannot routinely be interpreted as such.

PSYCHOMOTOR SPEED

Research to date has consistently demonstrated schizophrenic subjects to perform more slowly than control subjects on psychomotor tasks. Babcock (1930), who in her early studies found psychotic subjects to receive their lowest scores on simple tests of motor and mental speed, concluded that psychomotor retardation is the *primary* basis of intellectual deterioration in psychotic persons, and more recent data reported by Shapiro and Nelson (1955) lend support to such a view.

Shapiro and Nelson administered measures of vocabulary, problem-solving ability, problem-solving speed, psychomotor speed, and learning and retention to 20 each of normal, neurotic, schizophrenic, manic-depressive, and brain-damaged subjects. On all measures the schizophrenic, manic-depressive, and brain-damaged groups earned significantly lower scores than the normal and neurotic groups. However, when the groups were matched for psychomotor and problem-solving speed, they no longer differed significantly in vocabulary, problem-solving ability, or learning and retention. Additionally, Shapiro and Nelson found psychomotor speed to correlate more highly than any other of the test scores with independent estimates of the subjects' prognosis and degree of disturbance.

Shapiro and Nelson interpret their data as supporting Babcock's view that slowness in psychological functioning may underlie much of the intellectual impairment observed in psychotic persons. Further bolstering this position, Shapiro, Kessel, and Maxwell (1960) found in a later study of normal, schizophrenic, and brain-damaged subjects that speed of performance differentiated their psychotic from normal groups more clearly than other parameters of intellectual functioning.

As reviewed by Payne (1961, pp. 226–228), a number of other studies indicate that performance speed as measured on psychomotor tasks alone discriminates between psychotic and normal groups even more efficiently than the combined indices of psychomotor and problem-solving speed employed by Babcock and Shapiro et al. Extensive studies of psychomotor functioning in schizophrenia by Shakow and his co-workers and by King have clearly demonstrated that psychomotor retardation characterizes schizophrenic disturbance. As amplified below, however, these investigators have drawn different conclusions concerning the primacy of psychomotor retardation in schizophrenia, Shakow viewing it as a secondary consequence of inability to maintain set and King considering it a primary aspect of failure in adaptational capacity.

Psychomotor Retardation as a Secondary Consequence of Inability to Maintain Set

In two early studies Shakow and Huston (1936) and Huston, Shakow, and Riggs (1937) found chronic schizophrenics to perform significantly more slowly than normal subjects on measures of tapping speed and reaction time. Their measure of reaction time, in which subjects lifted a finger from a key in response to a cue provided by the examiner, differentiated the groups more clearly than did the tapping test, where the subjects performed independently of cues from the examiner. Huston et al. therefore suggested that the subnormal performance of the schizophrenic subjects was due not only to psychomotor retardation per se, but also in large measure to the limited capacity of the schizophrenics to *prepare* themselves to respond to the external cues.

Rodnick and Shakow (1940) subsequently devised an index of response preparation, called the *set index,* that efficiently discriminates schizophrenic from normal subjects. Instructing subjects first to press a key and then to release it as soon as a light flashed, Rodnick and Shakow studied response set by varying the time interval between the subject's pressing of the key and the appearance of his cue to release it, that is, the bulb flashing. They observed schizophrenic subjects to react more quickly to shorter *preparatory intervals* (*PI's*) than to longer *PI's* when the intervals were presented in a regular series, but to react more quickly to longer *PI's* when the intervals were irregularly programmed. Normal subjects, on the other hand, performed better on regular than on irregular series, regardless of the length of the *PI's* except for intervals of very long duration. The set index derived by Rodnick and Shakow from their subjects' scores discriminated the schizophrenics from the normals *without overlap*.

Several more recent investigations have replicated these various findings. Cromwell, Rosenthal, Shakow, and Zahn (1961) observed schizophrenic subjects to perform considerably more slowly than normal controls on the reaction-time task devised by Huston et al. (1937). In contrast to earlier hypotheses, however, Cromwell et al. noted schizophrenic performance to improve rather than to deteriorate as the experimenters imposed increasing numbers of conditions on the response task, that is, as they injected increasing numbers of external cues for which the subject was responsible. They suggest that it was not greater autonomy that allowed schizophrenic subjects to attain more nearly normal performance on tapping than reaction-time tasks in the early Shakow and Huston (1936) and Huston et al. (1937) studies, but rather the relatively automatic, repetitious nature of the tapping task, which, unlike the reaction-time measure, does not require the subject continually to adapt his response to new cues.

Other studies by Tizard and Venables (1956) and by Rosenthal, Lawlor, Zahn, and Shakow (1960) have confirmed slower reaction times in schizophrenic than in normal subjects and substantiated the capacity of the Rodnick and Shakow set index to discriminate efficiently between the two groups. Rosenthal et al. also found the set index to identify levels of disorganization within a group of schizophrenic patients, with the set index correlating .89 with ratings of the subjects' mental health. Zahn and Rosenthal (1964), subsequently investigating whether response preparation could discriminate acute as well as chronic schizophrenic subjects from normals, obtained a significant between-group difference in the set index that confirmed their hypothesis that impaired psychomotor functioning appears even in the early stages of schizophrenic disturbance.

In recent summaries of this work on schizophrenia, Shakow (1962, 1963) clearly states his view that although impaired psychomotor functioning characterizes schizophrenic disorder, the schizophrenic person is unable to perform efficiently on measures of psychomotor speed only as a secondary consequence of his difficulty in maintaining an adequate focus of attention and an adaptive set to respond.

Psychomotor Retardation as a Primary Aspect of Failure in Adaptational Capacity

In contrast to Shakow, King (1954) concludes from his extensive studies of psychomotor functions in schizophrenia that psychomotor retardation is a primary identifying characteristic of schizophrenia that results from basic impairments of adaptational capacity associated with the disorder. Administering measures of reaction time, tapping speed, and finger dexterity to 194 normal subjects, 90 chronic schizophrenics, and 50 "subacute" patients described as having neurotic or pseudo-neurotic schizophrenic disturbances, King found the chronic schizophrenics significantly psychomotorically retarded in comparison to both the normal and subacute groups on all three measures. The subacute group performed more like the normals than the chronic schizophrenics, but they were also consistently subnormal in psychomotor speed, primarily as a result of the relatively slow functioning of the pseudo-neurotic schizophrenic members of the subacute group.

King also observed that within his chronic schizophrenic group degree of retardation was related to degree of disturbance as judged from behavior ratings, hospital management criteria, and duration of disturbance. This finding has been confirmed by Weaver (1961), who was able with a battery of psychomotor tests to differentiate between more and less severely disturbed patients even within a group of hospitalized chronic schizophrenics.

King interprets his data as indicating that the impaired psychomotor performance of schizophrenic subjects is not a secondarily derived phenomenon but rather constitutes a *primary* functioning disturbance. He suggests that inasmuch as the ability to move is a basic adaptational capacity of animate organisms, impaired psychomotor functioning should be considered a salient aspect of the central failure of adaptation that defines schizophrenic disturbance. King would thus take issue with the Bleulerian notion that disturbances of motility in schizophrenia are secondary to other aspects of the disorder, and he presents an extensive review of the literature in defense of his position (King, 1954, pp. 122–150).

A number of studies have attempted to examine further whether psychomotor impairment in schizophrenia is a basic defect or a secondary phenomenon attributable to motivational variables. The method in these studies has been to stimulate or reward the schizophrenic subject by making escape from an aversive stimulus contingent on his executing the required psychomotor act. Experiments of this type by Cohen (1956), Stotsky (1957), Rosenbaum, Grisell, and Mackavey (1957), Lang (1959), and others have in the main yielded similar results: under motivating conditions schizophrenic subjects improve their psychomotor performance, but they improve relatively little in relation to the extent of their initial deficit and they do not attain normal functioning levels. [2]

There is thus experimental support both for the view that low motivation contributes to schizophrenic performance deficits on psychomotor tasks and the belief that some basic impairments of psychomotor capacity exist in schizophrenic persons beyond what can be accounted for by motivational variables. However, these studies leave unresolved the issue of whether those psychomotor impairments that cannot be accounted for by motivational variables are primary or secondary phenomena. Both the set notions of Shakow and the adaptational approach of King fit the data, and the apparent disagreement between their positions may be more semantic than real.

To summarize the studies of psychomotor speed in schizophrenia, two consistently demonstrated facts are (a) that schizophrenic subjects are psychomotorically retarded in comparison to normal persons and (b) that the degree of retardation is roughly associated with degree of disturbance. Recalling the earlier discussion of general intellectual level, however, it is pertinent to point out that there is a dearth of longitudinal data bearing on the actual onset and progression of psychomotor slowing in schizophrenia. The reported differences between early and long-term schizophrenic subjects constitute only indirect evidence for deterioration during the course of schizophrenic disturbance, and there have been no longitudinal studies of psychomotor functioning in schizophrenics to provide direct evidence relating to this question. Furthermore, there are no longitudinal data to indicate whether the psychomotor slowing of schizophrenic persons begins with the onset of their disorder, or, as with depressed intellectual ability, appears in a potentially schizophrenic person long before he becomes overtly disturbed, as one of the concomitants of the constitutional and experiential factors that predispose him to develop schizophrenia.

[2] For a fuller review of the work in this area the reader is referred to Yates (1961).

PERCEPTUAL CONSTANCY

The most frequently studied aspect of perceptual functioning in schizophrenic subjects is constancy, particularly for size.[3] Size constancy is defined by the degree to which a person persists in perceiving a given object in terms of its actual size despite differences in the size of the retinal images it casts as its distance from the perceiver changes. The more a subject's size estimates are determined by the actual size of an object rather than by the size of the retinal images it casts, the more nearly constant is his perception; the more his size judgments are influenced by the size of his retinal images, the more *underconstant* is his perceptual functioning and the lower are the constancy scores he earns on experimental measures; in the event that a person becomes so committed to the initial size of a stimulus that his size estimates disregard both his retinal image and actual changes in the size of the stimulus, his perceptual functioning is *overconstant* and he earns inappropriately high constancy scores.

The first experimental study of size constancy in schizophrenics was reported by Raush (1952), who hypothesized that paranoid schizophrenics, because of their characteristic inflexibility, would demonstrate higher constancy scores than normals, whereas nonparanoid schizophrenics, as a result of their disorganization, would display less size constancy than normals. Raush's data confirmed the presence of overconstancy in paranoid schizophrenics as opposed to normal subjects. However, although his nonparanoid schizophrenics were significantly less overconstant than the paranoid group, they also received higher constancy scores than the normals, contrary to his hypothesis.

Sanders and Pacht (1952) obtained similar results in a study of normal subjects and neurotic and schizophrenic patients who were being seen in an outpatient clinic. Their neurotic group demonstrated the most accurate size constancy, whereas their normal subjects tended to be somewhat influenced by retinal-image size, that is, were underconstant, and their schizophrenics were notably overconstant, that is, were reluctant to alter their size estimates in accord with changing retinal images even when it would have been appropriate to do so.

Lovinger (1956), however, suggests that these researchers demonstrated overconstancy among schizophrenics primarily because they

---

[3] For further reading on the performance of schizophrenic subjects on a variety of perceptual tasks the reader is referred to Eysenck, Granger, and Brengelmann (1957) and Ittelson and Kutash (1961).

sampled only relatively intact, well-integrated schizophrenic subjects. Hypothesizing that the impaired reality testing in schizophrenia should conduce to *decreased* rather than increased size constancy, Lovinger studied perceptual functioning in groups of nonpsychiatric hospital patients, open-ward schizophrenics judged to be in good reality contact, and closed-ward schizophrenics in poor reality contact. Consistent with his hypothesis, Lovinger's open-ward schizophrenics were essentially similar to the control subjects in size constancy, whereas the closed-ward schizophrenics displayed significant underconstancy in relation to the other two groups. In further contrast to Raush, Lovinger found no differences in size constancy associated with paranoid-nonparanoid distinctions.

Lovinger's findings have been confirmed in studies by Weckowicz (1957) and Hamilton (1953). Weckowicz observed significantly less perceptual constancy in a group of chronic schizophrenic patients than in nonpsychiatric patient groups, and Hamilton obtained significantly lower constancy scores from a group of chronic schizophrenic subjects than from neurotic and normal control groups, with no difference in constancy scores between paranoid and nonparanoid schizophrenic subjects.

Boardman, Goldstone, Reiner, and Himmel (1964) have proposed an integrative framework to account for these diverse findings. They proceed from the following two observations: (a) overconstancy has been noted primarily in studies of paranoid and remitted schizophrenics and underconstancy in chronic schizophrenics with poor reality contact; and (b) other data suggest that acute schizophrenic subjects are perceptually unstable and may be either underconstant or overconstant, depending on their reaction to such external variables as the nature of the stimulus and the conditions under which it is presented.

On the basis of these observations Boardman et al. hypothesize that perceptual constancy takes different forms in schizophrenia at different stages of disturbance: early schizophrenics suffer a loss of stability in their perceptual functioning, are influenced more by contextual stimuli than by internal conceptual standards, and are neither consistently underconstant nor consistently overconstant in their perceptions; with persistence or increasing severity of disturbance, however, the schizophrenic person withdraws his attention from external variables to autistic frames of reference and is consequently likely to demonstrate diminished perceptual constancy; but, in the event of remission or a developing paranoid orientation, both of which are characterized by an exaggerated focus on establishing and maintaining a definite hold on objective reality, overconstancy is likely to appear.

Though attractive, the Boardman et al. hypothesis still fails to encompass all reported findings. With regard to chronic schizophrenia, for example, Leibowitz and Pishkin (1961) obtained no differences in size constancy between a group of withdrawn schizophrenic patients with a mean length of hospitalization of 8.84 years and a group of normal controls, which suggests that the perceptual abilities involved in size matching are not necessarily affected by schizophrenic withdrawal.

In a study relevant to early schizophrenia, Harway and Salzman (1964) administered size-constancy measures to schizophrenic subjects within 48 hours after their admission to the hospital. Varying the availability to their subjects of distance cues, they found that these early schizophrenic subjects were more sensitive than normal controls to the degree of information available, which is consistent with the Boardman et al. hypothesis that early schizophrenics are particularly influenced by external cues. However, contrary to the Boardman et al. expectation, these early schizophrenics consistently received higher constancy scores than the normals regardless of the degree of information available. Furthermore, similarly to Lovinger and Hamilton, Harway and Salzman found no constancy differences between paranoid and nonparanoid schizophrenics. Harway and Salzman also replicated the earlier findings by Sanders and Pacht that neurotic subjects earn constancy scores higher than normal but lower than schizophrenic groups.

Given the limited state of current knowledge about perceptual constancy in schizophrenia, it is difficult to draw definitive conclusions. The available data suggest that whatever constancy disturbances accompany schizophrenia are more marked in chronic, long-term schizophrenics than in acute, early, remitted, or improved schizophrenics. However, the evidence in this regard, like that bearing on psychomotor speed, is based on comparative studies and is at best indirect. Longitudinal studies that could clarify changes in perceptual constancy associated with the onset and course of schizophrenic disturbance have not yet been reported. Also unknown is the extent to which any differences between schizophrenic and normal persons in perceptual constancy may be present as an aspect of schizophrenic predisposition before the onset of an overt schizophrenic disorder.

LEARNING ABILITY

A number of early investigators, having observed subnormal performance by schizophrenic subjects on tests of learning and retention, concluded that learning capacity is impaired in schizophrenia. [4] However, such inferences overlook the important difference between capacity and ability mentioned earlier in this chapter. As Shakow (1946, 1962) points out, capacity is the upper limit of a person's ability to perform under optimal conditions, whereas ability is his actual level of functioning given characterological and situational factors that prevent him from exercising his full potential. Shakow stresses, with regard to learning tasks, that the inferior performance of schizophrenics is not necessarily a reflection of inferior capacity to learn, but rather may result from the adverse influence of factors unrelated to basic learning capacity.

Three nonintellectual factors frequently posited to account for the impaired performance of schizophrenic subjects on learning tasks are poor cooperation, distractibility, and aversive motivation. Concerning cooperation, it has generally been observed that schizophrenic subjects are likely to improve their performance in direct relationship to the degree of rapport the examiner is able to achieve with them. Wittman (1937), for example, reports a median correlation of .75 between the performance of schizophrenic subjects on a variety of memory and reasoning tasks and ratings of their cooperativeness.

Huston and Shakow (1948, 1949) examined carefully the role of cooperation in performance on a pursuit rotor task in which subjects were required to keep a pointer fixed on a moving target. They found that, although schizophrenic subjects were less adept than normal and manic-depressive subjects in learning to execute this task, those among the schizophrenics who were classed as cooperative learned more readily than those who were not. Furthermore, the performance of the schizophrenic group improved over successive trials, presumably as they became more familiar with the examiner and more inclined to cooperate with him.

Huston and Shakow also noted that when some of their schizophrenic subjects were given prolonged practice on the pursuit rotor task, with considerable encouragement, their performance approached that of normal subjects. However, without such extensive practice and encouragement even the most cooperative schizophrenic subjects were inferior to the normals in learning ability, so Huston and Shakow concluded that freedom from distraction and positive motivation are also necessary for the schizophrenic subject to exercise his full learning capacity.

Consistent with the discussion in Chapter 4 of cognitive focusing,

---

[4] The early studies of learning in schizophrenic subjects are described by Hunt and Cofer (1944) and concisely summarized by Jones (1961).

a number of studies confirm that freedom from distraction, or *set maintenance,* is intimately related to the learning performance of schizophrenic subjects. Hall and Crookes (1951), for example, were able to trace the subnormal learning performance of early schizophrenic subjects to the interference of competing previously learned responses that the subjects were unable to eliminate from their response sets. Pascal and Swenson (1952) administered to psychotic, neurotic, and nonpatient groups a complex discrimination reaction-time problem in six trials, the last two of which were accompanied by white noise that persisted until the subject made the correct response. They found that whereas the patient groups were inferior to the normals on the first four trials, they performed equally as well on the last two. To the extent that the presence of the white noise may be considered to have focused the subjects' attention on the task at hand (see p. 155), the Pascal and Swenson data demonstrate that improved set tends to eliminate the apparent learning incapacity of schizophrenic subjects.

The role of motivational factors in the learning performance of schizophrenic subjects, however, is not yet clear. Studies by Garmezy (1952) and Smock and Vancini (1962) suggest that schizophrenic subjects are particularly dependent on positive encouragement in their efforts to utilize their learning capacity. Garmezy administered a discrimination learning task to schizophrenic and normal subjects under two conditions. In one condition the correct response was rewarded and in the other the correct response was rewarded and all incorrect responses were punished. The performance of the schizophrenic subjects was inferior to that of the normals in the reward-only condition, but declined even further with the addition of punishment. Smock and Vancini found schizophrenics who had been censured during practice trials on a memory task to display less reminiscence than schizophrenics who had been praised, even though both groups had originally learned equally well.

These findings are consistent with the previously mentioned Rodnick and Garmezy (1957) notion that schizophrenic performance deficits are attributable to the schizophrenic's sensitivity to social censure and need to avoid failure (see Chap. 9), but Bleke (1955) reports a study in which punishment during a discrimination task *facilitated* the reminiscence of schizophrenic subjects. As indicated in Chapter 9 and in a detailed review of relevant experimental work by Buss and Lang (1965, pp. 3–13), motivational frameworks do not appear as consistently and parsimoniously to account for schizophrenic performance as concepts of set and distractability. On the other hand, Garmezy's finding that punishment or reward for all responses actually handicapped his schizophrenic subjects' performance relative to a reward-only condition is contrary to set theory, which would predict best performance where there was most focusing on responses by either praise or censure.

Whereas the etiology of poor learning performance among schizophrenics has therefore not been definitively established, such performance decrements regularly accompany schizophrenia and appear related to the degree of disturbance present. In this latter regard, Peters (1953), Hall and Crookes (1951), and others provide evidence that chronic schizophrenics perform less well than acute or early schizophrenics on measures of learning ability. As is the case with psychomotor speed and perceptual constancy, however, there are no longitudinal studies that directly assess fluctuations in learning impairment associated with the onset, progression, and remission of schizophrenic disorder.

On the basis of an extensive review of relevant literature, Jones (1961) offers the following conclusions concerning learning ability in abnormal groups, none of which has been challenged by subsequent data: (a) psychotic patients of all types are capable of learning but perform less well than normal or neurotic persons on measures of learning ability; (b) this performance deficit may represent a secondary result of other personality defects rather than a true impairment of learning capacity; (c) paranoid schizophrenics are less likely than other schizophrenic subjects to display learning impairments; and (d) other things being equal, the degree of learning impairment is related to the chronicity and severity of disturbance.

► 12

SYNTHETIC FUNCTIONS

THE normal person is able to organize and integrate his thought processes, relation to reality, interpersonal skills, defensive resources, and intellectual capacities in the service of a stable and rewarding life pattern. Such integrating and organizing activity constitutes the synthetic functions of the ego and represents an individual's general ability to utilize his personality resources effectively. Schizophrenia is often characterized by disorganized and disharmonious personality functioning, the schizophrenic person having many reasonably intact islands of functioning that he cannot bridge and many latent adaptive talents that he is unable to exercise.

Although the synthetic functions of the ego overlap and summarize the various other functions treated in earlier chapters, synthesizing operations are uniquely reflected in two types of psychodiagnostic test score that have not been considered to this point. These types of score are specific Rorschach *indices of organizational activity* and certain *global Rorschach evaluations* that yield a single score for over-all ego adequacy.

INDICES OF ORGANIZATIONAL ACTIVITY

Fenichel (1938, pp. 77–78), in discussing ego strengths and weaknesses, indicates that "a strong ego is also strong in its organization . . . what is characteristic for the unifying tendency of the ego is the way in which it brings its various trends into harmony with one another." As Fenichel's view implies, schizophrenic ego impairment is suggested not by the absence of organizational activity, but by a pro-

219

clivity for inappropriate, ineffective, and unrealistic organizational acts. In other words, the *quality* of organizational activity is the critical dimension of ego-synthetic operations on which schizophrenic persons are likely to differ from normal individuals. Organizational activity can be assessed in the psychodiagnostic test battery by either of three widely used Rorschach scoring systems devised for this purpose, Beck's Z, Hertz' g and Friedman's Developmental Level (*DL*) approach. Clinical and experimental studies of these indices, as reviewed below, confirm that estimates of the quality of organizational acts facilitate the differential diagnosis of schizophrenia.

BECK'S Z

The first systematic procedure for evaluating the amount of organizational activity represented by a Rorschach protocol was outlined by Beck (1933), who recommended the organization score Z for all responses in which separate details are combined into a unitary percept. Z is scored for any W response, for any combination of either adjacent or nonadjacent details, and for any response in which white space is integrated into the percept. On the basis of responses given by 39 normal adults of superior intelligence, Beck derived a series of Z weights, ranging from one to six points, to be assigned for various types of organization responses occurring on the different cards. [1]

Its relationship to organizational activity notwithstanding, Beck's Z appears to have limited utility for diagnosing schizophrenia. Studies by Beck et al. (1950) and Sisson and Taulbee (1955) observed mean weighted Z scores of 22.48 and 24.03 in normal samples of 157 and 60 subjects, respectively. Schizophrenic groups have demonstrated Z scores above and below these normal values. Sixty schizophrenics reported by Beck (1954, p. 210) had a mean weighted Z of 18.90, whereas 60 schizophrenics studied by Sisson and Taulbee (1955) had a mean weighted Z of 27.38. In neither study were Z differences between normal and schizophrenic groups significant.

It is likely that Beck's system for assessing organizational activity

---

[1] The details of weighted Z scoring have recently been reviewed by Beck et al. (1961, pp. 46–65). It is questionable, however, whether Beck's Z weights add anything to a simple tabulation of the number of Z responses occurring in a record. Wilson and Blake (1950), scoring 104 Rorschach records both for Beck's weighted Z and for the unweighted frequency of Z responses, obtained a correlation approaching 1.00 between weighted Z and Z frequency. They conclude that the computation of weighted Z may be unnecessary in practice, and they provide a table for converting Z frequencies to weighted Z scores and comparing them with Beck's (1961, p. 232) normative data for weighted Z.

fails to discriminate schizophrenic from normal subjects because it does not encompass important qualitative scoring refinements. That is, Z is scored independently of the degree to which responses are accurately perceived and logically integrated and thus pertains strictly to the *amount* and not the *quality* of organizational activity. For example, whereas Beck scores all W as Z, accurately perceived W percepts occur more frequently in normal than schizophrenic subjects, and W— responses are given more often by schizophrenics than by normals (see Chap. 7). Similarly, amorphous and vague W's are associated with schizophrenia, but well-articulated W's are not (see Chap. 8). The Z index of organizational activity, in not differentiating these W subcategories, is too gross a score to discriminate schizophrenic from nonschizophrenic organizational activity. It is noteworthy, however, that Thiesen (1952) found a pattern consisting of both low Z (weighted Z less than 7.5, equivalent to less than four Z responses) *and* poor perceptual accuracy ($F+\%$ less than 69) to occur significantly more frequently in schizophrenic than in normal subjects.

The grossness of the Z index and the importance of scoring subcategories has also been revealed in efforts to validate Becks' (1947, p. 12) suggestion that Z accurately represents intellectual functioning and varies directly with intelligence. Wishner (1948) found a correlation of .54 between Z and Wechsler-Bellevue *IQ* in one study, but Taulbee (1955) concluded from the low correlation he obtained between Z and *IQ* in another study that Z is not a reliable indicator of intelligence. Goldfarb (1945) found no relationship between Z and Wechsler-Bellevue *IQ* in 30 normal adolescents, and McCandless (1949) reports no relationship between Z and the academic achievement of officer candidates in the military. Data presented on page 226 suggest that intelligence can be reliably estimated from organizational activity only by reference to subcategories of W response that are not differentiated by Z scoring.

HERTZ' g

The g index was developed by Hertz (1942; 1960, pp. 28–36) specifically to assess the qualitative features of organizational activity. Hertz scores g for the same response categories for which Beck scores Z, but she utilizes in addition the following three qualitative weights: (a) 1.5 for organizational activity involving accurately perceived original forms; (b) 1.0 for combinations of forms that are accurate but neither original, popular, nor vague; and (c) 0.5 for combinations of vague, popular, or inaccurately perceived forms.

Unfortunately, few clinical data are available to indicate the psychodiagnostic utility of the weighted g index. Hertz (1960, pp. 44–45) does report median weighted g scores for 40 college women (13.0), 25 depressed adults (5.6), 35 delusional schizophrenic adults (6.1), and 50 brain-injured adults (5.1), and the divergent values for these normal and schizophrenic subjects suggest that low weighted g may on occasion identify schizophrenia when depression and brain injury can be ruled out. However, because weighted g is based on equal weights for popular and perceptually inaccurate responses and according to Hertz is highly correlated with Z, further research with weighted g does not hold much promise for differential diagnosis.

Hertz (1960, pp. 53–54) in fact concludes that high weighted g scores are associated primarily with high energy, drive, and expansiveness and low scores with mental deficiency, retardation, deterioration, and depression, and that psychotic processes may operate either to raise or lower these scores. On the other hand, Hertz suggests that the subcategories of $g+$ and $g-$, scored respectively for organizational acts of good and poor perceptual accuracy, may have diagnostic value. Investigating this hypothesis, Hertz and Paolino (1960) found 35 schizophrenic subjects significantly more frequently than 35 neurotics to give organizational responses involving poor form, inappropriate and unrealistic combinations, and rare, unique, or bizarre concepts.

DEVELOPMENTAL LEVEL (DL)

The diagnostically most useful Rorschach index of organizational activity is the previously mentioned (see Chap. 8) Developmental Level (DL) scoring scheme devolved by Friedman (1952a, 1953) from the developmental psychology of Heinz Werner (1948). Werner postulates as one of the central elements of cognitive ontogenesis an increasing capacity to differentiate and integrate perceptual stimuli. Pointing out that limited ability to analyze and synthesize perceptual fields characterizes children, primitive peoples, and psychotic adults, Werner endorses a regressive view of psychopathologic phenomena (see p. 10).[2]

The use of the Rorschach test to study such perceptual development was first suggested by Dworetzki (1939), who felt that genetic studies of the Rorschach could shed light both on developmental trends and

---

[2] A concise outline of the comparative-developmental interpretation of schizophrenic phenomena is presented by Goldman (1962), who cites relevant research demonstrating the relationship of regression to schizophrenic impairments in several areas of cognitive functioning.

on the perceptual processes underlying response to the test. In a summary of her research with groups of children of various ages, Dworetzki (Meili-Dworetzki, 1956) presents evidence that certain Rorschach determinants and certain aspects of the manner in which Rorschach responses are organized vary systematically with age. Friedman's *DL* scoring scheme is basically an extension of Dworetzki's formulations, with increased focus on the developmental aspects of location choice and more extensive quantification of the frequency of organizational acts of various kinds.

DL SCORES AND SCHIZOPHRENIC DISTURBANCE

The core of *DL* scoring is Friedman's distinction between *genetically mature* and *genetically immature* percepts. The former represent definite, differentiated, and well-organized perceptual activity, whereas the latter reflect vague, diffuse, and poorly organized perceptual functioning. According to Friedman, genetically immature levels of perceptual integration are indicated by inaccurate, vague, and amorphous percepts and by such illogical organizational acts as Confabulation, Contamination, and Fabulized Combination responses. As previously reviewed in Chapters 5, 7, and 8, each of these genetically immature categories occurs more frequently in the records of schizophrenic than of normal subjects. To reflect the genetically mature perceptual functioning that is manifest in adaptive organizational activity, Friedman employs the three response categories of *plus-plus, plus,* and *mediocre,* as defined below.

Plus-Plus Responses. Plus-plus responses are percepts in which a single area of an inkblot is first differentiated into component parts and then logically reintegrated into a single, perceptually accurate response. Inasmuch as *plus-plus* responses involve the desynthesis of a unitary blot area, they can occur in association with W locations only on those cards that constitute a relatively solid, unitary stimulus, namely, Cards I, IV, V, VI, and IX, which Friedman calls the "unbroken" blots. Illustrative W++ responses are Card I seen as "Three people doing a balancing act" and Card V seen as "A donkey with a heavy load on its back." *Plus-plus* responses to a D location can be given to any of the common details and are illustrated by the following responses: Card I, center detail—"Two people embracing"; Card III, side red detail—"An acrobat swinging from a rope"; Card IX, green detail—"A man riding a motorcycle."

Normative data provided by Friedman (1952a), Siegel (1953), Frank (1951), Pena (1953), and Rosenblatt and Solomon (1954) reveal that *plus-plus* responses occur rarely in the records of normal, neurotic, schizophrenic, brain-damaged, and mentally retarded adults alike. The median frequency of both $W++$ and $D++$ percepts in all groups studied is zero (see Table 3). Although normal and neurotic subjects are more likely to give *plus-plus* responses than schizophrenic subjects, the differences between these groups in *plus-plus* responsivity is not significant. Hence the presence or absence of *plus-plus* responses, considered in isolation, helps neither to identify nor rule out schizophrenic impairment.

TABLE 3

MEDIAN PERCENTS OF GENETICALLY MATURE RORSCHACH RESPONSES IN DIFFERENT DIAGNOSTIC GROUPS[1]

Category	Normal	Neurotic	Paranoid Schizophrenia	Hebephrenic-Catatonic Schizophrenia	Brain-Damaged	Mentally Retarded
W++/W%	0(27.)[2]	0(17.)	0(17.)	0(10.)	0(7.)	0(4.)
D++/D%	0(13.)	0(13.)	0(10.)	0(0.)	0(7.)	0(0.)
W+/W%	13.0	0(20.)	0(—)[3]	0(43.)	0(43.)	0(9.)
D+/D%	18.0	9.5	13.0	10.5	15.5	0(13.)
W++ & W+/W%	22.5	—	0(—)	0(47.)	4.6	—
D++ & D+/D%	18.0	—	13.0	10.5	16.0	—
Wm/W%	50.0	50.0	41.5	31.5	46.4	50.0
Dm/D%	60.0	59.5	50.0	45.0	47.8	67.0
High W%	83.0	67.0	60.0	38.0	58.6	47.0
High D%	76.0	75.0	67.0	57.5	66.3	67.0

[1] Based on studies by Friedman (1952a, 1953), Frank (1951), Pena (1953), Siegal (1953), and Rosenblatt and Solomon (1954) involving a total of 230 adult subjects.
[2] Where median percent is zero, the percent of subjects giving one or more such response is indicated in parentheses.
[3] Data not available.

Plus Responses. *Plus* responses are percepts in which two or more discrete areas of an inkblot are integrated into a single perceptually accurate response. In contrast to *plus-plus* responses, *plus* responses to W locations can be scored only on those blots that are "broken," that is, in which there are discrete D areas separated by white space, namely,

Cards II, III, VII, VIII, and X. The following are illustrative $W+$ responses: Card II—"Two people having an argument"; Card VIII— "A medical illustration of human anatomy"; Card X—"An underwater scene."

Plus responses involving D locations are scored for any logical combination of two or more common details, provided some meaningful integration of them is indicated. For example, "two people" seen on Card III is not a *plus* response, but "Two people bending over to pick something up" is scored $D+$. Other illustrative $D+$ responses are the following: Card X, top center details—"Heads of two girls, making faces at each other"; Card X, top center details—"Two insects fighting"; Card X, center blue details—"Two men shaking hands."

Normative data indicate that *plus* responses occur more frequently than *plus-plus* responses in all groups studied, but the various reports do not provide a clear basis for determining whether $W+$ and $D+$ responses considered in isolation validly differentiate diagnostic groups. As can be seen in Table 3, the median reported percentage of $W+$ in all W responses ($W+/W\%$) is 13 for normal subjects and zero for neurotic, schizophrenic, brain-damaged, and mentally retarded subjects. Friedman (1953, p. 178) states that the difference between the normal and the hebephrenic-catatonic schizophrenic groups in $W+/W\%$ approaches significance; Siegel (1953, p. 156), however, treating the same data, describes this difference as insignificant, and neither author reports sufficient information to allow an independent statistical evaluation.

A similar situation obtains with regard to $D+/D\%$. According to Friedman, the difference between the median $D+/D\%$'s of the normals (18.0%; see Table 3) and the hebephrenic-catatonic schizophrenic (10.5%) is significant; according to Siegel, it is not. Furthermore, it can be seen that the neurotic subjects are even lower than the schizophrenics in both $W+$ and $D+$ tendency. Hence, although the $W+/W\%$ and $D+/D\%$ variables may identify some differences between normals and certain schizophrenics, they do not differentiate these schizophrenics from neurotic subjects.

However, pursuing further the possible diagnostic implications of the organizational activity represented by *plus-plus* and *plus* responses, Siegel presents additional data concerning the combined frequency of these scores. For the combined percentage of $W++$ and $W+$ responses in all W, Siegel found median values of 22.5% in normal subjects and 0.0% in both paranoid and hebephrenic-catatonic schizophrenic groups (see Table 3). The two schizophrenic groups differ significantly from the normals on this index, but not from each other.

Siegel's analysis of combined $D++$ and $D+$ percent revealed the normals to be higher, but not significantly so, than the two schizophrenic groups.

Siegel's data suggest that the combined W index for *plus-plus* and *plus* responses may validly capture differences in organizational activity between normal and schizophrenic persons. However, for clinical purposes the combination of these two scores with the category of *mediocre* responses, as amplified below, yields over-all indices of perceptual maturity that appear more efficiently than any of the other DL summary scores to differentiate diagnostic groups.

Before leaving the *plus* and *plus-plus* responses, it is of interest to note some additional findings that attest the crucial significance of scoring subcategories in clinical validating studies of psychodiagnostic tests. Blatt and Allison (1963) stress the importance in psychodiagnostic research of "revising and refining conventional scores so they more fully reflect . . . the subtle and vital differentiations made by the clinician," and they demonstrate their argument by comparing intelligence test scores with both gross $W\%$'s and combined $W++$ and $W+/W\%$'s. They found no relationship between Raven score and $W\%$ for their subjects, but the combined $W++$ and $W+$ index correlated significantly and positively with the intelligence scores. Repeating this study with a different intelligence criterion (WAIS IQ), Allison and Blatt (1964) observed no correlation ($-.08$) between $W\%$ and intelligence, but a significant relationship ($.57$) between intelligence and the combined percentage of $W++$ and $W+$ in all W.

Mediocre Responses. A *mediocre* response is a definite and perceptually accurate response given to a unitary Rorschach area but involving no explicit analysis or synthesis of the area. *Mediocre W* responses (Wm) can occur only on the unbroken blots, since any perceptually accurate W given to a broken blot is by definition a $W+$. Scored as Wm are such responses as "bat" to Card I, "butterfly" to Card V, and "animal skin" to Card VI. *Mediocre D* responses (Dm) may be given to any of the common Rorschach details and include such responses as the following: Card I, center detail—"The figure of a person"; Card III, center red detail—"Butterfly"; Card IX, green detail—"Man's head."

The normative data for *mediocre* responses (see Table 3) reveal definite differences between diagnostic groups, but again the significance of these differences is unclear. For $Wm/W\%$ the hebephrenic-catatonic schizophrenics (31.5%) are significantly lower than the normals (50.0%), but the paranoid schizophrenics (41.5%) differ significantly from neither the normal nor the hebephrenic-catatonic group.

In the case of $Dm/D\%$, the difference between the normals (60.0%) and hebephrenic-catatonic schizophrenics (45.0%) is significant according to Friedman (1953, p. 178) but not according to Siegel (1953, p. 157), and there again are insufficient data in their reports to allow independent statistical treatment.

Although it is therefore uncertain whether *mediocre* responses taken alone efficiently discriminate diagnostic groups, the *mediocre* percents, like the *plus-plus* and *plus* percents, tend to be higher among normal and neurotic subjects than among paranoid schizophrenics and higher among paranoid schizophrenics than among hebephrenic-catatonic schizophrenics. These trends suggest that combined indices based on all three categories might sufficiently differentiate among diagnostic groups to warrant applying them in the individual case.

Percent Genetically High Responses. The percents of *genetically high responses* are Friedman's combined indices for the three categories of mature perception. These indices include *high W%*, which is the combined percentage of $W++$, $W+$, and Wm in all W, and *high D%*, which is the combined percentage of $D++$, $D+$, and Dm in all D. As can be seen in Table 3, *high W%* and *high D%* vary similarly across the various diagnostic groups. Siegel (1953, p. 155) indicates that for both *high W%* and *high D%* the median values earned by normals subjects (83.0% and 76.0%, respectively) are significantly higher than those received by paranoid schizophrenics (60.0% and 67.0%, respectively), and paranoid schizophrenics in turn significantly exceed hebephrenic-catatonic schizophrenics (38.0% and 57.5%, respectively) in both indices.

These data suggest that a *high W%* below 60% and/or a *high D%* below 67% reflect a pathologic deficiency of ability to analyze and synthesize experience. In the absence of mental retardation or brain damage, with which such a deficiency might also be associated (see Table 3), a Rorschach record in which mature W's constitute less than 60% of W responses given and/or mature D's comprise fewer than two thirds of the total D's points to a schizophrenic impairment of organizational activity. The implications of the observed differences between paranoid and nonparanoid schizophrenics in *high W%* and *high D%* are considered further in Chapter 14.

RESEARCH WITH DEVELOPMENTAL LEVEL (DL) SCORES

Although there is little research bearing directly on the clinical efficiency of *high W%* and *high D%* criteria for diagnosing schizophrenia, a number of studies demonstrate that Rorschach *DL* scores validly reflect developmental stages and relate meaningfully to parameters of schizophrenic disturbance. Regarding ontogeny, Hemmendinger (1953) compared the *DL* scores of normal adults with those of 160 normal children in eight age groups from three to 10 years. He found fairly systematic age progressions from one age group to the next for both *high W%* (from a median of 22.2% for three-year-olds to 63.4% for ten-year-olds) and *high D%* (from 25.0% at age three to 61.5% at age ten). As Friedman (1953) and Siegel (1953) note, Hemmendinger's work lends construct validity to the *DL* scoring system, and, inasmuch as the *high W%*'s and *high D%*'s of the children resemble those earned by schizophrenics (see Table 3), his findings are consistent with the conception of schizophrenia as a regressive disorder.

Several studies of schizophrenic subjects have employed a weighted scoring scheme for *DL* devised by Becker (1956) that yields a single summary index of perceptual maturity. Becker assigns each response from one to six points according to the following schedule: four, five, and six points, respectively, for *mediocre, plus,* and *plus-plus* responses occurring in *W* or *D* locations; three points for vague *W*'s and perceptually accurate responses to rare details (*Dd+*, a category not originally scored by Friedman); two points for each instance of a minus, vague, amorphous, or confabulatory *D* response and each instance of a minus *Dd* response; and one point for all minus, amorphous, and confabulatory *W*'s, for all responses perseverated on three or more cards, and for all instances of a Contamination or Fabulized Combination response.

Becker cumulates these weighted scores and divides by the number of responses to get his summary *DL* index. In his first study with this index, Becker (1956) observed significant and high negative correlations between summary *DL* and scores received on the Elgin Prognostic Rating Scale, which is partially a measure of severity of disturbance (see Chap. 13), in both male (−.60) and female (−.68) hospitalized schizophrenics. In a later factor analytic study of *DL* scores and scores from the Elgin scale, Becker (1959) found *DL* to load −.46 on a factor labeled Schizophrenic Withdrawal and −.64 on a factor of Reality Distortion.

Other investigators have similarly noted significant relationships between the Becker *DL* index and aspects of schizophrenia. Lebowitz (1963) found a significant difference in summary *DL* scores between 20 paranoid schizophrenics (mean summary *DL* of 3.14) and 20 nonpsychiatric hospital patients (mean of 4.08). Levine (1959), comparing the admission Rorschach records of 24 psychiatric patients who remained continuously hospitalized for one year or more after admission with those of 24 patients who were discharged within one year of admission, found the mean summary *DL* of the discharged group (3.41) to have been significantly higher on admission than that of the group that remained hospitalized (3.04). Levine and Cohen (1962) found the summary *DL* index to approach a significant negative correlation with the number of months a group of 120 patients were hospitalized during a three-year period following their initial hospital admission.

Wilensky (1959) has suggested modifying Becker's scoring by assigning one point for rejections and determining summary *DL* from the average *DL* for each card rather than from the record taken as a whole. Wilensky found summary *DL* computed in this manner to correlate .82 with whether or not hospitalized schizophrenic subjects were assigned to an open or closed ward and .71 with independent ratings of these subjects' degree of social participation. However, because Wilensky reports a correlation of .95 between his and Becker's summary *DL* scoring, and Goldfried (1962) found a correlation of .89 between the two methods, it appears of little consequence which of the two is used to compute summary *DL*.

Although these results suggest that a single summary *DL* index may usefully identify deficiencies in organizational capacity associated with the presence and severity of schizophrenic disorder, further normative data are necessary to establish specific criteria for the clinical application of such an index. One question to which additional research needs be addressed is the degree to which the summary *DL* is related to intelligence. Goldfried (1962) obtained a significant correlation of .39 between Becker's *DL* index and *IQ* in a mixed sample of psychiatric patients; Friedman and Orgel (1964), on the other hand, report for 141 psychiatric patients that any significant correlations between *DL* scores and *IQ* drop out when *IQ*'s below 79 are eliminated. Further clarification of the *DL-IQ* relationship is necessary for accurate clinical interpretation of summary *DL* scores.

Also of note is an alternative system for scoring Developmental Level proposed by Phillips, Kaden, and Waldman (1959). Reverting to the earlier notions of Dworetzki, Phillips et al. extend a developmental framework to aspects of determinant as well as location choice scoring. Relatively little normative data are yet available concerning this revised and extended *DL* scoring system. In one study Friedman (1960) reports that Phillips' revised scoring system adds very little to the simpler Friedman scores in differentiating normal from paranoid and hebephrenic-catatonic schizophrenic subjects, but the relative diagnostic utility of the two systems has not as yet been carefully explored.

GLOBAL RORSCHACH EVALUATIONS

Finally noteworthy in connection with psychodiagnostic appraisal of ego-synthetic operations are three global Rorschach scoring schemes that yield summary indices of over-all ego adequacy. These are the Basic Rorschach Score developed by Buhler, Buhler, and Lefever; the Delta Index for pathological thinking devised by Watkins and Stauffacher; and the Rorschach Schizophrenic Score derived by Kataguchi. Experimental data concerning these indices are meager, and the methods of scoring them will not be detailed here. As reviewed below, however, each has been studied specifically with regard to diagnosing schizophrenic disturbance.

BASIC RORSCHACH SCORE (BRS)

The Basic Rorschach Score (*BRS*) was constructed by Buhler, Buhler, and Lefever (1949) expressly to quantify Rorschach scores in a manner that would differentiate clinically between diagnostic groups. To this end, Buhler et al. developed weights for numerical ranges of all location and determinant choices, various content scores, certain specific types of deviant response, and several combinations of these various scores. Positive weights are assigned to those ranges, scores, responses, and combinations considered indicative of good adjustment, and negative weights to those associated with poor adjustment. The total *BRS* is then the algebraic sum of the positive and negative weights assigned to each response.

In their validating study with 338 subjects representing five diagnostic categories Buhler et al. (p. 114) obtained the following mean *BRS* scores: normals—19.0, psychoneurotics—7.7; psychopaths—*minus* 4.5; organics—*minus* 13.4; and schizophrenics—*minus* 16.2. An analysis of variance revealed a significant between-groups difference. The *BRS* has not been widely applied to problems of individual diagnosis, and one study by Finney (1955) suggests that it may not be adequate for such use. Nevertheless, the attention devoted by Buhler et al. to *ranges* of various Rorschach scores and the extensive data included in their monograph recommend their work to the reader's attention.

DELTA INDEX

Watkins and Stauffacher (1952) utilized 15 categories of deviant Rorschach response outlined by Rapaport, Gill, and Schafer (1946, pp. 331–336) to develop a Delta Index for pathological thinking. They assigned weights ranging from .25 to 1.00 to responses representing Fabulization, Fabulized Combination, Confabulation, Contamination, autistic logic, peculiar verbalization, queer verbalization, vagueness, confusion, overelaborate symbolism, relationship verbalization, absurdity, deterioration color, and mangled or distorted concepts. The Delta Index is computed by dividing the sum of these weights by the total number of responses and converting the result to a percentage.

Watkins and Stauffacher initially assessed the Delta Index with groups of 25 normal, 25 neurotic, and 25 schizophrenic subjects. They found the neurotic group to receive a mean Delta significantly higher than the normals but significantly lower than the schizophrenics. Furthermore, all the normal subjects had Delta percents below 5, and a Delta of 10% or more characterized none of the normal subjects, only two of the neurotic subjects, and half of the schizophrenic group.

Several subsequent studies have validated the Delta Index for differentiating schizophrenic from normal groups. Powers and Hamlin (1955), for example, studying Delta in five subject groups, found a mean Delta sum of six in normals, 11 in anxiety neurotics, 21 in "latent" schizophrenics, 21 in paranoid schizophrenics, and 34 in catatonic schizophrenics. The between-groups difference in mean sum Delta was significant. Examining Delta percent, Powers and Hamlin found the 10% cutting score suggested by Watkins and Stauffacher unsatisfactory; however, a score of 21% Delta was exceeded by none of their normal and neurotic subjects but roughly half of their schizophrenics.

In other studies Pope and Jensen (1957) found the Delta Index to decrease in schizophrenic subjects in direct relationship to independent measures of their clinical improvement, and Quirk, Quarrington, Neiger, and Sleman (1962) further demonstrated the capacity of the Delta Index to differentiate psychotic from both normal and neurotic groups. However, adequate criteria for diagnosis in the individual case have not yet been established for this index.

RORSCHACH SCHIZOPHRENIC SCORE (RSS)

Kataguchi (1959) has attempted to develop from previously validated scoring systems a Rorschach score than can efficiently discriminate schizophrenic from normal and neurotic subjects in the individual case. Kataguchi first compared the Basic Rorschach Score and Delta Index of 30 schizophrenic with 30 normal and 30 neurotic subjects and confirmed that both scores can significantly discriminate a schizophrenic group. He then added to the BRS and Delta Index three other Rorschach scores frequently validated in clinical studies with schizophrenic subjects, $R+\%$, $W-\%$, and $\#P$, and devised a discriminant function for these five scores. The cutting score he derived for his global index accurately categorized 77% of his subjects as schizophrenic or nonschizophrenic. Kataguchi does not present any cross-validating data, however, nor has any appeared in the literature since his initial work.

PART THREE

  DIFFERENTIAL DIAGNOSIS
IN SCHIZOPHRENIA

► 13

ACUTE AND CHRONIC SCHIZOPHRENIA

THE distinction between acute and chronic schizophrenia evolved from the Bleulerian and Meyerian assertions that schizophrenia was not, as Kraepelin had maintained, exclusively a progressive and deteriorating condition. [1] Bleuler cited his extensive clinical experience to demonstrate that many patients who exhibit classical features of dementia praecox as defined by Kraepelin nevertheless recover sufficiently to resume their social and occupational roles. However, Bleuler did not dichotomize schizophrenia into recovering and nonrecovering categories, but rather regarded schizophrenia as a basically chronic condition (1911, pp. 206–208). He avowed, in fact, that he had never seen a schizophrenic patient in whom signs of the disturbance were not still visible, regardless of the degree of social restitution the patient had made (1911, p. 256).

Meyer (1907, 1910), on the other hand, argued that schizophrenia could occur as an acute "reaction" to environmental stress and have no necessarily chronic features. Bleuler later acknowledged such a possibility by suggesting that schizophrenia may encompass two classes of psychosis: one class is a "morbid reaction to an affective experience" that can be labeled "reactive" or "situational" psychosis, whereas the other class is conditioned by "a morbid process in the brain" and is a "process" or "progressive" psychosis (Bleuler, 1924, p. 173).

In Bleuler's view, however, these two classes of symptomatology intermingle and do not justify any diagnostic subdivision of schizophrenic disturbance. He therefore continued to maintain that, although

---

[1] Kraepelinian, Bleulerian, and Meyerian concepts of schizophrenia are summarized in Chapter 1.

psychological factors influence a schizophrenic patient's overt behavior, schizophrenic thinking derives solely from a "fundamental process" that remains unaffected by experience (Bleuler, 1930, p. 206). Nevertheless, he adds, "Improvements up to what is practically a recovery do not . . . contradict the diagnosis of a schizophrenia" (1930, p. 209).

Some writers have attempted to reconcile Bleuler's and Meyer's positions regarding recovery in schizophrenia with Kraepelinian concepts by suggesting diagnoses other than "true schizophrenia" for socially restituting patients. Milici (1939), for example, describes those instances of apparent schizophrenia that are characterized by sudden onset in response to precipitating stress and relatively early remissions as "postemotive schizophrenia." Paskind and Brown (1940) designate such cases "psychoses resembling schizophrenia," and Langfeldt (1937, 1951) labels them "schizophreniform psychoses." Other diagnostic categories that have been applied to apparently schizophrenic but rapidly recovering patients include "acute exhaustive psychosis" (Adland, 1947), "benign stupor" (Hoch, 1921), and "oneirophrenia" (Meduna, 1950). These several authors distinguish such syndromes from "typical schizophrenia," to which, following Kraepelin, they ascribe a chronic and progressive course. [2]

However, the view most widely propagated by the formulations of Bleuler and Meyer is that schizophrenia occurs in two forms, one that remits under favorable circumstances and one that persists regardless of the nature of intercurrent events. The recovering form of schizophrenia is commonly referred to as *acute* or *reactive* schizophrenia and the nonrecovering form as *chronic* or *process* schizophrenia. The identifying characteristics of these contrasting schizophrenic subtypes are amplified in the following summary of various criteria that have been employed to classify them.

CRITERIA FOR CLASSIFYING ACUTE AND CHRONIC SCHIZOPHRENIA

Consistent with the association of acute schizophrenia with recovery from disturbance and chronic schizophrenia with persistence of disturbance, the differential classification of these two conditions has traditionally been structured in terms of prognostic indices. Kant (1941, 1944) and Chase and Silverman (1943), for example, approached the acute-chronic distinction by comparing schizophrenic patients who

---

[2] For a more detailed historical review of efforts to label remitting schizophrenic disturbance, the reader is referred to Vaillant (1964b).

responded to treatment with patients who failed to respond. They found that schizophrenics most likely to recover had been disturbed for a relatively short time, were not severely disorganized, dissociated, or affectively blunted, and displayed a minimum of such accessory symptoms as delusions and hallucinations. Schizophrenics with a long history of disturbance and prominent primary and secondary symptomatology, on the other hand, were relatively unlikely to improve. These investigators concluded that duration and severity of symptoms are therefore useful bases for estimating prognosis and dividing schizophrenic patients into acute and chronic subgroups.

Since the work of Kant and Chase and Silverman a number of scales more detailed and readily quantifiable than their descriptive criteria have been developed to predict recovery and distinguish between acute and chronic status in schizophrenic patients. Wittman (1941) constructed the earliest such measure, the Elgin Prognostic Scale, by translating a number of previously reported positive and negative prognostic indicators into a series of rating scales. In several studies (Wittman, 1941, 1944; Wittman and Steinberg, 1944) Elgin Scale ratings of large numbers of hospitalized schizophrenic patients have predicted outcome with 80% accuracy, and, as reviewed by Higgins (1964), the Elgin Scale has frequently been used as the independent variable in comparative studies of acute and chronic schizophrenic subjects.

More recently, developmental, case history, and autonomic nervous system criteria for differentiating acute and chronic schizophrenia have been devised by Kantor, Wallner, and Winder; Phillips; and Meadow and Funkenstein, respectively. A brief review of these contributions will define the significant distinguishing features of acute and chronic schizophrenic disturbance.

DEVELOPMENTAL CRITERIA

Kantor, Wallner, and Winder (1953) chose from the literature a number of developmental variables that had previously been imputed to distinguish between the recovering-acute-reactive and nonrecovering-chronic-process types of schizophrenia. From these variables they compiled the following list of 23 dichotomies, each of which contrasts the process pole of a developmental dimension with an opposite pole associated with reactive schizophrenia:

From birth to age five: early psychological trauma vs. good psychological history; severe physical illness vs. good physical health; odd family members vs. normal family members.

From age five to adolescence: difficulties at school vs. well-adjusted at school; family troubles paralleled with sudden changes in patient's behavior vs. domestic troubles unaccompanied by behavior disruptions; introverted vs. extroverted behavior patterns; breakdown vs. adequate history of social, physical, and mental functioning; pathologic vs. normal siblings; overprotective or rejecting vs. normally protective, accepting mother; rejecting vs. accepting father.

Adolescence to adulthood: lack of heterosexuality vs. heterosexual behavior; insidious gradual onset of psychosis without pertinent stress vs. sudden onset of psychosis, occurring later, with stress present and pertinent; physical vs. verbal aggression; poor vs. good response to treatment; lengthy stay vs. short course in hospital.

Adulthood: massive vs. minor paranoid trends; little vs. much capacity for alcohol; no manic-depressive component vs. presence of manic-depressive component; failure under adversity vs. success despite adversity; discrepancy vs. harmony between ability and achievement; awareness vs. no sensation of change in self; presence vs. absence of somatic delusions; clash vs. harmony between culture and environment; and loss vs. retention of decency (nudity, public masturbation, etc.).

Kantor et al. found that ratings on these variables reliably separated schizophrenic patients into process and reactive groups and that patients rated *process* more frequently than those classed *reactive* displayed psychotic features on independent Rorschach testing. Kantor and Winder (1959) have subsequently stressed the developmental aspects of the process-reactive dichotomies constituting their scale. Arguing that the earlier in an individual's life he is subject to stress, the more damaging are the consequences for his later development, Kantor and Winder posit that differences between process and reactive schizophrenia can be effectively quantified in terms of the developmental level to which a schizophrenic person has regressed.

There is considerable support for such a developmental distinction between acute and chronic schizophrenia. Becker (1956), for example, who agrees with Kantor and Winder that process and reactive conditions represent different maturational levels of personality organization, reports high correlations (around .60) between scores on the Elgin Prognostic Scale and Rorschach Developmental Level (see Chap. 12). Fine and Zimet (1959) and Zimet and Fine (1959), assessing the Rorschach Developmental Level of the original Kantor et al. subjects, found a significant difference in maturational level between the process and reactive groups. Fifty-seven percent of the process schizophrenics' responses but only 20% of those given by the reactive schizophrenics fell in genetically immature scoring categories.

In Becker's (1959) view, however, process and reactive schizophrenia are not distinct, dichotomous syndromes but rather points on a developmental continuum. The process point, according to Becker, is characterized by relatively primitive levels of organization, lack of personality differentiation, narrow and mild interests, rigidity, lack of internal direction, and inability to establish normal heterosexual relations and independence; the reactive point is identified by a higher level of personality differentiation, a prepsychotic personality more nearly normal, more varied and intense interests, more apparent personal motivation and direction, and a greater tolerance for emotional stress preceding breakdown.

Wynne and Singer (1963b), utilizing the Werner principles of differentiation and integration (see p. 222), also present a developmental scheme for classifying schizophrenic persons. In their view a continuum from "amorphousness," which represents global, predominantly undifferentiated functioning, to "fragmentation," which indicates failure of hierarchic integration after attainment of some degree of clear differentiation, provides the most useful basis for classifying both the quality and severity of schizophrenic thought disorder.

CASE HISTORY CRITERIA

Closely related to the Kantor et al. criteria is a case-history scale developed by Phillips (1953) to predict the response of schizophrenic patients receiving shock therapy. Although the Phillips scale includes sections on premorbid history, possible precipitating factors, and current manifestations of disturbance, the section on premorbid history has been found to correlate almost perfectly with the full scale and by itself to predict validly the outcome of schizophrenia (Query & Query, 1964; Seidel, 1960).

The premorbid history section of the Phillips scale consists primarily of items dealing with personal adjustment, many of which overlap the developmental variables listed on page 237. In practice, therefore, there is little difference between the Kantor et al. and the Phillips criteria for differentiating subcategories of schizophrenia. On the other hand, the good premorbid and poor premorbid distinction stressed by Phillips figures prominently in the clinical evaluation of acute and chronic schizophrenia. [3]

AUTONOMIC NERVOUS SYSTEM CRITERIA

The possibility of differentiating between chronic and acute schizophrenic disturbance by measuring autonomic nervous system functioning originated with studies by Funkenstein, Greenblatt, and Solomon

---

[3] Garmezy and Rodnick (1959) review a number of studies employing the Phillips scale to classify acute and chronic schizophrenia.

(1950) and Meadow and Funkenstein (1952). These investigators observed a significant relationship between response to treatment and autonomic reaction to cholinergic stimulation in schizophrenic patients. Specifically, they found changes in systolic blood pressure subsequent to intramuscular injection of mecholyl to vary widely across schizophrenic subjects: those schizophrenics who displayed a marked fall in blood pressure following mecholyl injection tended to be highly anxious, to perform relatively well on tests of concept formation, and to respond favorably to treatment; schizophrenics with only minimal autonomic response, on the other hand, performed poorly on cognitive tests and had a guarded prognosis for recovery.

Meadow, Greenblatt, Funkenstein, and Solomon (1953) subsequently inferred from these findings two "polar types" of schizophrenia, one characterized by personality disorganization and poor prognosis and identified by minimal autonomic nervous system reactivity, and the other characterized by relatively good personality organization and prognosis and identified by marked autonomic nervous system reactivity. Following confirmation of these relationships between autonomic reactivity and prognosis in schizophrenia by Hirchstein (1955) and Geocaris and Kooiker (1956), King (1958) proposed integrating this phenomenon with rating-scale distinctions between acute and chronic schizophrenia. Classifying a sample of schizophrenic subjects as process or reactive according to the Kantor et al. criteria, King demonstrated that the reactive group displayed greater autonomic reactivity following mecholyl injection than the process group.

Zuckerman and Gross (1959), however, replicated King's study with directly opposite results: their process schizophrenics *exceeded* their reactive schizophrenics in blood-pressure drop following mecholyl injection. In the absence of further definitive research, the relationship between autonomic nervous system functioning and developmental criteria for classifying subcategories of schizophrenia remains unclear.

CEREBRAL PATHOLOGY AND THE ACUTE-CHRONIC DISTINCTION

Also relevant to the classification of acute and chronic schizophrenia are current views reminiscent of Bleuler's early distinction between morbidity of affective experience and morbidity of brain process (see p. 235). Brackbill (1956), for example, reviewing studies of brain functioning in schizophrenia, hypothesizes that those schizophrenic persons who display chronic and severe thought disturbance have some kind of structural brain damage, whereas those whose disturbance is acute and of relatively short duration are free from central nervous system pathology.

Brackbill and Fine (1956) investigated this hypothesis by comparing the incidence of Piotrowski's (1937, 1940) Rorschach indices for brain damage among 28 organic patients and 36 process and 24 reactive schizophrenic patients identified by the Kantor et al. criteria. They confirmed their prediction that process schizophrenics would perform more similarly to brain-damaged than to reactive schizophrenic subjects: 34% of the organics and 36% of the process schizophrenics but only 8% of the reactive schizophrenics demonstrated five or more of the 10 Piotrowski signs.

In view of the specific nature of the Piotrowski signs, however, the Brackbill and Fine data cannot be taken as conclusive evidence of brain damage in chronic schizophrenia. As previous discussions indicate, six of the 10 signs identify schizophrenic impairments of ego functions as well as cerebral pathology: perseveration (see pp. 35–38); automatic phrases (see p. 38); $F+\%$ below 70% (see pp. 109–110); $P\%$ below 25% (see pp. 117–118); M less than two (see pp. 158–159); and presence of $Cnam$ (see p. 190). Available evidence suggests that these Rorschach scores can derive from *either* functional disturbances of ego functioning associated with schizophrenia *or* basic perceptual dysfunctions associated with organic brain damage, and the fact that process schizophrenia and organicity share these phenomena does not necessarily demonstrate them to be genotypically similar.

Furthermore, a phenotypic similarity between brain-damaged and chronic schizophrenic subjects has not been unequivocally supported by experimental data. Some investigators have found chronic schizophrenics to make errors more similar to those of brain-damaged than acute schizophrenic subjects on learning and object-sorting tasks (Hall & Crookes, 1951; Tutko & Spence, 1962), but studies with two perceptual measures highly sensitive to organic impairment, the spiral aftereffect (SAET) and critical flicker frequency (CFF), have failed to affirm any relationship between brain damage and chronic schizophrenia. King (1962) reports no difference in CFF between normal and chronic schizophrenic subjects, and McDonough (1960) observed for both CFF and SAET that normal, process schizophrenic, and reactive schizophrenic subjects all earned similar scores and all differed significantly from brain-damaged subjects. From another point of view, Kety (1959) reviews the evidence concerning biochemical theories of schizophrenia and concludes that work in this area provides little support for dichotomizing schizophrenia into organic and functional categories.

Nevertheless, there remains considerable room for theory and research concerning the differential role of organic factors in schizophrenic disturbance. For example, whereas Costa and Vaughan (1962) and Vaughan and Costa (1962) point out that the psychodiagnosis of cerebral pathology rests as much on sensorimotor as on perceptual-cognitive measures, the comparative performance of acute and chronic schizophrenic subjects on such sensorimotor tests has not yet been carefully investigated. Furthermore, both Reitan (1962, pp. 425–426) and Meyer (1961, pp. 552–557), reviewing the literature on organic psychological deficit, stress that brain damage is not a unitary condition but rather comprises many diverse syndromes that have markedly heterogeneous patterns of psychological deficit.

Hence it may be that chronic schizophrenia, or perhaps all schizophrenic disturbance, is based on certain kinds of cerebral dysfunction that do not give rise to those patterns of perceptual-cognitive and sensorimotor deficit typically associated with brain damage. In other words, although it has been pointed out above that brain damage and chronic schizophenia may be phenotypically similar but genotypically different, it is equally reasonable to hypothesize that organic and schizophrenic conditions may be phenotypically different, though sharing certain common genotypic features.

Resolution of these issues must await further research in the behavioral sciences, but it is pertinent to note other recent contributions that stress the notion of a *continuum* rather than a *dichotomy* between acute and chronic schizophrenia. Belmont, Birch, Klein, and Pollack (1964), for example, present Rorschach data consistent with Brackbill's emphasis on organic dysfunction in process as opposed to reactive schizophrenia, but argue against viewing such differences as dichotomous. They compared the incidence in two groups of adult schizophrenic subjects of several Rorschach variables previously demonstrated by Birch and Belmont (1961) to identify brain damage. One schizophrenic group had a childhood history of marked behavior disorder and the other did not. The investigators found a greater frequency of the organic signs in the poor premorbid than among the good premorbid schizophrenics, but they also observed the good premorbid schizophenics to manifest these signs more often than normal controls.

Belmont et al. conclude from their data (a) that both organic and environmental features play a part in all schizophrenic disturbance, and (b) that chronicity is a function of the extent and kind rather than the mere presence of central nervous system pathology. Though they do not necessarily endorse Belmont et al.'s views concerning organic features, Herron (1962a) and Higgins (1964) similarly conclude from extensive reviews of the process-reactive literature that these labels are more accurately conceived as points along a continuum than as dichotomies.

DIFFERENTIAL PSYCHODIAGNOSIS OF ACUTE
AND CHRONIC SCHIZOPHRENIA

The various criteria employed to classify acute and chronic schizophrenia reveal a general consensus that chronic as opposed to acute schizophrenic persons become disturbed earlier and remain so longer, are more withdrawn and less responsive to environmental events, have a poorer history of social adjustment, and more prominently manifest identifying features of schizophrenia, that is, impaired ego functioning. These variables define the severity of a schizophrenic disturbance, and clinical and laboratory data as summarized below confirm the utility of the *severity of disturbance* dimension for distinguishing between acute and chronic schizophrenia. These data also identify a second dimension, *acceptance of disturbance,* that contributes independently of severity of disturbance to the differential diagnosis of acute-chronic status. The assessment of the acceptance and severity dimensions and their relationship to schizophrenia are outlined in the following sections.

SEVERITY OF DISTURBANCE

It has generally been demonstrated that chronic schizophrenics, as distinguished either by duration of disturbance or by one of the criteria reviewed in the previous pages, exhibit to a greater degree than acute schizophrenics most of the identifying features of schizophrenic ego impairment outlined in Chapters 4–12 of this book. With certain specific exceptions to be mentioned shortly, chronic schizophrenics deviate more from normal persons than do acute schizophrenics in their abilities to maintain cognitive focus, reason logically, form concepts at appropriate levels of abstraction, perceive realistically, employ adaptive defenses, utilize constitutionally determined potentials, and integrate their personality functioning.

Such differences between acute and chronic schizophrenic subjects in severity of impairment have been demonstrated in laboratory studies of concept formation, association, perception, and psychomotor skill. Regarding concept formation, for example, Chapman and Taylor (1957), Herron (1962b) and Sturm (1965) found chronic schizophrenic subjects to be more impaired than acute schizophrenics in assigning objects to appropriate conceptual categories; similar differential impairments between chronic and acute schizophrenics are reported by Herron (1962b) and Lewinsohn and Riggs (1962) on proverbs tests, and by Lewinsohn (1963) on the Shipley-Hartford conceptual scales.

Impaired abstraction correlates highly with disturbed association in schizophrenic subjects, according to a study by Meadow, Greenblatt, and Solomon (1953), and Judson and Katahn (1964) found that process schizophrenics, as identified by the Elgin scale, performed significantly less well than reactive schizophrenics on tests of association. Higgins, Mednick, and Philip (1965), administering word-association tests to hospitalized schizophrenic patients, observed a significant positive relationship between degree of associative disorder and chronicity of disturbance as inferred from length of hospitalization.

In other studies, Weckowicz (1960) noted greater perceptual impairments among chronic than acute schizophrenics as measured in an embedded figures test, and H. E. King (1954) found chronic schizophrenics significantly more impaired in psychomotor functioning than acute schizophrenics (see p. 211). On the basis of a thorough review of the experimental work in this area, Winder (1960, p. 239) concludes, "What research has been done suggests that acute and chronic groups differ from each other in psychomotor performance, perception, thinking, learning, intellectual efficiency, and physiological functioning, as well as in adequacy of premorbid adjustment."

These laboratory data imply that the more extremely a patient manifests psychodiagnostic indices of identifying features of schizophrenic disturbance, the more severe is his disorder and the more likely he is to be chronically rather than acutely disturbed. The major exceptions to this general principle are certain indices relating to variability and scatter of performance, which, for reasons to be explained in the discussion of *acceptance of disturbance,* tend to be more prominent in acute than in chronic schizophrenia.

Unfortunately, few clinical studies have compared in detail the psychodiagnostic test performance of acute and chronic schizophrenic subjects, and not all of the test variables described in Part Two of this book have been investigated for their capacity to discriminate efficiently between acute and chronic schizophrenia. On the other hand, such detailed psychodiagnostic comparisons are drawn in the early monograph by Skalweit (1934) and the two volumes by Rapaport, Gill, and Schafer (1945, 1946). These contributions, together with relevant data reported by Beck, Feshbach, and Legg (1962), Belmont, Birch, Klein, and Pollack (1964), Brackbill and Fine (1956), Cohen, Senf, and Huston (1956), Herron (1962b), Senf, Huston, and Cohen (1955), and Zimet and Fine (1959), suggest that the following test scores, grouped by related ego function, discriminate significantly between acute and chronic schizophrenic subjects:

COGNITIVE FOCUSING. Regarding impaired focus on essential stimuli, chronic are more likely than acute schizophrenics to overemphasize W and Dd locations and receive a correspondingly low D% on the Rorschach.

REASONING. Regarding overgeneralized and circumstantial thinking, chronic more frequently than acute schizophrenics give Confabulation and Contamination responses on the Rorschach.

CONCEPT FORMATION. Regarding uneven concept formation, chronic perform less well than acute schizophrenics on WAIS Similarities.

REALITY TESTING. Regarding perceptual inaccuracy, chronic are lower than acute schizophrenics in Rorschach $F+\%$ and $R+\%$; regarding poor judgment, chronic give fewer P on the Rorschach and receive lower scores on WAIS Comprehension than acute schizophrenics.

RELATION TO REALITY. Regarding indefinite ego boundaries, chronic more frequently than acute schizophrenics give amorphous and vague Rorschach responses.

OBJECT RELATIONS. Regarding deficient empatic capacity, chronic are lower than acute schizophrenics in frequency of M and H percepts on the Rorschach.

DEFENSIVE OPERATIONS. Regarding inadequate resources for integrating affective experience, chronic more frequently than acute schizophrenics give poorly controlled Rorschach color responses, especially C and Cnam.

AUTONOMOUS FUNCTIONS. Regarding impaired psychomotor speed, chronic are slower than acute schizophrenics on WAIS Digit Symbol.

SYNTHETIC FUNCTIONS. Regarding maladaptive organizational acts, chronic more frequently than acute schizophrenics give $W-$ and less frequently give $W+$ and $D+$ responses on the Rorschach.

There are as yet no established normative data for acute and chronic schizophrenic subjects that can be translated into quantitative differential diagnostic criteria for these and other test indices. The clinician must therefore judge subjectively whether the severity of disturbance present in a record is more consonant with an acute or a chronic schizophrenic disorder; in doing so he can follow the general principle that the more extremely a patient deviates from normal performance, the more likely he is to be chronically disturbed.

ACCEPTANCE OF DISTURBANCE

Acute and chronic schizophrenic persons differ in the degree to which they have accepted their psychological disorder, independently of the severity of their disturbance as defined by extent of ego impairment. The acutely disturbed schizophrenic is typically confused and distressed by his inability to think effectively, relate to reality, and communicate with people. He is anxious about his mental state, threatened by situations that expose his abnormality, and actively engaged in efforts to resolve his condition.

Chronic schizophrenia, in contrast, is characterized by considerable tolerance for what is an ingrained psychological disturbance. The chronic schizophrenic may be anxious about external circumstances, real or imagined, but he displays little concern about those features of his behavior that identify him as schizophrenic, and he rarely recognizes that any of his difficulties derive from aberrations within his own personality. In short, schizophrenic phenomena are seen as relatively *ego-alien* by the acute schizophrenic and as relatively *ego-syntonic* by the chronic schizophrenic.

Mednick (1958) formulates these differences between acute and chronic schizophrenic persons in awareness of and concern about their disturbance in terms of a learning-theory approach to schizophrenia. Mednick attributes the onset of schizophrenia to intolerable anxiety, and he conceives schizophrenic symptoms as efforts to eliminate anxiety-provoking thoughts from awareness. The acute schizophrenic, according to Mednick, tends to remain painfully cognizant of the disorganizing change in his behavior, and his anxiety is compounded by the thought, "I am going crazy."

With persistence of disturbance, Mednick continues, two phenomena mediate the transition from acute distress to chronic blandness. First, because schizophrenic symptoms have the drive-reducing feature of eliminating anxiety, they are continually self-reinforcing and over time acquire increasing secondary reward value. Second, the schizophrenic who remains disturbed is likely to develop additional techniques to eliminate whatever anxieties derive from his fear of being disturbed. As these two processes accelerate, Mednick concludes, the schizophrenic person becomes increasingly estranged from the external world and progressively less likely to manifest either awareness of his disturbance or disorganizing anxiety.

Feinberg and Garman (1961), finding that acute schizophrenic subjects made significantly more implausible errors than chronic schizophrenic subjects on the Raven Progressive Matrices, similarly suggest that "acutely ill patients have not yet learned to function in the presence of the mental changes induced by the disease." In other words, they add, the overt distress of the early schizophrenic pervades his functioning in all areas and impairs his performance even on such an impersonal, objective task as the Raven, whereas the chronic schizophrenic has sufficiently adapted to and focalized his disturbance so that he can function adequately on tasks not directly related to the inroads of his disorder. This hypothesis is consistent with another aspect of Mednick's learning-theory formulation: that the relatively high anxiety level of the acute schizophrenic promotes a greater degree of indiscriminate overgeneralization than that induced by the lesser anxiety of the chronic schizophrenic.

The association of disorganizing anxiety and inefficient task performance primarily with acute rather than chronic schizophrenia has been confirmed in many studies of response variability. With few exceptions acute schizophrenics are observed to perform less consistently than chronic schizophrenics from one moment to the next. Among experiments illustrating greater variability among acute than chronic schizophrenic subjects are studies by Reisman (1960) of card sorting, by Zlotowski and Bakan (1963) on a guessing task, and by Armitage, Brown, and Denny (1964) on a lever-pulling task.

An ego-alien view of symptoms and relatively variable performance thus identify nonacceptance of disturbance and help to discriminate acute from chronic schizophrenia. Both of these variables can be readily translated into psychodiagnostic test language.

Indices of Ego-Alien and Ego-Syntonic Attitudes. The degree to which a subject's attitude is ego-alien or ego-syntonic is usually revealed by his approach to the testing situation. As Waite (1961) points out, the more a schizophrenic subject gives his deviant responses with a sense of detachment and the less he is inclined to reflect on and criticize them even when encouraged to do so, (a) the less aware he is of his pathology, (b) the less he is struggling to alter his current status, and (c) the more likely he is to be chronically rather than acutely disturbed. Correspondingly, the greater the subject's concern about his disturbed responses and the more marked his appropriate critical judgment of them, the more likely he is to have an ego-alien, acute disturbance.

The following two descriptions quoted from test reports illustrate these different types of behavior. The first patient was a 26-year-old, acutely disturbed man being evaluated in an outpatient clinic, whose protocols revealed poor reality testing, limited interpersonal skill, and inadequate defensive resources. He was described as follows:

Mr. S was extremely anxious during the examination. In general his speech, though comprehensible, was pressured and punctuated with nervous laughter, and he expressly complained of being fearful in many situations, including the present one. On the tests he frequently decried his inability to perform adequately on tasks even before he had attempted them, and on several such occasions gentle persuasion aided him to persevere successfully where he had already given up. Gestures of dismay—literally throwing up his hands, rubbing his chin, and perplexedly scratching his forehead—were frequent and contributed further to the picture of a frightened, inadequate man who expected to fail and be punished for his ineptitude.

It should be stressed that this description is not *specific* to acute schizophrenic disturbance, nor does an ego-alien view of symptoms bear any unique relationship to schizophrenia. On the contrary, anxious or agitated subjects with many different types of ego-alien disturbance are likely to behave as this man did in the testing situation. However, given other data to suggest schizophrenic disturbance, such overt distress in response to examination becomes significant for discriminating acute from chronic schizophrenia.

The second, contrasting description is from a report on a 44-year-old woman examined during a brief hospitalization, whose test performance revealed gross thinking disturbances and who was considered chronically, though not incapacitatingly, disturbed:

Mrs. B's prominent thought disturbance appears chronic in nature but not particularly debilitating at this time. She performed comfortably in the test situation, and her difficulties in thinking seem to be ingrained features of her behavior that she can accept without becoming anxious about. Furthermore, her disturbance is not pervasive, and she was able to maintain a fairly high level of perceptual accuracy and to organize her experience in a fairly integrated manner. She was additionally able to maintain a fairly appropriate relationship with me, and the disturbed thinking evident on the tests was not clearly apparent in my extratest conversation with her."

Certain types of specific comments, whether given spontaneously or in response to inquiry about deviant responses, also facilitate the ego-alien/ego-syntonic distinction. Self-critical reflections like the following suggest nonacceptance of disturbance and a corresponding acute condition: "I guess it doesn't make much sense, but that's the idea that came to me"; "No, I just can't seem to get a clearer impression of it than that, I don't know what's wrong with me"; "I have the feeling that's not a very good answer, but I'm not sure what to do about it."

Comments of this type, however, need to be distinguished from the self-deprecatory recriminations of depressed subjects, who frequently disparage their efforts and bemoan their inadequacies. Aiding this distinction is the fact that the hypercritical comments of depressed persons are typically unselective and appended indiscriminately to good and poor responses alike. The expressed concern of the acutely disturbed schizophrenic, on the other hand, is most frequently addressed to those deviant responses that reveal his personality disorder. Negative critical comments accompanying good responses, then, are associated more with depression than with any form of schizophrenia, whereas anxiety and accurate criticism associated with deviant responses, particularly in the absence of deprecatory comments about good responses, are likely to differentiate acute from chronic schizophrenia.

In contrast, the following types of matter-of-fact, unconcerned, and unenlightening responses to inquiry about deviant responses are apt to characterize chronic rather than acute schizophrenic subjects: "Yes, that's right"; "It just looks that way"; "As far as I'm concerned that's the correct answer"; and even "Of course I've seen things like that, and I'm surprised to hear you haven't." Such responses clearly bear the ego-syntonic stamp of chronic disturbance.

Indices of Variable Performance. Turning from ego-syntonicity to variability, a number of specific WAIS and Rorschach indices associated with inconsistency and scatter have been demonstrated to differentiate acute from chronic schizophrenic subjects. Rapaport et al. (1945, pp. 302–303) report that acute schizophrenic subjects, as a consequence of their turmoil, confusion, and inefficiency, perform less well on most Wechsler subtests relative to their Vocabulary scores than chronic schizophrenic subjects, who are more bland, have "settled down with their psychosis," and "approach the tests in a more casual, nonanxious manner."

Thus, despite the fact that Rapaport et al.'s chronic schizophrenics were particularly low in Comprehension compared to the acute group, in general the more extreme the intertest scatter of their schizophrenic subjects, the more likely they were to be acutely rather than chronically disturbed. It is reasonable to expect that intratest scatter will similarly be more marked in acute than chronic schizophrenia, but such a possibility has not yet been investigated.

In view of these data concerning variable performance, intertest and intratest scatter are two specific exceptions to the general principle stated on page 244 that the more extreme manifestations of psychodiagnostic indicators of schizophrenia are associated with chronic rather than acute disturbance. A third exception to this principle are those Rorschach scores that identify heightened variability, particularly those related to variable response quality as defined on page 58. Specifically, sudden shifts in the perceptual and organizational qualities of responses, as from $W++$ to $W-$ percepts, point to acute rather than chronic status.

In a similar vein Sherman (1955) relates the dilation-constriction index of Rorschach variability to the distinction between acute and chronic schizophrenia. Sherman notes that schizophrenic subjects giving dilated records, that is, records with relatively high R, relatively low $F\%$, and a variety of determinants, are usually observed to be experiencing considerable conflict and distress. According to Sherman, Rorschach dilation in schizophrenia represents the schizophrenic subject's struggle with his circumstances and quest for a resolution of his condition; constriction, on the other hand, defined by relatively low R and relatively high $F\%$, is likely to represent distinterest in engaging the external world and lack of concern with altering modes of responding to it. Hence, Sherman concludes, dilation in schizophrenic subjects suggests acute status and constriction, chronic disorder.

It should be noted, however, that the implications of constriction for chronicity in schizophrenic subjects are most significant in records where guardedness is not in evidence. Suspicious or acutely anxious subjects not infrequently give constricted Rorschach records as a means of concealing from the examiner the nature of their thoughts and feelings. Such guardedness is usually accompanied by a high anxiety level during the testing, obvious efforts to withhold responses, and explicit statements of reluctance to cooperate. It is primarily in the absence of such features, that is, when a constricted record is given by a schizophrenic subject who appears comfortable and relaxed and is cooperating well with the test procedures, that chronic rather than acute disturbance is suggested.

THE ACUTE-CHRONIC DISTINCTION
AND PROGNOSIS IN SCHIZOPHRENIA

Before proceeding to case material illustrating the differential psychodiagnosis of acute and chronic schizophrenia, it is important to consider briefly the extent to which these categories of schizophrenic disturbance have been implicit in prognostic conceptualizations. Psychodiagnostic studies of prognosis in schizophrenia have consisted primarily of retrospective test comparisons between improving and nonimproving schizophrenic patients, and the variables suggested by these studies to have negative prognostic significance pertain with few exceptions to the severity of disturbance and acceptance of disturbance parameters of chronic schizophrenia delineated in pages 243–250.

In studies by Rees and Jones (1951) and Lipton, Tamerin, and Lotesta (1951), for example, insulin and electroshock-treated schizophrenics who improved were found more likely than unimproved subjects to have demonstrated before treatment such Rorschach factors as ample productivity with few rejections, the presence of good M responses, $F+\%$ greater than 70, and other scores similarly suggestive of mild rather than severe disturbance. In other investigations by Grauer (1953) and Winslow and Rapersand (1964) schizophrenics who responded favorably to electroconvulsive treatments had before the treatments displayed more prominently than nonresponding subjects Rorschach indices of anxiety, inner conflict, and inconsistency, all of which are associated with nonacceptance of disturbance.

It should be noted that, inasmuch as these Rorschach prognostic scores correspond essentially to an acute-chronic distinction, their relationship to favorable response in insulin and electroconvulsive therapy is not surprising. These somatic treatments have been widely observed to yield favorable outcomes primarily in patients who are acutely rather than chronically disturbed (Horwitz, 1959, p. 1496; Kalinowsky, 1959, p. 1512).

Piotrowski, who contributed several early Rorschach studies of response to insulin treatment (see Piotrowski & Lewis, 1952), has more recently cross validated a long-term prognostic index with quite different criteria: follow-up studies of the thought processes, psychosocial adjustment, and self-attitudes of schizophrenic patients (Piotrowski & Bricklin, 1958; Piotrowski & Bricklin, 1961). This index, however, like those in the outcome studies mentioned above, is heavily loaded with features that define severity of disturbance, including absence of M and H, perseveration, vague and inaccurate perception, indeterminate form, absurd explanations, and a queer response style.

Studies utilizing hospital discharge rather than rated improvement or follow-up evaluations as the prognostic criterion have also yielded test signs directly related to the acute-chronic distinction. Stotsky (1952), comparing continuously hospitalized and discharged schizophrenic patients, found the groups to have differed significantly on Rorschachs administered in the initial period of their hospitalization in $F+\%$, $R+\%$, P, M, CF, C, H, and presence of Po responses, with all differences indicating more severe disturbance among the group that remained continuously hospitalized. Seidel (1960) also contrasted discharged with nondischarged schizophrenic patients and found the former at the time of their admission to have earned significantly higher "ego strength" scores than the latter on the Rorschach Prognostic Rating Scale (Klopfer, Kirkner, Wisham, & Baker, 1951).

Drawbacks of Equating Prognosis with Chronicity. The fact that most psychodiagnostic studies have in essence vested prognostic judgments in acute-chronic differentiations has two important drawbacks for clinical practice. First, these studies cannot be expected to provide any basis for estimating the future course of the chronically disturbed schizophrenic. As reviewed by Windle (1952) and Fulkerson and Barry (1961), this gap has been painfully brought home in frequent inconclusive efforts to cross-validate many prognostic test indices. Both reviewers point out that this apparent impasse may derive from the researchers' failure to recognize that *different* prognostic contingencies may obtain for different subgroups of schizophrenic patients. Fulkerson and Barry suggest that effective prognostic use of tests may in fact require applying one set of scores to a patient to determine which of another set should be employed prognostically.

Zubin and Windle (1954) specifically propose that chronicity of disturbance is itself an important independent variable in evaluating prognostic data. In their paper and in a companion study by Windle and Hamwi (1953) the authors report interesting confirmatory data for this hypothesis. Administering a visual-motor test to chronic and early schizophrenic patients, they found that whereas among the early group there was a positive relationship between scores and likelihood of discharge, the reverse was true for the chronic group; among the chronic patients the mean attainment of those remaining in the hospital was significantly *higher* than among those who were out of the hospital at the time of follow-up one year after the testing.

Assessing these findings, Zubin, Windle, and Hamwi (1953) hypothesize that efficient test performance by early schizophrenics is prognostically favorable because it reflects minimal disturbance, but that effectual performance by chronically disturbed psychotics is prognostically *unfavorable* because any chronic patient who, despite his disturbance, can think with sufficient clarity to perform well on a cognitive test is so entrenched in his psychosis as to be hopeless. This intriguing possibility, though not yet fully validated, has important implications for the prognostic interpretation of test data and clearly demonstrates the pitfalls of confusing prognosis with the acute-chronic distinction.

The second drawback of imposing acute-chronic considerations on prognostic judgments is that these considerations may have little practical relevance in the individual case. Prognostic judgments cannot be formulated independently of the question, "Prognosis for what?" In prognosticating the likelihood of a patient's recovering from or continuing to suffer ego impairments, the labels *acute* and *chronic* are by definition prognostic judgments; in practice, however, occasions arise when answering this question is less important than estimating the patient's needs for extended hospitalization or his capacity for eventually resuming his life activities, and these outcomes may be relatively unrelated to whether a patient's ego functions are acutely or chronically disrupted.

For example, an acutely disturbed schizophrenic person who has experienced a sudden and calamitous breakdown may enter the hospital extremely distressed and floridly psychotic and require several months' care before he is ready for discharge. On the other hand, a chronically schizophrenic person who has been maintaining a reasonable degree of compensation may be hospitalized following a mild exacerbation of his disorder and within a few weeks be able to restitute his defenses sufficiently to allow him to return to his customary activities, even though his diagnosis remains *chronic schizophrenia*. Furthermore, prognosis for social restitution often hinges on such environmental factors as the demands made on a patient by the nature of his work and family responsibilities, the availability to him of supportive figures, and the possibilities for arranging adequate outpatient care, and none of these is necessarily related to whether the patient's schizophrenic condition is chronic or acute.

A great many studies have demonstrated the prognostic significance for psychologically disturbed persons of such nonpersonality variables as those mentioned above. Hollingshead and Redlich (1954), for example, found a strong relationship between lower socioeconomic class membership and a schizophrenic patient's likelihood of being and remaining hospitalized. Chapman, Day, and Burstein (1961) observed that marital status predicts hospital discharge for schizophrenics as well as the Elgin Prognostic Rating Scale does. Orr, Anderson, Martin, and Philpot (1955) found the discharge rate among a large group of state hospital patients to be influenced more by their length of hospitalization, education, and possession of immediate family than by their age, diagnosis, or nature of treatment received. Investigations by Freeman and Simmons (1963) and Cheek (1965) have confirmed that family tolerance for deviance is a critical factor in the posthospital adjustment of the schizophrenic person. Finally, attesting that chronic schizophrenia is far from equivalent to need for hospitalization, a recent report indicates that of all schizophrenic patients receiving psychotherapy in outpatient clinics in the United States, 32% carry a diagnosis of "chronic undifferentiated" (*Outpatient Psychiatric Clinics*, 1963).

These observations make clear that the distinction between acute and chronic schizophrenia, though important for treatment planning, may by itself have minimal predictive power for the future course of a patient's social rehabilitation. Chapman et al. (1961) suggest in this regard that, because the characteristics of adjustment probably vary in different subcultural groups, a given test score may have different prognostic significance for schizophrenic patients from varying social backgrounds. These complexities of prognosticating schizophrenic disturbance are by no means unique to the psychodiagnostic test battery, but apply generally to the question of prognosis in schizophrenia. As summarized by Huston and Pepernik (1958), numerous researchers have endeavored to predict outcomes in schizophrenia from hereditary, social, historical, and physiological test factors as well as from personality style and clinical signs and symptoms, yet early and recent reviews indicate that most such efforts have yielded poor results (Romano & Ebaugh, 1938; Vaillant, 1962, 1964a).

Although Vaillant (1962, 1964a) notes that previous research has failed to document any method for predicting the long-term clinical course of schizophrenics on admission, he nevertheless extracts from the literature, and to some extent validates, a prognostic scale based on seven characteristics previously observed to correlate fairly consistently with remission in schizophrenia. These seven prognostically favorable indices are acute onset, obvious precipitating factors, concomitant depression, nonschizoid premorbid adjustment, confusion, concern with death, and a positive heredity for affective psychosis. Vaillant concludes from his work that effective prognosis requires emphasis on longitudinal factors rather than on current clinical phenomena. Accordingly, accurate prognostic judgments are unlikely to derive merely from attention to a patient's personality structure as revealed on tests, but rather necessitate an integration of his personality structure with relevant aspects of his past history, current social situation, and expected future circumstances.

INTRODUCTION TO CASE STUDIES

The remainder of this chapter and sections of Chapters 14–18 are case studies illustrating differential psychodiagnosis of schizophrenia in the individual case. For previously stated reasons (see Preface) these protocols were chosen from case files of actually referred patients whose diagnostic status was sufficiently uncertain to warrant formal psychological examination. Hence the test material that follows is not representative of schizophrenic patients in general, but rather typifies schizophrenic patients concerning whom the psychologist is called on to venture differential diagnositic opinions.

Because the cases are selected to represent diagnostically uncertain patients referred for psychological consultation, they do not always fully and unequivocally demonstrate the identifying features of schizophrenic disturbance outlined in Part Two of this book. In some, where differential diagnostic impressions necessarily hinge on subtle psychodiagnostic indices, the experienced reader may lean toward formulations different from those proposed. Uncertainty and alternative inter-pretations are not to be decried in presentations of this kind, however, for they constitute the modal activity in clinical psychodiagnosis. The "easy" cases, those where the disturbances are marked and distinctive, are readily diagnosed on interview and rarely referred for psychologi-cal testing. Instead, the psychologist must routinely wrestle with the "difficult" case, in which equivocal data defy distillation and an ap-proximate diagnosis is a significant achievement.

The following case material illustrates the application of ego-psycho-logical concepts to differential diagnosis in schizophrenia, and the test data are discussed primarily with reference to parameters of schizo-phrenic disturbance. Although an adequate psychological examination should assess personality strengths as well as weaknesses and delineate areas of conflict, attitudes toward significant figures, and hierarchy of coping behaviors as well as nosology, these considerations are sacri-ficed here to an intensive focus on schizophrenic impairments of per-sonality functioning. These impairments are analyzed in the language of the ego-disturbance model of schizophrenia elaborated in Chapters 4–12. These concepts and the relationship of various test indices to them are not further defined or cross-referenced in what follows, but the reader can review them as necessary in relevant sections of the earlier chapters.

Included with each case are pertinent background and follow-up data that identify the patient's clinical status and primary concerns. Because these patients' test data were working records rather than protocols procured for teaching or research purposes, they are not complete. All the cases have full Rorschach records, but for most there is only a partial WAIS and for some a full set of drawings was not or could not be obtained. The following procedures are followed in pre-senting the WAIS, DAP, and Rorschach data:

WECHSLER ADULT INTELLIGENCE SCALE

For Information and Picture Completion correct items are indicated with a + and incorrect answers are quoted; for Arithmetic, Block De-sign, Picture Arrangement, and Object Assembly the time required and the credits given are indicated for each item; for Digit Span and Digit Symbol the total score is reported; and for Comprehension, Simi-larities, and Vocabulary all responses are quoted with the credit given them. The abbreviation "dk" is used for "don't know" replies. Inquiries appear in italics, and the notation (?) represents such routine requests for further information as "Could you explain further?" and "How do you mean?"

Following each subtest and the report of scale scores, aspects of the patient's response that identify schizophrenic disturbance are reviewed. At the end of each record is a summary discussion of the salient features of the WAIS protocol that suggest personality disorder and facilitate differential diagnosis in schizophrenia.

DRAW-A-PERSON

The figure drawings are presented with each case and discussed in the order in which the subject rendered them. As in the WAIS, the discussion is focused on those aspects of the test performance that identify differentiating features of schizophrenic disturbance.

RORSCHACH

The spontaneous associations and those parts of the inquiry that establish determinant choice or are otherwise relevant to differential diagnosis in schizophrenia are indicated for each card. The inquiry necessary to determine location choice is not routinely reported, and in some instances no inquiry of any kind was made. The examiner's comments appear in italics, and the notation ($?$) represents such routine questions as "What suggested it to you?" and "How do you mean?" The reaction time is noted for each card and the position in which the card was held is indicated for responses given in other than the standard $(\wedge)$ position. Location choices are described in terms of the standard $(\wedge)$ position regardless of the actual position employed; thus, a response given to the center red detail appearing at the bottom of Card II viewed in the $(\wedge)$ position is labeled "bottom center detail" or "bottom red" even for responses in the $(>)$, $(<)$, or $(\vee)$ position.

Location, determinant, content, and qualitative scores accompany each response. The scoring combines certain features of the several systems reviewed in Part Two that the author has found useful in his work. Location is scored according to Beck (see Chap. 4) with the addition of the Developmental Level scoring as outlined by Friedman (see Chaps. 8 & 12). The various locations are designated verbally rather than by Beck's number system, to spare the reader from having to refer to an accompanying chart; for the most part, however, the descriptions employed are those listed by Beck et al. (1961, pp. 25–30). Determinants and Populars are scored according to Klopfer, form level partially according to Beck and partially according to Piotrowski (see Chap. 7), and qualitative features according to the categories derived in Chapter 5 from the Rapaport and Holt systems. Barrier and Penetration scores as defined by Fisher and Cleveland (see Chap. 8) are also noted, with total scores determined from the standard 25 responses. Summary scores are presented at the end of each record, with $F+\%$ and $R+\%$ determined as recommended in Chapter 7 and *high W%* and *high D%*

computed following Friedman (see Chap. 12). Scoring decisions are not elaborated in the case presentations, and questions concerning scoring procedures should be referred to the various relevant sections of Part Two.

Following the Rorschach protocols, the implications of the data for impaired ego functioning and differential diagnosis in schizophrenia are discussed. In the service of parsimony, the responses are not analyzed in uniform detail: at some points considerable attention is paid to subtle nuances of the data; at other points, particularly where diagnostically relevant data abound, some pertinent aspects of the responses do not receive comment. Similarly, not all of the complexities and qualifications delineated in Part Two as influencing the interpretation of test indices are further specified in examining the data, nor is a detailed sequence analysis of the Rorschach records attempted. To include such extensive discussions in the following case studies would be unwieldy and would dilute the intended emphasis on psychodiagnostic variables relating to schizophrenic disturbance.

CASE STUDIES

The following four cases illustrate the differential diagnosis of acute and chronic schizophrenia and encompass a broad spectrum of both severity of disturbance and degree of incapacitation. Of the two acutely schizophrenic patients presented first, one is a young woman who was seen only for evaluation in an outpatient clinic and with no particularly adverse consequences declined an offer of continued clinic care, while the other is a man who required several weeks' hospitalization before he could fully resume his work and family responsibilities. The second two cases are quite dissimilar instances of chronic schizophrenia. One of these patients did not respond to intensive care in the psychiatric services of a general hospital and was ultimately certified to a state hospital. The other, a college student who sought help in connection with serious academic and interpersonal difficulties, was able to remain ambulatory and improve his adjustment despite persistent thought disorder and social inadequacy.

CASE 1

Case 1 is a 21-year-old single young woman who was examined in an outpatient clinic following a mild suicidal gesture. Although her gesture had been precipitated by an argument with her boyfriend and was reportedly intended to "get even" with him, she had been undergoing personality change for at least one month before the argument. During this time she had been observed to become increasingly short-tempered, arguing constantly with her friends and flying abruptly into combative and destructive rages. She had quit her job because she felt "nervous" and that her supervisor was too critical of her, and she had begun to hear nonexistent musical sounds and a voice telling her, "Everything is all right."

In the interview situation the patient spoke in a well-organized and coherent manner and related appropriately to the interviewer. However, she was noted to be restless and hyperactive, to smile and laugh to herself for no apparent reason, and at times to stare vacantly into space. These observations, together with her apparent hallucinatory experiences and her report that two of her sisters had been briefly hospitalized for what sounded like acute schizophrenic episodes, suggested that she might be suffering a schizophrenic disturbance and prompted referral for psychological examination.

WECHSLER ADULT INTELLIGENCE SCALE

Information

FLAG: +. BALL: +. MONTHS: +. THERMOMETER: Used to graph temperature. RUBBER: +. PRESIDENTS: Truman, Dewey, Eisenhower, Roosevelt. LONGFELLOW: He was a president, I think. WEEKS: +. PANAMA: +. BRAZIL: +. HEIGHT: +. ITALY: +. CLOTHES: +. WASHINGTON: It was last week. (?) The 23rd of February. HAMLET: +. VATICAN: dk. PARIS: This is just a guess—2,000 miles. EGYPT: Below Europe. (*Continent?*) I just know it's below the Mediterranean. YEAST: +. POPULATION: 71 million. SENATORS: dk. GENESIS: +. TEMPERATURE: dk. ILIAD: dk. BLOOD VESSELS: I only know of veins and arteries. KORAN: dk. FAUST: dk. RAW SCORE: 14.

The patient's responses to Information contain four subtle indications of impaired ability to maintain a consistently relevant focus of attention. First, she employs peculiar langauge in stating that a thermometer is used "to *graph* temperature." Second, she perseverates from PRESIDENTS TO LONGFELLOW by suggesting he "was a *president*." Third, her answer that Egypt is "below Europe" is an overly concrete association; she is apparently thinking of Egypt's position on a map rather than the relevant and more abstract concept of continental affiliation. Finally, she demonstrates scatter by answering GENESIS correctly after failing several much easier, factorially related items, including PRESIDENTS, VATICAN, and POPULATION. These lapses in ability to shift focus, exercise consistent cognitive efficiency, and direct association along relevant lines and in terms of conventional language point to disordered thinking.

Comprehension

ENVELOPE: Mail it (2). BAD COMPANY: It makes them seem bad (1). MOVIES: Tell the manager (2). TAXES: Because the money is needed to run the government (2). IRON: I wouldn't. (?) If I knew it was hot, I wouldn't strike. (?) It could mean that when you're mad you strike, because you have quick reflexes (0). CHILD LABOR: So children won't have to work under a certain age (0). FOREST: Start a fire—no, that's not right; get in an open space and wait for someone to come (0). DEAF: Because you can't learn to talk without hearing other people talk (2). CITY LAND: A lot of business and stuff makes the value of the land grow higher (1). MARRIAGE: Because it's against the law. (?) It's only sensible. (?) I don't believe in common-law marriage; if you love someone you should marry him; otherwise you could be living with anyone (0). BROOKS: No matter how little a person is they can put up a big squawk (0). SWALLOW: dk. RAW SCORE: 14.

As on Information, her responses though not grossly deviant demonstrate features of thought disorder. Her response to IRON is both dissociated and overly concrete: her first two comments, in which she insists "I wouldn't strike," are oblique to the question, "What does this saying mean?", and when she does attempt to explain the proverb, she interprets *strike* literally, associating being *hot* with being *angry*. She also evinces mild dissociation on MARRIAGE, where she loses focus on the question and expounds her peripherally related attitudes toward love and common-law marriage. In addition to her dissociation and impaired abstraction, her generally inconsistent performance suggests that intruding elements interfere with her cognitive efficiency. Noteworthy in this regard is her good response to DEAF following three consecutive zero-credit answers on less difficult items.

Also of interest is her uncertain and inadequate answer on FOREST. She correctly criticizes her initial response—"No, that's not right"—which indicates that consistent with acute status she has retained some capacity to take distance from her responses. Her eventual failure on this item, however, inasmuch as it is within her intellectual capacity, suggests some impairment of judgment.

Similarities

ORANGE: Fruits (2). COAT: Clothing (2). AXE: Tools (2). DOG: Animals (2). NORTH: Locations (1). EYE: Senses (2). AIR: Something that's needed (1). TABLE: Used together for eating (1). EGG: Grow into something (1). POEM: Man-made (1). WOOD: Alcohol comes from wood (0). PRAISE: It depends on the person; some may like it and some may dislike it (0). FLY: dk. (0). RAW SCORE: 15.

There is little evidence of impaired cognition in these responses. One exception to her otherwise adequate performance, however, is her answer on PRAISE, which is oblique to the request for a similarity and constitutes a subtle instance of dissociation.

Picture Completion

KNOB: +. TAIL: +. NOSE: +. HANDLES: +. DIAMOND: +. WATER: A hand to push it over. NOSE PIECE: +. PEG: +. OAR LOCK: A man. BASE THREAD: dk. STARS: It should be colored in. DOG TRACKS: Other foot. FLORIDA: The states aren't outlined. STACKS: Sails. LEG: +. ARM IMAGE: +. FINGER: dk. SHADOW: Is it that the man's hands are dirty? STIRRUP: Rider. SNOW: Doorknobs. EYEBROW: Nothing. RAW SCORE: 9.

These responses present additional evidence of the patient's difficulty in focusing her attention consistently on the relevant aspects of her experience. Although many of her errors are common to normal and patient groups, her answers on STARS, SHADOW, and SNOW are highly idiosyncratic and grossly irrelevant. She also continues here the scattered thinking noted on Information and Comprehension, succeeding on LEG and ARM IMAGE after failure on the easier, factorially related OAR LOCK and DOG TRACKS.

Block Design

ITEM 1: 5" (4). ITEM 2: 12" (4). ITEM 3: 13" (4). ITEM 4: 15" (4). ITEM 5: 24" (4). ITEM 6: 55" (4). ITEM 7: 105" (4). ITEM 8: 160" (0). RAW SCORE: 28.

On ITEM 8, after an initial unsuccessful effort, the patient became visibly upset, brushed the blocks aside, and bemoaned the fact that she could not function adequately. Following considerable encouragement, she resumed work and finally achieved the correct solution, but the remaining designs were omitted because of her poignant distress at this point. Her display of anxiety about instead of resignation to incapacity on this subtest is consistent with acute rather than chronic disorder.

Scale Scores

Information: 9. Comprehension: 8. Similarities: 11. Picture Completion: 7. Block Design: 9.

Discussion. This WAIS protocol is not grossly deviant, but it contains sufficient evidence of disordered thinking to suggest schizophrenia. The patient's perseveration on Information and her unusual errors on Picture Completion identify difficulty in attending flexibly to the appropriate stimulus elements of a situation; her three instances of subtle dissociation, her one instance of peculiar language, and her scatter on Information, Comprehension, and Picture Completion demonstrate the interference of irrelevant, intruding elements with her ability to maintain an efficient cognitive focus; and finally, her two instances of overly concrete association suggest she has difficulty thinking at appropriate levels of abstraction.

Evidence of disturbance is the exception rather than the rule in her protocol, however, which suggests that her disturbance is relatively mild and hence probably acute rather than chronic in nature. Acute status is further suggested by her overt test anxiety on Block Design and her variable, scattered performance on three of the subtests.

DRAW-A-PERSON

This woman's figure drawings are reproduced in Figures 13 and 14. The male figure, which she drew first, contains evidence of both disturbed reasoning and impaired ego boundaries. Illogical reasoning is demonstrated in her failure to eliminate the line of the body that shows through the arm, which results in an incongruous combination of visible with normally obscured details, that is, *transparency*. Indefinite ego boundaries are indicated in the broken contours of her drawing. The lines of the legs blur and disappear at the bottom of the figure, and close inspection reveals that many parts of the body contour are unconnected.

The patient's female drawing is less conclusive for schizophrenia. She begins rather well, closing up the lines of the figure and adequately differentiating the sex of her drawing by the ample use of hair. Subsequently, however, she absolutely refused to draw the rest of the figure and could not be cajoled into doing so. Significantly, she was markedly anxious and distressed at this point, and her refusal did not appear related to anger, disinterest, negativism, or a conviction that the drawing was complete as it stood. Hence, though her drawing omits major body parts, it is likely that these omissions derived more from concerns about her body and perhaps about feminine sexuality than from a gross disturbance of body imagery. Her overt anxiety during this task and her apparent awareness that her drawing was inadequate are further clues to an acute rather than chronic disturbance.

RORSCHACH

Card I 3″

1. (*Wm,S F+ Ad*) A wolf. (?) Just the way it looks. (*Parts?*) I see the ears, the eyes, the nose, and the mouth; it's just the head.
2. (*W—,S F— (Hd)*) ∨ A monster. (?) It's just the head part again, and I can see the eyes, nose, mouth, and ears.
3. (*D—,S F— Hd Peculiar*) ∨ Looks like two men [side details].

Figure 13

Figure 14

(?) There's one on each side, one head that is; here is the eye [white space], the nose [middle side projection], and the chin [bottom side projection]. (*Kind of men?*) They look ugly and disformed, with big chins.

4. (*Dm F+ (Hd)*) The other way it looks like two more men [side details]. (?) I can see two heads with big noses [upper side projection], little mouth, and indented chins. (*How look?*) Funny, like cartoon figures. (*Cartoon?*) It's their big noses, like cartoon figures on TV, and the way the hair stands up [top side detail].

5. (*Dd F+ A Autistic Logic*) I see bugs. (?) All these doodads [tiny specks on edge of blot] remind me of bugs. (?) Because they're small and there are a lot of them, so they're bugs.

Card II 4″

6. (*W—,S F— (Hd) Perseveration, Po*) It's a monster again. (?) I can see his mouth [center white], eyes [upper white], and nose [top center detail]; these [upper red] are electrical doodads on his head, and these [bottom red projections] are his fangs. (*Fangs?*) Because his mouth is right here and they're near his mouth.

7. (*Dm F+ A*) Two rabbits here [top red details].

8. (*Dd F— H Absurd Dd, Autistic Logic*) Two men [side "ear" detail]. (?) They look like villains. (*Villains?*) They just look mean; they've got the shape to be mean. (?) You can just tell, that's all.

9. (*Dd F+ A*) ∨ Two birds here [bottom corner detail], roosters I guess.

10. (*D— F— A*) A crab [bottom red detail].

11. (*D+ FM+ A P*) Two dogs. (?) It looks like two puppies playing together.

Card III 2″

12. (*Dm F+ H,Cg P-tendency Fluid*) Two men, and I can see their whole body; maybe they're women . . . no, they're men . . . no, they're women, because they have heels on. (*Women?*) Because they have heels and they got—uh—a chest like, so they're women. (*Describe further?*) I guess they remind me of chickens.

13. (*Dd F+ Ad*) ∨ Two eagles [torso portion of popular human figure]. (?) Actually it's just the head, the beak, and the neck.

14. (*D—,S F—,FC′ Hd*) I see a man in here [bottom center detail]. (?) It's just the head, with the eyes here [white space] and some protection here. (*Protection?*) The black reminds me of the black stuff people put under their eyes to prevent glare from the sun.

15. (*Dm F+ A P*) A butterfly.

16. (*Dm Fm+ H,Cg Fabulized*) > Two dead people, floating in

the water. (*Floating?*) Their clothes are shabby and just dangling, and they look pathetic; they're dead and they're a mess.

Card IV 3″

17. (*W— F— Ad Penetration*) Some sort of an animal, a dog maybe. (?) I can see the ears and face and long nose; the face looks all pushed in, like it had been hit or something.

18. (*Dm F+ Ad*) Two dogs, the heads again [toe part of "boot" detail].

19. (*Dm F+ Ad*) Two birds [upper side details].

20. (*D— F— Ad*) This [top detail] looks like part of a fish's head.

Card V 2″

21. (*Dm M+,C′F H Barrier, Fabulized, Autistic Logic*) Two people hiding [side details]. (?) They're hiding in the shadows; I can tell it's two people because I can see the head, eyes, nose, elbow, and legs; they're nice looking. (*Nice looking?*) Because they're young. (*Shadows?*) Because it's dark, and you can't see everything.

22. (*Wm F+ A P*) ∨ A butterfly.

23. (*Dm F+ Hd*) Two more heads [side details], and they have beards ["leg" detail], so they must be men.

24. (*S F+ Hd*) Two women [outline of white space along bottom of side detail]. (?) I see the heads of two women, with the nose here and the mouth here; it's just the shape of it.

Card VI 3″

25. (*Dm F+ Ad*) A cat, just the head of it [top detail].

26. (*Wm F+ Aobj P-tendency*) ∨ An animal skin. (?) Just the shape of it; the head is off, but here are the arms, the tail, and the legs.

27. (*W— F— A*) > A fish.

28. (*Dm F+ Hd*) Heads again, I don't know why I'm always seeing heads. (?) Right here [bottom portion of side detail] I can see a nose, a chin, and a forehead; it almost reminds me of the way George Washington's head looks, because of the way the nose is shaped [laughs].

Card VII 1″

29. (*Dm F+ Hd,Cg*) Here I see two Indians, two girls [upper side details]. (?) I can't see their legs, it's just the upper part; they have a nice shape, with dresses or skirts on.

30. (*Dm M+ Hd Fabulized*) ∨ This way it looks like two girls with no heads on, running [same as #29]. (*Running?*) They must be afraid to die, but they don't want to admit it, so they're running.

31. (*Dm F+ A*) ∨ Some kind of bug, with big wings [bottom detail].

Card VIII 3″

32. (*Wv CF At Penetration*) It's guts—the insides of a person. (?) That's the way it looks, mainly because of the colors. (*Specify?*) Nothing definite, really; it might be the intestines here [bottom detail], with the lungs in the blue, and maybe the stomach; but it's all mixed up and nothing is in the right place.

33. (*Dm F+ A P-tendency*) Two mountain lions on the sides, or maybe a bobcat, but with no tail.

Card IX 5″

34. (*Dm FC+ Hd Peculiar, Penetration*) Two dead men [side green details]. (*Dead?*) They're green with death. (?) They're decaying, it looks like. (*Parts?*) It's just the head, with the eyes, nose, and mouth here and something like a mole sticking out of the chin.

35. (*D— F— A*) Seahorses [orange details].

36. (*Dm F+ Hd Fabulized*) > Two more men or young boys [green details]. (*Young?*) It's their heads, and the way the nose looks and the hair is sticking up suggests they're young, and they look mischiefy [laughs].

Card X 4″

37. (*Dm F+ A*) I see a lot of different bugs and worms. (*Bugs?*) These [outer gray details] remind me of grasshoppers.

38. (*Dm F+ (H)*) And there are monsters here [top gray details]. (?) I can see the face and the body and doodads coming from their head; they're just different and strange looking.

39. (*Dm F+ A P-tendency*) And these are the worms down here [bottom green]. (?) It's their long and skinny form.

40. (*Dm M± (H) Fabulized, Fluid*) These things [side blue] are attacking somebody, and they look angry. (*Look?*) They look like they're going to kill somebody. (*What might they be?*) It looks like a wolf's head, but it's just something different . . . there are so many legs . . . it could be a man's head too . . . or a wolf's. (?) It just looks real mean.

41. (*Dd F— Hd*) ∨ A weird face. (?) The eyes are here [inner yellow], the mouth here ["wishbone" detail], and the nose here [inner blue]. (*Weird?*) I don't know, it just has a funny look to it.

Scores

R	41	M	3+1	H	5	F+%	64%
W	8(19%)	FM	1+1	(H)	2	R+%	68%
D	27(60%)	m	1	Hd	9	P	3+4
Dd+S	6(15%)	F	34	(Hd)	3	High W%	38%

		C'	0+2	A	14	High D%	81%
Fabulized	5	FC	1	Ad	6		
Autistic Logic	3	CF	1	Aobj	1	Barrier	1
Peculiar	2			At	1	Penetration	3
Fluid	2			Cg	0+3		
Perseveration	1						
Absurd Dd	1						
Position	1						

Discussion. The patient's Rorschach protocol contains evidence of several identifying characteristics of schizophrenia, although, as on her WAIS, the amount of disturbance present appears neither pervasive nor incapacitating. Most conclusive for schizophrenia is the thought disorder suggested by her impaired capacities to maintain effective cognitive focus and reason logically about relationships between events.

With regard to cognitive focusing, her elevated *Dd%* of 15 and her perseveration on response #6 reveal a tendency to attend to nonessential aspects of a situation and resist shifting attention as the situation changes. Additionally, her peculiar use of language in #3 (*disformed* men) and #34 (men *green with death*) and her deviant tempo (more responses to Card IX than to Card VIII) demonstrate the interference with her cognitive functioning of intruding elements that impair her abilities to communicate clearly and think consistently.

Disturbed reasoning appears in her many examples of overgeneralized and circumstantial thinking. Her overgeneralizing is partly attested by her five Fabulized responses, although in none of these does she evince any markedly unjustified elaboration or specification of her percepts. On the other hand, her absurd *Dd* in #8, where she assigns the highly specific personality attribute of *villainy* to the two tiny details she sees as men, clearly illustrates a propensity to infer highly overdrawn conclusions from minimal evidence.

Indicating circumstantially are her three instances of subtly autistic logic (#'s 5, 8, & 12) and her *Po* response on #6. On #5 she states that details are "bugs" because "they're small and there are a lot of them"; on #8 she justifies her perception of "villains" by stating "they've got the shape to be mean"; and on #21 she describes the people as nice looking "because they're young." Each of these explanations expresses predicate logic (e.g., "bugs are small and these dots small, so these dots are bugs") rather than conventional reasoning. Similarly, in her *Po* response on #6 her only justification for seeing one detail as "fangs" is its proximity to an area previously identified as a mouth.

This woman's Rorschach also demonstrates mild impairments in relation to reality, defensive resources, and ego-synthetic operations. Her perception is sufficiently inaccurate ($F+\%$ of 64 and $R+\%$ of 68) to suggest poor reality testing, and her occasionally fluid response style substantiates the figure drawing evidence of indefinite ego boundaries. Her use of color (1 FC, 1 CF, and 0 C', which indicates color stress) identifies inconsistent resources for integrating affective experience. Finally, although her *high D%* is within normal limits, her quite low *high W%* of 38 further confirms her difficulty in effectively organizing and integrating her personality functioning.

As noted above, however, these indices of impairment are neither gross nor pervasive in this patient's record, and she complementarily displays many areas of relatively intact functioning. Her repressive defenses are operating sufficiently well to prevent bizarre content from appearing in her record, and her retained *high D%* of 81 indicates she can function without perceptual or reasoning disturbance when she is able to restrict her attention to common, simple stimuli that do not require integrative activity. These features of her Rorschach performance point to a relatively mild condition consistent with an acute rather than chronic disturbance.

Summary. This young woman's test battery reveals tendencies toward dissociated, perseverated, overgeneralized, circumstantial, and scattered thinking. These features of thought disorder, together with her poor reality testing, indefinite ego boundaries, and inconsistent defensive resources, identify her as having a schizophrenic disturbance. However, her impairment is both relatively mild and ego-alien in nature: examples of deviant response are infrequent and subtle rather than pervasive or gross in her protocols, and she at times expresses concern about the adequacy of her performance. These aspects of her behavior are consistent with an acute rather than chronic condition.

CASE 2

This patient is a 34-year-old factory worker and father of six children who had no history of psychological disturbance before his current breakdown. His developmental years were unremarkable except for his close and extremely dependent relationship with his mother, and he described his childhood and adolescence as "happy" times. He left school at age 16 to work, married at age 19, and for the next 15 years experienced no major concern other than whether he could provide adequately for his growing family. Six weeks before his psychological examination he had suffered a mild respiratory illness, and his demanding, dependent reaction to his malaise had apparently exceeded his wife's tolerance. At the conclusion of a bitter argument she had told him to "grow up and be a father" or "get out."

Following this incident the patient decompensated rapidly and did not return to work after regaining his physical health. He remained at home, alternating between episodes of irritability and short-temperedness and periods of apathy and withdrawal. Concerned by his increasing inability to function, his wife eventually contacted their family doctor, who arranged immediate psychiatric hospitalization. On admission the patient's forlorn, lethargic, and tearful demeanor suggested a depressive reaction, but even after his depression lifted considerably during the first week of his hospital stay he continued to demonstrate unusual ideas about his health, a concrete style of thinking, and primitive, maladaptive defensive behaviors. Psychological examination was consequently requested to evaluate possible schizophrenic disturbance.

The patient remained in the hospital approximately six weeks, during which time he was noted to be fairly well aware of the extent to which he had decompensated. Following the alleviation of his initial acute depression he began to think positively about returning to his work and family, and a program of home visits and family interviews was instituted. After six weeks' care he was sufficiently recovered to leave the hospital and resume what had been his characteristic behavior patterns before his respiratory illness.

WECHSLER ADULT INTELLIGENCE SCALE

Information

RUBBER: +. PRESIDENTS: +. LONGFELLOW: + WEEKS: +. PANAMA: Westerly. BRAZIL: +. HEIGHT: +. ITALY: dk. (?) I just can't think . . . maybe France . . . no, that's not right. CLOTHES: They're heavier. WASHINGTON: February 12. HAMLET: dk. VATICAN: +. PARIS: No idea. EGYPT: Arabia. YEAST: (long silence) I dk, maybe something in the yeast. POPULATION: dk. RAW SCORE: 11.

These responses are not grossly deviant, but they nevertheless contain some evidence of impaired cognitive focusing in the form of blocking and dissociation. Suggesting blocking are his complaint of being unable to think on ITALY and his long silence on YEAST, during which he appeared to be struggling effortfully to focus his attention on the question. Such behavior could relate to depressive lethargy as well as to schizophrenic blocking, but other aspects of his test performance do not suggest a significant depressive component. Concerning dissociation, his ideas that France is the capital of Italy and Arabia the location of Egypt are loosely connected associations apparently based on unwarranted assumptions of identity between geographic terms.

Also noteworthy here is his appropriate criticism of his response to ITALY, inasmuch as a disturbed person's ability and willingness to reflect on his thoughts in this way suggest an ego-alien stance and acute rather than chronic status.

Comprehension

ENVELOPE: Put it in the mail (2). BAD COMPANY: They're likely to turn bad themselves (2). MOVIES: Report it to the manager (2). TAXES: To support the government (2). IRON: Do it first. (?) If you hear there is going to be an attack on the United States, if the United States is ready, it should attack first and get in the first move (0). CHILD LABOR: To protect the people. (?) If you have a child and it gets hurt, you'd be responsible, and you could lose everything you have (0). FOREST: Try to back-track (0). DEAF: Because they can't hear nothing to begin with (1). CITY LAND: It's more valuable for industry (1). MARRIAGE: If it didn't, you'd be living with anyone you wanted to (0). BROOKS: There's not much water in them; I never heard that one though. SWALLOW: dk. RAW SCORE: 14.

Consistent with his Information performance, he displays subtle dissociation on this subtest. In responding to inquiry on IRON and CHILD LABOR he wanders from the point and elaborates such specific, loosely related associations as the readiness of the United States to anticipate attack and the financial liability of a parent for his child's misadventures. In other respects his Comprehension performance is fairly good, with the possible exception of his poor response to FOREST, "back-track," which suggests impaired judgment. However, the relative difficulty of this item for him minimizes the significance of his inadequate response to it.

Similarities

ORANGE: Fruits (2). COAT: Clothes (2). AXE: Tools (2). DOG: Animals (2). NORTH: Directions (2). EYE: Senses (2). AIR: Both have moisture in them (0). TABLE: Furniture (2). EGG: Food (0). POEM: They're both objects (0). WOOD: Both can be used to burn (1). PRAISE: dk. (0). FLY: They're both outside (0). RAW SCORE: 15.

The only impairment of note on this subtest is the patient's somewhat uneven concept formation. In stating that air and water "both have moisture," he employs a narrow and overly specific categorization, whereas his classing poem and statue as "objects" is an inappropriately broad and overly general abstraction. However, the implication for thought disorder of his variability on these two items is mitigated by their relative difficulty for him.

Vocabulary

BED: Furniture to sleep on (2). SHIP: Boat (2). PENNY: Coin (2). WINTER: A season (1). REPAIR: Fix (2). BREAKFAST: A meal (1). FABRIC: Clothing or cloth (2). SLICE: To cut, or a piece (1). ASSEMBLE: Put together (2). CONCEAL: Hold back (0). ENORMOUS: Large amount (1). HASTEN: dk (0). SENTENCE: Words (1). REGULATE: Adjust (2). COMMENCE: Proceed (2). PONDER: dk (0). CAVERN: Caves (2). DESIGNATE: (long pause) dk . . . can't think of it (0). DOMESTIC: Famous (0). CONSUME: Report (0). TERMINATE: dk (0). OBSTRUCT: Destroy (0). RAW SCORE: 24.

His hesitation and vain effort on DESIGNATE suggest a further instance of the blocking noted on Information; it is likely that his subsequent answers to DOMESTIC, CONSUME, and OBSTRUCT, all of which he gave very quickly, were random guesses he employed to avoid the distress of further blocking he anticipated were he to strive to focus his attention on an accurate definition. He also displays some scatter here by correctly defining the relatively difficult words COMMENCE and CAVERN after failing the easier CONCEAL and HASTEN.

Digit Symbol

RAW SCORE: 40.

The patient worked diligently but slowly on this task, and, consistent with the implications of his scatter within Vocabulary, he seemed to have difficulty keeping his attention focused on what he was doing. At the conclusion of the task he appeared quite distressed and concernedly asked, "Did I do all right on that one?" This overt anxiety about the adequacy of his performance, like his self-critical reflection on Information, suggests an ego-alien view of symptoms and is consistent with acute status.

Picture Completion

KNOB: +. TAIL: + NOSE: Ears. HANDLES: +. DIAMOND: +. WATER: No hand to hold it. NOSE PIECE: +. PEG: Bow. OAR LOCK: A man to row the boat. BASE THREAD: +. STARS: Pole. DOG TRACKS: Man's other foot. FLORIDA: dk. STACKS: +. LEG: +. ARM IMAGE: Her other arm; is that the right answer? FINGER: +. SHADOW: His hand. STIRRUP: dk. SNOW: Part of the fence is broken. EYEBROW: The other eye. RAW SCORE: 9.

On this subtest he clearly exhibits the propensity for scattered, inconsistent cognitive effort that was minimally in evidence on Vocabulary and Digit Symbol. He succeeds on BASE THREAD but fails three easier, factorially related items, OAR LOCK, PEG, and WATER; he answers LEG correctly but misses the easier, factorially related DOG TRACKS and OAR LOCK; and he passes FINGER after failing the factorially related WATER. With the exception of SHADOW and EYEBROW, however, his errors are common types and do not compound the impairment revealed by his inconsistent performance.

Also of note here is his expressed concern about his answer on ARM IMAGE ("Is that the right answer?"), which is a further clue to his distress about his mental state and the acute nature of his condition.

Block Design

ITEM 1: 10" (4). ITEM 2: 14" (4). ITEM 3: 9" (4). ITEM 4: 20" (4). ITEM 5: 27" (4). ITEM 6: 44" (4). ITEM 7: 60" (4). ITEM 8: 150" (0). ITEM 9: Gives up after making little progress. RAW SCORE: 28.

On this subtest the patient continued to express great concern about the adequacy of his performance. Particularly on items 8 and 9, where he was least successful, he produced a stream of such anxious comments as, "I can't seem to do this one; is that all right, Dr.?" and "Should I be able to figure all of these out?"

Picture Arrangement

NEST: 3" (4). HOUSE: 5" (4). HOLD UP: 9" (4). LOUIS: CATOIM, 39" (0). ENTER: 20" (4). FLIRT: JNATE, 20" (0). FISH: EFJHGI, 35" (0). TAXI: SALUEM, 20" (0). RAW SCORE: 16.

Scale Scores

Information: 8. Comprehension: 8. Similarities: 11. Vocabulary: 7. Digit Symbol: 7. Picture Completion: 7. Block Design: 9. Picture Arrangement: 7.

Noteworthy in this profile is the discrepancy of four scale scores between Similarities and the factorially related Vocabulary. This degree of scatter between subtests, like the patient's variability within Vocabulary and Picture Completion, attests his inconsistent cognitive functioning and identifies the variability more frequently associated with acute than with chronic conditions. Additionally, the fact that his Block Design performance exceeds both his Picture Completion and Picture Arrangement scores begins to suggest relative inefficiency in interpersonal as opposed to impersonal situations. However, these latter scale score differences are not sufficiently large to demonstrate significant interpersonal aversiveness.

Discussion. The major indications of schizophrenia in this patient's WAIS are his subtle manifestations of disordered thinking. His blocking on Information and Vocabulary, his dissociative tendencies on Comprehension, and his scatter within Picture Completion and between

Vocabulary and Similarities identify the interference of intruding elements with his ability to establish and maintain a relevant focus of attention. However, the subtlety and infrequency of deviant responses in his record indicate mild rather than severe disturbance, which, together with his variability and abundant concern about his inadequate responses, is consistent with acute status.

DRAW-A-PERSON

The patient apologetically but firmly refused to attempt figure drawings. He became sufficiently agitated in response to the examiner's urging that it appeared unwise to insist that he execute this task. Although such refusal has several possible causes, including negativism, fear of rendering an inferior product, and blocking, the source of the patient's particular reluctance was not clearly established with him.

RORSCHACH

Card I 5″

1. (*Dm F+ A Peculiar*) Looks like a crab [top half of center detail]. (*?*) These paws up here [top center] reminded me of it; it's just the paws and the head.
2. (*W++ M+ H,Cg*) Could be a bunch of people. (*How look?*) It looks like they're wearing Halloween costumes, like witches' costumes; there are two on the outside and one in the middle and it's like they're dancing together, with their hands up.
3. (*Wv F± Ge*) A map. (*?*) It's just a funny shape. (*Map of any particular place?*) No, it could be anywhere.
4. (*Wm FM+ A P*) A bat flying. Is this how you want me to do these?

Card II 9″

5. (*D+ FM+,C A,Bl P*) I see two bears fighting. (*Fighting?*) Because there's blood here [bottom red], down on their feet.
6. (*Wm F+ H,Cg Fluid*) I don't know what else it could be . . . (long pause) . . . maybe it could be two people too. (*?*) Well, their heads are up here [top details]. (*Describe?*) I don't know how to. (*How look?*) It looks like . . . like they have costumes on, like that; they could be two turkeys . . . maybe they're turkeys, with heads like turkeys . . . no, they're people. Is that right?

Card III 8″

7. (*Dm F+ H P*) This one could also be two people. (*?*) Just the way they look, and the way the chests are they're probably women.
8. (*W FM−,C A,Bl Fabulized Combination, Penetration*) Looks like two deers. (*?*) The two deers are in the black parts; they could be

fighting, with blood here which could have come off their head or chest; it's probably male deers, because that looks like the way they fight. (*Blood?*) It just seemed that they were fighting, and because of the color of it.

Card IV 14″

9. (*Wm FM+ A Fabulized*) Looks like a big ape. (?) I can see the back part, the head, and the feet, with the arms sticking out at the side. (*Big?*) It just looks like a big one, and the way the arms are spread out it looks like he's going to attack somebody.

10. (*W— FM— A Barrier*) Could be a turtle. (?) It looks like a turtle laying down and crawling; the head [bottom center detail] is shaped like a turtle, and the back is too.

11. (*DW F— A Confabulation*) A frog. (?) Because this part up here [top detail] looks like the head of a frog.

Card V 37″

12. (*Wm FM+ A*) I have no idea what it is . . . the only thing I could say is just two deers laying down. (?) There's one on each side, with their rear parts out here.

Card VI 27″

13. (*W— F— A Penetration*) Looks like a fish cut open. How am I doing on these? (?) You can see the bones inside, like a fish cut through the center with gills here [lower detail] and the tail up here [upper detail].

Card VII 30″

14. (*W+ F+,FM Obj,A*) I have no idea what that is . . . haven't the slightest idea . . . all I can think of is one of those old-fashioned pictures, with a hinge in it, that folds at the bottom. (*Picture of what?*) Two people or two animals; maybe two bunnies looking at one another; the hinge part is at the bottom, and it reminds me maybe of a Christmas card that opens up; it's open now and the bunnies are the scene.

Card VIII 23″

15. (*Dm F+ A P-tendency*) A couple of lions on the outside.

16. (*Dm F+ Bt*) This center part at the top looks like a tree. (?) The way the branches are shaped, like a Christmas tree.

17. (*Dv CF Obj*) Could be a light, the center and bottom part of a light. (?) The top part of the light is here [blue detail], with a chain beneath it, and down here [pink and orange] is the bottom part with maybe candles on the outside; it just gets brighter and brighter. (*Main thing that suggests it?*) The brightness of it, the coloring.

Card IX 29″

18. (*D— F— Hd*) The red parts look like the palms of hands, with the thumbs here [upper-inner portions of red detail]. Is that okay?

19. (*D— F— At Po, Penetration*) Could be a person's throat, too. (?) The passageway is through here [center detail], and this [center portion of bottom red] could be part of the stomach, and all this green part the mouth. (*Stomach and mouth?*) I just thought of it because those parts are next to the throat part.

Card X 8″

20. (*Dm F+ A P*) First, I see two spiders.

21. (*Dm FM+ A Penetration*) Then there are two mice. [see #26 below]

22. (*Dm FM+ A Autistic Logic*) These are two birds in the center blue parts. (?) Because they're hanging on; the red could be tree bark, so it would be birds hanging on. (*Birds because they're hanging on?*) Yes, isn't that okay?

23. (*D— F— A Barrier*) Two snails [bottom green].

24. (*Dd FC— At Autistic Logic*) Could be two hearts [orange portion of inner yellow details]. (?) Because of the red dots in the center of the yellow. (?) I was taught in school that a spot in the center was just like your heart being in the center.

25. (*Dm F+ Obj*) Reminds me of three bells in the center ["wishbone" detail].

26. (*D F— Bt Fabulized Combination*) Could be a stick or a tree [top center detail]. (?) It looks like the mice [see #21 above] are chewing on this stick or tree. (*Look most like?*) A tree, with the mice chewing on it.

Scores

R	26	M	1	H	3	F+%	57%
W	11(42%)	FM	8+1	Hd	1	R+%	62%
D	14(54%)	F	15	A	14+1	P	4+1
Dd+S	1(4%)	FC	1	Obj	3		
		CF	1	Bt	2	High W%	54%
Fabulized		C	0+2	At	2	High D%	64%
Combination	2			Ge	1		
Autistic Logic	2			Cg	0+2	Barrier	2
Position	1			Bl	0+2	Penetration	4
Confabulation	1						
Fabulized	1						
Peculiar	1						
Fluid	1						

Discussion. This patient's Rorschach reveals multiple impairments of ego functioning, the most prominent of which are his disturbed reasoning and poor reality testing. His proclivity for illogical reasoning is indicated by his several examples of circumstantial, combinative, and overgeneral thinking. Illustrating circumstantiality are his autistic logic in responses #22 (birds *because they are hanging*) and #24 (heart *because it is in the center*) and his *Po* response in #19, where his combination of the "throat," "stomach," and "mouth" details on the basis of their juxtaposition grossly violates anatomical size and position relationships.

Demonstrating inappropriate combinative thinking are his one improbable (#8) and one impossible (#21) Fabulized Combinations. Response #8 is a loose and strained connection between the non-adjacent "deer" and "blood" details, and in #21 he maintains the mice are chewing on a "tree," even though the tree detail is smaller than those he sees as mice. Finally attesting reasoning disturbance is his Confabulation on #11, where he overgeneralizes from one portion of the blot that reminded him of a frog's head to a perceptually inaccurate impression of the entire blot as a frog.

This man's poor reality testing is disclosed (a) by his $F+\%$ of 57% and $R+\%$ of 62%, both of which are well below normal limits of perceptual accuracy; and (b) by his barely adequate number of Populars (four with one additional), which, especially in view of his failure to note the easy P on Card V, reflects difficulty in sharing conventional frames of reference. Primarily as a consequence of his frequent inaccurately perceived and illogically reasoned responses, his *high W%* (54%) and *high D%* (64%) also fall below normal expectancy and indicate deficient capacity to integrate experience effectively.

Supplementing these indications of disordered thinking and impaired reality testing is evidence of ineffective cognitive focusing and inconsistent defensive resources. Regarding cognitive focusing, the patient's Rorschach does not as clearly as his WAIS reflect inability to maintain an appropriate focus of attention, but, as on the WAIS, he exhibits occasional blocking. Significant for blocking are his long delay on #6, which is preceded and followed by explicit statements of difficulty persevering with the task ("I don't know how to"), and some of his long reaction times.

Particularly helpful in discriminating his schizophrenic blocking from depressive lethargy or poor cooperation is his 37" delay on Card V, one of the easiest cards to which to respond. Such difficulty on Card V, in the context of fairly good over-all responsivity (26 R in this case, with some variety of content and determinants) and frequent expressions of concern about doing well on the tests, is more consistent with blocking than with either depression or negativism. Finally, in connection with defensive resources, the patent's color use (1 FC, 1 CF, 0 C, indicating color stress) identifies a lack of consistent resources for integrating affective experience.

It is interesting to note that various indications of ego impairment are more marked in this man's Rorschach protocol than in that of the previous patient. His greater extent of disturbance explains in part why he required hospitalization, whereas the previous young woman was able to maintain an ambulatory adjustment. Even though he is relatively severely disturbed in comparison to Case 1, however, his concern about the adequacy of his responses, as evident in such questions as "How am I doing?" and "Is that right?" reveals an awareness of and struggle against the inroads of schizophrenic disturbance and points to acute rather than chronic disorder.

Summary. This patient's WAIS and Rorschach reveal blocking, scattered cognition, poor reality testing, inconsistent defensive resources, and a proclivity for circumstantial, combinative, and overgeneral thinking. The extent of these ego impairments in his protocols is sufficient to identify schizophrenia and to reflect his need for hospital care. On the other hand, the marked variability of his performance and his frequent expressions of concern about the adequacy of his responses suggest that his disturbance is acute rather than chronic in nature.

CASE 3

This patient is a 37-year-old widower and sporadically employed semiskilled laborer who was admitted to the hospital with paralyzing anxiety about a nonexistent rash on his penis. One of seven children in an economically marginal farm family, he had not completed high school until age 21 because of frequent family moves and a heavy burden of farming chores. During his developmental years he was noted to be shy and withdrawn, avoiding any heterosexual contacts and maintaining his only close relationship with a younger brother. He interrupted his last year in high school to enlist in the Navy, but was discharged within a few months because of "nervousness" and resumed his schooling.

Following graduation he worked briefly at various farming and laboring jobs. He married a woman several years older than himself, who reportedly dominated him in a maternal fashion and managed their household until her death one year before his hospital admission. For the few months preceding his admission he had been planning to marry another older woman he had met, and his fears of having a venereal disease with which he would infect his future wife became increasingly pronounced as the tentative date of this marriage approached.

On admission the patient's delusional preoccupation with his genitals and blatantly disorganized thinking left little doubt that he was seriously disturbed. However, he was reluctant to talk about himself, and only sparse background material became available during the initial period of his hospitalization. Psychological examination was consequently requested to clarify the possible contribution of schizophrenic, organic, and intellectual deficits to his condition. The test data revealed at least average intellectual capacity and no prominent features of organic brain damage. Because the relationship of the test data to differential diagnosis of cerebral pathology is not discussed in the following analysis, it is pertinent to state that other diagnostic procedures confirmed the psychologist's impression that gross organic pathology was not present.

The patient was tested during the first week of his hospital stay. His condition remained unchanged for the next few weeks, and a course of shock treatment was instituted. Failing to respond to 15 treatments, he continued to be highly disorganized and preoccupied with his delusional venereal disease. He was ultimately certified to a nearby state hospital for continued care.

WECHSLER ADULT INTELLIGENCE SCALE

Information

RUBBER: +. PRESIDENTS: Truman, Eisenhower, Roosevelt, and Goldwater. LONGFELLOW: +. WEEKS: +. PANAMA: +. BRAZIL: The southern tip of the continent of South America; so is Argentina, Peru, and Ecuador(+). HEIGHT: 5'9". ITALY: Venezuela. CLOTHES: They hold the heat; light-colored clothes are repellent of heat (+). WASHINGTON: +. HAMLET: Israel. VATICAN: A great Roman theater. PARIS: 1200 miles. EGYPT: Southern tip of Africa (+). YEAST: +. POPULATION: +. SENATORS: 48. GENESIS: +. TEMPERATURE: +. ILIAD: dk. BLOOD VESSELS: I don't know that, but in the skin there's epidermis and dermis. KORAN: dk. FAUST: dk. RAW SCORE: 16.

This Information performance is strikingly dissociated and perseverated. Perseveration appears first, in the patient's inability to shift his set from PANAMA to BRAZIL. After correctly describing the direction of travel between Chicago and Panama as "south," he states that Brazil is in the "southern" tip of South America. His continued preoccupation with *south* apparently leads him to offer another South American country, Venezuela, as the capital of Italy and incorrectly to locate Egypt in the "*southern* tip of Africa."

Related to dissociation is his considerable difficulty focusing his attention on what is essential and avoiding irrelevant and peripheral associations. On BRAZIL he extraneously lists several South American countries without being asked to do so; his suggesting "Venezuela" as the capital of Italy is not only perseverative but may also reflect an unwarranted assumption of identity between geographical terms; "Israel" as the author of Hamlet is a grossly irrelevant response that could derive only from a most devious and disconnected train of dissociation; finally, his description on BLOOD VESSELS of the layers of the skin is blatantly tangential and unrelated to the question at hand.

Two other noteworthy indications of disordered thinking in the patient's Information are his peculiar language usage on CLOTHES, where he describes light-colored clothing as "*repellent* of heat," and his marked scatter. He fails the easy PRESIDENTS item but succeeds on the factorially related and much more difficult POPULATION, GENESIS, and TEMPERATURE, and he passes EGYPT after failing the easier, factorially related HEIGHT, ITALY, and PARIS. Such pervasive proclivities for dissociated, perseverative, and scattered thinking demonstrate serious impairment of cognitive focusing capacities.

Comprehension

ENVELOPE: Turn it in to the post office or to an FBI agent (2). BAD COMPANY: It lowers their standards of living and their morals (1). MOVIES: Tell the usher or the movie director (2). TAXES: To help support the nation as a whole (2). IRON: Do it while it's hot; get your work done immediately and not wait until it cools off (1). CHILD LABOR: To protect the younger generation so they don't have to overwork (1). FOREST: By roads, different roads (0). DEAF: Because their equilibrium is gone, the sense of balance that controls their speech (0). CITY LAND: There's corporation taxes and you pay for the luxuries that you don't have in the country (1). MARRIAGE: To protect people, so there's no venereal disease, and to protect the welfare of the nation and their families (1). BROOKS: You can hear them better because they aren't stagnant and run more (0). SWALLOW: dk. RAW SCORE: 15.

Several of these answers combine correct with irrelevant elements and subtly confirm the dissociation noted on Information. He would deliver a lost envelope either to the post office or the FBI; he considers bad company adversely to affect standards of living as well as moral principles; and he adjudges city land costly not only because of its improvements but also as a result of corporation taxes. Additionally suggesting dissociation is his response on DEAF, where he appears to have answered in terms of the relationship between parts of the auditory apparatus and the balance sense ("because their equilibrium is gone").

Further evidence of his inability to direct his associations along conventional lines emerges in his somewhat peculiar and pretentious language on TAXES ("support the nation as a whole") and CHILD LABOR ("protect the younger generation") and in his perseverative tendency on MARRIAGE, where he earns partial credit for mentioning disease but appears to perseverate his previous ideas about protection from CHILD LABOR and about the nation's welfare from TAXES. Finally of note here is his inadequate response to FOREST, which points to impaired judgment.

Similarities

ORANGE: Fruits (2). COAT: Material, like clothing (2). AXE: Material used in lumbering (1). DOG: Animals (2). NORTH: Directions (2). EYE: Parts of the human body (1). AIR: Have to do with life; they're life-giving substances (2). TABLE: Made out of the same composition, made out of wood (0). EGG: Both are of food value (1). POEM: dk. (0). WOOD: Alcohol arrives from the same product as wood (0). PRAISE: They're not alike, as best I can see (0). FLY: Both of nature (1). RAW SCORE: 13.

Most notable here are additional instances of peculiar language usage. The phrases "made out of the same composition" on TABLE, "of food value" on EGG, and "arrives from the same product" on WOOD reflect some difficulty in formulating thoughts in conventional language. Additionally, his unusual description of axe and saw as "material," following his appropriate use of this word on COAT, constitutes another instance of perseveration and attests his inability to shift the focus of his attention to meet new situations adaptively.

Digit Symbol

RAW SCORE: 38.

The patient worked very unevenly on this subtest, and his manner of coding the digits suggested considerable preoccupation and limited ability to maintain focus on the task. He would code several numbers rapidly, then abruptly cease working and gaze fixedly at the page for several seconds, seemingly distracted, only to resume his efforts just as abruptly with a sudden burst of efficient coding.

Picture Completion

KNOB: +. TAIL: +. NOSE: Rest of her body. HANDLES: +. DIAMOND: +. WATER: Glass is only half full. NOSE PIECE: Part of his body. PEG:

Strings. OAR LOCK: +. BASE THREAD: The fixtures aren't all there. STARS: Pole. DOG TRACKS: dk. FLORIDA: The states. STACKS: There's no water. LEG: dk. ARM IMAGE: There's no lamp. FINGER: The guy doesn't have a shirt on. SHADOW: +. STIRRUP: +. SNOW: dk. EYEBROW: Her body isn't all there. RAW SCORE: 7.

The patient's performance on this subtest clearly demonstrates his previously noted incapacity to identify and attend consistently to the relevant and essential elements of his experience. His six uncommon errors (on NOSE, WATER, BASE THREAD, STACKS, ARM IMAGE, and FINGER) attest the idiosyncratic frames of reference with which he interprets situations, and his considerable scatter reveals inconsistent cognitive efficiency: he passes SHADOW after failing the easier, factorially related ARM IMAGE, LEG, and DOG TRACKS, and he succeeds on OAR LOCK after failing the easier, factorially related PEG and WATER.

Block Design

ITEM 1: 25" (4). ITEM 2: 45" (4). ITEM 3: 10" (4). ITEM 4: 12" (4). ITEM 5: 9" (4). ITEM 6: 37" (4). ITEM 7: 60" (4). ITEM 8: 90" (4). ITEM 9: 75" (5). ITEM 10: 140" (0). RAW SCORE: 37.

The patient's demeanor in executing Block Design contrasted markedly with his approach to the other subtests. On Block Design only did he put forth an efficient, organized, and consistent effort unmarred by digression, distractibility, or gross error. His strikingly adequate performance on this subtest suggests he is most comfortable in impersonal situations where he has neither to interact with another person nor attend to socially contextual matters. This implication of his behavior is consistent with interpersonal aversion.

Scale Scores

Information: 10. Comprehension: 9. Similarities: 10. Digit Symbol: 7. Picture Completion: 6. Block Design: 11.

Most striking in the patient's WAIS profile is his particularly low Picture Completion, which further confirms disordered thinking and relative ineptness in interpersonal situations. Specifically, the fact that his score on this subtest is well below his over-all level of performance attests impaired ability to focus his attention on the most relevant aspects of his experience; furthermore, the scatter of five scale scores between the factorially related Picture Completion and Block Design subtests is both an instance of scatter and further evidence of relatively efficient functioning on impersonal tasks and relatively disorganized performance in social contexts.

Discussion. This WAIS is notable for the striking evidence of disordered thinking apparent on all subtests except Block Design. The patient's frequent dissociative and perseverative excursions reveal considerable preoccupation and grossly impaired ability to attend consistently to the relevant aspects of his experience. Intrusions on his cognitive focusing are also apparent in the scatter of his performance, which is particularly extreme within the Information and Picture Completion subtests.

The extent of disordered thinking reflected in this record, in which almost every verbal response is marred by some irrelevance, peculiarity, or redundancy, indicates severe disturbance and suggests a chronic condition. Although the patient's variability is an exception to the expected picture in chronic disturbance, it would be difficult to reconcile the degree of his preoccupation and devastated cognition with an acute disorder. It is furthermore significant that at no point in his response to the WAIS did he express any of the critical judgment or ego-alien concern about test performance that marks the two previous cases of acute schizophrenia; rather, consistent with chronic status, he appears accustomed to and comfortable with what is an ingrained, ego-syntonic personality disturbance.

DRAW-A-PERSON

This patient's two figure drawings, reproduced in Figures 15 and 16, demonstrate gross distortion of body imagery, as manifest in omission of vital body parts that are relatively easy to draw and failure to indicate sexually differentiating characteristics. In neither drawing does the patient provide any designation of eyes, ears, shoulders, hands, or feet, and, although he identified the first figure he drew (Figure 15) as a woman, close inspection reveals little variation in sexually differentiating body contours between this figure and the male figure in Figure 16. In general these drawings are extremely primitive and, in a man of average intellectual capacity, point to severely impaired personality functioning.

Also of note is the heavy sketching in the crotch area of the female figure (Figure 15). To the extent that this dark coloring can be interpreted as representing pubic hair, it indicates both impaired reasoning, inasmuch as the hair is visible in what otherwise does not appear to be a nude figure, and inadequate repressive control of sexual ideation.

In executing these drawings the patient in no way intimated that he considered them other than perfectly accurate and acceptable productions. His blandness and lack of critical judgment on this test, like that he displayed on the WAIS, is, together with the primitive nature of his drawings, consistent with chronic rather than acute disturbance.

Figure 15

Figure 16

Card I 2″

1. (*W— F— A*) Looks like a spider. (?) Just the way it looks, with the legs.

2. (*D— F— Sex,At Peculiar*) Looks like an ovary [center detail]. (?) Just that it could be the womb of a woman.

Card II 2″

3. (*Dd F+ Sex,At Peculiar, Penetration*) That looks like a rectum [inner portion of bottom red detail]. (?) The way it opens up; it looks like the insides of a rectum of a human body.

Card III 5″

4. (*D— F— Sex,At Peculiar, Perseveration*) That looks like a woman's womb [bottom center detail].

5. (*D— F— Sex,At Peculiar*) It looks like a man's in a way, too [outer dark portions of bottom center detail]. (*How do you mean?*) It looks like where your two sacs are, like up in your scropia.

Card IV 8″

6. (*D— F— Sex,At Peculiar, Perseveration, Penetration*) Looks like a rectum of a person [bottom center detail]. (?) It looks like an opening.

Card V 2″

7. (*Wm F+ A P*) That one looks most like a bat.

Card VI 4″

8. (*Dm F+ A*) Looks sort of like a wasp up here [top detail].

9. (*D— F— Sex,At Peculiar, Perseveration*) Could be an oval of a woman [all of bottom detail] with the eggs coming down here [inner lighter details].

Card VII 5″

10. (*S F— Sex,At Peculiar, Perseveration*) That could be an oval of a woman (?) It just looks like an ovary.

11. (*Dm F+ Sex,At Penetration*) ⋁ A man's rectum here [bottom inner detail].

Card VIII 3″

12. (*D— F— A Perseveration*) That [upper gray detail] looks like a spider. (?) Just the way its limbs are.

13. (*Dm F+ A P-tendency*) This could be a pig here.

14. (*Da C Water*) This could represent water [blue detail]. (?) Because it's blue.

15. (*Dv CF Food Penetration*) This could represent an egg, a broken egg [bottom orange]. (?) Primarily because of the color of it.

Card IX 5″

16. (*Dd F— Sex,At Peculiar, Perseveration*) Could be an ovary of a woman [inner portion between green details]. (?) The way it looks.

Card X 5″

17. (*Dm F+ Sex,Hd*) Could be a man's penis here [top center detail]. (?) It just looks like one.

Scores

R	17	F	15	Hd	0+1	F+%	43%
W	2(11%)	CF	1	A	5	R+%	43%
D	12(71%)	C	1	Sex	10	P	1+1
Dd+S	3(18%)			Food	1		
				Water	1	High W%	50%
Peculiar	9			At	0+9	High D%	33%
Perseveration	6						
						Penetration	4

Discussion. This patient's Rorschach graphically demonstrates him to be unable to focus his attention consistently on essential aspects of his environment. His capacities for conventional Rorschach response are almost completely submerged by his inaccurately perceived, peculiarly phrased, and perseverative *Sex* responses, and his inordinate sexual preoccupation clearly exemplifies interpenetration of themes. Five of his 17 percepts (responses 2, 4, 9, 10, & 16) are female sexual anatomy responses, none of which is perceptually accurate and most of which involve unusual, redundant, or awkward language usage. He alternately refers to these parts as "an ovary," "a woman's womb," "an *oval* of a woman," and "an ovary of a woman." He also produces three "rectum" responses, one of which (#6) is inaccurately perceived and perseverated. An additional example of peculiar language usage is his reference in #5 to parts of the male sexual anatomy as "your *scropia*."

Although less dramatically apparent than the thought disorder revealed by his peculiarity, perseveration, and preoccupation, other ego impairments are reflected in the patient's record. His poor perceptual accuracy (F+% only 43) and limited capacity for sharing common ways of perceiving (only one P) identify markedly deficient reality testing. His failure to produce a single M or H response strongly supports the interpersonal aversion and social ineptness suggested by the WAIS. His overflowing sexual ideation indicates that his repressive defenses are grossly inadequate, and his use of color (0 *FC*, 1 *CF*, 1 *C*, 0 *C'*, demonstrating color stress) attests ineffective resources for integrating affective experiences. Finally, his low *high W%* (50%) and low *high D%* (33%) identify limited capacity for adaptive organizational activity.

The crippling extent of ego impairment this man exhibits in his Rorschach performance points to a severe and chronic condition. Consistent with chronic status is the fact that on the Rorschach, as on the other tests in the battery, he accompanied his deviant responses with negligible concern about their adequacy and minimal awareness of the disturbance they reflected. Although he appeared highly anxious about his delusional preoccupations, at no point did he question the basis of his fears or the intactness of his personality functioning.

Summary. This man presents gross evidence of dissociative, perseverative, and disorganized thinking, peculiar language usage, poor reality testing, withdrawal from interpersonal relationships, and limited defensive resources. He is able to focus his attention on little else than his delusional sexual concerns, and his anxieties appear directed primarily toward his imagined physical disease rather than the abnormalities of his cognitive and affective functioning. His marked impairment in several spheres of ego functioning, his lack of awareness of deviant aspects of his behavior, and the general degree of his constriction, preoccupation, and withdrawal identify him to have a chronic schizophrenic disturbance.

CASE 4

Case 4 is a 21-year-old college junior who sought psychotherapy to "help me establish my reference points." His request for treatment had been precipitated by the urging of his school authorities, who were perplexed by his extremely erratic academic and interpersonal behavior. His grades had ranged from A's to E's, and he had been noted alternately to withdraw from social contacts and to engage in persistent, presumptive, and sometimes offensive efforts to relate to his classmates and teachers, whom he usually ended by alienating. He himself complained of being unable to concentrate, suffering "feelings of blockage," and sensing a great distance between himself and other people.

This young man was the only child of distant and emotionally unresponsive parents who had always felt his only problem was shyness and who minimized the extent of his difficulties even during his subsequent treatment. Leading a quiet and solitary life, he had managed to get by without major incident until the time of his request for help, when he was about to be dropped from school for his erratic performance. His bleak social history, lack of object relations, poor social skills, inconsistent school performance, and peculiar language usage and reasoning on interview strongly suggested schizophrenia, and testing was requested primarily to assess the chronicity of the patient's condition.

In the year after the testing he continued in supportive outpatient psychotherapy, which helped him to adjust to a relatively undemanding job as a salesclerk following his suspension from college and to approach people in a somewhat less maladaptive manner. His basic style of language, thinking, and reasoning did not change during this period, however, and his therapist continued to view him as a chronically schizophrenic man.

WECHSLER ADULT INTELLIGENCE SCALE

Information

RUBBER: +. PRESIDENTS: +. LONGFELLOW: +. WEEKS: Fifty-two and some odd days (+). PANAMA: +. BRAZIL: +. HEIGHT: +. ITALY: +. CLOTHES: +. WASHINGTON: +. HAMLET: +. VATICAN: +. PARIS: 4,500 miles. EGYPT: +. YEAST: dk. POPULATION: +. SENATORS: +. GENESIS: +. TEMPERATURE: +. ILIAD: +. BLOOD VESSELS: +. KORAN: +. FAUST: +. ETHNOLOGY: +. APOCRYPHA: +. RAW SCORE: 27.

This extremely good Information performance reveals superior intellectual capacity but contains two mild indications of impaired cognitive focusing. First, in response to WEEKS the patient follows the correct answer with the irrelevant and unrequested addendum "and some odd days," as if his attention had inappropriately shifted from *weeks in a year* to *length of a year*. Second, inasmuch as he passes EGYPT and KORAN after failing the easier and factorially related PARIS and succeeds on TEMPERATURE after missing the less difficult, factorially related YEAST, his performance demonstrates scatter and suggests inconsistent cognitive efficiency.

Comprehension

ENVELOPE: Mail it (2). BAD COMPANY: It depends on the meaning of "bad"; if it means merely uncomfortable company, maybe you should put yourself in it; if it's bad because it's dull and boring, then you should avoid it because there will be no cross-communication (0). MOVIES: Alert the manager (2). TAXES: If you don't, you wind up in trouble; why do people agree to be part of a society that demands taxes, anyway; it's done, and you accept it, without ever questioning why it comes up (0). IRON: Don't hesitate to take advantage of opportunities (2). CHILD LABOR: In a capitalistic economy, the tendency has been for employers to appropriate the cheapest labor, which is children; work is not creative for them; it has a cash value, which offends our sense of humanity (0). FOREST: Try to find a path and follow it (1). DEAF: We learn to speak by imitation (2). CITY LAND: More people want to use it, and that determines its value (2). MARRIAGE: To have a record of who is married (2). BROOKS: People who are most bombastic are apt to be superficial (1). SWALLOW: One indication of a certain kind of thing does not indicate you're in the presence of the whole thing (2). RAW SCORE: 20.

The patient's performance on this subtest strikingly substantiates the dissociative tendencies tentatively suggested on Information. On BAD COMPANY, TAXES, and CHILD LABOR, items well within his demonstrated intellectual capacity, he fails to maintain focus on the issues most central to the question and wanders off into such tangential concerns as the tedium of boring companions, the passivity of submitting to taxation, and the creativity of work in a capitalistic economy. Even within the context of his associations his ideas follow a blurred and circuitous path, as when he suggests a relationship between the cash value of work and its offending "our sense of humanity."

Additionally, his scattered performance on this subtest confirms the inconsistent cognitive focusing noted on Information; his inadequate responses on BAD COMPANY, TAXES, and CHILD LABOR contrast with facile and accurate replies to several of the more difficult Comprehension items.

Similarities

ORANGE: Have to be peeled before they're eaten (1). COAT: Articles of apparel (2). AXE: Used as implements to cut (1). DOG: Mammals (2). NORTH: Directions (2). EYE: Sensory organs (2). AIR: Both are substances (0). TABLE: Pieces of furniture (2). EGG: They're starting cells in the reproductive process (2). POEM: Works of art (2). WOOD: Both exist (0). PRAISE: Reactions we can give to other people of their behavior (1). FLY: Living things (2). RAW SCORE: 19.

Although the patient responds concisely here, without the discursiveness that marred his efforts on Comprehension, he continues to reveal impaired thought processes. First, he again performs in a scattered and inconsistent manner: after failing AIR, he gives full-credit responses to four more difficult items, TABLE, EGG, POEM, and FLY. Second, he employs peculiar language in describing eggs and seeds as "starting cells." And third, he is inclined to uneven concept formation. He receives only partial credit on the easy ORANGE and AXE items because his answers, "have to be peeled" and "used as implements to cut," are somewhat concrete, narrow bases of comparison; on the other hand, he describes air and water as "substances" and states that wood and alcohol "exist," both of which are excessively broad, overinclusive categorizations.

Digit Symbol

RAW SCORE: 58

The patient worked consistently but rather slowly on this task, and his demeanor suggested that he felt neither any sense of urgency about coding rapidly nor any concern about the adequacy of his performance.

Picture Completion

KNOB: +. TAIL: +. NOSE: +. HANDLES: +. DIAMOND: +. WATER: +. NOSE PIECE: +. PEG: +. OAR LOCK: +. BASE THREAD: +. STARS: +. DOG TRACKS: +. FLORIDA: +. STACKS: The main mast. LEG: +. ARM IMAGE: +. FINGER: +. SHADOW: +. STIRRUP: Nothing. SNOW: +. EYEBROW: dk. RAW SCORE: 18.

There is little evidence of personality disturbance on this subtest, with the possible exception of the error on STACKS. "Main mast" is an uncommon error, and in relation to his success on the more difficult, factorially related FINGER, indicates some scatter.

Block Design

ITEM 1: 8" (4). ITEM 2: 4" (4). ITEM 3: 6" (4). ITEM 4: 10" (4). ITEM 5: 7" (4). ITEM 6: 12" (4). ITEM 7: 29" (6). ITEM 8: 38" (6). ITEM 9: 46" (6). ITEM 10: 90" (4). RAW SCORE: 46.

Most notable in the patient's response to Block Design, aside from his almost perfect score, was the manner in which he approached this task. More so than on any other subtest except possibly Information, he appeared highly interested in the materials and motivated to do well. He avidly awaited the presentation of each new stimulus card, executed the designs with alacrity, and appeared disappointed when the subtest was ended. As with the previous patient, whose most efficient WAIS performance also occurred on Block Design, this upsurge of interest and enhanced efficiency, even in the absence of significant quantitative differences between Block Design and other subtests, reflects greater comfort in impersonal than in interpersonal situations and is consistent with interpersonal aversion.

Scale Scores

Information: 17. Comprehension: 12. Similarities: 13. Digit Symbol: 11. Picture Completion: 13. Block Design: 15.

These scale scores reveal a fairly pronounced degree of scatter among factorially related subtests. The patient's Information exceeds both his Comprehension and Similarities scores by four or more points, and his Block Design similarly surpasses his Digit Symbol by four scale scores. This degree of variability suggests the interference of intruding elements with his ability to exercise his cognitive functions in a consistent and efficient manner.

Discussion. This WAIS protocol is noteworthy primarily for the patient's conspicuous dissociation and variability on the verbal subtests. His difficulty in maintaining a relevant and consistent focus of attention on Information and Comprehension, his tendency to alternate between overly specific and overly general concept formation on Similarities, and his scattered performance both within and among these subtests establish the presence of a thought disorder.

His WAIS performance is not particularly clear regarding the question of acute or chronic disturbance. On one hand, his near-perfect Information and Block Design scores attest considerable retention of functioning ability, and the inroads of his disordered thinking do not approach the pervasive cognitive devastation demonstrated by the previous chronically disturbed patient. On the other hand, at no point does he acknowledge the irrelevance of his tangential discursions, nor does he recognize or fret about his markedly scattered pattern of successes and failures. The implications, then, are of a disturbance that is both mild and ingrained, in which the ego impairments are not incapacitating but nevertheless are viewed ego-syntonically. His performance demonstrates the point made on page 253 that there may be no necessary relationship between chronicity and severity of schizophrenic disturbance.

DRAW-A-PERSON

Figures 17 and 18 are the drawings produced by this young man. Aside from their general grotesqueness, which may be attributable partly to limited drawing skill, they are marred by several formal features of indefinite ego boundaries and distorted body imagery. On both the contours of the body are broken and fragmented and the limbs recede into empty space. Of specific significance are the uncertain closure of the woman's arms, the open ends of the man's arms with no indication of hands, and the vague suggestion of the man's feet.

The implication of these drawings for personality disturbance is accentuated by the fact that, although the patient drew individual lines rapidly, he did not hurry to complete his drawings; rather, he studied them carefully while he was working on them and before pro-

Figure 17

Figure 18

nouncing them finished. His care in executing the drawings and his expressed satisfaction with them clarify that they are products of impaired reality sense rather than a hasty and abbreviated effort. Additionally, his apparent tolerance for the gross unreality of these drawings lends weight to the impression from the WAIS that his disturbance is ego-syntonic and chronic in nature.

RORSCHACH

Card I 3"

1. (*Wm F+ A P*) Looks like a bat. (?) The center of it is here, and the wings are on the side.

2. (*Wm F+ Em*) A coat of arms. (?) It's symmetrical and looks a little ornate; it's emblematical.

3. (*D— M—,Fc Hd,Sex,Cg Fabulized, Penetration*) A woman standing with her head way back and her arms up, imploring someone [center detail, but with unusual use of parts]. (?) We're looking at her from the front, and she's leaning way, way back; her breasts are here [top center details], and you can't see her head; she's clothed, and there's a difference in the darkness here, perhaps with her body showing through some flimsy material.

4. (*W++ M+ (H),Cg Fabulized, Barrier*) The whole thing could be a fairy tale; it sort of reminds me of three witches, like the scene from Macbeth. (?) They've just flown in, and their cloaks are still flying out; here are their heads and their caps.

Card II 3"

5. (*D+ FM+,C A,Bl P Fabulized*) It looks like two polar bears in the black, or grizzlies; they're dancing, maybe dancing to exhaustion; or it could be that they're fighting; that would explain the red part down here that would be blood on them; perhaps they're having a mating fight.

6. (*W+ M+ (H) Fabulized, Penetration*) The whole could be two people in mock anger, sticking out their tongues at each other in mock anger. (*Kind of people?*) They look like comic-strip characters; they're being snotty, but it's all in good fun.

7. (*W+ F+,mF Na,Water Barrier*) ∨ This way I see a cave, with the opening here [white space] and perhaps a waterfall up above it, with water spilling over the rocks and forming a pool. (*Waterfall?*) It just has a splashed look.

8. (*Wv M± (H),Ab Fabulized, Penetration*) > From this view the black parts look like some sort of abstract monster that's pursuing these two [upper red] and has just got this one [lower red] and squashed it.

(*Squashed?*) It's not a compact form; it looks all mangled and flattened out.

9. (*W— M— H Fabulized*) > The same way, the whole thing could be a policeman taking off down the highway after a speeder. (?) I can't get it from the picture itself; it just came from the other scene I described.

10. (*D— F— Sex,At*) This area could be a penis [top center detail].

11. (*Dd F+ Ad*) These could be animal horns [projections on bottom red detail].

12. (*Dv cF Food*) The coloring in the dark areas reminds me of soup. I'm bored with this one. (?) The way the colors of different intensity run into each other; the shadings just suggest a good, thick, homemade soup.

Card III 2″

13. (*D+ M+ (H),Cg P Barrier*) The first thing I see is two women; they look like they're staring at each other; it looks like they have beaks and reminds of a costume; I saw a play once in which there were people dressed up as magpies.

14. (*D— F— A*) The thing down here [bottom center detail] looks like a crab of some sort.

15. (*Dm Fm+ Ad Penetration*) A beheaded chicken hanging on a wall [outer red detail].

16. (*Dm Fm+ At Incongruous Combination, Perseveration-tendency*) Two kidneys, also hanging on a wall for some reason or other [center red detail].

17. (*Dm F+ A P*) The center red also reminds me of a butterfly.

18. (*Dd F+ Obj*) The top part of this [outer red detail] reminds me of the top of a guitar.

19. (*W+ M+,FK,Fm H,Obj*) > This way the black looks like a woman leaning over the water's edge and looking at her reflection; the reddish part is something floating in the water.

20. (*Dm F+ A*) Some kind of fish [leg part of popular human figure].

21. (*Dm F+ Em*) ∨ The black also gives a coat of arms effect, mainly because of its symmetry.

22. (*Dm F+ A*) And these black [popular human figure] look like two birds.

Card IV 15″

23. (*W++ F+,FK H,Cg,Bt Barrier*) It could be a clown with very big shoes on, and this [bottom center detail] would be a tree that's behind him.

24. (*Dm F+ Ad*) ∨ These are heads of otters [toe portion of "boot" detail].

25. (*Dm F+ Em,Ab*) ∨ This part [center detail between "boot" details] is one of those symbols of strength on coins, like the Italian symbol adopted by the fascists.

26. (*Dd F+ Obj Barrier*) ∨ A pot with a handle on it [heel of "boot" detail].

27. (*W— F— A*) A toad or a frog.

Card V 4″

28. (*Dm F+ Ad*) Two wolves, just their heads [outer portions of side details].

29. (*W++ M+,Fc H,Cg Fabulized, Autistic Logic, Barrier*) Two people leaning back to back. (*Describe?*) They're young, of medium build, with long hair and fleshy faces; they're just quietly sitting there leaning against each other without any impulse to move, because they're very tired; I think they're both women. (*Women?*) This could be the outline of the breast here, and they're wearing green sweaters. (*Green sweaters?*) That's what they ought to be wearing, big thick woolen ones. (?) I just want it that way, that's all.

30. (*Dd FM+ A Penetration*) This line [lower side projection] is a snake with its tongue sticking out.

Card VI 8″

31. (*W— F— Ar Barrier*) One of those turret things on a building.

32. (*W++ F+,mF Obj,Water Fabulized*) It looks like someone has thrown a clarinet or flute into the water; the whole dark line here [entire darker center detail] could be the instrument and the rest is the water splashing.

33. (*W— F— Obj Queer, Barrier*) A throne; I don't see the king sitting in it, but it looks like a throne, with all this regalia at the top.

34. (*D— F— A*) These two spots [inner lighter details] are two bugs.

35. (*Dm F+ Im*) > This part looks like a ship [half of lower portion].

36. (*Dm Fm+ Obj*) > A candle burning down; it's even on the sides, like those expensive kinds of candles that burn uniformly [lower side projection].

37. (*D— M—,FK H,Sex Perseveration, Queer*) ∨ This could be that woman from before [apparent reference to #3], with her hands raised up; there are her breasts; it's like it's being seen at a very long distance looking through something [bottom center detail].

38. (*Dd F+ Ad Peculiar*) The feelers of a catfish [top "whisker" details].

39. (*Dd M+ Hd*) This could be a man sticking his neck out, his head and neck [upper side projection].

40. (*Dd M— Hd Contamination, Fabulized*) Also here is his hand with his thumb pointing out [same detail as #39]; he's making some kind of statement, orating or imploring somebody to do something.

41. (*Dd F— Ge*) These two little spots are lakes, like on a map [tiny lighter dots in lower corners of bottom portion].

Card VII 11″

42. (*Dm F+ A*) Rabbits, with the ears up here [upper two thirds].

43. (*DW F— Obj Confabulation*) The ear parts of the rabbits look like antennas, which suggests the whole thing is a radarscope, although it doesn't look like one. (?)Yes, I'd say a radarscope, primarily because of these antennas.

44. (*Dm F+ Ad*) Elephants, with the trunk here [upper two thirds, with top detail as trunk]. (?) It's not all there, only half his body and his trunk.

45. (*D— M— Hd,Sex*) A naked woman with her legs spread apart [lower third]. (?) Just her legs, not the rest of her body.

46. (*Dd M— Sex,At Fluid, Fabulized Combination*) There's an *equals* sign in there for some reason [tiny darker lines at bottom of lower center detail]. (?) It looks like an *equals* sign, or it could be a penis approaching the body. (?) This could maybe be the vagina of the woman's body, with the penis approaching it, or it could be a finger.

47. (*W+ M+ H Fabulized, Queer*) It's two of the boys from Winken, Blinken, and Nod; they're looking at each other in utter amazement, sitting in the tub; they wonder where their brother is, because there should be three of them—who's writing this poem, anyway? Maybe they wonder which is Blinken and which is Nod.

Card VIII 4″

48. (*Dv CF Food*) The first thing it looks like is sherbet, because of the color [pink and orange details]. (?) It reminds me of raspberry and orange sherbet.

49. (*Wa C Ab*) Stained glass. (?) Nothing actually; it's just the color effect of it, like a kaleidoscope.

50. (*W+ FM+,FK A,Na P*) An animal of some sort, walking along a shoreline, with his reflection here.

51. (*Dm FC+ A*) A butterfly in this part [bottom orange]. (?) The shape of it and the fact that it's colored.

52. (*Dm F±,Fc Na*) Icebergs [blue detail]. (?) It just looks like a chunk of ice; it looks solid and chunky.

53. (*Dm F+ At Fabulized, Penetration*) The ribs of something,

after the meat has been taken off, after it's been skinned and eaten [center "rib" detail].

54. (*Dm F+ Na*) A mountain top [upper gray detail].

55. (*W+ F+ Em*) A nice emblem; it could all fit together, the animals, the butterfly, and everything, to make a nice emblem.

56. (*Da C Ab*) ∨ It looks like the world as seen through a kaleidoscope [pink and orange details]. (?) It's nonrepresentational; it's just attractive and pretty, and I was reacting to the colors and symmetry.

Card IX 4″

57. (*Dm F+ A*) This shape here [orange detail] is a moose.

58. (*Da C Ab*) This color reminds me of mint; it's green and it looks very, very cool [green details].

59. (*Dd F+ Obj*) These dim lines here [top center] remind me of a bowl, like the bowl at Ferris Park.

60. (*Dm F+ Ad*) A walrus, or the head of a walrus, in this part down here [pink detail].

61. (*Dd F+ Im*) These look like the head of a rake of some sort [inner green "finger" details].

62. (*Dv mF,cF,CF Smoke*) A fire; no, it's more like smoke than fire [orange details]. (?) Mainly because it looks wispy and flowing. (*Color?*) No, the color is not very precise; it's mainly the way it looks billowy and not very dense.

Card X 4″

63. (*Dm F+ Im*) A bicycle pump [top center detail].

64. (*Dv CF Bt*) ∨ Seaweed in the green part. (?) The coloration of it.

65. (*D+ FM+ A Penetration*) ∨ Some kind of bug [outer gray] sucking on whatever this yellow thing is.

66. (*D+ M+ H Fabulized*) ∨ The two blue [inner details] are men in their respective apartment houses, leaning over their balconies with glasses of beer and clinking them together.

67. (*Dd F+ Bt*) ∨ These two are walnuts [orange spots in inner yellow details].

68. (*Dv mF Water*) > The red is a flood coming on, or some waves at a shore. (?) It just looks like water washing over a shore.

Scores

R	68	M	15	H	7	F+%	77%
W	19(28%)	FM	4	(H)	4	R+%	75%
D	37(55%)	m	5+3	Hd	3	P	5
Dd+S	12(17%)	FK	0+3	A	14		

		F	37	Ad	8	High W% 63%	
Fabulized	12	Fc	0+2	Obj	7+2	High D% 65%	
Queer	3	c	1+1	Em	4		
Perseveration	2	FC	1	Na	3+1	Barrier	5
Contamination	1	CF	2+1	Ab	3+1	Penetration	4
Confabulation	1	C	3+1	Im	3		
Fabulized				Sex	2+3		
Combination	1			At	2+2		
Autistic Logic	1			Bt	2+1		
Incongruous	1			Food	2		
Peculiar	1			Water	1+2		
Fluid	1			Ge	1		
				Ar	1		
				Smoke	1		
				Cg	0+5		
				Bl	0+1		

Discussion. This lengthy Rorschach record encompasses virtually every type of deviation associated with a schizophrenic impairment of ego functioning but contrasts interestingly with the previous example of chronic schizophrenia (Case 3). Whereas little else than indications of disturbance are visible in the Rorschach of the previous patient, this young man complements his deviant responses with an abundance of well-organized, accurately perceived, and conventionally formulated responses. Thus, although his deviant responses occur with sufficient frequency to betoken personality disorder, they make up a relatively small proportion of his total response. This difference between the two records reveals in part why this young man was able to remain ambulatory while the previous patient, who exhibited no such complementary resources, was totally incapacitated.

More specifically, this patient's Rorschach is notable for his readiness to wander far afield into overgeneralized, illogical elaborations of his percepts that signify considerable autistic fantasy preoccupation. His 12 Fabulized responses range from such creative and mildly fanciful efforts as the discussion between Blinken and Nod in response #47 to the unusually specified impression in #5 of bears "dancing to exhaustion" and the totally unjustified fantasy in #9 of a policeman pursuing a speeder, for which he admits he can find no basis in the blot itself.

Although none of his Fabulized responses, considered singly, establishes pathologic thinking, the frequency of such elaborations in his record identifies a proclivity for excessive overgeneralization. Also graphically illustrating overgeneralized thinking is his Confabulation on #43, where he inaccurately maintains that Card VII resembles a "radarscope" solely because the top details "look like antennas."

Less frequent than his overgeneralizing but equally conclusive for disturbed reasoning are his several instances of combinative and circumstantial thinking. Significant for thought disorder are his incongruous combination of an object and an activity on #16 (kidneys "hanging on a wall"); his Fabulized Combination in #46, in which there is a highly unlikely size discrepancy between the "vagina" and "penis" details; his Contamination on #40, in which he interprets the same detail to represent both the head and the hand of the figure; and his expression of autistic logic in #29, where he maintains that the figures are wearing "green sweaters" because "that's what they ought to be wearing."

In addition to demonstrating disturbed reasoning, his Rorschach substantiates the ineffective cognitive focusing suggested by his WAIS performance. He becomes distracted by nonessential details ($Dd\%$ of 17) and has trouble shifting the focus of his attention (two perseverations); his communications are marred by the intrusion of irrelevant asides (e.g., "Who's writing this poem, anyway?" on #47) and other queer methods of formulating his responses (e.g., on #33, "A throne, but I don't see the king sitting in it," and on #37, "This could be that woman from before"); and at many points he shifts suddenly from accurately perceived and well-integrated to vague, shoddy, or autistic responses (e.g., the sequences in #'s 13–14, 31–32–33, & 45–46–47).

Also in evidence in the patient's Rorschach are impaired reality sense and inadequate defensive resources. Concerning reality sense, his occasional vague and amorphous percepts attest further the indefinite ego boundedness noted in his figure drawings. With regard to defenses, he evinces both insufficient repressive control of ideation and limited resources for integrating affective experience: his Sex responses, though not inordinately numerous for a record of 68 R, include two uncommon penis percepts (#'s 10 & 46), an uncommon breasts percept (#37), reference to nudity (#45), and allusion to sexual activity (#46), all of which identify repressive failure; his poorly controlled response to color (1 FC, 2 CF, 3 C, 0 C', demonstrating color stress) reveals serious incapacity to integrate emotional experience in a consistent and effective manner.

In addition to these several clear indices of personality disorder, however, his record includes sufficient numbers of adequately perceived and well-organized responses that his over-all reality testing is within normal limits ($F+\%$ of 77, $R+\%$ of 75, P of five) and his over-all organization scores (*high W%* of 63, *high D%* of 65) are not strikingly low. As noted above, therefore, although his disordered thinking and defensive inadequacy identify schizophrenia, he has retained certain adaptive capacities that allow him to function reasonably well in many circumstances. His strikingly variable performance, with numerous very good and numerous very poor responses, is, furthermore, notably consistent with his history of erratic behavior.

However, this patient's variability does not appear associated with an acute disorder. Rather, he presents a characteristically chronic picture of deeply ingrained disturbances for which he has considerable tolerance. He produced his Rorschach calmly and even with some relish, and he displayed no concern about his deviant responses even when their adequacy was questioned. On #43, for example, he blandly reaffirms his confabulated percept without considering its justification, and similarly bland is his comment on #12, "I'm bored with this one," which follows a fabulization he could not defend and an unusual *Sex* response.

Summary. This patient's test responses clearly demonstrate disturbances in association, reasoning, ideational control, affective integration, and reality sense. He appears to be a highly intellectualized, preoccupied, and withdrawn young man who lives primarily in a world of fantasy that he is reluctant to alter in favor of realistic considerations. The apparently fixed nature of his disturbance and his considerable tolerance for deviant thinking point to chronic disorder. On the other hand, his superior intellectual capacity and his not-infrequent demonstration of highly integrated and accurate interpretations of his experience contrast with the clear evidence of disorder and identify both his tendency toward erratic, inconsistent behavior and his capacity to maintain a marginal ambulatory adjustment despite his chronic disturbance.

▷ 14

PARANOID AND NONPARANOID SCHIZOPHRENIA

THE differential classification of schizophrenic disorders originated with Kraepelin's (1896) designation of paranoia, catatonia, and hebephrenia as three forms of a single disturbance, dementia praecox, rather than as separate pathologic entities. As reviewed in Chapter 1, Bleuler (1911) accepted Kraepelin's approach to differential classification but delineated *four* primary forms of schizophrenia: the paranoid form, characterized by delusions of grandeur, persecution, and reference; the catatonic form, identified by episodic stupor, immobility, and/or agitated hyperkinesis; the hebephrenic form, marked by shallow, inappropriate affect and deterioration of personal habits; and the simple form, a category introduced by Bleuler to describe those schizophrenic persons who present a socially withdrawn, affectively blunted picture undistinguished by prominent paranoid, catatonic, or hebephrenic features. Bleuler reported that among hospitalized schizophrenics catatonic and hebephrenic forms of the disturbance were equally frequent and more common than paranoid forms, and he hypothesized that simple schizophrenia, which was seldom seen in the hospital, was probably the most prevalent form of the disturbance among nonhospitalized schizophrenics.

Current diagnostic practices and research findings, however, identify a simple dichotomy between paranoid and nonparanoid forms of schizophrenia as the most meaningful classification of the disturbance. Reports from clinics and hospitals reveal that diagnoses of catatonic, hebephrenic, and simple schizophrenia are now rarely made and that most schizophrenic patients are designated either paranoid or undifferentiated. According to Katz, Cole, and Lowery (1964), for example, 76% of all schizophrenics admitted to state hospitals in New York are diagnosed paranoid, undifferentiated, or unascertained, and a Maryland state hospital reported for the year 1960 that 71% of schizophrenic patients were adjudged paranoid or undifferentiated, 25% catatonic, and less than 1% each hebephrenic and simple.

A paranoid-nonparanoid diagnostic dichotomy is equally apparent in reports from outpatient psychiatric clinics in the United States (*Outpatient Psychiatric Clinics*, 1963). Of some 17,000 schizophrenic patients terminated from these clinics during the year 1961, 38% were diagnosed undifferentiated, 36% paranoid, 6% catatonic, 5% simple, and 1% hebephrenic. It is evident that the current trend in subtyping schizophrenic disturbance is essentially to decide whether or not the patient demonstrates prominent paranoid features. [1] Accordingly, this chapter focuses on the identification of those distinctive features of paranoid disturbance that differentiate paranoid from nonparanoid forms of schizophrenia.

DISTINCTIVE FEATURES OF PARANOID DISTURBANCE

The prevailing diagnostic practice of dichotomizing schizophrenia into paranoid and nonparanoid forms is well founded in empiric data. Particularly significant in this regard is the many years' study of psychological deficit in schizophrenic persons recently summarized by Shakow (1962, 1963). Shakow concludes from abundant performance data on a variety of cognitive and psychomotor tests that schizophrenia is manifest in two distinctive and contrasting reaction patterns, one that

[1] It is relevant to speculate that the difference in diagnostic patterns between Bleuler's time and the present reflects neither changing diagnostic criteria nor a shift in symptom prevalence, but rather may be an artifact of the stage of disturbance and the setting in which schizophrenic patients are seen. Brill and Glass (1965) have recently suggested that the hebephrenic reaction pattern so commonly noted by Bleuler may represent an advanced stage of schizophrenic regression determined largely by the effects of long-term institutionalization and often appearing in schizophrenic patients who had earlier displayed prominent paranoid symptomatology. Because Bleuler dealt primarily with a chronic, institutionalized population, it is likely that he saw relatively few of those ambulatory or mildly disturbed persons in early stages of decompensation who more often become patients in clinics and hospitals today than they did a half century ago. In other words, though current clinicians might diagnose Bleuler's sample much as he did, his sample may have been less representative of the actual range of schizophrenic disturbance than is the present population of clinic and first-admission schizophrenic patients, who so frequently demonstrate paranoid disturbance.

appears to be associated with the traditional picture of paranoid disturbance and another that he considers to represent a hebephrenic type of syndrome.

The paranoid type of schizophrenic, according to Shakow's data, is an alert, vigilant person highly sensitive to personal reference, whose intellectual functioning is relatively preserved and who concentrates his energies on protecting his personality against the inroads of his environment. He governs his experience rigidly, imposing accurate limits on what he perceives and cautious strictures on how he responds. The hebephrenic type of schizophrenic, in contrast, is quite disturbed intellectually, venturesome and inaccurate rather than circumspect in his dealings with his environment, relatively defenseless in the face of external affront, and unresponsive to personal reference.

Additional research in a number of areas has confirmed the differential psychological impairments in paranoid and nonparanoid schizophrenia reported by Shakow. [2] Reviewing studies of intellectual deficit in schizophrenic subjects, Payne (1961, p. 209) concludes that IQ losses associated with paranoid schizophrenia are markedly less than those observed in other forms of the disturbance, and he cites other literature demonstrating that paranoid schizophrenics generally evince less psychomotor slowing and less cognitive deterioration than nonparanoid schizophrenics. Lothrop (1961), summarizing research on conceptual performance in schizophrenia, similarly notes that paranoid subjects have consistently been found to display less conceptual impairment than subjects with nonparanoid forms of schizophrenia.

Johannsen (1961) presents evidence to suggest significant differential impairment in social communication skills between paranoid and nonparanoid schizophrenic subjects. The performance of Johannsen's paranoid schizophrenic subjects on a button-pressing task remained unchanged when social feedback was introduced, whereas his nonparanoid schizophrenic subjects declined significantly in performance when confronted with necessity for interpersonal communication.

Before deriving far-reaching conclusions from these observed differences between paranoid and nonparanoid schizophrenics, however, it is reasonable to ponder whether they constitute a *basis for* or a *result*

[2] It should be noted that Shakow does not himself use the label nonparanoid to describe any of his subjects. Indeed, in Shakow's view nonparanoid schizophrenia is a gross and heterogeneous nosological category that with careful clinical observation and precise research methodology can be meaningfully subdivided into such groups as the hebephrenic and catatonic (Shakow, personal communication). To facilitate the integration of research and clinical literature in this presentation, however, nonparanoid is uniformly applied to all persons designated in the various reports as having other than a paranoid form of schizophrenia.

of diagnostic practice. It is conceivable that the outcomes of the above studies are partially determined by the fact that those schizophrenics who appear clinically to be alert, rigid, and sensitive and to have suffered relatively little intellectual, conceptual, or social impairment are diagnosed paranoid, whereas those who appear otherwise are assigned nonparanoid labels. For example, a sample of paranoid schizophrenics may be observed by the researcher to be relatively rigid because the clinician who designated them paranoid was reacting in part to his impression of their rigidity. However, such possible contamination of independent (clinical diagnosis) and dependent (test performance) variables notwithstanding, the clear congruence apparent in the literature between clinical impressions of differential paranoid symptomatology and the distinctive manifestation of paranoid patterns on the experimental techniques of the researcher argues for construct validity of these paranoid-nonparanoid distinctions.

It should also be noted that the reported differences between paranoid and nonparanoid schizophrenics in intellectual, conceptual, psychomotor, and social impairment mirror similar discriminating features of acute and chronic schizophrenic disturbance (see Chap. 13). Responding to this similarity, Johannsen, Friedman, Leitschuh, and Ammons (1963) examined whether the acute-chronic and paranoid-nonparanoid dimensions are sufficiently independent to justify considering them separately. Johannsen et al. classified 52 schizophrenic patients on the basis of four variables: acute-chronic status as defined by length of hospitalization; process-reactive as measured by the Kantor, Wallner, and Winder criteria (see pp. 237–238); see good-poor premorbid history as indicated by the Phillips scale (see p. 239); and paranoid-nonparanoid orientation as determined from independent staff diagnoses. The acute-chronic, process-reactive, and good-poor premorbid dimensions were found to correlate highly and significantly with each other but negligibly with the paranoid-nonparanoid dimension, which demonstrates that the first three of these dimensions are essentially similar and obtain whether a particular patient has a paranoid or nonparanoid disturbance.

In addition to demonstrating the differential psychological impairment of paranoid and nonparanoid schizophrenic persons reported by Shakow, empiric data also confirm that the behavioral orientations he observed distinguish two different personality types among schizophrenic subjects. These confirmatory data derive primarily from cogent conceptual analyses of the distinctive features of paranoid behavior, as expressed in terms of specific *cognitive dispositions* and particular constellations of *impulse and defense*.

COGNITIVE DISPOSITIONS IN PARANOID DISTURBANCE

A number of significant contributions indicate that paranoid and nonparanoid schizophrenic persons exhibit personality differences that are in part determined by their disparate cognitive dispositions. Mc-Gonaghy (1960), endorsing Bleuler's emphasis on associational disturbance in conceptualizing schizophrenic phenomena, points out that a person can deviate from normal associational patterns in either of two directions: he may develop a *strengthened* capacity to assign logical meanings to environmental events, with the result that he achieves "a triumph of logic over common-sense" and his established meanings firmly resist the influence of conflicting possibilities; or his ability to exclude logically irrelevant associations may become *weakened,* in which case his thought processes become vague and characterized by intuition rather than reasoning, and meaning eludes him. McGonaghy suggests that this first type of thinking provides the basis for paranoid disturbance, whereas the second is associated primarily with nonparanoid forms of schizophrenia.

Some experimental support for McGonaghy's hypothesis is adduced by Bower, Testin, and Roberts (1960). These investigators employed two Rorschach scoring scales, one a *disorganization* scale designed to measure loss of control and organization and the other an *arbitrary tightening* scale intended to assess exaggerated attempts at control. They applied their scales to five patient groups representing catatonic schizophrenia, paranoid schizophrenia, depressive reaction, obsessional neurosis, and personality-trait disturbance. Consistent with McGonaghy's hypothesis, Bower et al. found their nonparanoid schizophrenics to be notably high in disorganization and their paranoid schizophrenics to be particularly high in arbitrary tightening.

McGonaghy's cognitive approach to dichotomizing schizophrenic disturbance has recently been extended and further validated by Silverman (1964). Silverman bases his formulation on two principles of cognitive control, *scanning-control* and *cognitive filtering,* that have been identified by Gardner, Holzman, Klein, Linton, and Spence (1959) as reflecting relatively invariant characterological response dispositions. The scanning-control principle pertains to the extensiveness with which an individual scans stimuli from his perceptual fields, and the cognitive filtering principle defines the breadth of the categories with which a person organizes incoming information.

Silverman hypothesizes that paranoid schizophrenics, who are observed to be cautious, suspicious, and vigilant on one hand and rigid and inflexible on the other, are inclined to scan their environment extensively but filter their consequently abundant information input into relatively narrow conceptual categories. Nonparanoid schizophrenics, who tend more frequently than paranoids to be socially withdrawn, preoccupied, and emotionally impoverished and to be disorganized rather than overcontrolled, are believed by Silverman to engage in relatively little environmental scanning and to organize information into broad and diffuse conceptual categories. Administering measures of extensiveness of scanning and breadth of categorization to paranoid and nonparanoid schizophrenic subjects, Silverman obtained data consonant with these hypotheses.

Silverman attempts, in addition to his descriptive delineation of different cognitive dispositions in paranoid and nonparanoid schizophrenic persons, to formulate a genetic reconstruction of the developmental paths that eventuate in these diverse orientations. He traces extensive scanning to early-experienced reinforcement contingencies that foster hyperalertness to cues preceding or accompanying noxious psychological events, and he posits that narrow categorization is a protective measure particularly likely to be developed by extensive scanners. Because extensive scanning increases the amount of registered aversive input, Silverman reasons, the extensive scanner is saddled by a burden of unpleasurable experience that he strives to ease either by scanning less or by forcing his experience into narrow, delimited categories of meaning that are not anxiety-provoking. It is the persistence of early-determined extensive scanning and the narrow categorization it encourages that contribute to subsequent paranoid cognitive dispositions, Silverman concludes.

Arieti (1955, p. 139) similarly suggests a relationship between certain types of childhood experience and the development of a cognitive style that predisposes to paranoid disturbance. According to Arieti, the parents of paranoid patients "generally accuse the patients for their *intentions* or for *lying*." The child of such parents learns to defend himself in one or both of two ways, Arieti continues: he attempts to anticipate these accusations, which leads him to scan his environment extensively and contributes to his becoming an alert, anxious, and suspicious person readily inclined to perceive external threat; or he resorts to rationalizations and "pseudo-logical defenses" to protect himself against accusations, which fosters narrow concept categorization and contributes to the rigidity, grandiosity, and litigiousness that frequently characterize paranoid disturbance.

IMPULSE AND DEFENSE IN PARANOID DISTURBANCE

Considerable attention has been devoted to the interplay of specific impulses and defenses that conduce to paranoid rather than other forms of personality breakdown. In terms of defensive style, the major distinction between the paranoid and nonparanoid schizophrenic person is the former's reliance on the mechanism of *projection*, which, following Schafer (1954, p. 279), may be defined as "a process by which an objectionable internal tendency is unrealistically attributed to another person or to other objects in the environment instead of being recognized as part of the self."

Freud's Contribution. The term projection was introduced by Freud (1896) in one of his early papers to explain the distrust and delusions he observed in a paranoid woman. He suggested (p. 180) that in paranoia the individual seeks to protect himself against self-reproaches related to unacceptable thoughts or ideas by ascribing them to others; thus others and not himself have bad thoughts, and reproaches are delusionally perceived as coming from them rather than from himself.

In his later, classic study of the Schreber memoirs Freud (1911a) formulated in detail a relationship between paranoid disturbance and defenses instituted to deal with unacceptable homosexual impulses. He posited (p. 448) that paranoia in men stems from the unacceptable feeling, "I (a man) love him (a man)." According to Freud, this feeling can be contradicted in one of four ways: (a) denial of the verb, to yield "I *hate* him," which, also being an unacceptable thought, is transformed by projection into "*he* hates *me*" and provides the basis for persecutory delusions; (b) denial of the subject, resulting in "*she* loves him," which contributes to delusional jealousy and delusions of infidelity; (c) denial of the object, which produces "I love *her*" and may induce either erotomania or, when projected (i.e., "*she* loves *me*"), an exaggerated feeling of being loved; and (d) denial of the entire proposition, stated as "I do not love any one," which leads to the companion thought, "I love only myself," and results in exaggerated self-regard. The first two of these defensive reactions to unacceptable homosexual impulses can account for the perceptions of persecution and victimization observed in paranoid patients, whereas the latter two provide a basis for the grandiosity and megalomania frequently associated with paranoid disturbance.

Neofreudian Views. The contribution of projective mechanisms to paranoid symptomatology, as first explicated by Freud in these early papers, is a widely acknowledged phenomenon. Later writers, however, have explored more fully than Freud the relationship to paranoid tendencies of projective defense against other than primarily homosexual anxiety. Ovesey (1955), for example, suggests that relatively few cases of paranoid disturbance result directly from the projection of homosexual impulses, but rather that paranoid disturbance is a more general adaptational problem that often has only *pseudohomosexual* components.

According to Ovesey, whose presentation encompasses only masculine dynamics, the basic problem disposing a man to a paranoid orientation is a feeling of being a failure, that is, of being unable to adapt satisfactorily to his environment. A man who experiences such feelings of failure, Ovesey continues, is likely to compensate for them by seeking power and strength, a quest which requires him to compete with, defeat, and subjugate other men. The projection of such aggressive impulses leads a man to the paranoid expectation that other men seek to control, damage, and destroy him. Pseudohomosexual concerns often emerge in the course of these reflections because the thought, "I am a failure," readily translates into ideas of being something less than an adequate man and hence a homosexual. Therefore, Ovesey concludes, homosexual anxiety may appear in many paranoid patients without necessarily being the basic concern against which their projective defenses are instituted.

Other valuable contributions to the dynamics of paranoid mechanisms have been made by Sullivan (1956, pp. 145–165) and Salzman (1960). Sullivan describes a paranoid orientation as a "dynamism" characterized by a transfer of blame onto others and necessitated by "an awareness of inferiority of some kind." For Sullivan, "awareness of inferiority" is the anxiety that results when a person perceives himself as being incapable of establishing intimate and gratifying relationships with others, and "transfer of blame" is utilized to alleviate anxiety by persons who experience such interpersonal inadequacy. Regarding homosexual concern, Sullivan asserts that because problems of intimacy involve people, whether men or women, both homosexual and heterosexual longings may participate in the genesis of a paranoid disturbance. For Sullivan, therefore, the particular interpersonal rather than sexual content of anxiety determines differential personality disturbance.

Salzman also formulates paranoid pathology in terms of self-attitudes, but he offers a unique interpretation of the sequence of events in paranoid development. Though agreeing with Sullivan that the basic determinant of paranoid disturbance is a person's attempt to defend against low self-esteem, Salzman hypothesizes that the paranoid person's first pathologic reaction is not projection onto the environment of blame for his inadequacies, but denial and replacement of self-depreciation with a grandiose conviction of his capabilities and worth.

The unreality, grandiosity, and presumptousness of the behavior attending such a defensive reaction, Salzman continues, alienate and antagonize the potentially paranoid person's environment and provoke sufficient negative reaction to convince him that his surroundings are indeed hostile, unsympathetic, and untrustworthy. Homosexual concerns are relevant to these developments, Salzman adds, only in that homosexual inclinations and sexual inadequacy are culturally unfavored characteristics that may contribute to a person's feelings of personal unworthiness.

Relevant to Salzman's position is a suggestion by Bullard (1960) that homosexuality is a *result* rather than a *cause* of paranoid disturbance. Bullard views the paranoid person as one whose primary difficulties are suspiciousness of the motives of other people and difficulty forming intimate relationships with them. Bullard postulates that such patterns begin early in life and interfere with a person's ability to shift his object choice from homosexual to heterosexual companions during adolescence, when such a shift normally takes place. The potentially paranoid person is not primarily interested in homosexuality, Bullard continues, but fears making the shift to heterosexuality because, as a result of his projections, he anticipates rejection and ridicule in such a venture. Fearing and withdrawing from women, the potential paranoid is thus prone to increasing concern about being or being considered a homosexual.

Neither the issue of whether homosexual anxiety precipitates or results from paranoid attitudes nor the question of whether concern about being a homosexual is a cause or a consequence of more general feelings of inadequacy can be satisfactorily resolved from available data. However, regardless of which dynamic interpretation is preferred, the implications for phenomenology are the same: that homosexual preoccupation is often an observable concomitant of paranoid disturbance.

Empiric Findings. Empiric data confirm that specific homosexual concerns, though not especially frequent in schizophrenic persons, are more likely to be associated with paranoid than nonparanoid forms of the disturbance when they are present. Significant in this regard are studies by Klein and Horwitz (1949) and Norman (1948). Klein and Horwitz found that 85% of a sample of 80 paranoid schizophrenic men and women displayed one or more of the following types of sexual preoccupation: fear of sexual attack, fear of being maligned for having sexual thoughts, concern with infidelity of a mate, impression of self as fantasied love objects of others, and fear of being considered a sexual pervert, particularly a homosexual.

These fears correspond neatly to the various paranoid delusional patterns traced by Freud to underlying homosexual impulses (see p. 308). On the other hand, however, Klein and Horwitz reported that only one fifth of their cases demonstrated specific homosexual concerns. Norman, utilizing case-history and amytal interview data for 75 paranoid schizophrenic patients, observed conscious homosexual concerns in only 24% and evidence of latent homosexual conflicts in 31% of his sample; however, both such concerns were even less prevalent among a group of catatonic patients he studied.

In an experiment relevant to the association of homosexual concern with paranoid forms of schizophrenia Daston (1956) compared paranoid schizophrenic, unclassified schizophrenic, and normal subjects in tachistoscopic recognition of series of neutral, heterosexual, and homosexual words. For both neutral and heterosexual words he found the paranoid and unclassified schizophrenics to have slower recognition times than the normals. In recognizing homosexual words, however, the paranoid schizophrenics approached normal speed and were significantly faster than the unclassified schizophrenics. Daston interprets these data to indicate that sensitivity to homosexual stimuli is unrelated to schizophrenia in general but is enhanced in association with paranoid elaborations of the disturbance.

It is conservative to conclude, therefore, that homosexual concerns are not the central dynamic element in all cases of paranoid schizophrenia but do play a significant role in many. For diagnostic purposes it is accordingly reasonable to entertain a paranoid rather than nonparanoid hypothesis regarding those schizophrenic patients who exhibit prominent homosexual concerns.

In concluding this discussion of impulse and defense in paranoid schizophrenia, it is important to note that these various dynamic formulations, regardless of their accuracy, explain only the *how* and not the *why* of paranoid breakdown. Whether a paranoid reaction derives from a flight from homosexual impulses, a need to compensate for feelings of failure, an awareness of inadequate social skills, or a defense against low self-esteem, the presence of such sources of concern is sufficient to account only for a person's being anxious and seeking defensive measures; it does not explain why he selects projective rather than other compensatory mechanisms to deal with his anxiety. Indeed, a variety of psychopathologic reaction patterns may be precipitated by low self-esteem, feelings of failure, and inadequate social skills, and neither is specific to paranoid disturbance. The point of these observations is that the elucidation of differential symptom choice rests not with sources of anxiety but with such genetic formulations of response disposition as those outlined by Silverman and Arieti (see p. 307).

DIFFERENTIAL PSYCHODIAGNOSIS OF PARANOID
AND NONPARANOID SCHIZOPHRENIA

Whether differences between paranoid and nonparanoid schizophrenia are formulated in terms of intellectual-conceptual-psychomotor performance, cognitive dispositions, or the interplay of impulse and defense, the implications for paranoid phenomenology are the same: the paranoid person is an alert, sensitive, and vigilant individual whose personality integration is relatively intact; he perceives his environment as a hostile, potentially threatening place and is accordingly cautious and suspicious in his dealings with it; he views the motives of other people with uncertainty and misgivings and consequently hesitates to trust them, maintains a formal distance from others, and prefers to reflect upon rather than share his thoughts and feelings with anyone; and finally, he inclines to self-protective and self-aggrandizing maneuvers, particularly externalization of blame and depreciation of others, with which he seeks to avoid awareness of his fallibility and which in extreme forms are manifest in a pompous, litigious, and grandiose nature.

Psychodiagnostic indices of these various identifying features of paranoid disturbance may appear in the structure and content of a subject's test responses and in his general behavior during the test administration as well. *Structural, content,* and *behavioral* variables thus provide the framework for the following presentation of differential psychodiagnostic clues to paranoid disturbance.

STRUCTURAL VARIABLES

Prominent among the structural aspects of psychodiagnostic test performance that discriminate paranoid from nonparanoid disturbance are certain scores that reflect the relatively intact personality integration demonstrated among paranoid schizophrenics in the laboratory. Specifically, paranoid schizophrenics in comparison with various groups of nonparanoid schizophrenics have been observed on the Rorschach to receive higher $F+\%$'s (Rickers-Ovsiankina, 1938), higher *high* $W\%$'s and *high* $D\%$'s (Siegel, 1953), and fewer of the Piotrowski signs mentioned on page 241 (Eckhardt, 1961). However, relatively intact personality organization also relates to minimally severe disturbance (see pp. 243–245), and the relationship of relatively good personality integration to both paranoid and mild nonparanoid schizophrenic disturbance has two important implications for diagnostic practice.

First, because relative retention of personality functioning is consistent with but not unique to paranoid forms of schizophrenia, the differentiation between paranoid and mild nonparanoid schizophrenia must rest with test variables that are independent of severity of disturbance. Second, because a paranoid orientation may nevertheless attenuate some of the loss of function that would otherwise accompany a schizophrenic breakdown, high scores for perceptual accuracy and Developmental Level are less meaningful in ruling out schizophrenia in clearly paranoid than in nonparanoid subjects. In other words, adequate levels of $F+\%$, high $W\%$, and high $D\%$ may, in the Rorschach of a paranoid person, still be consistent with prominent schizophrenic disorder.

Those structural variables in the clinical battery that discriminate paranoid from nonparanoid schizophrenia independently of severity of disturbance are defined mainly by the Rorschach. Schafer (1948, pp. 80–81) suggests that paranoid alertness may on occasion be reflected in the WAIS by particularly well-retained Comprehension, Arithmetic, and Picture Completion scores, but there are also cases in which the paranoid person's scores on these three subtests are depressed by his tendency to distort the implications of social situations (the "paranoid pseudocommunity"; see Cameron, 1959, pp. 518–519) and his distrust of obvious, easily attained solutions. Rapaport, Gill, and Schafer (1945, p. 304) in fact conclude from their extensive comparisons among subgroups of schizophrenic subjects that the paranoid schizophrenic WAIS profile is roughly similar to that of the nonparanoid schizophrenic.

Hence WAIS clues to the differential diagnosis of paranoid schizophrenia appear primarily in the content and behavioral aspects of a subject's responses and not in the structure of his scores. Similarly for the DAP, differentiating indices of paranoid and nonparanoid schizophrenia involve mainly the content and behavioral variables of the test. The following discussion of structural variables thus centers around the Rorschach and reviews three of its parameters that contribute distinctions between paranoid and nonparanoid forms of schizophrenia: *location choice, experience balance,* and *constriction-dilation.*

Location Choice. With regard to location choice, schizophrenic subjects, as a consequence of their inability to focus consistently on the common, essential elements of a stimulus situation, not infrequently give relatively few D responses and correspondingly more W and/or Dd responses on the Rorschach (see Chap. 4). However, more specific data summarized by Hemmendinger (1960, pp.

65–66) suggest that paranoid and nonparanoid schizophrenic subjects are likely to deviate from normal $D\%$ in different directions. Hemmendinger's tables reveal that although both paranoid and hebephrenic-catatonic schizophrenic groups tend as expected to receive lower $D\%$'s than normal subjects, only the hebephrenic-catatonic group displays marked elevation of $W\%$, whereas the paranoid schizophrenics actually fall below the normals in $W\%$. On the other hand, it is primarily the paranoid group that exhibits marked $Dd\%$ elevation, with the hebephrenic-catatonic schizophrenics choosing relatively few Dd locations.

This distinctive preference among paranoid as opposed to nonparanoid schizophrenic persons for Dd locations can be conceptualized in terms of the caution, sensitivity, and concern about self-protection noted in the previous section to typify the paranoid defensive style. The Dd scoring category includes three major types of rare detail responses: tiny details, large arbitrary details that do violence to the blots' natural demarcations, and white space details. Each of these three types of response is suited to the paranoid subject's exaggerated needs to peruse his environment carefully and maintain his autonomy in the face of perceived external threat.

Specifically, the paranoid person is extremely sensitive to subtle nuances in his environment and prone to attach significance to the most inconsequential events; he is therefore more likely than the nonparanoid schizophrenic to focus his attention on tiny details, and he is particularly more likely to develop highly elaborate, overgeneralized interpretations of such Dd. The paranoid person distrusts the obvious, being unwilling to take things at their face value and inclined to seek for the "true" and "hidden" meanings in his experience; consequently he is likely to ignore the contours of the large common details and instead carve out his own boundaries for his percepts. Finally, as elaborated by Fonda (1960, p. 97), the paranoid person, struggling to protect his sense of separateness and integrity from encroachment, tends to exercise autonomy in part by rejecting the obvious figure-ground distinctions of the Rorschach blots in favor of S-determined responses.

In general, then, given a schizophrenic subject with unusual location choice, an elevated $Dd\%$ suggests paranoid and an elevated $W\%$ suggests nonparanoid forms of disturbance. The major exceptions to this psychodiagnostic guideline are those paranoid persons who are primarily grandiose and megalomanic rather than suspicious. The grandiose paranoid schizophrenic performs quite differently on tests from the suspicious paranoid: he is expansive where the suspicious paranoid holds back, blustery where the other is constrained, and self-assured where the latter frets about threats to his integrity.

In his location choice, therefore, the grandiose paranoid is less likely to concern himself with picayune and unusual details than he is to concentrate his efforts on complex W responses that satisfy his needs for ambitious undertaking and lofty achievement. The differential diagnosis of paranoid schizophrenics inclined to such W emphasis is usually not difficult, however, because the extent of grandiosity necessary to submerge what would otherwise be a paranoid person's anxious attention to detail is an extreme defensive pattern that leads to a multitude of content and behavioral indicators of paranoid disturbance.

Experience Balance. Rorschach (1921, p. 116) suggested in his original monograph that experience balance reflects a person's basic personality style and determines the nature of the symptomatology he displays on becoming schizophrenic. Employing Bleuler's subcategories of schizophrenia, Rorschach related simple schizophrenia to a *coartated* experience type (M and *Sum C* zero), catatonia to an *ambiequal dilated* type (M and *Sum C* equal, both greater than zero), hebephrenia to an *extratensive* type (*Sum C* greater than M), and paranoia to an *introversive* type (M greater than *Sum C*).

Although the utility of Rorschach's distinctions between simple, catatonic, and hebephrenic schizophrenic experience types has not been widely examined, there is considerable support for his view that a schizophrenic subject who prefers movement to color responses on the Rorschach is more likely to have a paranoid than a nonparanoid form of the disturbance. The relationship between introversive experience balance and paranoid tendencies is frequently noted clinically (Bohm, 1958, p. 275; Klopfer & Kelley, 1942, p. 361; Phillips & Smith, 1953, p. 84), and research studies have found significantly more M, FM, and m responses and significantly fewer color responses, especially CF and C, in paranoid than nonparanoid schizophrenic subjects (Rapaport et al., 1946, pp. 248, 255; Thomas, 1955).

Therefore, the more a schizophrenic subject emphasizes movement in his Rorschach responses and the less his affinity for color, the more likely he is to have a paranoid rather than nonparanoid disturbance. Obversely, the more his determinant choice tends to color rather than movement and to CF and C rather than FC, the greater is the likelihood that his disturbance is nonparanoid in nature.

The paranoid subject's interest in movement determinants and aversion to unstructured color responses is consistent with the distinctive defensive style that marks the paranoid personality. As Schafer (1954, p. 283) points out, the paranoid defensive style is primarily ideational in nature and revolves around careful observation and orderly reflection on the significance of environmental events (*extensive scanning* and *narrow categorization* in the language of cognitive disposition; see p. 306). Furthermore, a major focus of the paranoid person's attention is other people, whose actions he is intent on anticipating and whose motives he is struggling to discern. Inasmuch as these two characteristics of the paranoid defensive style, investment in ideational activity and attention to the motives of others, both contribute significantly to M emphasis on the Rorschach (see p. 156), it follows that paranoid persons are likely to display a proclivity for M responses.

The color aversion of paranoid persons can be traced to the frequency with which they project hostile impulses onto environmental figures and consequently mistrust them. Imputing calumny and malevolence to those about him, the paranoid individual is reluctant to reveal his thoughts and feelings, indisposed to spontaneous expression, and heedful lest his affects or his behavior escape his stringent control. Hence, inasmuch as response to color is related to emotional expression and unstructured color responses are related to spontaneous, unmodulated affective discharge (see Chap. 10), paranoid subjects are inclined either to avoid Rorschach color determinants entirely or to eschew CF and C responses in favor of a few FC.

Constriction-dilation. Schafer (1954) also observes, however, that the rock-ribbed behavioral controls self-imposed by particularly guarded and secretive paranoid subjects may induce them to refrain from M as well as color responses on the Rorschach. The result of such zealous defensive effort is a brief, constricted record limited primarily to F determinants and A and P contents. Rapaport et al. (1946, pp. 115–116) in fact found their paranoid schizophrenic subjects as a group to give fewer responses, higher percentages of both F and form-dominated percepts, and a greater relative frequency of A and P responses than their unclassified schizophrenics. By carefully restricting himself to a few F, A, and P responses, a suspicious paranoid subject can satisfy his urgent needs to control his environment and insulate himself against it; he avoids being influenced by the subtler nuances of the test stimuli, that is, non-F determinants, and he withholds impressions that would reveal his underlying impulses and attitudes, that is, non-A and non-P contents.

Constriction, therefore, as reflected in reduced R, high $F\%$ and form-dominance, and high $A\%$ and $P\%$, is likely in the context of a schizophrenic record to indicate a paranoid rather than nonparanoid form of disturbance. On the other hand, it is obvious from the previous discussion that such extreme constriction does not characterize all paranoid persons. Those with grandiose reaction patterns are likely to produce lengthy and expansive records, and many suspicious paranoid subjects attend carefully to the subtle nuances of the inkblots, employing M determinants freely and purposefully avoiding the obvious A and P percepts. Hence for those paranoids who incline to M and non-P responses differential diagnosis rests with variables other than constriction-dilation.

In concluding this discussion of Rorschach structural variables that discriminate paranoid from nonparanoid schizophrenia, it is important to note that Dd location emphasis, introversive experience balance, and a constricted approach are specific not to paranoid disturbance but rather to the ideational activity and emotional control that characterize the paranoid defensive style. These aspects of the paranoid style are shared by many persons who employ obsessive-compulsive defensive operations.[3] In practice, therefore, a differential diagnosis between paranoid schizophrenia and obsessive-compulsive neurosis usually cannot be made on the basis of these structural Rorschach variables but must be referred to indicators of schizophrenic ego impairment and to content and behavioral manifestations of projective defense, neither of which is consonant with obsessive-compulsive neurosis.

Finally, it is relevant to consider the effect of acute-chronic status on the relatively well-retained $F+\%$, high $W\%$, and high $D\%$, the introversive experience balance with many M's and little color use, and the generally constricted, controlled approach that discriminate paranoid from nonparanoid schizophrenic disturbance. The work of Skalweit (1934), Rapaport et al. (1946), Zimet and Fine (1959), and others (see pp. 244–245) suggests that increasing chronicity of schizophrenic disturbance is accompanied by decline in $F+\%$ and Developmental Level scores, decreasing frequency of M, enhanced color affinity (particularly for CF and C), and generally diminished controls.

Hence the effects of chronicity on the personality functioning of a paranoid schizophrenic person may tend to eliminate from his Rorschach performance many of the structural characteristics that would otherwise discriminate his performance from that of nonparanoid schizophrenics. Because the records of chronic paranoid schizophrenics are therefore not markedly dissimilar in structure from those of other chronic schizophrenics, the differential diagnosis of paranoid tendencies in instances of chronic disturbance rests primarily with the content and behavioral variables discussed below.

---

[3] For a comprehensive discussion of obsessive-compulsive defensive operations and their manifestations on the Rorschach, the reader is referred to Schafer (1954, pp. 332–423).

The projective defensive style that typifies paranoid forms of schizophrenia is reflected in characteristic test content that facilitates the differential diagnosis of this condition. Partly following Schafer (1954, pp. 288–289), these fantasy contents can be grouped according to three frequent concomitants of prominent projective defense: *experienced external threat, need for protection,* and *homosexual concern.*

Experienced External Threat. The paranoid person, as a consequence of the extent to which he projects hostility onto his environment, is prone to perceive aggressive intent in the actions of others, to consider himself under the scrutiny of potential accusers and adversaries, and to anticipate being the helpless victim of various animate and inanimate forces that wait to assail him. Each of these derivatives of projective defense has distinctive manifestations in fantasy productions that identify paranoid tendencies.

In relation to perception of aggressive intent, the paranoid person is likely to emphasize aggressive interactions between the animal and human figures he perceives on the Rorschach ("arguing," "fighting," "killing each other," "hate one another," etc.) and also to display uneasy concern that he is not privy to the mysterious and unfathomable motives of others, as in human percepts described as "cloaked," "hidden," or "obscured" and such elaborations as "I can't make out what they're doing" or "I'm unable to determine what kind of a person it is."

Subjects sensitive to being observed by potential malefactors often focus attention on scrutinizing organs and activities and on the trappings of accusation and indictment. Thus the paranoid person is likely to stress eyes, ears, and faces in his Rorschach percepts and on his figure drawings; to elaborate his fantasy productions with such verbs as "looking," "peering," "staring," and "spying"; and to report on the Rorschach such uncommon images as "fingerprint," "footprint," "lie-detector machine," and "wire-tapping device" and such unique persons as "detective," "policeman," and "judge." Responses of these kinds are particularly significant for paranoid concerns when they appear in dramatic or personalized combinations, such as "A pair of eyes peering out from behind a bush" or "A magistrate leveling an accusing finger at me."

Fear of victimization is revealed on the Rorschach by the attribution of dangerous qualities to fantasy images ("evil, sinister man," "deadly, poisonous insect," "threatening cloud of doom"), perception of victimizing agents ("trap," "snare," "executioner," "jailer"), and direct impressions of submission to overpowering forces ("a bird of prey swooping down on its victim," "a squashed animal that's been run over by a car," "a tree being uprooted by the wind"). Victimization responses, like those involving scrutiny, most clearly indicate paranoid ideation when they are self-referentially phrased, as in "A devil's face looking right at me," "A man with a gun coming toward me," and "A violent windstorm blowing down my house."

The content of WAIS as well as Rorschach responses can reveal these varieties of experienced external threat, as the following Comprehension answers illustrate: on BAD COMPANY, "You can't trust them and they'll take advantage of you"; on TAXES, "The FBI will track you down if you don't"; on CITY LAND, "It really doesn't, but the machinations of the big city bosses contrive to yield such a result." Each of these responses skirts the correct answer in favor of paranoid-type concerns about being deceived by friends, pursued by agents of the government, and abused by the misanthropy of influential persons.

It is important to recognize, however, that just as the structural Rorschach indicators of ideational activity and emotional control are not specific to paranoid disturbance (see p. 317), neither are these content clues to experienced external threat unique to paranoid schizophrenia. Rather, they identify the projection of hostile impulses that characterizes paranoid schizophrenia, and they are also likely to occur in certain nonschizophrenic states marked by projective maneuvers.

Persons with phobic neuroses, for example, typically invest their environment with dangerous potential and experience considerable external threat. However, although phobic subjects may therefore produce fantasy content similar to that of paranoid persons, the two groups can usually be differentiated by reference to the structure of their Rorschach records. As elaborated by Schafer (1954, pp. 203–210), phobic persons employ a primarily hysterical and repressive response style that rarely conduces to the *Dd* emphasis, introversive experience balance, and form-dominance associated with the paranoid's orientation toward ideational activity and emotional control. In addition, the previously noted self-referential elaborations of such content are far more likely to reflect paranoid schizophrenic than phobic concern with external threat, as are responses that involve overgeneralized thinking, inaccurate perception, or unusual locations, especially tiny details and white spaces.

Also inclined to fantasy content reflecting projection of hostile impulses are subjects with certain organic brain syndromes that are accompanied by prominent paranoid features. Paranoid delusions are common in amphetamine-induced psychoses (Weiner, 1964a) and in some alcoholic states (Noyes & Kolb, 1963, pp. 176–177), for example, and the psychologist's differential diagnostic opinion is not infrequently solicited concerning such cases. As in the case of phobic neurosis, the differential diagnosis can usually be referred to structural test variables, where the amphetamine psychotic displays a degree of affective discharge not consistent with paranoid schizophrenic disturbance (Weiner, 1965c) and delusional alcoholics are likely to manifest states of delirium or dementia not typical in schizophrenia (Bohm, 1958, p. 298).

Need for Protection. Need for protection and homosexual concern relate less specifically to projective defense than experienced external threat, but both contribute significantly to the differential diagnosis of paranoid and nonparanoid schizophrenia. As reviewed by Schafer (1954, p. 288), primarily suspicious-constricted and primarily megalomanic-expansive paranoid persons both experience urgent needs to protect their integrity, and their preferred techniques for protecting themselves against anticipated debasement and mortification are reflected in distinctive fantasy content.

The constricted paranoid seeks to insulate himself against environmental affront by erecting barriers between himself and others. He consequently is likely in his Rorschach percepts to emphasize concealment, armor, masks, hard-shelled animals, and other categories of the Barrier score as defined by Fisher and Cleveland (see pp. 130–132) and on figure-drawings to stress heavy, solid, reinforced body contours. Megalomanic paranoids, on the other hand, protect themselves by an inflated conviction of their potency and infallibility. They correspondingly tend on the Rorschach to emphasize images of status ("emblem," "coat of arms"), power ("king," "crown," "idol"), and excellence of one kind or another (reference to great historical, religious, and mythical figures—Julius Caesar, John F. Kennedy, Joan of Arc, Pope John, Zeus, Hercules, etc.) and on the DAP to render large, grandiose, muscular figures and such powerful, authoritarian persons as kings, queens, mythical gods, soldiers, and athletes.

The paranoid person protects his sense of security and worth not only by insulating himself against environmental aspersion and identifying with sources of power, but also by depreciating the potency and significance of external objects and events. Hence he is not unlikely to focus his imagery on depreciated as well as powerful and staunchly fortified figures. Such depreciatory tendencies usually appear in the Rorschach in the form of qualifications of human percepts that dehumanize them or otherwise belittle their capacity to influence, injure, or oppose the perceiver.

Significant in this respect are such (H) responses as "A man raising a sword, but he's only a statue," such Hd responses as "A powerful looking guy who doesn't have any arms to do anything with," and such adjectival fabulizations as "small," "weak," "stupid," "silly," "deformed," and "inept." Fantasies of this type serve to enhance the subject's feelings of safety; by establishing his superiority to the external figures he enervates them and reassures himself that other people lack sufficient resources to mount any serious threat against him.

Research with Content Indicators of Experienced External Threat and Need for Protection. Before considering test indices of homosexual concern that facilitate the differential diagnosis of paranoid schizophrenia, it is appropriate at this point to review some research data that bear on content indicators of experienced external threat and need for protection. These data cannot be considered independently of controversy concerning the extent to which projective test content reflects underlying personality dynamics, and a brief statement of this issue as it has been joined in reference to diagnostic utilization of the Rorschach and DAP is relevant to the studies that follow.

In Rorschach's (1921, pp. 122–123) view the content of a subject's fantasy productions seldom had significant implications for his personality dynamics. Most subsequent writers, however, have endorsed broader interpretations of Rorschach content variables than Rorschach employed. Most extreme in this regard is the approach advocated by Lindner (1946) and Brown (1953), who derive detailed inferences from particular combinations of specific contents and locations. According to Lindner, for example, the response "gorilla" to Card IV "is found among depressives and ruminating obsessives who experience strong guilt reactions and self-recriminations"; according to Brown, the center detail of Card I seen as a dress "signifies a sense of inner emptiness, great distance from people with inability to empathize with them, cathexis withdrawal, and feelings of depressed depersonalization."

Less specific but still far-reaching is the interpretive style employed by Phillips and Smith (1953, pp. 119–153) for Rorschach content and by Machover (1949) on the DAP. These writers consider fantasy content to represent general response dispositions the influence of which in the case of the Rorschach is not restricted to any exclusive locations. According to Phillips and Smith (1953, pp. 129–130), for example, an emphasis on "building" and "tower" contents anywhere in the Rorschach indicates masculine identification, mature and complex personality, active striving toward realistic aspirations, inferiority feelings derived from a relationship with a powerful and successful father figure, and feelings of inadequacy not justified by achievements; for Machover (1949, pp. 57–58), a long neck on a figure drawing reflects a sense of body weakness compensated for by a drive for physical power and aggression.

The Brown, Lindner, Machover, and Phillips and Smith styles of content analysis have been vigorously criticized by clinicians who prefer a more conservative approach and by researchers who have been unable to verify many such specific relationships between projective test fantasy and personality dynamics. Beck (1952, pp. 62–68), for example, argues that Rorschach content can be effectively interpreted only in such general categories as *anatomy, oral, religious,* and so forth, which provide "leads" for further investigation. Schafer (1954, pp. 114–139) similarly elaborates a thematic approach to content analysis in which specific fantasy becomes meaningful primarily in its relation to such broad orientations as *dependency, sado-masochism,* and *confused identification.*

The debate in which these writers have engaged (see especially Lindner, 1950; Brown, 1953; Shafer, 1954, pp. 118 & 142–143) has clarified for clinicians two important considerations in extrapolating from research findings to psychodiagnostic practice: first, the fact that many specific hypotheses derived on a one-to-one basis from particular content scores are not demonstrably valid does not necessarily imply that *all* such hypotheses are invalid; second, although certain specific content interpretations employed singly may have limited differential power or validity, these content scores in combination may constitute thematic patterns having considerable diagnostic utility. The following close inspection of research data in fact confirms that both certain specific fantasy contents and certain patterns of content scores related to experienced external threat and need for protection do differentiate paranoid from nonparanoid schizophrenic subjects.

Among the specific content indicators of paranoid orientation that have been examined experimentally are *eye, ear,* and *reinforced body contour* emphases. Wertheimer (1953), studying eye content in the Rorschach of 230 state hospital patients, found the frequency with which the word *eye* appeared in a protocol, expressed as a percentage of the total response, was not particularly dissimilar among paranoid schizophrenic (17.8%) and neurotic (16.4%) subjects. Although Wertheimer's word-count method ignores important differential contingencies that contribute to accurate clinical interpretation of eye and similar fantasy contents (see p. 318), his data do caution against one-to-one inferences from content category to diagnostic inference.

On the other hand, two additional features of Wertheimer's results justify some positive conclusions that have general implications for psychodiagnostic research. First, he found a notably lower eye index among a combined sample of simple, hebephrenic, and catatonic schizophrenic patients (11.1%) than in either his paranoid schizophrenic or neurotic groups. Second, when his subjects were independently rated for "degree of suspiciousness," mention of eyes was more frequently observed in the records of relatively suspicious patients than among less suspicious patients. These findings imply (a) that although prominent eye content may not discriminate paranoid schizophrenia from all other personality patterns, it does identify the suspiciousness associated with paranoid states and other conditions similarly marked by reliance on projective defense (see p. 319), and (b) that *within the context of a schizophrenic disturbance,* such content is likely to be associated with paranoid rather than nonparanoid symptomatology.

These conclusions apply similarly to DAP studies of paranoid indicators. Ribler (1957), for example, reports failure to confirm differences between paranoid and nonparanoid subjects in eye and ear emphasis on figure drawings, but his nonparanoid subjects were a mixed group of unclassified schizophrenics, anxiety neurotics, and normal controls. Because those anxious neurotic persons with phobic symptomatology share with paranoid schizophrenics a proclivity for projective defense, many of Ribler's nonparanoid subjects would be expected to demonstrate such indicators of experienced external threat as eye and ear emphasis (see p. 319). Inasmuch as Ribler does not deal separately with the subgroups of his nonparanoid sample, his data do not answer the crucial diagnostic question of whether *among schizophrenic persons* eye and ear emphasis on figure drawings discriminates paranoid from nonparanoid disturbance.

Reznikoff and Nicholas (1958) circumvented these diagnostic issues by examining the figure drawings of a sample of hospitalized patients independently rated for degree of paranoid behavior regardless of diagnosis. Consistent with predictions concerning need for protection, they found subjects with prominent paranoid tendencies significantly more often than relatively nonparanoid subjects to produce drawings with heavy over-all line emphasis and a particular reinforcement of the outer boundaries of the figures.

Unfortunately, Reznikoff and Nicholas minimize these findings because they were the only two of 25 variables tested for which statistically significant results were obtained. However, in disagreement with their statistical reasoning, it should be noted that their derived probability values for the over-all line emphasis and boundary reinforcement variables were .05 and .02, respectively; two significant results, one of them at the .02 level, is clearly beyond what might be expected to occur solely by chance among 25 comparisons, which randomly should yield only one result at the .04 level.

Although the Wertheimer, Ribler, and Reznikoff and Nicholas studies thus illustrate that the potential utility of specific fantasy content for differentiating paranoid from nonparanoid schizophrenia may be disabused by narrow interpretations of research findings, the bulk of available data nevertheless indicates that isolated, one-to-one content interpretations are less reliable than diagnostic inferences based on the combination of various content categories into thematic scores. Examining such a combination, DuBrin (1962) compared the incidence in paranoid schizophrenic, nonparanoid schizophrenic, and nonschizophrenic subjects of *paranoid content,* which he defined as eye, face, or mask responses given to either human, animal, or inanimate percepts during spontaneous association. He found considerable within-group variability in percentages of paranoid content thus defined, but median tests revealed significant differences among the groups for both paranoid content percentage and presence versus absence of paranoid content. Each of his 24 paranoid schizophrenics had some paranoid content in his protocol, and all but one exceeded the total population median in paranoid content percentage.

Employing an even broader thematic approach, Bower, Testin, and Roberts (1960) devised a paranoid schizophrenic content scale with weighted scores for the following types of responses: perception of excessively depreciated objects and/or excessive depreciation of objects; concern with a searching, nonwholistic sensory acuity and awareness; dangers inferred from signs, cues, and partial aspects of objects and situations; and sadomasochistic relations seen between objects. Comparing groups of paranoid schizophrenic, catatonic schizophrenic, depressed, obsessive, and character disordered subjects, Bower et al. found that paranoid schizophrenics earned higher scores than any other group on this scale.

The utility of a thematic combination of content indicators of need for protection in differentiating paranoid from nonparanoid schizophrenia has been demonstrated by the work of Fisher and others with the Rorschach Barrier scale (see pp. 130–136). Fisher and Cleveland (1958, p. 236) hypothesize that paranoid schizophrenics, in connection with their exaggerated needs to maintain their autonomy and body integrity, are likely to give unusually high Barrier scores in comparison to undifferentiated schizophrenics, and Fisher (1964a) cites research affirming that paranoid schizophrenics do tend to earn significantly higher Barrier scores than nonparanoid schizophrenics.

There is therefore fairly consistent though not yet abundant research evidence that thematic patterns encompassing several content indicators of perceived external threat and need for protection validly differentiate paranoid from nonparanoid schizophrenics. Furthermore, although comprehensive one-to-one relationships between specific test responses and paranoid schizophrenia may not be justified, there is some basis for expecting that, given the context of a demonstrated schizophrenic disorder, certain content signs even taken singly may discriminate validly between paranoid and nonparanoid forms of schizophrenia.

Homosexual Concern. As noted on page 311, there is reason to expect that the greater a schizophrenic person's preoccupation with homosexual concerns, the more likely he is to have a paranoid rather than nonparanoid disorder. This conclusion does not presume any specific cause-effect relationship, nor does it slight the possibilities (a) that many paranoid persons may manifest no such concerns and (b) that many nonschizophrenic, nonparanoid persons may experience major problems around homosexuality. On the other hand, it does imply that test patterns associated with homosexual tendencies will assist the differentiation of paranoid from nonparanoid disturbance in schizophrenic subjects. Both specific content scores and thematic patterns have been proposed that appear to indicate homosexual concern and to facilitate the differential diagnosis of paranoid schizophrenia.

The first formal scale for psychodiagnostic evaluation of homosexual concern was developed for the Rorschach by Wheeler (1949). Wheeler, relying heavily on earlier suggestions by Lindner (1946) and Due and Wright (1945), compiled 20 "homosexual" signs, 14 pertaining to specific responses given to certain locations and six involving general content categories. Wheeler was able with these signs to differentiate significantly two groups of nonhomosexual male clinic patients, one group who were judged by their therapists to have overt, suppressed, or repressed concerns about homosexuality and another group who had displayed no such concerns. Of these 20 signs, which are listed in Table 4, the 13 indicated by an asterisk were considered by Wheeler to be sufficiently consistent with the total scale to justify their individual use.

Later studies by Davids, Joelson, and McArthur (1956) and Hooker (1958) of the frequency of Wheeler's signs in overtly homosexual and heterosexual men found both the mean number of Wheeler signs and the mean percentage of the signs among total R to be significantly larger in homosexual than in heterosexual groups. However, because there was considerable variability within their groups and many of the signs taken individually did not validly discriminate between groups,

TABLE 4

WHEELER'S (1949) RORSCHACH INDICATORS OF LATENT HOMOSEXUALITY

No.	Location	Content
*1	Card I, W	Mask or human or animal-like face
2	Card I, lower center D	Male or muscular female torso
3	Card II, bottom center D	Crab or crab-like animal
4	Card III, popular	Humans with sexual specification confused
5	Card III, popular	Humans with uncertain sexual specification
*6	Card III, popular	Animals or animal-like (dehumanized)
*7	Card IV, W	Contorted, monstrous, or threatening human or animal
*8	Card V, W or center D	Human or humanized animal
9	Card VI, center or top D	Object, with implication of cleavage
*10	Card VII, W or top D	Female with derogatory specifications
*11	Card VIII, popular	Several incongruous alternatives or animal with incongruous parts
*12	Card X, top center D	Dehumanized human figure
*13	Card X, top center D	Animal attacking or fighting over central object
14	Card X, pink with center blue	Human, with blue as oral specification
*15	Any	Oral detail
*16	Any	Anal detail or specification
*17	Any	Humans or animals "back-to-back"
18	Any	Religious specification
*19	Any	Male or female genitalia
*20	Any	Feminine clothing

* Recommended by Wheeler for individual use.

these authors express grave reservations about the utility of Wheeler's scale for diagnosing overt homosexuality in men. On the other hand, it should be noted that the possible limitations of Wheeler's signs for identifying overt homosexuality do not necessarily impugn their diagnostic significance for paranoid tendencies, inasmuch as the conceptual relationships between homosexuality and paranoid disturbance involve *homosexual concern* and *latent* homosexuality, not *overt* homosexual practice (see p. 308).

Hooker (1958) also examined the relative preference of her homosexual and heterosexual subjects for a number of Rorschach content themes outlined by Schafer (1954, pp. 130–138), and she found several of them to occur significantly more often among the homosexual group. These differentiating themes, which encompass many of the Wheeler signs, are the following, with illustrative examples quoted from Schafer:

ANAL ORIENTATION AND PREOCCUPATION. Direct anal reference (anus, rectum, buttocks, feces, defecation, rear ends of creatures), anal contact and perspective (figures seen from behind or with backs turned, buttocks bumping or touching, persons back to back), dirt (mud, smear, stain), and assault or explosion (bleeding rectum, erupting lava, flaming tail of rocket).

FEMININE EMPHASIS. Feminine clothing and objects (brassiere, corset, jewelry, cosmetics), decorative objects and plants (vase, chandelier, pretty flowers), and careful attention to details of dress of female figures.

REFERENCE TO PERVERSIONS. Lesbians embracing, bestiality, transvestism, etc.

GENERAL SEXUAL IMAGERY. Heightened frequency of genital (penis, vagina), anal (anus, rectum), and oral (mouth, breasts) contents.

It should be noted that both the Wheeler signs and these thematic patterns are formulated in terms of male dynamics. Little comparable study has been made of Rorschach indices of homosexual concern in women. However, it appears significant that three of the Schafer themes associated with homosexuality in men, namely, feminine emphasis, reference to perversions, and increased sexual imagery, are considered by Schafer to represent feminine identification and fear of and rejecting attitudes toward masculine roles. There is therefore some basis for expecting that analogous evidence of masculine identification and rejecting attitudes toward feminine roles will be associated with homosexual concerns among women.

Several Rorschach indices of homosexual concern in women can be extrapolated from Wheeler's signs and Schafer's content themes. First, it is reasonable to expect that homosexually concerned women will share with latently homosexual men evidence of confused and uncertain sexual identification, prominent sexual imagery in general, and reference to perverse sexual activity. Second, the derogation of female figures and emphasis on feminine accoutrements observed in homosexual men might well be replaced in homosexually oriented women with flattering descriptions of female images ("beautiful," "slender," "well-dressed," "graceful," "cultured,"), derogatory specifications of masculine figures ("dumb," "crude," "clumsy," "ugly," "weak," "boorish," "helpless,"), and attraction to masculine roles, as indicated by an emphasis on such contents as implements, mechanical objects, and athletic events and participants. [4] Although the validity of such patterns

---

[4] Distinctions between *feminine* and *masculine* contents should be recognized as flexible and relative rather than absolute or exclusive. Persons with wide-ranging

for feminine homosexuality has not been carefully examined, an extensive case study by Fromm and Elonen (1951) does confirm the association of many such responses, particularly those derogating male figures, with female homosexuality.

Draw-a-Person indices of homosexual concern have not been explored as fully as these various Rorschach content categories. Although Machover (1949) suggests many DAP clues to homosexual tendencies, no formal homosexual scales comparable to the Wheeler signs have been developed for this test. Furthermore, representative studies by Barker, Mathis, and Powers (1953) and Grams and Rinder (1958) have revealed little consistent difference between homosexual and heterosexual subjects on various DAP clues proposed in the literature as homosexual indicators.

With regard to differential diagnosis, there is evidence that Rorschach indices of homosexual concern do contribute to the identification of paranoid tendencies in schizophrenic subjects. Aronson (1952), for example, obtained significantly different numbers and percentages of Wheeler signs from 30 paranoid, 30 nonparanoid psychotic, and 30 normal subjects. His paranoid group had a mean frequency of 7.10 signs (22.9% of total R), whereas the nonparanoid psychotic group on the average produced only 1.96 signs (8.5%) and the normals 1.10 signs (4.9%). With particular reference to the marked difference between his paranoid and nonparanoid psychotic groups, Aronson appropriately concludes that prominence of the Wheeler signs in the Rorschach of a psychotic subject enhances the likelihood of his having a paranoid disturbance.

Grauer (1954) subsequently took issue with Aronson's inferred co-variation of homosexual and paranoid tendencies, but the data Grauer reports actually tend to confirm the significance for paranoid disturbance of frequent Wheeler signs in the Rorschach records of schizophrenic subjects. Examining 31 paranoid schizophrenics, Grauer obtained a mean of 3.07 Wheeler signs (12.7% of total R), which he states does not differ significantly from the frequency of these signs in Aronson's nonparanoid psychotic group and thus refutes Aronson's hypothesis.

---

interests normally extend their activities beyond rigidly defined sex-appropriate roles; neither the man with horticultural interest nor the woman with a mechanical bent, for example, can automatically be assumed to be grappling with an uncertain sexual identification. Furthermore, the current zeitgeist, in which women are being increasingly encouraged to engage in many professional and recreational activities formerly reserved to men, is relevant to the interpretation of fantasy content. The inference of homosexual tendencies should be limited to those instances where traditionally opposite-sex interests clearly submerge any but minimal attention to sex-appropriate roles.

However, the t value Grauer lists for the mean difference in Wheeler signs between his paranoid schizophrenic and Aronson's nonparanoid psychotic group is 1.75, which represents a probability of chance occurrence of less than .10 for samples of this size (Snedecor, 1956, p. 46) and hence should not be unqualifiedly interpreted as controverting Aronson's work. Furthermore, because Grauer was in part replicating Aronson's study and thereby tacitly employing a unidirectional hypothesis regarding the test performance of paranoid persons, it is appropriate to apply a one-tailed test to his data. With a one-tailed test Grauer's t of 1.75 achieves the .05 probability level conventionally required for "significance" (see footnote, p. 30).

In a recent review of studies with the Wheeler scale, Meketon, Griffith, Taylor, and Wiedman (1962) conclude that, although the power of the scale is low, it has uniformly yielded results that are in the expected direction and justify its continued use. Meketon et al. also stress that Wheeler's signs, having been derived from a latently homosexual population, are likely to identify latent homosexuality more effectively than overt homosexuality and are therefore particularly relevant to paranoid conditions that are in part characterized by latent homosexual concerns. They support this hypothesis by presenting the following cumulated mean Wheeler percentage for approximately 550 subjects sampled in various previous studies: normal—6.2%; neurotic—8.2%; overt homosexual—13.2%; and paranoid—15.3%.

There is some research basis, then, for employing Wheeler-type signs to discriminate paranoid from nonparanoid disturbance in schizophrenic subjects. The Schafer themes identified by Hooker as relating significantly to homosexuality have unfortunately not been similarly studied in regard to the paranoid-nonparanoid distinction. In view of the overlap of these thematic patterns with Wheeler's signs, however, it is reasonable to expect that appropriate research would demonstrate their utility for discriminating paranoid from nonparanoid schizophrenic subjects. In practice, therefore, it appears justified to entertain a paranoid hypothesis concerning those schizophrenic men whose Rorschach content reveals anal orientation, rejection of masculine identity, and feminine identification, as illustrated above, and for those schizophrenic women who exhibit rejection of feminine identity and masculine identification.

BEHAVIORAL VARIABLES

A schizophrenic subject's approach to and comments about the testing situation often contribute to the identification of paranoid disturbance. Relevant behaviors of this type, all reflecting prominent reliance on projective defense, fall into three general categories: *externaliza-*

tion of blame, distrust of the motives and actions of others, and *cautious reluctance to commit oneself.*

Externalization of Blame. The subject who projects is likely to engage in two characteristic types of test behavior. First, he tends to attribute his difficulties with test items to the nature of the items themselves. Thus he may excuse his quandaries on WAIS Similarities with "There is no similarity," on Picture Completion with "There's nothing missing," and on Block Design with "There aren't enough blocks" or "It can't be done." Responses of this type also occur in nonparanoid contexts, primarily in connection with narcissistic and psychopathic forms of character disorder that are characterized by defenses against loss of self-esteem; their repetition, however, particularly when the subject is reminded that he is being asked for similarities, that in each picture there is something missing, and that the designs are soluble, points to a rigid, probably paranoid reliance on projective defense. Projective mechanisms are especially likely to be operating in subjects who express such responsibility-absolving comments even before attending to or reflecting on the tasks set for them.

Second, the externalizing subject often casts aspersions on the significance of the tests as a means of subverting, at least in his own eyes, any unfavorable inferences the examiner might draw from his responses to them. He is thus inclined to depreciate the value and/or validity of the examination by criticizing the materials ("That's a silly question"; "These cards are poorly made"), the concept of testing ("I've read that these tests really aren't any good"; "I'm sure all these questions really aren't telling you anything important about me"), and the examiner ("Are you fully qualified to give these tests?"; "I don't think you know enough about me to understand the situation").

In an interesting study of such behavioral indices of externalization of blame, Wiener (1957) compared the WAIS Similarities and Picture Completion performance of two groups of subjects, one that had been given instructions intended to increase distrust of the experimental situation and another that had received no such instructions. He found the "distrust" group significantly more frequently than the controls to respond that there was no similarity or that nothing was missing.

Distrust of the Motives and Actions of Others. The subject who projects is also prone to express considerable concern about the nature, purpose, and implications of the testing and unusual interest in the examiner's behavior during the test administration. He repetitively asks why the testing is needed, what it will reveal about him, how the results will be evaluated, and to whom they will be communicated. He attends to what the examiner is recording, expressing dismay that all of his asides and interjections are being written down, and he questions certain technicalities of the procedures ("I see there are other parts to that test; how come you didn't give them all to me?"; "Why didn't you ask me to explain about that response as you did about the others?"). He inquires why the tests are made as they are, by whom and where they are made, and to what kinds of persons they are given. Additionally, he is likely on the Rorschach to maintain the fiction that there is some specific meaning in each of the various cards that is hidden from or intended to deceive him, and he repetitively asks, "What is it really supposed to be?" These behaviors taken singly are not necessarily pathologic, but their persistence in the face of reasonable, straightforward answers bespeaks the suspiciousness and mistrust associated with projective defense.

Cautious Reluctance to Commit Oneself. Reflecting the reluctance accompanying projective mechanisms, the subject who projects tends to protect his flanks by familiarizing himself as much as possible with the nature of the test situation before making any commitment to it. Thus, in addition to asking many questions about the nature and purpose of the tests, he reads the backs of the Rorschach cards, notes from its title that the WAIS is an intelligence test, and repetitively requests instructions about what he is expected to do. Furthermore, the paranoid person's exaggerated concern with knowing the rules and avoiding any transgressions for which he could be penalized often inclines him to repeat on several Rorschach cards such queries as, "Just tell you what it looks like, that's what I'm supposed to do?", "Is it permissible to turn them?", and "Can I break it up into parts?" Although such requests for external support often appear in nonschizophrenic subjects, particularly those with prominent passive-dependent character features, their reiteration by a schizophrenic person points to paranoid cautiousness.

The relative prominence of these three categories of behavioral variables in paranoid persons usually reflects their differing preferences for megalomanic and suspicious behavior patterns. To the extent that a paranoid subject's defensive style is oriented primarily toward megalomania rather than suspiciousness, he tends to exhibit relatively little distrust or caution and to devote his major defensive energies to externalization of blame. Thus the megalomanic paranoid responds to the tests in a lofty, patronizing, and self-assured manner marked by pomposity and condescension, and, should the examiner in any way challenge or dent his self-aggrandizing, he is quick to counter by heaping invective and abuse on the tests, the tester, the hospital, clinic, or office, and the world in general. The predominantly suspicious paranoid, on the other hand, is less given to denounce his environment than he is to deal cautiously and distrustfully with it, and the more he feels threatened the more likely he is to resort to careful surveillance and deliberation rather than to testy rebukes.

In concluding this section, it should be stressed that these various behaviors, like the several structural and content indices of paranoid tendencies, are not unique to paranoid schizophrenia. First, each may occur in a normal context, and it is only their frequent repetition in the face of explanation and reassurance that suggests personality disturbance. Second, their maladaptive recurrence usually represents excessive reliance on projective defense, which may appear in phobic neurosis, certain organic psychoses, and some patterns of character disorder as well as in paranoid schizophrenia. The diagnostic significance of these behavioral variables in the current context is that, given schizophrenic disturbance, their prominence strongly suggests a paranoid rather than nonparanoid form of the disorder.

CASE STUDIES [5]

The following case studies illustrate the differential diagnosis of paranoid schizophrenia. The protocols presented contrast interestingly with the four in the previous chapter, each of which contains some paranoid features but exemplifies primarily nonparanoid disturbance. The two protocols in this chapter also differ from each other in a manner corresponding roughly to the distinction between suspicious and megalomanic forms of paranoid disturbance. At the same time, they demonstrate that in practice there may not be a sharp distinction between suspicious and megalomanic patterns of test response, but rather that many paranoid subjects combine features of both.

The first of these two patients produced constricted, carefully controlled protocols while employing a legalistic, pompous language style and attempting to maintain a superior relationship to the tests and the examiner. The second patient produced expansive test protocols, particularly on the Rorschach, but accompanied his responses with many suspicious comments. Thus the one patient was constricted-suspicious in the structure of his test performance but expansive-megalomanic in his behavior, whereas the other behaved suspiciously

[5] The format followed in presenting the case studies is described on pages 254–257.

while responding expansively. In relation to content variables, however, the two patients gave similar evidence of prominent projective defense.

CASE 1

This patient is a 41-year-old skilled machinist and part-time farmer who was admitted to the hospital after a three-week period of increasingly incapacitating anxiety. The owner of three small farms, he had become so preoccupied with fears that his property would be damaged by the elements or stolen by thieves that he was unable to eat, sleep, or work effectively at his job. Although not previously hospitalized, he had visited a psychiatrist sporadically over the previous two years, primarily to seek advice on how to curb his wife's imputed infidelity and lavish spending. He could offer no evidence for these accusations against his wife, nor were they in any way confirmed by her, and his psychiatrist had consequently concluded that he was suffering paranoid delusions. However, the patient had rejected a recommendation for treatment and did not seek formal help before the sudden exacerbation of symptoms that precipitated his hospitalization.

This man was the youngest of five children in an economically marginal family. He was the only one of his siblings to complete high school, and after graduation he had begun working and supporting his parents. Little known of his early life, except that he appears to have been a shy, sensitive, suspicious, and withdrawn child with few friends and that he was excused from military service on the grounds of "psychiatric inadequacy." His adult life was marked by uneven achievement. He earned sufficient money in his trade to have purchased the farm land on which he lived, but he frequently changed jobs and was seldom promoted to positions of responsibility.

His work difficulties stemmed primarily from continual conflict with supervisors, whose authority he resented and challenged and whom he considered to dislike him and intentionally make things difficult for him. Also significant was his wife's report that he exhausted himself around the farms doing extra work for which he was reluctant to hire anyone else because anyone he hired would have "ulterior motives." At the age of 34 he had married his wife after she became pregnant by him—"a compulsory arrangement because of child conception" in his words—and their marriage had been marked by strife and discord.

The patient was considered on admission to present paranoid symptomatology and to be suffering from an acute exacerbation of a chronic paranoid schizophrenic condition. Testing was requested to assess the validity of this diagnostic impression. The patient remained in the hospital for seven weeks, during which time he continued to be distressed and responded neither to psychotherapy nor medication. He was subsequently transferred to a nearby state hospital, where he remained for five months on a variety of treatments before recovering sufficiently to leave the hospital and return home.

WECHSLER ADULT INTELLIGENCE SCALE

Information

RUBBER: +. PRESIDENTS: +. LONGFELLOW: +. WEEKS: +. PANAMA: +. BRAZIL: +. HEIGHT: 5'2". ITALY: +. CLOTHES:+. WASHINGTON: February (?) 19. HAMLET: +. VATICAN: +. PARIS: +. EGYPT: +. YEAST: There are bacteria in the yeast; I don't know the exact process. POPULATION: +. SENATORS: +. GENESIS: I have never read it. (?) I'm not interested in the Bible. TEMPERATURE: +. ILIAD: +. BLOOD VESSELS: Veins, arteries, and the heart itself, which is also a blood vessel. KORAN: A book used in the Jewish faith. FAUST: I've forgotten; I know it's a French opera. ETHNOLOGY: dk. APOCRYPHA: dk. RAW SCORE: 20.

These responses are generally clear and relevant, but the scatter of success and failures suggests some inconsistency in the patient's cognitive functioning. After missing HEIGHT, he passes the factorially related, more difficult ITALY, PARIS, and EGYPT, and similarly within factorially related items he passes POPULATION and SENATORS after missing the relatively easy WASHINGTON and succeeds on TEMPERATURE after failing YEAST.

The quality of his response style on these items tentatively suggests pomposity and a focus on protective behaviors. He shows some inclination to demean the significance to him of what he does not know ("I'm not interested in the Bible"), to emphasize that he really does know many things (the author of Faust is "forgotten," but "I know it's a French opera"), and to attend to ambitious tasks ("I don't know the exact process"). Although none of these behaviors necessarily identifies paranoid schizophrenia, each is a subtle clue to a behavioral style that derives from reliance on projective defense and, in the context of a schizophrenic disturbance, suggests a paranoid rather than a nonparanoid orientation.

Comprehension

ENVELOPE: It would be my obligation to put it in a mailbox; a United States stamp gives it sanction (2). BAD COMPANY: So as not to learn bad habits (2). MOVIES: If I couldn't put it out myself, I'd call the owner or an employee of the theater (2). TAXES: Support the government (2). IRON: Take necessary action while the opportunity is there (2). CHILD LABOR: To keep unscrupulous people from exploiting children (1). FOREST: It's important how large the forest is; I'd try to walk in one definite direction, and I'd also climb a tree to see where I was (1). DEAF: They have no realization of what sound is, and they don't know how to use their vocal cords (0). CITY LAND: People live closer in the cities, and it's because of the relative distance between home and place of business. (?) If there are many homes in a neighborhood, the property is worth more for commercial reasons (0). MARRIAGE: So as to conform to legality; it's the moral law (0). BROOKS: Never heard it; I think it applies to people of low intellect creating a furor to gain self-interest (1). SWALLOW: You're not getting a complete thing just by having a mouthful of it or a small portion of it (1). RAW SCORE: 18.

These responses are not grossly deviant, but they subtly reveal both the inroads of dissociation and peculiar language on the patient's cognitive focusing and a legalistic, authoritarian attitude consistent with paranoid trends. Suggesting dissociation are his irrelevant comment on FOREST ("It's important how large the forest is"), his peculiar use of "having a mouthful" as equivalent to "small portion" on SWALLOW, and his condensed, difficult to follow explanation on CITY LAND. Although on CITY LAND he appears to have in mind some reasonable relationship between the proximity of potential patrons and the commercial value of business property, his references to "relative distance" and "many homes in the neighborhood" skirt loosely around such a possible explanation and fail to bring it into sharp focus.

Highly significant for paranoid orientation is his unusual addendum on ENVELOPE, "A United States stamp gives it sanction." Here and in his later concern with "moral law" on MARRIAGE he demonstrates a propensity to think in legalistic terms about authority, rules, and the dictates it is necessary to follow to escape punishment. Of related interest is his reference on CHILD LABOR to "exploiting" by "unscrupulous" persons; though neither irrelevant nor peculiar, this response, in contrast to the tenor of blander possible replies (e.g., "children should be in school"), suggests concern about uncharitable motives and unkindly actions that are attributed to others. As previously stated, such responses are not unique to paranoid schizophrenia, but in the setting of a schizophrenic disturbance they point to a paranoid condition.

Similarities

ORANGE: Citrus fruits (2). COAT: Wearing apparel (2). AXE: Cut wood (1). DOG: Have four legs, two eyes, and a mouth (1). NORTH: Both go in the same direction, halfway between them. (?) There are

45 degrees between north and west, which equals northwest, and that goes the same way (0). EYE: Two of the five senses (2). AIR: Contain hydrogen and oxygen in small amounts (1). TABLE: Usually have four legs (0). EGG: An egg is a seed, an unfertile seed (0). POEM: They meet on a philosophical basis. (?) If you make a statue of a man, he must be someone great, and usually a poem is written about someone great; they're monuments, both of them (1). WOOD: Alcohol is made from wood (0). PRAISE: There is no similarity (0). FLY: No similarity, other than that the membranes of a leaf and a fly's wings are both webbed (0). RAW SCORE: 10.

Most significant in these responses is the grossly disturbed reasoning they disclose. Although the patient eventually achieves a partially adequate answer on POEM ("monuments"), he precedes it with the flagrantly circumstantial conclusion that because both poems and statues often commemorate great men, "They meet on a philosophical basis." Even more difficult to follow is his tortuous logic on NORTH, where he apparently concludes that north and west are similar by virtue of sharing in common the 45-degree bisecting direction *northwest*.

In addition to this evidence of reasoning impairment, the patient also exhibits here some of the paranoid features noted on Information. His Similarities responses attest his inclination to approach situations carefully and to protect himself by parading his erudition where he is knowledgeable and externalizing his failures where he is not. He avoids excessive commitment by qualifying his responses (table and chair "*usually* have four legs"), he adds unrequired extra information (eye and ear are "two of the five senses"; air and water "contain hydrogen and oxygen in small amounts"), and he emphatically denies the existence of meaningful similarities on the last two items.

Picture Completion

KNOB: +. TAIL: +. NOSE: +. HANDLES: That one appears to be in order . . . but no windshield wipers. DIAMOND: +. WATER: +. NOSE PIECE: That would be something to ask a fellow who works in the spectacle business . . . I can see that a bridge across the nose is needed, though (+). PEG: Bow. OAR LOCK: Man to propel the boat. BASE THREAD: +. STARS: +. DOG TRACKS: His left foot. FLORIDA: The divisions of the states. STACKS: +. LEG: +. ARM IMAGE: Her right arm. FINGER +. SHADOW: +. STIRRUP: Rider. SNOW: It's a complete barnyard; I live on a farm. EYEBROW: It's complete. RAW SCORE: 12.

On this subtest the patient gives further evidence of the inconsistent cognitive focusing and paranoid orientation noted on the verbal subtests. Although, with the exception of "windshield wipers" on HANDLES, his errors are of types common to normal and patient groups, his over-all performance must still be regarded as markedly scattered. He passes WATER, BASE THREAD, STACKS, and FINGER after failing the factorially related, much easier HANDLES, and he similarly responds correctly on LEG and SHADOW after missing both OAR LOCK and DOG TRACKS.

Paranoid orientation is suggested here by further instances of his earlier observed inclination to deflect affronts to his self-esteem by demeaning the significance or denying the existence of situations in which he is not fully competent. Thus, although he has been instructed that these are pictures with important parts missing, he begins on HANDLES by asserting that the picture "appears to be in order" and later avers that SNOW and EYEBROW are "complete." Additionally significant regarding maintenance of self-esteem is his addendum on SNOW, "I live on a farm," in which he appears to be bolstering his position as if to add, "And I'm well qualified to identify when a barnyard is complete."

Further illustrating the patient's protective externalization is his initial response to NOSE PIECE. Although he was able eventually to answer this item, he preceded any effort to attend to the stimulus card with the complaint that it could more appropriately be presented to "a fellow who works in the spectacle business." Such aggressive criticism of test items is usually a rationalization designed to avoid embarrassment should the item be failed, and in a schizophrenic setting it implies paranoid disturbance.

Block Design

ITEM 1: 25" (4). ITEM 2: Fails first trial; 4" on second trial (2). ITEM 3: 8" (4). ITEM 4: 12" (4). ITEM 5: 4" (4). ITEM 6: 20" (4). ITEM 7: Test discontinued. PARTIAL RAW SCORE: 22.

The patient's response to this subtest was dramatic and informative. On ITEM 1 his solution was delayed by his insistence on matching all the sides of the sample design, even though he was instructed that only the top needed to be the same. Among possible interpretations of this behavior are distrust of the examiner, need to assert autonomy by doing it his own way, and an ambitious quest for a more perfect solution than is required, all of which are consistent with a projective defensive style.

On ITEM 2 he exhibited the more blustery, pompous facet of his defenses by refusing to attend to the examiner's demonstration and impatiently protesting, "I know how to do it." He prefaced his work on the task by asking, "Just on top?", which here is not only distrustful but also grossly inappropriate in view of the two-dimensional nature of the stimulus, and he then embarked on a series of abortive manipulations of the blocks that did not represent any significant progress toward a solution within the allotted time. After a second demonstration, he completed the design very quickly and, as his other times indicate, facilely executed the next four designs. His abject and unrationalizable failure on ITEM 2 following his blatant braggadocio had apparently undermined his defenses, however, for in spite of his easy success on ITEMS 3–6 he was markedly agitated and tremulous while working on them and began to complain in a somewhat feeble and subdued manner of uncontrollable nervousness. On ITEM 7, where he was unable to effect an immediate solution, he became so visibly wretched that the examiner elected to discontinue the subtest and allow him hopefully to restitute his defenses.

Scale Scores

Information: 12. Comprehension: 10. Similarities: 8. Picture Completion: 9. Block Design: 7 (minimal estimate).

The major relevant aspect of these scales scores is the four-point discrepancy between the factorially related Information and Similarities subtests. This intertest scatter complements the intratest scatter noted on Information and Picture Completion in identifying inconsistent cognitive efficiency and suggesting impaired capacity to maintain a relevant focus of attention.

Discussion. This very rich WAIS protocol clearly demonstrates schizophrenic ego impairments and a paranoid orientation. The patient's dissociated, peculiar, and condensed verbalizations on Comprehension and his scatter both within and between subtests strongly suggest the interference of intruding elements with his capacity to focus his attention effectively on the relevant information in his environment. This impairment of his cognitive focusing and the reasoning disturbance revealed by his circumstantiality on Similarities constitute compelling evidence of thought disorder.

With regard to paranoid tendencies, the patient's test behavior reflects an habitually cautious approach to situations, a proclivity to pompous bravado and externalization of blame when his competence is threatened, and a susceptibility to dissolution of his controls when he is unable successfully to rationalize his actions. Each of these behaviors is consistent with projective defensive style and concomitant paranoid orientation.

RORSCHACH

Card I 4″

1. (*Dm F+ Hd,Cg*) Part of a human being in the middle, in a dress. (*Parts?*) I see the torso and the legs, minus the feet, and the

neck and head; she's wearing a dress, and she looks like she'd be a little plump.

2. (*Wm F+ A*) Sea life or a winged insect; no, it's not an insect. (?) It just looks like a crustacea; it's the way it looks.

3. (*Wm,S F+,M (Hd)*) It could be a hobgoblin, with horns and holes there for the eyes. (?) The eyes and the mouth are here [white spaces], and the shape of the eyes and mouth suggest a hobgoblin; it has a rather nasty expression to it.

Card II 5″

4. (*D— F— Sex*) ∨ It looks like—it has the appearance of female organs, I believe, from what pictures I've seen of them [upper center black detail]. (?) It just has the look of that fleshy part, the clitoris I believe it's called.

4a. (*Dv CF Sex*) ∨ There may be one up here too [bottom center red]. (?) Because of the redness of the flesh; but this other part [reference to #4] looks more like it.

5. (*Dm F+ Ad*) ∨ Part of an insect, with antennas on the top [bottom center red]. (?) It's an insect, but with a part of it missing. (*Which part?*) The rear parts are missing.

Card III 12″

6. (*Dm F+ (Hd) Peculiar*) ∨ It could be like a man from Mars, like the pictures you see of them on TV [black portion]; the arms are up here and the face here [bottom center detail], but it's incomplete; there's nothing to propel it. (?) It just could be some sort of a being, with the eyes here [darker portions of "face" detail], and it's not complete because I can't see the legs. (*Propel?*) Because it doesn't have any legs.

Card IV 8″

7. (*Wm F+ A*) ∨ Perhaps we have some sea life here; it's the head of something [lower center detail], with eyes and antenna on it, and these [upper lateral details] could be its means of propelling itself.

Card V 3″

8. (*Wm F+ A P*) ∨ Now we have a butterfly, complete with antenna and wings, and that's all I'll say for it.

Card VI 20″

9. (*Dm F+,M Hd*) It's nothing . . . I don't see anything at all. (*What does it look most like to you?*) In its entirety it's nothing. (*What else could you say about it?*) Well, this part up here [uppermost detail], with the two light spots, could be a face with eyes, either facing me, uh, or . . . (?) I can't tell you anything more about it.

Card VII 1′ 30″

10. (W— F— H,Cg Barrier) It's nothing . . . no . . . it bears no similarity to anything I can think of. (*How would you describe the way it looks?*) Just as an inkblot. (*What is the closest it comes to looking like anything?*) Well, it could be that if the top parts were brought together, it could be a person with a large coat on.

Card VIII 21″

11. (Dm F+ Cg Barrier) ∨ It could be some sort of jacket here [pink and orange detail]. (?) It looks like shoulders, sleeves, and lapels in these parts.

12. (Dm F+ Ad P-tendency) > Here it could be a four-legged animal with a tail, but wait, there are only three legs. (*Kind of animal?*) On the order of a woodchuck or a weasel.

Card IX 20″

13. (Dd F+ Hd Queer) These were colored inks—were they lithographed or photolithed? There isn't much of anything here . . . no . . . it doesn't compare with any material thing or beings I've seen; but there does appear to be a pair of eyes in here [center green and white slits], but they're not proper eyes. (*Proper?*) No, they're not proper, because they close from the sides, the lids or hair of them is on the sides.

Card X Reject

It's a lot of pretty colors, but no creatures I can see . . . no . . . nothing. (*What does it look like to you?*) Nothing, nothing at all; just some varied and symmetrical colors. (*What would you say it reminds you of?*) Nothing . . . no [turns and studies from various angles], nothing.

13a. (S F+ (Hd)) (*Does any part of it look like anything to you?*) This part [center white space] coud be some peculiar comic strip character, with his eyes here [white spaces between pink and gray details], the nose here [center orange detail], but it wouldn't have a mouth.

Scores

R	13+2	M	0+2	H	1	F+%	85%
W	5(39%)	F	13+1	Hd	3	R+%	85%
D	7+1(54%)	CF	0+1	(Hd)	2+1	P	1+1
Dd+S	1+2(7%)			A	3		
				Ad	2	High W%	80%
				Cg	1+2	High D%	100%
Peculiar	1			Sex	1+1		
Queer	1					Barrier	2

Discussion. Several features of this Rorschach protocol demonstrate both schizophrenic disorder and paranoid tendencies. With regard to schizophrenia, the patient's brief, constricted record, though not reflecting gross ego impairment, does suggest impaired cognitive focusing, poor judgment, limited empathic capacity, and inadequate defensive resources. Specifically, difficulty in maintaining a relevant focus of attention is revealed by his peculiar language on response #6, where he speaks of legs as being used to "propel" a person; by his queer approach on #13, where instead of viewing the blot from a more advantageous position he describes eyes as closing "from the sides"; and by his deviant tempo (rejection of Card X after a response to Card IX).

Concerning judgment, the patient's inadequate number of Popular responses (one with one additional) indicates a marked inability or reluctance to share common ways of perceiving. Inasmuch as other scores relating to reality testing capacity are well-retained here ($F+\%$ and $R+\%$ are 85), it would appear that reluctance rather than inability is involved; nevertheless, his low P score implies that his actual judgments will tend to be idiosyncratic and maladaptive, and such reluctance to endorse conventional realities is additionally significant for paranoid trends.

The patient's handling of object relations similarly demonstrates both schizophrenic and paranoid qualities. His single H response and failure to produce any main M's connote limited capacity for close, empathic relationships with other people. Furthermore, his H response and one of the two additional M's he does give occur on cards to which he responded only after considerable encouragement (Cards VI and VII); it might be argued in view of the examiner's urging on these cards that they should be considered rejections, in which case the record would contain no H and only one additional M. On the other hand, to obtain adequate test data from such cautious and guarded patients as this man it is often necessary to employ gently phrased and carefully timed exhortation, and responses thus elicited usually contribute meaningfully to the summary scores of a brief record. Notice, however, that on Card X, to which the patient declined to respond after two general questions, rejection is scored and the percept he eventually gave in answer to a specific, leading question is considered additional.

Indicating defensive inadequacy is the patient's *Sex* response in #4. The mere presence of a *Sex* response in such a brief, constricted record suggests failure of repressive control over ideation, and the significance for such failure of this particular response is enhanced by the facts that (a) it is perceptually inaccurate and (b) it is a feminine sexual response given to an area that in the case of a sexual association is usually perceived as male rather than female genitalia.

Turning to evidence of paranoid tendencies, this record clearly illustrates the relatively well-retained ego functioning, cautious and constricted approach, sensitivity to scrutiny, critical and depreciatory view of the environment, and latent homosexual concerns that discriminate paranoid from nonparanoid forms of schizophrenia. Despite the schizophrenic impairments noted above and the fact that he was sufficiently disturbed to require several weeks hospitalization, this man has retained enough control to limit his responses almost exclusively to accurately perceived and logically reasoned percepts. Although the brevity of his record suggests he may have been withholding other, less adequate responses, his doing so would nevertheless imply an adaptive awareness of the inadequacy of such responses and the ability to suppress them in favor of percepts of good quality.

Caution and constriction emerge in many features of this patient's behavior as well as in his reluctance to use any determinants other than pure form ($F\%$ is 100). He leaves little doubt concerning his intention to control what he reveals to the examiner (on #8, "That's all I'll say for it"; on #9, after appearing about to reveal a significant idea associating with "facing me," "I can't tell you anything about it"). His comment on #13, "Were they lithographed or photolithed?", appears to reflect both an exaggerated need to familiarize himself with the test and an attempt to exchange his role as testee for that of intellectual observer. Finally, he conspicuously turns five of the cards to an inverse position before examining them. The primary determinants of such precipitous and emphatic card-turning, which include oppositional behavior, emphasis on asserting autonomy, and distrust of the position presented by the examiner, identify the cautious, self-protective approach to situations that characterizes the paranoid posture.

The patient evinces sensitivity to scrutiny primarily by his frequent references to eyes and faces in his percepts (#'s 3, 6, 7, 9, 13, & 13a). Such responses, emphasized by the allusion in #3 to the "nasty expression" on the face, identify a propensity to perceive in the environment the hazards of unsympathetic investigation and biased indictment. Associated with this man's perception of such threat is the depreciatory manner in which he formulates his human and animal percepts. Of his six associations to human figures, only one is an able-bodied, fully endowed H percept; three others are Hd responses with major parts missing (#'s 1, 9, & 13) and the other two are (Hd) responses (#'s 3 & 6) that are incomplete and dehumanized.

Furthermore, as the infirmity ascribed to the figure in #6 (no legs to "propel" himself) graphically implies, he appears to promote his own sense of security and impregnability by depreciating in fantasy the power and significance of others persons. Such *Hd* and (*Hd*) responses considered singly are not pathologic, but their frequency here in comparison to the single *H* identifies the patient's reluctance to measure other people accurately and grant them their full stature.

Finally significant for paranoid tendencies is the latent homosexual concern suggested by the frequency of Wheeler signs in this record. Response #'s 1, 4, and 6 provide three Wheeler signs (see Table 4), and #'s 10 and 11 suggest a fourth; in thematic language, these responses reflect uncertain sexual identity, pressing sexual fantasy, and feminine emphasis. Three Wheeler signs in this brief record constitutes a Wheeler percentage (23%) that in a schizophrenic context is highly likely to be associated with paranoid tendencies.

Summary. The thinking disorder suggested by this man's scatter, dissociation, and disturbed reasoning on the WAIS, together with the Rorschach evidence of limited capacity for adaptive object relationships and inadequate defensive resources, are consistent with schizophrenic disturbance. His relatively well-retained organizational and reality-testing capacities, however, suggest a paranoid rather than nonparanoid form of the disturbance, and this impression is clearly substantiated by his cautious, constricted, suspicious approach to his experiences, his self-aggrandizing proclivities to externalize blame for his difficulties and depreciate the objects in his world, and his latent homosexual concern.

CASE 2

This patient is a 19-year-old college sophomore who was admitted to the hospital for diagnostic study with a recent history of uncontrollable crying and temper outbursts. The first of these outbursts had occurred four months earlier when he had suddenly dissolved into tears while watching a fight scene in a movie—"It got to me, the way everyone was fighting without knowing why." He had subsequently sought help at the counseling center of the school he was attending, and a communication from that agency described his campus behavior as characterized by "resistance to established authority," "suspiciousness about the motives of people around him," "escape into daydreaming and fantasy," and "volcanic temper."

This young man's mother had died when he was eight years old, and he had been raised by a maternal aunt who had moved in with him and his father. The latter was a strict, authoritarian figure whose business affairs kept him away from the home much of the time. The patient apparently adjusted relatively well until he was 15, when his father remarried. He viewed the remarriage as "deceitful" and his stepmother as a "shrew," and he was supported in both opinions by his aunt. He bickered constantly with his stepmother and began to withdraw increasingly into solitary activities and daydreams, many of which had violently aggressive themes.

He was referred for testing to determine whether his breakdown was of schizophrenic proportions. After two weeks of hospitalization transfer to a psychiatric hospital oriented toward long-term intensive treatment was advised, but the young man's family rejected this recommendation. He subsequently returned to his home in a different community and was lost to follow-up.

WECHSLER ADULT INTELLIGENCE SCALE

Information

RUBBER: +. PRESIDENTS: +. LONGFELLOW: +. WEEKS: +. PANAMA: +. BRAZIL: +. HEIGHT: 5'2". ITALY: +. CLOTHES: +. WASHINGTON: dk, some time in February. HAMLET: +. VATICAN: +. PARIS: 2500 miles. EGYPT: Asia. YEAST: +. POPULATION: 75 million, I think. SENATORS: +. GENESIS: +. TEMPERATURE: dk. ILLIAD: +. BLOOD VESSELS: Veins . . . dk . . . something goes on by osmosis through the membranes. KORAN: +. FAUST: Shakespeare. ETHNOLOGY: dk. RAW SCORE: 19

These responses contain three indications of disordered thinking, the most prominent of which is the patient's considerably scattered cognitive efficiency. After failing HEIGHT and EGYPT, he succeeds on the factorially related and much more difficult KORAN, and he similarly passes GENESIS, ILLIAD, and KORAN after missing the easier, factorially related POPULATION. Second, his comment about "osmosis through the membranes" on BLOOD VESSELS is irrelevant to the question asked and suggests dissociation. Third, his reference to Shakespeare on FAUST, though not irrelevant, has a perseverative quality; faced with a literary question, he has difficulty shifting his focus from his previous accurate literary response on HAMLET.

Comprehension

ENVELOPE: Mail it (2). BAD COMPANY: They'll get you in trouble (1). MOVIES: Holler fire and look for the nearest fire box (0). TAXES: To keep the government going (2). IRON: If you have an advantage, use it (2). CHILD LABOR: So parents can't push kids out and start them working (0). FOREST: Look at something in the distance, like a tree, and go to that; I'd just try to keep in a straight line and walk my way out (1). DEAF: Because they've never heard anybody speak (1). CITY LAND: It's more valuable as a business prospect (1). MARRIAGE: To make sure they're married legally (1). BROOKS: People with not too many brains are usually the ones spouting off all the time on something they know nothing about (2). SWALLOW: It's like don't count your chickens; just because there's one indication of something, it doesn't mean the thing is going to come to pass (2). RAW SCORE: 19.

This Comprehension performance presents several subtle clues to thought disorder and some tentative suggestions of paranoid orientation. Most significant here is the patient's inclination to use language peculiarly, which suggests that he is estranged from conventional ways of directing his thought processes. Lost in a forest, he would "walk my way out," and city land is valuable "as a business prospect"; in conventional language, however, one *walks* or *makes his way*, but does not "walk my way," and land may *have prospects* but is seldom described as *being* a prospect. Though picayune, these semantic distinctions illustrate the detailed analysis of language usage that is often necessary to identify disordered thinking in mildly disturbed subjects.

With regard to paranoid orientation, the patient begins to vent here characteristic paranoid feelings of being put upon and abused by others. Bad company will "get you in trouble" and parents will "push kids out and start them working." Although these thoughts are not grossly unusual, they do contrast meaningfully with other possible ways of phrasing the same ideas without focusing on the misanthropy of others, for example, "to avoid trouble" rather than "*they'll* get you in trouble."

Similarities

ORANGE: Fruit (2). COAT: Clothing (2). AXE: Used in chopping wood (1). DOG: Four-footed animals (2). NORTH: Directions (2). EYE: Sensory . . . they have to do with the senses (2). AIR: Elements (1). TABLE: Articles of furniture (2). EGG: Both are ready to come to life under the proper conditions (1). POEM: Both are flowing. (?) You better change that; both are forms of art (2). WOOD: Both are used (0). PRAISE: Both are forms of justice (0). FLY: These are getting kind of ridiculous; both are made up of molecules (0). RAW SCORE: 17.

The patient's Similarities responses deviate only slightly from normal expectancy. His answer for egg and seed, "Both are ready to come to life," is somewhat awkwardly phrased, and his comment that poem and statue "are flowing" suggests an idiosyncratic or arbitrarily reasoned association, but his language peculiarity is minimal and he is able on inquiry to reject his "flowing" association in favor of an accurate response.

Significant for the nature of his disturbance, however, is his comment on FLY, "These are getting kind of ridiculous." Such a complaint, occurring in the context of three consecutively failed items, indicates a tendency to deny responsibility for situations that exceed his competence: it is the ridiculousness of the item, not his inability, that causes failure. This externalization of blame is consistent with a projective defensive style and affirms the paranoid orientation suggested on Comprehension.

Digit Symbol

RAW SCORE: 54

The patient performed consistently but somewhat slowly on this subtest. He appeared to learn the symbols quickly, so that he seldom found it necessary to refer back to the key, but he reproduced them deliberately and with care to fit each exactly within the confines of its respective square. His cautious approach here is consistent with, though not exclusively indicative of, paranoid preference for a wary and painstaking approach to externally imposed problems.

Picture Completion

KNOB: +. TAIL: +. NOSE: +. HANDLES: The opposite wheels. DIAMOND: +. WATER: +. NOSE PIECE: +. PEG: +. OAR LOCK: +. BASE THREAD: +. STARS: Correct beyond time limit. DOG TRACKS: The man's other foot. FLORIDA: +. STACKS: +. LEG: I'm not well enough acquainted with— oh, wait, there's a leg missing (+). ARM IMAGE: +. FINGER: +. SHADOW: +. SNOW: I can't see anything. EYEBROW: +. RAW SCORE: 17.

This subtest, like the preceding ones, is more notable for intactness than impairments of ego functioning. The patient makes few errors, and those he does commit are not unusual among normal subjects. Yet his responses nevertheless provide subtle clues to both disordered thinking and paranoid tendencies. First, his failures on the relatively easy HANDLES and DOG TRACKS, followed by successes on many more difficult and factorially related items, further demonstrate the scattered cognitive efficiency noted on his Information.

Second, his introductory response to LEG, "I'm not well enough acquainted with—," identifies another facet of self-protective behavior similar in significance to his previously observed cautious approach and externalization of blame. As if anticipating failure on this item, he prefaces his attention to it with a self-reassuring rationalization that he quickly breaks off as he realizes that he has found the correct solution after all. Such rationalizations of surmised deficiencies, pervasive to such a point that they precede realistic assessment of capacity to surmount challenge, suggest a paranoid emphasis on maintaining autonomy and self-esteem at all costs.

Block Design

ITEM 1: 5" (4). ITEM 2: 7" (4). ITEM 3: 4" (4). ITEM 4: 8" (4). ITEM 5: 9" (4). ITEM 6: 22" (4). ITEM 7: 27" (6). ITEM 8: 49" (5). ITEM 9: 93" (4). ITEM 10: 115" (4). RAW SCORE: 43.

The patient's facile, efficient, and consistent performance on this subtest contains no indications of personality disturbance, nor did he accompany his performance with any comments or behaviors significant for either schizophrenic or paranoid tendencies.

Scale Scores

Information: 12. Comprehension: 11. Similarities: 12. Digit Symbol: 10. Picture Completion: 12. Block Design: 13.

Discussion. The patient's generally consistent, well-organized WAIS performance indicates relatively intact cognitive functioning, but there are subtle indices in his protocol of disordered thinking and paranoid tendencies. His scatter within Information and Completion and his dissociative tendencies and peculiar language on Comprehension and Similarities reveal the interference of intruding elements with his capacity to maintain a consistent, conventionally formulated focus of attention on his experience. His focus on external aggression in Comprehension, externalization of blame for his difficulties on Similarities, cautious approach to Digit Symbol, and self-reassuring rationalization on Picture Completion suggest a paranoid orientation. None of these latter behaviors considered singly is pathologic, and taken together they represent an alert, careful, and self-protective approach to experience that may appear in connection with normal and neurotic as well as schizophrenic behavior patterns. Within the context of schizophrenic disorder, however, they point to a paranoid rather than nonparanoid form of the disturbance.

DRAW-A-PERSON

The patient's figure drawings, which appear in Figures 19 and 20, contain no prominent indications of schizophrenic ego impairment. All vital body parts are present, the body contours are clearly indicated and connected, and the sexuality of the figures is adequately differentiated. Striking in the drawings, however, are the heavy emphasis on the outlines of the body and the particularly dark shading of the eyes. The eyes are especially conspicuous in the male figure, who is drawn as if facing directly at the observer.

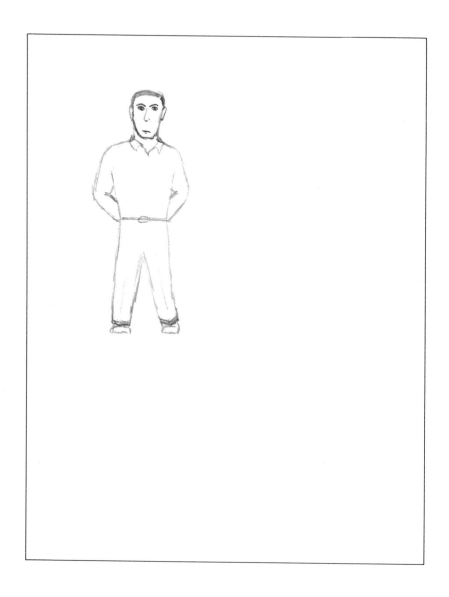

Figure 19

Figure 20

Such strong DAP emphasis on body outline, consistent with several features of the patient's WAIS behavior, suggests urgent needs to buttress himself against anticipated environmental affronts and to assert his autonomy in the face of perceived external threat. More speculatively, the stolid appearance of the male figure—heavily-trunked, feet firmly planted, arms held in check—may be interpreted as reflecting this young man's determination to resist adverse environmental pressures with careful control and firm resolve. These self-protective behaviors, together with the concern about scrutiny suggested by his eye emphasis, confirm the impression from the WAIS that schizophrenic disturbance in this man is more likely to assume paranoid than nonparanoid forms.

RORSCHACH

Card I 5″

1. (Wm $F+$ A P) A bat. (?) There's a suggestion of wings and antennae, and a body here in the center.

2. (Wm,S $F+,Fm$ $Mask$) $\vee$ Can I turn it? That doesn't help. Wait, this way it looks like a mask of some sort; yes, it looks like a death head. (*Death head?*) There's nothing in the eyes; it looks pathetic, like the masks they have around theaters, the frowning one.

3. (Wm,S $Fm+$ $Mask$) This way it looks like a smiling imp. (?) It's also a mask, an impish one; the eyes have an evil look about them, with an evil laugh to the mouth; there's a suggestion of horns up here.

4. (Wm $F+,m$ Ad) It might be a wolf's head. (?) It's the shape of a wolf's head; the ears are up here on the sides and there could be a muzzle here; there seems to be an evil glint in the eyes. [Subject watches the examiner's writing closely and continues to do so throughout the test.]

Card II 13″

5. (S,D $Fm+,CF$ Im,Fi) It looks like a flying saucer taking off. (?) The white in the center is the saucer and here is the exhaust [bottom center red]. (*Exhaust?*) The red looks like flame.

6. ($D+$ $M+$ H,Cg $Barrier$) Looks like two people squatting down playing patty-cake [entire side black details]. (?) Their hands are together up here, like in patty-cake. (*Kind of people?*) They look very shadowed, and their heads are scrunched down; maybe they have flowing robes on, and there are hoods to them. (*Men or women?*) I don't know; from their size and burliness I'd guess men; so I'm no sex fiend, huh?

7. ($D-$ $Fm-,m$ $H,Expl$ $Fabulized$) $\vee$ Two people being knocked

back by the force of an explosion. (?) The explosion is here [bottom center red] and the people here [side black details], and it's like their heads are being blown back; it could be two scientists, who have been working on some bomb or device, and it's just blown up in their faces. (*Explosion?*) It's the red, not the color but the way it goes off in all different directions.

8. (*D— F— Ad*) I can't see any possible use for these two things (upper red details); they look like two roosters' heads. (?) They just look like the heads of roosters or peacocks.

Card III 15″

9. (*Dm F+ A P*) ∨ Where did you ever dig these up? On this one, if I turn it this way, the red in the middle looks like a butterfly of sorts. (?) Just the general shape of it.

10. (*D—,S F— (H)*) ∨ If it were all filled up, this part [entire black] would look like some bug-eyed monster I've seen in science fiction movies, with the arms or tentacles up here [leg details of popular human figures]. (?) The arms are here and there's some apparatus sticking out of his head; the darker shapes are bug-eyes and the open space beneath them is his mouth.

11. (*D+ M+ H,Cg P Incongruous-tendency*) If it weren't for their beak-like appendages, these would look like two women, maybe on one of those hand-cars, pushing it along. (*Women?*) There's a suggestion of breasts there, and the edge of the skirt flying and high heels.

12. (*D++ M+ (H) Penetration*) These two red things [outer red] look like maybe some form of imps, hanging from a string; they're sticking their tongues out or smoking a cigar.

13. (*Dm F+,m Bt Peculiar*) ∨ This way, the same two red things look like disheveled flowers. (?) There's a stem; maybe they're a marigold, or a beat-up sunflower after a windstorm.

Card IV 11″

14. (*W— F— Ad Peculiar*) Looks like a lop-eared dog. (?) The darker parts in here [inner details] are where I see the eyes, and the ears are here on the sides; this [center lower detail] is the primitive idea of a muzzle, or a jutting of the nose; it's just the head that I see.

15. (*Wm Fm+ A Fabulized*) ∨ This way, some sort of flying creature, with a suggestion of wings; it looks like it's sitting down, regaining its composure, trying to regain its flight. (?) The feet are here [upper side details] and they're sticking up as they would if something like a bat were to sit down.

16. (*Wm M+ (H) Peculiar*) Something like a giant, falling, or how a person would look to an ant on a backward fall; I don't know what

this [reference to lower center detail] would have to do with it. (?) The feet are down here and the head up here, and it just looks like a giant tippled backwards.

17. (*Wm F+ Bt*) Some sort of leafy growth. (?) It's actually too symmetrical . . . but these might be leaves [sides] with a stalk here [bottom center detail].

Card V 3″

18. (*Wm FM+ A P Fabulized*) It looks like a bird or butterfly in the down-stroke of its flight.

19. (*W++ M+ H,Cg*) Looks like maybe a woman leaning up against a mirror, or two women leaning against each other. (?) The legs are at the sides; it looks more like two women leaning against each other; you can see their skirts here.

20. (*Dm M+ H,Cg Barrier*) ∨ Here we have the effect of a woman diving into the water with all her clothes on [entire side detail]. (?) She's in the water up to her shoulders; you can see a dress and the legs again; it's like a side view, and it reminds me of a woman because of the flowing thing here, a robe or dress.

Card VI 3″

21. (*Dm FM+ (Ad) Fabulized, Barrier*) An old tomcat [laughs], with his head and shoulders stuck up above some fence, giving out with a good yell; am I going too fast for you? (?) He's got his head way up [upper portion], yowling, and his whiskers are here; maybe it's a wolf, yes, like one of those Walt Disney characters.

22. (*Dm F+,m Aobj P-tendency*) It looks like a hide strung up to be tanned. (?) The shape of it.

23. (*Wm F+ A Penetration*) > A cat, maybe, that's been squashed under a wheel; what's the idea of showing me such gory pictures [laughs]?

24. (*Dd F— Ad*) ∨ This part [large arbitrary section of lower portion] looks like a fox terrier's head, because of the general shape; I notice the eyes in particular [tiny darker inner details], they're small and beady.

Card VII 6″

25. (*W+ M+ H,Cg*) My first impression is two adolescent girls doing some sort of modern dance together, with the contortions and all. (?) I see their skirts here and pony tails up here, that's what started me on the idea; there is also clear indication of arms, their faces, nose, and chin.

26. (*S F+ Bt*) ∨ The part in the center looks like a mushroom.

27. (*W*+ *M*+ *H,Cg*) ∨ Two girls again, with floozy hair; they're back to back, or against a mirror. (?) There could be a mirror here, and this girl with floozy hair is sort of looking over her shoulder at the mirror; her arm is out here, her skirt here, and her leg here.

Card VIII 3″

28. (*Dm FM*+ *A P*) Two sloths, climbing like up a tree; one on either side. (?) They look like sloths or muskrats, climbing, with their tails hanging down.

29. (*Dm FC*+ *Bt*) Some sort of pansy [orange and pink detail]. (?) The different colors of it and the way the petals are arranged.

30. (*D*−,*S FC*−,*FC' Hd*) An African native's painted-up face [upper gray and upper center white details]. (?) It's the way the hair streams out to the sides, and the eyes, these white spots; the nose is this painted part [darker center line in gray detail] above the mouth part. (*Colors play a part?*) Yes, you wouldn't see it if it weren't for the colors; it looks like a painted native face.

31. (*Dm F*+ *Na*) A bit of a mountain [upper gray detail].

32. (*S F*+ *A*) A sea gull [white portion between blue and pink-orange details]. (?) The way it's shaped.

33. (*D*−,*S M*− *Hd*) ∨ A smiling face, with a goatee [entire blot except for side pink]. (?) The goatee is this part [upper gray detail], with a broad smile here [white space between gray and blue details], and the eyes here [white between blue and pink-orange details]; his eyes are crinkled up and he's smiling, and he has a very nice smile.

34. (*Dm F*+,*M* (*Hd*) *Peculiar*) ∨ Another monster here [pink and orange detail]. (?) He has his hands out like this [gestures], and you can see eyes in there [inner details] and a long probiscus, which means nose, doesn't it? It's just the upper body part.

35. (*Wm F*+ *Fm*) < A vague suggestion of a coat of arms, as seen from the side, just the general shape of it.

Card IX 28″

36. (*Wm FC*+,*M,Fc Bt,H,Cg Contamination-tendency*) ∨ It looks like a humanized flower . . . or it could be just a flower by itself. (*Humanized?*) Don't you see it? These look like legs here [orange details], spread apart, with the hands on the hips, but they're leaves at the same time; the head is up here [pink detail], with a hat on, and that's the blossom part. (*Blossom?*) Well, the whole thing is a flower, with two leaves on the side, the stalk in the center, and the flower up here, just some pink, fluffy flower.

37. (*D*++ *M*+ *Hd,Fd Penetration*) > The upper portion of a man, eating [green detail]. (?) He's hunched over, like he's at the table; I see

his head and arm, like he's holding a spoon or fork, with his pinky out, just about to put food in his mouth.

38. (*Dd KF Cl*) < It looks like clouds here [outer lighter portion of orange detail]. (?) There are darkened sections like shadows in it, which suggests the rollingness of a cloud.

39. (*Dm FC+,Fc Cg Barrier*) ∨ This pink part that was part of the flower also looks like a pom-pom, or an ostrich feather, like a circus horse would wear. (?) The pink color of it and the shading in here, which helps make it look colored.

40. (*D+ M+,FC Hd,Bt Barrier*) Here is someone peeping out from between some foliage [green details with center portion between them]. (?) The green is the foliage, and here are the eyes here; it's sort of a face.

41. (*Dm Fm+ Im*) A little electrical equipment here [top center detail], like a melodrama movie; sparks are flying as from an electrical current.

42. (*D—,S F— Ad*) The head of a fish [both green details]. (?) The white dots are the eyes; you're looking at it straight forward.

Card X 4″

43. (*D— M— (A) Incongruous*) Looks like two frogs talking and looking at each other [upper center gray details].

44. (*Dd F— Hd*) A man with a more or less German moustache; just the face. (?) The eyes are here [inner yellow detail], and this [entire inner green portion] is the nose and moustache, curving and bristly like a German moustache.

45. (*Dm F+ A P*) Two crabs, fiddler crabs [outer blue], with the claws here [upper outer green].

46. (*Dm F+ A*) Two crickets [outer gray details].

47. (*S F— Ad*) A grasshopper's head. (?) The eyes are these spots [white between pink and inner blue portions] and here [white below inner blue] it has the form of a face, looking straight at it.

48. (*D— F— (A)*) ∨ Some sort of alien creature with big wings [entire lower green].

49. (*Dd M—,FC Hd*) ∨ A face; it looks like maybe it's painted up a little bit; also it has a goatee and it's smiling. (?) The goatee is here [entire upper gray portion], these are the eyes [inner yellow details], and the blue [inner blue] is the painted-up part on the cheeks. (*Color play a part?*) Yes, the blue is the paint.

50. (*Dd F+ Bt*) Two walnuts [inner orange dots in inner yellow details].

51. (*D+ FM+ A*) ∨ Two caterpillars, facing each other, sitting

way up [pink details]. (?) They're just sitting way back with their legs sticking out here.

52–53. (*Dd F+,M H; Dm F+ Art,Hd Fabulized Combination*) Some sort of pointy-headed man [tiny lower portion of upper center gray column] standing in front of an oblong statue of a face [rest of upper center gray]. (?) The man is very clear, particularly his eyes and mouth.

54. (*Dm F+ Ad P*) A fish—no—it's a rabbit, just the head.

Scores

R	54	M	13+3	H	8+1	F+%	70%
W	15(28%)	FM	5	(H)	3	R+%	73%
D	29+1(54%)	m	4+5	Hd	6+1	P	7+1
Dd+S	10+6(18%)	K	1	(Hd)	1		
		F	27	A	10	High W%	93%
		Fc	0+2	(A)	2	High D%	72%
Fabulized	4	C'	0+1	Ad	7		
Peculiar	4	FC	4+2	(Ad)	1	Barrier	3
Fabulized		CF	0+1	Bt	6+1	Penetration	1
Combination	1			Mask	2		
Incongruous	1			Im	2		
Incongruous-				Cg	1+7		
tendency	1			Art	1		
Contamination-				Na	1		
tendency	1			Aobj	1		
				Cl	1		
				Em	1		
				Fd	0+1		
				Fire	0+1		
				Expl	0+1		

Discussion. This lengthy, varied, and expansive Rorschach record contrasts interestingly with the guarded, constricted protocol of the previous patient but nevertheless shares with it many identifying features of paranoid orientation and schizophrenic disturbance. However, schizophrenia is indicated in this case by relatively few areas of impaired ego functioning. This young man's reality testing (*F+%* of 70, *R+%* of 73, *P* of 7) and organizational ability (*high W%* of 93, *high D%* of 72) are within normal limits, and he gives no evidence of withdrawal from interpersonal concerns (*M* and *H* are abundant), loss of repressive control (neither sexual nor blatant aggressive content is present), or difficulty integrating affective experience (neither pure C nor indications of color stress occur). Although his form-level scores might in some cases suggest mildly impaired perceptual accuracy, their significance in his 54-response record is attenuated by the normally expected inverse relationship between R and $F+\%$.

On the other hand, disturbances of cognitive focusing and reasoning are identified here by aspects of the patient's location choice and fantasy elaborations. Significant for impaired cognitive focusing are his frequent Dd and S responses (18%), which even in a record of this length reflect an inordinate attention to irrelevant aspects of experience, and his four peculiar responses (*"disheveled* flowers" in response #13, "the *primitive idea* of a muzzle" in #14, "a giant *tippled* backwards" in #16, and "a long *probiscus"* in #34). None of these responses is grossly unusual, and it is reasonable to question whether only four such minimally peculiar responses in a lengthy record justifies inferring thinking disturbance. Additionally, however, the patient's difficulty in framing his thoughts in conventional language appears in several other subtly unusual verbalizations (e.g., "the *rollingness* of a cloud" on #38, "looking at it *straight forward*" on #42), and it is problematic to account for repetitive instances of such awkward, idiosyncratic expressions in an intelligent, educated person whose native language is English without invoking an hypothesis of disordered thinking.

Reasoning disturbance appears in the patient's occasional recourse to illogical lines of inference. Though none of his four Fabulized responses (#'s 7, 15, 18 & 21) transcends the boundaries of normally imaginative fantasy, he several times indulges in irrational combinative thinking. Noteworthy in this regard are his Contamination-tendency on #36 ("humanized flower"), his incongruous perception in #11 of women with beak-like appendages pushing a handcar (although neither attribute is impossible, neither is particularly likely), and his Fabulized Combination in #'s 52–53, which involves the unlikely juxtaposition of a man and a statue of a face far exceeding the man in size.

The fact that these illogically reasoned responses are neither grossly bizarre nor pervasive does not in this case minimize the likelihood of schizophrenic ego impairment. Given the relative retention of personality integration that characterizes paranoid as opposed to nonparanoid forms of schizophrenia, and given a paranoid schizophrenic subject whose disturbance is mild and of recent onset, test protocols may be expected in which paranoid trends can be readily identified but evidence of schizophrenia is minimal. The relatively well-integrated Rorschach performance of this paranoid young man, whose acute upset was of recent onset but who was sufficiently disturbed to require hospitalization and be referred for continued residential care, appears a case in point.

Demonstrating a paranoid orientation in the patient's Rorschach record are numerous features of a projective defensive style. First, he is inclined to reflect carefully on experience and curtail spontaneous emotional expression. His introversive experience balance (13 M, Sum C of 2.0) and his emphasis on form-dominated color (4 FC, 0 CF, 0 C) indicate he favors circumspect musing to sharing his ideas with others, would rather think about things than do them, and prefers to restrict his emotional displays to formal, restrained, and isolated expressions of affect. Such an ideational orientation, though not unique to paranoid disturbance, provides the fertile soil in which paranoid frames of reference typically germinate and thrive.

Second, fairly specific to paranoid orientation is this man's readiness to construe in his environment sources of threat. He frequently attributes evil intent to external objects ("death-head" on #2, "evil look" on #3, "evil glint" on #4, "monsters" on #'s 10 & 34), and he often expresses concern that other persons' motives are disguised from him (masks on #'s 2 & 3, hooded and "shadowy" people on #6). Also, consistent with a vigilant and suspicious nature, he exhibits considerable preoccupation with scrutinizing and being scrutinized by his environment. Notable in this regard are the "bug-eyed monster" on #10, the "beady eyes" on #24, and the 13 other responses in which he calls attention to the eyes of figures on inquiry; the faces on #30 ("painted-up"), #44 ("German"), and #'s 33 and 49 ("smiling"); and the especially significant response on #40, "Someone peeping out from behind some foliage." Finally attesting the trepidation with which he views his environment are his perceptions of victimization and helplessness in the face of external forces (men "being knocked back" by an explosion in #7, the aftermath of a windstorm in #13, a cat squashed by a wheel in #24, and his general emphasis on m determinants).

Third, the patient combats his fears and suspicions with a number of characteristically paranoid protective maneuvers. By interspersing his Rorschach responses with a number of derogatory comments that demean the significance of the test for him, he strives to absolve his responsibility for anything amiss in his responses. When he has difficulty interpreting details, he "can't see any possible use" for them (#8); after two perceptually inaccurate responses with which he appeared dissatisfied, he asks, "Where did you ever dig these up?" (#9); and after the only response in which he seemed to lose control of underlying aggressive impulses (#23, cat "squashed under a wheel"), he adroitly affixes the blame on the examiner: "What's the idea of showing me such gory pictures?" Further demonstrating his need to disengage himself from the influence of the tests and the examiner is the oppositional, autonomy-asserting behavior he exhibits in selecting four main and six additional S locations.

Also consistent with paranoid protective maneuvers are the patient's frequent human and animal detail responses (6 *Hd*, 7 *Ad*) and dehumanized and mythical human and animal figures (3 (*H*), 1 (*Hd*), 2 (*A*), 1 (*Ad*)). These percepts, in concert with his derogating asides, reflect a tendency to maintain feelings of well-being by critically depreciating the power and status of external objects: as in his jocular comments about the test, the patient appears to defend himself by making fun of others around him.

Finally relevant to the dynamics of paranoid disturbance is the number of responses in this young man's record that suggest feminine orientation, including in particular his six *botany* percepts and his frequent specification of clothing details. Both these responses and the anal orientation in his "back-to-back" reference on #17 are consistent with homosexual concern. On the other hand, his record contains only six of the Wheeler signs (signs #1, 7, 10, 15, 17, & 20; see Table 4), which constitute less than 12% of his 54 responses. Though he therefore displays only moderate evidence of latent homosexuality, his tentative anal and feminine orientation nevertheless points to paranoid rather than nonparanoid disturbance.

Summary. This young man's test performance is notable for the relatively intact relation to reality, capacity for object relations, defensive resources, and organizational skills he manifests in spite of the fact that he was sufficiently disturbed clinically to require hospital care. Nevertheless, his inconsistent cognitive efficiency and dissociative tendencies on cognitive testing, as well as his peculiar language usage and illogical reasoning on both the WAIS and the Rorschach, suggest thought disorder, and his response style throughout the test battery identifies marked paranoid tendencies. He approaches situations cautiously, is prone to perceive external threat, is concerned about being scrutinized by his environment, prefers to reflect on his experience rather than share his thoughts and feelings with others, and protects his integrity by externalizing blame for his difficulties and depreciating the significance of people and events. This case interestingly demonstrates that minimal personality disorganization may be sufficient basis for inferring schizophrenic disorder in persons with prominent paranoid features.

▷ 15

INCIPIENT AND REMITTING SCHIZOPHRENIA

AN important and frequently overlooked consideration in evaluating schizophrenic disturbance, particularly in its acute forms, is the *phase* in which it is manifest. Schizophrenia occurs primarily in three phases, *incipient*, *overt*, and *remitting*. The incipient phase of schizophrenia is a period of early decompensation characterized by increasing personality disintegration and movement toward an impending psychosis; it is a stage of disturbance at which unequivocal diagnosis is often difficult, but at which early detection can foster preventive measures that avert further decompensation. Overt schizophrenia is that phase of frank psychosis that has been illustrated by the case material in Chapters 13 and 14. Remitting schizophrenia is a phase of recovery from overt schizophrenia that is marked by restitutive efforts and progressive personality redintegration; it is the stage of disturbance at which such important therapeutic measures as decrease in supervision, discharge from hospital, and return to work can be most effectively implemented.

The differential diagnosis of incipient, overt, and remitting disturbance thus has substantial implications for the schizophrenic person's anticipated course and therapeutic management. The notion of phase applies primarily to acute and not chronic conditions, however, because it concerns decompensation into and recovery from schizophrenia. Although chronic schizophrenic persons may experience periods of relative symptom exacerbation and quiescence, their basic schizophrenic disorder does not pass through incipient and remitting phases. Rather, as outlined in Chapter 13, chronic schizophrenics typically manifest signs of disturbance from early life on and continue to do so even during periods of social restitution. This is not to say that chronic schizophrenia does not like acute schizophrenia occur in other than overt forms; nonovert forms of chronic schizophrenia, typically defined as *borderline* or *pseudoneurotic* disorders, are discussed in Chapter 16.

This chapter focuses on the identification of incipient and remitting phases of schizophrenic disturbance and their differentiation from both acute overt and chronic schizophrenia. A variety of clinical clues to the early detection of incipient schizophrenia appears in the literature, many of them deriving from psychoanalytic conceptualizations of the regressive shift that accompanies movement from a normal to a schizophrenic adaptation. Fenichel (1945, pp. 418–419), for example, suggests that inasmuch as schizophrenic regression involves a withdrawal of cathexes from external objects and a corresponding narcissistic hypercathexis of the ego, such characteristic hypochondriacal phenomena as exaggerated somatic complaints, alterations in body-image, and feelings of estrangement and depersonalization are often the earliest precursors of schizophrenic decompensation.

Chapman and Reese (1953) infer from psychoanalytic conceptions that the transitional point between normality and schizophrenia represents a middle ground between love of a heterosexual object and love of oneself. They hypothesize that homosexual object choice constitutes such an intermediate step in the regression from normal object relatedness to schizophrenic narcissism and that developing homosexual interest may therefore be an early clue to incipient schizophrenia.

In support of their hypothesis Chapman and Reese report observing a higher incidence of homosexual indicators in the Rorschach records of six patients who were developing schizophrenic psychosis than in the records of six normal control subjects they examined. However, because Chapman and Reese did not include a sample of overtly schizophrenic subjects in their work, it is not possible to determine whether the relatively high incidence of homosexual indicators in their incipiently schizophrenic subjects was in any way specific to the incipient phase of schizophrenia or was rather a function of schizophrenia in general (or perhaps of paranoid schizophrenia; see pp. 325–329).

Other contributions to the clinical identification of incipient schizophrenia have been made by Miller (1940), who suggests that many persons approach overt schizophrenia in stages of minor maladjustments and neurotic compromises that transiently resemble typical neurotic syndromes; and by Mace, Koff, Chelnek, and Garfield (1949), who consider marked preoccupation the major clue to early schizophrenia in patients presenting with prominent neurotic features. However, the almost ubiquitous conclusion drawn in the literature in this area is that the accurate diagnosis of incipient schizophrenia is a challenging task and one in which recourse to sensitive psychodiagnostic measures is particularly crucial and valuable (Gurvitz & Miller, 1952; Whitman, 1954).

Aside from such possibly unique features of incipient schizophrenia as the above authors suggest, and the general notion that remitting schizophrenia is a recovering state, the literature provides no conceptual formulation of the relationships between incipient, overt, and remitting schizophrenia from which appropriate extrapolation to psychodiagnostic data can be made. In the following section such a general formulation is proposed and extended to differentiating test parameters.

A CONCEPTUALIZATION OF INCIPIENT AND REMITTING SCHIZOPHRENIA

A diagnostically heuristic formulation of the incipient and remitting phases of schizophrenic disturbance requires two sets of differential parameters: (a) parameters on which both incipient and remitting schizophrenia can be differentiated from chronic forms of schizophrenia that do not appear in these phases; and (b) parameters on which incipient and remitting schizophrenia can be discriminated from acute overt schizophrenia and from each other. Three parameters that can be defined to satisfy these requirements are *acceptance of disturbance, differential control,* and *severity of disturbance.*

ACCEPTANCE OF DISTURBANCE

Acceptance of disturbance has previously been delineated (see pp. 245–250) as central to the distinction between acute and chronic schizophrenic disorder. In brief, acceptance of disturbance is defined by an ego-syntonic view of symptoms, with either total unawareness of or considerable tolerance for manifestations of deviant behavior and with referral of adjustment difficulties to environmental rather than to intrapersonal defects. Nonacceptance of disturbance, on the other hand, consists of an active struggle by the disturbed person against what he perceives as ego-alien phenomena, with keen sensitivity to and marked distress about manifestations of his personality malfunctioning. As elaborated in Chapter 13, acceptance of disturbance in schizophrenic persons is associated primarily with chronic disorder, whereas nonacceptance of disturbance is an identifying feature of acute status.

It is proposed to view incipient and remitting schizophrenia as sharing with acute disorder the identifying characteristic of nonacceptance of disturbance. In both incipient and remitting states there is movement and struggle, in the one case the struggle to *retain* personality integration in the face of powerful disorganizing influences, and in the other the struggle to *regain* personality integration in the aftermath of an overt psychotic episode. Both phases are likely to be marked by overt distress, in one the fear of the impending disaster lying ahead and in the other the dread of the already experienced psychotic state still lurking tentatively in the wake. Incipient and remitting schizophrenia are thus acute, tenuous states that may eventuate in either a nonschizophrenic or overt schizophrenic adjustment.

Conceptualizing incipient and remitting schizophrenia as acute conditions marked by nonacceptance of disturbance differentiates them both from chronic overt schizophrenia as described in Chapter 13 and from the chronic nonovert forms of schizophrenia considered in Chapter 16. Although these latter conditions, that is, the borderline and pseudoneurotic forms of schizophrenia, resemble incipient schizophrenia in certain respects (see Chap. 16), they differ from the incipient and remitting phases of acute schizophrenia in being defined in part by acceptance of disturbance and minimal awareness of schizophrenic pathology.

DIFFERENTIAL CONTROL

Whereas nonacceptance of disturbance differentiates incipient and remitting from chronic schizophrenia, the parameter of differential control provides a basis for discriminating these conditions from each other and from acute overt schizophrenia. Control is used here to represent the degree to which an individual can prevent indications of schizophrenic ego impairment from becoming manifest in his behavior. For nonschizophrenic and overtly schizophrenic persons the adequacy of such control is evident: the nonschizophrenic person presumably has no schizophrenic ego impairments and so manifests none, whereas the overt schizophrenic is identified by his inability to avert public disclosure of his personality disturbance.

It is proposed that incipient and remitting schizophrenic persons are neither free from nor powerless to restrain emergent schizophrenic phenomena, but rather characteristically employ partial patterns of control. Whereas overt schizophrenia may be construed as a state in which control over the manifestation of ego impairments is *lost*, the incipient schizophrenic person is in the process of *losing* and the remitting schizophrenic of *regaining* such control. With these controls viewed as internal restraints imposed by a person on the content of his thoughts, feelings, and actions, the following paradigm may be suggested:

The incipient schizophrenic, who is losing his internal controls, is able to perform relatively adaptively in clearly defined situations that provide him specific external directives; the more ambiguous are his circumstances and the more he is forced to seek directions from within, however, the more likely are his words and actions to reveal his developing disturbance. The remitting schizophrenic, who is regaining his controls, functions most effectively in open-ended contexts that allow him freedom to govern his behavior according to those methods of control he has succeeded in restituting; when confronted with specific demands that transcend or controvert his nascent internal controls, however, he is relatively unable to prevent the remnants of his disturbance from gaining ascendance. The overt schizophrenic, who has already lost but not yet appreciably begun to regain his internal controls, is likely, with some variation, to manifest his disturbance in both ambiguous and clearly defined situations; he thus seldom displays clearly either of the differential patterns of partial control that characterize incipient and remitting schizophrenia.

This paradigm of differential control can be readily extrapolated to the psychodiagnostic test battery. Situations that present specific external directives and transcend internal controls are represented by such structured tests as the WAIS, whereas projective tests like the Rorschach and DAP force an individual to seek internal direction while allowing him to determine his responses in terms of his preferred methods of control. Consequently, the following specific implications of differential control for test performance in incipient, overt, and remitting schizophrenia obtain:

Incipient Schizophrenia. Incipient schizophrenic persons are likely to evince personality disturbance primarily on the projective portions of the test battery. The unstructured nature of the Rorschach and DAP, with their vaguely specified instructions and lack of right-or-wrong standards, leaves the incipient schizophrenic to his inadequate internal resources, and, because neither test provides him prominent footholds with which to cling to his crumbling controls, his deviant thoughts and feelings will have ready access to overt expression.

Struggling to retain his slipping controls, however, the incipient schizophrenic is bolstered by the external structure of the WAIS, on which his task is clearly defined to him and his responses fall into definite right-wrong categories. He is consequently better able on the WAIS than on projective tests to resist the inroads of his personality disturbance and may frequently respond to the WAIS in an orderly, well-integrated fashion. Hence the combination of relatively intact WAIS and relatively disturbed Rorschach and DAP performance suggests incipient disorder.

Overt Schizophrenia. The overt schizophrenic exhibits neither that differential pattern of disturbance associated with incipient disorder (see above) nor that characterizing remitting disturbance (see below). Inasmuch as he is neither losing nor regaining control, the degree to which his environment is structured has less influence on his behavior than it has for incipient and remitting schizophrenic persons. The overt schizophrenic thus typically displays disturbance on both the structured (WAIS) and projective (Rorschach and DAP) tests in the clinical battery.

Remitting Schizophrenia. Remitting schizophrenics are likely to manifest relatively little disturbance on projective tests, but to give clear indications on the WAIS of the overt psychosis from which they are recovering. The remitting schizophrenic utilizes the freedom and self-determination of the Rorschach and DAP situations to impose upon his test responses whatever techniques and methods of control he has been able to re-establish. On these tests he can modulate and censor his responses, even to the extent of rejecting Rorschach cards and drawing stick figures, without doing great violence to the reality of the testing situation: "I have no imagination" and "I just can't draw" are defensive but not bizarre means of dealing with these tests.

The WAIS, on the other hand, allows little such latitude for the remitting schizophrenic to employ his tenuously developing restitutive efforts. Here he must respond to specific questions and tasks posed by the examiner, and he can conceal the vicissitudes of his cognitive functioning only by refusing or pleading inability to respond; however, both refusal and inability are anathema to the remitting schizophrenic, who is striving to recover his sense of personal adequacy and to impress others with his cooperativeness and improvement. Whereas lack of imagination and limited drawing talent are not abnormal and furnish the remitting patient a not-too-ungracious exit from a revealing Rorschach and DAP performance, neither refusal nor total inability to respond on straightforward verbal and perceptual-motor tasks, particularly on items clearly within the subject's intellectual capacity, can be regarded by either subject or examiner as adaptive behavior.

Hence the very WAIS structure that bolsters the ineffective internal controls of the incipient schizophrenic threatens to dissolve those internal controls the remitting schizophrenic has so painstakingly restituted. It is primarily on the WAIS rather than on the projective tests, therefore, that the remitting subject tends to display personality disturbance. However, reflecting the controls exercised by the remitting schizophrenic in unstructured settings, he performs in a characteristically guarded fashion on the projectives. He is particularly inclined to produce a banal and constricted Rorschach record, with few R, terse verbalization, and obvious and unelaborated percepts (see pp. 316–317).

SEVERITY OF DISTURBANCE

Severity of disturbance, like acceptance of disturbance, has previously been presented as a differential index to acute-chronic status in schizophrenia (see pp. 243–245). Briefly, the more extremely a schizophrenic subject demonstrates test indices of the various identifying features of schizophrenic ego impairment (with certain specific exceptions; see Chap. 13), the more likely he is to be chronically rather than acutely disturbed. Incipient and remitting schizophrenia, being acute rather than chronic conditions, are accordingly characterized by relatively minimal deviation even at those points in the test battery where evidence of schizophrenia is most readily elicited.

In most cases the two previously defined parameters of acceptance of disturbance and differential control serve adequately to differentiate incipient and remitting schizophrenia, and reference to severity of disturbance is superfluous. However, for schizophrenic subjects who present differential patterns of control on various parts of the test battery but do not unequivocally display either tolerance for or concern about manifestations of their disturbance, severity of disturbance contributes significantly to the differential diagnosis.

Specifically, severity of disturbance is a major diagnostic parameter for those subjects who respond adaptively to the WAIS and deviantly to the Rorschach but do not present clear indications of either an ego-alien or ego-syntonic view of their behavior. In such instances Rorschach evidence of relatively mild disturbance enhances the likelihood of an acute disorder and suggests incipient schizophrenia, whereas a flagrantly deviant Rorschach points to chronic disturbance and is in such a context consistent with borderline rather than incipient schizophrenia (see Chap. 16).

CLINICAL AND RESEARCH FINDINGS IN INCIPIENT
AND REMITTING SCHIZOPHRENIA

The preceding conceptualization of incipient and remitting schizophrenic disturbance implies the following psychodiagnostic distinctions: the schizophrenic subject who displays more indications of ego impairment on the Rorschach and DAP than on the WAIS is likely to be in an incipient phase of disorder; the schizophrenic whose deviant responses appear primarily on the WAIS and whose Rorschach and

DAP, although guarded and banal, are relatively free from gross disturbance is usually in a remitting phase of disturbance; and the schizophrenic who has difficulty maintaining his personality integrity on structured and projective tests alike is most probably overtly schizophrenic. Available clinical and research evidence, as reviewed below, is consistent with these hypothesized relations between diminishing controls, incipient schizophrenia, and particular susceptibility to disturbed response on projective tests on one hand, and between restituting controls, remitting schizophrenia, and primary impairment on structured tests on the other.

FINDINGS IN INCIPIENT SCHIZOPHRENIA

Clinical studies demonstrate that incipient schizophrenic subjects tend to be relatively mildly disturbed and to display their disturbances primarily on the projective portions of the test battery.

The data of Rapaport, Gill, and Schafer (1945, pp. 302–306; 1946) revealed milder impairment among preschizophrenic than acute overt schizophrenic subjects in Wechsler indices of concentration, concept formation, and scatter, whereas on the Rorschach these preschizophrenic subjects were more similar to acute schizophrenic than to normal control subjects in $Dd\%$, $F+\%$, and $R+\%$, in numbers of C and Sex responses, and in frequency of Fabulization, Fabulized Combination, Confabulation, Contamination, peculiar, and queer responses, all of which are salient indicators of ego impairment. On the basis of these data and his clinical experience, Schafer (1948, pp. 88–90 & 263) concludes with regard to incipient schizophrenia that Wechsler responses are "generally quite orderly," whereas the Rorschach "almost always indicates the early stage of the process of disorganization." He adds that any accumulation of disturbed responses on the Wechsler points to a fully developed rather than incipient psychosis.

Piotrowski (1945) similarly asserts that primary intellectual deficiencies are seldom manifest in incipient schizophrenia and hence that measures of intellectual functioning will not reveal the extent of disorder in the incipient phase of the disturbance. On the other hand, Piotrowski continues, incipient schizophrenia can be disclosed by an examination of the subject's emotional life, particularly as it is revealed on the Rorschach test.

Pursuing this hypothesis, Piotrowski developed and refined a Rorschach formula, called *alpha*, which is intended to differentiate between neurosis and early, mild, incipient, and pseudoneurotic forms of schizophrenia (Piotrowski & Lewis, 1950; Piotrowski & Berg, 1955; Piotrowski & Levine, 1959). The alpha formula is based on an elaborate system of scoring weights, the essence of which is that, among patients presenting serious problems of clinical diagnosis, those whose Rorschach records are characterized by few W's, few color responses, and a surplus of light shading (*Fc, cF,* and *c*) over chromatic (*FC, CF,* and *C*) responses are likely to be schizophrenically rather than neurotically disturbed, particularly if their $F+\%$ falls below 70.

Although Piotrowski and his co-workers have had some success in cross-validating the alpha formula, recent work by Abrams (1964) suggests that alpha may occur with equal frequency among early, advanced, and chronically hospitalized schizophrenic patients and may measure a *form* rather than a *stage* of disturbance. Therefore, although alpha appears clearly to differentiate schizophrenia from neurosis, further work is needed to determine whether it is in any way unique to incipient schizophrenic disturbance.

FINDINGS IN REMITTING SCHIZOPHRENIA

Several longitudinal studies of schizophrenic persons confirm that the remission process is reflected in increasingly adaptive performance, primarily on the projective rather than the structured portions of the test battery. As noted in Chapter 11, little work has been reported on fluctuations in cognitive functioning during the course of schizophrenic disorder. However, there is evidence from studies by Benjamin (1944) that structured cognitive examination continues to disclose ego impairment during the remitting phase of a schizophrenic disturbance. Benjamin concluded from his work with proverbs and other structured tests that their inclusion in the clinical battery is valuable particularly because even marked clinical improvement in schizophrenic subjects is not accompanied by the disappearance from such tests of indications of formal thinking disorder.

In contrast, repeated projective testing of schizophrenic subjects has revealed marked diminution of indications of ego impairment concomitant with clinical improvement. The most significant DAP work in this area is reported by Modell (1951), who obtained several hundred drawings from a sample of primarily schizophrenic state-hospital patients over a one-year period. Modell found the figure drawings of patients who at the end of the year were judged clinically to be recovering from regressed states to differ from those of nonrecovering patients in two dimensions, *body image maturation* and *sexual maturation.* These two dimensions correspond closely to the DAP indicators of indefinite ego boundaries and distorted body imagery outlined in Chapter 8 as indices of deficient reality sense.

Specifically, the body image maturation observed by Modell in the

DAP's of remitting schizophrenic patients consisted of improved differentiation of the figures, with the incompleteness and openendedness of the drawings they had rendered during regressed states giving way to clear indication of important body parts, generally increased detail, and closed body boundaries. The sexual maturation evinced by the recovering subjects was defined by enhanced differentiation of appropriate sexual characteristics. Modell's work confirms the expectation that a schizophrenic subject is likely to manifest less disturbance in his figure drawings during remission than during the overt phase of his disorder.

Also pertinent to the course of body boundary concern in phases of schizophrenic disturbance is a study by Cleveland (1960) of Rorschach Barrier and Penetration scores. Cleveland found a significant relationship between decline in Penetration score and likelihood of hospital discharge in an initial study of schizophrenic subjects. In a cross-validating sample he obtained the following additional results: of 45 schizophrenic patients tested on admission and again just before discharge, 33 who were regarded as improved demonstrated a significant mean reduction in Penetration, from 3.97 to 1.97; 12 rated unimproved had no significant reduction in Penetration; and 14 of the improved patients who were rated "markedly improved" also had a significant mean increment in Barrier score, from 1.82 to 3.55. These data confirm that remitting schizophrenia is in part characterized by relative absence in the Rorschach protocol of content indicators of disturbed body boundaries.

Further delineating Rorschach changes in remitting schizophrenia is a longitudinal study by Goldman (1960) of the 45 schizophrenic patients whose protocols were used by Cleveland in the above study. Goldman made a number of comparisons between the admission and predischarge Rorschachs of these patients, in regard to shifts in their interpersonal relations, perception of the world, and ability to deal with emotions.

Specifically, Goldman hypothesized that the recovering schizophrenics would demonstrate the following phenomena: (a) an increased capacity for adaptive interpersonal relationships, as indicated by an increase in M and H responses and a relative increase in the ratio of FC responses to the sum of CF and C responses; (b) a more accurate and comfortable style of perceiving the world, as disclosed by an improved $F+\%$, an increase in P, fewer signs of tension in the content, and a decrease in rejections, denials, and self-references; and (c) enhanced ability to deal with the expression and control of emotion, as measured by more optimum $F\%$ and percent of responses to Cards VIII-X, a shift in the $FC:CF:C$ distribution in the direction of increased control, and a relative increase in form-dominated over nonform-dominated responses.

Goldman found that all of these hypothesized shifts, with the exception of the P, rejection-denial-self-reference, and form-dominance indices, were significantly more likely to characterize her restituting than her nonrecovering schizophrenic subjects; of the three nonsignificant indices, only P failed at least to approach the conventional .05 level. Her data thus confirm the expectations both that the Rorschach records of restituting schizophrenics are likely to be relatively free from indices of ego impairment and that such freedom from pathologic indicators is achieved in part by an emphasis on control of emotional expression and censoring of distressing content.

A longitudinal study by Rickers-Ovsiankina (1954) further confirms the likelihood of a conventional but stereotyped and overcontrolled Rorschach in remitting schizophrenia. Rickers-Ovsiankina re-examined after a period of years 38 schizophrenic patients, 19 of whom were considered to have improved and 19 whose condition was considered unchanged. The improved schizophrenic subjects displayed a significant increase in $F+\%$ and $A\%$ and a near-significant increase in $P\%$ between their first and second testings, and they were significantly more likely than the unchanged schizophrenics to shift their color use toward a more optimum balance of FC over CF and C responses.

In summarizing the implications of her findings, Rickers-Ovsiankina (1954, p. 116) makes the following clear statement of Rorschach expectations in remitting schizophrenia:

> Moreover these people have achieved better inner control and more concern for standards of the outer world. This regulating and inhibiting factor is strong enough to check autistic thinking and to block any freer emotional expression. By leaning heavily on the conventional and commonplace, they manage to keep on "the safe side" in their behavior and thereby insure surface adjustment. The Rorschach material demonstrates convincingly, however, that this outer appearance in most cases is bought at the price of bleaching and restriction of inner life.

Beck's S-3 Schizophrenia. In concluding this discussion, it is helpful in conveying the "feel" of the Rorschach likely to be produced by a remitting schizophrenic subject to consider the schizophrenic reaction patterns identified on the basis of trait analysis by Beck (1954), with particular attention to the S-3 type he describes.

In summarizing the results of his investigation, Beck (1954, p. 131) concludes that the S-3 type of schizophrenia "stands by itself," "is characterized by a defensive exterior and a brittle internal condition," and is primarily of interest in "being a pattern to which some patients turn from some other schizophrenia." Beck does not specifically refer to this S-3 condition as a remitting phase of schizophrenia, but his description of it corresponds closely to the recovering stage as conceptualized earlier in this chapter. Furthermore, the defining Rorschach characteristics Beck reports for S-3 are thoroughly consistent with the guarded, controlled picture that typifies remitting schizophrenia.

Of 120 descriptive traits observed by Beck in patterns of schizophrenic disturbance, the following five most prominently describe the S-3:

THINKING IS COHERENT. This trait is manifest in the Rorschach by absence of items indicating severe dysfunction; specifically, $F+\%$ is not below 55, irregular or confused sequence is not present, and neither DW, Po, $Z-$, nor inconsequential Dd responses occur.

ATTITUDES ARE RIGID AND CRAMPED. This pattern is indicated by low R and Z, high $F\%$ and $A\%$, rejection trends without complete rejection, and excessive qualifications of responses.

BREADTH OF INTEREST IS NARROWED. This trait is indicated by a notably narrow and stereotyped range of content.

BREADTH OF ACHIEVEMENT IN GENERAL SOCIAL ADAPTATION IS LIMITED. This trait is revealed by an R lower than expectation in view of other indicators such as intelligence, by constricted focus of attention on obvious locations, namely, D's and easy W's, and by higher $A\%$ and lower Z than the subject's intelligence would lead one to expect.

THINKING IS LOGICAL. This trait is defined by a sequence that is orderly to the point of being rigid.

It is significant to note from Beck's tables (1954, pp. 76–79) that these traits are among the least likely of the 120 in the identified schizophrenic universe to characterize the categories of "advanced" schizophrenia noted by Beck, the S-1 and S-2 patterns. These two patterns appear to represent overt schizophrenic disturbance and are characterized in the main by indices of intellectual disruption and affect-dominated behavior, respectively, most of which seldom play a significant role in S-3. The resemblance of S-3 to remitting schizophrenia suggests that the above Rorschach indices help to define the cautious, constricted protocols that often accompany remission.

CASE STUDIES [1]

The following case studies illustrate incipient and remitting schizophrenic disturbance. The first is a young woman who was seen in an

[1] The format followed in presenting the case studies is described on pages 254–257.

outpatient setting at an early phase of her disturbance when her diagnostic status and treatment needs were in doubt. She became increasingly disturbed in the weeks following the testing and was eventually hospitalized with an overt schizophrenic reaction. The second patient is a man who had been hospitalized with an acute paranoid schizophrenic reaction and was referred for testing when his clinical improvement raised question concerning his readiness for discharge.

CASE 1

This patient is a 23-year-old single school teacher with a four-year history of transient episodes of depersonalization and feelings of unreality. She was able in spite of feeling estranged from her environment and uncertain about the reality of her existence to complete her college degree and maintain a reasonable social adjustment. However, the frequency of such feelings increased markedly soon after she began her first teaching job, and she shortly became extremely anxious, disorganized, and fearful of losing control of herself. She consulted a psychiatrist at this point and was admitted to the hospital, where she remained for five weeks. The hospital staff considered her to have a hysterical character disorder and a propensity for dissociative reactions, and a course of intensive psychotherapy was recommended as the treatment of choice.

She was subsequently seen in twice-weekly, insight-oriented psychotherapy for eleven months. During this period she was able to resume working, although she continued to complain of feeling "tired," "dead," and "in a fog." This course of treatment was terminated when her therapist, expecting to leave the community, transferred her care to a colleague. To her new therapist the patient reported not only her persistent feelings of depersonalization and unreality—"I'm not seeing things clearly, they seem to be foggy or misty and as if I'm not there" —but also unusual and distorted perceptions of ordinary objects around her—stove, chair, door, and so forth. Her second therapist continued to view her as neurotically disturbed, but he was sufficiently concerned about her degree of distress and possible instability to discontinue intensive psychotherapy in favor of supportive treatment on a once-weekly basis.

For the following three months, however, her condition continued to decline. She became increasingly inhibited in her behavior, preoccupied with suicidal fantasies, and unable to assume any responsibilities outside her home. At this point she was referred for psycho-

logical examination to clarify her diagnostic status and personality resources. Three weeks after the testing she experienced an episode of
acute dread that she would lose control and slash her wrists, and she
was rehospitalized.

During this second hospitalization she expressed, in addition to the
depersonalization, derealization, and distorted perceptions reported
at earlier stages of her disturbance, some visual hallucinations and such
unusual ideas of reference as a feeling that things about her would
bend if she touched them. The hospital staff now agreed that she was
schizophrenically disturbed. Over the subsequent two months she responded only minimally to psychotherapy, medication, and a brief
trial of electroconvulsive therapy, and she was then committed for
continuing care to a state hospital. She remained at the state hospital
for several months as an inpatient and for two years in an aftercare
program before being discharged as improved.

WECHSLER ADULT INTELLIGENCE SCALE

Information

RUBBER: +. PRESIDENTS: +. LONGFELLOW: +. WEEKS: +. PANAMA: +.
BRAZIL: +. HEIGHT: (pause) dk. (*Estimate?*) 5'6" (+). ITALY: +.
CLOTHES: +. WASHINGTON: +. HAMLET: +. VATICAN: +. PARIS: (pause)
dk. (*Estimate?*) I never could tell distance very well. EGYPT: +. YEAST:
There's a bacteria or chemicals of some kind that do it, I'm not sure.
POPULATION: +. SENATORS: +. GENESIS: +. TEMPERATURE: +. ILIAD: +.
BLOOD VESSELS: Arteries, veins, and—I dk. KORAN: +. FAUST: It's about
the devil, I know, but I can't recall the author. ETHNOLOGY: It has
something to do with people, with their living places and something
like that. APOCRYPHA: dk. RAW SCORE: 23.

Although the patient's responses are for the most part efficient and
well-organized, she does evince sufficient blocking, scatter, and peculiar language to suggest difficulty maintaining consistent cognitive
focus. Blocking was evident primarily in certain features of her test
behavior that are not fully apparent in the content of her responses.
She answered each question in a careful and deliberate manner, and
from her furrowed brow, intense concentration, and halting speech it
appeared that only with considerable effort could she direct her attention toward the identification and report of even easy answers. Her
correct response on HEIGHT after considerable delay is a case in point.

Such slow reaction times and effortful concentration can relate to
depression as well as to blocking, but the fact that during the testing
as a whole she exhibited neither generally slowed reaction times nor
impoverished ideation emphasizes blocking rather than depression as
the source of her behavior here. On the other hand, it is important to

note that her deliberate efforts end in a predominance of accurate, conventionally expressed responses. Her ability thus to submerge whatever deviant or irrelevant thoughts may be interfering with her thinking is consistent with what would be expected in incipient schizophrenia. That is, she is able to utilize the external structure of test items to control the emergence of deviant thoughts or impulses.

The scatter and peculiarity in her performance are minimal but should not be overlooked. Her errors on PARIS and YEAST are inconsistent with her success on more difficult, factorially related items, EGYPT and KORAN in one case and TEMPERATURE in the other. Even more subtle is her unusual reference to the "living places" of people on ETHNOLOGY. Although this choice of words is not markedly deviant, her phrase is awkward and stilted in comparison with such more conventional expressions as "dwelling places" or "simply "places where they live."

These observations notwithstanding, the patient's Information performance reveals largely intact cognitive functioning and above average or superior intellectual ability. Furthermore, the impairments noted are significant not because they are sufficient evidence of overtly disordered thinking, but because they represent the kinds of subtle and minimal clues that are crucial to the recognition of early and mild phases of schizophrenic disturbance.

Comprehension

ENVELOPE: Mail it (2). BAD COMPANY: So you don't get into trouble (1). MOVIES: Tell the manager (2). TAXES: So there's money to run the government (2). IRON: You should act at the most opportune time (2). CHILD LABOR: So parents won't exploit their children (1). FOREST: I'd try to keep walking in a straight line until I came to the end of it (1). DEAF: Because they haven't heard words or sounds and aren't able to copy them (2). CITY LAND: More people want land in the city (2). MARRIAGE: So that no one is married to more than one person at a time (1). BROOKS: (pause) I know what I want to say, but . . . the water isn't deep . . . I don't know, that's all I can think of (0). SWALLOW: Swallows come in the summer, but just because you see one doesn't mean that it's summer (1). RAW SCORE: 21.

The patient's performance on this subtest is with one exception concise, relevant, and insignificant for impaired ego functioning. The exception is her hesitant and ineffective attempt to focus her thoughts on BROOKS, which further exemplifies the blocking noted on Information.

Similarities

ORANGE: Fruit (2). COAT: Clothing (2). AXE: Tools (2). DOG: Animals (2). NORTH: Directions (2). EYE: Part of anatomy; features of the head (1). AIR: They're both made of the same elements (1). TABLE:

Furniture (2). EGG: Beginnings of life (2). POEM: Have to do with art (2). WOOD: dk (0). PRAISE: Ways of behaving toward someone (0). FLY: dk (0). RAW SCORE: 18.

As on Comprehension there is little in the patient's responses here to suggest personality disorder. The only possible clue to ego impairment is the slightly uneven level of her concept formation. Her partial-credit responses to EYE and AIR are somewhat overly narrow categorizations, based respectively on anatomical location and chemical composition, whereas her response to PRAISE, "ways of behaving," is an overly broad generalization. Her variability in this regard is minimal, however, and it is remarked here more for didactic than for diagnostic purposes.

Picture Completion

KNOB: +. TAIL: +. NOSE: +. HANDLES: +. DIAMOND: Correct beyond time limit. WATER: Someone to pour the water. NOSE PIECE: Nothing is missing . . . no, wait (correct beyond time limit). PEG: +. OAR LOCK: +. BASE THREAD: Correct beyond time limit. STARS: Pole. DOG TRACKS: +. FLORIDA: +. STACKS: +. LEG: +. ARM IMAGE: The rest of the chair and the woman's arm. FINGER: Nothing. SHADOW: +. STIRRUP: Saddle horn. SNOW: Nothing. EYEBROW: +. RAW SCORE: 12.

The patient's response to Picture Completion is somewhat deceptive, suggesting at first glance considerably more disturbance than is confirmed by a close inspection of her performance. Though her gross pattern of successes and failures is markedly scattered, none of her nine errors represents either a conspicuous focus on irrelevant details or an idiosyncratic view of social situations. Three of the items she answers correctly but beyond the acceptable time limit, on two she reports nothing missing, and on the other four she makes types of errors commonly observed in normal as well as patient groups.

On the other hand, her spotty performance does contain some minimal clues to personality disturbance. The fact that she required more than the allotted time to respond on three items that she was eventually able to answer correctly further attests the blocking noted on Information and Comprehension. The possibility that depression rather than blocking was preventing her from mustering her cognitive skills in these three instances is unlikely, inasmuch as her reaction times on this subtest were neither generally slowed nor particularly related to item difficulty. Additionally, her errors on WATER and ARM IMAGE, even though common, reflect inconsistency in her ability to maintain her focus of attention, for she succeeds on more difficult items factorially related to each: PEG, OAR LOCK, and FLORIDA in relation to WATER, and SHADOW in relation to ARM IMAGE.

Additionally, it should be noted that on two occasions and nearly on a third she evades responsibility for making a response by asserting that nothing is missing. This type of denial of the instructions (i.e., the statement, "I am going to show you some pictures in which *there is some important part missing*") is, as noted in Chapter 14, consistent with the defensive reliance on externalization of blame that characterizes paranoid tendencies. Her behavior in this regard, then, provides a tentative clue that paranoid trends may be participating in her current adjustment.

Scale Scores

Information: 14. Comprehension: 13. Similarities: 12. Picture Completion: 9.

Discussion. The WAIS administration was terminated after Picture Completion because of the patient's considerable distress at this point. Obvious to the examiner was the heavy toll her effortful performance was taking of her psychological reserves. The most salient characteristic of this WAIS protocol, in fact, is the extent to which this young woman, though revealing glimpses of impaired thinking, manages by dint of great effort to keep such impairments in check and to maintain an accurate, conventional, and relevant response pattern. Although such indices of impaired cognitive focusing as blocking and intratest scatter are present, her performance is sufficiently intact that it would be difficult to infer schizophrenic disturbance from her WAIS alone.

However, the facts that (a) her WAIS performance is relatively intact and (b) she is making obvious efforts to control her responses at the expense of marked anxiety and distress about her functioning suggest that, should other data demonstrate schizophrenic disturbance, the phase of her disorder is probably incipient rather than overt at this time.

DRAW-A-PERSON

The patient was reluctant to execute the figure drawings, and only after considerable encouragement did she agree to render the single figure reproduced in Figure 21. Although the sketchiness of her drawing might suggest a disinterested and hasty effort, it is significant that she concentrated intently on this task and drew the lines of her figure with painstaking care. Her attitude toward her performance was also of considerable interest. She was noticeably tense and anxious during the test, which suggested it was difficult for her and that she was dissatisfied with the quality of her efforts. Nevertheless, when at the end of her work she was asked, "Would you like to add anything further to it?", she replied, "No, that's all I can do."

Figure 21

Particularly because the patient applied herself diligently to her drawing and was encouraged to elaborate her final product, the gross incompleteness of Figure 21 has significant implications for personality disturbance. First, she leaves major gaps between the lines of the trunk, arms, and legs and fails to close the ends of the arms and legs. Such clear breaks of the body contour reflect indefinite, poorly demarcated ego boundaries and suggest that this young woman is having marked difficulty maintaining a sense of her own reality as a single, unique, and integral person.

Second, she omits many vital body parts, including hands, feet, and all the features of the head, which points to a confused and uncertain body image. Some of these body parts are more difficult to draw correctly than others, but overriding such a consideration in this case is the fact that the patient makes no effort even to approximate these organs and achieves a basically well-proportioned drawing as far as she goes. Hence not limited drawing talent but rather a distorted view of her body and its functions appears responsible for her deviant performance. This distorted body imagery shares with her indefinite ego boundaries major implications for impaired reality sense.

It is further noteworthy that the patient's DAP performance is considerably less adequate than what might normally be expected in view of her reasonably conventional, efficient, and well-organized effort on the WAIS. This discrepancy, which implies some personality disturbance that she can control fairly well on structured tasks but cannot as adequately compensate in the setting of a projective test, is consistent with incipient schizophrenic disorder.

Rorschach

Card I 6″

1. (D+ M+ H,Cg *Peculiar, Barrier*) It looks like two of those men who used to be head people; they're in the middle part, standing with their hands up together and with hoods over their heads. (*Head people?*) I mean executioners, because of their hoods and all.

2. (Wm,S F+,m *Mask Fabulized*) It looks like—a—mask, the whole thing. (*Kind of mask?*) I see eyes, a mouth, and ears, and these side parts are what goes around the face. (*How look?*) Evil. (?) Because of the eyes. (?) They just look evil; and the mouth makes it look horrible, like evil laughing; as if there would be fire behind the eyes and mouth. (*What suggests fire?*) I don't know.

3. (Wm,S FC′+ Ad) It looks almost like a cat, too, a black cat; but mostly it looks like those men with the hoods. (*Parts?*) I see ears, a face, a mouth, teeth, and a nose in the center; it's just the head.

Card II 14″

4. (*D+ M+,FC′ H,Cg Barrier*) It looks like people in some kind of hoods [black details]; it's some kind of ritual, and they have their hands together and are squatting down, like in some kind of ritual. (*Kind of people?*) Their backs are turned, and they're in some type of dark cloaks with hoods; I can't see what they look like. Their arms are here [upper center] and the space here is a space between them.

5. (*Da C Fire Fabulized Combination*) This may be a fire in front of them. (?) The red is fire [bottom red]. (*What about the red part suggests fire?*) It also looks like lungs, too, but more like fire. It's just that it's red and it seems like a fire. (*Relate to people?*) It looks like it goes with the people.

6. (*D— FM— Ad*) These things [upper red] don't look like anything. They could be some odd kind of bird, just the head of it; heads of birds, and they're looking at one another.

Card III 5″

7. (*Dm F+ (H) Incongruous*) They're like two funny things, half person and half bird, with something in between them like a basket. (*Half person and half bird?*) That's the way it is; the heads look like beaks, and the bodies are like people; but the feet are like the claws of a bird, and the arms are like wings.

8. (*Dm FC+ Cg P Barrier*) Oh, I don't like this card [patient shudders]! Here it looks like a bow. (?) It looks like a red bow; it's tied like a red bow, and it's a little frayed. (*What not like about this one?*) I don't mind it so much now.

Card IV 3″

9. (*D+ F+,M (H),Cg Fabulized, Barrier*) It looks like two clowns, back to back; they're tired. (*Tired?*) Their faces are tired. (?) They're just tired, so tired they don't care; I don't know how you tell, but they just are. (*Clowns?*) Because of the big feet, and they look like they have clowns' suits on.

10. (*Dm F+ (H)*) The whole thing looks sort of like a gorilla or a monster; the arms are odd, though; they're limp, and it almost seems like they're not even exactly arms. (?) It looks mainly like a monster, with the head here, these strange arms at the side, and the feet at the bottom. (*Whole thing?*) No, this part [lower center detail] is not a part of it.

Card V 62″

11. (*D— F—,M (Hd),Cg Barrier*) These [two halves of upper "head" detail] look like two men, back to back; they remind me of wise

sages from a long time ago, with tall hats and beards; they sort of look like Santa Claus, too; they look more like Santa Claus. (?) It resembles Santa Claus, but not his whole body; you can see part of his body and here [upper projection] are his hat, his face, and his beard.

12. (*Dm M+ H,Cg*) These are like women lying down here [entire side portions]. They're not sleeping, but just lying down. (?) I can see the head, arms, and legs, one on each side; they're not sleeping because you can see the eyelash open, I mean the eye open. (*Women?*) You can see her legs, which means she has a dress on.

13. (*Dm F+ Ad*) The whole doesn't look like anything, but it does make me think of an ostrich; I don't know why. Just this part here [bottom detail] is it, is part of the legs of an ostrich.

Card VI 6″

14. (*Dm F+ Obj*) The top part looks like the top of a totem pole.

15. (*D— F— Ad Barrier*) It reminds me of seals. (?) It's also the top part; there are whiskers, the head, and a fin; it's not the whole seal, just parts of it.

16. (*Dm F+ Aobj P-tendency*) It's sort of like an Indian skin rug [entire lower portion]. (?) It just seems like a rug; I've seen them on floors, animal skins used as rugs.

17. (*Dd M—,FC' Hd,Cg,Rel Fabulized, Barrier*) This looks like people from the days in Egypt when they wore white cloth around their heads with a band in it; there's just the head here, looking away; it's like a figure from Bible times [upper corner of right half of lower portion, adjacent to center column]. (?) I see a face here, with the eye in this spot, the white cloth and the band here, and it looks like it's looking away; just the head part.

18. (*Dd F+ (Hd),Cg Barrier*) These look like elves [middle side areas of lower portion], with pointed hats [upper side projection] and a beard here [lower side projection], a funny little beard. The whole thing doesn't look like anything. (?) Because of the eyes, nose, and beard. (*Funny?*) It's just an odd, funny elf.

Card VII 4″

19. (*W+ M+ H Fabulized*) It's two women; they're angry at each other and turning around quickly, so that their hair flies up and around.

20. (*Dm F+ Ad*) I think of a rabbit, but I really don't see one there; maybe it's the ear of a rabbit [top detail]; yes, this looks like a rabbit ear; but mostly it's the women.

21. (*Dd F+ Ad*) Faces, funny faces; it's like an animal's face, in the middle [lower outer corner of middle side detail]; there are two of them, there are always two (*Funny?*) It just looks kind of silly . . .

silly . . . the noses are funny, and there's not much mouth; the ears are funny, like animal's ears.

Card VIII 5″

22. (*Dm FM*+ *A P*) These look like prehistoric animals, climbing. (?) They're lumbering along, and they're large and ugly.

23. (*Dd M*— *Hd,Cg,Rel Absurd Dd, Barrier*) A Chinese woman right here, in this little part [tiny orange projection in center between pink and blue details]; she's like she's kneeling and dressed in costume. (*Chinese?*) I can see it from her hair, the way she's wearing it, and she has a costume with those wide sleeves on like Chinese wear; it looks like she might be praying; I can't see her legs and it looks like she's kneeling.

24. (*Dd F*—,*M Art*,(*H*) *Fabulized*) These look like statues here [narrow areas of gray area on either side of and running parallel to upper center column]; they look like Romans, like Roman men with their arms raised up high. The rest of it doesn't look like anything. (*Roman?*) The way the heads look; I can see laurel leaves on their heads.

Card IX 37″

25. (*D*— *F*—,*C,FK Art,Rel Autistic Logic*) It made me think of a Christmas card; this part here [upper center column] looks like a modern picture of a Madonna, so modern that it's not very pretty; and there's blue light behind it. The whole thing doesn't look like anything else; just that little part is anything. (?) It looks sort of stretched out and not too real. (*Christmas?*) The blue light behind it suggests Christmas. (*Not pretty?*) It's not pretty because it's modern.

Card X 11″

26. (*Dm M*+ (*A*) *Fabulized, Incongruous*) Funny little animals talking to one another, and they're angry [top gray details]. (*Kind of animals?*) No particular kind, just odd animals.

27. (*Dm F*+ *Ar*) I think of the Eiffel tower [entire upper gray]; that's silly, it doesn't really look too much like that.

28. (*Dm F*+ *A P Fabulized*) It looks like a great big lobster in a book I had when I was little, with a great big claw.

29–30. (*Dm FM*+ *Ad P; Dv CFarb Obj Incongruous, Fabulized Combination*) A rabbit that's grinning and has great big eyes; there's something on the sides of his head, almost like green hair, but that doesn't belong to the rabbit. (?) It's got great big eyes, and a mouth; it's just the head part; these on the side look like green hair, and the rabbit's right here, too, but they just don't go together. (*Are they separate?*) No, the hair is attached to the rabbit.

31. (*Dm F+ Obj*) A wishbone [middle orange detail].

32. (*D— F— A Autistic Logic*) And these look like little seahorses here [inner yellow details]. (?) They just look like one. (*Little?*) Because they're small in relation to the rest of the things on the card.

Scores

R	32	M	7+3	H	4+1	F+%	72%
W	3(9%)	FM	3	(H)	3	R+%	73%
D	24(75%)	m	0+1	Hd	2	P	4+1
Dd+S	5(16%)	FK	0+1	A	3+1		
		F	18	(A)	1	High W%	100%
		C′	1+2	(Hd)	2	High D%	67%
Fabulized	7	FC	1+1	Ad	7		
Incongruous	3	CF	1	Obj	3	Barrier	8
Fabulized		C	1+1	Art	2		
Combination	2			Cg	1+6		
Autistic Logic	2			Mask	1		
Peculiar	1			Ar	1		
Absurd Dd	1			Fire	1		
				Rel	0+3		

Discussion. Noticeably gone from this young woman's Rorschach protocol is the effortful but adaptive control that marked her WAIS performance. She makes some attempt to check her associations, as in responses #13 and #20, where she restricts her imagery to only one portion of what are commonly seen as more complete figures,[2] but in general she is either unwilling or unable to avoid a freely associative record that demonstrates both disordered thinking and paranoid tendencies.

Although indications of personality disturbance do not pervade her record, the patient sufficiently exhibits illogical reasoning and maladaptive cognitive focusing to identify thought disorder. Lapses in cogntive focusing appear in her inordinate attention to unusual and irrelevant aspects of her experience (*Dd%* of 16), in her peculiar language usage ("head men" in #1), and in three subtle dissociative episodes in which she responds obliquely to inquiry.

These three instances of dissociation aptly illustrate the manner in which subtle discontinuities in the verbal exchange between subject

[2] Such responses, following Rorschach (1921, pp. 40–41), may be scored as *Do* or *oligophrenic* details. Rorschach observed these responses to be associated in persons of normal intelligence with anxiety and compulsive mechanisms of control.

and examiner may reveal mild or incipient thought disorder. On #2 the patient is asked, "What kind of mask does it look like?" and she responds by tangentially specifying the parts she sees; in #4, when asked what *kind* of people she has seen, she replies with a loosely related description of their position and clothing; on #5 she is asked what suggests fire and irrelevantly responds, "It also looks like lungs," before she addresses herself to the matter of the fire. These discontinuities do not approach the blatant dissociation observed in overtly schizophrenic subjects, but they do exemplify an important type of diagnostic clue to mildly or incipiently disturbed thinking.

Several examples of inappropriately overgeneralized, combinative, and circumstantial thinking in the patient's responses demonstrate illogical reasoning. Indicating overgeneralization are her seven Fabulized and one absurd *Dd* responses. Three of her seven fabulizations (#'s 9, 19, & 26) are merely fanciful attributions of feeling states to her perceived figures and are not significant for thought disorder. However, two others are elaborations for which there is little external justification (#2, "as if there would be fire behind the eyes and mouth"; #28, "a *great big* lobster"), and in the remaining two tiny details are utilized as sufficient basis for detailed specification of her percepts (in #17 the people are *Egyptians* because of the suggestion of white cloth around their heads; in #24 the statues are *Roman* because of the minuscule indication of laurel leaves on their heads).

Her proclivity for overgeneralized thinking is most vividly apparent in her absurd *Dd* response on #23, where from an extremely minute detail with few distinguishing features she infers a human figure with sexual and racial characteristics ("Chinese woman"), affecting a particular kind of hair style and dress ("wide sleeves"), and engaged in a specific activity ("praying"). Taken together, the patient's overgeneralizations indicate that she is inclined to jump from minimal evidence to overdrawn conclusions about the meaning of her experience.

Revealing inappropriate combinative thinking are the patient's three incongruous and two Fabulized Combination responses. Her incongruous percepts illustrate three of the different forms that such combinations may take: she produces an unnatural composite of human and animal details in her "half person and half bird" response on #7; in #26 she posits an impossible combination of an object (animal) and an activity (talking); and she reports an arbitrary integration of color and form in her "green hair" response in #30.

Her two Fabulized Combinations arbitrarily link images she does not quite interrelate but nevertheless cannot keep logically separate. In #'s 4–5 she concludes that the fire "goes with the people," even though such a conclusion, in view of the juxtaposition of the details, implies the highly unlikely circumstance of the people standing in the fire. In #'s 29–30 she struggles with the realization that "rabbit" and "green hair" do not naturally occur together, but she is unable to avoid specifying that "the hair is attached to the rabbit."

Finally suggestive of reasoning impairment is her tendency to autistic logic in #'s 25 and 32. In #25 she asserts that the Christmas card is not pretty "because it's modern." Although the aesthetic quality of modern art could be debated, the patient is not engaging here in such an abstract discussion; rather, she appears to conclude that being modern is an adequate and automatic basis for being unattractive, and such a circumstantial conclusion transcends the boundaries of conventional logic. Similarly, in #32 she infers that the seahorses are "little" because of their circumstantial relationship to other, larger details of the inkblot.

Additionally identifying the patient's schizophrenic disturbance and her particular difficulty in maintaining her controls in the context of unstructured situations are Rorschach indications of ineffective integration of affective experience. Her one main and one additional pure C responses represent breakdown of integrative ability, and her general color use ($1\ FC$, $1\ CF$, $1\ C$) constitutes color stress and reveals inconsistent defensive resources for handling emotional stimulation.

Further delineating this young woman's current condition are a number of structural and content aspects of her Rorschach that point to paranoid trends. Her prominent introversive experience balance and elevated $Dd\%$ are consistent with the ideational orientation that differentiates paranoid from nonparanoid forms of schizophrenia, and the content of her responses suggests considerable reliance on projective defense. She frequently attributes aggressive intent to her environment ("executioner" on #1, "evil laughing" on #2, women "angry at each other" on #19, "angry" animals on #26); she appears concerned about being under the scrutiny of others (evil eyes on #2, "looking at one another" on #6, faces on #21); she expresses feelings that the motives of others are hidden from her and difficult to discern (cloaked, hooded figures, "can't see what they look like" on #'s 1 & 4, mask on #2); and she demonstrates exaggerated concern with insulating her body against the environment (eight Barrier responses).

More speculatively, there is some suggestion that she is having difficulty accepting a feminine sexual identity. This possibility emerges from a number of responses that depreciate male figures ("clowns" in #9, monster with "limp arms" in #10, elves with a "funny little beard" on #18) and the homosexual ideation probably underlying her percept in #12 of two women lying down in adjacent positions and "not sleeping." These indications of ideational orientation, reliance on projective defense, and difficulty with sexual identity suggest that further decompensation in this woman might well proceed along paranoid lines.

Summary. In her contrasting performance on various parts of the test battery this young woman gives evidence of an incipient schizophrenic disorder. She responds in an orderly and well-integrated fashion to the WAIS, although her blocking and overt distress on this test suggest she is struggling against unacceptable, ego-alien personality aberrations that she manages to submerge only with considerable effort. On the DAP and Rorschach, however, she is unable to prevent minimal but clear evidence of dissociation, illogical reasoning, impaired reality sense, and inadequate defensive resources from emerging. Her ability to control her behavior better in structured than unstructured situations, her anxious awareness of her personality malfunctioning, and her relatively mild extent of disturbance indicate that her schizophrenic disorder is in an incipient phase.

CASE 2

This patient is a 30-year-old professional man who had no history of psychological disturbance until six months before his psychological examination. Having accepted a new position, he had left his wife and two children behind to make living arrangements in the community to which they would be moving. While by himself for a two-week period, he had begun to ruminate about past events, particularly previous situations when he had taken new jobs that had subsequently proved unsatisfactory. He continued to be preoccupied with explaining to himself these past misadventures even after his family joined him, and he soon developed feelings of reference about newspaper and television content, which he interpreted to have special significance for him. Several weeks of burgeoning delusional and referential ideas culminated in his thinking one day that he heard on the radio that his wife and children were in danger, upon which he rushed home after work and refused to leave the house for the next several days.

At the instigation of his employers he was then seen by a psychiatrist, who recommended hospitalization. On admission the patient was extremely suspicious and guarded, questioning staff persons about their credentials and complaining that he had no way to ascertain if they were really who they said they were. Although a long hospital course was envisioned for this man, he responded surprisingly well to medication and psychotherapy. Within a week he was seemingly in good control of himself and expressed eagerness to return home.

He was referred for psychological examination at this point to assess the nature of his apparent remission. Following the testing he was started on a graduated program of increasingly frequent home visits, on which he did well, and he was totally discharged two weeks later. He was followed supportively after his discharge, and in the 18 months until the time of this writing he has not required further hospital care.

WECHSLER ADULT INTELLIGENCE SCALE

Information

RUBBER: +. PRESIDENTS: +. LONGFELLOW: +. WEEKS: +. PANAMA: +. BRAZIL: +. HEIGHT: +. ITALY: +. CLOTHES: +. WASHINGTON: Sometime in February, I'm not sure when. HAMLET: +. VATICAN: +. PARIS: +. EGYPT: +. YEAST: Cataleptic action, some chemical action. POPULATION: +. SENATORS: +. GENESIS: +. TEMPERATURE: +. ILIAD: +. BLOOD VESSELS: I can't remember what they're called. KORAN: It has something to do with the Jewish Bible. FAUST: dk. ETHNOLOGY: +. APOCRYPHA: dk. RAW SCORE: 23.

There is little in these responses to suggest personality disturbance. The patient responds concisely and relevantly to almost every item. Three mildly deviant features of his performance can be noted for future reference, however. First, he employs peculiar language on YEAST, using *cataleptic* where he apparently means *catalytic*. Such an error in technical terminology does not by itself identify disordered thinking, but it should alert the examiner for subsequent idiosyncratic communications.

Second, he evinces some minimal scatter within factorially related items, passing POPULATION and SENATORS after missing WASHINGTON and succeeding on TEMPERATURE after failing YEAST. Third, in his response on BLOOD VESSELS, "I can't remember what they're called," he exhibits some of the self-aggrandizement (i.e., "it's not that I don't know, but just that I can't remember") that characterizes the paranoid defensive stance.

Comprehension

ENVELOPE: I'd mail it (2). BAD COMPANY: It may lead them to be bad, like one sour apple may spoil the basket, I guess (2). MOVIES: Let someone in charge know, without raising a panic (2). TAXES: To help support the government (2). IRON: Do something before it's too late (2). CHILD LABOR: To protect young children from abuse in labor; do you write all this down? (1). FOREST: If the sun were out, I'd get a shadow from a tree (1). DEAF: They never heard the sounds, I guess (1). CITY LAND: It's more in demand (2). MARRIAGE: To make sure of their age and check for diseases (1). BROOKS: If there isn't much there, like if someone doesn't know much, they make a lot of noise (2). SWALLOW: Just because one thing happens, that doesn't mean a lot of things are going to happen; what kind of writing is that you're doing—it looks like a different language (2). RAW SCORE: 24.

On this subtest the patient gives considerable substance to the language peculiarity and paranoid orientation tentatively inferred from his Information performance. He states that child-labor laws are needed "to protect young children from abuse *in labor*"; lost in a forest, he would "get a shadow from a tree"; and he asserts that persons born deaf seldom talk because "they never hear the sounds." Each of these responses communicates enough of the sense of a correct answer to receive some credit; yet the first two involve unusual phraseology (being *in labor* conventionally has meanings other than being in a work situation, and a person may *observe* or *look for* a shadow, but he does not *get* one), whereas the third is a highly elliptical expression (hear sounds *of what*, one might wonder). These awkward and peculiar phrases indicate that the patient has difficulty formulating his thoughts in conventional language.

Paranoid tendencies appear here in the patient's prominent concern about the actions and motives of the examiner. At one point he asks whether everything he says is being recorded, and later, apparently having closely observed the examiner's rapid, abbreviated notations, he questions what kind of writing it is and states that it looks like a different language. Comments of this type relect the caution, suspiciousness, and fear of being misused that characterize the paranoid position.

Finally of note is the patient's added comment on BAD COMPANY, "One sour apple may spoil the basket." Aside from the fact that this expression deviates from the usual "*bad*-apple-in-a-*barrel*" manner of stating this aphorism, it is significant that the saying itself is not meaningfully related to the reasons why bad company should be avoided. Contrasting with his good capacity to explain the relatively difficult proverbs BROOKS and SWALLOW, his tangential response here suggests some dissociation.

Similarities

ORANGE: Fruits (2). COAT: Clothes (2). AXE: Used to chop trees, or to carpent, if there's such a word (1). DOG: Animals (2). NORTH: Directions (2). EYE: Senses (2). AIR: Things we need to live (2). TABLE: Furniture (2). EGG: They're both the beginnings of some step of development (2). POEM: Art (2). WOOD: Alcohol comes from wood (0). PRAISE: They're opposites (0). FLY: That's a good one; both are not human is all I can say (0). RAW SCORE: 19.

The patient's Similarities performance, like his response on Information and Comprehension, is generally efficient and accurate. The only clue to cognitive disturbance here is his neologism on AXE, *carpent*, which further confirms the tendency to peculiar language usage noted on Comprehension. However, his spontaneous critical judgment of his response—"If there's such a word"—somewhat mitigates its pathologic significance and reveals him to be actively engaged in assessing his own behavior and attempting to respond along conventional lines. In other words, he appears aware of and reluctant to accept his manifestations of personality disturbance.

Also of interest here is the patient's approach on the last two items, the difficulty of which apparently exceeded his intellectual capacity. On both items he endeavors to cushion his failure with protective measures of a type not infrequently observed in paranoid subjects. On PRAISE he absolves himself from any responsibility for identifying a similarity by unequivocally asserting there is none—"They're opposites." On FLY he admits being unable to answer adequately but subordinates his admission to a disarming introductory comment, "That's a good one," by which he employs evaluation of the item to take distance from his role as a testee.

Digit Symbol

RAW SCORE: 42.

The patient worked consistently but methodically on this subtest, and his performance was generally unremarkable. He seemed comfortable and composed during the coding, and his relatively low score resulted primarily from the care and deliberation with which he drew the symbols, fitting each one neatly within the confines of its respective square.

Picture Completion

KNOB: +. TAIL: +. NOSE: +. HANDLES: Correct beyond time limit. DIAMOND: +. WATER: No one is holding up the pitcher. NOSE PIECE: +. PEG: The jobby you play the violin with. OAR LOCK: +. BASE THREAD: A socket. STARS: +. DOG TRACKS: He should have a gun if he's hunting. FLORIDA: +. STACKS: +. LEG: dk. ARM IMAGE: +. FINGER: Nothing. SHADOW: +. STIRRUP: A rider. SNOW: dk. EYEBROW: dk. RAW SCORE: 11.

This extremely inconsistent and scattered performance contrasts markedly with the patient's efficient approach on the previous subtests. His almost random pattern of successes and failure bears little relationship to the difficulty of the various items within their factorial groupings: he passes OAR LOCK and FLORIDA after missing WATER; ARM IMAGE and SHADOW after missing DOG TRACKS; and STACKS after missing BASE THREAD. The degree of his scatter clearly indicates the intrusion of interfering elements on his ability to focus his attention consistently on the relevant aspects of his experience. The pathologic significance of his relatively inept performance here was enhanced by the fact that he attended carefully to the task, studying the cards at length and formulating his responses with considerable deliberation.

Block Design

ITEM 1: 5″ (4). ITEM 2: Unsuccessful on first trial; second trial in 4″ (2). ITEM 3: 6″ (4). ITEM 4: 13″ (4). ITEM 5: 12″ (4). ITEM 6: 36″ (4). ITEM 7: 43″ (4). ITEM 8: 60″ (5). ITEM 9: 58″ (6). ITEM 10: 110″ (4). RAW SCORE: 41.

On this subtest the patient restituted the efficient functioning that had characterized his efforts before the Picture Completion. Except for his difficulty orienting himself to the task on ITEM 2, he assembled the blocks quickly and confidently and injected no extraneous comments.

Scale Scores

Information: 14. Comprehension: 16. Similarities: 13. Digit Symbol: 9. Picture Completion: 8. Block Design: 12.

Most notable in these scale scores, aside from the superior intellectual capacity they suggest, is the low Picture Completion score. In relation to his significantly higher Block Design score, the patient's Picture Completion performance indicates intertest scatter and complements the inconsistency observed within his Information and Picture Completion. The Picture Completion and Block Design discrepancy also discloses that his personality integration is more adversely affected by social than impersonal contexts.

Discussion. Although this highly intelligent man responds to the WAIS in a generally orderly and relevant fashion, his occasionally peculiar language on the verbal scales, scattered efficiency between and within subtests, and particular susceptibility to performance decrements in socially contextual settings identify inconsistent cognitive focusing and interpersonal aversion, both of which characterize schizophrenic disturbance. Additionally, his suspicious, guarded approach, especially as reflected in his extratest comments, points to paranoid tendencies.

The extent of his disturbance on the WAIS is mild, however, and the pathologic significance imputed here to many subtle, almost unremarkable features of his performance might be difficult to justify were it not for the fact that just one week before the testing he had presented a clear clinical picture of flagrant, overt, paranoid schizophrenia. The patient's mildly pathologic WAIS is by itself equivocal concerning phase of disturbance. Such a record in combination with a relatively poorly controlled, more extremely deviant Rorschach would point to incipient schizophrenia, as illustrated in the preceding case. Accompanied by an even better controlled, more conventionally oriented Rorschach, however, his WAIS would be consistent with a remitting phase of disturbance, in which schizophrenic tendencies emerge primarily under the stress of specific, structured environmental demands.

DRAW-A-PERSON

The patient's figure drawings are presented in Figures 22 and 23. They are somewhat primitive products of a man apparently minimally blessed with artistic talent, yet it is significant that they are relatively free of indications of impaired reality sense. With regard to ego boundaries, for example, the body contours on both of his drawings are unbroken and fairly continuous. Those minor line gaps present, as in the lines of the woman's skirt (Figure 23), are not of the same proportion as the discontinuities noted in previous illustrations (see Figures 5 & 6) and do not imply indefinite ego boundaries.

These drawings are also unmarred by evidence of distorted body imagery. All the vital parts of the bodies, including arms, legs, hands, feet, eyes, and ears, are indicated, and the patient employs hair and clothing details adequately to differentiate the sex of his two figures. Additionally, although the emphasis in the male figure on the eyes and the ears, with the pupil and external meatus indicated, is consistent with paranoid suspiciousness, these DAP features are less clearly indicative of paranoid tendencies than his behavior on the WAIS. His improved functioning on this projective test relative to his performance on the more structured WAIS begins to suggest the enhanced capacity for control in unstructured situations that characterizes remitting schizophrenic disturbance.

RORSCHACH

Card I 3″

1. (*Wm F+ A P Peculiar*) I don't know, it looks like some kind of bug. I had some of these cards in psychology courses in school. Is all this confidential? (*Anything else?*) No, just a bug, or maybe a bat. (?) I'd say it's a bat, with the wings on the side and some sort of antlers here [top center details].

Figure 22

Figure 23

Card II 4″

2. (*Dm F+ Ad P*) Two little bears or dogs on the sides; I don't know what they're doing. [Pause] I don't see anything else. (*Encouragement*) I—uh—gee, they just look like blotches to me . . . I can't even—uh—I don't know, unless these [reference to upper red] are sort of—no, they're nothing. (?) Just a couple bears, because of the shape; the mouth and the head are here, and the shoulders; it's just the upper part of it, and the paws are chopped off.

Card III 2″

3. (*D+ M+ H P Autistic Logic*) It looks like a couple of natives, standing and beating a drum; a couple of Indians or natives. (*Natives?*) We're all natives of someplace; I should have said natives in Africa. (*Natives in Africa?*) I don't know what suggests it; just the way they're beating the drums, like in the movies; they have no feathers, so they're not Indians. (*Men or women?*) Women, because it looks like a bosom here.

4. (*Dm F+ A P*) The center looks like a butterfly. (?) The shape, the body with two wings.

5. (*Dm F+,Fm Ad Fabulized*) These on the side [outer red] sort of look like chickens, with their heads chopped off, sort of hung up for a feast.

Card IV 2″

6. (*Wm F+ A Queer*) That looks like my friend the bat; he's sort of upside down, though, but he looks like a pretty good bat to me. (?) It looks like an upside-down bat; if I turn the card [reverses position] —that's funny, this way [∨] it doesn't look like a right-side-up bat.

Card V 2″

7. (*Wm F+ A P*) It looks like a butterfly or a moth, and that's all. (?) The wings and the things out in front; it's the general appearance is all.

Card VI 5″

8. (*Dm F+,Fm Aobj P-tendency Fabulized*) I don't know, it looks like a rug or something, hung up; like someone went out and shot something and hung it up in a den to display it; the bottom part of it mainly. (?) The shape of it.

9. (*Dm F+ Obj*) The top part looks like some kind of totem pole. (?) It looks like some sort of idol or something like that; a pagan idol, like something from one of those horror movies.

Card VII 12″

10. (W+ M+ (H),Cg Barrier) I have no impression whatsoever. Well, looking close I can see two elves; they're looking at one another, standing on rocks; they appear to have tails and big feathers on their heads. (?) This could be the tail [side projection] and this a hat or feather [top detail], with the face here; one is staring at the other; yes, it looks like a sleeping-cap up here; they look like little statuettes you might put on your table.

Card VIII 3″

11. (D+ FM+ A,Bt P) It looks like a couple of mountain lions, climbing up the side of a mountain, and maybe grabbing a branch here at the top [side projections of upper gray]. (?) It looks like something from the cat family, but—actually, now it looks more like a mouse than a cat, or some rodent. (Mountain?) No, I don't really see a mountain there; it's mainly an impression of the rodents climbing and grabbing a branch.

Card IX 15″

12. (Dm F+ (H),Cg Barrier) I really don't see too much of any- thing here, just a big blob. Well, really stretching my imagination, it could be a couple of witches up here [orange details], with pointed caps, long fingers, and a big nose. (Witches?) The way they look, with those caps and the long fingers.

13. (Dm F+ Ad) These two on the side [green details] look like hippopotamuses, with their foot here and mouth here. (?) Because of the big mouth; the eye is here, and one foot; the other foot is chopped off, and it's not the whole thing, but just the front part of a big animal.

14. (Dv CF,cF Food Penetration) The bottom part [pink] could be a couple of cotton candies. (?) They're pink, and they have a flow- ing, rounded look like they're twisted around something. I recently remember buying my son a cotton candy.

Card X 4″

15. (Dm F+ A P) The blue looks like a spider or some such thing.

16. (D+ M+ (H)) The top [upper gray details] look like some men from Mars, looking each other in the eye, staring at each other. (?) They look like they're staring each other down; I can see a mouth, eye, couple of feet, and a tail on each one.

17. (D+ F+,mF Obj,Wa Peculiar, Penetration) The pink parts look like a water fountain or spout, like you'd see in a park; each one is flowing out some water. (?) They look like two little figures or statu-

ettes, like you'd see with water flowing out of their mouths; I don't really see water, unless I stretch it to include this [inner blue]; it's mainly the statue part I see.

18. (*Dm FC+ A P Peculiar*) The green part looks like some worms or snails or something like that. (?) They look squiggly, and because of the fact that they're green; they could be some green worms.

Scores

R	18	M	3	H	1	F+%	100%	
W	4(22%)	FM	1	(H)	3	R+%	100%	
D	14(78%)	m	0+2	A	7	P		8+1
		F	12	Ad	3			
		cF	0+1	Obj	2	High W%	100%	
Peculiar	3	FC	1	Aobj	1	High D%	93%	
Fabulized	2	CF	1	Food	1			
Queer	1			Cg	0+2	Barrier		2
Autistic Logic	1			Bt	0+1	Penetration		2

Discussion. Consistent with expectation in remitting schizophrenia, this man's Rorschach (a) reveals glimpses of underlying personality disturbance but is relatively free from gross indicators of schizophrenic impairment, (b) achieves over-all integration at the expense of marked banality, constriction, and guardedness, and (c) is better controlled and more adaptive than his reaction to the WAIS.

The only features of the patient's protocol that reflect his recently flagrant schizophrenic condition are infrequent, minimal indications of maladaptive cognitive focusing and inadequate resources for integrating affective experience. Difficulty maintaining a consistently relevant focus of attention appears in his three peculiar and one queer responses and in his deviant tempo. His peculiar responses confirm the proclivity for unusual language usage noted on the WAIS: on #1 he speaks of a bat as having *antlers* when his intended meaning is *antennae;* on #17, in reporting a statue that "is *flowing out* some water," he incorrectly uses *flow* as a transitive verb (note, however, that he corrects himself on inquiry by stating "with water flowing out"); and on #18 he describes the worms as "squiggly," which is apparently a neologistic condensation of *squirm* and *wriggle.*

Queer is scored for his unusual response style on #16. First he states, "That looks like my friend the bat," and then, without turning the card to a more advantageous position, he describes it as an "upside-down bat." Since bats not unusually appear in upside-down positions, his response is less strikingly queer than those in which objects are unnaturally and with no justification described as upside-down in preference to turning the card (e.g., "an upside-down tree"); on the other hand, it is noteworthy that when he does turn the card, he is unable to see a "right-side-up bat." Further attesting an unusual focus of attention is his deviant tempo (more responses to Card IX than to Card VIII), which, like the scatter noted on the WAIS, identifies inconsistent cognitive efficiency.

Concerning inadequate affective integration, finally, it is significant that the patient's color use (1 *FC*, 1 *CF*, 0 *C'*) constitutes color stress and suggests that he lacks a stable pattern of emotional reactivity. The only other suggestion of schizophrenic ego impairment in this record is the patient's autistic logic on #3, where he considers the figures "natives" because "they are beating drums." The implied predicate syllogism here is that since natives beat drums and these figures are beating drums, these figures are natives. However, at no other points does he employ circumstantial or highly overgeneralized reasoning.

The patient's Rorschach thus identifies some features of schizophrenic disturbance, but its few deviant responses stray only slightly from normal expectation. Most salient in this man's performance, in fact, is his rigid overemphasis on accurate and obvious percepts. His *F+%* and *R+%*'s of 100, *high W%* of 100 and *high D%* of 93, and eight *P*'s demonstrate a compelling need to attend strictly to narrowly interpreted conventional reality. His exacting reality testing and precise organizational efforts, together with his high percentages of F (67%), A (56%), and P (44%) responses, clearly exemplify the type of constricted, controlled Rorschach performance typically exhibited by remitting schizophrenic persons.

The patient's Rorschach also illustrates the primary characteristics of Beck's S-3 type of schizophrenia, which appears to represent a recovering phase of disturbance (see pp. 369–370). First, as noted above, his thinking is coherent and logical, and neither inaccurate perception nor grossly disturbed reasoning is in evidence. Second, rigid and cramped attitudes as defined in Beck's work are strikingly apparent in his record. For an intelligent and apparently thoughtful and reflective man, he gives relatively few responses (*R* of 18) and confines them largely to F, A, and P percepts.

Furthermore, although he does not reject any cards, the patient displays rejection trends on four occasions. On Cards I, VI, VIII, and IX, to each of which he eventually gives responses with little encouragement, his initial comments, respectively, are "I don't know," "I don't know," "I have no impression whatsoever," and "I really don't see much of anything here, just a big blob." He also excessively qualifies many of his responses. His verbalizations are liberally sprinkled with such noncommittal addenda as *"sort of* looks like" (#5), "a rug *or some-thing"* (#8), "a spider *or some such thing"* (#15), etc. His rejection tendencies and noncommittal approach are consistent with (a) concern about revealing possible deviant thoughts and attitudes and (b) ability to avoid such revelations at the price of a cautious and equivocal approach to experience.

The other two primary features of S-3 schizophrenia, narrow breadth of interest and limited breadth of achievement, are also prominent in the patient's record. As already noted from his high *P%* and *A%*, his range of content is banal and stereotyped, particularly in relation to his intellectual capacity, and similarly significant in view of his intelligence is his location-choice emphasis on *D* and easy *W* responses.

Further identifying the phase of this man's disturbance is the fact that his efforts at control are more pronounced and successful in his Rorschach than on his WAIS. He appears better able to maintain his personality integration when he is given freedom to determine his own style and rate of response, as he is on projective testing, than when he is forced to fit his behavior to the specific structures and demands of such situations as the WAIS subtests. This type of discrepancy between structured and projective test performance, in favor of the latter, points to a remitting phase of disturbance.

Finally, the patient's Rorschach responses demonstrate further the several paranoid characteristics observed in his WAIS and DAP. His repeated reference to handicapped figures that have been the object of aggressive assault ("paws are chopped off" on #2; "heads chopped off" in #5; something "shot" and "hung up" on #8; "foot is chopped off" in #13), his concern with being scrutinized (faces "staring" at each other in #10; "looking each other in the eye . . . staring each other down" in #16), and his question on #1, "Is all this confidential?", suggest paranoid mistrust and experience of external threat.

In many ways, in fact, his guarded, constricted Rorschach record is not markedly dissimilar from that produced by the first overtly paranoid schizophrenic man presented in Chapter 14 (see pp. 338–343). Significantly differentiating the two records, however, are the overtly schizophrenic patient's lone *P* and his inability to prevent a deviant *Sex* response from emerging; this remitting patient, in contrast, focuses his attention carefully on *P* percepts and allows no unusual images to transcend his controls.

Summary. This patient displays sufficient tendencies toward peculiar language usage and scattered cognitive efficiency to indicate disordered thinking and suggest schizophrenic disturbance. However, evidence of his disturbance is minimal and appears primarily in his response to the WAIS. On the Rorschach and DAP he presents relatively little indication of ego impairment, but rather achieves a well-integrated response at the expense of considerable constriction, banality, and rigidity. The combination of his improved performance on projective as opposed to structured tests, his obvious, effortful struggle to achieve such improvement, and his reasonably adaptive over-all performance suggests that his schizophrenic disturbance is in a remitting phase.

► 16

BORDERLINE AND PSEUDONEUROTIC SCHIZOPHRENIA

THE preceding chapter has considered two nonovert forms of schizophrenia, the transitional phases of increasing decompensation into (incipient) and progressive recovery from (remitting) overt schizophrenia. In view of the shifting level of adjustment and active struggle against personality disorganization observed in incipient and remitting schizophrenic disturbances, these conditions are categorized in Chapter 15 as acute disorders. Schizophrenia also appears in nonovert forms that are chronic in nature and, unlike incipient and remitting schizophrenia, comprise neither transitional nor ego-alien phenomena. Two types of chronic nonovert schizophrenia, *borderline* and *pseudoneurotic,* are the subject of this chapter.

Borderline and pseudoneurotic are two of many nosological terms that have been proposed to identify fairly stable personality states in which schizophrenic features are implied but not overtly manifest in the normal course of events. Bleuler (1911, p. 239) originally suggested for persons who thus manage to conceal underlying schizophrenic disorder with a facade of socially conventional behavior the diagnosis *latent schizophrenia,* and in later years Federn (1952, Chap. 7) and Bychowski (1953, 1957) among others have endorsed this diagnostic label. Bychowski (1957) in particular has spelled out the meaning of latent schizophrenia:

The term does not mean . . . a simple dialectical statement to the effect that everybody . . . is a potential psychotic. . . . What we mean, more precisely, is a group of individuals whose psychic structure is such that it provides a background for a prospective psychosis. This of course does not in any way imply that the prospective psychosis has to become manifest; it may become so if certain additional factors are given.

Some writers have questioned the diagnostic practicability of the concept of *latent* schizophrenia on the grounds that latent schizophrenia cannot be diagnosed while the patient is latently disturbed (e.g., Hoch & Cattell, 1959). The essence of this criticism is that if latent schizophrenia is to be defined by a social facade that prevents any manifestations of underlying schizophrenia from appearing, then the diagnosis of *latent* schizophrenia can be made only in retrospect for patients in whom previously dormant schizophrenic symptomatology emerges. As Bychowski (1957) and Bellak (1958, p. 57) cogently observe, however, the term latent schizophrenia, if appropriately employed, is not solely a retrospective diagnosis. Rather, it designates a nonovert condition that may not be demonstrable by ordinary clinical investigation but *can be revealed* at any time by such special procedures as free-associative interviews and psychodiagnostic testing.

Zilboorg (1941, 1956), concerned about the therapeutic nihilism attached by many clinicians to a diagnosis of schizophrenia, introduced the concept of *ambulatory* forms of schizophrenia to promote the recognition that schizophrenic disturbance can occur in persons who nevertheless remain able to maintain a social adjustment and do not require hospital care. The term ambulatory is often applied to the same kinds of patients designated by Federn and Bychowski as latent schizophenics. Kutash (1957), for example, refers to ambulatory forms of schizophrenia as conditions marked by primary paralogical processes but in which the "damaged ego" maintains some type of "homeostasis that averts disintegration and prevents surrender to distorted thought processes."

However, as Hoch and Cattell (1959) point out, the diagnostic specificity of ambulatory schizophrenia has been attenuated by the widespread application of this term to schizophrenic persons of all types who happen not to be hospitalized. Zilboorg (1957) has objected to tying ambulatory schizophrenia to such a fully external criterion, but, despite Zilboorg's plea, it is nevertheless the case that discharged hospital patients as well as those who never require hospitalization are frequently described as ambulatory.

Among other diagnostic labels recommended in the literature for persons with underlying schizophrenic disturbance who manage to maintain a superficially adequate adjustment are *abortive schizophrenia* (Mayer, 1950), *minimal* or *moderate schizophrenia* (Gaw, Reichard, & Tillman, 1953), *pseudopsychopathic schizophrenia* (Dunaif & Hoch, 1955), *subclinical schizophrenia* (Peterson, 1954), and *schizophrenic character* (Schafer, 1948). The two terms most frequently applied to such pathologic states in clinical diagnostic practice are *borderline schizophrenia* and *pseudoneurotic schizophrenia,* and the following discussion of chronic nonovert schizophrenia focuses on these terms.

THE CLINICAL PICTURE OF BORDERLINE AND PSEUDONEUROTIC SCHIZOPHRENIA

BORDERLINE SCHIZOPHRENIA

Borderline schizophrenia has a long clinical history, but for many years it was derided as an inexact concept that related more closely to the uncertainty of clinicians than to the condition of their patients. Analyses of borderline disturbance by Fenichel (1945, pp. 443–446) and Knight (1953), however, have demonstrated its diagnostic import. Fenichel points out that the term borderline does *not* mean merely that the issue of whether a particular patient is neurotically or psychotically disturbed cannot be resolved. Rather, he contends, borderline state describes a specific and unique clinical picture in which a mixture of neurotic and psychotic mechanisms is in evidence: "There are neurotic persons who, without developing a complete psychosis, have certain psychotic trends, or have a readiness to employ schizophrenic mechanisms whenever frustrations occur" (p. 443).

Knight presents a concise and lucid statement of diagnostic and psychodynamic considerations in borderline schizophrenia. He introduces his formulation by rejecting as untenable the following three frames of reference, each of which, he argues, leads to diagnostic errors and confounds in particular the accurate appraisal of borderline disturbances: (a) a disturbed person has either "broken with reality" or he has not; (b) neurosis and psychosis are mutually exclusive conditions; and (c) various psychopathologic states are determined by the fixated level of psychosexual genesis to which a patient regresses.

Knight avers, in disagreement with these three beliefs, that borderline states occur precisely because (a) the relation to reality can go through various stages of bending without breaking; (b) it is possible for neurotic and psychotic mechanisms to develop in the same individual; and (c) the clinical picture of a psychological disorder is determined not by the stage of the ego's regression but by the nature of the particular defenses the person erects to maintain an adaptive relationship with his environment. Knight conceives borderline schizophrenia as a disturbance in which ego functions are differentially rather than globally impaired: integrative ability, concept formation, judgment, realistic planning, and repressive control over primary process fantasy are usually severely impaired, he suggests, whereas conventional environmental adaptation and superficial object-relatedness remain relatively intact.

Knight elaborates three identifying characteristics of borderline schizophrenia that facilitate its differential diagnosis. First, the clinical picture in borderline schizophrenia is determined by the particular defenses the patient is employing to compensate for his underlying disturbance; depending on which defenses he employs, the borderline schizophrenic will present any one or combination of several neurotic complaints, including hysterical, phobic, obsessive-compulsive, and psychosomatic symptoms.

Second, it is to such neurotic symptoms rather than to his impaired ego functioning that the borderline schizophrenic typically attributes his difficulties. The borderline patient is usually unaware or uncritical of emerging manifestations of his schizophrenic condition; although he may be anxious about his presenting neurotic complaints, his view of his schizophrenic tendencies is thus ego-syntonic. According to Knight, borderline disturbance is strongly suggested when a patient with prominent neurotic complaints and apparent underlying schizophrenic tendencies neither displays anxiety and embarrassment about nor attempts to correct his deviant verbalizations and behavior.

Third, although close observation will usually reveal that the borderline patient demonstrates on interview such features of thought disorder as blocking, peculiar language, and circumstantial reasoning, these deviations are likely to escape notice in most well-structured settings. On the other hand, the more a borderline schizophrenic is presented with an unstructured situation, as in a free-associative interview or on projective tests, and in Knight's words thus "abandoned to his own fantasies," the more readily he will produce evidence of his underlying schizophrenic disturbance.

There is general support among clinicians for Knight's dynamic and diagnostic formulations of the borderline state. Schmideberg (1959), for example, shares with Knight and Fenichel the view that borderline schizophrenia is a distinct clinical entity but occurs in a variety of forms that combine features of normal, neurotic, psychotic, and psychopathic behavior patterns. In defending her assertion that borderline schizophrenia should be regarded as a clinical entity, Schmideberg calls attention to frequent observations that the borderline patient generally remains substantially the same throughout his life:

He is stable in his instability, whatever ups and downs he has, and often even keeps constant his pattern of peculiarity. As the borderline condition rarely ushers in a schizophrenia, it should not be regarded as a prepsychotic condition . . . (pp. 398–399).

Schmideberg's reference to the stability of borderline schizophrenic disturbance and Knight's allusion to the ego-syntonic stance of the borderline patient describe the major bases for distinguishing border-line from incipient schizophrenia. In his relatively stable course and his acceptance of schizophrenic symptomatology, the borderline schizo-phrenic demonstrates two criteria for *chronic* disturbance outlined in Chapter 13; the incipient schizophrenic, on the other hand, is charac-terized by a variable course and opposition to schizophrenic phenom-ena, both of which identify *acute* disorder (see Chap. 15). The acute-chronic basis for differentiating between borderline and incipient schizophrenia is clearly stated by Bellak (1958, pp. 55–56) in the following remarks:

The diagnosis of borderline schizophrenia is indicated if the condition de-scribed refers to an apparently *stable* condition of functioning, perhaps of even lifelong duration, and without signs of deterioration . . . relating to a character formation with many unfortunate defensive traits that are likely to make a person appear quite peculiar . . . yet never develop a frank psychosis. If this same picture of dubious functioning is present, but accompanied by signs of increasing lability of mood, progressive inability of impulse control, increasing emergence of the primary process, and increasing crumbling of defenses, then we are dealing with incipient schizophrenia . . . .

Bellak adds that these distinctions identify the diagnostic importance of assessing the stability as well as the nature and quality of a patient's defensive patterns.

The inverse relationship in borderline schizophrenia between degree of external structure and amount of disturbance manifest, as discussed by Knight, is similar to that observed in incipient disturbance (see Chap. 15) and discriminates both borderline and incipient from overt schizophrenia. This nonovert feature of borderline schizophrenia is also delineated by Forer (1950, p. 302):

The latent schizophrenic is a person who, because of a faulty system of internal cues, is pathologically dependent upon external cues. When . . . he becomes imbedded in an environmental situation which provides him with reliable and valid cues to behavior and makes minimum demands upon his capacity to judge, decide, and interpret external stimuli, he may . . . appear normal, displaying no psychotic behavior in his interpersonal relationships. . . . When such individuals are forced away from the protection of structured situ-ations, their psychotic potential becomes manifest in psychotic episodes. . . .

In a review of clinical findings in patients defined as having border-line, ambulatory, or latent schizophrenic disturbance, Weiner (1958, pp. 147–151) concurs that "it is possible to define this group of patients so that a rather clear-cut clinical picture emerges." The literature summarized by Weiner confirms that this clinical picture is characterized by (a) a primary associational disturbance frequently demonstrable only in an unstructured interview situation or on psychodiagnostic tests, (b) marked compensatory neurotic mechanisms of one kind or another, (c) superficially adequate social behavior, and (d) a disinclination to view symptoms as being unusual or strange.

PSEUDONEUROTIC SCHIZOPHRENIA

Pseudoneurotic schizophrenia is a form of borderline schizophrenic disturbance uniquely characterized by simultaneous defensive recourse to a number of neurotic behavior patterns. The concept of pseudoneurotic schizophrenia was heralded in papers by Kasanin and by Polatin and Hoch. Kasanin (1944) referred to "so-called 'neurotic' schizophrenic cases in which there is a history of elaborate neurotic defenses erected by the patient in an attempt to solve his personal problems"; Polatin and Hoch (1947) discussed the importance of utilizing certain diagnostic clues to identify underlying schizophrenia in types of patients who are mistakenly viewed as chronic, severe neurotics.

Hoch and Polatin (1949) were the first to formulate pseudoneurotic schizophrenia as a definite clinical entity. In their paper and in a later contribution by Hoch and Cattell (1959) pseudoneurotic schizophrenia is described as a pathologic condition combining several symptoms of schizophrenia with a special type of secondary symptomatology and a fairly stable course. According to these authors, some pseudoneurotic patients may improve their adjustment with therapy and others may become progressively disabled, but there is no evidence that the syndrome is by nature a transitional state.

Although Hoch and Cattell recommend replacing the concept of borderline schizophrenia with pseudoneurotic schizophrenia, there is some advantage to fine differential diagnosis in retaining both concepts. Pseudoneurotic schizophrenia as defined by these authors shares with the prevailing conceptions of borderline schizophrenia the three identifying characteristics of underlying ego impairment, neurotic compensatory mechanisms that provide some social adaptability, and a chronic, stable course. On the other hand, it is primarily in regard to pseudoneurotic schizophrenia that recourse to a mixed, multifaceted neurotic defensive pattern is delineated as a salient phenomenon.

Borderline schizophrenia may thus be conceived as the general class of disturbances in which a neurotic pattern partially conceals underlying schizophrenic tendencies, and pseudoneurotic schizophrenia as a specific form of borderline disturbance marked by simultaneous operation of a gamut of neurotic behavior patterns. It is accordingly proposed here to apply the diagnosis of borderline schizophrenia to those patients who compensate for their underlying ego disturbance by exaggerated reliance on *one or another* of such nonpsychotic syndromes as anxiety, hysterical, phobic, or obsessive-compulsive neurosis and to reserve the designation of pseudoneurotic schizophrenia for those who defensively employ a concurrent mixture of *several* of these symptom patterns and/or psychosomatic and psychopathic phenomena as well.

Hoch, Polatin, and Cattell actually require for the diagnosis of pseudoneurotic schizophrenia two phenomena in addition to evidence of underlying schizophrenia and pan-neurotic compensatory mechanisms: a high level of diffuse anxiety (*pan-anxiety*) and a readily expressed preoccupation with sexual matters (*pan-sexuality*). However, both heightened anxiety about neurotic complaints and the access to conscious awareness of primitive sexual and aggressive impulses generally characterize borderline disturbances as defined here; hence it is primarily the presence of pan-neurotic symptomatology that warrants the diagnosis of pseudoneurotic disturbance in a person with a chronic nonovert form of schizophrenia.

PSYCHODIAGNOSTIC INDICES OF BORDERLINE AND PSEUDONEUROTIC SCHIZOPHRENIA

As reviewed in the preceding section, borderline and pseudoneurotic schizophrenia are defined by (a) combination of underlying schizophrenic disturbance with overt manifestations of neurotic or characterological disorder, (b) the particular susceptibility of these surface mechanisms to dissolution in unstructured settings, and (c) a stable, ego-syntonic course in which neither concern about nor struggle against schizophrenic phenomena is apparent. These features of borderline and pseudoneurotic states have three major implications for differential psychodiagnosis.

First, borderline and pseudoneurotic subjects, being nonovertly disturbed, will similarly to incipient schizophrenics tend to perform fairly conventionally on structured portions of the test battery (the WAIS) but be relatively unable to prevent schizophrenic phenomena from emerging in their response to projective tests (Rorschach and DAP). Second, borderline and pseudoneurotic schizophrenics, being chronically disturbed, will in contrast to incipient subjects exhibit considerable tolerance for and acceptance of their deviant test responses. Third, in relation to the severity of disturbance associated with chronic disorder, borderline and pseudoneurotic subjects will tend to display particularly deviant behavior at those points in the testing where their compensatory mechanisms are breached (i.e., the projectives); in this respect also their performance diverges from the relatively mild disturbance evinced by incipient schizophrenics even on projective testing.

Each of these implications has been widely confirmed by clinical observation. With regard to differential performance on structured and projective tests, Brown, as quoted by Bychowski (1953), states on the basis of his experience, "The better the performance on a structured test in contrast to a poor functioning on an unstructured test such as a Rorschach, the greater the likelihood of latency," whereas, "the poorer the structured performance in conjunction with a bizarre Rorschach, the greater the likelihood of an overt, reality-distorting psychosis."

The expectation that the borderline schizophrenic subject will produce a relatively orderly, efficient WAIS and markedly pathologic projective test protocols is further attested by the experience of Forer (1950), Shapiro (1954), Schafer (1954, p. 66), and Stone and Dellis (1960). The latter report an intensive psychodiagnostic study of over 200 patients with borderline or pseudoneurotic disturbance. They found these patients almost without exception to show no gross thought disturbance on "surface" tests, including the WAIS, but to reveal marked thinking disturbance and an accumulation of other schizophrenic indices on such "depth" tests as the Rorschach.

Concerning tolerance for deviant response, Fisher (1955) observed in a careful analysis of Rorschach reaction patterns among borderline schizophrenic patients that his subjects uniformly exhibited comfortable acceptance of the pathology present in their records. Fisher's borderline subjects not only expressed patently bizarre ideas without becoming anxious about them, but also willingly discussed their deviant responses on inquiry, remaining unconcerned even when the bases of their percepts were questioned. Schafer (1948, pp. 218–233) presents a detailed case history of a borderline schizophrenic patient (*schizophrenic character* in Schafer's terminology) in which he similarly calls attention to the diagnostic significance for borderline disturbance of the marked blandness with which the subject regarded his highly deviant thoughts and behavior in unstructured settings.

In relation to severity of disturbance, considerable discrepancy between a reasonably intact social presentation and a strikingly deviant Rorschach performance has frequently been remarked in borderline patients. First to call attention to the value of the Rorschach in diagnosing borderline disturbance was Rorschach himself (1921, pp. 120–121), who concluded from his work that the test often identifies underlying schizophrenic tendencies in persons with otherwise barely perceptible personality disturbance and even in some subjects who have never demonstrated such psychopathology but who have schizophrenic parents or siblings.[1]

Rorschach (1921, pp. 155–158) includes in his case material the protocol of a woman with "nervous exhaustion" whose Rorschach performance, in marked contrast to her apparently responsible and productive life adjustment, comprised numerous blatantly schizophrenic phenomena, including an $F+\%$ of 56, a $Dd\%$ of 31, seven *Sex* responses, self-referential Fabulizations, and several peculiarly phrased and illogically reasoned percepts. Rorschach suggests that this woman exemplifies latent psychosis, and he adds that latent schizophrenic subjects are not unlikely to produce records even more deviant from normal performance than those obtained from overt schizophrenics.

Several contributions concur with Rorschach's observations of particularly deviant projective test behavior in borderline schizophrenia. McCully (1962) and Stone and Dellis (1960) both comment on the frequency among borderline schizophrenic persons of an impressive lack of relationship between the extent of psychopathology manifest on projective tests and the relatively adequate adjustments suggested by the clinical picture. Mercer and Wright (1950) and Zucker (1952) present some interesting case material that further confirms the tendency of borderline subjects to produce a surprising frequency of deviant response on the Rorschach, a frequency not unusually exceeding that associated with overt schizophrenia.

In practice, then, it is indicated to diagnose as borderline schizophrenic those persons who respond in a fairly orderly and adaptive fashion to the WAIS but whose Rorschach and DAP protocols clearly embrace identifying features of schizophrenic disturbance, and who in addition display acceptance of and tolerance for such deviant responses

---

[1] This early observation by Rorschach bears an interesting relationship to Meehl's (1962) recent speculations on schizophrenic etiology. As reviewed on page 7, Meehl considers overt schizophrenia to result from the unfortunate combination of a genetically inherited schizophrenic disposition and psychologically adverse environmental experiences. Meehl labels *schizotypes* those persons who inherit a schizophrenic genotype but as a consequence of favorable experimental factors are able to avert schizophrenic disturbance. Meehl suggests that schizotypic persons nevertheless suffer an underlying neural integrative defect, called *schizotaxia*, evidence of which can be elicited by careful diagnostic study. Rorschach's patients who had schizophrenic relatives and displayed deviant Rorschach performance even though they had never been overtly disturbed neatly correspond to the schizotypic group postulated by Meehl.

as emerge. Patients whose ego impairments pervade their WAIS as well as their projective test performance are likely to be overtly rather than nonovertly schizophrenic; those whose superiority of WAIS to projective test performance suggests nonovert disturbance but who exhibit awareness of and concern about the inadequacy of deviant responses typically are experiencing incipient rather than borderline schizophrenia.

Finally, those borderline persons whose defenses against overt schizophrenia encompass a wide variety of neurotic behavior patterns, as reflected in test evidence of hysterical, phobic, and obsessive-compulsive tendencies, should be diagnosed pseudoneurotic. Test indices of various neurotic defensive patterns are alluded to in various parts of this book and in the case studies that follow; for a detailed treatment of defensive styles as reflected on the Rorschach the reader is recommended to Schafer's (1954) chapters on repression (pp. 193–230), projection (pp. 279–331), and obsessive-compulsive defensive operations (pp. 332–423).

CASE STUDIES [2]

The following two cases demonstrate borderline schizophrenic disturbance. Both patients had applied for clinic help with concerns they did not relate to underlying schizophrenic disturbance. The first patient was troubled by difficulty in concentrating, which she attributed to guilty ruminations about sexual indiscretions, and the second presented with phobic and anxiety symptoms she associated with a variety of somatic complaints. Both patients were maintaining a reasonable social adjustment and neither required hospital care. The first patient displayed a primarily ideational defensive style, whereas the second exhibited a mixed defensive pattern consistent with pseudoneurotic schizophrenia.

CASE 1

This 22-year-old single woman was near completion of a course in secretarial school when occasional crying spells and difficulty concentrating brought her for psychological help. She readily reported that her distress stemmed from her concern that other people, by looking

---

[2] The format followed in presenting the case studies is described on pages 254–257.

into her eyes, could see that she was "bad." She had begun to view herself as "bad" four years earlier when, as a college freshman, she had become illegitimately pregnant. She had left school at that time and been cared for by her family, who had repetitively expressed to her their conviction that she had done an "evil" thing that could have derived only from basic "badness."

Although the patient was upset that her badness was evident to those around her, she did not regard as in any way peculiar the extra-sensory powers she thus ascribed to others. Rather, she appeared to accept as a logical reality that her evil was self-evident, and she requested help not to alter her thinking but to conduct her life better, particularly her sexual activities, so that she might redeem her good name. She was currently involved in an unsatisfactory sexual affair in which she was aware of being exploited, but she felt unable either to break off the affair or to understand why she had allowed herself to become embroiled in it in the first place.

Aside from her peculiar thought about her transparent badness and her depressive ruminations about sexual misconduct, this young woman was maintaining a reasonably adequate social adjustment. Her school performance was excellent, she was effectually responsible for her everyday affairs, and she had aroused no concern among her family, friends, and associates as to her personality integration. After initial evaluation in the office she was begun in intensive psychotherapy. However, her rapid production of deeply personal material in the initial sessions raised question whether her ego resources might be insufficient to tolerate an insight-directed approach, and psychological consultation was arranged to assess this possibility.

Subsequent to the testing she was seen in supportive psychotherapy for some 13 months, to the present time. Her therapist continued to view her as having a borderline schizophrenic disturbance, but he was able to help her effect major improvements in her life adjustment, including advancement in her secretarial work and establishment of more stable and gratifying interpersonal relationships than she had previously enjoyed. At the time of this writing the frequency of her sessions had been reduced from weekly to biweekly meetings, and her therapist was optimistic concerning her future course.

WECHSLER ADULT INTELLIGENCE SCALE

Information

RUBBER: +. PRESIDENTS: +. LONGFELLOW: +. WEEKS: +. PANAMA: +. BRAZIL: +. HEIGHT: +. ITALY: +. CLOTHES: +. WASHINGTON: dk. HAMLET: +. VATICAN: A building in Rome. PARIS: Six thousand miles. EGYPT:

Asia. YEAST: +. POPULATION: dk. SENATORS: dk. GENESIS: +. TEMPERA-
TURE: 120°. ILIAD: +. BLOOD VESSELS: +. KORAN: The Bible for some
religion, but I don't know which one. FAUST: dk. ETHNOLOGY: dk.
APOCRYPHA: dk. RAW SCORE: 18.

This relevant, orderly Information performance contains no indication of ego impairment. At first glance the patient's efforts may appear
somewhat inconsistent and scattered, but in only one of the several
groups of factorially related items does her pattern of success and failure violate order of difficulty, namely, the group including POPULATION,
GENESIS, TEMPERATURE, and ILIAD. In all other respects she displays
adaptive and efficient cognitive focusing on this subtest.

Comprehension

ENVELOPE: Mail it (2). BAD COMPANY: You're known by the company
you keep (1). MOVIES: Get up and find someone, like the manager, and
report it (2). TAXES: It's the government's main source of income (2).
IRON: Do things when the opportunity presents itself (2). CHILD LABOR:
So children can't be made to work (0). FOREST: Walk toward the sun
(1). DEAF: You learn to speak by listening to other people (2). CITY
LAND: There's less land per person (1). MARRIAGE: One reason is you
need a medical exam to get it, which prevents the spread of congenital
disease (1). BROOKS: People who talk all the time really have nothing
to them (1). SWALLOW: I'll have to guess; does it mean that the summer
is made up of more than one part? (0). RAW SCORE: 19.

As on Information, the patient responds relevantly to the various
items, expressing her thoughts in conventional language and maintaining a fairly consistent and logical frame of reference. Thus to this point
in the WAIS she has presented no evidence of ego impairment.

Similarities

ORANGE: Fruit (2). COAT: Clothing (2). AXE: Tools (2). DOG: Animals (2). NORTH: Directions (2). EYE: Organs of sense (2). AIR: Elements (1). TABLE: Furniture (2). EGG: Beginnings of something (1).
POEM: They're in memory of something (1). WOOD: That's a good question . . . they're not alike, as far as I can see (0). PRAISE: They're both
human acts (0). FLY: They're living (2). RAW SCORE: 19.

The patient continues here to demonstrate intact cognitive functioning and freedom from indices of disordered thinking. Her responses on
EGG ("beginnings of something") and PRAISE ("human acts") are somewhat overly general, but since these items are at the limits of her demonstrated intellectual capacity, her slightly inappropriate level of abstraction on them has little significance for uneven concept formation.

Digit Symbol

RAW SCORE: 68.

The patient worked rapidly and consistently on this subtest and gave no evidence of difficulty focusing her attention on the task.

Picture Completion

KNOB: +. TAIL: +. NOSE: +. HANDLES: +. DIAMOND: +. WATER: +. NOSE PIECE: +. PEG: Bow. OAR LOCK: A person. BASE THREAD: +. STARS: Pole. DOG TRACKS: +. FLORIDA: +. STACKS: dk. LEG: +. ARM IMAGE: Her other arm. FINGER: +. SHADOW: +. STIRRUP: +. SNOW: +. EYEBROW: +. RAW SCORE: 16.

In the scatter of her successes and failures on this subtest the patient gives her first indication of possible thinking disturbance. She passes BASE THREAD and FLORIDA after missing the easier, factorially related PEG, and similarly within factorially related groups of items she passes DOG TRACKS, LEG, SHADOW, and SNOW after missing the relatively easy OAR LOCK and succeeds on FINGER after failing STACKS. Although this degree of scatter identifies inconsistent cognitive focusing, the pathologic implications of her disorderly response to this subtest are somewhat mitigated by the fact that all of her errors are types of errors commonly observed in normal as well as patient groups.

Block Design

ITEM 1: 10″ (4). ITEM 2: 6″ (4). ITEM 3: 4″ (4). ITEM 4: 5″ (4). ITEM 5: 10″ (4). ITEM 6: 19″ (4). ITEM 7: 21″ (6). ITEM 8: 43″ (6). ITEM 9: 56″ (6). ITEM 10: 105″ (4). RAW SCORE: 46.

As the patient's time-to-completion and near-perfect score reflect, she attacked this subtest with relish and achieved the correct solutions with considerable facility.

Scale Scores

Information: 11. Comprehension: 11. Similarities: 13. Digit Symbol: 13. Picture Completion: 11. Block Design: 15.

The only suggestion of personality disturbance in these scale scores is the four-point difference between Picture Completion and Block Design. In view of the factorial relatedness of these two subtests, the patient's discrepant performance on them constitutes intertest scatter and complements her scatter within Picture Completion in identifying inconsistent cognitive focusing. Second, the fact that she does so much better on the impersonal, abstract Block Design task than when she is dealing with the socially contextual stimuli of the Picture Completion subtest suggests she is inclined to experience disorganizing concerns primarily in interpersonal settings and hence may be interpersonally aversive.

Discussion. This WAIS record is almost entirely free from indications of schizophrenic disturbance. The patient displays some scatter within Picture Completion and between Picture Completion and Block Design, but otherwise her performance is orderly, relevant, and reality-oriented. It would therefore be inadvisable, if not totally unjustified, to diagnose schizophrenia from this record. The patient's generally appropriate and conventional response to the various subtests indicates she is likely to relate reasonably adaptively to daily life situations, particularly those that are well structured and impersonal.

DRAW-A-PERSON

The patient's figure drawings appear in Figures 24 and 25. In terms of their formal structure, her drawings are generally intact. She connects the major lines of the body contour, for the most part indicates the important parts of the body, and adequately differentiates the sex of her figures by appropriate use of hair and clothing details.

On the other hand, each of her drawings contains a peculiarity that is not consistent with expectation in a subject who produces as intact a WAIS as she does. On the male drawing there is a blatant and uncorrected transparency, with the lines of the belt and the leg or trousers showing through the arm, and on her female drawing she has neglected to indicate the hands. These indices of illogical reasoning (the incongruous combination of normally visible and normally invisible details) and impaired reality sense (omission of a major body part) are more suggestive of ego defect than most aspects of her WAIS performance. Nevertheless, her DAP is more notable for the personality strengths than the weaknesses it reflects, and to this point in the test data schizophrenia has yet to be clearly demonstrated.

RORSCHACH

Card I 4″

1. (*Wm FC′+ A P*) A bat. Do you want more things? (?) It has black wings, and black wings always suggest a bat to me.

2. (*Dm M+ H,Cg,Rel Fabulized Combination, Barrier*) Two priests with long flowing gowns blowing in the wind [two halves of center detail]. (?) I see their heads and their two arms raised in prayer; they almost look like they're Siamese twins. (*Siamese twins?*) The way they're joined together.

3. (*W M— H,Cg,Sex Fabulized, Fabulized Combination, Autistic Logic*) A woman undressing in the wind. (?) This looks like the woman

Figure 24

Figure 25

here [center detail, but unusually specified]; her hips, legs, and feet are here [inner darker portion of lower center], these are her hands up here, and I guess these [upper innermost details] could be her breasts. (*How look?*) Like she's undressing, and undressing in the wind because her clothes are all over the place [side details].

4. (*Wm,S F+ Mask Incongruous*) A mask; that's all. (?) There are two eyes and a mouth [white space], and the part in the middle [inner darker portion of lower center] is the tongue.

Card II 14″

5. (*W—,S F—,C Sex,At,Bl Penetration*) A diagram of the female reproduction system . . . during menstruation. I don't see anything else. (?) It looks like a vagina here [lighter pink middle section of lower red] and the uterus here [center white]; the rest is a little misplaced, but these are the ovaries [upper red details] and the shaded part is the muscle tissue that's around. (*Menstruation?*) The reddish is like blood.

Card III 5″

6. (*D+ M+ H,A,Sex P Autistic Logic, Penetration*) Two men, and they're fighting over the—I don't know what it is—an animal of some sort. (?) Their arms are here, and their hands are holding onto what's between them, an animal. (*Kind of animal?*) A female animal. (?) Because this [center white dot in "animal" detail] looks like the opening to the vagina.

7. (*Dm F+ A P*) A butterfly in the middle. (?) The way it's shaped.

8. (*Dm M+ H*) Two women, lying on the floor [outer red details]. (?) They just look like women might look lying on the ground, that's all.

9. (*WS— F— A Autistic Logic, Penetration*) In a way, the whole thing looks like a butterfly, with transparent wings [entire blot, including arbitrarily demarcated surrounding white space]. (?) I just used my imagination, and that's the way it came out. (*Transparent?*) Because of what I couldn't see.

10. (*W—,S F— Mask Perseveration*) It looks like another mask, a Halloween mask. (?) The mouth is here [lower white], the tongue here [lower center black], the nose here [center red], the ears here [outer red], and the eyes here [head details of popular human figures].

Card IV 8″

11. (*Wm F+ Bt*) A desert plant. (?) It looks like a cactus; there are little spines on it down here [lower center detail], a pretty flower part up here, and leaves on the sides.

12. (*W++ M+ H,Obj Penetration*) A man getting a drink from a water fountain. (?) The water fountain is this part [lower center

detail], and his feet and legs are here; he's bending over and drinking.

13. (*W— F—,Fc Hd*) The back of a woman's hair. (?) This could be her neck [lower center detail], and the rest is the hair coming down, parted in the back, with the stray locks on the sides. (*Hair?*) It just looks curly, sort of.

Card V 3″

14. (*Wm FC′+ A P*) A bat. (?) Because of the wings, the black wings.

15. (*W— M—,FC′ H,Obj Barrier*) Four men, sitting with their backs against something, talking. (?) I see four heads here [projections along upper edge of side details] and legs sticking out the sides; because it's dark here, I can't see the rest of the men, but it suggests they're on the other side of something, leaning against it.

16. (*Dm F+ A*) This part [center detail] looks like a rabbit.

17. (*D— M— H,Sex Fabulized, Queer*) And on the sides are two couples making out. (?) It looks like a man with his arm around someone; this looks like a man's head here [upper side projection] and this looks like a woman's leg here, and the rest just looks like they've got their arms around each other.

Card IV 3″

18. (*W F+ Aobj Contamination*) A cat, made into a bearskin rug. (?) Because this part [lower portion] reminds me of a bearskin rug, and this part [upper portion] reminds me of a cat, with whiskers.

19. (*D++ FK+,C′F Na Barrier*) Two mountains, with a river running between them [lower portion]. (?) It's a mountain and a river, as if I were looking at it from a long ways above; this looks like water in the middle, dirty water. (*Dirty?*) Because it's black.

20. (*D+ M+ Sex, At Penetration*) Sexual intercourse. (?) This is the man's organ [center portion of upper detail], going into the woman [side portions of upper detail].

Card VII 3″

21. (*W+ M+ (A),Cg Incongruous, Barrier*) Two poodle dogs, dressed up as little girls, dancing together. I don't see anything else.

Card VIII 4″

22. (*Dd F+,mF,C Na*) A volcano. (?) The main thing is that this top part [upper gray] looks like a mountain; this [blue detail] reminds me of something cold and these [side pink] of something hot, like it would be lava about to burst through the top. (*Cold and hot?*) The color; the blue looks like ice and the pink like subdued fire.

23. (*DdD M— H,Cg Fabulized, Confabulation*) Two women, sitting

on the ground, with lots of presents around them [orange and pink detail]. (?) They don't really look like women, I suppose, but that's what I thought of, because it looks like heads looking up here [pink details] and these are feet sticking out [bottom side projections of orange details]; and the rest of the area looks like it could be presents, furs and things.

24. (*D M— H,Sex Contamination, Fabulized Combination*) And two men that look very much like rats, walking away from the women, and they're carrying their organs. (?) These [side pink] would be the men, but they look like rats. (*Connected with the women?*) Yes, they're going away and leaving them. (*Organs?*) Well, they look like they don't have any clothes on, and these things [purplish details in upper, outer corners of blue] look like they might be their organs, sexual organs, they're carrying.

Card IX 4″

25. (*W M+,m H,Cg,Sex Fabulized, Fabulized Combination*) Two women doing a striptease. (?) The pink part looks like a bare woman, the green looks like clothes falling off, and the pink looks like clothes already taken off. (*Bare?*) You can see her hips, and her arms stretched out, and a breast here.

26. (*Dd M+,FC′ Hd,Cg,Rel Fabulized, Fabulized Combination, Autistic Logic, Barrier*) A mother hiding behind something and looking up; there's a halo over her head, and she's crying; and she looks like she's going to be angry. (?) This is the mother's dress [pink], her neck [portion where side green adjoin], her eyes [center white slits], and her white hair [upper middle]. (*Crying?*) It looks like there are teardrops in there. (*Mother?*) Because of the puffed sleeves on the dress, it looks like a typical old-fashioned mother. (*Angry?*) These green things remind me of storm clouds.

27. (*Wa C Fire*) Fire. (?) The orange and the green look like parts of a flame, and the pink just looked hot.

28. (*Da Csymb Ab*) And the green also reminds me of envy.

Card X 4″

29. (*Dm F+ A P*) Two spiders.

30. (*D+ FM+ A,Obj*) Two funny little bugs fighting over a stick [upper gray portion].

31. (*Dm F+ A*) Two crabs [outer gray].

32. (*Dd FCarb— Hd,Cg Incongruous, Barrier*) An old man with long pink hair and a funny hat. (?) His eyes are here [inner yellow], his moustache here [lower green], his hair is the pink, and the top part is his hat.

33. $(D+ M+ Hd)$ Two women talking and crying. (?) These parts [upper portion of pink details] look like women's faces; it's just the face.

Scores

R	33	M	14	H	10	F+%	67%
W	15(45%)	FM	1	Hd	4	R+%	67%
D	15(45%)	m	0+2	A	8+1	P	5
Dd+S	3+3(10%)	FK	1	(A)	1		
		F	12	Sex	2+5	High W%	40%
		Fc	0+1	Mask	2	High D%	74%
Fabulized	5	C'	2+2	Na	2		
Fabulized		FC	1	Aobj	1	Barrier	5
Combination	5	C	2+2	Bt	1	Penetration	4
Autistic Logic	4			Fire	1		
Incongruous	3			Ab	1		
Contamination	2			Cg	0+6		
Confabulation	1			Obj	0+3		
Queer	1			At	0+2		
Perseveration	1			Rel	0+2		
				Bl	0+1		

Discussion. This young woman's highly deviant Rorschach performance encompasses virtually the full range of schizophrenic ego impairments and contrasts markedly with her adaptive WAIS response. More fully than many of the overtly schizophrenic subjects discussed in Chapters 13 and 14, she presents evidence here of inefficient cognitive focusing, illogical reasoning, impaired reality testing, inadequate defensive operations, and maladaptive organizational activity.

With regard to cognitive focusing, this young woman tends to overlook the obvious details in her experience ($D\%$ of only 45, which is significantly low in a record of above average length) in favor of a focus on unproductive global interpretations (15 W, only six of which are of good quality). On one occasion she makes no effort even to differentiate figure from ground in her perception (WS on #9), and in another instance she fails to shift her frame of reference appropriately (perseverated *mask* response on #10). She additionally demonstrates an extremely variable level of attention to her environment in her deviant tempo (more responses to Card V than to either IV or VI, and more to Card IX than to VIII), her sudden shifts from accurate and well-integrated to bizarre and autistic responses (e.g., the sequence of #'s 12–13 & 18–19), and her inconsistent mixture of formal and slang terminology ("sexual intercourse" on #2, "making out" on #17).

Illogical reasoning is a pervasive characteristic of her responses. She displays overgeneralized thinking in her five Fabulized responses (woman *undressing* in #3, man and woman *making out* in #17, objects seen as *presents* in #23, women *doing a striptease* in #25, and woman seen as *old-fashioned mother* in #26) and one Confabulation (women because of their heads and feet on #23). Although these elaborations might derive from a normally active imagination, the patient's additional instances of inappropriate combinative and circumstantial thinking leave little doubt that her embellishments are associated with an underlying thought disorder.

Her combinative responses in fact illustrate most of the various forms such paralogical integrations take. In her three incongruous percepts she combines images with unlikely parts (mask with a *tongue* on #4), unlikely activities (dogs *dancing* on #21), and unlikely colors (*pink* hair on #32). In her five Fabulized Combinations she infers unusual links between adjacent stimuli (the priests in #2 are "Siamese twins" because "they're joined"), she interrelates percepts bearing unlikely size and positional relationships (the women in relation to their clothing on #'s 3 & 25, the men in relation to the women in #24), and she combines natural and supernatural elements not in reality seen together (mother with a halo on #26). Finally, and especially conclusive for thought disorder, she produces two Contaminations, the "cat made into a bearskin rug" in #18 and the "men that look very much like rats" in #24. These two responses, together with her similar tendency on #21 ("dogs dressed up as little girls"), reveal that she has great difficulty maintaining logical distinctions between overlapping features of her experience.

Demonstrating circumstantial thinking are her four instances of autistic logic. In #3 she infers wind "because clothes are all over the place"; in #6 she apparently reasons, "Females have an opening (vagina), this animal has an opening, therefore this animal is female"; in #9 she offers the highly autistic explanation that her percept is transparent "because of what I couldn't see"; and in #26 she concludes that the figure is angry because of the circumstance of adjacent "storm clouds."

From the patient's summary scores it can be concluded that her reality testing is impaired and her organizational activity maladaptive. Her $F+\%$ of 67 and especially her $R+\%$ of 67 reflect pathologic perceptual inaccuracy, and her *high* $W\%$ of only 40 mirrors limited capacity to synthesize experience effectively in such unstructured settings as the Rorschach blots represent.

Finally, the patient's use of pure C and her frequent, unusual sexual associations make clear that she has difficulty integrating her affective responses and adequately controlling her ideational activity. Her two main and five additional *Sex* responses are significant more for their content than for their number, however: her references to nudity (#'s 24 & 25), sexual intercourse (#20), and menstruation (#5) are highly unusual Rorschach associations that strongly imply a pathologic failure of repressive control.

This Rorschach, then, patently establishes that, in spite of her adaptive performance on the WAIS, this young woman has an underlying schizophrenic disturbance. This pattern of WAIS-Rorschach discrepancy is consistent with both borderline and incipient schizophrenia, but the likelihood that her disturbance is borderline rather than incipient in nature is enhanced by two prominent differences between her Rorschach performance and that of the incipiently schizophrenic young women presented in Chapter 15 (see pp. 377–384).

First, at no time does this patient communicate her deviant responses with any reluctance or concern about their adequacy. To the contrary, she was notably relaxed and nonchalant throughout the testing. Hence, unlike the blocked and anxious woman studied in Chapter 15, this patient appears, to an extent consistent with chronic disorder, to accept her schizophrenic tendencies and tolerate their manifestations. Second, the degree of disturbance present in her Rorschach far exceeds the minimal evidence of ego impairment observed in the previous incipiently schizophrenic patient. It is thus the combination of severe but calmly accepted disturbance on the Rorschach and a reasonably conventional WAIS performance that identifies borderline schizophrenia in this woman.

Also revealed by this woman's Rorschach are the compensatory mechanisms she employs to maintain her social adjustment. From her experience balance (14 *M, Sum C* of 3.5) and detailed, integrative response elaborations, it is clear that she is an ideationally oriented person whose primary approach to her experience is to impose on it her own well-developed structure of needs and attitudes. Her two main and two additional pure *C* responses suggest she is occasionally prone to impulsive behavior and volatile affective outbursts, but her minimal use of other color determinants indicates that intellectual rather than expressive defenses dominate her life style. She is thus likely to display a ruminative, obsessive-compulsive behavior pattern. Furthermore, it should be observed that her fantasy elaborations and introversive experience balance are in many respects similar to features of paranoid orientation noted in Chapter 14. It is therefore reasonable to expect that, in the event of increasing personality disturbance, her decompensation would probably proceed along paranoid lines.

Summary. This young woman responds to the WAIS in an appropriate and conventional manner but on the projective tests presents gross evidence of disordered thinking, impaired reality testing, and inadequate defensive resources. This discrepancy between an adaptive reaction to a structured situation and a pathologic response in an unstructured setting, together with the fact that she displays considerable tolerance for such marked manifestations of personality disturbance as appear, points to a borderline schizophrenic condition.

CASE 2

This patient is a 39-year-old married mother of two teenage children who applied to a psychiatric clinic for help in connection with persistent somatic concerns for which no organic basis had been demonstrated. Since witnessing her sister-in-law's fatal heart attack several months earlier, she had become increasingly fearful that she, too, was on the verge of cardiac arrest. During this time she had experienced frequent anxiety attacks, with palpitation and tremulousness, had had difficulty eating and sleeping, and had grown reluctant to leave her house lest she somehow aggravate her "condition."

The patient's husband was a recently retired career army man, and she had prevailed on him to remain at home and relieve her of her domestic responsibilities. Although she reported that she and her husband were happily married, she readily detailed a long history of premarital and extramarital sexual promiscuity on both their parts. She expressed no concern about her numerous sexual affairs, however, but considered them a satisfying way of "tying men to me."

The patient's manner on interview was quite striking. Though an attractive woman with a decidedly feminine figure, she typically wore severe, man-tailored suits. She was expressive and histrionic in talking about herself and at one point, while speaking of a previous injury, began to lift her skirt, saying, "Do you want to see my scars?" Although she spoke logically and coherently and overtly was seeking help only to rid herself of her somatic complaints, her mixed pattern of phobic and hypochondriacal attitudes, anxiety and depressive reactivity, labile and seductive manner, and indiscriminate sexual promiscuity raised concern about the possibility of underlying schizophrenic disturbance.

She was subsequently referred for psychological examination, following which she was discouraged from further psychological investigation of her difficulties and was treated with medication and supportive techniques focused on her somatic symptoms. During the first year of this program, to the present, she has responded well, with decreasing somatic concern and anxiety and an improved capacity to assume domestic and social responsibility.

WECHSLER ADULT INTELLIGENCE SCALE

Information

RUBBER: +. PRESIDENTS: +. LONGFELLOW: +. WEEKS: +. PANAMA: +. BRAZIL: +. HEIGHT: +. ITALY: +. CLOTHES: +. WASHINGTON: February 12. HAMLET: dk. VATICAN: It's connected with the Catholic religion. (?) It's a church or monastery or something, that's all I know. PARIS: 2000 miles. EGYPT: It's near the Mediterranean sea. (*Continent?*) Asia. RAW SCORE: 13.

The patient performs consistently and relevantly here, and her responses contain no indications of personality disturbance.

Comprehension

ENVELOPE: Drop it in a mail box (2). BAD COMPANY: You're judged by the company you keep (1). MOVIES: You should notify the manager, but I've never really been put to the test, so I don't know if I would panic (2). TAXES: There are many reasons, because we like to have nice streets, and police, and nice schools, and things like that (1). IRON: Do something when you have the opportunity to do it (2). CHILD LABOR: Because they would be working rather than going to school, and businessmen would take advantage of them and work them for low wages (2). FOREST: I'd think about where the sun was shining, and I'd also look for familiar objects (1). DEAF: Because they can't hear sound and therefore don't know how to form sound (1). CITY LAND: The demand for it is higher, because you have an established community with many advantages and facilities (2). MARRIAGE: To control the type of person getting married, especially for health reasons (1). BROOKS: Someone making a lot of noise is not necessarily a deep thinker (1). SWALLOW: Just because you see the first swallow come back, it doesn't mean that summer is here (1). RAW SCORE: 21.

As on Information the patient responds in a conventional and efficient manner and manifests no indications of ego impairment. It is of some interest, however, to note the variable defensive style that begins to appear. In contrast to the limited intellectual interest suggested by her low average Information performance, she employs here some formal, almost pedantic language, as in her reference on CITY LAND to "an established community with many facilities and advantages."

Similarities

ORANGE: Fruit (2). COAT: Clothing (2). AXE: Instruments of strength to cut (1). DOG: Animals (2). NORTH: Directions (2). EYE: Senses (2). AIR: Elements (1). TABLES: Instruments you use (0). EGG: Both produce (1). POEM: Both have a meaning (1). WOOD: dk (0). PRAISE: It would be far-fetched to try to make them alike (0). FLY: They're both up in the air is all I could think of (0). RAW SCORE: 14.

Of interest here is the patient's peculiar designation of axe and saw as "instruments of strength." This stilted expression bears out the pedantic language quality noted on Comprehension, and she perseveratively employs the notion of *instrument* in her overly general response to TABLE, "instruments you use." Aside from these minimal indices of peculiar language and excessively broad concept formation, however, her responses otherwise provide no evidence of personality disturbance.

Picture Completion

KNOB: +. TAIL: +. NOSE: +. HANDLES: +. DIAMOND: +. WATER: A hand to hold the pitcher. NOSE PIECE: +. PEG: +. OAR LOCK: +. BASE THREAD: +. STARS: dk. DOG TRACKS: +. FLORIDA: +. STACKS: It's not right; an ocean liner shouldn't have sails. LEG: +. ARM IMAGE: +. FINGER: This guy has one big arm and one little arm. SHADOW: +. STIRRUP: +. SNOW: +. EYEBROW: +. RAW SCORE: 17.

The patient's Picture Completion response is somewhat less adaptive than her behavior on the preceding verbal subtests, but only minor indications of cognitive dysfunction emerge. One of the four items she misses, WATER, is considerably easier than several other factorially related items she passes, including PEG, OAR LOCK, BASE THREAD, and FLORIDA. Although her failure on WATER thus constitutes some scatter, none of her other errors is inconsistent with order difficulty within factorial groups of items.

Two of her errors are sufficiently unusual to suggest some difficulty in maintaining focus of attention. Although she is asked to identify missing parts in the pictures, she responds with irrelevant and inaccurate criticisms on STACKS ("an ocean liner shouldn't have sails") and FINGER ("one big arm and one little arm"). It is also of interest that this woman who refers to "this guy" on FINGER is the same woman who spoke of "established community" on Comprehension and "instruments of strength" on Similarities; the implication is again of a varying defensive style reflected in a shifting quality of language usage.

Scale Scores

Information: 9. Comprehension: 13. Similarities: 10. Picture Completion: 12.

The only tentative clue to personality disorder in these scale scores is the four-point discrepancy between Information and Comprehension, which is an example of intertest scatter and, like her scatter and irrelevance within Picture Completion, suggests inconsistent cognitive efficiency.

Discussion. This WAIS protocol is virtually free from indications of schizophrenic ego impairment. With the exception of extremely subtle and tentative suggestions of peculiar language, broad concept formation, and inconsistent focus of attention, there is no basis on this test for entertaining an hypothesis of schizophrenic disturbance.

DRAW-A-PERSON

The patient's figure drawings appear in Figures 26 and 27. Her stylized drawings are sketchy at points, particularly in the discontinuous lines of the woman's arms, but in general she draws with some skill and gives no indications of inadequate ego boundaries or distorted body imagery. Of considerable interest, however, is the concern about sexual identification suggested by her drawings. Even conservatively interpreted, her male drawing is markedly feminized, whereas her drawing of the woman, though clearly feminine and so attired as particularly to identify her femininity, appears a more solid, competent, and mature person than the male. Although these features of her drawings do not identify ego impairments, they do suggest that uncertain sexual identification and possible latent homosexual concerns may be prominently influencing her behavior patterns.

RORSCHACH

Card I 8″

1. (*Wm F+ A P*) A weird kind of butterfly. (?) It's got a body and two wings on the sides, and it just looks weird.

2. (*Dd F+ A*) And here it looks like a spider [upper half of center detail].

3. (*D— Fc—,Fk At,X-ray Penetration*) An X-ray section of the spine [center detail]. (?) Because of the roundness of it, the way it seems to be rounded the same way on both sides.

4. (*Wm,S F+ Mask*) It could be a Halloween face. (?) It has like jack-o-lantern eyes, and a mouth, and maybe with teeth cut in; you know how grotesque they are sometimes; and these up on the sides could be the ears on the mask.

Card II 2″

5. (*W— M—,FC',Fc (A),Cg Incongruous, Barrier*) It looks like two roosters dancing in the barnyard with black feather robes on.

6. (*Dm F+,Fm At Fabulized*) ∨ Can I turn it? It doesn't look

Figure 26

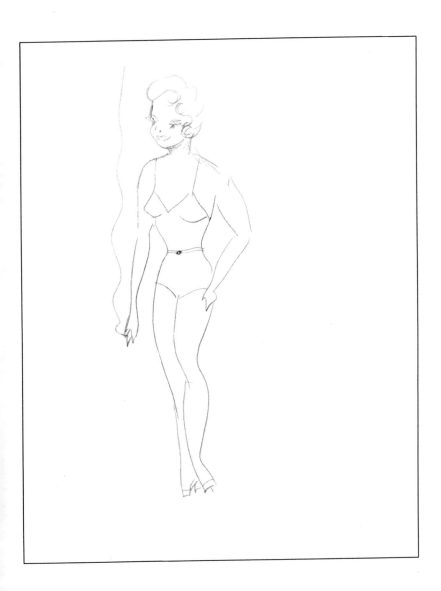

Figure 27

like much this way. (*Encouragement*) A pelvic bone [black details].
(?) It just looks like two bones coming out, two loosely hanging bones.

Card III 7"

7. (*W+ M+,FC H,Cg P Fabulized*) This looks like two women dancing; they're holding fans, or dancing over a pot, or perhaps it's a nightclub show; yes, a nightclub show, and these red things are part of the act. (*Women?*) Because of their protruding breasts, hairdo, high heels, and short skirts. (*Red things?*) Just some red background decorations that go with the act.

8. (*D— M— Hd,At Incongruous, Penetration*) ∨ A man, from halfway down, bent over with his heels showing, but it doesn't include the red. (?) A man crouching, or in a squat; you can see his feet ["head" detail of poular human figure], his knees, his thighs ["leg" detail of popular], and here [center black] a cutaway that shows his bone structure.

9. (*Dv CF Bl Fabulized*) ∨ I don't know about the red spots smeared around; they resemble spattered blood, like there has been violence around.

9a. (*Dm F+ Cg P*) ∨ And now this center red also looks like it could be a bow tie.

9b. (*Dm F+ A*) ∨ And this side red look like seahorses somewhat; but I favor the violence.

Card IV 2"

10. (*Wv F± Obj*) Something one might see under a microscope. (*What?*) Nothing in particular; it just has the appearance of something horrible.

11. (*D— F— AAt*) A bone structure [lower center detail]. (?) Because of the spiny things; it looks like it might be the bone of a turkey neck.

12. (*Wv cF Na*) A fossil of some sea life. (?) Just the way it's so indistinct; and even though it's not 3-D, but just one-dimensional, it's like it has ridges and things.

12a. (*W— FC'— Ad Penetration*) Going way out, it could be a monster's face, with these pits [inner details] for eyes, and here [lower portion] is where the mouth and jaw have rotted away; maybe it's a black dog, yes, the face of a black dog with the mouth and chin missing.

Card V 1"

13. (*Wm FM+ A P*) It looks like a bat, a bat that would be flying.

Card VI 2"

14. (*W— F—,FC' Sex,At,Bl Fabulized, Self-reference, Penetration*) The first impression I get is the vagina of a woman, but upside down;

this way [∨] I get the vagina [middle detail of lower portion] and the anus [middle portion of upper detail], and maybe some scar tissue. (?) I have two little lips at the top of my vagina, just like these [reference to bottom inner projections], and a long narrow opening like this, skinny, with hair around. (*Hair?*) The rest of it is like black hair, like mine. (*Scars?*) Scars from having children, like I have, and maybe there's some blood around; I bleed a lot when I have children.

15. (*Wm FC+,Fm Aobj P*)It could be a fur off an animal, stripped off and hung up; the head is gone, but the tail is intact.

Card VII 3″

16. (*W M+,FK (A),Obj Peculiar, Incongruous, Fabulized Combination*) It looks like a little poodle dog dancing on a hassock, with his reflection on the other side.

17. (*Wm F+ Cg Barrier*) It could be a necklace, or one of those necklace collars you tie around sweaters.

17a. (*W+ M+,Fc H,Cg Barrier*) ∨ I see something else this way. It could be those Russian-type dancers, with big fur hats on, dancing back to back, and with big boots on.

Card VIII 4″

18. (*W FC'−,M,C (Hd),Cg,Fire Contamination, Fabulized Combination, Barrier*) It's a pretty arrangement of colors. The gray at the top could be a monster of ice. (?) His nose is here [upper center white] and the gray is the top of his head; it's like a drawing in a horror story. (*Ice?*) Because he's gray, the color of ice; and maybe the blue is his cape and the rest down here could be hell fire he's lording it over. (*Fire?*) Because of the orange and red color.

19. (*Dm FCarb+ A P-tendency Incongruous, Fabulized Combination*) The side could be a red bear. (*Red bear?*) Well, they're red, that's all; I don't know why; and they look like polar bears, so they go with the ice.

20. (*Wm F+ Em Barrier*) The whole thing could be the crest on a shield.

21. (*W− F− Hd,Cg*) ∨ This way it could be a skeleton laughing with big hollow sockets where his eyes were [pink], the blue socket for his mouth, the red as ears, and the gray as his chin; it looks like a mask on a doctor, like in surgery. (*Look more like?*) Let's say a mask; the blue is the mask, with the eyes here [pink], chin here [gray], and this [orange] as the head.

Card IX 9″

22. (*Wv CF Art*) Nothing, except a smear of paint; it looks like

someone was trying to do something with water colors and just smeared them all around.

Card X 2″

23. (*D— FCarb— Ad Incongrous*) It looks like quite a few little monsters or imaginary animals. This [bottom green] looks like an animal with long green ears, green eyes, and whiskers. (*Kind of animal?*) It could be a rabbit's head, with these long green ears (uses popular "worms" as ears).

24. (*Dm FC′+ (H)*) Two little black devils at the top. (*How look?*) They have ugly feet and bodies with no neck, short fat legs, and antennae on their heads.

25–26. (*Dm F+ A P; D— FCarb— Ad Incongruous, Fabulized Combination*) Some kind of a crab with a green claw.

27. (*Wv CF Bt*) A cutaway of flowers of some sort. (*?*) There is a stem, and the neck of the flower, and the petals; inside is the stamen; the rest out here are all the colored leaves and maybe other flowers.

Scores

R	27+5	M	4+2	H	1+1	F+%	70%	
W	16+2(59%)	FM	1	(H)	1	R+%	57%	
D	10+2(37%)	m	0+2	Hd	2	P	5+1	
Dd+S	1+1(4%)	k	0+1	(Hd)	1			
		FK	0+1	A	5+1	High W%	44%	
		F	11+2	(A)	2+1	High D%	40%	
Incongruous	6	Fc	2+2	Ad	2			
Fabulized	4	c	1	At	2+2	Barrier	4	
Fabulized		C′	2+3	Cg	1+6	Penetration	3	
Combination	4	FC	3+1	Bl	1+1			
Peculiar	1	CF	3	Obj	1+1			
Contamination	1	C	0+1	Sex	1			
Self-reference	1			Mask	1			
				Em	1			
				AAt	1			
				Aobj	1			
				Art	1			
				Na	1			
				Bt	1			
				Fire	0+1			
				X-ray	0+1			

Discussion. This woman's Rorschach protocol, like that of the previous patient, reveals an extent of personality disturbance strikingly at variance with her WAIS performance. Her orderly, efficient response to the more structured part of the testing is replaced here by multiple indications of unusual cognitive focusing, illogical reasoning, impaired relation to reality, weakened defensive control, and maladaptive organizational activity.

With regard to her thinking processes, her minimal attention to the obvious aspects of her experience ($D\%$ only 37) and her many instances of inappropriately overgeneralized and combinative thinking identify thought disorder. Although her four Fabulized responses are not inconsistent with a normally active imagination, her bizarre self-reference in response #14, where she draws highly specific comparisons between the appearance of the blot and the anatomical structure of her own genitals, clearly demonstrates inappropriate loss of distance from the card and pathologic overgeneralization in terms of personalized associations.

Further attesting reasoning disturbance are the patient's six incongruous, four Fabulized Combination, and one Contamination responses. She incongruously combines objects with actions (rooster *dancing* in #16), external with internal details (man with his bone structure showing in #8), and colors with forms ("red bear" on #18, "green ears" on #23, and "green claw" on #26). She infers between juxtaposed percepts relationships that are largely unjustified by the size, position, or nature of the figures seen ("dogs dancing on a hassock" on #16, the monster lording it over the hell fire in #18, the bears that "go with the ice" on #19, and the crab with the claw on #26). Finally, her Contamination in #18, "monster of ice," reveals her inability to keep her associations, in this case "monster" and "ice," logically distinct.

Concerning her perceptual functioning, the inaccuracy of the patient's percepts ($F+\%$ of 70, $R+\%$ of only 57) and her predilection for vague, poorly differentiated percepts (four Wv responses) identify significantly impaired relation to reality. Her reasoning and perceptual disturbances are jointly reflected in her notably low organizational scores (*high* $W\%$ of 44, *high* $D\%$ of 40), both of which are well below normal limits. Finally indicating ego impairment is the failure of repressive control reflected by the unusual sexual association noted above.

The patient's Rorschach, then, clearly demonstrates schizophrenic disturbance. Three additional features of the data reveal her to have a pseudoneurotic form of schizophrenia: first, her disturbed Rorschach performance is balanced by her adaptive response to structured tests; second, at no point during her Rorschach does she evince concern about the quality or adequacy of her markedly deviant responses; and third, as elaborated below, she displays a mixed and highly variable defensive style.

Concerning defensive style, this woman exhibits a striking breadth of response dispositions that exceeds any observed in the previous case illustrations. On occasion she appears a reflective, imaginative person who takes considerable pleasure in ideational activity and in a detailed analysis of her experience. Relevant in this regard are her four main and two additional M responses, the large number of diverse content categories she employs, and her extensive, far-reaching fantasy elaborations. At other times, however, she seems to favor affective rather than ideational channels of expression and to prefer a superficial, nonanalytic approach to her experience. Pertinent here are her $Sum\ C$ of 4.5 and her satisfaction with a number of vague, poorly defined responses (e.g., "something . . . nothing in particular" on #10, "it's so indistinct" on #12).

In addition to evincing these features of both ideational and repressive defensive styles, the patient uses achromatic color and shading determinants in several responses and makes a number of references to anatomy and to "weird," "grotesque," and "horrible" aspects of her percepts. Extrapolations to possible neurotic symptom choice from these various structural and content characteristics of her Rorschach response—reflection and active fantasy, superficiality and labile emotionality, reaction to shading and achromatic color, and attention to anatomy and external danger—would include phobic and obsessive reactions, hysterical and conversion phenomena, and anxiety and depressive affect. The patient's mixed defensive style is thus consistent with pan-neurotic phenomena, and this mixed pattern, in combination with the primary emergence of her disturbance in unstructured settings and her apparent comfort with and ego-syntonic view of her personality structure, points to pseudoneurotic schizophrenic disturbance.

Summary. This patient responds consistently and adaptively to the WAIS and reasonably well on the DAP, but in the unstructured setting of the Rorschach test she produces multiple indications of disordered thinking and impaired relation to reality. She also displays a variable pattern of ideational and expressive defenses and evinces dispositions to a wide variety of neurotic phenomena. Her relatively good functioning in structured situations and loss of control in unstructured settings, together with her mixed defensive style and her notable tolerance for manifestations of her underlying disturbance, is consistent with a pseudoneurotic form of schizophrenic disturbance.

17

SCHIZO-AFFECTIVE DISORDER

SCHIZO-AFFECTIVE disorder is an overt form of schizophrenia in which features of primary affective disturbance intermingle or alternate with fundamental symptoms of schizophrenic ego impairment. Bleuler (1911, pp. 208–211) included affective disturbances among the accessory symptoms of schizophrenia and described the occurrence in schizophrenia of both melancholic and manic conditions, the former as manifest in depressive affect and inhibition of thought and action and the latter as reflected by euphoria, flights of ideas, and hyperactivity. In regard to differentiating such a mixture of schizophrenic and affective symptomatology from manic-depressive psychosis, Bleuler (1911, p. 304) taught the following:

All the phenomena of manic-depressive psychosis may also appear in our disease; the only decisive factor is the presence or absence of schizophrenic symptoms. Therefore, neither a state of manic exaltation nor a melancholic depression, nor the alternation of both states has any significance for the diagnosis. Only after careful observation may we conclude that we are dealing with a manic-depressive psychosis.

The presence of marked affective disturbance and an atypical course of exacerbation and recovery in apparently schizophrenic patients is reported in other early contributions by Dunton, Hoch, and Hunt and Appel. Dunton (1910) called attention to "cyclic forms of dementia praecox" characterized in part by recurring periods of "excitement" and "stupor." In his view such "cyclic" patients represented a unique form of dementia praecox that was closely allied to manic-depressive psychosis but could best be conceived as a link between schizophrenic and manic-depressive disturbance. Hoch (1922) discussed a group of patients who similarly were clearly schizophrenic and also displayed prominent affective disturbance, but he questioned whether, in light of their usual early recovery, such persons should be diagnosed dementia praecox.

Hunt and Appel (1936) presented 30 patients with mixed schizophrenic and manic-depressive features in whom they noted the following common characteristics: early age of onset, neuropathic heredity, mixed cycloid and schizoid personality traits, heightened incidence of somatization, serious precipitating factors in the onset, and frequent persecutory trends and hallucinations. Like Dunton, Hunt and Appel described the conditions of such patients as "psychoses lying midway between schizophrenia and manic-depressive psychosis."

Other writers have agreed more closely with Bleuler that persons who exhibit features of both manic-depressive and schizophrenic disorder are basically schizophrenic. Lewis and Hubbard (1931) and Lewis and Piotrowski (1954), for example, affirm Bleuler's view that manic-depressive psychosis can be accurately diagnosed only by the elimination of schizophrenic possibilities, and they report data demonstrating that most patients who initially present such mixed symptomatology are eventually diagnosed schizophrenic. Lewis and Piotrowski outline 10 clinical signs that in their experience differentiate schizophrenia from manic-depressive psychosis and from neurosis: physical sensations with dissociation; delusions regarding others; delusions regarding physical objects; feelings of physical isolation and personal unreality; inability to concentrate; feeling of having changed; speech disturbance and intellectual blocking; repetitive, uncontrolled anxiety-provoking thoughts; ideas of reference and/or feelings of being controlled by inimical outside forces; and maintenance or increase of seclusiveness after hospitalization.

These various clinical observations were first formulated as the *schizo-affective* syndrome by Kasanin in a 1933 paper, "The Acute Schizo-affective Psychoses." Kasanin takes issue in this paper with the Bleulerian view that all manic-depressive symptoms may appear in schizophrenia, and he suggests instead that a new clinical entity, *schizo-affective disorder*, is necessary to categorize those patients who present with concurrent schizophrenic and affective disturbance. Kasanin conceives schizo-affective disorder as a dramatic psychotic episode that emerges primarily in fairly young, socially integrated individuals who precipitously undergo severe emotional stress. The psychosis, according to Kasanin, lasts a few weeks to a few months and is followed by recovery. Although Kasanin's view of schizo-affective disorder as a clinical entity is tacitly endorsed in this chapter, his argument with Bleuler is not joined; rather, as stated above, schizo-affective disorder is regarded here as a form or subcategory of schizophrenic disturbance.

Little in the way of further conceptualization or research data has been added to the literature on schizo-affective disorder since these early contributions. Nevertheless, occasional case reports demonstrating the unique clinical picture and cyclic course of this condition have appeared (e.g., Solow, 1953), and schizo-affective disorder is not infrequently diagnosed even in outpatient settings, where in 1961 it constituted 6% of all schizophrenic diagnoses (*Outpatient Clinic Report*, 1963).

PSYCHODIAGNOSTIC INDICES OF SCHIZO-AFFECTIVE DISORDER

Inasmuch as schizo-affective disorder comprises both schizophrenic and affective components, its psychodiagnosis rests with concurrent test evidence of schizophrenic ego impairment and manic and/or depressive tendencies. Psychodiagnostic indicators of identifying characteristics of schizophrenic disturbance are detailed in previous chapters, and it remains here to review briefly the salient test indices of manic and depressive states.

TEST PERFORMANCE IN MANIC STATES

Manic states, as discussed in detail by Arieti (1959b) and Noyes and Kolb (1963, pp. 306–310), are characterized primarily by elated mood, stream of thought, and increased psychomotor activity. Manic persons are accordingly remarkable for their joyous excitement; infectious good humor, garrulity, rapid flights of ideas, restless hypermotility, and energetic undertakings. Such companion phenomena as grandiose scheming, exuberant philanthropy, and gregarious sociability also participate in manic disturbance. These identifying features of mania are reflected in a number of structural, content, and behavioral test variables, particularly on the Rorschach.

As delineated by Rorschach (1921), Bohm (1958, pp. 277–279), Phillips and Smith (1953, p. 84), and others, manic tendencies affect Rorschach performance in several specific respects. Consistent with their active ideation and expansive emotional style, manic subjects tend to produce large numbers of responses embracing a wide variety of content and determinant categories. They employ both movement and color freely, extend their interpretations far beyond conventional *A* and *P* percepts and obvious *D* locations, and embellish their responses with numerous fanciful specifications, combinations, and peripheral associations.

These Rorschach characteristics, however, can relate either to primarily manic pathology or to the thought pressure, reasoning impairment, and loss of affective control that accompany schizophrenic disturbance (see Chaps. 4, 5, & 10). It is therefore important to interpret them in terms of salient differences between schizo-affective disorder and manic psychosis outlined by Bleuler (see p. 431) and applied to Rorschach data by Klopfer and Spiegelman (1956, pp. 308–310). Specifically, both manic-depressive and schizo-affective subjects produce an overflow of movement and color responses. On the other hand, Klopfer and Spiegelman point out, whereas the manic-depressive subject is likely to produce few bizarre responses and to indulge in minus form-level associations only through carelessless or lack of effort, schizo-affective persons mirror their schizophrenic ego impairments in bizarre content that violates the reality of the blots. Nonpsychotic subjects with cycloid or hypomanic personality patterns are similarly inclined to dilated records but not to minus form-level elements. Hence it is the infusion of the manic response pattern with elements of primary disturbances of reasoning and reality testing that differentiates schizo-affective disorder from manic psychosis.

Turning to Rorschach content, manic tendencies are usually reflected in fantasy productions associated with excessive reliance on the mechanism of denial. As conceptualized by Schafer (1954, pp. 250–255), manic disturbance is largely defined by the defensive patterns and euphoria that result from prominent use of denial. The hypomanic person maintains an exaggerated feeling of well-being by denying the existence of any thought, action, or event that might reflect adversely on his adequacy, veracity, or security. However, Schafer adds, because defense by denial is typically unstable, the hypomanic person is frequently subject to near-conscious awareness of anxiety- and guilt-provoking reflections that precipitously render him prone to depression and irritability in the face of challenge.

Correspondingly, the unstable hypomanic defensive pattern conduces to Rorschach content indicating denials, that which is being denied, and the defensive instability itself. As elaborated by Schafer, denial appears in an emphasis on images of innocence, abundant supply, potency, serenity, gaiety, and hope, as exemplified respectively by such imagery as "angels," "bulging picnic basket," "virile man," "peaceful landscape," "children playing," and "a colorful festival." The denied concerns are likely to emerge in contrasting images of guilt ("hell"), aggression ("bombs exploding"), helplessness ("weak old man"), gloom ("dark clouds"), and despair ("broken," "worn," and "useless" objects).

The hypomanic subject's defensive instability is mirrored in frequent fluctuations between the denials and the denied, with rapidly shifting characterizations of Rorschach cards and responses. Thus, the hypomanic subject embellishes his responses with many intrinsic denials ("a very pleasant-looking witch"; "two men fighting, but they really like each other"); with vacillations between response to and description of the cards (Card V—"it's a bat, but not a very good one; the shape is off and I don't like the colors; if we could square off the wings a little and enlarge the body and give it some oranges and reds we'd have one of those real pretty butterflies you see when you're outdoors"); and with highly fabulized, symbolic injections of personal feelings (Card X—"this is a beautiful card, with everyone helping everyone else; the blue symbolizes friendship, and they're holding the pink together; and all the others are watching, and they're happy that everything is going so well").

In regard to behavioral variables, Schafer (1954, p. 254) makes the following significant observations on the Rorschach response of persons who display an attentuated manic, or hypomanic, emotional tone:

> In general, the hypomanic may be expected to be emotionally overresponsive to the tester, to the inkblots, and to his own responses. He will run the gamut from interest, gaiety, excitement, and pleasure to intense anxiety, self-reproaches, irritability, and possibly even tears. When euphoric features are prominent, the record should contain, in addition, puns, quips, self-references, and rambling tending toward irrelevancy and chain-thinking. In general, there should be a driven out-pouring of words, associations, digressions, and emotions.

Little specific attention has been paid in the literature to comparable DAP and WAIS indices of manic disturbance. Machover (1949) comments on the tendency of manic subjects to draw large, expansive figures (p. 90) and spontaneously to write on or identify their drawings (p. 141), but she does not systematically outline any uniquely manic drawing patterns. Mania is not indexed by Wechsler (1958) and is observed by Schafer (1948, p. 23) to occur too infrequently in clinical psychological practice to be described in terms of a generalized Wechsler pattern. However, as the case study in this chapter illustrates, the WAIS allows ample opportunity for the affectively disturbed subject clearly to reveal a diagnostic pattern of flighty ideation and rampant emotionality.

TEST PERFORMANCE IN DEPRESSED STATES

The depressive phase of manic-depressive psychosis and depressed states in general are characterized by dysphoric mood, retarded and impoverished ideational processes, and psychomotor slowing and inertia. As elaborated by Arieti (1959b) and Noyes and Kolb (1963, pp. 310–313), depression is the antithesis of mania, replacing euphoria with melancholia, expansiveness with inhibition, and hyperactivity with lethargy. As noted by Schafer (1948, pp. 57–61), the test performance of depressed subjects is correspondingly marked by (a) retarded perceptual, associative, and motor processes, (b) inhibited emotional reactivity, (c) irritability or negativism, and (d) pervasive expressions in test content and behavior of gloomy preoccupations and feelings of guilt, inadequacy, and despair.

The salient test findings in depressed states include the following: the WAIS usually reflects impairments in tasks requiring active reasoning, prolonged concentration, or psychomotor facility, with virtually all subtests inferior to Information, Similarities, and Vocabulary (Rapaport, Gill, & Schafer, 1945, pp. 308–310); the DAP figures tend to be small and drawn low on the page and to convey oral emphasis and impressions of impotence and lassitude, as in seated figures (Machover, 1949, pp. 43, 65, 89, & 91); and the Rorschach record is likely (a) to be meager and unimaginative, with few R and a focus on Dm, $F+$, A, and P responses, (b) to reveal little capacity for either productive fantasy or emotional expression, with few M and color responses, and (c) to comprise themes of somatic preoccupation, discouragement, and self-recrimination (Klopfer & Kelley, 1942, pp. 393–396; Rapaport et al., 1946; Schafer, 1948, pp. 57–61; Bohm, 1958, pp. 253–265). On all three tests, in addition, the depressed subject will display delayed reaction times and terse, abbreviated verbalization. [1]

In concluding this section it is important to observe that a differential diagnosis between schizo-affective disorders in which the affective state is depressed and psychotic depression frequently cannot be made from psychodiagnostic tests alone. Psychotically depressed patients share with depressed schizo-affective subjects the lethargy and dysphoria associated with depression and the general personality disintegration and functioning disability that attend a psychotic extent of disturbance, and both types of patients typically display test indices of impaired reality testing and inadequate defensive resources.

Among euphoric patients, those with schizo-affective disorder differ from manic psychotics in that they exhibit disordered thinking as well as poor reality testing and unstable defenses (see p. 48). However,

---

[1] It is suprising to note that the few contributions referenced here constitute the bulk of the psychodiagnostic literature on depression, exclusive of segmental research reports. An integrated presentation of differential psychodiagnosis in depressive states, developed in terms of psychopathologic conceptions of depression and evaluated in light of extant research findings, has not come to the author's attention.

as a consequence of the inhibition and limited responsivity that derive from depressed affect, the dissociation and bizarre fantasy elaborations that otherwise differentiate schizo-affective disorder from manic-depressive psychosis are unlikely to appear in the test performance of the depressed schizo-affective subject. In other words, the impoverishing effect of a depressive state on ideational and emotional expression often masks the differences in ego structure between the depressed schizo-affective and the psychotically depressed subject.

As Schafer (1948, p. 60) remarks, the appearance of colorful or strained integrative responses in an otherwise inhibited, stereotyped record will occasionally distinguish a depressed schizophrenic from a psychotically depressed state. However, in the absence of previous historical data that might shed light on the patient's diagnostic status, the decision as to whether or not a severely depressed patient also suffers from schizophrenic disorder usually must await a sufficient lifting of his depression to allow him to respond fully to psychodiagnostic tests. This diagnostic impasse is outlined in detail by Mercer (1949), who presents two cases in which repeated testing identified a basically schizophrenic disorder in patients whose initial depressive state concealed their schizophrenia and precluded differential diagnosis from psychotic depression.

CASE STUDY [2]

The following case illustrates schizophrenic disturbance accompanied by prominent affective features, and the patient's protocols reflect both marked ego impairment and hypomanic tendencies. The patient is a 29-year-old married mother of three living sons who first began to manifest psychological disturbance 10 years before the testing when her second-born child, also a boy, died in infancy from complications associated with a congenital disorder. From that time she was observed to undergo mood swings from mild depression to periods of considerable gaiety and industriousness. Three years before this examination she had reacted with a depressive episode to a serious accident incurred by her oldest son, who recovered only after lingering near death for several days. One and one half years after this incident she gave birth to her youngest child, following which she became obsessed with the persistent and unshakeable feeling that she must make amends to her obstetrician for major injustices she erroneously believed herself to have done him.

[2] The format followed in presenting the case studies is described on pages 254–257.

In the year preceding her admission to the hospital the patient engaged in unusual behavior with increasing frequency. Allowing a close friend to borrow a handbag, she bitterly complained on its return that it had been switched for a cheaper model, and she abruptly terminated this friendship of many years' duration. Preoccupied with thoughts about her obstetrician, she filled pages of note paper with paragraphs concerning him, including such repetitive statements as, "I'm a very good girl and Dr. C will take care of me." Finally, on the day before her admission, she impulsively invited all of her neighbors in for coffee, which she had not made, and subsequently barred the door with her person and denied them permission to leave. When her husband arrived home and interceded, she dashed frantically through the house cutting various electrical wires with a scissors.

On admission to the hospital the following day she was noted to be extremely agitated and hyperactive and to speak with tremendous pressure. She also described a number of delusional ideas, including feelings that her acquaintances were undergoing personality change and that her husband and family were about to suffer great harm at the hands of the communists. Although her degree of disturbance was clearly of psychotic proportions, there was some initial question concerning differential diagnosis between schizophrenic and manic-depressive disorder. Psychological testing was requested in this connection.

The patient regained some control during five weeks' care in the psychiatric unit of a general hospital but appeared to require further inpatient treatment. She was subsequently transferred to a nearby state hospital, where she remained an additional two months as an inpatient and five months on convalescent outpatient care before being discharged as improved.

WECHSLER ADULT INTELLIGENCE SCALE

Information

RUBBER: +. PRESIDENTS: +. LONGFELLOW: He was a poet; maybe I better put on my glasses (+). WEEKS: +. PANAMA: +. BRAZIL: +. HEIGHT: 5'5", and for a man it's about 5'8", and I don't know what it would be for children (+). ITALY: +. CLOTHES: +. WASHINGTON: February 14 . . . no, February 12; Lincoln was born on the 14th. HAMLET: +. VATICAN: +. PARIS: No idea. (*Estimate?*) You mean by air, or what—plane, auto, boat travel, it makes a difference. (?) I'd say 15,000 miles. EGYPT: Asia. YEAST: Some explosive power within it. POPULATION: 63 million. SENATORS: dk. GENESIS: +. TEMPERATURE: 120°. ILIAD: +. BLOOD VESSELS: Arteries and veins are all I know. KORAN: +.

FAUST: Dante comes to mind, he wrote about hell; I don't remember, though. ETHNOLOGY: dk. APOCRYPHA: dk. RAW SCORE: 18.

The patient's responses are most notable for the many disorganized thoughts that intrude on her verbalizations more rapidly than she can assess their relevance to the task at hand. On HEIGHT she volunteers unsolicited data concerning the average man and becomes concerned with the rather esoteric question of the average height of children; on PARIS she irrelevantly attends to the manner of travel rather than the measured distance between the cities and includes reference to a highly unlikely trip from Paris to New York "by auto"; and on WASHINGTON her attempt to account for both Washington and Lincoln interferes with her efforts to answer what in view of her total score should be a relatively easy item for her.

These tangential asides are consistent with a flight of ideas, and in two other cases she displays dissociation as well. Following LONGFEL-LOW she states, "I'd better put on my glasses," although nothing in the apparent nature of the test or the examiner's behavior provided reasonable basis for such a conclusion; in fact, she had at this point in the examination completed a visual test (the Bender-Gestalt) during which she had not worn her glasses. Also suggesting dissociation is her response of "Dante" to FAUST. Although this response is by itself a reasonable guess, her further explanation reveals she may have derived it from an inappropriate assumption of identity on the basis of similarity; *Faust* has a devil in it, devils go with hell, "Dante wrote about hell," therefore "Dante comes to mind."

In addition to thought pressure and dissociative tendencies, the patient's responses also demonstrate some peculiar language usage and scatter. She peculiarly describes YEAST as having "some explosive power within it," and she produces an inconsistent pattern of successes and failures. However, the three items that contribute to her inconsistency, namely, the relatively difficult GENESIS, ILIAD, and KORAN that she passes, are factorially interrelated; hence it is only within one group of items, those loading on a factor of General Information, that her attainment is uneven.

Comprehension

ENVELOPE: Mail it (2). BAD COMPANY: Your own character would be weakened; birds of a feather flock together, you know, and a good apple can be spoiled by the bad; look what's happening in all those teenage groups, it's a terrible thing (2). MOVIES: Report it to the usher; I saw one once in a movie over in Mudville, only they were able to put it out pretty well (2). TAXES: To support the government, so they can supply the people with the things they need (2). IRON: While everything is ready, it will work better; that is, iron can be worked better when it's hot; now, with a patient like me, I have problems and I need to be helped quickly (1). CHILD LABOR: To protect the children; in the old days they were overworked and had no way to deal with authority (1). FOREST: Stay in one spot and figure out the directions from the sun; I sense my way out of places without knowing directions, I do it all the time, so I'm sure I could find my way out (2). DEAF: Because they aren't able to imitate the sounds others make (2). CITY LAND: There are more facilities in the city, all the services that make living comfortable (1). MARRIAGE: For the sake of society; things would get out of hand and people wouldn't stick to their word if there were no licenses; a wife and children need protection; I know of one case where a man just walked out and left his family with no money at all (1). BROOKS: If it's shallow you can hear the ripple of water going over the rocks; the noise echoes more easily (1). SWALLOW: Swallows are a rare bird; there's that song about swallows going back to Capestrano, it's a religious song; but they're rare, and seeing one doesn't mean that many are expected (0). RAW SCORE: 21.

The patient's verbosity alone on this subtest confirms the thought pressure noted on Information. Here again she is unable to limit her focus of attention to the relevant aspects of her experience but rather ranges far afield into personalized and tangential associations. Her personalized references to having seen a fire on MOVIES, being able to find her way on FOREST, and a case in point on MARRIAGE, as well as her expression of concern about teenage groups on BAD COMPANY, represent the type of free-flowing ideation that characterizes both schizophrenic thought pressure and manic flight of ideas.

In three other instances the patient's responses interestingly illustrate the differentiation between flights of ideas associated with manic-depressive psychosis, in which loosely related thoughts emerge in a rapid stream but bear some comprehensible relationship one to the other, and thought pressure associated with schizo-affective disorder, in which successive thoughts are dissociated rather than logically related. Her comment on BAD COMPANY that "birds of a feather flock together" has nothing directly to do with her preceding statement concerning the adverse influence of bad company; her association on IRON, "Now, with a patient like me, I need help quickly," is in no way related to her previous explanation of the proverb, and on SWALLOW, although her thoughts are somewhat interrelated, she introduces her only relevant attempt to explain the proverb with totally irrelevant observations on the rarity of swallows and songs about them. Her performance, then, includes features of both manic flightiness and schizophrenic dissociation.

Similarities

ORANGE: Fruit (2). COAT: Clothing (2). AXE: Tools for making things (2). DOG: Animals; actually, they're a higher order of animals; a dog is a good servant to a man and a lion is lion-hearted; in other words, they both have good traits (2). NORTH: Directions (2). EYE: Sense organs of the body (2). AIR: Both are necessary for the human body (2). TABLE: They're implements to use, invented by man for his comfort (0). EGG: They're reproductive (2). POEM: They're monuments to someone great (1). WOOD: Alcohol comes from wood (0). PRAISE: Praise encourages people and punishment discourages them; both could be used for a good end (0). FLY: Both are living things (2). RAW SCORE: 19.

In this subtest the patient exerts more adaptive control over her ideation than on Information and Comprehension and produces a number of concise, accurate answers. Nevertheless, her uneven concept formation here provides further evidence of thought disorder. On DOG, the one item on which she does become involved in an extraneous elaboration of her response, she concretely applies the concept of lion-heartedness to lions and infers from it that lions, like dogs, have good traits. Overly broad as well as overly narrow conceptual categorizations appear on other items. She vaguely and overinclusively describes table and chair as "implements . . . invented by man for his comfort" and praise and punishment as "used for good ends," whereas she too exclusively restricts poem and statue to the category of "monuments to someone great."

Picture Completion

KNOB: +. TAIL: +. NOSE: +. HANDLES: The chrome on the side and the other tires. DIAMOND: There should be numbers in all four corners. WATER: +. NOSE PIECE: +. PEG: +. OAR LOCK: +. BASE THREAD: There's just too much inside it. STAR: The rest of the pole. DOG TRACKS: He doesn't have a gun. FLORIDA: +. STACKS: The guns on the top. LEG: There should be dark red lines on the shell. ARM IMAGE: +. FINGER: +. SHADOW: +. STIRRUP: The rider and the saddle horn. SNOW: There's no haystack. EYEBROW: Her collar. RAW SCORE: 11.

The patient's performance here is markedly idiosyncratic and scattered and strongly suggests thought disorder. Her previously noted inability to focus her attention on the relevant aspects of her experience stands out sharply here in her 10 errors, only two of which are common types of error. Her answers on HANDLES, DIAMOND, BASE THREAD, DOG TRACKS, STACKS, LEG, SNOW, and EYEBROW are all unusually irrelevant and identify the frequent interference of tangential associations with her attention to obvious and significant aspects of her experience. Of particular interest is her response on STACKS, "guns on the top," which is not only unusual and irrelevant but appears to be a perseveration of her thought about a gun on DOG TRACKS.

Concerning scatter, the patient's irregular sequence of successes and failures indicates marked inconsistency in the efficiency of her cognitive focusing. In several cases she passes relatively difficult items after failing much easier, factorially related items: she passes ARM IMAGE and SHADOW after failing DOG TRACKS; WATER, PEG, and OAR LOCK after failing HANDLES; and FINGER after failing BASE THREAD and STACK.

Block Design

ITEM 1: 4″ (4). ITEM 2: 5″ (4). ITEM 3: 8″ (4). ITEM 4: 9″ (4). ITEM 5: 18″ (4). ITEM 6: 53″ (4). ITEM 7: 30″ (6). ITEM 8: Patient became unable to function; test discontinued. RAW SCORE: 30.

The patient attacked this subtest with breezy self-confidence and, as her times to completion attest, completed the first five designs quickly and efficiently. On ITEM 6, however, when she was unable to effect a solution within the first 10–15 seconds, she became visibly upset, complained of feeling nervous, and undertook a long series of haphazard trial and error placements until she happened on the correct solution. On ITEM 7 she regained her composure and performed well, but on ITEM 8, where she again encountered difficulty, her defenses collapsed dramatically. For several minutes she worked agitatedly and ineffectually on the task without making any progress toward the correct solution. During this period she became increasingly distraught and repetitively mumbed, "I just can't do it, I just can't do it." The subtest was discontinued at this point to spare her further distress.

The patient's initially adept performance on the Block Design suggested she might be particularly well able to function in such an impersonal context, but her rapid collapse on the subtest defers to subsequent data the question of whether she can adapt better to impersonal than interpersonal contexts. On the other hand, her sudden surrender to incapacitating dismay at the first indication of difficulty, following her previously unbounded self-confidence, identifies defensive instability and is consistent with the abrupt shifts from exuberant self-assurance to abject despair that characterize affective disturbance.

Scale Scores

Information: 11. Comprehension: 13. Similarities: 13. Picture Completion: 8. Block Design: 9.

Discussion. The patient's WAIS performance clearly reveals components of both schizophrenic and affective disturbance. Her dissociation on Information and Comprehension, her scatter on Information and Picture Completion, her shifting levels of abstraction on Similarities, and her idiosyncratic frames of reference on Picture Completion identify impaired cognitive focusing and uneven concept formation and point to schizophrenic thought disorder. Her flights of ideas on the verbal subtests, her expansive mood and rapid speech, and her sudden shift from enthusiasm to dejection in the face of minimal frustration on Block Design are consistent with a picture of unstable hypomanic defense. It is primarily the evidence of thought disorder that relates her affective disturbance to a schizo-affective rather than manic-depressive disorder.

DRAW-A-PERSON

The patient's figure drawings are presented in Figures 28 and 29. Immediately striking is their extremely small size, which is somewhat contrary to expectation in a subject who approached the testing in a gay, expansive mood as this woman did. It is conceivable, however, that her tiny figures represent her underlying image of herself as a small, weak, unworthy person and that her superficial self-assurance is a defense by denial against such a devalued self-percept.

On close inspection the drawings provide several indications of impaired reality sense. Even if their primitive quality is attributed to limited artistic ability, there still remain in them inaccuracies and inconsistencies that denote distorted body imagery. In the drawing of the female figure one of the girl's legs appears in an impossible position, extending beyond the lateral boundary of the skirt with the knee joint appearing to hang in mid-air. On the male figure, after apparently attempting to represent hair on the man's arm, the patient indicates his sleeves as extending to the wrists. She thus produces a transparency, with the hair unrealistically showing through the sleeves. Similarly incongruous on the male figure is the patient's clear rendition on one foot of the top of the shoe and her failure on the other foot to indicate any demarcation between leg and shoe. These incongruities and distortions demonstrate both some impairment of her reasoning capacity and the likelihood that she holds some inaccurate views of her body and its functions.

Figure 28

444

Figure 29

RORSCHACH

Card I 2″

1. (*Wm F+ A P*) A butterfly or a bird or an owl. (?) It looks most like a butterfly; the body is here and the wings are here, but it's out of proportion.

2. (*Dm F+ Hd,Cg Barrier*) The middle part looks like a woman, with her collar up here. (?) She's wearing a dress with a buckle on it, and she has no head.

3. (*Dm F+ (H)*) These side parts are wings or a dwarf's head or Snow White [upper side portion]; there's a long nose like Cyrano or Pinnochio. (*Most like?*) A dwarf's head.

4. (*Dm F+ Hd,Cg Barrier*) An animal's claws [upper inner details]. (?) They look like a crab's claws or pincers, or they could be the side view of a child's hands with mittens on, that's what it's more like.

5. (*Dd F+ (Hd)*) Here it looks like an angel's wings [top one-third of blot].

6. (*Dm M+,Fc Hd,Cg Incongruous, Penetration*) It could be a dress here [darker portion of lower middle]; you can see the contour of a woman's body through it. (?) It's just the lower part of a woman from the back; she's looking out in the other direction and you can see the back of her legs.

Card II 2″

7. (*Da C Bl*) The red [upper red] looks like blood.

8. (*W— FC—,Fc Sex,At Peculiar, Penetration*) Female anatomy, the insides of the body from the waist down; the female reproductive organs [black details] and the digestive tract [upper center] are here, and the red and black shadings have a lot to do with it; the top red could be lungs, and in the sides these could be muscles and eggs in the female during the fertilized period [reference to indistinct inner detail].

9. (*Dm F+ Obj*) The top look like two hand puppets [upper red].

10. (*D— F— A Contamination-tendency*) An insect, with a front on it like an airplane or a spear; these could be the wings on the side [entire black portion].

11. (*Dd,S F—,CF Na Fabulized, Peculiar*) Someone could be building, building a road that's going down here through this red nature, through these bushes [road is center white and inner portion of bottom red; bushes are remainder of bottom red].

12. (*Dd FC+ Fd*) The bottom could be red candy canes or icicles [tiny projections from bottom red]. (*More like?*) Candy cane.

13. (*D F+ Na Contamination*) Rockheads. (?) They just look like

rock and they look like heads [side black].

14. (*Dv CF,mF Fire Penetration*) ∨ This way it could be fireworks or volcanoes shooting up out of the earth [bottom red]. (?) The color is like you'd see.

15. (*Dd FC— (Hd)*) ∨ Snakes, or ducks, or a devil's head; the inner part is a devil's head, with red horns [inner portion and tiny projections of bottom red].

16. (*Dm F+ Ad P*) Two dogs' heads.

Card III 2″

17. (*Dm F+ At*) It looks like a baby, an embryo; the two red things [outer red] are babies with the umbilical cord.

18. (*D— F— Sex,At Perseveration, Penetration*) Female sex organs [lower center portion]; the two ovaries are on the sides and the birth canal is in the middle.

19. (*Dm M+ (H) P-tendency Incongruous*) Two ballet dancers doing one of their fancy numbers; they have legs with claws on them, or the leg of an insect or a bug. (*Claws?*) Yes, they have claws on their legs, that's the way it looks.

20. (*D— M— Hd Self-reference*) And in the corner here are eyes looking at you ["head" detail of popular human figures].

Card IV 4″

21. (*Dd F— Ad*) A scary head; a head of an animal with the eyes and the ears showing [top center is head; upper side details are ears]. (*Scary?*) It just looks like something I wouldn't want to run into, because it would frighten me.

22. (*Dm F+ A*) Or it could be snakes [upper side details]; I don't like snakes.

23. (*Dm F+ Cg*) Two feet or boots [lower side details]; they look like old men's boots. (*Old?*) They look sort of old and ragged.

24. (*D— F— Ad Fabulized*) The head of a mouse or a young calf [lower center detail]; it has two eyes that are big and warm-looking.

25. (*Dd F— Cg Confabulation, Barrier*) The top part looks like a Queen Victoria dress with a high collar [indistinct upper center area]. (?) Mainly because this part [top center detail] looks like the collar.

Card V 3″

26. (*Wm F+ A P*) A butterfly, but its body is bigger than its wings; the feelers are up here and the legs down here.

27. (*Dm F+ Ad*) An animal's head, with an eye and a nose [upper projections on side details]. (*Kind?*) It looks more like a monkey's head

on one side and a dog's head on the other.

28. (*Dm F+ A*) Snakes here on the ends.

Card VI 2"

29. (*D— Fk— X-ray,At Penetration*) It reminds me of lungs, seen through an X-ray [entire lower portion].

30. (*Dm F+ Obj*) The top is a totem pole—no, it's more like a bug —no, like a totem pole.

31. (*Dm F+ Hd Fabulized*) The head of an old king, with his beard sticking out [outer edge of middle side portion].

32. (*Dd F+ Ad*) It looks like insects' feelers here [tiny projections in bottom center area].

33. (*D F— Sex,At Confabulation, Perseveration, Incongruous, Penetration*) These two little things look like eggs [egg-shaped details at middle bottom], so that could be the birth canal up here [center column], and this [remainder of lower portion] could be the rest of the reproductive system, with these black spots being the inner parts of human cells [reference to tiny inner black dots].

34. (*Dm F+ Ad*) The head of an animal [uppermost detail].

35. (*Dm FM+ A Self-reference*) And it looks like a bird looking at you [upper portion]; there are two eyes and a beak, but it needs bigger wings.

Card VII 2"

36. (*Dm F+ Sex,At Penetration*) It's similar here again; all of these have a center part that looks like the sex organs of a female [dark center bottom detail].

37. (*Dm F+ Hd*) The heads of little boys [upper side details].

38. (*D— F— Ad*)> The head of a snake [top projections].

39. (*W+ Fm+ Na*) Rocks balanced on other rocks.

40. (*Dm F+ (Hd)*) The head of a puppet or cartoon figure (middle side detail).

41. (*Dd FM— Ad Fabulized, Penetration*) A member of the cat family, ready to spring to the attack [lower outer corner of middle side detail]. (?) It's just his head, with his mouth open like he's going to attack.

42. (*Dd F— (Hd)*) This tiny part here [upper outer projection of middle side detail] could be the head of a woman or mermaid; but I don't believe in mermaids.

43. (*Dd Fm— A Fabulized*) This inner part [indistinct lateral portion of bottom detail] looks like a rabbit in cramped quarters, like he's just been caught in a basket.

Card VIII 2″

44. (*Dm FCarb+ A P-tendency Incongruous*) There are animals on the side; they look like that dark, black animal even though they're red; panthers, I mean, but they have heads of mice. (?) They would look like red panthers, but the heads would be mice heads.

45. (*D— F— Sex,At Perseveration, Penetration*) Organs; it could be a diagram of anatomy, the insides; it would be the insides of a female; the blue would be the lung cavity and the yellow the sex organs, but it's not in as much detail as on the other cards.

46. (*Wv FK± Ge*) The whole thing like a map or like an aerial view. (*Place?*) It's no place in particular, but just a view of anywhere.

Card IX 2″

47. (*DW F— Sex,At Confabulation, Perseveration, Penetration*) The insides of people again, anatomy; the thin lines running all through it could be the nerves of the body. (?) The main thing that suggested it was that this part [center portion of bottom pink] is the female sexual parts.

48. (*Dd M+ (Hd) Fabulized, Barrier*) It looks like the head of a ghost peering through a keyhole [lower portion of center light area]; it's Caspar, the friendly ghost.

49. (*D— F— Ad*) A baby bird or a chicken, as it looks in the egg just before it's born; it's just the head [side portions of bottom pink].

50. (*Dd F— Al*) The orange on the green looks like Chinese writing [reference to tiny overlapping portions of orange and green details].

Card X 2″

51. (*D— F— At Perseveration, Peculiar*) Lungs, with the rib cavity between them [entire upper gray].

52. (*D F+,FC Ad,Cg P Fabulized Combination*) The bottom looks like a rabbit; its head is here and these long green things could be part of its dress.

53. (*Dm FM+ A*) Two mice hanging [side details of upper gray].

54. (*Dm F+ A P*) These two blue things look like crabs or spiders.

55. (*D— F— At Perseveration*) Nerves, all the black things on the outside [outer gray details] looks like nerves of the body.

56. (*Da C Na*) Here it looks like the sun, the face of the sun, with yellow sunbeams [inner yellow].

57. (*D— FC— At*) This reminds me of the digestive tract [pink detail]. (?) Because it's red.

58. (*Dd F+ Hd*) Faces here, with a high forehead [top portion of pink details]; they look like the heads of two little children.

Scores

R	58	M	4	H	0	F+%	60%
W	6(11%)	FM	3	(H)	1	R+%	57%
D	38(65%)	m	2+1	Hd	7	P	5+2
Dd+S	14(24%)	k	1	(Hd)	6		
		FK	1	A	10	High W% 50%	
		F	39	Ad	10	High D% 55%	
Fabulized	6	Fc	0+1	Sex	6		
Perseveration	6	C'	0+1	At	4+7	Barrier	2
Incongruous	4	FC	5+1	Na	4	Penetration	6
Confabulation	3	CF	1	Cg	2+3		
Peculiar	3	C	2	Obj	2		
Self-reference	2			Bl	1		
Contamination	1			Fire	1		
Contamination-				Al	1		
tendency	1			Ge	1		
Fabulized				Fd	1		
Combination	1			X-ray	1		

Discussion. This lengthy Rorschach record demonstrates virtually every major identifying feature of schizophrenic disturbance. With regard to cognitive focusing, the patient reveals by her elevated Dd% (24%) and her six perseverative responses, four of which involve sexual anatomy, that she is easily distracted by irrelevant aspects of her experience and often unable to shift the focus of her attention flexibly to meet the demands of new situations. In addition, her three peculiar responses ("*fertilized* period" instead of *fertile* period on #8; "red nature" corrected to "red bushes" on #11; and "lungs with the rib cavity," an apparent confusion of *lung cavity* and *rib cage*, on #51) and her deviant tempo (more responses to Card IX than to Card VIII) indicate inconsistent cognitive functioning.

Concerning reasoning, the patient engages liberally in inappropriately overgeneralized and combinative thinking. Beyond the normally active fantasy demonstrated by her six Fabulized responses (#'s 11, 24, 31, 41, 43, & 48), her two self-reference responses and three Confabulations reflect a pathologic tendency to draw overgeneralized conclusions about the meaning of her experience. On #'s 20 and 35 she sees eyes and birds "looking at you" (*you* apparently meaning herself), and she inaccurately interprets a relatively large area of Card IV as a "dress" because the uppermost part looks like a "collar" (#25), an area of Card VI as "the reproductive system" because the tiny bottom details resemble "eggs" (#33), and all of Card IX as "insides" because the bottom center is "the female sexual parts" (#47).

Inappropriate combinative thinking appears in her four incongruous, one Fabulized Combination, one Contamination, and one Contamination-tendency responses. Twice she attributes transparent effects to her percepts (the woman's body showing through the dress on #6 and the "inner parts of cells" on #33), thus unrealistically combining normally visible and normally invisible details; twice she creates unnatural composite figures (people with claws on their legs in #19; panther with head of a mouse on #44); and additionally on #44 she endorses an arbitrary combination of color and object, "red panther." In her Fabulized Combination on #52 she describes the improbable circumstance of a *clothed* rabbit, and in her Contamination and Contamination-tendency responses, the "rockheads" on #13 and the insect "with an airplane or a spear" for a front on #10, she is grossly unable to maintain logical distinctions between normally discrete percepts.

Regarding concept formation, the patient generally keeps her Rorschach performance within appropriate levels of abstraction. However, her *Al* responses on #50, the "Chinese writing," is a highly symbolic percept that even among subjects giving very long records seldom occurs except in association with an inclination to overly symbolic interpretation of experience at the expense of inadequate attention to concrete and practical considerations.

Turning to reality testing, this woman discloses in her low $F+\%$ (60) and low $R+\%$ (57) that her perceptual accuracy is significantly impaired. Her reality sense also appears weak, with her high Penetration score of six, much of it derived from anatomy percepts, suggesting major concerns about the integrity of her body boundaries.

Capacity for object relatedness is also notably lacking in the patient's Rorschach. Particularly critical for limited interpersonal skills is the total absence from her long record of a single *H* response. Her four *M*'s are given to other than *H* contents, and her ratio of *H* to $(H)+Hd+(Hd)$ responses is a highly unusual 0:14. This ratio implies that, although she may frequently reflect on interpersonal concerns, she is afraid or unable to deal with people in an open, intimate, and trusting manner; it is as though she promotes her feeling of safety by construing people only in terms of their component parts or as cartoon, caricatured, or puppet-like images of themselves.

Defensive operations function with only sporadic success in the patient's Rorschach response. She is unable to prevent sexual preoccupation from pervading her responses, and four of her six *Sex* responses (#'s 8, 18, 33, & 47) are perceptually inaccurate and uncommon among normal subjects. In addition to her weakened repressive control over sexual ideation, she has difficulty regulating her emotional response. Her two pure *C* responses and her combination of one *CF* with no *C'*, which indicates color stress, reveal that she is inclined toward volatile affective outbursts and lacks any consistent pattern for integrating her affective experience.

Concerning synthetic capacity, finally, the patient's scores for organizational activity (i.e., her *high W%* of 50 and *high D%* of 55) are well below normal limits and confirm her propensity for maladaptive organizational efforts.

These numerous indications of impaired ego functioning clearly demonstrate schizophrenic disturbance in this woman. Regarding the differential diagnosis for which she was referred, it is significant that whereas a manic-depressive subject might share her evidence of impaired relation to reality and weakened defensive resources, the prominent thought disorder and impaired capacity for social relatedness she displays are not consonant with manic psychosis.

On the other hand, the patient's Rorschach performance does bear out her WAIS indications of a significant affective component in her disturbance. Her very brief reaction times, large number of responses, wide use of determinant and content categories, and frequently shifting associations are consistent with the flights of ideas noted on the WAIS. Such response breadth alone is of course insufficient to identify hypomanic ideational activity. Highly intellectual subjects, in their effort to produce a meaningful document, often approach the Rorschach in an ambitious, deliberate, and studious manner and achieve lengthy, complex records (see for example pp. 294–299). This woman, however, in typical hypomanic fashion, dashed off her 58 responses with little hesitation or reflection, little effort to study the various parts of the cards from different positions, and little interest in attaining meaningful integrations of her responses.

The patient also exhibits flighty ideation in her Rorschach on the many occasions in which she jumps from one thought to another and laces her responses with personal asides. Among relevant examples of such behavior are #1 ("a butterfly or a bird or an owl"), #15 ("snakes, or ducks, or a devil's head"), and #30 ("a totem pole . . . a bug . . . a totem pole"), and her comments that an animal "would frighten me" (#21), that she doesn't like snakes (#22), and that she doesn't believe in mermaids (#42).

Further identifying the affective component in her disturbance are concurrent fantasy images suggesting both concern about and denial of unpleasant thoughts and experiences. A number of her responses reflect depressive trends, with possible guilt feelings, and the projection of hostility onto her environment, with consequent tendencies to perceive external danger and threat. Significant in these regards are her percepts of "fireworks or volcanoes shooting up" (#14), "devil's head" (#15), "eyes looking at you" (#20), "scary head" (#21), "old and ragged" boots (#23), "a bird looking at you" (#35), animal "ready to spring to the attack" (#41), "ghost peering through a keyhole" (#48), and "faces" (#58).

In contrast to these responses, many of her images suggest denial of dysphoric and aggressive concerns and a focus on that which is inno-cent, productive, and happy. Of considerable interest in this connection is her repeated emphasis on feminine fertility, as revealed by references to ovaries (#18), birth canal (#'s 18 & 33), and fertilized eggs (#8) and her two percepts of embryos (#'s 17 & 49). Similarly suggesting denial are her "Snow White" (#3) and "angels' wings" (#5), which pertain to innocence, and her references to candy cane (#12) and the calf "with warm-looking eyes" (#24), which relate to abundance and succor. Finally of note are several percepts in which threats are posed and denied within a single response, such as #44, where the panther is given the head of a mouse, and #48, where the "peering ghost" turns out to be "Caspar, the friendly ghost."

Summary. Throughout her test response this woman displays features of both schizophrenic and affective disturbance. On projective tests she demonstrates disordered thinking, impaired reality testing, poor object relatedness, and unstable defensive resources, which together with evi-dence on her WAIS of maladaptive cognitive focusing and uneven con-cept formation clearly attest overt schizophrenic disturbance. At the same time, her rapid speech and reaction times, expansive ideation, and sudden shifts from enthusiasm and images of peace and contentment to dejection and images of danger and decay disclose a prominent affec-tive component in her condition. The coexistence of these cognitive and affective disturbances indicates that she has a schizo-affective disorder.

► 18

SCHIZOPHRENIA IN ADOLESCENCE

THE differential diagnosis of schizophrenia in a behaviorally disturbed adolescent is a unique and difficult problem, primarily because adolescence is normally an unsettled period during which changing sexual and social demands antiquate previously adaptive response patterns, and successful solutions to the complexities of adult living hover mysteriously beyond the pale. As sensitively depicted by Sullivan (1953, pp. 263–310) and Erikson (1956, pp. 77–102), the adolescent must wrestle simultaneously with his relationship to himself, his parents, and his peers; with his needs to feel secure but also to endanger his security by risking intimate engagement in friendships and heterosexual associations; with responsibilities for demonstrating his capacity for independence and for deciding on his life goals; and with the perplexing task of identifying to himself exactly what kind of person he is—his sex, his interests, his capacities, and his worth.

With the onset of the hormonal changes that usher in puberty, the child of yesterday is thus confronted with myriad uncertainties with which at best he is poorly equipped to deal. Even assuming that previous positive developmental experiences have provided him a reasonably integrated personality structure and some confidence in his ability to meet new challenges, he still must develop frames of reference for interpreting the new experiences his maturation thrusts upon him, and he must learn virtually from scratch a repertoire of techniques for handling problems of sexuality, independence, and career planning.

Normal adolescence is consequently a time of great uncertainty and of urgent quest for knowledge, a time when loose ends are left unraveled and numerous roles are experimentally explored. The adolescent undergoes a several-year hiatus between his integrated child and adult behavior patterns, during which he struggles along with an indefinite view of himself as a person, with rapidly shifting patterns of interests, activities, moods, and passions, and with premature attempts to consolidate some organized conception of his world, typically by highly invested, intensely endorsed, and far-reaching conclusions about the meanings of his experience.

These normal adolescent phenomena can readily conduce to idiosyncratic frames of reference, overgeneralized and circumstantial thinking, a fluid, indefinite sense of body image and boundaries, and strained efforts to control ideation and integrate emotional response. In short, it is apparent that several identifying features of schizophrenic disturbance in adults, including unusual cognitive focusing, impaired reasoning, poor reality sense, and ineffective defensive operations, may accompany adjustment difficulties in adolescents who are by no means approaching a schizophrenic decompensation.

These seemingly pathologic features of normal adolescent development are eloquently described by Anna Freud (1958), who observes that adolescent phenomena "come close to symptom formation of the neurotic, psychotic, or dissocial order and merge almost imperceptibly into borderline states." She continues as follows (pp. 275–276):

I take it that it is normal for an adolescent to behave for a considerable length of time in an inconsistent and unpredictable manner; to fight his impulses and to accept them; to ward them off successfully and be overrun by them; to love his parents and to hate them; to revolt against them and to be dependent on them; to be deeply ashamed to acknowledge his mother before others and, unexpectedly, to desire heart-to-heart talks with her; to thrive on imitation of and identification with others while searching unceasingly for his own identity; to be more idealistic, artistic, generous, and unselfish than he will ever be again, but also the opposite: self-centered, egoistic, calculating. Such fluctuations between extreme opposites would be deemed highly abnormal at any other time of life. At this time they may signify no more than that an adult structure of personality takes a long time to emerge, that the ego of the individual in question does not cease to experiment and is in no hurry to close down on possibilities.

On the other hand, recent studies of normal adolescents by Offer, Sabshin, and Marcus (1965) and Silber, Hamburg, Coelho, Murphey, Rosenberg, and Pearlin (1961) make clear that by no means do such apparently pathologic phenomena inevitably accompany adolescent development. To the contrary, these studies indicate that many young people, though grappling with problems of independence, heterosexuality, and academic and vocational planning, remain able to relate reasonably well to their parents, respond to their experiences with fairly stable affective patterns, and effectively pursue productive goals.

The problem for differential diagnosis is therefore not that normal adolescents resemble schizophrenics, which they do not. Rather, it is that, because of the nature of adolescent processes as described above, even mild adjustment disturbances in this life period may be manifest in schizophrenic-like thinking and behavior. Accordingly, the following sections focus specifically on the distinction between schizophrenic and nonschizophrenic disorder in *behaviorally disturbed* adolescents.

CLINICAL STUDIES OF ADOLESCENT SCHIZOPHRENIA

Although the literature on schizophrenia in adolescence is sparse, the possibility that mildly deviant phenomena during this period of life can be mistaken for schizophrenic disturbance has long been recognized in clinical practice. Among the earliest relevant contributions is a 1929 paper by Kasanin and Kaufman, who describe their careful examination of 21 hospitalized children whose presenting symptoms closely resembled schizophrenic psychoses as observed in adults. Five of these children, three aged 14 and two aged 15, were reclassified by Kasanin and Kaufman as "reactive psychosis," inasmuch as they had experienced a sudden upsurge of deviant behavior following some emotional trauma, had not previously presented evidence of schizophrenia, and subsequently recovered with a long period of stable adjustment.

Although these five reclassified adolescents might by present standards be diagnosed as having suffered an acute schizophrenic reaction, others of the supposedly schizophrenic children whom they studied were reclassified into categories of hysterical and psychopathic disorder. Kasanin and Kaufman also refer to much earlier observations, extending back into the 19th century, that the "tantrums" of children may mimic adult schizophrenia and necessitate careful differential diagnosis.

More recently, Warren and Cameron (1950) have attempted to identify differential diagnostic considerations in adolescents who display apparent schizophrenic disturbance but eventually prove to have been undergoing only transient reactions to specific adolescent crises. They noted in a number of such boys they studied that the onset of distress coincided neatly with the arousal of sexual interests and increasing frequency of erections, whereas in such girls decompensation corresponded closely with the menarche. The bizarre thought content of both the boys and girls they observed was transparently related to such sexual concerns.

Warren and Cameron were also impressed that these adolescent patients, despite their sexual preoccupations, exhibited good affective rapport with others and well-integrated personality functioning. They accordingly concluded from their observations that three factors helping to rule out schizophrenia in behaviorally disturbed adolescents are (a) a relatively transparent, simple connection between intercurrent events and the content of the disturbance, (b) retained capacity for warm interpersonal relatedness, and (c) freedom from personality disintegration.

A number of writers have similarly sought to delineate clinical phenomena that accurately discriminate adjustment reactions from schizophrenia in disturbed adolescents. Neubauer and Steinert (1952) confirmed two of the Warren and Cameron hypotheses in a group of 25 schizophrenic adolescents. They noted that these schizophrenic adolescents, in contrast to the nonschizophrenic youngsters studied by Warren and Cameron, demonstrated major disturbances of affect, particularly as manifest in marked apathy or depression, and considerable personality disorganization, as revealed in inability to plan effectively and disruption of such basic biological rhythms as eating and sleeping.

Warren (1949), assessing clinical and background data in 50 adolescents consecutively admitted to a hospital for "mental breakdown," found that the most significant factor differentiating those of the group who were eventually considered psychotic from those who turned out not to have psychotic disturbance was the degree to which typical adolescent concerns colored the formers' symptoms: the more the adolescent's disturbed thinking, affect, or behavior revolved around adolescent developmental difficulties, the less likely he was to be schizophrenic. Among the particularly adolescent phenomena reflected in the symptomatology of Warren's nonschizophrenic adolescents were increased distance from parents or siblings, increased independence or overdependence, overt or fantasied sexuality or fears thereof, homosexuality, excessive anxiety over menstruation, neglect of personal hygiene or appearance, increased self-consciousness and introspection, and excessive idealism.

Spotnitz (1961), in a review of the difficulties of differentiating schizophrenic from adolescent problems, recommends as an especially reliable index the duration of symptoms. Spotnitz points out that schizophrenic-like adolescent states are by nature transitory, and that when grossly disturbed behavior persists for several weeks or months a diagnosis of schizophrenia rather than adolescent adjustment reaction is usually indicated. Formulating other clues to differential diagnosis, Spotnitz suggests that the disturbed adolescent who responds to frustration by self-directed rather than object-directed aggression and/or who resorts to prominent braggadocio and mendacity to gain admiration and attention is particularly likely to be schizophrenic.

Keiser (1944), who concurs that psychological conflicts in adolescence may produce behavioral disturbances that are differentiated from schizophrenia only by the patient's rapid recovery, describes two other phenomena he has found useful in making the differential diagnosis among adolescent girls. First, he suggests that among girls who claim not to love or be loved by their families, those who express hope that they err in this belief, who recognize evidence that they are mistaken, and display needs and efforts to be loved are relatively unlikely to be schizophrenic; on the other hand, schizophrenia is more likely when such girls exhibit a cold, hard attitude, remain, regardless of contrary evidence, unshakeably convinced that they hate and are hated, and neither express love not attempt to elicit its expression by others.

Second, Keiser observes that the manner in which disturbed adolescent girls avoid, deny, or protest their feminine identity may facilitate differential diagnosis of schizophrenia. He suggests that such protests expressed in the wish to be a boy, in masculine affectations and interests, or even in homosexuality may occur in nonschizophrenic adolescent turmoil. Schizophrenic disturbance is indicated, however, when teenage girls uncompromisingly demand to be allowed to function as men, as if fully expecting they can become men, and thus deny the fact that their sexuality is fixed and immutable.

Finally of interest is a report by Burns (1952) of two behavior patterns that heralded the onset of schizophrenic disturbance in adolescents he observed: withdrawal and hypersensitivity. Concerning withdrawal, Burns suggests that the adolescent who becomes increasingly withdrawn from people into solitary activities, from emotional expression into a blunted affective tone, and from his work into declining performance in school and recreational pursuits may well be approaching a schizophrenic decompensation. With regard to hypersensitivity, he concludes that an increased inability to tolerate the give-and-take of lively peer relationships, especially when so extreme as to result in a school phobia, is an ominous sign for nascent severe psychopathology.

As further summarized by Edelston (1949) and Weiner (1958, pp. 171–172), these and other contributions indicate that the clinical distinction between schizophrenic and nonschizophrenic reactions in disturbed adolescents devolves on two complementary considerations: on one hand, the longer a disturbed adolescent's symptoms persist, the more they pervade his functioning, and the less readily they are explicable, the more likely he is to be schizophrenic; on the other hand, the more an adolescent has retained capacities for social rapport and appropriate affective response, the less personality disintegration he displays, and the more the content of his difficulties is clearly traceable to typical adolescent concerns, the less is the likelihood of schizophrenia.

PSYCHODIAGNOSIS OF ADOLESCENT SCHIZOPHRENIA

Nonschizophrenic adolescents are observed to respond to developmental crises with idiosyncratic frames of references, overgeneralized and circumstantial inferences, indefinite ego boundaries, abstract preoccupations, uncertain body imagery, inconsistent affective patterns, and ready access to consciousness of primitive sexual and aggressive fantasies. It is hence reasonable to expect that nonschizophrenic adolescents may display a number of the various psychodiagnostic indices of inconsistent cognitive focusing, impaired reasoning, uneven concept formation, poor reality sense, inadequate defensive operations, and limited organizational skill (see Chaps. 4, 5, 6, 8, 10, & 12). This possibility, that nonschizophrenic adolescents will manifest in the test battery many personality characteristics associated in adult subjects with schizophrenic disturbance, greatly complicates the psychodiagnosis of schizophrenia in a behaviorally disturbed adolescent.

However, the previously reviewed literature provides two guidelines for this differential diagnosis. First, as elaborated below, the more these test indices of ego impairment pervade an adolescent's battery and the more they defy surface explicability, the greater the likelihood of schizophrenia. Second, inasmuch as neither reality testing nor object relatedness is among those ego functions normally affected by adolescent developmental difficulties, indices of impairment in these areas (see Chaps. 7 & 9) will have similar pathologic implications for adolescents as for adults.

PERVASIVENESS AND INEXPLICABILITY OF DEVIANT RESPONSES

The significance of *pervasiveness* and *inexplicability* of deviant responses for schizophrenia in adolescents involves three diagnostic principles. First, although a nonschizophrenic adolescent may in one or another portion of the test battery display one or another disturbance in thinking, reasoning, reality sense, defensive operations, and synthesis, the greater the number of these disturbances he reveals and the more tests on which they appear, the more likely is the presence of schizophrenic disturbance. Thus, for example, the adolescent who displays some strained reasoning on the WAIS items, *or* some indefinite body boundaries on the DAP, *or* some abstract preoccupations or unusual fantasy on the Rorschach may not be schizophrenic, even though any one of these behaviors would raise the question of schizophrenia in an adult subject; however, the adolescent who evidences impairment in all three of these respects may well be schizophrenic.

Second, although the evidence for several identifying features of schizophrenic disturbance should be interpreted more liberally in adolescent than in adult subjects, it remains the case for adolescents as for adults that the more a subject's thinking, reasoning, self-image, and ideational and affective controls transcend adaptive limits, the more likely he is to be schizophrenically disturbed. Hence, for example, moderately unusual location choice, flighty ideation, and fairly scattered cognitive efficiency may not suggest schizophrenia in an adolescent, but a Rorschach record with 50% *Dd*, instances of gross dissociation, and complete collapse of cognitive efficiency indicates schizophrenia as much in adolescents as in adults. Similarly, whereas instances of clearly incongruous responses and Fabulized Combinations in adolescent Rorschachs may not imply schizophrenia, repetitive Contaminations and blatantly autistic logic do. In other words, although different standards obtain for interpreting certain indices of impaired ego functioning in adolescent and adult protocols, there are still limits of severity for these deviations beyond which they point to schizophrenia even among adolescent subjects.

Third, the less clearly an adolescent's unusual responses reflect typical developmental concerns (i.e., the more they are inexplicable), the more likely he is to be schizophrenically disturbed. Unusual or bizarre responses relating to aggression, sexuality, or relationships to parents, as well as deviant responses to test stimuli that commonly elicit concerns in these areas, fall within the range of nonschizophrenic adolescent phenomena. On the other hand, deviant test responses that arise in what appear to be neutral situations, and/or are proffered by the subject without personal involvement or embellishment, usually have similar pathologic implications for adolescents and adults. This distinction between explicable and inexplicable deviation is clarified further in the case illustrations that follow.

REALITY TESTING AND OBJECT RELATEDNESS

Inasmuch as the capacities for reality testing and object relatedness have not been observed to suffer impairment in the course of normal adolescent development, it follows that test indices of perceptual inaccuracy, poor judgment, limited emphatic capacity, and interpersonal aversion will identify schizophrenic ego impairment similarly for adolescent and adult subjects. Specifically suggesting schizophrenia in adolescent subjects, then, are low $F+\%$, low $R+\%$, and low P on the Rorschach, deficient Comprehension performance on the WAIS, absence of M or H on the Rorschach, and prominent Picture Completion-Block Design discrepancy on the WAIS.

RESEARCH FINDINGS IN THE PSYCHODIAGNOSIS
OF ADOLESCENT SCHIZOPHRENIA

Although the research literature on psychodiagnosis of schizophrenia in adolescence is sparse, available reports generally confirm the expectations derived from clinical observations of adolescent personality processes. That normal adolescents do produce many types of responses consonant with schizophrenia in adult subjects is substantiated in an extensive normative study by Ames, Metraux, and Walker (1959). Among Rorschach responses occurring in 700 records of normal children between the ages of 10 and 16, Ames et al. found considerable numbers of vague, fluid, fabulized, and confabulated percepts, incongruously combined and contaminated images, and violently aggressive specifications (p. 287). They noted that their 16-year-old subjects in particular displayed marked abstract preoccupation and free-associative response elaborations that ranged far afield into past and future circumstances impinging on images, conflict and interaction between forces, symbolic interpretationse of colors and shapes, and even self-referential Fabulizations (pp. 241–246).

The Ames et al. normal adolescents thus clearly exhibited illogical reasoning, abstract preoccupation, vague ego boundaries, and limited repression of aggressive impulses, all of which in adults identify schizophrenic ego impairments. Ames et al. accordingly conclude that these Rorschach indices are not necessarily associated with schizophrenia in adolescents, and they stress that only deviation from *normative adolescent test patterns* provides adequate basis for inferring personality disturbance in adolescent subjects.

Further attesting the presence in normal adolescents' Rorschachs of responses considered deviant for adults are studies by Rychlak and O'Leary (1965) and Silverman, Lapkin, and Rosenbaum (1962). Rychlak and O'Leary collected Rorschach data on 562 11- to 18-year-old boys and girls who represented a cross-section of socioeconomic and geographic backgrounds. They evaluated in their study the frequency of several categories of "unhealthy" content in these normal adolescents' protocols. For one large sample of 13- to 18-year-olds, for example, they assessed responses for the following nine categories of "unhealthy" content: Blood-Guts, Death-Decay, Destructive Tools, Disguise, Fur, Tension-Turbulence, Sex, Smoke-Cloud-Dough-Mud, and Stereotyped Cultural Fears.

In five samples composing their population Rychlak and O'Leary found the mean number of responses to range from 24.05 to 28.26 and the mean percentage of "unhealthy" content responses from 17.21% to 21.92%. Their data thus suggest that 15–20% of a normal adolescent's Rorschach is likely to consist of content usually considered "unhealthy" in the interpretation of adults' records. They also report from their findings that roughly 75% of normal adolescent subjects can be expected to give one or more such "unhealthy" response for every 10 in their records.

Furthermore, Rychlak and O'Leary adduce evidence that even an increasing percentage of these unhealthy contents does not necessarily bode ill for social adjustment. Among their adolescents the percentage of unhealthy content was in fact *significantly* and *positively* related to scores for superego strength and will-power on a personality inventory and to a sociometric index of popularity. Two interesting implications of these findings are that (a) within these categories of "unhealthy" contents even extreme deviation from normal adult standards is not pathologic for adolescents and (b) the total absence of such "unhealthy" content scores in an adolescent subject may actually signify some disturbance. This second implication requires careful cross-validation, but it is conceptually reasonable to hypothesize that if these "unhealthy" contents mirror an adolescent's struggle with normal developmental enigmas, their absence from an adolescent protocol may indicate chronic immaturity or pathologic withdrawal from the activities, interactions, and preoccupations of normal adolescence.

Silverman et al. studied Rorschach performance of 40 11- to 18-year-old adolescents tested in a residential treatment center. Their sample included 20 schizophrenic adolescents and 20 adolescents with neurotic and characterological disorders who matched the schizophrenics in age, intelligence, and sex. Silverman et al. scored these adolescents' Rorschachs according to the Holt manual for primary process thinking (Holt & Havel, 1960), which encompasses many of the indices of thought disorder presented in Chapters 4, 5, and 6 of this book.

Silverman et al. analyzed their data with a *density* scoring, in which the subject's Rorschach score for the formal aspects of primary process thinking was computed as a ratio of the number of primary process scores to the total number of responses. The density scoring differs from the percentage-of-response scoring employed by Rychlak and O'Leary in that, because a single Rorschach response can receive more than one primary process score, the density values represent the percentage among total responses of deviant *scores,* rather than of deviant *responses.* The Silverman et al. *nonschizophrenic* adolescents received a mean density score for formal primary process variables of 43.30; in other words, these nonschizophrenic adolescents averaged a frequency of roughly nine formal primary process scores for every 20 responses they gave. These data further confirm the expectation that nonschizophrenic adolescents may produce many responses that in an adult subject would identify schizophrenic thought disorder.

However, consistent with the hypothesis on page 460 concerning severity of disturbance, Silverman et al. found that extreme deviations in these formal variables do identify schizophrenia even in adolescents. In contrast to the 43.30% mean density score for formal aspects of primary process thinking in their nonschizophrenic adolescents, Silverman et al.'s schizophrenic adolescents had a significantly larger mean density score of 74.15%. This result supports the principle that, although formal indices of thinking disorder should be interpreted more liberally for adolescent than for adult subjects, when pervasive they nevertheless have pathologic implications for adolescents as well as for adults.

On the other hand, affirming the Rychlak and O'Leary report, Silverman et al. found no direct relationship in their subjects between extent of *content* representations of primitive sexual and aggressive impulses and likelihood of schizophrenia. For the Holt content indices of primary process thinking they obtained almost identical mean density scores of 20.45% and 19.50% in the schizophrenic and nonschizophrenic subjects, respectively. Content indices of primitive sexual and aggressive impulses thus appear to occur as frequently in nonschizophrenic as in schizophrenic adolescents and not by themselves to constitute a differential diagnostic index.

Finally, normative data provided by Ames et al. confirm in part the expectation that the variability among nonschizophrenic adolescents does not extend to impairments of reality testing and object relatedness. Of considerable value in evaluating adolescent psychopathology is an Ames et al. table (1959, pp. 26–28) indicating percentile scores on a large number of Rorschach variables for age groups from 10 to 16 years. For two variables related to reality testing, $F+\%$ and P, their table reveals considerable similarity between sexes and across age groups. The $F+\%$ interquartile ranges, representing the twenty-fifth and seventy-fifth percentiles, are the following for the various age groups: age 10, 83–92%; age 11, 86–93%; age 12, 83–93%; age 13, 83–94%; age 14, 85–93%; age 15, 83–94%; and age 16, 82–93%. The interquartile ranges for P are 5–8 for ages 10, 11, 12, and 14, 6–8 for age 13, and 5–7 for ages 15 and 16. These data indicate that adolescents normally display good perceptual accuracy and adequate recognition of conventional modes of response, which confirms that low $F+\%$ and low P have similar implications for pathologically impaired reality testing in adolescent and adult subjects.

The Ames et al. results for M and H justify the same conclusion regarding capacity for interpersonal relationships. Failure to give M falls at the tenth percentile for the Ames et al. adolescents, and, with the exception of 15-year-old boys, in all of the Ames et al. groups fewer than 10% of the subjects avoided H responses entirely. The interquartile ranges for M are 1–4 for age 12 and 1–3 for all other age groups, and for $H\%$ the total group interquartile range is 11–26%. It consequently is indicated to entertain an hypothesis of pathologically deficient empathic capacity for adolescents as for adults when M and H responses fail to appear.

Unfortunately, little work has been done with differential WAIS and DAP indices of adjustment reaction and schizophrenia in adolescence. Of interest, however, is a significant contribution by Machover (1961), who discusses the psychodiagnosis of schizophrenia in adolescents with a representative test battery. Machover concurs with two principles outlined here: (a) that adolescents normally evince in test protocols a number of disturbances related to the vicissitudes of adolescent development, including oedipal concerns, a sense of dissociation between the outer self and inner feelings, sexual tensions, pressures toward disorganized acting out, preoccupation with masturbation and castration anxiety, somatic concerns, and confusion concerning sexual roles and identity; and (b) that the key to identifying schizophrenia in adolescents lies accordingly in the structure and not the content of their thought processes.

Machover additionally suggests that the more alert and the less anxious is an adolescent who presents test evidence of cognitive disruption, the more likely he is to be schizophrenically disturbed; on the other hand, accompanying anxiety, embarrassment, and dissatisfaction rather than blandness mitigate the pathologic significance of an adolescent's disturbed responses. Included in Machover's paper are three case reports of schizophrenic and nonschizophrenic adolescents that are recommended to the reader wishing to review case material in addition to that which follows.

CASE STUDIES [1]

The following two cases illustrate the differential diagnosis between schizophrenia and nonschizophrenic adjustment difficulty in behaviorally disturbed adolescents. The first case is a girl who was seen in connection with family conflicts and rebellious behavior and was not considered schizophrenic; the second is a boy whose dramatic symptomatology and subsequent course were fairly conclusive for schizophrenic disturbance. Both test batteries include many features that are associated with schizophrenic ego impairments in adult but not necessarily in adolescent subjects; however, they also differ from each other in certain crucial respects that determine differential diagnostic judgments.

CASE 1

This patient is a 16-year-old girl whose parents brought her against her wishes for a psychiatric consultation when they were no longer able to tolerate her behavior. The family graphically depicted undeclared adolescent-parent warfare over issues of independence and social mores. The parents were distressed primarily by their daughter's association with known delinquent youths, her at least verbal endorsement of sexual promiscuity, and her recalcitrance to their efforts to legislate her behavior in any way. Their request for help had been precipitated by the patient's threat to commit suicide if they persisted in demanding that she terminate her relationship with a boy she was currently dating and of whom they heartily disapproved.

The patient was tight-lipped and petulant on interview and did not provide a clear picture of the extent to which her actual behavior was deviant. However, because she spoke in a consistently logical and relevant manner, alluded to extensive and apparently gratifying social relationships, and had no history of previous psychological disturbances, a diagnosis of schizophrenia was not entertained. Psychological examination was nevertheless requested to aid in identifying the underlying needs and attitudes that were contributing to her difficulties with her parents and to assess the nature of her behavioral controls, particularly in regard to whether she was a suicidal risk.

WECHSLER ADULT INTELLIGENCE SCALE

Information

RUBBER: +. PRESIDENTS: +. LONGFELLOW: +. WEEKS: +. PANAMA: +. BRAZIL: +. HEIGHT: +. ITALY: +. CLOTHES: +. WASHINGTON: In Febru-

---

[1] The format followed in presenting the case studies is described in pages 254–257.

ary, I don't know the date. HAMLET: +. VATICAN: +. PARIS: dk. EGYPT: +. YEAST: The cells multiply. POPULATION: I'm not sure (*Estimate?*) 24 billion? I don't know. SENATORS: +. GENESIS: +. TEMPERATURE: 112°? I don't know. ILIAD: +. BLOOD VESSELS: Red corpuscles, white corpuscles, and—I don't know. KORAN: A holy book, of the Hindus. FAUST: Oh, I studied that; some old English guy. ETHNOLOGY: dk. APOCRYPHA: dk. RAW SCORE: 19.

The patient's Information responses are somewhat scattered, with her errors on PARIS and POPULATION contrasting with her success on much more difficult, factorially related items as EGYPT in the first case and SENATORS, GENESIS, and ILIAD in the second. Otherwise there is no suggestion of personality disorder here.

Comprehension

ENVELOPE: Mail it (2). BAD COMPANY: It wouldn't be a good idea; it would hurt my reputation (1). MOVIES: Get an usher and tell him (2). TAXES: To support the government (2). IRON: Do something while you've got the ambition and feel like doing it. (1). CHILD LABOR: To keep children from working too hard and hurting themselves (1). FOREST: Look at the sun and follow that direction (2). DEAF: You learn to talk by copying what you hear other people say (2). CITY LAND: It's more scarce (1). MARRIAGE: To make sure you're not married already? I don't know [giggles] (1). BROOKS: Stupid people talk a lot (2). SWALLOW: You can have one good thing go wrong, but that doesn't mean everything will (1). RAW SCORE: 22.

As on Information, there is little here to suggest impaired ego functioning. It is of interest to note, however, that the patient's personal association to her own reputation on BAD COMPANY and her giggling on MARRIAGE are probably related to typical adolescent concerns about social impressions and sexual activity and thus reflect her involvement with such concerns.

Similarities

ORANGE: Grown in tropical climates (1). COAT: Clothing (2). AXE: Tools (2). DOG: Animals (2). NORTH: Directions (2). EYE: Senses (2). AIR: Matter (0). TABLE: Furniture (2). EGG: Basic elements in forming something else (1). POEM: Work of an artist (2). WOOD: Come from trees (0). PRAISE: Expressions of some emotions (1). FLY: dk. RAW SCORE: 17.

As on the previous subtests, the patient responds in a relevant and efficient manner, with the exception of her somewhat concrete answer on ORANGE. Although in contrast to this answer her response of "matter" on AIR is overly general, there is no other evidence on this subtest to suggest uneven concept formation.

Digit Symbol

RAW SCORE: 68.

Picture Completion

KNOB: +. TAIL: +. NOSE: +. HANDLES: +. DIAMOND: I don't know anything about cards. WATER: +. NOSE PIECE: +. PEG: A string. OAR LOCK: +. BASE THREAD: Filament. STARS: +. DOG TRACKS: Part of his leg. FLORIDA: dk. STACKS: The top part of the ship. LEG: +. ARM IMAGE: Her arm. FINGER: +. SHADOW: I can't see his hand, but I don't know if that's it. STIRRUP: Saddle horn. SNOW: Part of the fence. EYEBROW: Can't see anything. RAW SCORE: 10.

On this subtest the patient displays moderate scatter within factorial item groups, passing LEG after failing DOG TRACKS, OAR LOCK after missing PEG, and FINGER after erring on BASE THREAD and STACKS. All of her errors, however, are of types that occur commonly in normal as well as patient groups.

Block Design

ITEM 1: 6" (4). ITEM 2: 8" (4). ITEM 3: 8" (4). ITEM 4: 8" (4). ITEM 5: 10" (4). ITEM 6: 14" (4). ITEM 7: 29" (6). ITEM 8: 95" (4). ITEM 9: 119" (4). ITEM 10: 135" (0). RAW SCORE: 38.

Picture Arrangement

NEST: 3" (4). HOUSE: 3" (4). HOLD UP: 6" (4). LOUIE: 50" (4). ENTER: 35" (4). FLIRT: 30" (4). FISH: 60" (4). TAXI: AMLUES, 60" (0). RAW SCORE: 28.

Scale Scores

Information: 12. Comprehension: 14. Similarities: 12. Digit Symbol: 13. Picture Completion: 8. Block Design: 11. Picture Arrangement: 12.

The patient's low Picture Completion in relation to her performance on the other perceptual and manipulative subtests constitutes some intertest scatter, but her scale scores do not otherwise raise concern about her ego functioning. Her Block Design-Picture Completion discrepancy might suggest relative cognitive ineptness in interpersonal as opposed to impersonal situations, but her well-retained Picture Arrangement score tends to offset this possible index of interpersonal aversion and her relatively high Comprehension score reflects good capacity for realistic social judgments.

Discussion. Aside from this girl's scatter within and between subtests there is little evidence of personality disturbance in her WAIS protocol. Her inconsistency can be readily interpreted within the framework of normal adolescent variability, and she displays no other ego impairments here that might suggest schizophrenia.

DRAW-A-PERSON

The patient's figure drawings are presented in Figures 30 and 31. The drawings are somewhat sketchy and it is possible to see in them many points at which the body lines are incompletely or inaccurately drawn. The sketchiness and lack of detail in her drawings suggest indefinite ego boundaries and concerns about her body functions, both of which are frequently associated in adults with a schizophrenic impairment of reality sense but correspond closely to normal adolescent concerns about identity and body image. Furthermore, her drawings in spite of their sketchiness depict the human form without any gross distortions and include such sexually differentiating details as the hair, narrow waist, and skirt indicated for the woman.

RORSCHACH

Card I 5″

1. (*Wm F+ A P*) The whole form looks like an eagle. (?) The wings are on the sides and the body in the center.

2. (*Dm F+ Hd,Cg Incongruous-tendency, Barrier*) In here [center detail] it looks like a fat lady, with two heads instead of one [laughs]; I see two hands up at the top and the legs and feet down here; but I don't really see heads, just these two bumps up here. (?) I see the hands and the legs, but there is no head there; a lady without a head, but the body looks like a fat lady. (*Fat?*) Well, it looks almost as if—wait, it could be a short lady with just a big skirt on, like she could have a good figure in here.

Card II 12″

3. (*Dm F+ Hd*) ∨ These look like feet [upper red]. (*Feet of?*) A person. (*Kind of person?*) A boy; they're kind of big. (*Big?*) They look thick and wide.

4. (*D— F— Ad*) ∨ The head of an animal, of a lizard or something [upper center detail]. (?) It looks like a mouth there and eyes.

4a. (*D— FM— A Fabulized*) ∨ And maybe the whole black thing could be a bird, like it was coming down on a person; I hate birds, can't stand them. (*Bird?*) These look like wings, and it looks big and mean.

5. (*Wv CF,mF,C′F Expl*) ∨ It looks sort of like an explosion, I guess. (?) It's the black, that looks like smoke, and exploding into fire. (*Fire?*) The orange suggest it.

Figure 30

469

Figure 31

Card III 5″

6. (*D+ M+ H P Fabulized*) It looks like two people, each one cooking something over the same fire. (*Describe people?*) They look like they have low mentality. (?) The way their nose or jaw protrudes. (*Men or women?*) Women, I think. (?) Uh—the way their head looks, and—uh—they have a chest on them.

7. (*D— FC— At Fabulized, Fabulized Combination, Penetration*) This sounds far-fetched—maybe they're mean people who have no hearts and these [center red] are their hearts outside of them (*Hearts?*) Because of the color and shape of them.

8. (*Da Csymb Ab,Bl Fabulized Combination*) They could be cannibals, and they have blood on their minds, represented by these [outer red]. (?) The redness.

Card IV 6″

9. (*Dm F+ A*) This part looks like a caterpillar [lower center detail]. (?) The way the head of it looks, and the spikes that stick out of it are like a caterpillar.

10. (*W— F— A Perseveration*) It looks like wings on it again, like a bird.

Card V 1″

11. (*Wm F+ A P*) It looks like a bat; that's all I can think of, just a bat. (?) It's got wings, feet, and a head, and it looks just like those crummy bats look.

Card VI 5″

12. (*Dm F+ A Incongruous-tendency*) Up here it looks like some kind of animal, maybe a mouse—with wings on it [upper portion]; I don't see anything else. (?) It just looks like a mouse, but it has wings on it, everything has wings. (*Mouse with wings?*) I guess it would be better as a bird. (*Rest look like?*) Nothing, it just looks like a blob of ink; there's something down here at the bottom, but it doesn't remind me of anything.

Card VII 7″

13. (*D+ F+,mF Ar,Smoke Fabulized, Autistic Logic*) It looks like a factory with smoke coming out of it right here [factory is bottom center detail; smoke is darker central area just above factory]. (*Factory?*) This part just looks like a factory. (*Smoke?*) It's just coming out of the roof; what else would come out of the roof of a factory?

14. (*Dm F+ A*) > Looking at it this way these look like lions [upper two-thirds]. (?) It just looks like some animal with a big head.

14a. (*D M+ (H),Ar Fabulized Combination*) Also, that factory part could be a haunted house with a witch crawling out of the ceiling.

Card VIII 8″

15. (*Dm F+ A P-tendency*) Looks like two raccoons or something on the side; nothing else. (*Rest look like?*) I don't know; it's just spots of yellow and pink and blue and gray.

Card IX 15″

16. (*Da Csymb,mF Ab,Fire Fabulized Combination*) I don't really see anything; maybe just something falling into a fire, with the red standing for fire. (*Something?*) I don't know what; the main thing about it is the red, the fire, on the bottom, (*What falling?*) I don't know; maybe the green part, that's the biggest. (*Green look like anything?*) No.

Card X 4″

17–18. (*Wm F+ A; Dm F+ A P*) It looks like a lot of insects [upper gray, bottom green, outer brown and yellow] and a couple spiders.

19. (*D++ FC+,Fm At*) This looks like red corpuscles floating around in lymph or something [inner yellow]. (?) It looks like a laboratory picture of the red corpuscles.

Scores

R	19+2	M	1+1	H	1	F+%	83%
W	5(26%)	FM	0+1	(H)	0+1	R+%	80%
D	14(74%)	m	0+4	Hd	2	P	4+1
		F	13	A	9+1		
		C′	0+1	Ad	1	High W%	60%
Fabulized	3+1	FC	2	At	2	High D%	71%
Fabulized		CF	1	Ab	2		
Combination	3+1	C	2	Ar	1	Barrier	1
Incongruous-				Expl	1	Penetration	1
tendency	2			Fire	0+1		
Perseveration 1				Bl	0+1		
Autistic Logic 1				Cg	0+1		

Discussion. Though not markedly deviant in any respect, this girl's Rorschach contains indications of thought disorder and inconsistent defenses that in an adult subject would suggest at least mild schizophrenic ego impairment. In relation to disordered thinking, she perseverates the concept of bird from response #1 to #10, and she fabulizes her percepts with specific characteristics in three instances and inappropriate combinations on three other occasions. Particularly deviant by adult standards are her strained integration of people "with hearts outside of them" and "blood on their minds" in #'s 6, 7, and 8 and her circumstantiality on #13, where she sees "smoke" because, "What else would come out of the roof of a factory?" Further suggesting disordered thinking are her *Ab* responses on #'s 8 and 16, in which she displays more concern with the symbolic than the actual meaning of her experience.

Concerning defensive inadequacy, the patient's two *Csymb* responses and her combination of two *FC* and one *CF* with no *C'* responses, which constitutes color stress, suggest she has difficulty integrating her emotional experiences and lacks any consistent pattern of affective expression.

On the other hand, several other aspects of her Rorschach indicate that her thinking and defensive impairments are probably not associated with schizophrenia. First, her reality testing ($F+\%$ of 83, $R+\%$ of 80, and P of 4) is within normal limits. Second, her attention to interpersonal concerns (one main and one additional M) is adequate, particularly in view of the fact that her failure to give more than a single M response seems at least partly attributable to an apparently crystallizing repressive defensive style. Repressive orientation is reflected in her affinity for color (*Sum C* is 5.0), her labile personal expressions ("I hate birds" on #4a; "crummy bats" on #11), and the frequency with which she unreflectively accounts for many of her percepts with such phrases as "just looks like it."

Third, her fantasy points to considerable involvement in normal adolescent concerns. A generally high level of inner turmoil is disclosed by her four *m* determinants and contents like "explosion" on #5, and specific anxieties about approaching adult sexuality are mirrored in her attention to the woman's figure on #2 and her embarrassment in describing female anatomy on #6. There is thus ample basis for attributing her difficulties in thinking and defensive operations to the ferment and inconsistency characteristic of nonschizophrenic adolescent crises. This fact, together with her unimpaired reality testing and interpersonal interests, militates against the likelihood of schizophrenic disturbance.

Summary. This adolescent girl displays a somewhat scattered and inconsistent WAIS performance, a poor sense of body boundaries on the DAP, and Rorschach manifestations of impaired reasoning, abstract preoccupation, and inconsistent defensive resources. At the same time, however, she evidences normal adolescent concerns to which most of these disturbances can be attributed, and she demonstrates no impairment of reality testing or of capacity for adaptive interpersonal relationships. In view of the circumscribed and explicable nature of the disturbance present in her protocols, there is little basis for considering her schizophrenic.

CASE 2

This patient is a 16-year-old boy who already had a long history of psychological contact by the time he was seen on this occasion. At the age of nine he had been brought by his parents to a child-guidance clinic for advice concerning his immaturity, unhappiness, and withdrawal from peers. Although family treatment was recommended at that time, neither the boy's father, a cold, rigid, authoritarian professional man, nor his mother, a dependent woman who relied on her son for an emotional closeness she felt lacking in her marriage, considered his problems serious enough to warrant pursuing the matter further.

Four years later the father again visited the agency to discuss transferring his son from parochial to public school, and again the agency strongly recommended treatment. At this time they noted that the boy was markedly suspicious, had few friends, engaged in a number of compulsive rituals, and had violent temper outbursts. The parents continued to resist the agency's advice, however, maintaining that the boy was just "cussed" and "ornery." Finally, when the patient was 16, his school authorities became concerned about changes in his behavior and insisted the parents take action. He had abruptly replaced his previous withdrawal with intense efforts to relate socially with his peers, efforts that had proved painfully frustrating and unsuccessful, and he had additionally begun to manifest unusual posturing and a rigid gait and to write bizarre and disorganized compositions.

On initial interview the patient complained of people not liking him and described a number of compulsive rituals that governed much of his activity. Although he spoke in an orderly and coherent manner, his history and the school report suggested schizophrenic disturbance, and psychological consultation was requested to clarify his diagnosis. Supportive psychotherapy was instituted following the testing, but over the next three months the patient's condition continued to decline. He developed blatant ideas of reference, including the conviction that his fellow students were laughing at and talking about him, and he received failing grades in all his courses.

The patient was subsequently hospitalized in the psychiatric unit of a general hospital, where for one month he displayed unabated paranoid ideation, autistic orientation, and ritualistic behavior. He was then transferred to a nearby state hospital, where he remained an additional two months before being discharged. In the four-year period between his discharge and this writing, he has been rehospitalized twice and has been for all but a few months of the time under either clinic or inpatient psychiatric care. His diagnosis throughout all of these clinic and hospital contacts has been paranoid schizophrenia.

WECHSLER ADULT INTELLIGENCE SCALE

Information

RUBBER: +. PRESIDENTS: +. LONGFELLOW: +. WEEKS: +. PANAMA: +. BRAZIL: +. HEIGHT: +. ITALY: +. CLOTHES: Light colors are more porous, let in more air. WASHINGTON: He died in 1799, was born in the middle of the year, 1732. (*Date?*) dk. HAMLET: +. VATICAN: +. PARIS: 5,000 miles. EGYPT: Middle East. (*Continent?*) Europe. YEAST: +. POPULATION: 250 million. SENATORS: +. GENESIS: Can't place it. TEMPERATURE: +. ILIAD: +. BLOOD VESSELS: The small intestine, the big intestine, and there's a lot of arteries around the heart. KORAN: +. FAUST: It's poetry; I'll say Hemingway. ETHNOLOGY: dk. APOCRYPHA: dk. RAW SCORE: 19.

The patient's Information response is marred by extreme scatter and a number of unusual and irrelevant responses. Contrary to order of difficulty within factorially related items, he passes TEMPERATURE, ILIAD, and KORAN after failing POPULATION and GENESIS, passes YEAST and TEMPERATURE after missing CLOTHES, and passes SENATORS after erring on WASHINGTON.

Even this extent of inconsistency might be consonant with non-schizophrenic adolescent variability, but the patient's unrealistic, idiosyncratic responses to CLOTHES, WASHINGTON, and BLOOD VESSELS raise serious question about the adequacy of his cognitive functioning. In inaccurately stating on CLOTHES that light-colored clothing is cool because it is porous, he illogically implies a necessary relationship between the color and porosity of a fabric; he irrelevantly gives the years of Washington's birth and death when asked for his birthday and then is unable even closely to approximate the date; and he peculiarly includes the intestines in his effort to name blood vessels.

Comprehension

ENVELOPE: Locate the owner; if I couldn't locate him I'd put it in the lost and found (1). BAD COMPANY: They're a bad influence; the company you keep is what you are (2). MOVIES: I'd go to the phone and call the fire department (1). TAXES: People have no choice, they have to pay taxes; they help the government to pay for things (2). IRON: Do it right now, before it's too late (2). CHILD LABOR: Kids should be in school, they're too young to work (1.) FOREST: Get to a clearing and send up a signal; it's really safer to tell someone where you're going to be and how long you'll be gone (0). DEAF: It affects the speech system somehow; they can't comprehend words because they can't hear them (1). CITY LAND: It's more populated and there isn't as much of it (2). MARRIAGE: To have proof of marriage (1). BROOKS: People sometimes make a lot of noise with no reason for it (1). SWALLOW: You should have more of what you started out to do (0). RAW SCORE: 18.

Most significant here is this boy's poor performance on all three of the "What would you do . . ." items (ENVELOPE, MOVIES, and FOREST). He would put an addressed envelope "in the lost and found," "call the fire department" on seeing smoke and fire in a theater, and "send up a signal" if lost in the forest. His poor judgment on these items suggests poor reality testing capacity, which is as significant in adolescents as in adults for schizophrenic ego impairment. Also of note on FOREST is his tangential association to the importance of keeping others informed of one's whereabouts, which like some of his Information answers is loosely related to the point of the question and suggests some dissociation.

Similarities

ORANGE: Fruits (2). COAT: They cover the body (1). AXE: Both can cut (1). DOG: Their physical structure is alike, and both can bark, too (1). NORTH: Points of direction (2). EYE: Two of the five senses that we have (2). AIR: We learned in science that we live in an ocean of air, and there's water in air (0). TABLE: Furniture (2). EGG: They go through a maturing process and develop through time into a finished product (1). POEM: I can't see any way they're alike (0). WOOD: I don't see any relationship between them (0). PRAISE: If you do something right you get praise, and if you do something wrong you get punishment; either way, you wind up wishing you hadn't done it (0). FLY: There's no relationship (0). RAW SCORE: 12.

The patient demonstrates some uneven concept formation here, with narrow categorizations on COAT ("cover the body"), AXE ("cut"), and DOG ("bark") and an overly inclusive categorization on EGG ("develop through time into a finished product"). However, more significant for thought disorder than his variable abstracting are his blatantly circumstantial reasoning on AIR, where he apparently concludes that *air* and *water* are alike in that both occur in oceanic form, and his irrelevant conclusion on PRAISE, "Either way, you wind up wishing that you hadn't done it," which bears little logical relationship to his previous statement. These responses identify an extent of disordered thinking beyond what usually can be attributed to nonschizophrenic adolescent phenomena.

Picture Completion

KNOB: +. TAIL: Nothing. NOSE: +. HANDLES: The other wheels. DIAMOND: The two little diamonds shouldn't be there. WATER: Someone holding it. NOSE PIECE: Shoulders. PEG: Bow. OAR LOCK: A person. BASE THREAD: Something in the top. STARS: +. DOG TRACKS: +. FLORIDA: Labels. STACKS: Nothing. LEG: Scales. ARM IMAGE: The woman's legs. Subtest discontinued. RAW SCORE: 4.

The patient reveals strikingly idiosyncratic frames of reference on this subtest, failing in all but four instances to focus his attention on the obvious and most relevant omissions in the pictures. His errors on even very easy items and his particularly unusual and uncommon answers on DIAMOND, NOSE PIECE, LEG, and ARM IMAGE suggest deviant cognitive focusing beyond the limits of nonschizophrenic adolescent idiosyncracy. The final five items of the subtest might have yielded additional unusual interpretations, but in view of the patient's persistently ineffective performance the subtest was discontinued after ARM IMAGE.

Block Design

ITEM 1: 10" (4). ITEM 2: 18" (4). ITEM 3: 14" (4). ITEM 4: 17" (4). ITEM 5: 25" (4). ITEM 6: Correct beyond time limit. ITEM 7: 80" (4). ITEMS 8 and 9: No progress toward solution. RAW SCORE: 24.

After executing the first five designs with relative ease, the patient encountered some difficulty with ITEM 6 and after 40 seconds flatly stated, "It can't be done." Encouraged to persevere, he declined saying, "There's no way to do it." After succeeding on ITEM 7, he approached ITEM 8 and ITEM 9 in an ineffectual and disorganized manner, at times stringing four and five blocks in a row, and he made no progress toward solving them in several minutes' time.

Scale Scores

Information: 12. Comprehension: 10. Similarities: 9. Picture Completion: 4. Block Design: 7.

Discussion. In his irrelevant and idiosyncratic associations, strained reasoning, uneven concept formation, and scattered performance, this boy displays several personality characteristics that, although significant for disturbed thinking in adults, often fall within the range of normal adolescent behavior. However, the *extent* to which he displays these various phenomena suggest disturbance beyond what could be attributed to adolescent developmental difficulties alone. Further indicating serious personality disturbance are his poor judgments on Comprehension, which suggest impaired reality testing and have equally serious implications for adolescent as for adult subjects.

It should also be noted that several of his comments reflect the needs for protection and externalization of blame that often accompany paranoid trends (see Chap. 14). Significant here are his denials of similarities and missing parts on Similarities and Picture Completion, respectively, and his insistence that a block design was insoluble.

DRAW-A-PERSON

Only one figure drawing was available for this boy, and it appears in Figure 32. A second drawing was not obtained because of the inordinate length of time he spent on this figure, working with total absorption for almost 20 minutes and appearing completely oblivious of the examiner's presence. The drawing is free from gross indices of impaired reality sense. His figure is complete in major body parts, adequately differentiated with regard to sex, and firmly connected at all boundary points. The somewhat unusual space indicated in the neck he identified as "an adam's apple." Although he therefore does not manifest indefinite ego boundaries or distorted body imagery here, his drawing does have some implications for the paranoid orientation tentatively suggested by his WAIS performance. The heavy lines, picayune detailing, unusual eye emphasis, and broad shoulders of his figure suggest several identifying characteristics of paranoid tendencies, including needs to emphasize autonomy and body integrity, a focus on strength and resoluteness (note the clenched fists), and a concern with scrutinizing and/or being scrutinized by the environment.

RORSCHACH

Card I 5″

1. (*Wv,S F+ Na Fabulized, Barrier*) ∨ A rock formation. (?) It looks like rock, with hollow spaces between it, like man created it; nature formed it that way, but man must have made it hollow. (?) Mainly the jagged shape of it.

2. (*Dr,S F— Obj*) ∨ Something like a pumpkin [large, indistinct area, excluding most of outer projections]. (?) Because of the triangular shape of the eyes, and the nose.

3. (*Wm,S F+,Fc Ad Fabulized, Peculiar, Barrier*) An India cat, cheetah, or tiger, something fierce [turns card over and reads back; does so on each subsequent card]. (?) I see the ears, the mouth, and

Figure 32

the tongue, just the head, and it might be fur out here. (*Fierce?*) The way the eyes look.

Card II 5″

4. (*W—,S F— At Peculiar, Penetration*) ∨ Parts of the body—the hipbone, the structured part around the legs, the rib cage, the abdominable cavity, and the lungs; that's it, a diagram from here [points to his neck] to here [points to his knee]. (*?*) These are the lungs [lower red], this is the rib cage [entire black portion], this is the hipbone [upper red], and the center space is the abdominable cavity. (*?*) It's just the shape of it, that's like a sketch from the crotch to the neck.

4a. (*Dv,S F± Na Barrier*) ∨ And the black could be two pillars of rock, with trees and bushes at the top and a gorge between them.

Card III 2″

5. (*D+ M+ H P*) Maybe two people dancing, it sure looks like it; meeting each other or dancing. (*?*) I just know I wouldn't want to meet anyone that way. (*?*) The way they're standing up, sort of weird. (*Sex?*) I can't tell, but they look about the same.

6. (*Dm F+ At Penetration*) ∨ The rib cage [bottom center detail]. (*?*) Just the structure of it.

6a. (*Dv cF Obj Barrier*) ∨ And this looks like fur on either side of the rib cage, but not connected with it.

Card IV 3″

7. (*Wm FM+ A*) ∨ It looks like a bat, like you see in caves; a head, and great big wings spread out.

8. (*W— F— A Autistic Logic*) Holding it this way, it's like under a microscope, an enlarged fly. (*?*) I can't explain just why. (*Enlarged?*) It's just that it fills most of the card.

8a. (*W++ FM+ A,Cg*) It also could be a huge ape walking towards a tree or something; there are shoes there, but of course an ape wouldn't have shoes.

Card V 8″

9. (*Wm FM+ A P*) Another insect; it looks like a bat with its wings spread out. (*?*) It looks like it's flying.

10. (*Wv F± Na*) And it also looks like a rock formation.

Card VI 6″

11. (*Wm F+ A Autistic Logic*) Another insect again, under a microscope; I don't know what kind of insect. (*Microscope?*) It's just because of the size of it again.

12. (*Dm F+,Fc Aobj P-tendency*) An animal rug out on the floor, like a bear rug. (*?*) Just the shape of it, with the arms out here.

Card VII 2″

13. (*W+ M+ Hd Fabulized*) It looks like two women saying good-bye to each other [laughs]—I'd better not say it. (*Encouragement*) Well, like in dances, they're—uh—well, they're bumping each other. (*Where?*) That's the part I'd better not say. It's this part of the body [rubs buttocks], and you see all of them except their legs.

14. (*Wv F± Na*) A weird rock formation, with pillars of rock.

15. (*W—,S F— At Perseveration, Penetration*) ∨ A diagram of the chest cavity, showing the bone structure.

15a. (*Wm F+ H,Cg Barrier*) ∨ It also looks like two show girls, wearing ornamental hats.

Card VIII 6″

16. (*Wm F+ At Penetration*) ∨ The chest cavity, showing the lungs and ribs. (?) The lungs are here [orange and pink], the rib cage is the middle part, and the pelvis is down here [gray detail].

17. (*Dm FM+ A P*) A couple of animals, bears, climbing up something.

Card IX 9″

18. (*W— F— At Perseveration, Penetration*) ∨ The chest cavity. (?) It's the inner part of the upper part of the body; the rib cage is here [green], the lungs here [red], and the spinal cord and hipbone are here [upper center and orange].

Card X

19. (*D— F— At Perseveration, Penetration*) It looks like the same thing again, the top part [upper gray] is the rib cage, with the neck muscles and the trachea in the middle, and the red part might be the legs.

20. (*Dm F+ A P*) And the blue spots might be a spider or something.

Scores

R	20+4	M	2	H	1+1	F+%	50%
W	13+2(65%)	FM	2+2	Hd	1	R+%	65%
D	6+2(30%)	F	16+2	A	6+1	P	4+1
Dd+S 1+6(5%)		Fc	0+2	Ad	1		
		c	0+1	At	6	High W%	46%
				Na	3+1	High D%	83%
Fabulized	3			Obj	1+1		
Perseveration	3			Aobj	1	Barrier	2
Peculiar	2			Cg	0+2	Penetration	6
Autistic Logic	2						

Discussion. This boy, like the nonschizophrenic girl presented in pages 468–473, displays in his Rorschach a number of ego disturbances that are associated with schizophrenia in adults but are not necessarily pathologic in adolescent subjects. He reveals idiosyncratic and inconsistent cognitive focusing, with unusual location choice (W% of 65, D% of 30), three perseverations (#'s 15, 18, & 19, all involving anatomy), and peculiar language (*"India* cat" in #3, *"abdominable* cavity" in #4); he exhibits circumstantial reasoning in two instances of autistic logic (#'s 8 & 11) in which he interprets his percepts as "enlarged" because the blots fill most of the cards; and, in contrast to the emphasis on body integrity in his figure drawing, he discloses here in his frequent vague responses, six Penetration scores, and many and perseverative anatomy contents that he suffers an uncertain sense of body boundaries and preoccupation with the nature and security of his body and its functions.

These several disturbances are no more striking in this boy's Rorschach than in the record of the previous nonschizophrenic girl. However, he additionally demonstrates reality testing impairments that did not mar her performance and are ominous for schizophrenia. His perceptual accuracy is well below normal limits ($F+\%$ of 50, $R+\%$ of 65) and confirms the implication of his poor judgment on WAIS Comprehension for reality testing deficiencies that cannot be attributed solely to adolescent developmental difficulties.

Also differentiating his Rorschach from that of the previous patient is the manner in which he approached the task. Consistent with his self-absorption on the DAP, he delivered his Rorschach responses in a flat, uninflected voice and seldom engaged the examiner in eye contact or direct discussion. Moreover, he remained affectively bland throughout the test without in any way overtly reacting to the content of his imagery. This apathy and uncritical acceptance of associations, in contrast to the previous girl's lively affective behavior in relation to the examiner and to her test productions, enhances the likelihood that he is schizophrenically disturbed.

Finally, the patient corroborates in his Rorschach the paranoid tendencies suggested by his WAIS and DAP performance. His six additional *S* locations and his reversals of Cards I, II, IV, and IX immediately on having them handed to him reflect exaggerated emphasis on asserting autonomy and resisting external influence. Second, his reading the backs of the cards and several questions he raised about the purpose of an intercom box on the examiner's desk (e.g., "I sure hope it's not on so people can listen in") point to a cautious, suspicious orientation to his experience. Third, such percepts as the "fierce eyes" on #3 and the "weird" people whom "I wouldn't want to meet" on #5 indicate concerns about the scrutiny and motivations of persons in his world.

Summary. This boy exhibits on his WAIS and Rorschach a number of personality characteristics that identify schizophrenic disturbance in adults but frequently occur within the context of nonschizophrenic adolescent phenomena, including scattered and inconsistent cognitive focusing, strained and circumstantial reasoning, uneven concept formation, and uncertain reality sense. However, the following additional features of his test response indicate disturbance beyond the limits of nonschizophrenic adolescent variability: (a) evidence of impaired reality testing, with poor judgment and inaccurate perceptions; (b) the fact that disordered thinking pervades his test battery, intruding on his performance even on the relatively structured WAIS items; and (c) a persistent affective blandness, uncritical acceptance, and self-absorption that characterized his test behavior. Complementing these indications of schizophrenic disturbance is a degree of concern about autonomy and safety and of reliance on projective defense that is consistent with paranoid tendencies.

PART FOUR

 CONCLUSION

► 19

SCIENTIFIC AND PROFESSIONAL ISSUES
IN PSYCHODIAGNOSIS

THIS concluding chapter concerns the relationship of psychodiagnostic practice to the psychologist's roles as scientist and professional, with particular reference to the reliability and validity of what he does and the status and rewards he realizes in doing it. Many of psychology's most informed and imaginative writers have addressed themselves to these issues, and psychodiagnosis has in the course of these discussions reaped full measures of attack and defense, abuse and praise, and, on occasion, unmitigated scorn and undying allegiance. The following sections outline several foci of such debate and briefly review extant psychometric and professional bases for employing psychodiagnostic techniques.

RELIABILITY OF PSYCHODIAGNOSTIC TESTS

A basic scientific requirement of measuring instruments is that they measure reliably. Some psychologists take exception to this premise, arguing that reliability considerations are irrelevant or inappropriate to the evaluation of clinical techniques (see Holzberg, 1960, pp. 361–362). The standard definitions of test reliability challenge the tenability of such a position, however. According to Cronbach (1949a, p. 59), for example, a reliability coefficient expresses "the accuracy of measurement." Gulliksen (1950, p. 22) defines the index of reliability as the correlation of true and observed scores. Viewed from these definitions, disavowal of reliability concerns in psychodiagnostic testing is equivalent to disregard for whether the tests accurately measure personality functioning, that is, whether they yield scores that closely approximate the subject's "true" scores. Disregard for accuracy is not easily reconcilable with usual scientific aims.

Its consequent importance notwithstanding, however, reliability has proved an elusive concept in psychodiagnostic research, with neither the nature of personality functioning nor the psychometric structure of the clinical test battery lending itself well to traditional methods of reliability study. Nevertheless, there are, as summarized below, data attesting both the *intrinsic reliability* and *interjudge agreement* attainable with the psychodiagnostic techniques discussed in this book.

INTRINSIC RELIABILITY

It follows from the definition of reliability as the correspondence between true and obtained scores that a measure is reliable to the extent it (a) remains constant when the phenomenon being measured can be assumed to have remained constant and (b) changes when there is good reason to believe that the true score has changed. This operational definition of intrinsic reliability is particularly relevant to the psychodiagnostic situation, in which stability and change are central concerns, and there is evidence to suggest that psychodiagnostic tests have considerable potential for satisfying this reliability criterion.

The fullest psychodiagnostic study of personality stability and change is reported by Harrower (1958), who administered the WAIS, DAP, Rorschach, and four other tests to a large number of patients on two separate occasions. Employing rating scales to derive a single adjustment-level score for her patients, Harrower observed the course of their measured adjustment over short and long retest intervals, during brief and intensive psychotherapy, and following positive and negative environmental events. Although aspects of Harrower's rating methodology and data treatment are subject to criticism (see Singer, 1960), her results impressively demonstrate (a) little change in adjustment score where little change in "true" adjustment would be expected and (b) increasing change as there was increasingly good reason to expect change to have occurred.

Specifically, Harrower observed virtually no change in adjustment score among patients retested after a 30-day interval during which no significant environmental event had transpired and among patients who had undergone brief psychotherapy and been rated by their therapists as unimproved. She found moderate gains in adjustment score among patients retested after one uneventful year and among patients who were considered by their therapists to have benefited from brief psychotherapy. She noted marked adjustment-score gains in patients undergoing intensive psychotherapy or who had experienced a definitely positive environmental change. And, finally, she discovered marked losses in patients who were referred for retesting at a time when their therapists reported noticeable worsening of their condition. The clear congruence in Harrower's data between change or lack of change in psychodiagnostically assessed adjustment and "true" adjustment level as inferred from external criteria significantly demonstrates the potential reliability of the psychodiagnostic battery.

Nonpersonality Variance. Complementing Harrower's work are numerous investigations of the extent to which test scores fluctuate in the absence of related true score changes. Researchers have operationalized the possibility that psychodiagnostic tests may pick up large amounts of error rather than true variance by assessing the covariance of test performance with factors irrelevant to a subject's personality, including such nonpersonality variables as examiner attributes, methods of test administration, transitory situational parameters, and conscious or unconscious response sets.

Experimental findings defining the susceptibility of psychodiagnostic tests to such sources of error variance, though somewhat mixed, generally suggest that, *within the context of a conventional clinical examination,* the reliability of the test battery is not seriously attenuated by the influence of nonpersonality variables. For the WAIS, for example, Masling (1959) found only small differences between responses elicited by examiners trained to assume "warm" and "cold" testing roles, and Nichols (1959), manipulating subjects' involvement and success experience, observed test scores to be only minimally affected by minor variations in testing procedure and differences in subjects' test-taking attitudes. In a DAP study Holtzman (1952) found no variability in drawings attributable to the examiner's personality, sex, or physical appearance.

However, as reviewed by Masling (1960) and Miller (1953), a number of Rorschach studies have reported influences on test performance of overtly and covertly induced sets, situational factors, and examiner variables. Nevertheless, the Rorschach literature on nonpersonality factors does not on the whole seriously challenge the test's reliability in the clinical diagnostic situation. A table prepared by Zax, Stricker, and Weiss (1960) from an integrative summary of relevant research reveals that investigations of various nonpersonality influences on some 30 Rorschach variables have as a group yielded considerably more *nonsignificant* than significant differences. Of specific interest is that among Rorschach variables particularly resistant to extraneous influences are

$Dd\%$, $F+\%$, M, H, and pure C, each of which figures prominently in the identification of schizophrenic ego impairment (see Chaps. 4, 7, 9, & 10).

Going beyond their table, Zax et al. point out that most of the studies that have demonstrated significant set and situational influences on Rorschach test performance involve artifacts having no counterpart in the clinical setting. For example, instructing subjects to see people in action (Hutt, Gibby, Milton, & Pottharst, 1950), informing them that certain location choices are associated with intelligence (Abramson, 1951), or subjecting them to electric shock (Eichler, 1951b) or immobilization (Singer, Meltzoff, & Goldman, 1952) will affect their Rorschach scores, but none of these procedures is compatible with recommended clinical practice. A similar observation applies to some studies of examiner influence on Rorschach response. Gross (1959) and Wickes (1965), for example, found that examiners can elicit increased numbers of certain kinds of responses by reacting to them in a positive way, as by nodding or saying "Good," but such intentionally induced operants are usually avoided by the skilled examiner.

On the other hand, the possibility that clinically germane error variance may derive from unconscious examiner influence, as through inadvertent behavior, personality style, or physical appearance, has not yet been thoroughly studied with the Rorschach. Work by Lord (1950) has suggested that Rorschach performance may be affected by a subject's reaction to the examiner's basic personality dynamics even when he attempts to conceal them by assuming various roles. Masling (1965) has recently demonstrated that examiners in whom sets are induced can influence their subjects to respond according to these sets without either the subject or the examiner recognizing the influence that is being exerted. Masling concludes that testing is basically an interpersonal process in which the examiner must necessarily attune himself as best he can to his influence on his subject's behavior.

Masling also reports, however, that despite great efforts to induce examiner bias in his study, the subjects still derived their information more from the stimulus characteristics of the blots than from the attitudes of their examiners. Furthermore, as Zax et al. (1960) point out, Rorschach variations thus far observed in relation to examiner variables have been statistical ones involving certain scoring dimensions that may or may not have interpretive significance when the test is used in clinical diagnosis. In other words, although examiner influence appears to be a well-established phenomenon, there is as yet no evidence to indicate that the effects of examiner influence either override the impact of the test stimuli or otherwise impair the reliability of diagnostic inferences drawn from the configuration of Rorschach scores and behavior in the clinical setting.

In general, then, there is no compelling evidence that the clinical test battery, administered for clinical purposes in a conventional clinical setting, is inordinately influenced by nonpersonality factors that would constitute error variance, and studies of personality change indicate that the psychodiagnostic battery can accurately measure individual adjustment.

Traditional Reliability Methods. Assessments of psychodiagnostic tests by traditional test-retest, split-half, and alternate-form reliability methods have proved difficult to design and interpret. First, because psychodiagnostic tests are expected to reflect personality change as well as personality consistency over time, test-retest correlations may provide little information concerning their reliability; high test-retest correlation in subjects who had undergone meaningful personality change, for example, would indicate unreliable measurement. It may be argued that some personality variables are stable and enduring and that for these variables test-retest correlations are appropriate reliability indicators regardless of the nature of intercurrent events, but personality research has not yet achieved consensus concerning which, if any, personality variables are so fixed and immutable.

On the other hand, test-retest methods have been applied to WAIS, DAP, and Rorschach protocols of subjects for whom little personality change could be surmised over the retest interval, and several such studies have yielded encouraging results. Guertin, Rabin, Frank, and Ladd (1962, p. 2) summarize reports of respectable test-retest reliabilities for both full scale and subtest scores on the WAIS. For the DAP Starr and Marcuse (1959) obtained good reliability on five of seven DAP characteristics studied with both immediate and one-month retest, and Guinan and Hurley (1965) found clinician-judges able to match almost without error sets of figure drawings done by a group of normal subjects on two occasions five weeks apart.

Holzberg and Wexler (1950b), readministering the Rorschach to chronic schizophrenic subjects after a three-week interval, report good reliabilities for a number of variables. In a unique study Griffith (1951) controlled for the memory factors that often inflate test-retest reliability estimates by administering the Rorschach twice to a group of severely amnestic patients with Korsakoff psychosis. Though they had no recollection of their testing one day earlier, Griffith's subjects produced very similar protocols on retesting.

Second, split-half and alternate-form reliability studies of psychodiagnostic tests have been complicated by difficulties in identifying efficacious splits and constructing appropriate alternate forms. Although they are therefore not trouble free, these methods have provided additional estimates of WAIS and Rorschach reliability. For the WAIS Wechsler (1958, pp. 101–103) reports respectable split-half reliabilities for verbal, performance, and many subtest IQ's, although the somewhat large errors of measurement for certain subtests have specific implications for their clinical interpretation (see pp. 34, 121, & 166). From data summarized by Guertin et al. (1962, p. 3), however, it appears that alternate-form reliability studies comparing the WAIS with the Wechsler-Bellevue have yielded mixed results, although the most careful studies have demonstrated reasonable reliabilities at least for full scale and verbal IQ scores.

For the Rorschach respectable split-half reliabilities are reported for alternate-card comparisons by Hertz (1934) and for alternate-response comparisons by Stein (1961). Buckle and Holt (1951) and Eichler (1951a), conducting alternate-form examinations with the Behn-Rorschach blots, observed extremely close response congruencies between the two forms. It should be noted in regard to the Rorschach that some writers, independent of their convictions regarding its use, are unsympathetic with any such statistical treatment of the test and relegate it to a psychometric wasteland. Block (1962), for example, details numerous psychometric inadequacies of the Rorschach that in this judgment prevent its development as any but a purely empirical technique. Murstein (1960) labels the test a "psychometric sow's ear." These views are not shared by such other contributors as Gleser (1963, p. 399), however, whose stance is that more definitive Rorschach reliability research awaits specific improvements in psychometric methodology.

The literature does contain reliability studies less promising than those mentioned here, particularly concerning the Rorschach, and the research in this area is beset with many problems of conceptualization and design beyond the scope of this discussion. For a broader treatment of these matters the reader is referred to Holzberg (1960), MacFarlane and Tuddenham (1951, pp. 35–42), and Zubin, Eron, and Schumer (1965, pp. 181–193), whose contributions are addressed primarily to the Rorschach but are generally applicable to the psychodiagnostic test battery.

INTERJUDGE AGREEMENT

Interjudge agreement is defined by the reliability of the users of a test and of the conclusions they draw from it. Interjudge agreement as such has no direct bearing on the previously considered issue of intrinsic reliability: whether or not judges can agree on the scores or interpretations they assign to a test reflects on the judges and not on the test's intrinsic potential for accurately measuring a given phenomenon. Interjudge agreement is nevertheless an important psychometric consideration, because the utility of any test, no matter how excellent its intrinsic reliability, is negligible if its nature precludes good consensus among judges trained in its use. As reviewed below, available evidence indicates that experienced, comparably trained clinicians can achieve good agreement on the scores and interpretations they assign to the tests in the clinical battery.

With regard to scoring, the WAIS, by virtue of its generally objective content and detailed guidelines (Wechsler, 1955), seldom presents major difficulties. Walker, Hunt, and Schwartz (1965) observed minimal scoring disagreement even on Comprehension, which is one of the least objectively scored WAIS subtests. Walker et al. found two judges able to agree completely in their scoring of 75% of 500 Comprehension responses. Giving the remaining 25% of ambiguous responses to five experienced clinicians, they found at least four of the five to achieve complete scoring agreement on more than half of these difficult-to-score answers. Furthermore, in most cases where the clinicians did not concur, their disagreements were of only one-point magnitude. Although Walker et al. express concern that the agreement was not greater than it was in their study, this degree of scoring consensus for Comprehension, a relatively subjective WAIS subtest, strongly suggests that the WAIS as a whole can be reliably scored.

For DAP scoring Lehner and Gunderson (1952) found good agreement among judges rating each of 21 graphic traits on 10 descriptive categories, and Lewinsohn and May (1963) obtained an interrater reliability of .85 among judges rating figure drawings for their over-all quality on a nine-point scale. Harris (1963, p. 90) reports similar consistency among trained judges in scoring children's drawings along a number of dimensions. Although for the Rorschach the literature includes disparate assessments of interjudge scoring agreement, the over-all picture as summarized by Zubin et al. (1965, p. 185) indicates that "a fairly high degree of reliability can be achieved when there is pre-training and supervised practice with respect to a *specific scoring system.*"

Encouraging evidence of reliability is also reported for test interpretations, particularly those that pertain to personality adjustment. In several WAIS studies by Hunt and his co-workers, as summarized by Hunt (1959), trained clinicians achieved good agreement in rating verbal responses for degree of schizophrenia reflected. As these ratings became more difficult to make, furthermore, the clinicians demonstrated increasingly superior agreement in comparison to naive judges. Albee and Hamlin (1949, 1950), utilizing paired comparisons in one study and a criterion rating scale in another, obtained considerable agreement among judges asked to assess level of adjustment from DAP protocols. Examining Rorschach interpretations, Krugman (1942) reported perfect accord among judges asked to match pairs of independently made interpretations of a series of Rorschach records, and in a separate study she noted a high percentage of agreement among judges in matching scored Rorschach records with their interpretations.

These findings clearly indicate that problems of interjudge agreement in scoring and interpreting psychodiagnostic tests, though sometimes at issue, are neither insurmountable nor an inescapable hindrance to the tests' effectiveness in the hands of adequately trained and experienced clinicians.

VALIDITY OF PSYCHODIAGNOSTIC TESTS

Test validity, which is traditionally defined as the degree to which it is known what a test measures or predicts (Cronbach, 1949a, p. 48), is an imprecise term that cannot be meaningfully applied to psychodiagnostic tests without careful specification. As stressed by Jenkins (1946) and many later writers, the question of whether a test is valid can be asked only in terms of "Valid for what?", and, as explicated by Cronbach and Meehl (1955), the validity of a test is relative to the *kind* of validity appropriate to its use, whether *content, concurrent, predictive,* or *construct.*

The validity question relevant to the subject matter of this book is whether psychodiagnostic tests are valid for differential diagnosis in schizophrenia, and the kind of validity conceived in this presentation as appropriate for such use of tests has involved *constructs:* wherever possible, diagnostic guidelines have been deduced from conceptual links between schizophrenic ego impairments and psychological test behaviors. Some of the substantiating research cited in the various chapters has similarly represented a construct approach to validation, although many of the data that can be adduced to support the construct validity of the test battery for diagnosing schizophrenia are themselves derived from concurrent validity studies, in which test indices are empirically related to external diagnostic criteria.

In considering further some general issues of test validity, it is necessary to recognize that test validity is a metonymical expression, the use of which should not obscure its true meaning. Strictly speaking, a *test* is itself neither valid nor invalid; only *scores* and *interpretations* derived from tests are more or less valid. Accordingly, issues concerning the validity of psychodiagnostic tests are grouped below under the categories of *test scores* and *test interpretations*.

VALIDITY OF PSYCHODIAGNOSTIC TEST SCORES

The concurrent or construct validity of various psychodiagnostic test scores related to schizophrenia has been substantiated in previous chapters by reference to pertinent concepts and available research data. However, this literature treatment has been illustrative rather than complete, and it is indicated to review here several clinical and methodological considerations that generally affect the adequacy of psychodiagnostic research. As indicated below, insufficient regard for many of these considerations is often noted to yield data apparently, but not in fact, challenging the validity of test scores.

Clinical Considerations. Two major clinical considerations in psychodiagnostic research are test score refinements and subcategories of schizophrenic diagnosis. As introduced early in this book (see p. 32) and restated at several relevant points, sophisticated clinical diagnosis proceeds from many subtle variations in test scores to numerous shadings of nosology. Consequently, studies that lump test scores (e.g., all Rorschach W responses regardless of form level or degree of differentiation) and schizophrenic subjects (e.g., acute with chronic or paranoid with nonparanoid schizophrenics) give short shrift to extremely important distinctions made by clinicians in their use of psychodiagnostic techniques.

That such discrepancies between research design and clinical practice have contributed to misleading failures in validational research is widely affirmed. Concerning gross categorization of schizophrenia, Rabin, King, and Ehrmann (1955) and Lang and Buss (1965, pp. 98–99) indicate that much of the equivocal research literature in all lines of schizophrenic investigation may be the result of failure adequately to specify and control various parameters of the subjects' disturbances. With regard to test scores, Klinger and Roth (1965) adduce evidence from Rorschach studies to demonstrate that (a) in many validity investigations Rorschach scores have not been applied as clinicians actually use them and (b) the more similarly to clinical practice such scores have been employed in research, the more consistently the researchers have obtained stable validities.

The implications of these clinical considerations for adequate psychodiagnostic research are further discussed by Ainsworth (1954) and Arbit and Lakin (1959). Ainsworth stresses how frequently neglected in Rorschach validation studies is the importance of refined hypotheses and close simulation of standard clinical practice. Arbit and Lakin, surveying DAP methodology in various researches and among practicing clinicians, confirm the presence of marked disparities between actual clinical use of DAP variables and their application in numerous investigations purporting to invalidate the test.

Methodological Considerations. Adequate psychodiagnostic research requires, in addition to sufficient specification of test scores and diagnostic categories, appropriate statistical treatment and clinically relevant interpretation of data. With regard to statistical treatment, the reliability of probability estimates for test scores often depends on whether parametric or nonparametric data analysis is employed. Cronbach (1949b), for example, exploring in detail possible sources of error in the application of statistical methods to Rorschach variables, points out that any computations based on addition of scores, including t and F significance tests, may yield distorted probability estimates because Rorschach data do not satisfy the interval scale and normal distribution assumptions traditionally required for such procedures. He recommends nonparametric analysis of Rorschach data, and he concludes that although procedural errors have in some instances led to unwarranted claims of significance, at other times "failure to apply the most incisive statistical test has led workers to reject significant relationships" (p. 425).

Even if, as recently suggested by Anderson (1961) and Boneau (1960), interval scale and normal distribution prove unnecessary to reliable parametric data treatment, research designs employing such limited parametric analyses as group mean comparisons may for other reasons still underestimate the validity of psychodiagnostic test scores. Frank, Corrie, and Fogel (1955) and Harper (1950), for example, note that group mean comparisons do not take sufficient account of the possible heterogeneity within diagnostic categories, and these writers suggest that many inconsistent results in WAIS studies have resulted from reliance on such limited comparisons. Hammer (1959), discussing DAP research, adds the significant observation that mean group comparisons are particularly inappropriate for assessing the validity of test variables on which either very high *or* very low scores may have pathologic implications.

Hammer also calls attention to the importance of adequate sampling in psychodiagnostic research, and he describes the extent to which limited sampling may obscure the practical validity of diagnostic indices that are rare even in pathologic groups. For example, a score that appears in none of 50 normal subjects and only two of 50 schizophrenics will not realize a statistically significant differentiation among these 100 subjects, but this score may without exception be pathognomonic for schizophrenia in any subject in whom it occurs. Only with samples sufficiently large to include a reasonable number of such rare signs can investigators meaningfully assess their validity.

Related to Hammer's point is the necessity in validity studies of psychodiagnostic test scores for clinically relevant interpretations of statistical outcomes. Often overlooked in such studies is the fact that the absence of a purported pathologic score is not equal in significance to its presence. As pointed out early in this book (see p. 32), for example, not all schizophrenic persons manifest a full range of ego impairments, nor do all schizophrenics with a given ego impairment manifest the full range of test scores associated with that impairment. Rather, the psychodiagnosis of schizophrenia rests essentially with the hypothesis that schizophrenic disturbance is conceptually related to a number of test behaviors, each of which characterizes some schizophrenics and is unlikely to appear in normal persons.

Hence, that many schizophrenics fail to exhibit a given test score does not preclude its being a valid index of schizophrenic ego impairment for those subjects in whom it occurs, nor does a study finding no difference between schizophrenics and normals in a test score necessarily invalidate that score as a schizophrenic indicator, providing it is prominent in neither group. Only the observation that many nonschizophrenic subjects definitely display a presumably schizophrenic index invalidates that index.

This assertion should not be construed to imply that all test signs can be assumed indicative of everything until proved otherwise. The point is rather that psychodiagnostic hypotheses about schizophrenia that are logically derived from theoretical conceptions of ego disturbance and test behavior are tenable until empirical data prove them inaccurate, and inaccuracy is defined not by failure to identify all schizophrenic subjects or to differentiate between all samples of schizophrenic and nonschizophrenic subjects, but by the frequent occurrence of hypothesized schizophrenic indices among nonschizophrenic subjects.

This formulation merely restates in specific terms the appropriate procedures in scientific discovery as delineated by Popper (1959), who holds that the verification of a logically derived theorem rests with its resistance to disproof: "We shall take it as falsified only if we discover a *reproducible effect* which refutes the theory" (p. 86). Such a perspective on the validity issue in psychodiagnostic research rebuts the not-infrequent citation of studies in which some schizophrenic subjects fail to manifest certain test signs usually considered pathognomonic for schizophrenia (e.g., Wittenborn & Sarason, 1949) as evidence that the test is an invalid diagnostic tool.

VALIDITY OF PSYCHODIAGNOSTIC TEST INTERPRETATIONS

For many clinicians the validity of psychodiagnostic tests is best assessed in regard not to the scores but the interpretations they prompt. Zubin (1954) and Zubin et al. (1965, pp. 193–237), extensively assessing Rorschach validation research, conclude that most of the "failures" in these studies are attributable to reliance on "atomistic" evidence, whereas global evaluations of Rorschach behavior have been more successfully validated. The clinical and methodological considerations outlined in the previous section on test scores suggest that *inappropriate* atomistic approaches, rather than atomism, may be responsible for many of these apparent failures. More to the point of Zubin's position, however, is evidence concerning the effectiveness of global interpretations in the psychodiagnosis of schizophrenia.

Early studies by Benjamin and Ebaugh (1938) and Garfield (1947) found clinicians estimating schizophrenia from Rorschach protocols able to achieve a high percentage of agreement with independent clinical diagnoses, and Kahn and Jones (1965) have recently demonstrated that experienced clinicians can meaningfully estimate severity of psychopathology from human figure drawings. On the other hand, the literature abounds with reports of the failure of global test interpretations to correlate significantly with various criteria. There is evidence, for example, that Rorschach interpretations do not validly predict performance in aviation school (Holtzman & Sells, 1954) or graduate training in clinical psychology (Kelly & Fiske, 1951) and do not even correspond well with diagnostic labels assigned from anamnestic data when the protocols are interpreted blindly (Little & Shneidman, 1959).

It is therefore important to clarify that most of the latter types of study, though often cited to denigrate psychodiagnostic instruments, are pertinent neither to their use in actual clinical practice nor to their validity for assessing schizophrenia. In the first place, these studies involve prediction from psychodiagnostic tests to complex life situations that are influenced not only by personality variables but also by environmental factors that may be subject to unanticipated change. As elaborated in Chapter 13, with reference to estimating prognosis in schizophrenia (see pp. 251–254), prediction to such multiply determined future events cannot reasonably be expected of psychodiagnostic tests and does not accurately reflect their general validity.

The necessity for appropriate criteria in validational research is treated further by Harris (1960, pp. 414–417), who in regard to global predictive studies with the Rorschach pointedly remarks, "It is just such unrelenting research with exceedingly complex criteria that helps to provide abundant support for the negative appraisals of the Rorschach technique which appear so often in general literature on psychology." On the other hand, Harris observes, "There is little question, even among severe critics of the Rorschach method, that in a large percentage of the classical cases of the various psychiatric disorders, particularly schizophrenia, the Rorschach test provides rather clear-cut diagnostic evidence of the disorder."

Also relevant to the implications of global predictive studies for test validity is the previously made distinction between that which is intrinsic to a test and that which is a function of its user's skill (see pp. 492–493). The significance of this distinction for validational research is clearly illustrated in a study by Chambers and Hamlin (1957), who asked 20 clinicians to assign sets of five Rorschach records, one each, to the five diagnostic categories of involutional depression, paranoid schizophrenia, anxiety neurosis, brain damage, and adult mental deficiency. Although these 20 clinicians as a group achieved significantly greater-than-chance accuracy in their judgments, Chambers and Hamlin express concern about the diagnostic utility of the Rorschach technique because the judges distinguished with only 50% accuracy among the four categories of depression, neurosis, schizophrenia, and brain damage. However, Chambers and Hamlin also report that five of their judges made *no* diagnostic errors at all and that an analysis of variance revealed a significant between-judge effect. Rather than as a challenge to the intrinsic diagnostic validity of the Rorschach, then, their data can be interpreted as attesting the power of the test in the hands of skilled clinicians.

Even with appropriate criteria and skilled clinicians, however, psychodiagnostic research can meaningfully answer validity questions only to the extent that its design approximates clinical practice. With few exceptions, negative studies of the validity of test interpretations have employed blind analyses of protocols and/or predictions from single tests (e.g., Cohen, 1955), neither of which meets this requirement. Although blind analysis and single-test predictions have established merit in teaching and nonapplied research, they are not congruent with sophisticated clinical practice and cannot adequately reflect its validity.

As stressed throughout this book, the clinician must frame his test interpretations in terms of a subject's demeanor and approach to the testing, clarifications and elaborations elicited on inquiry, and the circumstances precipitating the psychological consultation. Stripped, as he is in a blind interpretation, of important contextual data, of the opportunity to observe his patient's behavior, and of the chance to resolve by inquiry his uncertainties about the intended meaning of his subject's responses, the clinician operates with only a portion of the data necessary to accurate clinical appraisal.

Similarly emphasized in this book is the utility for clinical psychodiagnosis of a test *battery* measuring complementary features and levels of personality functioning. Restriction to a single test, just as blind diagnosis, deprives the clinician-judge of essential information and forces him to function as he seldom would in practice. The extent to which blind diagnosis and single-test designs obfuscate psychodiagnostic research is further explicated by Lebovits (1964), who demonstrates the ease with which validity studies bearing little relationship to clinical practice and yielding apparently negative results can be generated. Some additional issues bearing on the validity of test interpretations are considered in the following section on clinical and statistical prediction (see pp. 503–507).

It is important to note at this point, however, that validational research with psychodiagnostic techniques confronts many thorny design problems beyond the considerations mentioned thus far. In particular, such studies are seldom able to satisfy criteria for both meaningful control groups and adequate independence of variables. With regard to control groups, for example, investigations in which test batteries are administered to clearly schizophrenic and clearly nonschizophrenic subjects may yield differential indicators that are theoretically significant but have little practical value in the clinical situation, where psychodiagnosis must address fine and subtle pathologic distinctions among persons of uncertain diagnostic status. To solve this problem many investigators utilize actual clinical files of persons referred for psychological consultation, in which case they guarantee that their obtained results will be representative of and meaningful for clinical practice.

However, this type of sampling risks another difficulty: the contamination of the dependent variables (test indices) with the independent variables (diagnostic status) of the study. Such contamination arises because, in an actual clinical setting where patients are referred for psychological examination to resolve diagnostic dilemmas, the opinions derived by the psychologist from his test data usually influence the diagnostic label eventually attached to the patient. With patients who have been tested for pressing clinical purposes, therefore, the investigator may be hard pressed to develop a criterion of diagnostic status that is fully independent of the test data. On the other hand, the more he attempts to evade this difficulty by turning away from cases in which the tests played an integral role in establishing the diagnosis, the less relevant are his data to the more challenging judgments clinicians are asked to make.

There is no ready escape from this Scylla and Charybdis. The experimental difficulty might be surmounted by arranging to withhold psychodiagnostic opinions on referred patients of uncertain status pending their diagnosis on other bases, but such a procedure might violate patient-care principles and transgress administrative and ethical codes. A partial solution to this apparent impasse was effected in a study by Weiner (1961a), reviewed in Chapter 10, in which he was able to demonstrate that the test variables he was studying had not participated significantly in the psychologists' evaluations of schizophrenia in his sample of referred patients. However, Weiner's success was the fortuitous result of the fact that the variables he was examining happened not to be conventional schizophrenic indicators, and his method would probably be less successful in a study concerned with widely used and endorsed pathognomonic test scores.

This discussion notwithstanding, the fact that sampling of known groups and possible contamination of variables *may* obfuscate the meaning of a validational study does not imply that they necessarily *will*. Improved research designs and replicating studies are needed to establish more firmly the validity for schizophrenia of the psychodiagnostic indicators presented in this book, but need for further research is not grounds for disregarding previous work or anticipating its contradiction by future findings.

UTILITY OF VALID SCORES AND INTERPRETATIONS

Also important in evaluating psychodiagnostic research is the fact that validity alone, defined for present purposes as a significant relationship between a test score or interpretation and a parameter of schizophrenic disturbance, may or may not be equivalent to *utility* for that score or interpretation. The utility of a test in a given instance is differentiated from its validity by two considerations, *population base rates* and *appropriate efficiency weightings* for "hit" and error categories.

In terms of population base rate considerations, as delineated by Meehl and Rosen (1955), a score that validly differentiates schizophrenic from nonschizophrenic subject samples is diagnostically *useful* only to the extent that the percentage of correct judgments ("hits") it achieves significantly exceeds the proportion of schizophrenic subjects in the population from which the samples are drawn. For example, a score correctly classifying 60% of a subject sample as schizophrenic or nonschizophrenic may be a non-chance discriminator, if chance is defined as a 50-50 probability; however, if this 60% hit rate is realized among newly admitted patients in a hospital setting where typically 70% of all patients admitted are schizophrenic, it would be more efficient simply to label *all* new patients schizophrenic than to rely on the 60% accurate test.

Hence, to measure utility for a population as well as validity within a sample, psychodiagnostic researchers need either (a) to ensure by careful selective sampling that the expected frequencies against which they compare their obtained results are commensurate with population base rates or (b) to employ total block sampling, as by assessing all patients admitted to a hospital during a given time period. When either of these methods is used to obtain samples that accurately represent the population from which they are drawn, base-rate considerations are built into the data and efficiency is commensurate with the validity observed.

Statistical efficiency must often be tempered by extrastatistical values that attend diagnostic judgments, however. Even if labeling all patients admitted to a hospital *schizophrenic* were statistically more efficient than available clinical techniques, for example, most clinicians and hospital administrators would have grave reservations about such a procedure. Such nonstatistical considerations define the role of appropriate efficiency weightings. As spelled out by Hathaway (1959, pp. 196–198), efficiency weightings are determined by the values conventionally attached to the phenomenon being differentiated. That is, the relative significance of false negative and false positive determinations produced by a test varies with whether the test is being used to identify a positively or a negatively valued phenomenon.

To illustrate, in assessing such a positively valued attribute as scholastic aptitude, a college admissions committee is likely to be less distressed if its selection method allows a few students who cannot perform adequately to be accepted (false positives) than if it denies educational opportunities to qualified students (false negatives). On the other hand, for such negatively valued phenomena as pathologic states false positive estimates are often more serious deterrents to a test's use than false negatives. An examiner is usually less concerned when a test or test score fails to identify a schizophrenic or brain-damaged person, for example, than he is when it falsely assigns a subject to a nosological category.

The greater import of false positive than false negative judgments in clinical diagnosis, which is also discussed in Chapter 4 (see p. 32), is summarized in a remark by Hathaway (1959, p. 198) that psychodiagnostic tests are best used as "successive hurdles in probability." The major point of the "successive hurdles" conception is that the combination of a number of test variables, each of which correctly identifies some schizophrenics (true positives) without picking up nonschizophrenics (false positives), produces a highly efficient test battery; correspondingly, as long as a test index does not contribute numerous false positives, its utility is not necessarily vitiated by a high yield of false negatives. A variable occurring in all of 50 schizophrenics but in 25 of 50 nonschizophrenics as well will foster an appreciable number of unfortunate diagnostic errors, whereas a variable occurring in only a few schizophrenics but in *no* nonschizophrenics makes no unfortunate errors of commission and may be combined with other similar variables in a "successive hurdles" fashion that progressively reduces errors of omission. This approach to clinical psychodiagnosis is also described by Wechsler (1958, pp. 167–168), who advocates diagnosis by the "method of successive seives."

CLINICAL AND STATISTICAL PREDICTION

The clinician's ability to derive reliable and valid interpretations from psychodiagnostic tests cannot be considered independently of whether such efforts are worth the time he devotes to them. This question was first posed in detail by Meehl (1954), whose book, *Clinical versus Statistical Prediction,* has stimulated much constructive reflection on the utility of clinical techniques. Meehl distinguishes between methods in which clinicians make predictions and methods in which judgments are actuarially determined from scores, and his basic argument is that prediction to a given criterion should be vested in whichever of the two methods achieves the most favorable empirical result.

Reviewing 20 studies in which both clinical and actuarial methods were employed to predict aspects of personality functioning, Meehl reports that with only one exception predictions made actuarially proved either equal or superior to clinicians' judgments. Meehl concludes from his survey that the most scientifically and pragmatically justifiable goal for psychodiagnostic practice and research is the further development of actuarial guidelines and the elimination of wasteful, inefficient engagement by professional persons in psychodiagnostic activity. Elsewhere Meehl (1956) states, "Transition from psychometric pattern to personality description is an automatic, mechanical, 'clerical' kind of task, proceeding by the use of explicit rules set forth in the cookbook," and he avers that in this process the clinician is a "costly middleman" whose services can and should be dispensed with.

At issue with Meehl's conclusion, however, are several bases for regarding them as (a) ungeneralizable to psychodiagnosis in schizophrenia, (b) derived from inappropriately designed studies, and (c) phrased in terms of a dichotomy that in clinical practice may be more apparent than real. Concerning first the generalizability of his conclusions, Meehl (1954, p. 119) himself notes that the studies on which his impressions are founded all involve prediction either of recovery from a major psychosis, success in some kind of training or schooling, or recidivism among prisoners. None compares the correlation of clinical and actuarial diagnoses of schizophrenia or any other pathologic condition with external diagnostic criteria.

In reference to the design of the studies Meehl surveys, it is neither surprising nor distressing that the clinicians in these researches predicted relatively poorly from test protocols to such complex events as prognosis, school success, and recidivism. As reviewed in pages 498–499, the capacity of a clinician to predict complex life phenomena from blind test analyses has little to do with his ability to identify psychopathologic states or with the perspicacity with which he can predict a patient's future course given broad knowledge of his past history and current life circumstances as well as his personality structure.

By requiring both clinicians and formulas to work from the same set of test data, studies of the type to which Meehl refers automatically stack the deck against the clinician, who is forced to draw conclusions without benefit of much of the information to which his judgmental powers are attuned in actual clinical situations. This point, which is basically similar to the issue of blind diagnosis raised on page 500, is elaborated further by Holt (1958, 1961). Holt confirms that typical clinical-actuarial studies have in effect pitted the usual operation of the actuarial method against contrived, sheer guesswork operations on the part of clinicians.

Meehl (1957), acknowledging certain defects in the design of many clinical-actuarial studies, nevertheless challenges clinicians who are convinced that the right kind of study will demonstrate the validity of clinical judgment to *do* the right kind of study. This challenge has gone largely unmet until a recent contribution by Lindzey (1965). Lindzey was able to demonstrate clear superiority of clinician's blind judgments over actuarial treatment of TAT protocols in differentiating homosexual from nonhomosexual prison inmates. However, as Meehl (1965) has since noted, Lindzey's results are achieved in part by the same kind of deck-stacking, in reverse, for which earlier studies have been criticized. Lindzey utilized actuarial scores for homosexuality developed with a college population to make the prediction to the prison population, and he thus made rather harsh demands on the statistical method.

On the other hand, Lindzey's study does corroborate the generally accepted fact that clinical methods have greater flexibility and capacity for generalization than statistical methods, the efficiency of which often dissipates as even slight differences in the population or purposes for which they were derived are introduced. It is accordingly widely agreed among persons involved in the clinical-actuarial controversy that, no matter what the eventual utility of actuarial methods in clinical assessment may be, there remain broad areas of prediction for which no formulas have yet been worked out and for which clinical judgment is the most effective procedure available.

A second important methodological drawback of the studies on which Meehl bases his position is their scant regard for the skill of the clinicians making the various predictions. As pointed out by Hunt and Thorne (1958), it is illogical to expect either that all clinicians make equally valid judgments or that all the judgments of a single clinician are of equal validity. Experimental work by Kostlan (1954) and Oskamp (1962) affirms that not only do clinicians vary in their diagnostic skills, with accuracy of judgment being positively related to experience, but patients and test protocols differ in the accuracy with which they can be assessed. Hence, as mentioned on page 499, there is little merit in discussing the potential validity of clinical judgments without specifying the success of the individual judges and the factors related to their differential success. Although Meehl (1954, p. 114) alludes to the inadequate information about the skills and qualification of the clinicians in the studies he reviews, he does not attenuate his conclusions in deference to this important consideration.

Transcending these confrontations of clinical and statistical prediction is a broader argument that this distinction itself is of limited theoretical and practical significance. Without compromising Meehl's concern with justifying the psychologist's activity, it is possible to construe the clinician himself as the measuring instrument and to evaluate by actuarial methods the merit of his efforts. Such an approach is endorsed by Hunt (1959), who points out that emphasis on and respect for actuarial justification of psychodiagnostic activity neither obviates nor is antithetical to clinical judgment.

The controversy between clinical and actuarial methods of psychodiagnosis can also be seen in relation to the general issue of whether personality study is best conceived as a nomothetic science, concerned with general principles applicable to the control and prediction of human behavior, or as an idiographic discipline, devoted to the understanding of individual persons as unique psychological systems. This matter is considered at length in an important paper by Holt (1962). Holt reviews historically the disparate views (a) that personology is an artistic endeavor to which the methods of natural science are irrelevant and (b) that personality study is an orderly, objective investigation from which idiosyncratic impressions are to be eliminated. He rejects both views as deleterious to the advancement of knowledge, and points out that the process of discovering and verifying knowledge obviously encompasses stereotyped notions of both nomothetic and idiographic approaches, that is, both the intuitive grasp of individual occurrences and the establishment of general principles to account for such occurrences.

Holt's renunciation of an essential nomothetic-idiographic polarity in personality research leads him to conclude that the clinical-actuarial dichotomy is a badly formulated anachronism that for practical purposes is more apparent than real. Meehl (1957), however, denies that research and clinical contexts are analogous. He argues that whereas both formulas and intuition are integral aspects of scientific discovery, clinical practice involves merely making the best possible decision on the basis of what is known. When a formula is known to yield the most accurate predictions to a given criterion, Meehl continues, the formula should be used; when there is no such formula, clinicians must "use our heads."

Holt (1961) in turn vigorously disputes Meehl's position in this respect. He contends that no basic procedural distinctions can be drawn between research and clinical activities. In his view clinical judgment, like research, is scientific in that it represents a *disciplined analysis of data:* a clinician arrives at a diagnostic judgment by first erecting numerous hypotheses from his knowledge of personality functioning and psychopathologic processes and then proceeding to verify or discard these hypotheses in light of the data elicited by his techniques.

Clinical judgment is thus, according to Holt, a disciplined inquiry to which both statistical and intuitive operations are intrinsic. Elsewhere Holt (1958, p. 12) insists that the appropriate goal for psychodiagnostic research "is not to find the proper sphere of activity for clinical predictive methods and for statistical ones" but is rather to seek "optimal combinations of actuarially controlled methods and sensitive clinical judgment for any particular predictive enterprise."

The presentation in this book has not attempted to resolve the clinical-actuarial issue. The diagnosis of schizophrenia has been presented as a clinical judgment, but the judgment has been referred to a host of component decisions, some of which are determined by idiographic clinical impressions, others by generally observed clinical phenomena, and still others by fairly well-established normative tables. It may be an individual matter whether this approach is interpreted as solely clinical, as clinical *and* statistical, or as using formulas when they are available and clinical judgment where they are not. For a fuller discussion of the justification and utility of clinical methodology, the reader is referred to contributions by Garfield (1963) and Hunt and Jones (1962).

PROFESSIONAL ISSUES IN PSYCHODIAGNOSTIC PRACTICE

It is fitting to conclude this book with a brief polemic regarding the professional status and rewards of psychodiagnostic practice. Derogation of psychodiagnostic activity has achieved no finer edge than that honed by Meehl (1960, p. 26), who caps his assessment of the clinical method with the following remarks:

My advice to fledgling clinical psychologists is to construct their self-concept mainly around "I am a researcher" or "I am a psychotherapist," because one whose self-concept is mainly "I am a (test oriented) psychodiagnostician" may have to maintain his professional security over the next few years by not reading the research literature, a maneuver which has apparently proved quite successful already for some clinicians.

Meehl's foray has elicited many a psychodiagnostic "Ouch!", but there are adequate bases for retorting, "En garde!" First, the contention that ignorance of the literature is necessary to psychodiagnostic self-respect and that a psychologist is therefore better off as a therapist takes adequate cognizance of neither the psychodiagnostic nor the psychotherapeutic literature. As outlined in the previous sections of this chapter, one's appraisal of psychodiagnostic research depends on how carefully and with what frame of reference he peruses it, and there is considerable empirical evidence attesting the scientific merit of psychodiagnostic activity.

However, if, because inconsistent findings and conflicting interpretations of studies dot the literature, one is still inclined to reservations about psychodiagnostic techniques, he hardly improves his footing by shifting to psychotherapeutic ground, at least not in relation to the literature as evaluated in the following cheerless summary:

With the single exception of the psychotherapeutic methods based on learning theory, results of published research with military and civilian neurotics, and with both adults and children, suggest that the therapeutic effects of psychotherapy are small or non-existent, and do not in any way add to the specific effects of routine medical treatment, or to such events as occur in the patient's everyday experiences (Eysenck, 1961b, p. 720).

Eysenck's conclusion is quoted here not to endorse it; the author shares with such writers as Strupp (1963) an entirely different interpretation of the literature and a positive view of the effectiveness of psychotherapy. Rather, Eysenck's opinion is aired to demonstrate that Meehl's stance denies to psychodiagnosticians the latitude it allows psychotherapists: to endure with respect and seek increased knowledge despite the fact that the literature provides neither unqualified endorsement nor unequivocal encouragement. Also pertinent is Eysenck's remark that his conclusions about psychotherapy "are simply a summary of the existing literature and may have to be changed when further more adequate studies are reported" (p. 719). Meehl in his 1960 critique does not entertain the possibility of such reassessments, and there is considerable post-1960 literature to suggest he might well have done so. Neither science nor practice benefits from prematurely closed issues.

Perhaps more to the point than these somewhat *ad hominem* arguments is the fact that current mental health movements appear to be dating Meehl's emphasis on therapy and research as the only professionally secure functions for the clinician. In the face of the expanding focus on primary and secondary prevention and early detection of psychological disturbance in communities and institutions (e.g., Bennett, 1965; Yolles, 1966), the psychologist trained and identified solely as a psychotherapist can make only a limited contribution to the persons or agencies that might enlist his assistance. Rather than as a purveyor of a specific skill, the clinician is better identified as a *psychologist* with many skills, as diagnostician, therapist, consultant, and researcher, which he offers as the occasion and his interests direct.

Demands for psychodiagnostic services do not, however, automatically negate the frequent complaint that psychodiagnosis is a low-status activity, a menial and routine undertaking that subordinates the psychologist to other professional persons. Yet from the factors usually contributing to devalued identity among psychodiagnosticians, many of which are analyzed in excellent papers by Rosenwald (1963, 1965), it is clear that psychodiagnosticians may often be underlings not by virtue of their stars but by their own doing.

Specifically, the psychologist will derive status and satisfaction from his psychodiagnostic activities to the extent that he defines and establishes his role in them as that not of *tester,* but of *expert diagnostic consultant.* The clinician who accepts a brief written request as adequate basis for examining a patient and confines his report to a summation of personality structure and dynamics as revealed by his examination is a *tester;* he is treating psychodiagnosis as a laboratory procedure and cannot expect to be regarded by himself or by persons requesting his services as other than a subordinate auxilliary.

The psychodiagnostic *consultant,* in contrast, neither employs his skills for routine or unspecified purposes nor perceives tests as the sole basis of his response to a diagnostic referral, any more than a neurologist replies to a consultation request by producing an electroencephalographic record. The psychodiagnostic consultant, versed in psychodynamics and psychopathology as well as in psychodiagnostic techniques, expects to discuss with anyone seeking his opinion the nature of the case and the reason for the referral. He expects to inquire into aspects of the patient's history and symptomatology that he considers relevant to the diagnostic questions at issue. And he anticipates discussing in his report not only the patient's personality structure and dynamics as inferred from the tests, but also (a) the relationship of the test findings to aspects of the patient's observed behavior, (b) the degree to which the test data explain or fail to account for perplexing elements of the patient's symptomatology, (c) the congruence of the test and the clinical data as well with various diagnostic possibilities, and (d) indications from all available information of possible future courses the patient's adjustment and behavior might take in response to various kinds of foreseeable circumstances.

By practicing in this thorough and expert manner, the psychodiagnostician establishes himself as a consultant. In this role he shares the prestige and satisfactions enjoyed by consultants in most fields of endeavor, where the consultant, far from being an auxilliary or subordinate person, is a skilled professional who, on the basis of his expertise in a given area, is called in to deal with complex problems that cannot adequately be resolved by those who request his help. Dissatisfaction in such a role would certainly relate to the psychologist's interests and skills rather than to any limits of prestige intrinsic to psychodiagnostic activity.

REFERENCES

Abel, T. A. Figure drawing and facial disfigurement. *Amer. J. Orthopsychiat.*, 23:253–264, 1953.

Abrams, S. A validation of Piotrowski's alpha formula with schizophrenics varying in duration of illness. *Amer. J. Psychiat.*, 121: 45–47, 1964.

Abramson, L. S. The influence of set for area on the Rorschach test results. *J. consult. Psychol.*, 15:337–341, 1951.

Adland, M. L. Review, case studies, therapy, and interpretation of the acute exhaustive psychoses. *Psychiat. Quart.*, 21:38–69, 1947.

Ainsworth, M. D. Problems of validation. In B. Klopfer, M. D. Ainsworth, W. G. Klopfer, & R. R. Holt, *Developments in the Rorschach technique.* Vol. I. *Technique and theory.* Yonkers-on-Hudson: World Book, 1954. Pp. 405–500.

Aita, J. A., Armitage, S. G., Reitan, R. M., & Rabinowitz, A. The use of certain psychological tests in the evaluation of brain injury. *J. gen. Psychol.*, 37:25–44, 1947.

Albee, G. W., & Hamlin, R. M. An investigation of the reliability and validity of judgments inferred from drawings. *J. clin. Psychol.*, 5:389–392, 1949.

Albee, G. W., & Hamlin, R. M. Judgment of adjustment from drawings: the applicability of rating scale methods. *J. clin. Psychol.*, 6:363–365, 1950.

Albee, G. W., Lane, E. A., Corcoran, C., & Werneke, A. Childhood and intercurrent intellectual performance of adult schizophrenics. *J. consult. Psychol.*, 27:364–366, 1963.

Alden, P., & Benton, A. L. Relationship of sex of examiner to incidence of Rorschach responses with sexual content. *J. proj. Tech.*, 15: 231–234, 1951.

Allison, J., & Blatt, S. J. The relationship of Rorschach whole responses to intelligence. *J. proj. Tech. & Pers. Assess.*, 28: 255–260, 1964.

Ames, L. B., Metraux, R. W., & Walker, R. N. *Adolescent Rorschach responses.* New York: Hoeber, 1959.

Anastasi, A., & Foley, J. P. A survey of the literature on artistic behavior in the abnormal. III. Spontaneous productions. *Psychol. Monogr.*, 52 (Whole No. 237), 1941.

Anastasi, A., & Foley, J. P. An experimental study of the drawing behavior of adult psychotics in comparison with that of a normal control group. *J. exp. Psychol.*, 34:169-194, 1944.

Anderson, N. H. Scales and statistics: parametric and nonparametric. *Psychol. Bull.*, 58:305–316, 1961.

Arbit, J., & Lakin, M. Clinical psychologists' diagnostic utilization of human figure drawings. *J. clin. Psychol.*, 15:325–327, 1959.

Arieti, S. *Interpretation of schizophrenia.* New York: Brunner, 1955.

Arieti, S. Schizophrenia: the manifest symptomatology, the psychodynamic and formal mechanisms. In S. Arieti (Ed.), *American handbook of psychiatry.* New York: Basic Books, 1959a. Pp. 455–484.

Arieti, S. Manic-depressive psychosis. In S. Arieti (Ed.), *American handbook of psychiatry.* New York: Basic Books, 1959b. Pp. 419–454.

Armitage, S. G., Brown, C. R., & Denny, M. R. Stereotypy of response in schizophrenics. *J. clin. Psychol.*, **20**:225–230, 1964.

Aronson, M. L. A study of the Freudian theory of paranoia by means of the Rorschach test. *J. proj. Tech.*, **16**:397–411, 1952.

Atkinson, J. W. The achievement motive and recall of interrupted and completed tasks. *J. exp. Psychol.*, **46**:381–390, 1953.

Ausubel, D. P. Personality disorder *is* disease. *Amer. Psychologist*, **16**:69–74, 1961.

Babcock, H. An experiment in the measurement of mental deterioration. *Arch. Psychol.*, **18**:No. 117, 1930.

Babcock, H. *A short form of the Babcock examination for the measurement of mental deterioration.* Chicago: Stoelting, 1933.

Babigian, H. M., Gardner, E. A., Miles, H. C., & Romano, J. Diagnostic consistency and change in a follow-up study of 1215 patients. *Amer. J. Psychiat.*, **121**:895–901, 1965.

Baker, G. Diagnosis of organic brain damage in the adult. In B. Klopfer, *Developments in the Rorschach technique*. Vol. II. *Fields of application*. New York: Harcourt, Brace, & World, 1956. Pp. 318–375.

Baldwin, I. T. The head-body ratio in human figure drawings of schizophrenic and normal adults. *J. proj. Tech. & Pers. Assess.*, **28**:393–396, 1964.

Barker, A. J., Mathis, J. K., & Powers, C. A. Drawing characteristics of male homosexuals. *J. clin. Psychol.*, **9**:185–188, 1953.

Bateson, G., Jackson, D. D., Haley, J., & Weakland, J. Toward a theory of schizophrenia. *Behavioral Sci.*, **1**:251–264, 1956.

Beck, A. T., Feshbach, S., & Legg, D. The clinical utility of the Digit Symbol test. *J. consult. Psychol.*, **26**:263–268, 1962.

Beck, S. J. Personality diagnosis by means of the Rorschach test. *Amer. J. Orthopsychiat.*, **1**:81–88, 1930a.

Beck, S. J. The Rorschach test and personality diagnosis. *Amer. J. Psychiat.*, **10**:19–52, 1930b.

Beck, S. J. Configurational tendencies in Rorschach responses. *Amer. J. Psychol.*, **45**:433–443, 1933.

Beck, S. J. *Personality structure in schizophrenia*. New York: Nervous and Mental Disease Monograph, 1938.

Beck, S. J. The Rorschach test in psychopathology. *J. consult. Psychol.*, **7**:103–111, 1943.

Beck, S. J. *Rorschach's test*. Vol. II. *A variety of personality pictures*. New York: Grune & Stratton, 1947.

Beck, S. J. Rorschach F plus and the ego in treatment. *Amer. J. Orthopsychiat.*, **18**:395–401, 1948.

Beck, S. J. *Rorschach's test*. Vol. I. *Basic processes*. (2nd ed.) New York: Grune & Stratton, 1950.

Beck, S. J. *Rorschach's test*. Vol. III. *Advances in interpretation*. New York: Grune & Stratton, 1952.

Beck, S. J. *The six schizophrenias*. New York: American Orthopsychiatric Association, 1954.

Beck, S. J. SR-2: affect autonomy in schizophrenia. *Arch. gen. Psychiat.*, **2**:408–420, 1960.

Beck, S. J., Beck, A. G., Levitt, E. E., and Molish, H. B. *Rorschach's test*. Vol. I. *Basic processes*. (3rd ed.) New York: Grune & Stratton, 1961.

Beck, S. J., Rabin, A. I., Thiesen, J. W., Molish, H. B., and Thetford, W. N. The normal personality as projected in the Rorschach test. *J. Psychol.*, 30:241–298, 1950.

Becker, W. C. A genetic approach to the interpretation and evaluation of the process-reactive distinction in schizophrenia. *J. abnorm. soc. Psychol.*, 53:229–236, 1956.

Becker, W. C. The process-reactive distinction: a key to the problem of schizophrenia? *J. nerv. ment. Dis.*, 129:442–449, 1959.

Bell, J. E. *Projective techniques.* New York: Longmans, Green & Co., 1948.

Bellak, L. A multiple-factor psychosomatic theory of schizophrenia. *Psychiat. Quart.*, 23:783–795, 1949.

Bellak, L. Toward a unified concept of schizophrenia. *J. nerv. ment. Dis.*, 121:60–66, 1955.

Bellak, L. The schizophrenic syndrome: a further elaboration of the unified theory of schizophrenia. In L. Bellak (Ed.), *Schizophrenia: a review of the syndrome.* New York: Logos, 1958. Pp. 3–63.

Belmont, I., Birch, H. G., Klein, D. F., & Pollack, M. Perceptual evidence of CNS dysfunction in schizophrenia. *Arch. gen. Psychiat.*, 10:395–408, 1964.

Bender, L. Childhood schizophrenia. *Psychiat. Quart.*, 27:663–681, 1953.

Benjamin, J. D. A method for distinguishing and evaluating formal thinking disorders in schizophrenia. In J. S. Kasanin (Ed.), *Language and thought in schizophrenia.* Berkeley: Univ. California Press, 1944. Pp. 65–88.

Benjamin, J. D., & Ebaugh, F. G. The diagnostic validity of the Rorschach test. *Amer. J. Psychiat.*, 94: 1163–1178, 1938.

Bennett, C. C. Community psychology: impressions of the Boston conference on the education of psychologists for community mental health. *Amer. Psychologist*, 20:832–835, 1965.

Beres, D. Ego deviation and the concept of schizophrenia. *Psychoan. Stud. Child*, 11:164–235, 1956.

Berger, L., Bernstein, A., Klein, E., Cohen, J., & Lucas, G. Effects of aging and pathology on the factorial structure of intelligence. *J. consult. Psychol.*, 28:199–207, 1964.

Berkowitz, M., & Levine, J. Rorschach scoring categories as diagnostic "signs." *J. consult. Psychol.*, 17:110–112, 1953.

Berman, S., & Laffal, J. Body type and figure drawing. *J. clin. Psychol.*, 9:368–370, 1953.

Bernstein, L. The interaction of process and content on thought disorders of schizophrenic and brain-damaged patients. *J. gen. Psychol.*, 62:53–68, 1960.

Birch, H. G., & Belmont, I. Functional levels of disturbance manifested by brain-damaged (hemiplegic) patients as revealed by Rorschach responses. *J. nerv. ment. Dis.*, 132:410–416, 1961.

Birren, J. E. Psychological examination of children who later became psychotic. *J. abnorm. soc. Psychol.*, 39:84–96, 1944.

Blatt, S. J., & Allison, J. Methodological considerations in Rorschach research: the W response as an expression of abstractive and integrative strivings. *J. proj. Tech.*, 27:267–278, 1963.

Blaufarb, H. A demonstration of verbal abstracting ability in chronic schizophrenics under enriched stimulus and instructional conditions. *J. consult. Psychol.*, 26:471–475, 1962.

Bleke, R. Reward and punishment as determiners of reminiscence effects in schizophrenic and normal subjects. *J. Pers.*, 23:479–498, 1955.

Bleuler, E. (1911) *Dementia praecox or the group of schizophrenias*. New York: International Universities Press, 1950.

Bleuler, E. *Textbook of psychiatry*. New York: Macmillan, 1924. Translated from the 4th German edition.

Bleuler, E. The physiogenic and psychogenic in schizophrenic. *Amer. J. Psychiat.*, 10:203–211, 1930.

Block, W. A. Psychometric aspects of the Rorschach technique. *J. proj. Tech.*, 26:162–172, 1962.

Boardman, W. K., Goldstone, S., Reiner, M. L., & Himmel, S. Constancy of absolute judgments of size by normals and schizophrenics. *J. abnorm. soc. Psychol.*, 68:346–349, 1964.

Bohm, E. *Rorschach test diagnosis*. New York: Grune & Stratton, 1958.

Bolles, M., & Goldstein, K. A study of the impairment of "abstract behavior" in schizophrenic patients. *Psychiat. Quart.*, 12:42–65, 1938.

Boneau, C. A. The effects of violations of assumptions underlying the *t*-test. *Psychol. Bull.*, 57:49–64, 1960.

Bower, P. A., Testin, R., & Roberts, A. Rorschach diagnosis by a systematic combining of content, thought process, and determinant scales. *Genet. psychol. Monogr.*, 62:105–183, 1960.

Brackbill, G. A. Studies of brain dysfunction in schizophrenia. *Psychol. Bull.*, 53:210–226, 1956.

Brackbill, G. A., & Fine, H. J. Schizophrenia and central nervous system pathology. *J. abnorm. soc. Psychol.*, 52:310–313, 1956.

Brecher, S. The Rorschach reaction patterns of maternally overprotected and maternally rejected schizophrenic patients. *J. nerv. ment. Dis.*, 123:41–52, 1956.

Brenner, C. The nature and development of the concept of repression in Freud's writings. *Psychoan. Stud. Child*, 12:19–46, 1957.

Brill, N. Q., & Glass, J. F. Hebephrenic schizophrenic reactions. *Arch. gen. Psychiat.*, 12:545–551, 1965.

Brockway, A., Gleser, G. C., & Ulett, G. A. Rorschach concepts of normality. *J. consult. Psychol.*, 18:259–265, 1954.

Brodsky, M. Interpersonal stimuli as interference in a sorting task. *J. Pers.*, 31:517–533, 1963.

Brody, M. B. A survey of the results of intelligence tests in psychosis. *Brit. J. med. Psychol.*, 19:215–257, 1942.

Brown, F. An exploratory study of the dynamic factors in the content of the Rorschach protocol. *J. proj. Tech.*, 17:251–279, 1953.

Brown, M., & Bryan, G. The altitude quotient as a measurement of intellectual potential. *J. clin. Psychol.*, 13:137–140, 1957.

Bruner, J. S. & Goodman, C. C. Value and need as organizing factors in perception. *J. abnorm. soc. Psychol.*, 42:33–44, 1947.

Buchheimer, A. The development of ideas about empathy. *J. counsel. Psychol.*, 10:61–70, 1963.

Buckle, D., & Holt, N. Comparison of Rorschach and Behn inkblots. *J. proj. Tech.*, 15:486–493, 1951.

Buhler, C., Buhler, K., & Lefever, D. W. *Development of the Basic Rorschach Score*. Los Angeles: Buhler, Buhler, & Lefever, 1949.

Bullard, D. M. Psychotherapy of paranoid patients. *Arch. gen. Psychiat.*, 2:137–141, 1960.

Burgemeister, B. B. *Psychological techniques in neurological diagnosis.* New York: Harper & Row, 1962.

Burns, C. Pre-schizophrenic symptoms in pre-adolescents' withdrawal and sensitivity. *Nerv. Child,* 10:120–128, 1952.

Buss, A. H., & Lang, P. J. Psychological deficit in schizophrenia: I. Affect, reinforcement, and concept attainment. *J. abnorm. Psychol.,* 70:2–24, 1965.

Bychowski, G. Disorders in the body-image in the clinical pictures of psychoses. *J. nerv. ment. Dis.,* 97:310–334, 1943.

Bychowski, G. *Psychotherapy of psychosis.* New York: Grune & Stratton, 1952.

Bychowski, G. The problem of latent psychosis. *J. Amer. Psychoan. Assoc.,* 1:484–503, 1953.

Bychowski, G. Psychic structure and therapy of latent schizophrenia. In A. N. Rifkin (Ed.), *Schizophrenia in psychoanalytic office practice.* New York: Grune & Stratton, 1957. Pp. 124–139.

Cameron, N. Reasoning, regression, and communication in schizophrenics. *Psychol. Monogr.,* 50 (Whole No. 221), 1938.

Cameron, N. Schizophrenic thinking in a problem-solving situation. *J. ment. Sci.,* 85:1012–1035, 1939a.

Cameron, N. Deterioration and regression in schizophrenic thinking. *J. abnorm. soc. Psychol.,* 34:265–270, 1939b.

Cameron, N. Experimental analysis of schizophrenic thinking. In J. S. Kasanin (Ed.), *Language and thought in schizophrenia.* Berkeley: Univer. California Press, 1944. Pp. 50–63.

Cameron, N. *The psychology of behavior disorders.* Boston: Houghton Mifflin, 1947.

Cameron, N. Paranoid conditions and paranoia. In S. Arieti (Ed.), *American handbook of psychiatry.* New York: Basic Books, 1959. Pp. 508–539.

Cameron, N. *Personality development and psychopathology.* Boston: Houghton Mifflin, 1963.

Carluccio, C., Sours, J. A., & Kolb, L. C. Psychodynamics of echo-reactions. *Arch. gen. Psychiat.,* 10:623–629, 1964.

Cass, W. A., & McReynolds, P. A contribution to Rorschach norms. *J. consult. Psychol.,* 15:178–184, 1951.

Cavanaugh, D. K. Improvement of schizophrenics on concept formation tasks as a function of motivational change. *J. abnorm. soc. Psychol.,* 57:8–12, 1958.

Cavanaugh, D. K., Cohen, W., & Lang, P. J. The effect of "social censure" and "social approval" on the psychomotor performance of schizophrenics. *J. abnorm. soc. Psychol.,* 60:213–218, 1960.

Chambers, G. S., & Hamlin, R. M. the validity of judments based on "blind" Rorschach records. *J. consult. Psychol.,* 21:105–109, 1957.

Chambers, J. L. Perceptual judgment and associative learning ability of schizophrenics and nonpsychotics. *J. consult. Psychol.,* 20:211–214, 1956.

Chapman, A. H., & Reese, D. G. Homosexual signs in the Rorschachs of early schizophrenics. *J. clin. Psychol.,* 9:30–32, 1953.

Chapman, J., & McGhie, A. A comparative study of disordered attention in schizophrenia. *J. ment. Sci.,* 108:487–500, 1962.

Chapman, L. J. Distractibility in the conceptual performance of schizophrenics. *J. abnorm. soc. Psychol.,* 53:286–291, 1956.

Chapman, L. J. Intrusion of associative responses into schizophrenic conceptual performance. *J. abnorm. soc. Psychol.,* 53:374–379, 1958.

Chapman, L. J. Confusion of figurative and literal usages of words by schizophrenics and brain damaged patients. *J. abnorm. soc. Psychol.*, 60:412–416, 1960.

Chapman, L. J. A reinterpretation of some pathological disturbances in conceptual breadth. *J. abnorm. soc. Psychol.*, 62:514–519, 1961.

Chapman, L. J., Day, D., & Burstein, A. The process-reactive distinction and prognosis in schizophrenia. *J. nerv. ment. Dis.*, 133:383–391, 1961.

Chapman, L. J., & Taylor, J. A. Breadth of deviate concepts used by schizophrenics. *J. abnorm. soc. Psychol.*, 54:118–123, 1957.

Chase, J. M. A study of the drawings of a male figure made by schizophrenic patients and normal subjects. *Character & Pers.*, 9:208–217, 1941.

Chase, L. S., & Silverman, S. Prognosis in schizophrenics treated with Metrazol or insulin. *J. nerv. ment. Dis.*, 98:464–473, 1943.

Cheek, F. E. Family interaction patterns and convalescent adjustment of the schizophrenic. *Arch. gen. Psychiat.*, 13:138–147, 1965.

Chodorkoff, B., & Mussen, P. Qualitative aspects of the vocabulary responses of normals and schizophrenics. *J. consult. Psychol.*, 16:43–48, 1952.

Cleveland, S. E. Body image changes associated with personality reorganization. *J. consult. Psychol.*, 24:256–261, 1960.

Cleveland, S. E., Fisher, S., Reitman, E. E., & Rothaus, P. Perception of body size in schizophrenia. *Arch. gen. Psychiat.*, 7:277–285, 1962.

Cohen, B. D. Motivation and performance in schizophrenia. *J. abnorm. soc. Psychol.*, 52:186–190, 1956.

Cohen, B. D., Senf, R., & Huston, P. E. Perceptual accuracy in schizophrenia, depression, and neurosis and effects of amytal. *J. abnorm. soc. Psychol.*, 52:363–367, 1956.

Cohen, J. Factors underlying Wechsler-Bellevue performance of three neuropsychiatric groups. *J. abnorm. soc. Psychol.*, 47:359–365, 1952.

Cohen, J. The efficacy of diagnostic pattern analysis with the Wechsler-Bellevue. *J. consult. Psychol.*, 19:303–306, 1955.

Cohen, J. The factorial structure of the WAIS between early adulthood and old age. *J. consult. Psychol.*, 21:283–290, 1957a.

Cohen, J. A factor-analytically based rationale for the WAIS. *J. consult. Psychol.*, 21:451–457, 1957b.

Cooper, R. Objective measures of perception in schizophrenics and normals. *J. consult. Psychol.*, 24:209–214, 1960.

Costa, L. D., & Vaughan, H. G. Performance of patients with lateralized cerebral lesions. I: Verbal and perceptual tests. *J. nerv. ment. Dis.*, 134:162–168, 1962.

Craddick, R. A. The self-image in the Draw-a-Person test and self-portrait drawings. *J. proj. Tech.*, 27:288–291, 1963.

Cromwell, R. L., Rosenthal, D., Shakow, D., & Zahn, T. P. Reaction time, locus of control, choice behavior, and descriptions of parental behavior in schizophrenic and normal subjects. *J. Pers.*, 29:363–379, 1961.

Cronbach, L. J. *Essentials of psychological testing.* New York: Harper, 1949a.

Cronbach, L. J. Statistical methods applied to Rorschach scores: a review. *Psychol. Bull.*, 46:393–429, 1949b.

Cronbach, L. J., & Meehl, P. E. Construct validity in psychological tests. *Psychol. Bull.*, 52:281–302, 1955.

Cutter, F. Sexual differentiation in figure drawings and overt deviation. *J. clin. Psychol.*, 12:369–372, 1956.

Daston, P. G. Perception of homosexual words in paranoid schizophrenia. *Percept. mot. Skills,* 6:45–55, 1956.

Daston, P. G., & McConnell, O. L. Stability of Rorschach penetration and barrier scores over time. *J. consult. Psychol.,* 26:104, 1962.

Davids, A., Joelson, M., & McArthur, C. Rorschach and TAT indices of homosexuality in overt homosexuals, neurotics, and normal males. *J. abnorm. soc. Psychol.,* 53:161–172, 1956.

Davidson, H., & Klopfer, B. Rorschach statistics: Part I. Mentally retarded, normal, and superior adults. *Rorschach Res. Exch.,* 2:164–169, 1937–1938.

Davis, R. H., & Harrington, R. W. The effect of stimulus class on the problem-solving behavior of schizophrenics and normals. *J. abnorm. soc. Psychol.,* 54:126–128, 1957.

DeVos, G. A quantitative approach to affective symbolism in Rorschach responses. *J. proj. Tech.,* 16:133–150, 1952.

Dimmick, G. B. An application of the Rorschach ink-blot test to three clinical types of dementia praecox. *J. Psychol.,* 1:61–74, 1935–1936.

Draguns, J. G. Responses to cognititve and perceptual ambiguity in chronic and acute schizophrenics. *J. abnorm. soc. Psychol.,* 66:24–30, 1963.

DuBrin, A. J. The Rorschach "eyes" hypothesis and paranoid schizophrenia. *J. clin. Psychol.,* 18:468–471, 1962.

Due, F. O., & Wright, M. E. The use of content analysis in Rorschach interpretation. I. Differential characteristics of male homosexuals. *Rorschach Res. Exch.,* 9:169–177, 1945.

Dunaif, S., & Hoch, P. H. Pseudopsychopathic schizophrenia. In P. H. Hoch & J. Zubin (Eds.), *Psychiatry and the law.* New York: Grune & Stratton, 1955. Pp. 169–195.

Dunton, W. R. The cyclic forms of dementia praecox. *Amer. J. Insanity,* 66:465–476, 1910.

Dworetzki, G. Le test de Rorschach et l'evaluation de la perception. *Archives de Psychologie,* 37:233–396, 1939.

Eckhardt, W. Piotrowski's signs: organic or functional. *J. clin. Psychol.,* 17:36–38, 1961.

Edelston, H. Differential diagnosis of some emotional disorders of adolescence. *J. ment. Sci.,* 95:961–967, 1949.

Eichler, R. A comparison of the Rorschach and Behn-Rorschach ink-blot tests. *J. consult. Psychol.,* 15:185–189, 1951a.

Eichler, R. Experimental stress and alleged Rorschach indices of anxiety. *J. abnorm. soc. Psychol.,* 46:344–355, 1951b.

Eliseo, T. S. Figurative and literal misinterpretations of words by process and reactive schizophrenics. *Psychol. Rep.,* 13:871–877, 1963.

Elmore, C. M., & Gorham, D. R. Measuring the impairment of the abstracting function with the Proverbs Test. *J. clin. Psychol.,* 13:263–266, 1957.

Engel, G. L. *Psychological development in health and disease.* Philadelphia: Saunders, 1962. Chap. XXIII.

Epstein, S. Overinclusive thinking in a schizophrenic and a control group. *J. consult. Psychol.,* 17:384–388, 1953.

Eriksen, C. W. Perceptual defense as a function of unacceptable needs. *J. abnorm. soc. Psychol.,* 46:557–564, 1951.

Erikson, E. H. The problem of ego identity. *J. Amer. Psychoan. Assoc.,* 4:56–121, 1956.

Estes, S. G. Deviations of Wechsler-Bellevue subtest scores from vocabulary level in superior adults. *J. abnorm. soc. Psychol.*, **41**:226–228, 1946.

Evans, R. B., & Marmorston, J. Psychological test signs of brain damage in cerebral thrombosis. *Psychol. Rep.*, **12**:915–930, 1963.

Evans, R. B., & Marmorston, J. Rorschach signs of brain damage in cerebral thrombosis. *Percept. mot. Skills*, **18**:977–988, 1964.

Eysenck, H. J. Classification and the problem of diagnosis. In H. J. Eysenck (Ed.), *Handbook of abnormal psychology*. New York: Basic Books, 1961a. Pp. 1–31.

Eysenck, H. J. The effects of psychotherapy. In H. J. Eysenck (Ed.), *Handbook of abnormal psychology*. New York: Basic Books, 1961b. Pp. 697–725.

Eysenck, H. J., Granger, G. W., & Brengelmann, J. C. *Perceptual process and mental illness*. New York: Basic Books, 1957.

Federn, P. *Ego psychology and the psychoses*. New York: Basic Books, 1952.

Feffer, M. H. The influence of affective factors on conceptualization in schizophrenia. *J. abnorm. soc. Psychol.*, **63**:588–596, 1961.

Feifel, H. Qualitative differences in the vocabulary responses of normals and abnormals. *Genet. Psychol. Monogr.*, **39**:151–204, 1949.

Feinberg, I., & Garman, E. M. Studies of thought disorder in schizophrenia. II. *Arch. gen. Psychiat.*, **4**:191–201, 1961.

Feldman, M. J., & Drasgow, J. A. A Visual-Verbal Test for schizophrenia. *Psychiat. Quart. Suppl.*, **25**:55–64, 1951.

Feldman, M. J., Gurrslin, C., Kaplan, M. L., & Sharlock, N. A preliminary study to develop a more discriminating F+ ratio. *J. clin. Psychol.*, **10**:47–51, 1954.

Feldman, M. J., & Hunt, R. G. A relation of difficulty in drawing and ratings of adjustment based on human figure drawings. *J. consult. Psychol.*, **22**:217–220, 1958.

Feldstein, S. The relationship of interpersonal involvement and affectiveness of content to the verbal communication of schizophrenic patients. *J. abnorm. soc. Psychol.*, **64**:39–45, 1962.

Fenichel, O. (1938) Ego strength and ego weakness. In H. Fenichel & D. Rapaport (Eds.), *Collected papers of Otto Fenichel*. Second Series. New York: Norton, 1954. Pp. 70–80.

Fenichel, O. *The psychoanalytic theory of neurosis*. New York: Norton, 1945.

Fessel, W. J. Interaction of multiple determinants in schizophrenia. *Arch. gen. Psychiat.*, **11**:1–18, 1964.

Fey, E. T. The performance of young schizophrenics on the Wisconsin Card Sorting Test. *J. consult. Psychol.*, **15**:311–319, 1951.

Fine, H. J., & Zimet, C. N. Process-reactive schizophrenia and genetic levels of perception. *J. abnorm. soc. Psychol.*, **59**:83–85, 1959.

Fink, S. L., & Shontz, F. C. Inference of intellectual efficiency from the WAIS vocabulary subtest. *J. clin. Psychol.*, **14**:409–412, 1958.

Finney, B. C. The diagnostic discrimination of the "Basic Rorschach Score." *J. consult. Psychol.*, **19**:96, 1955.

Fisher, J., Gonda, T., & Little, K. B. The Rorschach and central nervous system pathology. *Amer. J. Psychiat.*, **111**:486–492, 1955.

Fisher, S. Some observations suggested by the Rorschach test concerning the ambulatory schizophrenic. *Psychiat. Quart. Suppl.*, **29**:81–89, 1955.

Fisher, S. A further appraisal of the body boundary concept. *J. consult. Psychol.*, **27**:62–74, 1963.

Fisher, S. Body image and psychopathology. *Arch. gen. Psychiat.*, **10**:519–529, 1964a.

Fisher, S. The body boundary and judged behavioral patterns in an interview situation. *J. proj. Tech. & Pers. Assess.*, 28:181–184, 1964b.

Fisher, S., & Cleveland, S. E. *Body image and personality.* Princeton: Van Nostrand, 1958.

Fisher, S., & Fisher, R. L. Body image boundaries and patterns of body perception. *J. abnorm. soc. Psychol.*, 68:255–262, 1964.

Fisher, S., & Seidner, R. Body experiences of schizophrenic, neurotic, and normal women. *J. nerv. ment. Dis.*, 137:252–257, 1963.

Fiske, D. W., & Baughman, E. E. Relationships between Rorschach scoring categories and the total number of responses. *J. abnorm. soc. Psychol.*, 48:25–32, 1953.

Fiske, D. W., Rice, L. Intra-individual response variability. *Psychol. Bull.*, 52:217–250, 1955.

Flavell, J. H. Abstract thinking and social behavior in schizophrenia. *J. abnorm. soc. Psychol.*, 52:208–211, 1956.

Fonda, C. P. The white-space response. In M. A. Rickers-Ovsiankina (Ed.), *Rorschach Psychology.* New York: Wiley, 1960. Pp. 80–105.

Forer, B. R. The latency of latent schizophrenia. *J. proj. Tech.*, 14:297–302, 1950.

Fortier, R. H. The response to color and ego functions. *Psychol. Bull.*, 50:41–63, 1953.

Frank, G. H. The WB and psychiatric diagnosis: a factor analytic approach. *J. consult. Psychol.*, 20:67–69, 1956.

Frank, G. H., Corrie, C. C., & Fogel, J. An empirical critique of research with the Wechsler-Bellevue in differential psychodiagnosis. *J. clin. Psychol.*, 11:291–293, 1955.

Frank, I. K. Perceptual structuralization in certain psychoneurotic disorders. Unpublished doctoral dissertation, Boston University, 1951.

Freeman, H. Physiological studies. In L. Bellak (Ed.), *Schizophrenia: a review of the syndrome.* New York: Logos, 1958. Pp. 174–215.

Freeman, H. E., & Simmons, O. G. *Mental patient comes home.* New York: Wiley, 1963.

French, E. G., & Hunt, W. A. The relationship of scatter in test performance to intelligence level. *J. clin. Psychol.*, 7:95–98, 1951.

Freud, A. (1936) *The ego and the mechanisms of defence.* New York: International Universities Press, 1946.

Freud, A. Adolescence. *Psychoan. Stud. Child*, 13:255–278, 1958.

Freud, S. (1894) The defense neuro-psychoses. *Collected papers.* Vol. I. London: Hogarth, 1953. Pp. 59–75.

Freud, S. (1896) Further remarks on the defense neuro-psychoses. *Collected papers.* Vol. I. London: Hogarth, 1953. Pp. 155–182.

Freud, S. (1900) *The interpretation of dreams.* New York: Basic Books, 1955.

Freud, S. (1911a) Psycho-analytic notes upon an autobiographical account of a case of paranoia (dementia paranoides). *Collected papers.* Vol. III. London: Hogarth, 1953. Pp. 390–470.

Freud, S. (1911b) Formulations regarding the two principles in mental functioning. *Collected papers.* Vol. IV. London: Hogarth, 1953. Pp. 13–21.

Freud, S. (1914) On narcissism: an introduction. *Collected papers.* Vol. IV. London: Hogarth, 1953. Pp. 30–59.

Freud, S. (1915) Repression. *Collected papers.* Vol. IV. London: Hogarth, 1953. Pp. 84–97.

Freud, S. (1923) *The ego and the id.* London: Hogarth, 1947.

Freud, S. (1924a) Neurosis and psychosis. *Collected papers.* Vol. II. London: Hogarth, 1953. Pp. 250–254.

Freud, S. (1924b) The loss of reality in neurosis and psychosis. *Collected papers.* Vol. II. London: Hogarth, 1953. Pp. 277–282.

Freud, S. (1926) *The problem of anxiety.* New York: Norton and the Psychoanalytic Quarterly Press, 1936.

Freud, S. (1937) Analysis terminable and interminable. *Collected papers.* Vol. V. London: Hogarth, 1953. Pp. 316–357. Quoted from *Standard edition,* Vol. XXIII. London: Hogarth and the Institute of Psycho-analysis, 1964. Pp. 216–253.

Freud, S. (1938) *An outline of psychoanalysis.* New York: Norton, 1949.

Friedman, A. S. Minimal effects of severe depression on cognitive functioning. *J. abnorm. soc. Psychol.,* **69**:237–243, 1964.

Friedman, H. Perceptual regression in schizophrenia. *J. genet. Psychol.,* **81**:63–98, 1952a.

Friedman, H. A comparison of a group of hebephrenic and catatonic schizophrenics with two groups of normal adults by means of certain variables of the Rorschach test. *J. proj. Tech.,* **16**:352–360, 1952b.

Friedman, H. Perceptual regression in schizophrenia. *J. proj. Tech.,* **17**:171–185, 1953.

Friedman, H. A note on the revised Rorschach development scoring system. *J. clin. Psychol.,* **16**:52–54, 1960.

Friedman, H., & Orgel, S. A. Rorschach developmental scores and intelligence level. *J. proj. Tech. & Pers. Assess.,* **28**:425–428, 1964.

Fromm, E. O., & Elonen, A. S. The use of projective techniques in the study of a case of female homosexuality. *J. proj. Tech.,* **15**:185–230, 1951.

Fromm-Reichmann, F. Transference problems in schizophrenics. *Psychoan. Quart.,* **8**:412–426, 1939.

Fromm-Reichmann, F. On schizophrenia. Part III of D. M. Bullard (Ed.), *Psychoanalysis and Psychotherapy: selected papers of Frieda Fromm-Reichmann.* Chicago: Univer. Chicago Press, 1959. Pp. 117–274.

Fulkerson, S. C., & Barry, J. R. Methodology and research on the prognostic use of psychological tests. *Psychol. Bull.,* **58**:177–204, 1961.

Funkenstein, D. H., Greenblatt, M., & Solomon, H. C. A test which predicts the clinical effects of electric shock treatment on schizophrenic patients. *Amer. J. Psychiat.,* **106**:889–901, 1950.

Gardner, G. E. The learning ability of schizophrenics. *Amer. J. Psychiat.,* **11**: 247–252, 1931.

Gardner, G. E. Rorschach test replies and results in 100 normal adults of average I. Q. *Amer. J. Orthopsychiat.,* **6**:32–60, 1936.

Gardner, R. W., Holzman, P. S., Klein, G. S., Linton, H. B., & Spence, D. P. Cognitive control: a study of individual consistencies in cognitive behavior. *Psychol. Issues,* **1**:No. 4, 1959.

Garfield, S. L. The Rorschach test in clinical diagnosis. *J. clin. Psychol.,* **3**:375–381, 1947.

Garfield, S. L. Wechsler-Bellevue patterns in schizophrenia. *J. consult. Psychol.,* **12**:32–36, 1948.

Garfield, S. L. An evaluation of Wechsler patterns in schizophrenia. *J. consult. Psychol.,* **13**:279–287, 1949.

Garfield, S. L. The clinical method in personality assessment. In J. W. Wepman

& R. W. Heine (Eds.), *Concepts of personality*. Chicago: Aldine, 1963. Pp. 474–502.

Garmezy, N. Stimulus differentiation by schizophrenic and normal subjects under conditions of reward and punishment. *J. Pers.*, **20**:253–276, 1952.

Garmezy, N., & Rodnick, E. H. Premorbid adjustment and performance in schizophrenia: implications for interpreting heterogeneity in schizophrenia. *J. nerv. ment. Dis.*, **129**:450–466, 1959.

Gaw, E. A., Reichard, S., & Tillman, C. How common is schizophrenia? *Bull. Menninger Clin.*, **17**:20–28, 1953.

Geocaris, K. H., & Kooiker, J. E. Blood pressure responses of chronic schizophrenic patients to epinephrine and mecholyl. *Amer. J. Psychiat.*, **112**:808–813, 1956.

Giedt, F. H., & Lehner, G. F. J. Assignment of ages on the Draw-a-Person test by male psychoneurotic patients. *J. Pers.*, **19**:440–448, 1951.

Gilbert, J. G., & Hall, M. R. Changes with age in human figure drawing. *J. Gerontol.*, **17**:397–404, 1962.

Gilhooly, F. M. The relationship between variability and ability on the Wechsler-Bellevue. *J. consult. Psychol.*, **14**:46–48, 1950a.

Gilhooly, F. M. Correction of "The relationship between variability and ability on the Wechsler-Bellevue." *J. consult. Psychol.*, **14**:329, 1950b.

Gilliland, A. R. Differential functional loss in certain psychoses. *Psychol. Bull.*, **37**:439, 1940.

Gilliland, A. R., Wellman, P., & Goldman, M. Patterns and scatter of mental abilities in various psychoses. *J. gen. Psychol.*, **29**:251–260, 1943.

Ginett, L. E., & Moran, L. J. Stability of vocabulary performance by schizophrenics. *J. consult. Psychol.*, **28**:178–179, 1964.

Glasner, S. Benign paralogical thinking. *Arch. gen. Psychiat.*, **14**:94–99, 1966.

Gleser, G. C. Projective methodologies. *Annu. Rev. Psychol.*, **14**:391–422, 1963.

Glick, B. S. Homosexual panic: clinical and theoretical considerations. *J. nerv. ment. Dis.*, **129**:20–28, 1959.

Goldfarb, W. Organizational activity in the Rorschach examination. *Amer. J. Orthopsychiat.*, **15**:523–528, 1945.

Goldfried, M. R. Some normative data on Rorschach developmental level "card pull" in a psychiatric population. *J. proj. Tech.*, **26**:283–287, 1962.

Goldman, A. E. Symbolic representation in schizophrenia. *J. Pers.*, **28**:293–316, 1960.

Goldman, A. E. A comparative-developmental approach to schizophrenia. *Psychol. Bull.*, **59**:57–69, 1962.

Goldman, R. Changes in Rorschach performance and clinical improvement in schizophrenia. *J. consult. Psychol.*, **24**:403–407, 1960.

Goldstein, K. Methodological approach to the study of schizophrenic thought disorder. In J. S. Kasanin (Ed.), *Language and thought in schizophrenia*. Berkeley: Univer. California Press, 1944. Pp. 10–39.

Goldstein, K. Concerning the concreteness in schizophrenia. *J. abnorm. soc. Psychol.*, **59**:146–148, 1959.

Goodenough, F. L. *Measurement of intelligence by drawings*. Yonkers, New York: World Book Co., 1926.

Goodstein, L. D., Guertin, W. H., & Blackburn, H. C. Effects of social motivational variables on choice reaction time of schizophrenics. *J. abnorm. soc. Psychol.*, **62**:24–27, 1961.

Gorham, D. R. A proverbs test for clinical and experimental use. *Psychol. Rep.*, **2**:1–12, 1956a.

Gorham, D. R. Use of the proverbs test for differentiating schizophrenics from normals. *J. consult. Psychol.*, 20:435–440, 1956b.

Gorham, D. R. Additional norms and scoring suggestions for the Proverbs Test. *Psychol. Rep.*, 13:487–492, 1963.

Grams, A., & Rinder, L. Signs of homosexuality in human figure drawings. *J. consult. Psychol.*, 22:394, 1958.

Grauer, D. Prognosis in paranoid schizophrenia on the basis of the Rorschach. *J. consult. Psychol.*, 17:199–205, 1953.

Grauer, D. Homosexuality in paranoid schizophrenia as revealed by the Rorschach test. *J. consult. Psychol.*, 18:459–462, 1954.

Griffith, R. M. The test-retest similarities of the Rorschachs of patients without retention, Korsakoff. *J. proj. Tech.*, 15:516–525, 1951.

Griffith, R. M., Estes, B. W., & Zerof, S. A. Intellectual impairment in schizophrenia. *J. consult. Psychol.*, 26:336–339, 1962.

Gross, L. R. Effects of verbal and nonverbal reinforcement in the Rorschach. *J. consult. Psychol.*, 23:66–68, 1959.

Guertin, W. H. An inverted factor-analytic study of schizophrenia. *J. consult. Psychol.*, 16:371–375, 1952.

Guertin, W. H., Frank, G. H., & Rabin, A. I. Research with the WB Intelligence Scale, 1950-1955. *Psychol. Bull.*, 53:235–257, 1956.

Guertin, W. H., Rabin, A. I., Frank, G. H., & Ladd, C. E., Research with the Wechsler intelligence scales for adults, 1955–60. *Psychol. Bull.*, 59:1–28, 1962.

Guinan, J. F., & Hurley, J. R. An investigation of the reliability of human figure drawings. *J. proj. Tech. & Pers. Assess.*, 29:300–304, 1965.

Guirdham, A. On the value of the Rorschach test. *J. ment. Sci.*, 81:848–870, 1935.

Gulliksen, H. *Theory of mental tests.* New York: Wiley, 1950.

Gurvitz, M. S., & Miller, J. A. Some theoretical and practical aspects of the diagnosis of early and latent schizophrenia by means of psychological testing. In P. H. Hoch & J. Zubin (Eds.), *Relation of psychological tests to psychiatry.* New York: Grune & Stratton, 1952. Pp. 189–207.

Guttmacher, M. S. Critique of views of Thomas Szasz on legal psychiatry. *Arch. gen. Psychiat.*, 10:238–245, 1964.

Hackfield, A. W. An objective interpretation by means of the Rorschach test of the psychobiological structure underlying schizophrenia, essential hypertension, Graves' Syndrome, etc. *Amer. J. Psychiat.*, 92:575–588, 1935.

Hall, K. R. L., & Crookes, T. G. Studies in learning impairment: I. Schizophrenic and organic patients. *J. ment. Sci.*, 97:725–737, 1951.

Hamilton, V. Size constancy and cue responsiveness in psychosis. *Brit. J. Psychol.*, 54:25–39, 1953.

Hamlin, R. M., & Jones, R. E. Vocabulary deficit in improved and unimproved schizophrenic subjects. *J. nerv. ment. Dis.*, 136:360–364, 1963.

Hammer, E. F. Critique of Swensen's "Empirical evaluations of human figure drawings." *J. proj. Tech.*, 23:30–32, 1959.

Hanfmann, E., & Kasanin, J. S. Conceptual thinking in schizophrenia. *Nerv. ment. Dis. Monogr.*, No. 67, 1942.

Harper, E. A. Discrimination of the types of schizophrenia by the Wechsler Bellevue scale. *J. consult. Psychol.*, 14:290–296, 1950.

Harrington, R., & Ehrmann, J. C. Complexity of response as a factor in the vocabulary performance of schizophrenics. *J. abnorm. soc. Psychol.*, 49:362–364, 1954.

Harris, A. J., & Shakow, D. The clinical significance of numerical measures of scatter on the Stanford-Binet. *Psychol. Bull.*, 34:134–150, 1937.

Harris, A. J., & Shakow, D. Scatter on the Stanford-Binet in schizophrenic, normal, and delinquent adults. *J. abnorm. soc. Psychol.*, 33:100–111, 1938.

Harris, D. B. *Children's drawings as measures of intellectual maturity.* New York: Harcourt, Brace, & World, 1963.

Harris, J. G. Validity: the search for a constant in a universe of variables. In M. A. Rickers-Ovsiankina (Ed.), *Rorschach psychology.* New York: Wiley, 1960. Pp. 380–439.

Harrower, M. *Personality change and development.* New York: Grune & Stratton, 1958.

Hartmann, H. (1939) *Ego psychology and the problem of adaptation.* New York: International Universities Press, 1958.

Hartmann, H. Comments on the psychoanalytic theory of the ego. *Psychoan. Stud. Child.*, 5:74–96, 1950.

Hartmann, H. The metapsychology of schizophrenia. *Psychoan. Stud. Child.*, 8:177–198, 1953.

Harway, N. I., & Salzman, L. F. Size constancy in psychopathology. *J. abnorm. soc. Psychol.*, 69:606–613, 1964.

Hathaway, S. R. Increasing clinical efficiency. In B. M. Bass & I. A. Berg (Eds.), *Objective approaches to personality assessment.* Princeton, N. J.: D. Van Nostrand, 1959. Pp. 192–203.

Haywood, H. C., & Moelis, I. Effect of symptom change on intellectual function in schizophrenia. *J. abnorm. soc. Psychol.*, 67:76–78, 1963.

Heath, E. B., Albee, G. W., & Lane, E. A. Predisorder intelligence of process and reactive schizophrenics. *Proceedings Amer. Psychol. Assoc.*, 1965. Pp. 223–224.

Heath, R. G. A biochemical hypothesis on the etiology of schizophrenia. In D. D. Jackson (Ed.), *The etiology of schizophrenia.* New York: Basic Books, 1960. Pp. 146–156.

Hecker, E. Die Hebephrenie. *Virchow's Archiv. f. pathol. Anat., Physiol., und klin. Medizin*, 52:394–431, 1871.

Helfand, I. Role taking in schizophrenia. *J. consult. Psychol.*, 20:37–41, 1956.

Hemmendinger, L. Perceptual organization and development as reflected in the structure of Rorschach test responses. *J. proj. Tech.*, 17:162–170, 1953.

Hemmendinger, L. Developmental theory and the Rorschach method. In M. A. Rickers-Ovsiankina (Ed.), *Rorschach psychology.* New York: Wiley, 1960. Pp. 58–79.

Herron, W. G. The process-reactive classification of schizophrenia. *Psychol. Bull.*, 59:329–343, 1962a.

Herron, W. G. Abstract ability in the process-reactive classification of schizophrenia. *J. gen. Psychol.*, 67:147–154, 1962b.

Herron, W. G. The disease controversy: closing open issues. *Psychol. Rep.*, 13:79–84, 1963.

Hertz, M. R. The reliability of the Rorschach ink-blot test. *J. appl. Psychol.*, 18:461–477, 1934.

Hertz, M. R. The Rorschach ink-blot test: historical summary. *Psychol. Bull.*, 32:33–66, 1935.

Hertz, M. R. The scoring of the Rorschach ink-blot method as developed by the Brush foundation. *Rorschach Res. Exch.*, 6:16–22, 1942.

Hertz, M. R. *Frequency tables for scoring responses to the Rorschach inkblot test.* Cleveland: Western Reserve Univer. Press, 1951.

Hertz, M. R. The organization activity. In M. A. Rickers-Ovsiankina (Ed.), *Rorschach psychology.* New York: Wiley, 1960. Pp. 25–57.

Hertz, M. R., & Paolino, A. F. Rorschach indices of perceptual and conceptual disorganization. *J. proj. Tech.,* **24**:370–388, 1960.

Higgins, J. The concept of process-reactive schizophrenia: criteria and related research. *J. nerv. ment. Dis.,* **138**:9–25, 1964.

Higgins, J., Mednick, S. A., & Philip, F. J. Associative disturbance as a function of chronicity in schizophrenia. *J. abnorm. Psychol.,* **70**:451–452, 1965.

Hirchstein, R. The significance of characteristic autonomic nervous system responses in the adjustment, change, and outcome in schizophrenia. *J. nerv. ment. Dis.,* **122**:254–262, 1955.

Hoch, A. *Benign stupors: a study of a new manic-depressive reaction type.* New York: Macmillan, 1921.

Hoch, A. Acute psychoses with symptoms resembling dementia praecox. *Amer. J. Psychiat.,* **78**:365–372, 1922.

Hoch, P. H., & Cattell, J. P. The diagnosis of pseudoneurotic schizophrenia. *Psychiat. Quart.,* **33**:17–43, 1959.

Hoch, P. H., & Polatin, P. Pseudoneurotic forms of schizophrenia. *Psychiat. Quart.,* **23**:248–276, 1949.

Hollingshead, A. B., & Redlich, F. C. Schizophrenia and social structure. *Amer. J. Psychiat.,* **110**:695–701, 1954.

Holt, R. R. Gauging primary and secondary process in Rorschach responses. *J. proj. Tech.,* **20**:14–25, 1956.

Holt, R. R. Clinical *and* statistical prediction: a reformulation and some new data. *J. abnorm. soc. Psychol.,* **56**:1–12, 1958.

Holt, R. R. Recent developments in psychoanalytic ego psychology and their implications for diagnostic testing. *J. proj. Tech.,* **24**:254–266, 1960.

Holt, R. R. Clinical judgment as a disciplined inquiry. *J. nerv. ment. Dis.,* **133**:369–382, 1961.

Holt, R. R. Individuality and generalization in the psychology of personality. *J. Pers.,* **30**:377–404, 1962.

Holt, R. R., & Havel, J. A method for assessing primary and secondary process in the Rorschach. In M. A. Rickers-Ovsiankina (Ed.), *Rorschach psychology.* New York: Wiley, 1960. Pp. 263–315.

Holtzman, W. H. The examiner as a variable in the Draw-a-Person Test. *J. consult. Psychol.,* **16**:145–148, 1952.

Holtzman, W. H., & Sells, S. B. Prediction of flying success by clinical analysis of test protocols. *J. abnorm. soc. Psychol.,* **49**:485–498, 1954.

Holtzman, W. H., Thorpe, J. S., Swartz, J. D., & Herron, E. W. *Inkblot perception and personality.* Austin: Univer. Texas Press, 1961.

Holzberg, J. D. Reliability re-examined. In M. A. Rickers-Ovsiankina (Ed.), *Rorschach psychology.* New York: Wiley, 1960. Pp. 361–379.

Holzberg, J. D., & Deane, M. A. The diagnostic significance of an obejctive measure of intratest scatter on the Wechsler-Bellevue Intelligence Scale. *J. consult. Psychol.,* **14**:180–188, 1950.

Holzberg, J. D., & Wexler, M. The validity of human form drawings as a measure of personality deviation. *J. proj. Tech.,* **14**:343–361, 1950a.

Holzberg, J. D., & Wexler, M. The predictability of schizophrenic performance on the Rorschach test. *J. consult. Psychol.*, 14:395–399, 1950b.

Hooker, E. Male homosexuality in the Rorschach. *J. proj. Tech.*, 22:33–54, 1958.

Horwitz, W. A. Insulin shock therapy. In S. Arieti (Ed.), *American handbook of psychiatry*. New York: Basic Books, 1959. Pp. 1485–1498.

Hozier, A. Q. On the breakdown of the sense of reality: a study of spatial perception in schizophrenia. *J. consult. Psychol.*, 23:185–194, 1959.

Hunt, J. McV. Psychological experiments with disordered persons. *Psychol. Bull.*, 33:1–58, 1936.

Hunt, J. McV., & Cofer, C. N. Psychological deficit. In J. McV. Hunt (Ed.), *Personality and the behavior disorders.* Vol. II. New York: Ronald, 1944. Pp. 971–1032.

Hunt, R. C., & Appel, K. E. Prognosis in the psychoses lying midway between schizophrenia and manic-depressive psychosis. *Amer. J. Psychiat.*, 93:313–339, 1936.

Hunt, W. A. An actuarial approach to clinical judgment. In B. M. Bass & I. A. Berg (Eds.), *Objective approaches to personality assessment.* Princeton, N. J.: D. Van Nostrand, 1959. Pp. 169–191.

Hunt, W. A., French, E. G., Klebanoff, S. G., Mensh, I. N., & Williams, M. The clinical possibilities of an abbreviated individual intelligence test. *J. consult. Psychol.*, 12:171–174, 1948a.

Hunt, W. A., French, E. G., Klebanoff, S. G. Mensh, I. N., & Williams, M. Further standardization of the CVS individual intelligence scale. *J. consult. Psychol.*, 12:355–359, 1948b.

Hunt, W. A., & Jones, N. F. The experimental investigation of clinical judgment. In A. Bachrach (Ed.), *Experimental foundations of clinical psychology.* New York: Basic Books, 1962. Pp. 26–51.

Hunt, W. A., & Thorne, F. C. Clinical judgment vs. statistical prediction. *J. clin. Psychol.*, 14:439–440, 1958.

Huston, P. E., & Pepernick, M. C. Prognosis in schizophrenia. In L. Bellak, (Ed.), *Schizophrenia: a review of the syndrome.* New York: Logos, 1958. Pp. 531–542.

Huston, P. E., & Shakow, D. Learning in schizophrenia. *J. Pers.*, 17:52–74, 1948.

Huston, P. E., & Shakow, D. Learning capacity in schizophrenia. *Amer. J. Psychiat.*, 105:881–888, 1949.

Huston, P. E., Shakow, D., & Riggs, L. A. Studies of motor function in schizophrenia: II. Reaction time. *J. gen. Psychol.*, 16:39–82, 1937.

Hutt, M. L., Gibby, R. G., Milton, E. O., & Pottharst, K. The effects of varied experimental "sets" upon Rorschach test performance. *J. proj. Tech.*, 14:181–187, 1950

Ittelson, W. H., & Kutash, S. B. (Eds.), *Perceptual changes in psychopathology.* New Brunswick, N. J.: Rutgers Univer. Press, 1961.

Jackson, W., & Carr, A. C. Empathic ability in normals and schizophrenics. *J. abnorm. soc. Psychol.,* 51:79–82, 1955.

James, R. E. Precipitating factors in acute homosexual panic (Kempf's disease). *Quart. Rev. Psychiat. Neurol.,* 2:530–533, 1947.

Jastak, J. Ranking Bellevue subtest scores for diagnostic purposes. *J. consult. Psychol.,* 17:403–410, 1953.

Jenkins, J. G. Validity for what? *J. consult. Psychol.,* 10:93–98, 1946.

Johannsen, W. J. Responsiveness of chronic schizophrenics and normals to social and nonsocial feedback. *J. abnorm. soc. Psychol.,* 62:106–113, 1961.

Johannsen, W. J., Friedman, S. H., Leitschuh, T. H., & Ammons, H. A study of certain schizophrenic dimensions and their relationship to double alternation learning. *J. consult. Psychol.,* 27:375–382, 1963.

Johnson, R. C., Weiss, R. C., & Zelhart, P. F. Similarities and differences between normal and psychotic subjects in response to verbal stimuli. *J. abnorm. soc. Psychol.,* 68:221–226, 1964.

Jones, H. G. Learning and abnormal behavior. In H. J. Eysenck (Ed.) *Handbook of abnormal psychology.* New York: Basic Books, 1961. Pp. 488–528.

Jones, L. W., & Thomas, C. B. Studies on figure drawings. *Psychiat. Quart. Suppl.,* 35:212–261, 1961.

Judson, A. J., & Katahn, M. Levels of personality organization and production of associative sequences in process-reactive schizophrenia. *J. consult. Psychol.,* 28:208–213, 1964.

Jung, C. G. (1903) *The psychology of dementia praecox.* New York: Nervous and Mental Disease Monograph, 1936.

Jung, C. G. On the psychogenesis of schizophrenia. *J. ment. Sci.,* 85:999–1011, 1939.

Kahlbaum, K. L. *Gruppierung der Psychischen Krankheiten.* Danzig: Kafemann, 1863.

Kahlbaum, K. L. *Die Katatonie oder das Spannungsirresein.* Berlin: Hirschweld, 1874.

Kahn, M. W., & Jones, N. F. Human figure drawings as predictors of admission to a psychiatric hospital. *J. proj. Tech. & Pers. Assess.,* 29:319–322, 1965.

Kalinowsky, L. B. Convulsive shock therapy. In S. Arieti (Ed.), *American handbook of psychiatry.* New York: Basic Books, 1959. Pp. 1499–1520.

Kant, O. Differential diagnosis of schizophrenia in the light of concepts of personality stratification. *Amer. J. Psychiat.,* 97:342–357, 1940.

Kant, O. A comparative study of recovered and deteriorated schizophrenic patients. *J. nerv. ment. Dis.,* 93:616–624, 1941.

Kant, O. The evaluation of prognostic criteria in schizophrenia. *J. nerv. ment. Dis.,* 100:598–605, 1944.

Kantor, R. E., Wallner, J. M., & Winder, C. L. Process and reactive schizophrenia. *J. consult. Psychol.,* 17:157–162, 1953.

Kantor, R. E., & Winder, C. L. The process-reactive continuum: a theoretical proposal. *J. nerv. ment. Dis.,* 129:429–434, 1959.

Kasanin, J. S. The acute schizoaffective psychoses. *Amer. J. Psychiat.,* 90:96–126, 1933.

Kasanin, J. S. The disturbance of conceptual thinking in schizophrenia. In J. S. Kasanin (Ed.), *Language and thought in schizophrenia.* Berkeley: Univer. California Press, 1944. Pp. 41–49.

Kasanin, J. S., & Hanfmann, E. An experimental study of concept formation in schizophrenia. I: Quantitative analysis of the results. *Amer. J. Psychiat.,* 95:35–52, 1938.

Kasanin, J. S., & Kaufman, M. R. A study of the functional psychoses in childhood. *Amer. J. Psychiat.,* 9:307–384, 1929.

Kataguchi, Y. Rorschach schizophrenic score (RSS). *J. proj. Tech.,* 23:214–222, 1959.

Katz, M. M., & Cole, J. O. A phenomenological approach to the classification of schizophrenic disorders. *Dis. nerv. Syst.*, 24:147–154, 1963.

Katz, M. M., Cole, J. O., & Lowery, H. A. Nonspecificity of diagnosis of paranoid schizophrenia. *Arch. gen. Psychiat.*, 11:197–202, 1964.

Keiser, S. Severe reactive states and schizophrenia in adolescent girls. *Nerv. Child*, 4:17–25, 1944.

Kelly, E. L., & Fiske, D. W. *The prediction of performance in clinical psychology.* Ann Arbor: Univer. Michigan Press, 1951.

Kety, S. S. Biochemical theories of schizophrenia. *Science*, 129:1528–1532, 1590–1596; 1959.

Kety, S. S. Recent biochemical theories of schizophrenia. In D. D. Jackson (Ed.), *The etiology of schizophrenia.* New York: Basic Books, 1960. Pp. 120–145.

Kimball, A. J. History of form-level appraisal in the Rorschach. *J. proj. Tech.*, 14:134–152, 1950a.

Kimball, A. J. Evaluation of form-level in the Rorschach. *J. proj. Tech.*, 14:219–244, 1950b.

King, G. F. Research with neuropsychiatric samples. *J. Psychol.*, 38:383–387, 1954.

King, G. F. Differential autonomic responsiveness in the process-reactive classification of schizophrenia. *J. abnorm. soc. Psychol.*, 56:160–164, 1958.

King, G. F. An interpersonal conception of Rorschach human movement and delusional content. *J. proj. Tech.*, 24:161–163, 1960.

King, H. E. *Psychomotor aspects of mental disease.* Cambridge, Mass.: Harvard Univer. Press, 1954.

King, H. E. Two-flash and flicker fusion thresholds for normal and schizophrenic subjects. *Percept. mot. Skills*, 14:517–518, 1962.

Kinross-Wright, V., & Kahn, E. On schizophrenia and the schizophrenic. *Amer. J. Psychiat.*, 114:703–706, 1958.

Klein, G. S. The personal world through perception. In R. R. Blake & C. V. Ramsey (Eds.), *Perception: an approach to personality.* New York: Ronald, 1951. Pp. 328–355.

Klein, H. R., & Horwitz, W. A. Psychosexual factors in paranoid phenomena. *Amer. J. Psychiat.*, 105:697–701, 1949.

Klinger, E., & Roth, I. Diagnosing schizophrenia with Rorschach color responses. *J. clin. Psychol.*, 20:386–388, 1964.

Klinger, E., & Roth, I. Diagnosis of schizophrenia by Rorschach patterns. *J. proj. Tech., & Pers. Assess.*, 29:323–335, 1965.

Klopfer, B. *Developments in the Rorschach technique.* Vol. II. *Fields of application.* New York: Harcourt, Brace, & World, 1956.

Klopfer, B., Ainsworth, M. D., Klopfer, W. G., & Holt, R. R. *Developments in the Rorschach tecnique.* Vol. I. *Technique and Theory.* Yonkers-on-Hudson: World Book, 1954.

Klopfer, B., & Kelley, D. M. *The Rorschach tecnique.* Yonkers-on-Hudson: World Book, 1942.

Klopfer, B., Kirkner, F., Wisham, W., & Baker, G. Rorschach Prognostic Rating Scale. *J. proj. Tech.*, 15:425–428, 1951.

Klopfer, B., & Spiegelman, M. Differential diagnosis. In B. Klopfer, *Developments in the Rorschach technique.* Vol. II. *Fields of application.* New York: Harcourt, Brace, & World, 1956. Pp. 281–317.

Knight, R. P. Borderline states. *Bull. Menninger Clin.*, 17:1–12, 1953.

528   References

Knopf, I. J. Rorschach summary scores in differential diagnosis. *J. consult. Psychol.*, **20**:99–104, 1956.

Kolb, L. C. Disturbances of the body-image. In S. Arieti (Ed.), *American handbook of psychiatry*. New York: Basic Books, 1959. Pp. 749–769.

Korchin, S. J. Form perception and ego functioning. In M. A. Rickers-Ovsiankina (Ed.), *Rorschach psychology*. New York: Wiley, 1960. Pp. 109–129.

Kostlan, A. A method for the empirical study of psychodiagnosis. *J. consult. Psychol.*, **18**:83–88, 1954.

Kotkov, B., & Goodman, M. The DAP tests of obese women. *J. clin. Psychol.*, **9**:362–364, 1953.

Kraepelin, E. (1896) *Dementia praecox and paraphrenia*. Chicago: Chicago Medical Book Co., 1919. Translated from the 8th edition of *Lehrbuch der Psychiatrie*, Vol. 3.

Krapf, E. E. The Bleulerian concept of schizophrenia and the comparative approach. *J. nerv. ment. Dis.*, **138**:332–339, 1964.

Krugman, J. A clinical validation of the Rorschach with problem children. *Rorschach Res. Exch.*, **6**:61–70, 1942.

Kutash, S. B. Ambulatory (borderline) schizophrenia: psychodiagnostics and implications for psychological data. *Amer. J. Orthopsychiat.*, **27**:667–676, 1957.

Laing, R. D., & Esterson, A. *Sanity, madness, and the family*. Vol. I. *Families of schizophrenics*. New York: Basic Books, 1964.

Landau, M. F. Body image in paraplegia as a variable in adjustment to physical handicap. Unpublished doctoral dissertation, Columbia Univer., 1960.

Lane, E. A., & Albee, G. W. Childhood intellectual development of adult schizophrenics. *J. abnorm. soc. Psychol.*, **67**:186–189, 1963.

Lane, E. A., & Albee, G. W. Intellectual differences between schizophrenic adults and their siblings. *J. abnorm. soc. Psychol.*, **68**:193–195, 1964.

Lang, P. J. The effect of aversive stimuli and reaction time in schizophrenia. *J. abnorm. soc. Psychol.*, **59**:263–268, 1959.

Lang, P. J., & Buss, A. H. Psychological deficit in schizophrenia: II. Interference and activation. *J. abnorm. Psychol.*, **70**:77–106, 1965.

Lang, P. J., & Luoto, K. Mediation and associative facilitation in neurotic, psychotic, and normal subjects. *J. abnorm. soc. Psychol.*, **64**:113–120, 1962.

Langfeldt, G. Schizophrenic psychoses: 4 cases. *Encephale*, **2**:183–201, 1937.

Langfeldt, G. The diagnosis of schizophrenia. *Amer. J. Psychiat.*, **108**:123–125, 1951.

Leach, W. W. Nystagmus: an integrative neural deficit in schizophrenia. *J. abnorm. soc. Psychol.*, **60**:305–309, 1960.

Lebovits, B. On empty bathtubs: a reply to Meehl. *J. proj. Tech. & Pers. Assess.*, **28**:307–313, 1964.

Lebowitz, A. Patterns of perceputal and motor organization. *J. proj. Tech.*, **27**:302–308, 1963.

Lehner, G. F. J., & Gunderson, F. K. Reliability of the graphic indices in a projective test (the Draw-a-Person). *J. clin. Psychol.*, **8**:125–128, 1952.

Lehner, G. F. J., & Silver, H. Age relationships on the Draw-a-Person test. *J. Pers.*, **17**:199–209, 1948.

Leibowitz, H. W., & Pishkin, V. Perceptual size constancy in chronic schizophrenia. *J. consult. Psychol.*, **25**:196–199, 1961.

Lemkau, P. V., & Crocetti, G. M. Vital statistics of schizophrenia. In L. Bellak

(Ed.), *Schizophrenia: a review of the syndrome.* New York: Logos, 1958. Pp. 64–81.

Levine, D. Rorschach genetic-level and mental disorder. *J. proj. Tech.,* **23**:436–439, 1959.

Levine, D., & Cohen, J. Symptoms and ego strength measures as predictors of the outcome of hospitalization in functional psychoses. *J. consult. Psychol.,* **26**:246–250, 1962.

Levine, K. N. *A comparison of graphic Rorschach productions with scoring categories of the verbal Rorschach record in normal states, organic brain disease, neurotic and psychotic disorders.* New York: Archives of Psychology, 1943.

Levine, M., & Spivack, G. *The Rorschach index of repressive style.* Springfield, Ill.: Charles C. Thomas, 1964.

Levinson, B. M. Cultural pressure and WAIS scatter in a traditional Jewish setting. *J. genet. Psychol.,* **93**:277–286, 1958.

Levy, B. I., Lomax, J. V., & Minsky, R. An underlying variable in the clinical evaluation of drawings of human figures. *J. consult. Psychol.,* **27**:308–312, 1963.

Levy, S. Figure drawing as a projective test. In L. E. Abt & L. Bellak (Eds.), *Projective psychology.* New York: Knopf, 1950. Pp. 257–297.

Lewinsohn, P. M. Use of the Shipley-Hartford conceptual quotient as a measure of intellectual impairment. *J. consult. Psychol.,* **27**:444–447, 1963.

Lewinsohn, P. M., & May, J. A technique for the judgment of emotion from figure drawings. *J. proj. Tech.,* **27**:79–85, 1963.

Lewinsohn, P. M., & Riggs, A. The effect of content upon the thinking of acute and chronic schizophrenics. *J. abnorm. soc. Psychol.,* **65**:206–207, 1962.

Lewis, J. M., Griffith, E. C., Reidel, A. F., & Simmons, B. A. Studies in abstraction: schizophrenia and orality. *J. nerv. ment. Dis.,* **129**:564–567, 1959.

Lewis, N. D. C. The practical value of graphic art in personality studies. I. An introductory presentation of the possibilties. *Psychoan. Rev.,* **12**:316–322, 1925.

Lewis, N. D. C., & Hubbard, L. D. The mechanisms and prognostic aspects of the manic-depressive-schizophrenic combinations. *Assoc. Res. nerv. ment. Dis.,* **11**:539–608, 1931.

Lewis, N. D. C., & Piotrowski, Z. A. Clinical diagnosis of manic-depressive psychosis. In P. H. Hoch & J. Zubin (Eds.), *Depression.* New York: Grune & Stratton, 1954. Pp. 25–38.

Lidz, T., & Fleck, S. Schizophrenia, human integration, and the role of the family. In D. D. Jackson (Ed.), *The etiology of schizophrenia.* New York: Basic Books, 1960. Pp. 323–345.

Lindner, R. M. Content analysis in Rorschach work. *Rorschach Res. Exch.,* **10**:121–130, 1946.

Lindner, R. M. The content analysis of the Rorschach protocol. In L. E. Abt & L. Bellak (Eds.), *Projective psychology.* New York: Knopf, 1950. Pp. 75–90.

Lindquist, E. F. *Design and analysis of experiments.* Boston: Houghton Mifflin, 1953.

Lindzey, G. Seer versus sign. *J. exp. Res. Pers.,* **1**:17–26, 1965.

Lipton, M. B., Tamerin, S., & Lotesta, P. Test evidence of personality change and prognosis by means of the Rorschach and Wechsler-Bellevue tests on 17 insulin-treated paranoid schizophrenics. *Psychiat. Quart.,* **25**:434–444, 1951.

Little, K. B., & Shneidman, E. S. Congruencies among interpretations of psycho-

530   References

logical test and anamnestic data. *Psychol. Monogr.*, **73** (Whole No. 476), 1959.

Lord, E. Experimentally induced variations in Rorschach performance. *Psychol. Monogr.*, **64** (Whole No. 316), 1950.

Lorenz, M. Problems posed by schizophrenic language. *Arch. gen. Psychiat.*, **5**:406–410, 1961.

Lorr, M., Klett, C. J., & McNair, D. M. *Syndromes of psychoses.* London: Pergamon, 1963.

Lothrop, W. W. Psychological test covariates of conceptual deficit in schizophrenia. *J. consult. Psychol.*, **24**:496–499, 1960.

Lothrop, W. W. A critical review of research on the conceptual thinking of schizophrenics. *J. nerv. ment. Dis.*, **132**:118–126, 1961.

Lovinger, E. Perceptual contact with reality in schizophrenics. *J. abnorm. soc. Psychol.*, **52**:87–91, 1956.

Lubin, A., Gieseking, C. F., & Williams, H. L. Direct measurement of cognitive deficit in schizophrenia. *J. consult. Psychol.*, **26**:139–143, 1962.

McCandless, B. R. The Rorschach as a predictor of academic success. *J. appl. Psychol.*, **33**:43–50, 1949.

McConnell, O. L., & Daston, P. G. Body image changes in pregnancy. *J. proj. Tech.*, **25**:451–456, 1961.

McCully, R. S. Certain theoretical considerations in relation to borderline schizophrenia and the Rorschach. *J. proj. Tech.*, **26**:404–418, 1962.

McDonough, J. M. Critical flicker frequency and the spiral aftereffect with process and reactive schizophrenics. *J. consult. Psychol.*, **24**:150–155, 1960.

Mace, N. C., Koff, S. A., Chelnek, I., & Garfield, S. L. Diagnostic problems in early schizophrenia. *J. nerv. ment. Dis.*, **110**:336–346, 1949.

MacFarlane, J. W., & Tuddenham, R. D. Problems in the validation of projective techniques. In H. H. Anderson & G. L. Anderson (Eds.), *An introduction to projective techniques.* New York: Prentice-Hall, 1951. Pp. 26–54.

McGhie, A., & Chapman, J. Disorders of attention and perception in early schizophrenia. *Brit. J. med. Psychol.*, **34**:103–116, 1961.

McGinnies, E. Emotionality and perceptual defense. *Psychol. Rev.*, **56**:244–251, 1949.

McGonaghy, N. Modes of abstract thinking and psychosis. *Amer. J. Psychiat.*, **117**:106–110, 1960.

Machover, K. *Personality projection in the drawing of the human figure.* Springfield, Ill.: Charles C. Thomas, 1949.

Machover, S. Diagnostic and prognostic considerations in psychological tests. In S. Lorand & H. I. Schneer (Eds.), *Adolescents.* New York: Hoeber, 1961. Pp. 301–345.

McKeever, W. F., & Gerstein, A. I. Base rate data on Rorschach card rejections. *J. clin. Psychol.*, **15**:425–427, 1959.

McNemar, Q. On WAIS difference scores. *J. consult. Psychol.*, **21**:239–240, 1957.

Madison, P. *Freud's concept of repression and defense, its theoretical and observational language.* Minneapolis: Univer. Minnesota Press, 1961.

Mahrer, A. R., & Bernstein, L. A proposed method for measuring potential intelligence. *J. clin. Psychol.*, **14**:404–409, 1958.

Masling, J. M. The effects of warm and cold interaction on the administration and scoring of an intelligence test. *J. consult. Psychol.*, **23**:336–341, 1959.

Masling, J. M. The influence of situational and interpersonal variables in projective testing. *Psychol. Bull.*, **57**:65–85, 1960.

Masling, J. M. Differential indoctrination of examiners and Rorschach responses. *J. consult. Psychol.*, **29**:198–201, 1965.

Mason, C. F. Pre-illness intelligence of mental hospital patients. *J. consult. Psychol.*, **20**:297–300, 1956.

Matarazzo, J. D. A postdoctoral residency program in clinical psychology. *Amer. Psychologist*, **20**:432–439, 1965.

Matarazzo, J. D., & Mensh, I. N. Reaction time characteristics of the Rorschach test. *J. consult. Psychol.*, **16**:132–139, 1952.

Matthews, C. G., Guertin, W. H., & Reitan, R. M. Wechsler-Bellevue subtest mean rank orders in diverse diagnostic groups. *Psychol. Rep.*, **11**:3–9, 1962.

Mayer, W. Remarks on abortive cases of schizophrenia. *J. nerv. ment. Dis.*, **112**:539–542, 1950.

Mayman, M. Review of the literature on "scatter." In D. Rapaport, M. Gill, & R. Schafer, *Diagnostic psychological testing*. Vol. I. Chicago: Year Book Publishers, 1945a. Pp. 548–558.

Mayman, M. Review of the literature on the Babcock test. In D. Rapaport, M. Gill, & R. Schafer, *Diagnostic psychological testing*. Vol. I. Chicago: Year Book Publishers, 1945b. Pp. 558–561.

Mayman, M., Schafer, R., & Rapaport, D. Interpretation of the Wechsler-Bellevue intelligence scale in personality appraisal. In H. H. Anderson & G. L. Anderson (Eds.), *An introduction to projective techniques*. New York: Prentice-Hall, 1951. Pp. 541–580.

Meadow, A., & Funkenstein, D. H. The relationship of abstract thinking to the autonomic nervous system in schizophrenia. In P. H. Hoch & J. Zubin (Eds.), *Relation of psychological tests to psychiatry*. New York: Grune & Stratton, 1952. Pp. 131–149.

Meadow, A., Greenblatt, M., Funkenstein, D. H., & Solomon. H. C. Relationship between capacity for abstraction in schizophrenia and physiologic response to autonomic drugs. *J. nerv. ment. Dis.*, **118**:332–338, 1953.

Meadow, A., Greenblatt, M., & Solomon, H. C. "Looseness of association" and impairment in abstraction in schizophrenia. *J. nerv. ment. Dis.*, **118**:27–35, 1953.

Mednick, S. A. A learning theory approach to research in schizophrenia. *Psychol. Bull.*, **55**:316–327, 1958.

Meduna, L. J. *Oneirophrenia*. Urbana, Ill.: Univer. Illinois Press, 1950.

Meehl, P. E. *Clinical versus statistical prediction*. Minneapolis: Univer. Minnesota Press, 1954.

Meehl, P. E. Wanted—a good cookbook. *Amer. Psychologist*, **11**:263–272, 1956.

Meehl, P. E. When shall we use our heads instead of the formula? *J. counsel. Psychol.*, **4**:268–273, 1957.

Meehl, P. E. The cognitive activity of the clinician. *Amer. Psychologist*, **15**:19–27, 1960.

Meehl, P. E. Schizotaxia, schizotypy, schizophrenia. *Amer. Psychologist*, **17**:827–838, 1962.

Meehl, P. E. Seer over sign: the first good example. *J. exp. Res. Pers.*, **1**:27–32, 1965.

Meehl, P. E., & Rosen, A. Antecedent probability and the efficiency of psychometric signs, patterns, or cutting scores. *Psychol. Bull.*, **52**:194–216, 1955.

Meer, B. The relative difficulty of the Rorschach cards. *J. proj. Tech.*, **19**:43–53, 1955.

532   References

Meili-Dworetzki, G. The development of perception in the Rorschach. In B. Klopfer, *Developments in the Rorschach technique*. Vol. II. *Fields of application*. New York: Harcourt, Brace, & World, 1956. Pp. 104–176.

Meketon, B. W., Griffith, R. M., Taylor, V. H., & Wiedman, J. S. Rorschach homosexual signs in paranoid schizoprhenics. *J. abnorm. soc. Psychol.*, 65:208–284, 1962.

Menninger, K. Toward a unitary concept of mental illness. In B. H. Hall (Ed.), *A psychiatrist's world*. New York: Viking, 1959. Pp. 516–528.

Mensh, I. N., & Matarazzo, J. D. Rorschach card rejection in psychodiagnosis. *J. consult. Psychol.*, 18:271–275, 1954.

Mercer, M. Diagnostic testing in two cases of schizophrenic depression. *J. Psychol.*, 28:147–160, 1949.

Mercer, M., & Wright, S. C. Diagnostic testing in a case of latent schizophrenia. *J. proj. Tech.*, 14:287–296, 1950.

Merrill, R. M., & Heathers, L. B. Deviations of Wechsler-Bellevue subtest scores from vocabulary level in university counseling-center clients. *J. consult. Psychol.*, 16:469–472, 1952.

Meyer, A. (1907) Fundamental concepts of dementia praecox. In A. Lief (Ed.), *The commonsense psychiatry of Dr. Adolf Meyer*. New York: McGraw-Hill, 1948. Pp. 184–192.

Meyer, A. (1910) Dynamic interpretation of dementia praecox. In A. Lief (Ed.), *The commonsense psychiatry of Dr. Adolf Meyer*. New York: McGraw-Hill, 1948. Pp. 247–259.

Meyer, V. Psychological effects of brain damage. In H. J. Eysenck (Ed.), *Handbook of abnormal psychology*. New York: Basic Books, 1961. Pp. 529–565.

Milgram, N. A. Preference for abstract versus concrete word meanings in schizophrenic and brain-damaged patients. *J. clin. Psychol.*, 15:207–212, 1959.

Milgram, N. A. Cognitive and empathic factors in role-taking by schizophrenic and brain damaged patients. *J. abnorm. soc. Psychol.*, 60:219–224, 1960.

Milici, P. Postemotive schizophrenia. *Psychiat. Quart.*, 13:278–293, 1939.

Miller, D. R. Prediction of behavior by means of the Rorschach test. *J. abnorm. soc. Psychol.*, 48:367–375, 1953.

Miller, W. R. The relationship between early schizophrenia and the neuroses. *Amer. J. Psychiat.*, 96:889–896, 1940.

Miner, J. B., & Anderson, J. K. Intelligence and emotional disturbance: evidence from Army and veterans' administration records. *J. abnorm. soc. Psychol.*, 56:75–81, 1958.

Modell, A. H. Changes in human figure drawings by patients who recover from regressed states. *Amer. J. Orthopsychiat.*, 21:584–596, 1951.

Molish, H. B. The popular response in Rorschach records of normals, neurotics, and schizophrenics. *Amer. J. Orthopsychiat.*, 21:523–531, 1951.

Monroe, J. J. The effects of emotional adjustment and intelligence upon Bellevue scatter. *J. consult. Psychol.*, 16:110–114, 1952.

Moran, L. J. Vocabulary knowledge and usage among normal and schizophrenic subjects. *Psychol. Monogr.*, 67 (Whole No. 370), 1953.

Moran, L. J., Gorham, D. R., & Holtzman, W. H. Vocabulary knowledge and usage of schizophrenic subjects: a six-year follow-up. *J. abnorm. soc. Psychol.* 69:246–254, 1960.

Moran, L. J., Moran, F. A., & Blake, R. R. An investigation of vocabulary performance of schizophrenics: I. Quantitative level. *J. genet. Psychol.*, **80**:97–105, 1952a.

Moran, L. J., Moran, F. A., & Blake, R. R. An investigation of vocabulary performance of schizophrenics: II. Conceptual level of definitions. *J. genet. Psychol.*, **80**:107–132, 1952b.

Morel, B. A. *Traité des maladies mentales.* Paris: Victor Masson, 1860.

Moriarity, D., & Kates, S. L. Concept attainment of schizophrenics on materials involving social approval and disapproval. *J. abnorm. soc. Psychol.*, **65**:355–364, 1962.

Murstein, B. I. Factor analyses of the Rorschach. *J. consult. Psychol.*, **24**:262–275, 1960.

Murstein, B. I. *Theory and research in projective techniques.* New York: Wiley, 1963.

Nathan, P. E. A comparative investigation of schizophrenic and normal conceptual performance. *J. nerv. ment. Dis.*, **138**:443–451, 1964.

Neubauer, P. B., & Steinert, J. Schizophrenia in adolescence. *Nerv. Child.*, **10**:128–134, 1952.

Nichols, R. C. The effect of ego involvement and success experience on intelligence test scores. *J. consult. Psychol.*, **23**:92, 1959.

Nichols, R. C., & Strümpfer, D. A factor analysis of Draw-a-Person test scores. *J. consult. Psychol.*, **26**:156–161, 1962.

Norman, J. P. Evidence and clinical significance of homosexuality in 100 unanalyzed cases of dementia praecox. *J. nerv. ment. Dis.*, **107**:484–489, 1948.

Noyes, A., & Kolb, L. C. *Modern clinical psychiatry.* (6th ed.) Philadelphia: Saunders, 1963.

Offer, D., Sabshin, M., & Marcus, D. Clinical evaluation of normal adolescents. *Amer. J. Psychiat.*, **121**:864–872, 1965.

Olch, D. R. Psychometric patterns in schizophrenics on the Wechsler Bellevue intelligence test. *J. consult. Psychol.*, **12**:127–136, 1948.

Olson, G. W. Failure and subsequent performance of schizophrenics. *J. abnorm. soc. Psychol.*, **57**:310–314, 1958.

Orbach, C. E., & Tallent, N. Modification of perceived body and of body concepts. *Arch. gen. Psychiat.*, **12**:126–135, 1965.

Orme, J. E. Rorschach sex response in a psychiatric population. *J. clin. Psychol.*, **18**:301–302, 1962.

Orme, J. E. Rorschach alphabetical and geometrical responses. *J. clin. Psychol.*, **19**:459–460, 1963.

Orme, J. E. A study of Weiner's Rorschach schizophrenic indicators. *J. clin. Psychol.*, **20**:531–532, 1964.

Orr, W. F., Anderson, R. B., Martin, M. P., & Philpot, D. F. Factors influencing discharge of female patients from a state mental hospital. *Amer. J. Psychiat.*, **111**:576–582, 1955.

Oskamp, S. The relationship of clinical experience and training methods to several criteria of clinical prediction. *Psychol. Monogr.*, **78** (Whole No. 547), 1962.

Outpatient Psychiatric Clinics: Special Statistical Report, 1961. Bethesda, Maryland: National Institute of Mental Health, 1963.

Ovesey, L. Pseudohomosexuality, the paranoid mechanism, and paranoia: an adaptational revision of the classical Freudian theory. *Psychiatry*, **18**:163–173, 1955.

Pasamanick, B., & Knobloch, H. Epidemiologic studies on the complications of pregnancy and the birth process. In G. Caplan (Ed.), *Prevention of mental disorders in children.* New York: Basic Books, 1961. Pp. 74–94.

Pascal, G. R., Ruesch, H. A., Devince, C. A., & Suttell, B. J. The study of genital symbols on the Rorschach. *J. abnorm. soc. Psychol.,* **45**:286–295, 1950.

Pascal, G. R., & Swenson, C. Learning in mentally ill patients under conditions of unusual motivation. *J. Pers.,* **21**:240–249, 1952.

Paskind, J. A., & Brown, M. Psychosis resembling schizophrenia occurring with emotional stress and ending in recovery. *Amer. J. Psychiat.,* **96**:1379–1388, 1940.

Payne, R. W. Cognitive abnormalities. In H. J. Eysenck (Ed.), *Handbook of abnormal psychology.* New York: Basic Books, 1961. Pp. 193–261.

Payne, R. W., Mattusek, P., & George, E. I. An experimental study of schizophrenic thought disorder. *J. ment. Sci.,* **105**:627–652, 1959.

Peck, R. E. Circumstantial schizophrenia. *Psychiat. Quart.,* **36**:655–664, 1962.

Pena, C. D. A genetic evaluation of perceptual structurization in cerebral pathology. *J. proj. Tech.,* **17**:186–199, 1953.

Peters, H. N. Multiple choice learning in the chronic schizophrenic. *J. clin. Psychol.,* **9**:328–333, 1953.

Peterson, D. R. The diagnosis of subclinical schizophrenia. *J. consult. Psychol.,* **18**:198–200, 1954.

Phillips, L. Case history data and prognosis in schizophrenia. *J. nerv. ment. Dis.,* **117**:515–525, 1953.

Phillips, L., Kaden, S., & Waldman, M. Rorschach indices of developmental level. *J. genet. Psychol.,* **94**:267–285, 1959.

Phillips, L., & Smith, J. G. *Rorschach interpretation: advanced technique.* New York: Grune & Stratton, 1953.

Piotrowski, Z. A. On the Rorschach method and its application in organic disturbances of the central nervous system. *Rorschach Res. Exch.,* **1**:23–40, 1936–1937.

Piotrowski, Z. A. The Rorschach inkblot method in organic disturbances of the central nervous system. *J. nerv. ment. Dis.,* **86**:525–537, 1937.

Piotrowski, Z. A. Positive and negative Rorschach organic reactions. *Rorschach Res. Exch.,* **4**:147–151, 1940.

Piotrowski, Z. A. Experimental psychological diagnosis of mild forms of schizophrenia. *Rorschach Res. Exch.,* **9**:189–200, 1945.

Piotrowski, Z. A. *Perceptanalysis.* New York: Macmillan, 1957.

Piotrowski, Z. A. The movement score. In M. A. Rickers-Ovsiankina (Ed.) *Rorschach psychology.* New York: Wiley, 1960. Pp. 130–153.

Piotrowski, Z. A., & Berg, D. A. Verification of the Rorschach alpha diagnostic formula for underactive schizophrenics. *Amer. J. Psychiat.,* **112**:443–450, 1955.

Piotrowski, Z. A., & Bricklin, B. A long term prognostic criterion for schizophrenics based on Rorschach data. *Psychiat. Quart. Suppl.,* **32**:315–329, 1958.

Piotrowski, Z. A., & Bricklin, B. A second validation of a long-term Rorschach prognostic index for schizophrenic patients. *J. consult. Psychol.,* **25**:123–128, 1961.

Piotrowski, Z. A., & Levine, D. A case illustrating the concept of the alpha schizophrenic. *J. proj. Tech.,* **23**:223–236, 1959.

Piotrowski, Z. A., & Lewis, N. D. C. An experimental Rorschach diagnostic aid for some forms of schizophrenia. *Amer. J. Psychiat.,* **107**:360–366, 1950.

Piotrowski, Z. A., & Lewis, N. D. C. An experimental criterion for the prognostication of the status of schizophrenics after a three-year interval based on Rorschach data. In P. H. Hoch & J. Zubin (Eds.), *Relation of psychological tests to psychiatry.* New York: Grune & Stratton, 1952. Pp. 51–72.

Pious, W. L. The pathogenic process in schizophrenia. *Bull. Menninger Clin.,* 13:152–159, 1949.

Polatin, P. Schizophrenia. *Med. Clinic N. Amer.* 32:623–629, 1948.

Polatin, P., & Hoch, P. H. Diagnostic evaluation of early schizophrenia. *J. nerv. ment. Dis.,* 105:221–230, 1947.

Pope, B., & Jensen, A. R. The Rorschach as an index of pathological thinking. *J. proj. Tech.,* 21:54–62, 1957.

Popper, K. R. *The logic of scientific discovery.* New York: Basic Books, 1959.

Powers, W. T., & Hamlin, R. M. Relationship between diagnostic category and deviant verbalization on the Rorschach. *J. consult. Psychol.,* 19:120–125, 1955.

Pruitt, W. A., & Spilka, B. Rorschach empathy-object relationship scale. *J. proj. Tech. & Pers. Assess.,* 28:331–336, 1964.

Query, J. M., & Query, W. T. Prognosis and progress: a five-year study of forty-eight schizophrenic men. *J. consult. Psychol.,* 28:501–505, 1964.

Quirk, D. A., Quarrington, M., Neiger, S., & Sleman, A. G. The performance of acute psychotic patients on the index of pathological thinking and on selected signs of idiosyncracy on the Rorschach. *J. proj. Tech.,* 26:431–441, 1962.

Rabin, A. I. Test score patterns in schizophrenic and nonpsychotic states. *J. Psychol.,* 12:91–100, 1941.

Rabin, A. I. Differentiating psychometric patterns in schizophrenia and manic-depressive psychosis. *J. abnorm. soc. Psychol.,* 37:270–272, 1942.

Rabin, A. I. Fluctuations in the mental level of schizophrenic patients. *Psychiat. Quart.,* 18:78–92, 1944.

Rabin, A. I. The use of the WB scales with normal and abnormal persons. *Psychol. Bull.,* 42:410–422, 1945.

Rabin, A. I., & Guertin, W. H. Research with the WB test: 1945–1950. *Psychol. Bull.,* 48:211–248, 1951.

Rabin, A. I., & King, G. F. Psychological studies. In L. Bellak (Ed.), *Schizophrenia: a review of the syndrome.* New York: Logos, 1958. Pp. 216–278.

Rabin, A. I., King, G. F., & Ehrmann, J. C. Vocabulary performance of short-term and long-term schizophrenics. *J. abnorm. soc. Psychol.,* 50:255–258, 1955.

Rapaport, D. (Ed.) *Organization and pathology of thought.* New York: Columbia Univer. Press, 1951a.

Rapaport, D. The autonomy of the ego. *Bull. Menninger Clin.,* 15:113–123, 1951b.

Rapaport, D. The structure of psychoanalytic theory. *Psychological Issues,* 2 (Whole No. 2), 1960.

Rapaport, D., Gill, M., & Schafer, R. *Diagnostic psychological testing.* Vol. I. Chicago: Year Book Publishers, 1945.

Rapaport, D., Gill, M., & Schafer, R. *Diagnostic psychological testing.* Vol. II. Chicago: Year Book Publishers, 1946.

Rappaport, S. R. Intellectual deficit in organics and schizophrenics. *J. consult. Psychol.,* 17:389–395, 1953.

Rappaport, S. R., & Webb, W. An attempt to study intellectual deterioration by premorbid and psychotic testing. *J. consult. Psychol.,* 14:95–98, 1950.

Rashkis, H. A., & Singer, R. D. The psychology of schizophrenia. *Arch. gen. Psychiat.,* 1:406–416, 1959.

Raush, H. L. Perceptual constancy in schizophrenia. *J. Pers.,* 21:176–187, 1952.

Rees, W. L., & Jones, A. M. An evaluation of the Rorschach test as a prognostic aid in the treatment of schizophrenia by insulin coma therapy, electronarcosis, electroconvulsive therapy, and leucotomy. *J. ment. Sci.,* **97**:681–689, 1951.

Reichard, S., & Schafer, R. The clinical significance of scatter on the Bellevue scale. *Bull. Menninger Clin.,* **7**:93–98, 1943.

Reid, J. R. The myth of Doctor Szasz. *J. nerv. ment. Dis.,* **135**:381–386, 1962.

Reisman, J. M. Motivational differences between process and reactive schizophrenics. *J. Pers.,* **28**:12–25, 1960.

Reitan, R. M. Certain differential effects of left and right cerebral lesions in human adults. *J. comp. psysiol. Psychol.,* **48**:474–477, 1955.

Reitan, R. M. Psychological deficit. *Annu. Rev. Psychol.,* **13**:415–444, 1962.

Reznikoff, M., & Nicholas, A. L. An evaluation of human-figure drawing indicators of paranoid pathology. *J. consult. Psychol.,* **22**:395–397, 1958.

Reznikoff, M., & Tomblen, D. The use of human figure drawings in the diagnosis of organic pathology. *J. consult. Psychol.,* **20**:467–470, 1956.

Ribler, R. I. Diagnostic predictions from emphasis on the eye and ear in human figure drawings. *J. consult. Psychol.,* **21**:223–225, 1957.

Richman, J. The effect of the emotional tone of words upon the vocabulary responses of schizophrenics. *J. gen. Psychol.,* **56**:95–119, 1957.

Rickers-Ovsiankina, M. A. The Rorschach test as applied to normal and schizophrenic subjects. *Brit. J. med. Psychol.,* **17**:227–257, 1938.

Rickers-Ovsiankina, M. A. Some theoretical considerations regarding the Rorschach method. *Rorschach Res. Exch.,* **7**:41–53, 1943.

Rickers-Ovsiankina, M. A. Longitudinal approach to schizophrenia through the Rorschach method. *J. clin. exp. Psychopath.,* **15**:107–118, 1954.

Rickers-Ovsiankina, M. A. Synopsis of psychological premises underlying the Rorschach. In M. A. Rickers-Ovsiankina (Ed.), *Rorschach psychology.* New York: Wiley, 1960. Pp. 3–22.

Rieman, G. W. The effectiveness of Rorschach elements in the discrimination between neurotic and ambulatory schizophrenic subjects. *J. consult. Psychol.,* **17**:25–31, 1953.

Rodnick, E. H., & Garmezy, N. An experimental approach to the study of motivation in schizophrenia. In M. R. Jones (Ed.), *Nebraska symposium on motivation.* Lincoln, Nebr.: Univer. Nebraska Press, 1957. Pp. 109–184.

Rodnick, E. H., & Shakow, D. Set in the schizophrenic as measured by a composite reaction time index. *Amer. J. Psychiat.,* **97**:214–225, 1940.

Roe, A., & Shakow, D. Intelligence in mental disorders. *Ann. N. Y. Acad. Sci.,* **42**:361–490, 1942.

Rogers, L. S. Differences between neurotics and schizophrenics on the Wechsler-Bellevue Scale. *J. consult. Psychol.,* **15**:151–153, 1951.

Romano, J., & Ebaugh, F. G. Prognosis in schizophrenia. *Amer. J. Psychiat.,* **95**:583–594, 1938.

Romano, J., & Engel, G. L. Delirium. I. Electroencephalographic data. *Arch. Neurol. Psychiat.,* **51**:356–377, 1944.

Rorschach, H. (1921) *Psychodiagnostics.* (5th ed.) Bern: Hans Huber, 1942.

Rosenbaum, G., Grisell, J. L., & Mackavey, W. R. Effects of biological and social motivation on schizophrenic reaction time. *J. abnorm. soc. Psychol.,* **54**:364–368, 1957.

Rosenblatt, B., & Solomon, P. Structural and genetic aspects of Rorschach responses in mental deficiency. *J. proj. Tech.,* **18**:496–506, 1954.

Rosenthal, D. Theoretical overview. In D. Rosenthal (Ed.), *The Genain quadruplets*. New York: Basic Books, 1963. Pp. 505–579.

Rosenthal, D., Lawlor, W. G., Zahn, T. P., & Shakow, D. The relationships of some aspects of mental set to degree of schizophrenic disorganization. *J. Pers.*, 28:26–38, 1960.

Rosenthal, D., Zahn, T. P., & Shakow, D. Verbal versus manual reaction time in schizophrenic and normal subjects. *Quart. J. exp. Psychol.*, 15:214–216, 1963.

Rosenwald, G. C. Psychodiagnostics and its discontents. *Psychiatry*, 26:222–240, 1963.

Rosenwald, G. C. Physicalism and psychodiagnosis. *Psychiat. Quart.*, 39:16–31, 1965.

Rosenzweig, S. Fantasy in personality and its study by test procedures. *J. abnorm. soc. Psychol.*, 37:40–51, 1942.

Rubin, H., & Lonstein, M. A cross-validation of suggested Rorschach patterns associated with schizophrenia. *J. consult. Psychol.*, 17:371–372, 1953.

Rychlak, J. F., & O'Leary, L. R. Unhealthy content in the Rorschach responses of children and adolescents. *J. proj. Tech. & Pers. Assess.*, 29:354–368, 1965.

Sacks, J. M., & Lewin, H. S. Limitations of the Rorschach as a sole diagnostic instrument. *J. consult. Psychol.*, 14:479–481, 1950.

Salzman, L. Paranoid state—theory and therapy. *Arch. gen. Psychiat.*, 2:679–693, 1960.

Salzman, L. F., Goldstein, R. H., Atkins, R., & Babigian, H. Conceptual thinking in psychiatric patients. *Arch. gen. Psychiat.*, 14:55–59, 1966.

Sanders, R. S., & Pacht, A. R. Perceptual size constancy of known clinical groups. *J. consult. Psychol.*, 16:440–444, 1952.

Sanderson, H. Norms for "shock" in the Rorschach. *J. consult. Psychol.*, 15:127–129, 1951.

Sandifer, M. G., Pettus, C., & Quade, D. A study of psychiatric diagnosis. *J. nerv. ment. Dis.*, 139:350–356, 1964.

Sandler, J., & Ackner, B. Rorschach content analysis: an experimental investigation. *Brit. J. med. Psychol.*, 24:180–201, 1951.

Sarason, S. B. *The clinical interaction*. New York: Harper, 1954.

Saunders, D. R. A factor analysis of the PC items of the WAIS. *J. clin. Psychol.*, 16:146–149, 1960a.

Saunders, D. R. A factor analysis of the Information and Arithmetic items of the WAIS. *Psychol. Rep.*, 6:367–383, 1960b.

Schachtel, E. G. On color and affect. *Psychiatry*, 6:393–409, 1943.

Schachtel, E. G. Subjective definitions of the Rorschach test situation and their effect on test performance. *Psychiatry*, 8:419–448, 1945.

Schafer, R. *The clinical application of psychological tests*. New York: International Universities Press, 1948.

Schafer, R. *Psychoanalytic interpretation in Rorschach testing*. New York: Grune & Stratton, 1954.

Schafer, R. Bodies in schizophrenic Rorschach responses. *J. proj. Tech.*, 24:267–281, 1960.

Schilder, P. *The image and appearance of the human body*. London: Kegan Paul, 1935.

Schmideberg, M. The borderline patient. In S. Arieti (Ed.), *American handbook of psychiatry*. New York: Basic Books, 1959. Pp. 398–416.

Schmidt, H. O., & Fonda, C. P. The reliability of psychiatric diagnosis: a new look. *J. abnorm. soc. Psychol.*, 52:262–267, 1956.

Schmidt, L. D., & McGowan, J. F. The differentiation of human figure drawings. *J. consult. Psychol.*, 23:129–133, 1959.

Schwartzman, A. E., & Douglas, V. I. Intellectual loss in schizophrenia: Part I. *Canad. J. Psychol.*, 16:1–10, 1962.

Searles, H. *The nonhuman environment.* New York: International Universities Press, 1960.

Seidel, C. The relationship between Klopfer's Rorschach Prognostic Rating Scale and Phillips' Case History Prognostic Rating Scale. *J. consult. Psychol.*, 24:46–49, 1960.

Senf, R., Huston, P. E., & Cohen, B. D. Thinking deficit in schizophrenia and changes with amytal. *J. abnorm. soc. Psychol.*, 50:383–387, 1955.

Shakow, D. The nature of deterioration in schizophrenia. *Nerv. Ment. Dis. Monogr.*, 70:1–88, 1946.

Shakow, D. Some psychological features of schizophrenia. In M. L. Reymert (Ed.), *Feelings and emotions.* New York: McGraw-Hill, 1950. Pp. 283–290.

Shakow, D. Segmental set: a theory of the formal psychological deficit in schizophrenia. *Arch. gen. Psychiat.*, 6:1–17, 1962.

Shakow, D. Psychological deficit in schizophrenia. *Behav. Sci.*, 8:275–305, 1963.

Shakow, D. The role of classification in the development of the science of psychopathology with particular reference to research. *Bull. Menninger Clin.*, 30:150–161, 1966.

Shakow, D., & Huston, P. E. Studies of motor function in schizophrenia: I. Speed of tapping. *J. gen. Psychol.*, 15:63–106, 1936.

Shapiro, D. Special problems of testing borderline psychotics. *J. proj. Tech.*, 18:387–394, 1954.

Shapiro, D. A perceptual understanding of color response. In M. A. Rickers-Ovsiankina (Ed.), *Rorschach psychology.* New York: Wiley, 1960. Pp. 154–201.

Shapiro, M. B., Kessell, R., & Maxwell, A. E. Speed and quality of psychomotor performance in psychiatric patients. *J. clin. Psychol.*, 16:266–271, 1960.

Shaprio, M. B., & Nelson, E. H. An investigation of the nature of cognitive impairment in cooperative psychiatric patients. *Brit. J. med. Psychol.*, 28:239–256, 1955.

Shaw, B. "Sex populars" in the Rorschach test. *J. abnorm. soc. Psychol.*, 43:466–470, 1948.

Shereshevski-Shere, E., Lasser, L. M., & Gottesfield, B. H. An evaluation of anatomy content and F+ percentage in the Rorschachs of alcoholics, schizophrenics, and normals. *J. proj. Tech.*, 17:229–233, 1953.

Sherman, L. J. Sexual differentiation on artistic ability? *J. clin. Psychol.*, 14:170–171, 1958a.

Sherman, L. J. The influence of artistic ability on judgments of patient and non-patient status from human figure drawings. *J. proj. Tech.*, 22:338–340, 1958b.

Sherman, M. H. A comparison of formal and content factors in the diagnostic testing of schizophrenia. *Genet. Psychol. Monogr.*, 46:183–234, 1952.

Sherman, M. H. The diagnostic significance of constriction-dilation on the Rorschach. *J. gen. Psychol.*, 53:11–19, 1955.

Shimkunas, A. M., Gynther, M. D., & Smith, K. Abstracting ability of schizophrenics before and during phenothiazine therapy. *Arch. gen. Psychiat.*, 14:79–83, 1966.

Siegel, E. L. Perception in paranoid schizophrenia and the Rorschach. *J. proj. Tech.*, 17:151–161, 1953.

Siegel, M. G. The diagnostic and prognostic validity of the Rorschach test in a child guidance clinic. *Amer. J. Orthopsychiat.*, 18:119–133, 1948.

Siegel, S. *Nonparametric statistics.* New York: McGraw-Hill, 1956.

Siipola, E. M. The influence of color on reactions to inkblots. *J. Pers.*, 18:358–382, 1950.

Silber, E., Hamburg, D. A., Coelho, G. V., Murphey, E. B., Rosenberg, M., & Pearlin, L. I. Adaptive behavior in competent adolescents. *Arch. gen. Psychiat.*, 5:354–365, 1961.

Silverman, J. Scanning-control mechanism and "cognitive" filtering in paranoid and non-paranoid schizophrenia. *J. consult. Psychol.*, 28:385–393, 1964.

Silverman, L. N., Lapkin, B., & Rosenbaum, I. S. Manifestations of primary process thinking in schizophrenia. *J. proj. Tech.*, 26:117–127, 1962.

Singer, J. L. What do we know of projective techniques? *Contemp. Psychol.*, 5:76–77, 1960.

Singer, J. L., Meltzoff, J., & Goldman, G. D. Rorschach movement responses following motor inhibition and hyperactivity. *J. consult. Psychol.*, 16:359–364, 1952.

Singer, R. D. Organization as a unifying concept in schizophrenia. *Arch. gen. Psychiat.*, 2:61–74, 1960.

Sisson, B. D., & Taulbee, E. S. Organizational activity on the Rorschach Test. *J. consult. Psychol.*, 19:29–31, 1955.

Sisson, B. D., Taulbee, E. S., & Gaston, C. O. Rorschach card rejection in normal and psychiatric groups. *J. clin. Psychol.*, 12:85–88, 1956.

Skalweit, W. *Konstitution und Prozess in der Schizophrenie.* Leipzig: Georg Thieme, 1934.

Small, L. *Rorschach location and scoring manual.* New York: Grune & Stratton, 1956.

Smith, A. Mental deterioration in chronic schizophrenia. *J. nerv. ment. Dis.*, 139:479–487, 1964.

Smock, C. D., & Vancini, J. Dissipation rate of the effects of social censure in schizophrenics. *Psychol. Rep.*, 10:531–536, 1962.

Snedecor, G. W. *Statistical methods.* (5th ed.) Ames, Iowa: Iowa State College Press, 1956.

Solow, R. A. Chronic cyclic schizo-affective psychosis. *Bull. Menninger Clin.*, 17:13–19, 1953.

Sommer, R., Dewar, R., & Osmond, H. Is there a schizophrenic language? *Arch. gen. Psychiat.*, 3:665–673, 1960.

Spence, J. T., & Lair, C. V. Associative interference in the verbal learning performance of schizophrenics and normals. *J. abnorm. soc. Psychol.*, 68:204–209, 1964.

Spotonitz, H. Adolescence and schizophrenia: problems in differentiation. In S. Lorand & H. I. Schneer (Eds.), *Adolescents.* New York: Hoeber, 1961. Pp. 217–237.

Starr, S., & Marcuse, F. L. Reliability in the Draw-a-Person test. *J. proj. Tech.*, 23:83–86, 1959.

Stein, H. An evaluation of Rorschach reliability through the alternate response method. *J. clin. Psychol.*, 17:241–245, 1961.

Stone, H. K., & Dellis, N. P. An exploratory investigation into the levels hypothesis. *J. proj. Tech.*, 24:333–340, 1960.

Stotsky, B. A. A comparison of remitting and nonremitting schizophrenics on psychological tests. *J. abnorm. soc. Psychol.*, 47:489–496, 1952.

Stotsky, B. A. Motivation and task complexity as factors in the psychomotor responses of schizophrenics. *J. Pers.,* **25**:327–343, 1957.

Strümpfer, D., & Nichols, R. C. A study of some communicable measures for the evaluation of human figure drawings. *J. proj. Tech.,* **26**:342–353, 1962.

Strupp. H. H. The outcome problem in psychotherapy revisited. *Psychotherapy,* **1**:1–13, 1963.

Sturm, I. E. Overinclusion and concreteness among pathological groups. *J. consult. Psychol.,* **29**:9–18, 1965.

Sullivan, H. S. *Conceptions of modern psychiatry.* Washington: William Alanson White, 1946.

Sullivan, H. S. *The interpersonal theory of psychiatry.* New York: Norton, 1953.

Sullivan, H. S. *Clinical studies in psychiatry.* New York: Norton, 1956.

Sullivan, H. S. *Schizophrenia as a human process.* New York: Norton, 1962.

Sundberg, N. D. The practice of psychological testing in clinical services in the United States. *Amer. Psychologist,* **16**:79–83, 1961.

Swenson, C. H. Sexual differentiation on the Draw-a-Person test. *J. clin. Psychol.,* **11**:37–41, 1955.

Swenson, C. H. Empirical evaluations of human figure drawings. *Psychol. Bull.,* **54**:431–466, 1957.

Szasz, T. S. A contribution to the psychology of schizophrenia. *Arch. Neurol. Psychiat.,* **77**:420–436, 1957a.

Szasz, T. S. The problem of psychiatric nosology. *Amer. J. Psychiat.,* **114**:405–413, 1957b.

Szasz, T. S. *The myth of mental illness.* New York: Hoeber-Harper, 1961.

Tamkin, A. S. Rorschach card rejection by psychiatric patients. *J. consult. Psychol.,* **22**:441–444, 1958.

Taulbee, E. S. The use of the Rorschach test in evaluating the intellectual levels of functioning in schizophrenics. *J. proj. Tech.,* **19**:163–169, 1955.

Taulbee, E. S., & Sisson, B. D., Rorschach pattern analysis in schizophrenia: a cross-validation study. *J. clin. Psychol.,* **10**:80–82, 1954.

Taylor, I. A., Rosenthal, D., & Snyder, S. Variability in schizophrenia. *Arch. gen. Psychiat.,* **8**:163–168, 1963.

Teuber, H. L. Neuropsychology. In M. R. Harrower (Ed.), *Recent advances in diagnostic psychological testing.* Springfield, Ill.: Charles C. Thomas, 1950. Pp. 30–52.

Thiesen, J. W. A pattern analysis of structural characteristics of the Rorschach test in schizophrenia. *J. consult. Psychol.,* **16**:365–370, 1952.

Thomas, H. F. The relationship of movement responses on the Rorschach to the defense mechanism of projection. *J. abnorm. soc. Psychol.,* **50**:41–44, 1955.

Thorp, T. R., & Mahrer, A. R. Predicting potential intelligence. *J. clin. Psychol.,* **15**:286–288, 1959.

Tizard, J., & Venables, P. H. Reaction time responses by schizophrenics, mental defectives, and normal adults. *Amer. J. Psychiat.,* **112**:803–807, 1956.

Tolor, A. Abstract ability in organics and schizophrenics. *J. proj. Tech. & Pers. Assess.,* **28**:357–362, 1964.

Trapp, C. E., & James, E. B. Comparative intelligence ratings in the four types of dementia praecox. *J. nerv. ment. Dis.,* **86**:399–404, 1937.

Trehub, A., & Scherer, I. W. Wechsler-Bellevue scatter as an index of schizophrenia. *J. consult. Psychol.,* **22**:147–149, 1958.

Tulchin, S. H. The pre-Rorschach use of inkblot tests. *Rorschach Res. Exch.,*

4:1–7, 1940.

Tutko, T. A., & Spence, J. T. The performance of process and reactive schizophrenics and brain-injured subjects on a conceptual task. *J. abnorm. soc. Psychol.,* **65**:389–394, 1962.

Vaillant, G. E. The prediction of recovery in schizophrenia. *J. nerv. ment. Dis.,* **135**:534–543, 1962.

Vaillant, G. E. Positive prediction of schizophrenic remission. *Arch. gen. Psychiat.,* **11**:509–518, 1964a.

Vaillant, G. E. An historical review of the remitting schizophrenias. *J. nerv. ment. Dis.,* **138**:48–56, 1964b.

Vaughan, H. G., & Costa, L. D. Performance of patients with lateralized cerebral lesions. II: Sensory and motor tests. *J. nerv. ment. Dis.,* **134**:237–243, 1962.

Vernon, P. E. The Rorschach Ink-Blot Test. (Bibliography No. I). *Brit. J. med. Psychol.,* **13**:89–118, 179–200, 271–291, 1933.

Vernon, P. E. The significance of the Rorschach test. *Brit. J. med. Psychol.,* **15**:199–217, 1935.

Vigotsky, L. Thought in schizophrenia. *Arch. Neurol. Psychiat.,* **31**:1063–1077, 1934.

Vinson, D. B. Responses to the Rorschach test that identify schizophrenic thinking, feeling, and behavior. *J. clin. exp. Psychopathol.,* **21**:34–40, 1960.

Von Domarus, E. The specific laws of logic in schizophrenia. In J. S. Kasanin (Ed.), *Language and thought in schizophrenia.* Berkeley: Univer. California Press, 1944. Pp. 104–114.

Waite, R. R. The intelligence test as a diagnostic instrument. *J. proj. Tech.,* **25**:90–102, 1961.

Walker, R. E., Hunt, W. A., & Schwartz, M. A. The difficulty of WAIS Comprehension scoring. *J. clin. Psychol.,* **21**:427–429, 1965.

Walker, R. G. An approach to standardization of Rorschach form-level. *J. proj. Tech.,* **17**:426–436, 1953.

Warner, S. J. An evaluation of the validity of Rorschach popular responses as differentiae of ambulatory schizophrenia. *J. proj. Tech.,* **15**:268–275, 1951.

Warren, W. Abnormal behavior and mental breakdown in adolescence. *J. ment. Sci.,* **95**:589–624, 1949.

Warren, W., & Cameron, K. Reactive psychosis in adolescence. *J. ment. Sci.,* **96**:448–457, 1950.

Watkins, J. G., & Stauffacher, J. C. An index of pathological thinking in the Rorschach. *J. proj. Tech.,* **16**:276–286, 1952.

Watson, C. G. Intratest scatter in hospitalized brain-damaged and schizophrenic patients. *J. consult. Psychol.,* **29**:596, 1965.

Weaver, L. A. Psychomotor performance of clinically differentiated chronic schizophrenics. *Percept. mot. Skills,* **12**:27–33, 1961.

Wechsler, D. *Measurement of adult intelligence.* (3rd ed.) Baltimore: Williams & Wilkins, 1944.

Wechsler, D. *Manual for the Wechsler Adult Intelligence Scale.* New York: Psychological Corp., 1955.

Wechsler, D. *The measurement and appraisal of adult intelligence.* (4th ed.) Baltimore: Williams & Wilkins, 1958.

Weckowicz, T. E. Size constancy in schizophrenic patients. *J. ment. Sci.,* **103**:475–486, 1957.

Weckowicz, T. E. Perception of hidden pictures by schizophrenic patients. *Arch.*

gen. Psychiat., 2:521–527, 1960.

Weckowicz, T. E., & Blewett, D. B. Size constancy and abstract thinking in schizophrenia. J. ment. Sci., 105:909–934, 1959.

Weckowicz, T. E., & Sommer, R. Body image and self-concept in schizophrenia. J. ment. Sci., 106:17–39, 1960.

Weiner, H. Diagnosis and symptomatology. In Bellak, L. (Ed.), Schizophrenia: a review of the syndrome. New York: Logos, 1958. Pp. 107–173.

Weiner, I. B. Cross-validation of a Rorschach checklist associated with suicidal tendencies. J. consult. Psychol., 25:312–315, 1961a.

Weiner, I. B. Three Rorschach scores indicative of schizophrenia. J. consult. Psychol., 25:436–439, 1961b.

Weiner, I. B. Rorschach tempo as a schizophrenic indicator. Percept. mot. Skills, 15:139–141, 1962.

Weiner, I. B. Differential diagnosis in amphetamine psychosis. Psychiat. Quart., 38:707–716, 1964a.

Weiner, I. B. Pure C and color stress as Rorschach indicators of schizophrenia. Percept. mot. Skills, 18:484, 1964b.

Weiner, I. B. Rorschach color stress as a schizophrenic indicator—a reply. J. clin. Psychol., 21:313–314, 1965a.

Weiner, I. B. Follow-up validation of Rorschach tempo and color use indicators of schizophrenia. J. proj. Tech. & Pers. Assess., 29:387–391, 1965b.

Weiner, I. B. Rorschach clues in the differential diagnosis of amphetamine psychosis. Read at Eastern Psychological Association meetings, Atlantic City, N. J., 1965c.

Wells, E. L., & Kelley, C. M. Intelligence and psychosis. Amer. J. Insan., 77:17–45, 1920.

Wender, P. H. Dementia praecox: the development of the concept. Amer. J. Psychiat., 119:1143–1151, 1963.

Werner, H. Comparative psychology of mental development. (rev. ed.) New York: Follett, 1948.

Wertheimer, M. On the supposed behavioral correlates of an "eye" content response on the Rorschach. J. consult. Psychol., 17:189–194, 1953.

Wexler, M. The structural problem in schizophrenia: the role of the internal object. In E. B. Brody & F. C. Redlich (Eds.), Psychotherapy with schizophrenics. New York: International Universities Press, 1952. Pp. 179–201.

Wheeler, W. M. An analysis of Rorschach indices of male homosexuality. J. proj. Tech. & Rorschach Res. Exch., 13:97–126, 1949.

Whiteman, M. The performance of schizophrenics on social concepts. J. abnorm. soc. Psychol., 49:266–271, 1954.

Whiteman, M. Qualitative features of schizophrenic thought in the formation of social concepts. J. nerv. ment. Dis., 124:199–204, 1956.

Whitman, R. M. The use of the Rorschach test in schizophrenia. Psychiat. Quart. Suppl., 28:26–37, 1954.

Whitmyre, J. W. The significance of artistic excellence in the judgment of adjustment inferred from human figure drawings. J. consult. Psychol., 17:421–424, 1953.

Wickes, T. A. Examiner influence in a testing situation. J. consult. Psychol., 20:23–26, 1956.

Wiener, G. The effect of distrust on some aspects of intelligence. J. consult. Psychol., 21:127–130, 1957.

Wilensky, H. Rorschach developmental level and social participation of chronic schizophrenics. *J. proj. Tech.*, **23**:87–82, 1959.

Will, O. A. Process, psychotherapy, and schizophrenia. In A. Burton (Ed.), *Psychotherapy of the psychoses.* New York: Basic Books, 1961. Pp. 10–42.

Wilson, G. P., & Blake, R. R. A methodological problem in Beck's organizational concept. *J. consult. Psychol.*, **14**:20–24, 1950.

Winder, C. L. Some psychological studies of schizophrenia. In D. D. Jackson (Ed.), *The etiology of schizophrenia.* New York: Basic Books, 1960. Pp. 191–247.

Windle, C. Psychological tests in psychopathological prognosis. *Psychol. Bull.*, **49**:451–482, 1952.

Windle, C., & Hamwi, V. An exploratory study of the prognostic value of the Complex Reaction Time Test in early and chronic psychotics. *J. clin. Psychol.*, **9**:156–161, 1953.

Wing, J. K. A simple and reliable sub-classification of chronic schizophrenia. *J. ment. Sci.*, **107**:862–875, 1961.

Winslow, C. W., & Rapersand, I. Postdiction of the outcome of somatic therapy from the Rorschach records of schizophrenic patients. *J. consult. Psychol.*, **28**:243–247, 1964.

Wishner, J. Rorschach intellectual indicators in neurotics. *Amer. J. Orthopsychiat.*, **18**:265–279, 1948.

Wishner, J. Factor analyses of Rorschach scoring categories and first response times in normals. *J. consult. Psychol.*, **23**:406–413, 1959.

Wittenborn, J. R. Symptom patterns in a group of mental hospital patients. *J. consult. Psychol.*, **15**:290–302, 1951.

Wittenborn, J. R., & Sarason, S. R. Exceptions to certain Rorschach criteria of pathology. *J. consult. Psychol.*, **13**:21–27, 1949.

Wittman, P. An evaluation of opposed theories concerning the etiology of so-called "dementia" in dementia praecox. *Amer. J. Psychiat.*, **93**:1363–1377, 1937.

Wittman, P. A scale for measuring prognosis in schizophrenic patients. *Elgin State Hosp. Papers*, **4**:20–23, 1941.

Wittman, P. Follow-up on Elgin Prognosis Scale results. *Illinois Psychiat. J.*, **4**:56–59, 1944.

Wittman, P., & Steinberg, L. Follow-up of an objective evaluation of prognosis in dementia praecox and manic-depressive psychoses. *Elgin State Hosp. Papers*, **5**:216–227, 1944.

Wolfson, W., & Weltman, R. E. Implications of specific WAIS picture completion errors. *J. clin. Psychol.*, **16**:9–11, 1960.

Wyatt, F. Some remarks on the place of cognition in ego psychology. *J. proj. Tech.*, **17**:144–150, 1953.

Wynne, L. C., & Singer, M. T. Thought disorder and family relations in schizophrenia. I. A research strategy. *Arch. gen. Psychiat.*, **9**:191–198, 1963a.

Wynne, L. C., & Singer, M. T. Thought disorder and family relationships of schizophenics. II. A classification of forms of thinking. *Arch. gen. Psychiat.*, **9**:199–206, 1963b.

Yacorzynski, G. K. An evaluation of the postulates underlying the Babcock deterioration test. *Psychol. Rev.*, **48**:261–267, 1941.

Yates, A. J. The use of vocabulary in the measurement of intellectual deterioration —a review. *J. ment. Sci.*, **102**:409–440, 1956.

Yates, A. J. Abnormalities of psychomotor functions. In H. J. Eysenck (Ed.), *Handbook of abnormal psychology.* New York: Basic Books, 1961. Pp. 32–61.

Yolles, S. F. The role of the psychologist in comprehensive community mental health centers. *Amer. Psychologist*, 21:37–41, 1966.

Zahn, T. P., & Rosenthal, D. Preparatory set in acute schizophrenia. *Amer. Psychologist*, 19:495, 1964. (Abstract)

Zax, M., Stricker, G., & Weiss, J. H. Some effects of non-personality factors on Rorschach performance. *J. proj. Tech.*, 24:83–93, 1960.

Zilboorg, G. Ambulatory schizophrenias. *Psychiatry*, 4:149–155, 1941.

Zilboorg, G. The problem of ambulatory schizophrenias. *Amer. J. Psychiat.*, 113:519–525, 1956.

Zilboorg, G. Further observations on ambulatory schizophrenia. *Amer. J. Orthopsychiat.*, 27:677–682, 1957.

Zimet, C. N., & Fine, H. J. Perceptual differentiation and two dimensions of schizophrenia. *J. nerv. ment. Dis.*, 129:435–441, 1959.

Zlotowski, M., & Bakan, P. Behavioral variability of process and reactive schizophrenics in a binary guessing task. *J. abnorm. soc. Psychol.*, 66:185–187, 1963.

Zubin, J. Failures of the Rorschach technique. *J. proj. Tech.*, 18:303–315, 1954.

Zubin, J., Eron, L. D., & Schumer, F. *An experimental approach to projective techniques*. New York: Wiley, 1965.

Zubin, J., & Windle, C. Psychological prognosis of outcome in the mental disorders. *J. abnorm. soc. Psychol.*, 49:272–281, 1954.

Zubin, J., Windle, C., & Hamwi, V. Retrospective evaluation of psychological tests as prognostic instruments in mental disorders. *J. Pers.*, 21:342–355, 1953.

Zucker, L. J. The psychology of latent schizophrenia: based on Rorschach studies. *Amer. J. Psychother.*, 6:44–62, 1952.

Zucker, L. J. *Ego structure in paranoid schizophrenia*. Springfield, Ill.: Charles C. Thomas, 1958.

Zuckerman, M., & Gross, H. J. Contradictory results using the mecholyl test to differentiate process and reactive schizophrenia. *J. abnorm. soc. Psychol.*, 59:145–146, 1959.

AUTHOR INDEX

SUBJECT INDEX

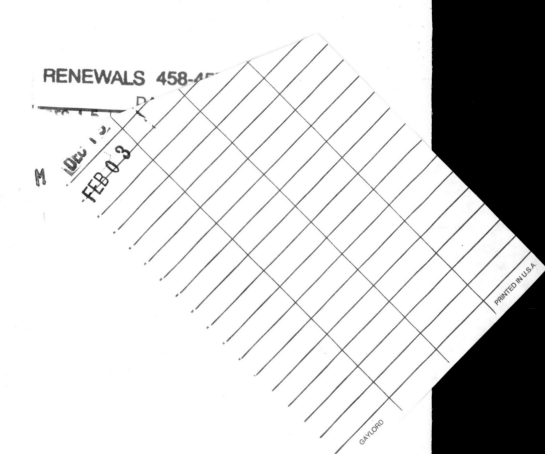